KV-422-232

004196

Boundaries and Easements

Boundaries and Easements

Fifth Edition

By

Colin Sara

BA (Oxon) of Gray's Inn, Barrister

SWEET & MAXWELL

 THOMSON REUTERS

First Edition (1991) by Colin Sara
Second Edition (1996) by Colin Sara
Third Edition (2002) by Colin Sara
Fourth Edition (2008) by Colin Sara
Fifth Edition (2011) by Colin Sara

Published in 2011 by
Sweet & Maxwell, 100 Avenue Road, London NW3 3PF
Part of Thomson Reuters (Professional) UK Limited
(Registered in England & Wales, Company No.1679046. Registered Office and
address for service: Aldgate House, 33 Aldgate High Street, London EC3N 1DL)

For further information on our products and services, visit
www.sweetandmaxwell.co.uk

Typeset by LBJ Typesetting Ltd of Kingsclere
Printed and bound in Great Britain by
Antony Rowe, CPI Group (UK) Ltd, Croydon, CRO 4YY

No natural forests were destroyed to make this product;
only farmed timber was used and re-planted.

A CIP catalogue record for this book
is available from the British Library

ISBN 978 0 414 04806 5 (Hardback)

Acknowledgments

I would like to thank St Catherine's College, Oxford, my *alma mater*, and the Bodleian Library, Oxford, for their support on my research visits; the Librarian and staff of Bristol Law Society Library, for their help and welcome; my former colleagues at the Bar for all the nice things they have said about the previous Editions and, of course, my wife Isobel and all my family and friends for their encouragement throughout this sometimes daunting project.

I also wish to thank the Stationery Office for permission to reproduce the following:

Land Registry Forms 313, SIM, PN1, OC1, ADV1, ADV2, DB, HC1, K3, K4.

Preface to the Fifth Edition

When I started preparing this Fifth Edition I wondered for a minute whether it was still relevant and important in the modern world. After all, the volume of legislation relating to this area in the last few years has not been that great.

However, as I looked through the authorities I realised first of all how many Court of Appeal judgments there are. The percentage of the Court of Appeal's work-load which is made up of boundary and easements disputes is amazingly high, between 10 and 20 per cent. This has unsurprisingly led to numerous judicial comments about the triviality of many disputes and ways of avoiding it.

"There are too many calamitous neighbour disputes in the Court."[1]
But, as Sir John Mummery has said:

> "It should be emphasised that in the civil justice system the parties to these local property disputes are just as entitled to have them decided according to the same high standards as parties in every other kind of case. Contested rights about property of modest value can matter as much to the parties as large sums or big issues matter to the parties in more complex cases. The cases are often as human in their impact on daily lives as those about the fundamental rights in the Human Rights Act 1998. The users of the civil justice system will rightly judge it on the quality of the courteous care and attention, the procedural fairness and the impartial adjudication that it aims to achieve in all proceedings".[2]

A person's house is his most valued possession and any perceived or actual attack on it or its garden is taken very personally. Practitioners have always moaned about boundary disputes, which seem less "sexy" than murder or massive commercial disputes, but the minutiae of these cases often says more about Britain today that an argument about share options.

Now the Law Commission has entered the fray with a full Report "Making Land Work: Easements, Covenants and Profits à Prendre"

---

[1] *Bradford v James* [2008] EWCA Civ 837.
[2] *Wilkinson v Farmer* [2010] EWCA Civ 1148 at para.5.

complete with a draft bill. The recommendations (which are considered in the course of the text) are, however, aimed more at simplifying the system and making it fairer than in avoiding disputes. Indeed, much of judicial development has tended towards preferring justice to certainty.

The truth is that boundary disputes have existed since Cain murdered Abel and are a perfect example of the rule of law overriding direct action.

Preparing this edition has done nothing to dampen my enthusiasm for an area of law which is both intellectually satisfying and important to many people (even if some of them are very annoying).

The law is as stated at June 30, 2011.

Preface to the First Edition

The aim of this book is to provide in one volume all the material which a practitioner would require to conduct an action involving a boundary dispute or an easement claim. For most members of the bar, the words "I've got a boundary dispute for you" create more a sense of apprehension than joy. I suspect most solicitors feel a similar sense of dread when a client begins to tell them the sorry tale. I found, however, over 20 years of practice, that boundary and easements disputes are rewarding both for the legal issues raised and the social history they uncover. The evidence in a prescriptive claim to a right of way can often unfold the history of a tiny corner of the country over a period of up to 100 years, moving from visits by the vicar on horseback, through carrying water from the well, up to the arrival of combine harvesters and satellite dish deliveries.

The reason why boundaries and easements have been treated together in one book is because that is how they often arise in practice. Many is the time when a claim to a way, or a right of support or a right to take water through a pipe is coupled with a claim to ownership of the disputed way or of land nearby. That is why they are often lumped together as "boundary disputes".

I appreciate, of course, that the law of boundaries and the law of easements do not often overlap. That is why the book is divided into two different sections. However, the jurisdiction and procedural issues are largely common between the two topics and are accordingly dealt with in a third section.

In setting out to write a book for practitioners I was determined to state the law as it is, without historical analysis and, therefore, to cite the latest case rather than the oldest. My original intention was to ensure that every case cited came from this century, but as I delved into the more obscure corners of the law I realised that many points had simply not been covered for 100 years. This led me to read not only the modern authorities, but some at least of the older ones. As I did so, my admiration for the late 19th century judges grew. Their English is clear, their grasp of the basic concepts secure and they come across as practical men who understand the ways of the world. The same can often be said of those who grace the bench today, but not always, and there are many 19th century quotations which I have omitted with regret, in favour of a more modern pronouncement.

The book, therefore, tries to provide the necessary information for someone preparing or presenting a case about boundaries or easements.

It does not, of course, cover every aspect of court practice, but neverthe-less tries to address not only the legal problems which may arise, but also some of the practical problems of case preparation, procedural steps and remedies which are peculiar to this kind of litigation. It is not primarily aimed at the specialist practitioner, rare in this field anyway, but at barris-ters and solicitors who find themselves dealing with such cases from time to time and want a book to which they can turn to answer their questions. Only time will tell whether it has achieved this aim.

I would like to thank my publishers for the help, support and encour-agement they have given me as I ploughed through the necessary research, composition and checking and to thank Elizabeth Burroughs for preparing the index, and Mike Bowden for preparing the tables.

Colin Sara

May 1991

Contents

Part I: Boundaries

Chapter Four: Boundaries of Registered Land

Chapter Five: Adverse Possession

Chapter Six: Party Structures

Chapter Seven: Highways

Chapter Eight: Water Boundaries

Part II: Easements

Part III: Remedies

Part IV: Precedents

Abbreviations

CCR   County Court Rules
CPR   Civil Procedure Rules
RSC   Rules of the Supreme Court

Table of Cases

Table of Statutes

Table of Statutory Instruments

Part I:
Boundaries

Chapter One
The Conveyance

1. The original conveyance

When a book has been in existence for 20 years, it is a good idea to look **1.01** afresh to see whether it is starting from the right place. By now nearly all boundary disputes involve registered land, the title of which derives from the fact of registration rather than a good root of title. However, it is apparent from the recent authorities that boundary disputes still turn, more often than not, on the history of the properties and the words used to describe what is or is not included.

It is tempting to start from the process of registration and omit the word "Conveyance". However, a glance of the Law List will show that solicitors still list their specialisms as "conveyancing" and the leading periodical is still called the "Conveyancer".

More importantly the fact that most titles are now registered has not obviated the need for boundary disputes because, even following the introduction of a better system for fixing boundaries through the Land Registry Adjudicator,[1] most boundaries on registered titles are not precise and are still subject to the general boundaries rule. The inter-relationship between boundaries of registered and unregistered land has, in many ways, added to the complexity of resolving boundary disputes. The system for fixing boundaries introduced by the Land Registration Act 2002[2] may affect the way in which boundary disputes are conducted in the future, but it will be a very long time before all boundaries are re-registered as fixed boundaries. It is still appropriate, therefore, to start a book on Boundaries and Easements with consideration of the Conveyance, especially as it was in conveyances, rather than transfers, that so many of the boundaries that lead to litigation, started life.

Whatever the date of registration, the primary source of the boundary line between any[3] two properties is the conveyance whereby their ownership was divided. While many building plots have been laid out in recent years, there are also many boundaries which go back hundreds if not thousands of

---

[1] Sections 107 to 114 of the Land Registration Act 2002 and Ch.4 below.
[2] Rule 122 of the Land Registration Rules 2003.
[3] *Steward v Gallop* [2011] 1 P. & C.R. 347.

years. Nevertheless the first step when presented with a boundary dispute is to try to identify and inspect this first conveyance[4] or transfer. This may seem obvious, but it is by no means universally practised. Many is the boundary dispute where the parties seem to think it enough to look at their own Land Certificate or conveyance without looking back further.[5]

Registration of title is not intended to change the boundary with adjoining properties. A boundary dispute may arise on first registration, or on a transfer or simply where an owner or occupier has decided to annex land in the belief that he is entitled to do so or even in the hope that he will get away with it. Even if the Land Certificate or Transfer appears to be plain, it may conflict with the neighbouring title. Therefore it may be necessary to go behind the registration to discover the true and original boundary. The specific problems of Land Registration are dealt with in Chapter Four. However, the basic principles are the same whether the land is registered or unregistered.

1.02   One of the difficulties in respect of registered land is that the registration is sufficient proof of ownership and registration is the basis of title. As a result earlier deeds may not be available. Even where title deeds are available from before the registration, it is easy, when representing a client, to assume that his initial conveyance is the governing one. However, experience has shown that errors can creep into conveyances and it is important, having found the client's first conveyance, to compare it with the initial conveyance of the other party who may have bought from a common vendor. If the land was conveyed to the other party first, it is of no value to the client to show that the vendor purported to convey the same land again two days later[6] (except perhaps on a claim against the vendor for breach of covenant of title or misrepresentation).

When perusing deeds, particularly plans, it is always advisable to look at the original. Photocopying may often cover over points which appear on the original and, in some cases, the colouring put onto the photocopy plan may not correspond with the original. It is particularly dangerous to rely on abstracts without checking against the originals where available.

2.   The parcels

1.03   The relevant part of the conveyance for establishing the boundary is the parcels clause (i.e. from "ALL THAT"). This clause will often refer to the plan, but it is a mistake to go straight to the plan without

---

[4] *Alan Wibberley Building Ltd v Insley* [1999] 1 W.L.R. 894 per Lord Hoffman at 895h; (1999) 78 P. & C.R. 327.

[5] "Thus the relevant conveyance is that from Sudemoor to Mr Longstaff. Unfortunately, it was not adduced in evidence" per Vice Chancellor in *Konstantinidis v Townsend* [2003] EWCA Civ 538 at [3]. One of many examples of this is *Frazer v Martin* [2010] 1 P. & C.R. 268 where the disputed land was omitted from the filed plan by mistake.

[6] *Scarfe v Adams* [1981] 1 All E.R. 843.

discovering what other descriptions are contained in the parcels clause and what reference, if any, is made to the plan.

Descriptions in the parcels are many and various, but a number of elements are commonly found.

(a)   The name of the property

Where a property has existed as an entity before the conveyance it is **1.04** logical to suppose that the extent of the conveyance corresponds to the previously existing entity. Over the last hundred years or so there has been a massive movement towards individual home ownership. Accordingly, a property conveyed has often been previously tenanted. The description of the property therefore as, for example, "the property known as Vine Cottage"[7] is of real importance. In such a case it will be important to establish what was the extent of "the property known as Vine Cottage" at the time of the first conveyance.[8] Was the shed at the bottom of the garden a woodshed used in conjunction with Vine Cottage or was it a communal wash-house used by everyone in the terrace? It does not, of course, necessarily follow that the vendor intended to convey to the purchaser the full extent of the property previously occupied as such or indeed that the purchaser had not agreed to purchase some additional land, but the extent of the property as it existed at the date of the first conveyance is an important starting point.

(b)   The description

Various descriptions are used in conveyances. Examples are "dwelling- **1.05** house", "messuage", "curtilage" and "appurtenances", but there are other less legalistic descriptions, such as "TOGETHER WITH the garden, coach-house and garage erected thereon". Generally the construction is a matter of common-sense. However, several terms have been the subject of judicial interpretation.

"Dwelling-house" is not restricted to that part of the property in which the inhabitants actually dwell. It includes the cellars below the property, even if used for something else,[9] "as well as the foundations and surface of the earth on which the house stands".[10] It might, however, be used to exclude something separate from the dwelling-house, such as a shop which formed part of the building and was otherwise within the description in the parcels. It is not necessary that the house be occupied. Empty and derelict buildings remain dwelling-houses as long as they

---

[7] Cf. *Neilson v Poole* (1969) 20 P. & C.R. 909. "If one enquired what property was 'known as' Bridge House" the answer would have been that it included the disputed land", *Frazer v Martin* [2010] 1 P. & C.R. 268.

[8] *Freeguard v Rogers* [1999] 1 W.L.R. 375 at 381 per Peter Gibson L.J.

[9] *Grigsby v Melville* [1974] 1 W.L.R. 80; [1973] 3 All E.R. 455.

[10] per Stamp L.J.

retain their physical structure and character.[11] Conversely a dwelling-house need not be a whole house. Any unit of occupation such as a flat can be a dwelling-house.

"Messuage" is commonly used in conjunction with "dwelling-house". Although it does not necessarily add to the definition,[12]

> "a house and messuage differ in that a house cannot be intended other than the matter of a building, but a messuage shall be said all the mansion place and the curtilage shall be taken as parcel of the messuage".[13]

It therefore includes "not only the house itself, but the outbuildings, courtyard, garden and adjacent land used and occupied with it".[14] According to this definition "curtilage" is included within "messuage".

1.06   The meaning of "curtilage" was defined by Buckley L.J. in *Methuen-Campbell v Walters*[15] as being something intimately associated with the house or other building.

> "This may extend to ancillary buildings, structures or areas such as outhouses, a garage, a driveway, a garden and so forth".

Whether or not particular land is within the curtilage is a question of fact. The fact that land is used in conjunction with the house is not enough, especially where it is separated off. Thus a paddock, which may provide a useful amenity or convenience for the occupant of the house, is not within the curtilage of the house.[16]

> "For land to be curtilage to a church, both must be occupied together in a physical sense their title not being such as to conflict with them belonging together."[17]

"Curtilage" does not only apply to a single dwelling. A block of flats, for example, may have its own curtilage.[18] The curtilage of a flat includes the curtilage of the premises of which it forms part. So a sixth floor attic store-room, used in conjunction with a second floor flat can be regarded as being within the curtilage of that flat.[19]

---

[11] *Re 1–4 White Row Cottages, Bewerley* [1991] Ch. 441; [1991] 3 W.L.R. 229.

[12] *Fenn v Grafton* (1836) 2 Bing N.C. 617 per Tindall C.J. at 618–95.

[13] 5 Termes de la Ley quoted with approval by Tindall C.J. in *Fenn v Grafton* (1836) 2 Bing. N.C. at 617, 619.

[14] *Royal Sydney G.C. v Fed. Comm of Taxation* (1950) 91 C.L.R. 610 at 625.

[15] [1979] Q.B. 525 at 543.

[16] *Methuen-Campbell v Walters* [1979] Q.B. 525; [1979] 1 All E.R. 606.

[17] *Re St. John's Church* [1967] P. 113.

[18] *Dartmouth Court Blackheath Ltd. v Berisworth Ltd* [2008] EWHC 350 (Ch), [2008] 1 P. & C.R. DG 23.

[19] *Cadogan v McGirk* [1996] 4 All E.R. 643; (1997) 73 P. & C.R. 483.

A "house" need not necessarily be a dwelling-house nor is a dwelling-house necessarily a house. It is easier to recognise a house when you see one than to define it. Whereas a flat can be a dwelling-house it cannot be a house:

> "It seems to me as impossible to hold that a single tenement is a house as it would be to hold that a suburban villa is a castle."[20]

The difficulties of trying to find a definition of a house, as opposed to a flat, for the purposes of the Leasehold Reform Act 1967 are demonstrated by *Malekshad v Howard de Walden Estate*[21] where the House of Lords exercised its collective mind in applying a definition of a house which applied where a building was divided vertically (like a semi-detached house or a terrace house). But what about a house which has a basement which goes under the house next door? Surely that is still a house? Not, it seems, on the definition in the 1967 Act.

Equally   **1.07**

> "I do not think that a tower block of flats would reasonably be called a house. But I think a four-storied building like the present one is reasonably called a house."[22]

This is so even if the house is in multiple occupation.

Although the word "garden" is often used in conveyances it has not often been the subject of judicial consideration. The Oxford English Dictionary definition is "an enclosed piece of ground devoted to the cultivation of flowers, fruit or vegetables". Many readers surveying neighbouring gardens, if not their own, might doubt that definition. In *Cresstock Investments Ltd v Commons Commissioner*,[23] that definition was significantly extended, as least in relation to land excluded from a common:

> "Frequently parts of a large garden are left wild and uncultivated. They remain available for cultivation and use and form part of the garden."

It is suggested that there are two factors, one that it is "enclosed", though this will not necessarily mean a fence, and the other that it is ancillary to the dwelling-house. There is also the negative factor that it must not be used for grazing or farming,[24] though it may include an orchard which is

---

[20] per Salmon L.J. in *Okereke v Brent LBC* [1967] 1 Q.B. 42 at 61.
[21] [2003] 1 A.C. 1013.
[22] per Lord Denning M.R. in *Lake v Bennett* [1970] 1 Q.B. 663.
[23] [1992] 1 W.L.R. 1088; [1993] 1 All E.R. 213.
[24] *Re Land at Freshfields* 91 L.G.R. 502; (1993) 66 P. & C.R. 9.

ancillary to the house, rather than a commercial operation.[25] Thus it would not include fields abutting the garden of a country house "in which those who dwell in the house may walk or play".[26]

1.08   A conveyance of land will usually include the buildings erected thereon:

> " 'Land' includes land of any tenure ... buildings or parts of buildings (whether the division is horizontal, vertical or made in any other way) and other corporeal hereditaments . . .".[27]

However, this presumption can be countered where the clear intention of the parties was to the contrary. Thus in a lease which described the demised premises as "the land and buildings constructed thereon", a rent review clause which referred to "the land" was construed to mean the land valued as in its undeveloped state.[28]

"Building" is not defined in the Law of Property Act. In relation to planning development it is defined in s.336(1) of the Town and Country Planning Act 1990 as including "any structure or erection". It will include, for example, a chalet.[29] However, it was accepted in that case that by agreement buildings such as chalets can be separated from the land so that they remain in the ownership of the licensees.

"Appurtenances" includes what is within the curtilage of a parcel of land[30] but also incorporeal hereditaments and anything which "belongs to or is usually enjoyed with the property".[31] Thus, in respect of a flat, it would include a storeroom or outhouse used in connection with the flat, even though it was not within the curtilage of the flat itself.[32] Where the context indicates it, this wider definition supersedes the older, strict definition of "appurtenance" as referring only to incorporeal hereditaments.[33]

On the other hand, "an 'outhouse' is an outbuilding or outside building in the grounds of or adjoining a principal building".[34] It does not, therefore, include any room, such as a storeroom, which is outside the curtilage of the flat itself, but still inside the principal building. Equally, a block of garages adjacent to a block of flats, but which is not directly connected to the ownership of the flats may not be appurtenant to the block.[35]

---

[25] *Sir Richard Storey v Commons Commissioner* (1993) 66 P. & C.R. 206.
[26] *Re Land at Freshfields* (1993) 66 P. & C.R. 9 per Warner J. at [13].
[27] Law of Property Act 1925 s.205(1)(ix).
[28] *Braid v Walsall MBC* (1999) 78 P. & C.R. 94.
[29] *R. v Swansea City Council Ex p. Elitestone Ltd* (1993) 66 P. & C.R. 422; [1993] 2 P.L.R. 65.
[30] *Methuen-Campbell v Walters* [1979] Q.B. 525; *Frazer v Martin* [2010] 1 P. & C.R. 268.
[31] *Methuen-Campbell v Walters* [1979] 1 Q.B. 525.
[32] Leasehold Reform, Housing and Urban Development Act 1993 s.62(2) and *Cadogan v McGirk* [1996] 4 All E.R. 643; (1997) 29 H.L.R. 294.
[33] *Trim v Sturminster Rural DC* [1938] 2 K.B. 508; *Frazer v Martin* [2010] 1 P.& C.R. 268
[34] *Cadogan v McGirk* [1996] 4 All E.R. 643; (1997) 73 P. & C.R. 483 at 489 per Millett L.J.
[35] *Dartworth Court Blackheath Ltd v Berisworth Ltd* [2008] EWHC 350 (Ch); [2008] 2 P. & C.R. 3.

"Forecourt" is a term usually associated with commercial premises. Despite its apparent reference to the front of the premises, it has been held to "encompass an outer court, which was not located at the front of the building or at a road frontage".[36]

(c)   Occupation

It seems often to have been assumed that to describe a property as **1.09** "ALL THAT property known as Vine Cottage and formerly in the occupation of Enoch Cribbins" would be enough to define its precise boundaries for posterity. It may be very hard to discover precisely what property Enoch Cribbins occupied. Identifying the former occupier, however, does serve to complement the description emanating from the name of the property and in rural areas where numbers and names of properties have often changed over the years it may be the only way of identifying which of the various parcels of land shown on a later plan was being referred to, though this is more often the case in respect of minor rights and incumbrances referred to in the deeds.

The identification of the former occupier has an additional value in that it provides a basis for finding out who would be a likely witness as to the extent of the property. Enoch Cribbins may well be remembered in the village and someone will know where his relatives live. His relatives in turn may well remember playing in the garden or using the shed.

(d)   Measurement

Measurements contained in the parcels or the plan may be either **1.10** dimensions or areas or even lines drawn between two points of uncertain identity.[37] Either have their pitfalls. To begin with they may simply be wrong. Equally it may be almost impossible to establish a datum point. Area measurements, anyway, can only be used as a check since they cannot establish the shape of the property. Furthermore there is more than one way of measuring the area of a piece of land and two surveyors will not necessary reach the same result. Nevertheless, it is important not to ignore the measurements and areas, whether shown in the body of the conveyance[38] or the plan. In *Cook v J D Wetherspoon Plc*[39] there was a stark conflict between the Transfer plan as scaled up (which showed a boundary at 30') and the measurement written on the plan (40'). The Court of Appeal accepted that this showed a clear ambiguity on the face of the

---

[36] per Kitchin J. in *Roadside Group Ltd v Zara Commercial Ltd* [2010] EWHC 1950 (Ch); [2011] 1 P. & C.R. DG5.
[37] See *Joyce v Rigolli* [2004] EWCA Civ 79 where the crucial boundary was between two points "C" and "D" which could not be precisely identified.
[38] *Wigginton & Milner v Winster Engineering Ltd* [1978] 1 W.L.R. 1462; [1978] 3 All E.R. 436.
[39] [2006] EWCA Civ 330; [2006] 2 P. & C.R. 18.

Transfer and decided between the two on the basis of the topography on the land, in the form of the edge of the concrete car park.

(e)   Ordnance Survey numbers

1.11   Even before land had to be registered with a site plan referring to Ordnance Survey number, farmland was normally conveyed by reference to such numbers often set out in a schedule. If properly drafted, the parcels should explain which edition is being used. The first edition dated from 1880 to 1881 and the second edition is 1903–4.[40] Since then there have been numerous new editions and revisions. It is important to establish, therefore, which edition is being referred to. It is not necessarily the one which was current at the time of the conveyance. Where it is not expressly stated in the parcels, it can usually be established by the numbers themselves, as the numbers are usually changed between editions though often not on revisions. It may also be necessary to see which edition is actually used as the basis of the plan even where there is no mention of the Ordnance Survey anywhere in the parcels. It is important to note than an Ordnance Survey number mentioned in the body of the deed will take priority over an "identification only" plan.[41] The Ordnance Survey map, therefore, may well be crucial in deciding the boundary at the time of the original conveyance.

With regard to registered land, the starting point will be the plan shown on the Land Certificate. The Ordnance Survey general map is now held on computer and is subject to continuous revision. This means that there is a possibility that the plans used on registration of contiguous land will differ. This is an especial risk where the boundary dispute relates to an incursion which has taken place after the registration of one parcel of land, but before the registration of the other. However, since compulsory registration has now been extended to all land and most dealings with land,[42] the appropriate Ordnance Survey map will be crystallised at the time of the registration.

(f)   The plan

1.12   The significance of the plan in comparison with other conveyancing documents has been the subject of many authorities.[43] Some general principles can be formulated, but they are by no means easy to apply to any particular facts.

A plan may be referred to in the parcels or may simply be bound into the conveyance. Where it is referred to in the parcels, the weight to be

---

[40] For a full explanation of the way in which Ordnance Survey maps are drawn up, see J.R.S. Booth, *Public Boundaries & Ordnance Survey 1840–1980* (Southampton: Ordnance Survey 1980).

[41] *Wigginton & Milner v Winster Engineering Ltd* [1978] 1 W.L.R. 1462; [1978] 3 All E.R. 436.

[42] Land Registration Act 2002 s.4.

[43] Most recently, *Strachey v Ramage* [2008] 2 P. & C.R. 154.

given to it in comparison with other elements in the parcels will depend on the terms of the reference. A general incorporation such as "as shown on the plan annexed hereto" will give the plan equal weight to the other aspects of the conveyance and, where there is ambiguity, extrinsic evidence can be used.

Frequently plans are incorporated with the words "for the purposes of **1.13** identification only more particularly delineated on the plan annexed hereto". Megarry J. in *Neilson v Poole*[44] has pointed out the incompatibility of these two phrases. How can a plan only to be used for identifying the property be said to delineate it? However, whatever may be achieved by critical analysis of the phrase there is no doubt that the words "for the purpose of identification only" relegate the plan to a subordinate position in comparison with other elements of the parcels. The law was authoritatively stated by Buckley L.J. in *Wigginton & Milner v Winster Engineering*[45]:

"When a court is required to decide what property passed under a particular conveyance, it must have regard to the conveyance as a whole, including any plan which forms part of it. It is from the conveyance as a whole that the intention must be ascertained. To the extent that the conveyance stipulates that one part of it shall prevail over another part of it, in the event of there being any contradiction between them in the ascertainment of the parties' intention, the court must of course give effect to that stipulation. So if the conveyance stipulates that the plan shall not control the description of the parcels, the court must have due regard to that stipulation; but insofar as the plan does not conflict with the parcels I can see no reason why, because it is described as being 'for identification only', it should not be looked at to assist in understanding the description of the parcels. The process of identification is in fact the process of discovering what land was intended to pass under the conveyance, and that is the precise purpose which the plan is said to serve. Accordingly, so long as the plan does not come into conflict with anything which is explicit in the description of the parcels, the fact that it is said to be 'for the purposes of identification only' does not appear to me to exclude it from consideration in solving problems which are left undecided by what is explicit in the description of any parcel."

The inter-relationship between the wording of the conveyance, the plan and the surrounding circumstances was considered recently in *Strachey v*

[44] *Neilson v Poole* (1969) 20 P. & C.R. 909 at 915–6.
[45] *Wigginton & Milner v Winster Engineering Ltd* [1978] 1 W.L.R. 1462; [1978] 3 All E.R. 436. See for example *Johnson v Shaw* [2004] 1 P. & C.R. 123, where the judgment of Peter Gibson L.J. is quoted and *Seeckts v Derwent* [2004] EWCA Civ 393 where it is expressly followed.

Ramage.[46] In some cases the parcels clause gives no real clue about the boundary apart from the reference to the plan. However, where, as in *Strachey*, there is a specific reference in the conveyance to a "boundary fence" and there is a fence in existence which is different from the "identification only" plan, then it is all the easier to override the plan in favour of the physical boundary.

One feature of plans, often seen, but not previously commented on in the authorities, is the presence of "T" marks (not to be confused with tie marks (*f*) in OS maps[47]). A "T" mark is used to show which side own the boundary fence. These were used in *Seeckts v Derwent*[48] as an important, and finally decisive, piece of evidence.

It is easy to concentrate too heavily on the plan. In *Hatfield v Moss*[49] the roof area was held to be included in a demise of the top floor, even though it was not expressly mentioned in the parcels and it was outside the area shown by the red line on the plan. The Court of Appeal was more swayed by the fact that there was access to the roof space from the flat demised than about the details of the parcels. In *Druce v Druce*[50] express terms of the description took priority over an "identification only" plan.

Furthermore plans may or may not be to scale and, in any event, it must be remembered that scaling up from small plans is always dangerous and that even where a scale is mentioned this may simply have been copied from some other document e.g. a plan annexed to a conveyance may be a reduced photocopy of a scale plan. Most conveyancing plans are not drawn up by surveyors, but conveyancing clerks.

The courts may huff and puff[51] but judges have learnt over the years that plans, however neat and well drawn they may seem, can be misleading and that notional lines drawn on the ground on the basis of plans have less validity than actual lines that appear from features that can be seen.[52]

A rather more sympathetic approach to the problems faced by conveyancers can be found in *Seeckts v Derwent*.[53] Very often conveyancers have more important concerns than the precise line of the boundary and the Law Commission[54] has warned against the exercise

---

[46] [2008] 2 P. & C.R. 154.
[47] See para.2.10 below.
[48] *Seeckts v Derwent* [2004] EWCA Civ 393. "In my view it is not possible to disregard the ordinary understanding of the T-marks. The natural implication is that they were intended to represent existing boundary features and that those features were to belong to Clock House" per Carnwath L.J. at para.28.
[49] *Hatfield v Moss* [1988] 2 E.G.L.R. 58.
[50] *Druce v Druce* [2003] EWCA Civ 535; [2004] 1 P. & C.R. 26.
[51] *Scarfe v Adams* [1981] 1 All E.R. 843.
[52] *Willson v Greene* [1971] 1 W.L.R. 635; (1971) 22 P. & C.R. 697; *Hatfield v Moss* [1988] 2 E.G.L.R. 58.
[53] *Seeckts v Derwent* [2004] EWCA Civ 393.
[54] Law Commission, *Land Registration for the Twenty-First Century: A Conveyancing Revolution* (London: The Stationery Office, 2001) Law Com. No. 271.

"... the process of fixing a boundary will all too likely create a boundary dispute where none had existed"

3. Construing the parcels

Each of the elements set out above can be important in construing the **1.14** parcels. Any judge seeking to construe the parcels will be keen to carry out the intention of the parties to the conveyance as he sees them. It is, therefore, dangerous to rely too heavily on rules of construction. The court will always try not to construe a deed in a way which creates an absurdity. If the line as drawn goes through someone's living room, or if it involves depriving one person of a playroom to which the other will then have no access[55] the court will take pains to reject it, whatever the rules of construction suggest.[56] A boundary fence which differs from the plan is bound to encourage the court to relegate the plan to what the parties intended.[57] The question is "What would the reasonable layman think he was in fact buying?",[58] though the answer to this question may well be that the "reasonable" purchaser does not think the same as the "reasonable" vendor.

Nevertheless the central rule of construction is the same in all branches of the law. In *Chartbrook Ltd v Persimmon Homes* the House of Lords[59] once again approved the central rule of construction set out by Lord Hoffmann in *Investors Compensation Scheme Ltd v West Bromwich Building Society (No.1)*[60]:

"Interpretation is the ascertainment of the meaning which the document would convey to a reasonable person having all the background knowledge which would reasonably have been available to the parties in the situation in which they were at the time of the contract."

This qualifies the traditional conveyancing principle that where the parcels are clear, extraneous evidence will not be allowed to show that the intention of the parties was different. In *Chartbrook Ltd v Persimmon Homes*[61] Lord Hoffman clarified the extent to which "background" evidence will be

---

[55] *Hatfield v Moss* [1988] 2 E.G.L.R. 58.
[56] See *Cook v J D Wetherspoon Plc* [2006] EWCA Civ 330; [2006] 2 P. & C.R. 18, where the measurement written on the plan would have gone through a building, while scaling the strip of land from the plan made perfect sense.
[57] *Strachey v Ramage* [2008] 2 P. & C.R. 154.
[58] per Butler Sloss L.J. in *Topliss v Green* [1992] EGCS 20 quoted with approval in *Seeckts v Derwent* [2004] EWCA Civ 393.
[59] [2009] 1 A.C. 1101; [2010] 1 P. & C.R.162.
[60] [1998] 1 W.L.R. 896 at 912.
[61] *Chartbrook Ltd v Persimmon Homes* [2009] UKHL 38; [2009] 1 A.C. 1101; [2010] 1 P. & C.R. 162.

allowed to contradict the clear terms of the Conveyance. In many ways that was, in reality, an example of mistake, but the case re-emphasised again how Courts are reluctant to interpret documents against common-sense:

> "The general rule ... is that there are no conceptual limits to what can properly be regarded as background".[62]

The House of Lords did, however, re-affirm the rule in *Prenn v Simonds*[63] that pre-contractual negotiations are inadmissible. However, despite pressure to try to limit the extent of evidence which can be called to cast doubt on the interpretation of the words of the conveyance, Lord Hoffman still insisted that even pre-contractual documents, which are not facts but assertions by the parties, can be referred to as "background".

What all these different formulations show is that the rules of construction are used by the judiciary to do justice between the parties, even at the expense of certainty. Although there are some cases where a more restrictive approach has been taken[64] the overall approach in recent years has been to allow extensive evidence to be called and then to decide on all the information before the court, albeit giving precedence to the conveyancing documents.

The parcels may comprise the five elements set out above or indeed any other description that seemed relevant to the draftsman.[65] If "the property known as Vine Cottage" does not correspond to the plan then there is an ambiguity. If the property formerly occupied by Enoch Cribbins does not correspond with the measurements set out in the plan then there is an ambiguity. If the boundary fence is not where the boundary is shown on the plan then there is an ambiguity.[66]

All the recent authorities seem to show that it is very rare that any piece of evidence, whether from the plan, the topography of the land or evidence about what the parties think the boundary is will be excluded from presentation in the case, even if this means that the time taken to hear the case is extended.

The various kinds of evidence which may be used where the conveyance does give rise to ambiguity are considered in Chapter Two.

---

[62] per Lord Hoffmann at [33].
[63] [1971] 1 W.L.R. 1381.
[64] e.g. *Horn v Phillips* [2003] EWCA Civ 1877.
[65] Such as the tie marks referred to above.
[66] *Strachey v Ramage* [2008] 2 P. & C.R. 154.

Chapter Two
Extrinsic Evidence

As set out in Chapter One, where the original conveyance is not avail- **2.01** able or where the parcels are not clear, either because they leave room for doubt or because they are self-contradictory, it is possible to look at extrinsic evidence. In practice it will be rare, where a boundary dispute has arisen, for the deed to be so clear as to brook no argument since presumably the other party has an argument of some sort to put forward in support of his case. So it would be a brave solicitor who prepared a case on the basis of a conveyance without checking it against other evidence, and a brave advocate who relied solely on the terms of conveyance without seeking to adduce any other evidence.

1.   Other deeds

If the operative conveyance is not the first registration or a registered **2.02** transfer it is likely that, since the operative conveyance, one or both of the parcels of land have been registered. Before registration there will have been other conveyances, mortgages, assents, deeds of release, etc. Some of these may not be part of the deeds as such, for they may be disposals of part of the land and will only be referred to in memoranda attached to or endorsed on the deeds. They may or may not be noted on the Register and may have been lost. Equally the party in dispute may not be the owner of the whole of the land conveyed by the operative conveyance, and that conveyance itself may be held by a third party, leaving the party with only an abstract or a note on the Register. Another possibility is that other properties may have been conveyed at the same time as the conveyance which falls to be construed.

It used to be considered that subsequent conveyances cannot be used to resolve ambiguities in the operative conveyances and this appeared to have been re-affirmed in *Beale v Harvey*.[1] However, consideration of this principle in a series of more recent cases[2] leads to the conclusion that no

---

[1] [2003] EWCA Civ 1883; [2004] 2 P. & C.R. 18.
[2] *Ali v Lane* [2007] 1 P. & C.R. 438; *Haycocks v Neville* [2007] EWCA Civ 78; [2007] 1 E.G.L.R 78 and *Bradford v James* [2008] EWCA Civ 837.

such rule can be relied on. This, however, is subject to the proviso that the subsequent evidence must be of "probative value".[3]

The traditional basic principle is still that subsequent conveyances cannot be used to resolve ambiguities in the operative conveyance. In *Beale v Harvey*,[4] Peter Gibson L.J. expressly found that the principle applied (at least in theory) in commercial cases[5] applies equally to conveyances, even though the issue was expressly left open in *Wigginton & Milner Ltd v Winster Engineering*.[6] Subsequent agreements may be binding boundary agreements, but cannot affect the interpretation of the original conveyance. However, as a matter of common-sense, the way people act after they have entered into a transaction may well be indicative of what they intended at the time. *Bradford v James*,[7] without referring in terms to *Beale v Harvey* expressly decided that,

> "extrinsic evidence of surrounding circumstances and subsequent acts, though not admissible to contradict or vary the 1976 Conveyance plan, is admissible to clarify the aspects of it relating to the position of the boundary".[8]

In *Ali v Lane*[9] the Court of Appeal considered the whole issue of extrinsic evidence including subsequent deeds and conveyances. Carnworth L.J. referred to a dictum of Megarry J.[10] that there is

> "good reason for tending to construe the (original) conveyance as having done what the parties appear to have treated it as doing",

but neither approved or disapproved the dictum.[11] Lord Hoffman's questionable distinction, in *Chartbrook v Persimmon Homes*[12] (which does not directly confront the issue of subsequent deeds) between "background" and probative evidence may well be used to enable parties to call evidence about how the original conveyance has been interpreted in subsequent deeds.

2.03   It is important to note, however, that at best subsequent conveyances and other documents can only be used to assist in construing what the

---

[3] per Carnworth L.J. in *Ali v Lane* at [37].
[4] *Beale v Harvey* [2003] EWCA Civ 1883; [2004] 2 P. & C.R. 18.
[5] *Whitworth Street Estates (Manchester) Ltd v James Miller & Partners Ltd* [1970] A.C. 583.
[6] *Wigginton & Milner Ltd v Winster Engineering* [1978] 1 W.L.R. 1462; [1978] 3 All E.R. 436 at 446g.
[7] *Bradford v James* [2008] EWCA Civ 837.
[8] per Mummery L.J. at [29].
[9] *Ali v Lane* [2007] 1 P. & C.R. 438.
[10] In *Neilson v Poole* (1969) 20 P. & C.R. 909.
[11] *L Schuler AG v Wickman Machine Tool Sales Ltd* [1974] A.C. 235; [1973] 2 W.L.R. 683.
[12] *Chartbrook v Persimmon Homes* [2010] 1 P. & C.R. 16.

parties meant by the original conveyance.[13] They cannot unilaterally alter the extent of the land thereby conveyed unless they amount to a boundary agreement or give rise to an estoppel.[14]

There are also older authorities that restrict the use of recitals. While the operative part of the conveyance can be seen as an act of the parties, the recitals are simply statements of fact. It has been held that such statements have no evidential value[15] unless the recital is twenty years old, in which case there is a statutory rebuttable presumption that what it says is true.[16] However, these decisions were all made before the Civil Evidence Acts 1968 and 1995, and it seems clear that any recital is hearsay evidence and can be admitted after the necessary notices or at the court's discretion.[17]

2. Abstract of title

The word processor and scanner has superseded the recondite art of **2.04** drafting abstracts of title, replacing them with an epitome of the relevant conveyances, death certificates, etc. However, it is easy to forget that less than 50 years ago the typist, and even before that the copywriter, had to prepare laborious abstracts setting out the relevant parts of the various conveyances, all expressed in indirect speech ("thereby" for "hereby", etc.) and in a kind of shorthand.

A purchaser who does not receive the old title deeds on completion (because they are or were needed for some retained land) is entitled only to a verified abstract going back to the root of title, together with an acknowledgment for production of deeds on demand. The abstract has no special evidential status and can only be adduced in evidence as a copy. However, in those cases where the title still includes an abstract, it is always worth checking the abstract against the original especially or all too often plans have become detached and stapled back in the wrong place.

3. Contracts and particulars

There is no doubt that the extrinsic evidence can include non- **2.05** conveyancing documents created before the conveyance.[18]

"Among the dirt of aspirations, proposals and counter-proposals there may gleam the gold of a genuine consensus on some aspect of

---

[13] *Ali v Lane* [2007] 1 P. & C.R. 438.
[14] *Ali v Lane* [2007] 1 P. & C.R. 438.
[15] *Bristow v Cormican* (1877-78) L.R. 3 App. Cas. 641 at 662 per Lord Blackburn.
[16] Law of Property Act 1925 s.45(6).
[17] Civil Evidence Act 1995 s.2, CPR Pt 33.
[18] *Scarfe v Adams* [1981] 1 All E.R. 843 at 849b.

the transaction expressed in terms which would influence an objective observer in construing the language used by the parties in their final agreement".[19]

The most significant of these documents is the contract. A change between the contract and the conveyance[20] may indicate that the parties changed their minds,[21] but where there is an ambiguity it may be the first step towards resolving it. Preliminary inquiries and their replies, auction particulars, architects' plans, estate agents' particulars, etc. come further down the scale, but again they can be invaluable in the difficult process of elucidating the operative conveyance and resolving ambiguities. Equally, where the conveyance is clear they can be used as showing a common intention justifying rectification. It must also be remembered that estate agent's particulars and the replies to preliminary enquiries can often be used to found a concurrent action against the vendor for misrepresentation. In these circumstances, the vendor is added as a second defendant in a claim for damages in case the main action fails. The fear of a claim against him in damages may also help to ensure his co-operation.

4. Documents subsequent to the conveyance

2.06   The problems that relate to abstracts apply equally to all documents produced subsequent to the operative conveyance strictly they cannot help to resolve ambiguities in the governing conveyance, but in practice a subsequent conveyance of the same land in slightly different terms may help to resolve a difficulty.[22] Again, however, it is important to remember that a person cannot convey land that he does not own and therefore that if the governing conveyance, properly construed, does not include the land in dispute, the fact that a subsequent conveyance purported to convey it is irrelevant.

5. Statutory declarations

2.07   Where title deeds are lost or missing, or the title is based on adverse possession, a statutory declaration made by a person with direct knowledge of the land is an acceptable means of establishing title to the satisfaction of a purchaser. As a result, statutory declarations are often treated as if they had some special status in boundary disputes. In fact, however,

---

[19] per Lord Hoffman in *Chartbrook v Persimmon Homes* [2010] 1 P. & C.R. 162 at [32].

[20] *Beale v Harvey* [2003] EWCA Civ 1883; [2004] 2 P. & C.R. 18.

[21] See for example *Chadwick v Abbotsford Properties* [2004] EWHC 1058 (Ch); [2005] 1 P. & C.R. 10.

[22] See *Ali v Lane* [2007] 1 P. & C.R. 438 where the court looked at measurements on related, but subsequent, conveyances to decide on the boundaries and dimensions in the conveyance in dispute.

this is far from the case. Statutory declarations were brought into existence by the Statutory Declarations Act 1835 as an alternative to affidavits. While the courts have power to allow evidence to be given by affidavit, this only applies to affidavits sworn for the purpose of the particular proceedings and headed accordingly. Therefore, strictly, a statutory declaration cannot be treated as an affidavit in the case.

An affidavit prepared for previous proceedings can be used against the person who made it,[23] but normally the statutory declaration is intended to be used in support of the title. It seems, therefore, that before the Civil Evidence Act 1968 the law was correctly stated by Williams on *Vendor and Purchaser*:

> "statutory declarations as to matters of title are not admissible as evidence in litigation unless against the deponent or his privies in estate, blood or law".[24]

Fortunately this problem has been resolved by the Civil Evidence Act 1995, since now statutory declarations, like any other signed statement, can be given in evidence as admissible hearsay evidence providing that the necessary notices are given.

A statutory declaration, therefore, has the same status as any other signed statement, except that its comparatively solemn execution may be seen by the court as giving it additional weight. However, if the deponent is still alive the other side may require his or her attendance to be cross-examined.[25]

6.   Other documents

There is an almost unlimited variety of other documents which may be **2.08** found in the deeds: Searches and Local Searches, Local Authority Enquiries, grants and releases of easements, planning applications and permissions[26] and applications for grants. All these can be useful once the initial hurdle of admitting extrinsic evidence is overcome.

7.   Maps

Reference has already been made to the use of Ordnance Survey maps **2.09** in conveyances. However, where there is ambiguity in the conveyance, contemporaneous maps are often useful in identifying the property

---

[23] *Pritchard, Executrix of Daniel Pritchard, Deceased v Bagshawe and Two Others* (1851) 11 C.B. 459; *Slatterie v Pooley* (1840) 6 M. & W. 664.

[24] Williams, *Vendor and Purchaser*, 3rd edn, p.128.

[25] CPR r.33.4.

[26] *Scott v Martin* [1987] 1 W.L.R. 841; [1987] 2 All E.R. 813; *Stock v David Wilson Homes (Anglia)* [1993] N.P.C. 83.

conveyed or resolving ambiguities. Many older conveyances do not contain a map at all, but rely on a very general description. In such a case a contemporaneous map may be the most objective way of establishing the boundaries and extent of the property.

It is rarely necessary to go any further back than the tithe maps of the middle of the nineteenth century. These can usually be inspected at County Record Offices, though the coverage of the country is not complete. Some are available online. They do not have the authority or accuracy of Ordnance Survey maps, but as they established liability to tithes it is certain that they did not depart too far from the truth.

In relation to land adjoining highways the turnpike maps may also be of use. If the land has been the subject of enclosure there may also be maps relating to this process, but these are likely to go back to the eighteenth century and it is rarely necessary to go back so far.

2.10   The Ordnance Survey is undoubtedly the published map to which any person seeking to establish a boundary will turn first. Although it has strictly no special evidential status it is produced under statutory authority[27] and is generally regarded as authoritative.

When the last Edition was printed, the Ordnance Survey was in the process of setting up the Digital National Framework (DNF) which is to be linked into the Land Registry mapping system.

The idea is that an accurate up-to-date map of the current position should be available without the need for private survey. This can then be compared with the historical evidence available, both older maps and measurements on deeds. The negative for the future will be the difficulty of ensuring that the information obtained from the Ordnance Survey is the same as that available at the time of the conveyance or transfer. The OS website, however, gives the impression that this plan is no nearer completion than it was four years ago.

In the meantime, there is however no significant change in the way the Ordnance Survey is operating. As far as the maps are concerned, they still use lines, areas and symbols. The Ordnance Survey calculates acreages from the middle of the hedge or ditch.[28] This means a conveyance of "O.S. Number 193" will include that land to the middle of the hedge or ditch, providing, of course, that the vendor owned the whole of it. Tie marks ("ʄ") are used to indicate which parcels of land are included in a particular Ordnance Survey number (lines with a tie mark are not boundaries between O.S. numbers), though where the map shows detailed boundaries there is not always room for the tie mark. "T" marks are used on

---

[27] Survey (Great Britain) Acts 1841–1870 repealed in relation to Berwick-upon-Tweed and the Isle of Man by Statute Laws (Repeals) Act 1993 Sch. 1, Pt. XIII.
[28] *Fisher v Winch* [1939] 1 K.B. 666; [1939] 2 All E.R. 144.

conveyance plans to indicate who owns the boundary,[29] but the Ordnance Survey maps have never been concerned with the ownership or occupation of land, only with identifying features on the ground. The significance of the fact that an alleged boundary line was also a parish boundary line was considered in *Scammell v Dicker*.[30]

Apart from the Ordnance Survey it must be remembered that local councils hold the definitive map of footpaths, bridleways and byways[31] and also maps of public highways maintained at the public expense.

Rule 33.6 of the Civil Procedure Rules provides that where plans, photographs and models are to be used in evidence, notice of this must be given by the date for serving witness statements.

8. Photographs

Photographs and video recordings are real evidence. "Real evidence is **2.11** evidence afforded by the production of physical objects for inspection or other examination by the court."[32] This means that photographs speak for themselves and it is not necessary to show who took them. Strictly it is the negatives that are the real evidence, and the prints that are produced from them are to that extent secondary evidence,[33] but in practice prints are normally accepted in evidence without further proof. By r.33.6 of the Civil Procedure Rules notice must be given that photographs are to be used in evidence at the same time as witness statements are served.

Many of the country's more substantial properties have been the subject of aerial photographs and there are many thousands of snapshots, wedding photographs, etc. hidden away. Although it may not always be easy to date such photographs, they have the considerable advantage that they are not susceptible to the vagaries of memory. An old photograph of a disputed feature is of far more use than the testimony of someone who claims to remember it. Many boundary disputes have been won or lost on the basis of a single old photograph showing that, for example, the old shed really was where the plaintiff says it was. The chance of such photographs being forgeries seems remote.

Photographs are, of course, extrinsic evidence and can only be used where there is ambiguity or uncertainty in the operative conveyance, but they rank amongst the most important elements of such evidence.

---

[29] *Seeckts v Derwent* [2004] EWCA. Civ 393 and see para.1.12 above.
[30] [2006] 1 P. & C.R. 52.
[31] See below, Ch. 9.
[32] per Simon P. in *Owners of the Sapporo Maru v Owners of the Statue of Liberty (The Sapporo Maru and The Statue of Liberty)* [1968] 1 W.L.R. 739; [1968] 2 All E.R. 195 at196F quoting E. Cockle, *Cases & Statutes on Evidence*, 10th edn (London: Sweet & Maxwell, 1963), p.348.
[33] *R. v Ali (Maqsud)* [1966] 1 Q.B. 688; [1965] 2 All E.R. 464 at 469C.

2.12   Straying onto the question of presentation, it is perhaps worth reminding practitioners that old prints can be inexpensively reproduced as photographic prints or as colour photocopies and not as black and white photocopies, whether or not the negatives are available. A neatly produced album of photographs will have far more impact than a single copy produced from the witness's inside pocket.

With the increasing use of video camcorders, it is likely that they will increasingly be used to show where the boundary was at a particular time, or to show activities carried on by parties on the disputed land. It seems likely that they will be treated in the same way as photographs.

Another use of camcorders and photographs is to show activities carried on by the other party on the disputed land or on their own land. This is real evidence and therefore normally admissible, but the position is complicated by the Human Rights Act 1998 and art.8 of the European Convention on Human Rights which provides, "Everyone has the right to respect for his private and family life, his home and his correspondence". By s.6 of the Human Rights Act 1998 a court must act in a way that is compatible with this provision. People are entitled to expect that they can do what they like on their own property without being photographed and recorded. On the other hand the tradition of the English courts has been to allow evidence to be adduced however it is obtained. The criminal courts have tended towards admitting surveillance evidence where it is obtained in the course of the investigation,[34] but there is a difference between the need for surveillance "for the prevention of disorder or crime" as provided for in the derogation and allowing surveillance in pursuance of a private dispute.

It seems likely that the counter-argument would be that the submission of this evidence is necessary for a fair trial within art.6, but there were indications before the Human Rights Act that the courts might not take kindly to surreptitious recording.[35]

9.   Publications

2.13   It may be only rarely that there is relevant published material apart from the Ordnance Survey and tithe maps. However, in a case where evidence is limited there are occasions when an antiquarian has mentioned the property in dispute in a way which sheds light on the boundary. Strictly books and publications are hearsay evidence. They are, however, specifically admissible by virtue of s.7(2)(a) of the Civil Evidence Act 1995; it is not, therefore, necessary to go through the procedures required by Court Rules before hearsay evidence can be tendered.[36]

---

[34] See *R. v Mason* [2002] EWCA Crim 385; [2002] 2 Cr. App. R. 38 and *R. v McLeod* [2002] EWCA Crim 989.
[35] *Ventouris v Mountain* (No.2) [1992] 1 W.L.R. 887; [1993] 3 All E.R. 414.
[36] CPR Pt 33.

10.   The site

(a)   Relevance

Often the most important piece of extrinsic evidence is the topography **2.14**
of the site itself. This can be used to resolve ambiguities in the conveyance
document,[37] or to identify the meaning of descriptions. Even when the
conveyance is unambiguous, it is still necessary to translate
the description in the parcels into an actual boundary on the land.[38] The
importance of the topography is receiving increasing recognition in
the authorities.

The site visit is an essential part of the ritual hearing of a boundary
dispute and I have seen a judge, armed with an aerosol, marking the trees
and posts which represented the boundary. It is therefore essential that an
adviser should see the site well before the issue comes to trial, as plans
and photographs can be misleading.

This process of identification can go beyond simply finding a wall,
hedge or trees. A little detective work can often uncover a few buried
stones remaining from an old wall or unevenness in a field representing
a destroyed hedge.

Where two parcels of land are being divided for the first time there may
be no feature to identify the boundary. It is normal practice then to peg
out the proposed boundary. In *Willson v Greene*[39] the line so pegged out
and showing a kink in the boundary line took priority over an "identification only" plan showing the boundary as a straight line. This applied not
only to the first conveyance, in which the purchaser specifically agreed
the pegs, but also (on the issue of breach of covenant of title) to the second
conveyance where the pegs had been seen by the purchaser but not, it
seems, specifically agreed.

The same conclusion was reached in *Clarke v O'Keefe*[40] even though the **2.15**
land was registered and the plan was not supplied "for the purpose of
identification only", although it did show only general boundaries. The
principles were succinctly set out by Lord Hoffman in *Alan Wibberley
Building Ltd v Insley*[41]:

> "The Land Registry uses maps based upon the Ordnance Survey
> which are, of course, usually very accurate. For example, if one field
> is divided from another by a natural feature such as a hedge, the line

---

[37] *Cook v JD Wetherspoon Plc* [2006] EWCA Civ 330; [2006] 2 P. & C.R. 18.
[38] See *Bradford v James* [2008] EWCA Civ 837 where the dog leg on the plan needed to be
explained and therefore gave rise to an ambiguity.
[39] [1971] 1 W.L.R. 635; (1971) 22 P. & C.R. 697.
[40] (2000) 80 P. & C.R. 126.
[41] [1999] 1 W.L.R. 894.

on the Ordnance Survey will indicate the middle line of the hedge. But the effect of the general boundaries rule is that the owner of a field shown on the filed plan only by reference to the Ordnance Survey map does not necessarily own it up to the middle line of the hedge. The precise boundary must, if the question arises, be established by topographical and other evidence."

(b)   Surveys

2.16   Expert evidence is often adduced to explain the conveyance and the plan. The whole process of expert evidence has been changed by the Woolf Reforms, affected by the Civil Procedure Rules 1998. The Practice Direction 35 for experts and assessors, together with the Protocol attached, now applies. The expressed aim is to limit the use of oral evidence to that which is reasonably required. It sets out a number of general obligations placed on experts, in particular their obligation to be truly independent and to prepare a proper written report, addressed to the Court and not the parties and giving details of their qualifications. The Protocol itself sets out in considerable detail the steps that parties who wish to instruct an expert should take. The Protocol also encourages the use of single joint experts. The Rules, meanwhile, still remain in place.

Experts have an overriding duty to the court to help the court on the matters within their expertise.[42] The aim is to bring experts within the same kind of obligation as is owed by counsel and solicitors, (and to try to avoid or at least restrict the increasingly partisan approach. For example,) they can now write directly to the court asking for directions.

Before an expert can give evidence, the party who wants to use him must apply for permission to do so.[43] The court must restrict expert evidence to that which is reasonably required to resolve the proceedings[44] and can then limit the fee recoverable as costs.[45]

The evidence will be given in a written report. There is then a new procedure for written questions to experts.[46] The expert's answers are then treated as part of his report. The Court can require that the experts meet for discussions.

2.17   There has been a change in the approach to joint experts. The Practice Direction clearly contemplates that it is best to appoint a single expert to avoid the cost and contention of having two experts arguing with each

---

[42] CPR r.35.3.
[43] CPR r.35.4.
[44] CPR r.3, 5.1.
[45] CPR r.35.4(4).
[46] CPR r.35.6.

other.[47] However, that approach was challenged in *D (A Child) v Walker*[48] and, more specifically, has been criticised in relation to contentious boundary disputes in *Childs v Vernon*[49] where Toulson L.J. said:

> "The task of a single joint expert in this type of case was going to be very difficult unless his role was quite strictly defined".[50]

If a joint expert is used the Court should set out exactly what he is to do. The complaint in that case was that he had taken part in discussions with the parties and their counsel. The recommendation to use only one joint expert, however, is still there in the Practice Direction.

In practice joint experts are still used in boundary disputes[51] and such use may be effective in reducing costs and avoiding unnecessary differences of opinion. If there is a joint expert the parties should be careful not to seek to influence him and, in particular, not to have discussions with him in the absence of the other party.[52] Usually, if a joint expert is appointed, leave will not be given for another expert.[53]

The new, more formalised, approach to expert evidence indicated by the new Practice Direction risks disguising the limited role of experts in boundary disputes. While such evidence can sometimes be useful and a proper large scale map of the site is often invaluable, care should be taken about the use of such evidence. Surveyors are trained to carry out calculations from information given. They do not necessarily understand the subtleties of "identification only" plans. It is dangerous and often futile to seek to scale up the sort of small scale plan found on conveyances. The "identification only" tag is designed specifically to prevent this. Even where a plan is not expressly "for the purpose of identification only", it must be remembered that it stands to be interpreted in conjunction with any other description in the parcels or from extrinsic evidence. The courts appear to be moving away from reliance on small-scale plans, even when they are not expressed to be for identification only. This specifically relates to Land Registry Plans, which are not tiny and come from the Ordnance Survey. In *Alan Wibberley Building Ltd v Insley*[54] the House of Lords allowed the hedge and ditch presumption to override the Land Registry Plan, where the boundary was shown as running along the middle of the ditch. This followed in the same line as *Clarke v O'Keefe*[55]

---

[47] "[W]here possible, matters requiring expert evidence should be dealt with by only one expert" CPR PD 35 para.1.
[48] *D (A Child) v Walker* [2000] 1 W.L.R. 1382; [2001] H.R.L.R. 1.
[49] [2007] EWCA Civ 305.
[50] *Childs v Vernon* [2007] EWCA Civ 305 at [6].
[51] e.g. *Childs v Vernon* [2007] EWCA Civ 305.
[52] *Childs v Vernon* [2007] EWCA Civ 305 at [18].
[53] *Edwards v Bruce & Hyslop (Brucast) Ltd* [2009] EWHC 2970 (QB).
[54] *Alan Wibberley Building Ltd v Insley* [1999] 1 W.L.R. 894; (1999) 78 P. & C.R. 327.
[55] *Clarke v O'Keefe* (2000) 80 P. & C.R. 126, but decided in 1997.

where staking out of the land overrode a Land Registry Plan. This contrasts with the earlier case of *Rhone v Stephens*[56] (which was not cited) where a plainly mistaken plan, too late to be rectified, took precedence over common sense. The *Clarke v O'Keefe* approach has been taken in nearly all subsequent cases.

2.18   Reliance on the visible features rather than the plan applies particularly where there are traditional boundary features such as walls, fences, hedges, ditches or trees, or even a means of access to the roof spaces.[57] It must be remembered, however, that boundary features can change. A fence may be replaced by a wall. Someone may plant a hedge. The basic rule is that once established, the boundary remains the same unless there is something which can be regarded as a boundary agreement or adverse possession.[58] Where a boundary has been artificially created, there is a greater likelihood that the plan will be relied on.

Similar problems apply in cases of measurements expressed in the parcels or on the plan. Measurements in the parcels are often qualified by the words "or thereabouts" which does not render them useless, since such approximations are recognised by the law,[59] but does prevent an over-exact extrapolation. Where such measurements are not so qualified they gain added significance, but again more general descriptions in the parcels may prevail if the result of putting measurements on the ground is to produce a meaningless boundary. Where the measurements are on an "identification only" plan, their significance is again reduced and they become just one element in the extrinsic evidence to be considered by the court.

It is necessary to remember too that measurement of land is difficult; bends and kinks are not necessarily covered properly in the measurements, an error in the original datum point can destroy the whole hypothesis and different surveyors can produce different measurements from the same land, particularly where the measurement is of areas. However, it is equally wrong to ignore a measurement of dimensions or area contained in a conveyance. The support of the area measurement for one of two alternative interpretations of a plan or description may tip the balance in its favour.

In the end, it is for the judge to make the decision and he is perfectly entitled to reject the views of the expert or experts and develop his own line of reasoning.[60]

---

[56] [1994] 2 A.C. 310; [1994] 2 W.L.R. 429 HL.
[57] See *Hatfield v Moss* [1988] 2 E.G.L.R. 58.
[58] *Haycocks v Neville* [2007] EWCA Civ 78; [2007] 1 E.G.L.R. 78.
[59] *Jolliffe v Baker* (1883) 11 Q.B.D. 255 at 273-274 per Watkin Williams J. See *Horn v Phillips* [2003] EWCA Civ 1877 where Jacob L.J. saw no uncertainty in a reference to "or thereabouts" in the governing description.
[60] *Haycocks v Neville* [2007] EWCA Civ 78.

It is suggested, therefore, that surveyors should be instructed in the first instance to produce a plan of the land as it is and should then be given full details of the various conveyances, the history of the property and the allegations before being asked to carry out measurements on the property.

11.   Boundary features

In resolving a boundary dispute it is very often important not only to **2.19** identify the feature which represents the boundary, but also to ascertain who owns it. The boundary may be a hedge, a fence, a wall, a stream, a shed, a house or may simply be pegged out. Most of these features have substantial width whereas a boundary, like any other line, theoretically has no width. Except in cases of party walls and other party boundaries,[61] the boundary features can either be owned entirely by one adjoining owner or the boundary may run along inside it.

In deciding who owns the boundary feature, it is important to discover whether the operative conveyance was by reference to the Ordnance Survey map. The practice of the Ordnance Survey is to draw the lines along the centre of hedges and other features, unless they are of such a width as to justify a double line (often the case with tracks).

The basic principle is that where land in common ownership is conveyed by reference to an Ordnance Survey map then the boundary must be as shown in the Ordnance Survey map.[62]

Normally this does not cause a problem since the Ordnance Survey map seeks to follow apparent boundaries. However, there is always a danger that this principle will come into conflict with the presumption that where there is a hedge and a ditch the boundary will be on the far side of the ditch from the hedge.[63]

In dealing with this conflict, it is important to distinguish between titles **2.20** where property in common ownership is divided by an operative convey-ance, as happened in *Fisher v Winch*,[64] and a situation where there are two lines of conveyances relating to an ancient boundary, as happened in *Alan Wibberley Building Ltd v Insley*.[65] The House of Lords in the latter case upheld the principles of the hedge and ditch rule in respect of ancient boundaries, even where one party had a conveyance by reference to

---

[61] See Ch.6.
[62] *Fisher v Winch* [1939] 1 K.B. 666; [1939] 2 All E.R. 144.
[63] *Alan Wibberley Building Ltd v Insley* [1999] 1 W.L.R. 894; [1999] 78 P. & C.R. 327; *Steward v Gallop* [2011] 1 P. & C.R. 347.
[64] [1939] 1 K.B. 666; [1939] 2 All E.R. 144.
[65] [1999] 1 W.L.R. 894; [1999] 78 P. & C.R. 327, see also *Hall v Dorling* (1997) 74 P. & C.R. 400.

Ordnance Survey maps.[66] Lord Hoffman[67] apparently distinguished *Fisher v Winch* on the basis of who was making the claim. However, it is perhaps more accurate to concentrate on the operative conveyance. In that case, there was no operative conveyance and therefore the court was faced with two parallel titles.

This principle, therefore must be used with some care, because properties originally conveyed by some other description may have Ordnance Survey descriptions added to the parcels in some subsequent conveyance. If the original operative conveyance either included or excluded the boundary hedge, it follows that a subsequent vendor either could not convey more than he owned, or alternatively is presumed to have intended to convey all of the land he owned and not to retain half a hedge.

Even where it is clear that the operative conveyance is by reference to Ordnance Survey numbers, the authorities are still not absolutely clear. In *Fisher v Winch*[68] land previously in common ownership, though occupied by separate tenants, was conveyed by reference to Ordnance Survey numbers to one of the former tenants. The boundary features between the two parcels of land were a hedge and a ditch. Despite the clarity of the parcels' clause, evidence was admitted that one of the former tenants had cleared out the ditch, indicating that it was occupied with his parcel of land. Although this evidence was rejected as insufficient, Greene M.R. did not go so far as to say that it was irrelevant. He said that it was properly referred to but:

> "Even if, contrary to my view of the evidence, there was sufficient evidence that she was in occupation of that particular ditch, the effect of the conveyance was not necessarily to convey it to her."[69]

It seems therefore that the use of Ordnance Survey numbers in an operative conveyance, while an indication that the boundary is in the middle of the hedge or other feature, is not conclusive.

Where the conveyance is not by reference to Ordnance Survey maps, the two essential factors are inferences about the purpose for which the boundary feature was originally constructed, and evidence about who has maintained it.

12.   Inferences and presumptions

2.21   If a person has a house with a large garden he may wish to surround it with a wall or a hedge. It is reasonable to suppose that he will build

---

[66] See para.2.21 below.
[67] At 900e.
[68] [1939] 1 K.B. 666; [1939] 2 All E.R. 144.
[69] *Fisher v Winch* [1939] 1 K.B. 666 at 673.

28

the wall or plant the hedge on his own land. In respect of agricultural land, it used to be the practice to dig a ditch whose outer edge was at the boundary, to toss the earth inwards to form an earthwork and then to plant a hedge on top of the earthwork. This must in turn go back to the days when people built stockades round their land to protect it from wild animals and human invaders. A ditch outside a stockade is the traditional form of such defences. The so-called "hedge and ditch rule" was affirmed and qualified by the House of Lords in *Alan Wibberley Building Ltd v Instey*[70] where Lord Hoffman[71] explained its rationale and extent:

> "It should be noticed that this rule involves two successive presumptions. First, it is presumed that the ditch was dug after the boundary was drawn. Secondly, it is then presumed that the ditch was dug and the hedge grown in the manner described by Lawrence J.[72] If the first presumption is displaced by evidence which shows that the ditch was in existence before the boundary was drawn, for example, as an internal drainage ditch which was later used as a boundary when part of the land was sold, then there is obviously no room for the reasoning of Lawrence J. to operate."

In examining the boundary features, therefore, an adviser should look for continuity in the wall or hedge. If it seems to be surrounding the property of one of the parties, or surrounding property of which his land once formed part, then this is an indication that the boundary feature belongs with that land. Where the feature is a hedge and a ditch, it will be necessary to look at the purpose of the ditch. If it is part of a drainage system it may be assumed that it pre-dates the boundary.[73] If it surrounds the property, then the "hedge and ditch" rule is more likely to apply. Where a fence is built on the boundary, there is a presumption that the fence itself is owned by the landowner on whose side of the paling the fence post stands.[74] This is because it is assumed that he will foot the post on his own land and then attach the paling on the far side of the posts, so as to have maximum use of his own land.

This intention may be particularly clear where the boundary feature is a building. Of course, it is not uncommon for buildings to be penthouses attached to an existing boundary wall, which may even belong to the adjoining owner. However, where the building seems to have been built complete, there must be a strong inference that the person who built the building built it entirely on land he owned.

---

[70] *Alan Wibberley Building Ltd v Instey* [1999] 1 W.L.R. 894; (1999) 78 P. & C.R. 327.
[71] At 897e.
[72] *Vowles v Miller* (1810) 3 Taunt. 137 at 138.
[73] *Steward v Gallop* [2011] 1 P. & C.R. 347.
[74] *Howe v Hawkes* [2002] EWCA Civ 1136.

2.22   It might be thought that the presumption would go further than this, since a person building a house or other building would find it difficult to construct it right on his boundary without trespassing on adjoining land, and might then have difficulties in keeping it in repair. However, this does not seem to be the case. Quite apart from terraces and semi-detached houses, which are by definition built right up to the boundary line, there are many, many buildings built right on the edge of the plot and it seems that the protection to the owner, if he wishes to repair his land, is an implied easement to enable him to go onto his neighbour's property to effect the repairs,[75] though ownership of the house will be extended to include the eaves and footings, but not the air space above and below them.[76]

2.23   The problems caused by the need to repair, demolish or improve buildings which are close to the boundary were addressed in the Access to Neighbouring Land Act 1992. This enables a person who needs to enter onto adjoining land for the purpose of carrying out works to apply to the court for an access order.

There is no restriction on the person who makes the application. He does not need to show that he owns or has any interest in the land and "the land" includes the whole of a party wall.[77] However, he must show that "the works are reasonably necessary for the preservation of the whole or any part of the dominant land"[78] though such works may incidentally involve alteration, adjustment or improvements or the demolition of buildings.[79] The order can be refused if the disturbance or hardship caused renders it unreasonable to make an order.[80] The Act is dealt with more fully later.[81]

13.   Maintenance

2.24   Against these various indications from the nature of the land and the features constructed on it, evidence will commonly be available of the practice of the occupiers in repairing and maintaining the feature. Hedging and ditching is an important part of agricultural operations and even in a domestic context walls have to be re-pointed and hedges have to be cut.

The significance of such evidence has not been fully considered. Essentially it is evidence of how the neighbours regarded the ownership of the land. It cannot override a clear provision in the parcels, but

---

[75] *Ward v Kirkland* [1967] Ch. 194; [1966] 1 W.L.R. 601.
[76] *Truckell v Stock* [1957] 1 W.L.R. 161.
[77] *Dean v Walker* (1997) 73 P. & C.R. 366.
[78] Neighbouring Land Act 1992 s.1(2).
[79] Neighbouring Land Act 1992 s.1(5).
[80] Neighbouring Land Act 1992 s.1(3).
[81] See para.6.31 et seq.

evidence that the person of the appropriate side of a ditch maintained it can support the proposition that the hedge and ditch rule applies.[82] So, where the parcels do not make clear who owns the boundary feature, evidence of maintenance has to be considered in conjunction with all the inferences from the site itself.

Such evidence is not necessarily conclusive. A farmer may dig out a ditch in order to keep his land well drained, without any consideration of whether he owns the ditch. Equally he may do so because it is more convenient for him to do the work from his side of the hedge than to require his neighbour to come through and possibly damage his land. Similar arguments may apply to cutting his side of the hedge and even doing some re-laying of the hedge. A domestic owner may re-point his side of the garden wall to stop it falling down, without seeking thereby to claim ownership of half of it or may replace a fence with a wall in a slightly different position without intending to change the boundary.[83]

14. Vertical and horizontal boundaries

The proposition that, in the absence of evidence to the contrary,[84] a boundary, in theory, runs down to the centre of the earth and up to the sky has recently been re-affirmed, following detailed and wide-ranging consideration, by the Supreme Court in *Bocardo SA v Star Energy UK Onshore Ltd.*[85] And despite comments to the contrary by Lord Wilberforce in *Commissioner for Railways v Valuer-General*[86] there is no reason to doubt that it is the law in England. However, the proposition does not apply to the airways.[87] **2.25**

In *Bocardo SA v Star Energy UK Onshore Ltd*[88] the general rule was challenged in respect of deep oil wells, but the Supreme Court upheld it even in cases where the stratum was so deep as to be out of range from the ground.

The basic vertical nature of the boundary is also qualified by the need to include the footings and the eaves as being within the ownership of the house owner, although not the air space above the footings and below the eaves.[89]

The growth of trees and other plants have no direct effect on vertical boundaries. Just as a boundary can go through the middle of a hedge or

---

[82] *Hall v Dorling* (1997) 74 P. & C.R. 400.
[83] *Kupfer v Dunne* [2003] EWCA Civ 1549.
[84] e.g. in *Rhone v Stephens* [1994] 2 A.C. 310; [1994] 2 W.L.R. 429.
[85] [2010] UKSC 35; [2011] 1 A.C. 380.
[86] [1974] A.C. 328; [1973] 2 W.L.R. 1021.
[87] "The air is a highway" *US v Causby* (1946) 328 US 256.
[88] [2010] UKSC 35.
[89] *Truckell v Stock* [1957] 1 W.L.R. 161.

to either side of it, so the trunk of a tree may be part of the boundary or on either side of it.

Strictly speaking the overhanging branches of a tree amount to trespass and, accordingly, the adjoining owner has the right to chop them back and remove the boughs.[90] The House of Lords in 1894 was very concerned about the difficulty this would cause and indicated that legislation might be necessary if this became common, but up to now, 115 years later, such legislation has not proved necessary, despite the provisions in the Anti-Social Behaviour Act 2003 dealing with oppressively high hedges and avenues.

There is, furthermore, no prescriptive right of overhang, comparable to the right of eavesdrop. So, however long the tree has been there, the right to cut it back survives.[91] Frequently, however, ownership is divided horizontally as well as vertically. Although flats are usually conveyed by reference to long leases rather than freeholds, this is purely a conveyancing device and does not mean that boundaries are unimportant. The Commonhold and Leasehold Reform Act 2002 has set out a new alternative system for blocks of flats and other similar structures. The common parts are held by a registered company, controlled by the flat owners, who are themselves registered as unit holders. However, it is still necessary to decide on the boundaries of the common parts, and the boundaries of the units between themselves and the common parts. Although, like long leasehold flats this is registered conveyancing, the registration is still of general boundaries and there is still the possibility of disputes in the same way as with long leases of flats. Equally, many older properties in urban areas have rooms over adjoining properties and over old passageways.

2.26   In principle there is no difference between a horizontal and a vertical boundary. Ownership and possession of property is three-dimensional. Where the boundary is not simply a line on a plan, several problems are created.

Firstly where there is a conveyance or a demise of a room, a flat, or a storey, the outside wall enclosing the property conveyed or demised, together with any fixtures attached to the outside, is included[92] unless a contrary intention is shown.[93] This, for example, allows the owner to attach an advertisement to the outside of his part of the wall.[94] The effect

---

[90] *Lemmon v Webb* [1894] 3 Ch 1.
[91] *Davies v Yadegar* (1990) 22 H.L.R. 232; [1990] 09 E.G. 67. A right to build higher than normal by obtaining bonus floor site ratios can be a proprietary right, as in *Uniting Church in Australia Property Trust (NSW) v Immer* (No. 145) Pty. [1992] A.L.M.D. 2318; [1992] C.L.Y. 551.
[92] *Sturge v Hackett* [1962] 1 W.L.R. 1257.
[93] *Davies v Yadegar* (1990) 22 H.L.R. 232; [1990] 09 E.G. 67.
[94] *Carlisle Café Co v Muse Bros* (1897) 67 L. J. Ch. 53.

of this principle on rights of support is dealt with later.[95] As far as internal walls are concerned "it seems to be clear that some part of the wall is included in the demise" or conveyance.[96]

It may also be necessary to decide exactly where the horizontal boundary runs between the different levels. A conveyance of a passageway (and therefore a room) normally includes the floor under it and not just the air space above the floor.[97] Equally the ceiling is included. It has not, however, yet been finally decided exactly where the line is to be drawn. The ceiling after all, is attached to the floor above. In *Sturge v Hackett*,[98] it was held that the flat must have extended

> "to at least the underside of the floor joists to which his ceiling was attached. It is unnecessary to decide whether it extended half-way through the thickness of the floor joists or to the top side of them."

It is submitted that structurally the ceiling is attached to the floor above, rather than vice versa, and accordingly that the logical point for the boundary is the under-side of the joists. Thus where the landlord has installed a false ceiling leaving a void, the space will normally be included in the lower flat.[99]

Where the conveyance or demise is of the top floor of the premises the question may arise as to who owns, or is in possession of, the roof. This is a matter of construction of the conveyance and different words may be interpreted in different ways. In *Cockburn v Smith*[100] it was held that a demise of "all that suite of rooms known as . . ." which suite of rooms formed part of the top floor, did not include the roof.

> "The contention that because the rooms include the walls therefore they include the roof also is one which I cannot assent to."[101]

It would appear from this case that generally where there is a demise or conveyance of part of premises where the lessor or vendor retains possession of common parts, the roof will not be included in the assurance unless there is something specific to indicate that it is included. Otherwise, the assurance of the top flat just includes the ceiling of that flat and the rafters and roof are retained by the lessor.[102]

---

[95] See Ch.19.
[96] *Phelps v London Corp* [1916] 2 Ch. 255 at 263, per Peterson J.
[97] *Phelps v London Corp* [1916] 2 Ch. 255.
[98] *Sturge v Hackett* [1962] 1 W.L.R. 1257; [1962] 3 All E.R. 166.
[99] *Graystone Property Investment Ltd v Margulies* (1984) 47 P. & C.R. 472; *Munt v Beasley* [2006] EWCA Civ 370.
[100] [1924] 2 K.B. 119.
[101] *Cockburn v Smith* [1924] 2 K.B. 119 at 128 per Bankes L.J.
[102] *Douglas-Scott v Scorgie* [1984] 1 W.L.R. 716; [1984] 1 All E.R. 1086 at 1088.

2.27   The case of *Strandley Investments v Barpress*[103] decided the fairly obvious proposition that a demise of a whole building includes the roof. However, the brief consideration of the issue in *Tennant Radiant Heat Ltd v Warrington Development Corp*[104] seems to indicate that a lease of one unit in a block of warehouses will be construed, in the absence of indication to the contrary, to include that part of the roof which runs over the unit demised. Furthermore it is likely that on those rare occasions when a flat or part of a house is disposed of freehold or even leasehold, so that nothing is retained by the vendor, the courts would try to ensure that the roof was not accidentally retained by the vendor or lessor.[105] However, it is submitted that despite *Tennant Radiant Heat Ltd v Warrington*[106] (above), in most cases, unless there is some express reference to the roof, it will remain the property of the lessor. In the normal case where the freehold is held by a maintenance company, the ownership of the roof will pass to the maintenance company.

A conveyance of the roof will usually include a conveyance of the roof space, but this will not necessarily be the case. The lessor may wish to retain the roof but be happy for the lessee of the top flat to use the loft.[107]

If the roof and roof space is included, the tenant has the right, subject to any relevant covenants, to extend upwards, since the air-space above is included, but not sideways.[108]

Ownership of the roof or other parts of the property is quite separate from an obligation to repair. The conveyance or demise may include a covenant to keep various parts in repair, which may or may not be enforceable.[109] In the absence of such a covenant the party who does not own the roof or wall, but is suffering as a result of its disrepair has to rely on his rights in tort.[110]

15.   Witnesses

2.28   It may seem inappropriate to leave to last the crucial extrinsic evidence in nearly all boundary disputes. Most of the various elements set out above depend on the sworn testimony of witnesses to prove them. Such evidence will be adduced at the hearing.

The Woolf Reforms implemented in the Civil Procedure Rules 1998, which apply to both High Court and county courts, have changed the whole climate of court procedure. To what extent they have changed the

---

[103] [1987] 1 E.G.L.R. 69.
[104] [1988] 1 E.G.L.R. 41.
[105] *Hatfield v Moss* [1988] 2 E.G.L.R. 58.
[106] [1988] E.G.L.R. 41.
[107] *Hatfield v Moss* [1988] 2 E.G.L.R. 58.
[108] *Davies v Yadegar* (1990) 22 H.L.R. 232; [1990] 09 E.G. 67.
[109] *Rhone v Stephens* [1994] 2 A.C. 310; [1994] 2 W.L.R. 429.
[110] *Bradburn v Lindsay* [1983] 2 All E.R. 408.

nature and relevance of oral testimony is another matter. The success of a claim or defence still depends both on care in preparation and the performance of the witnesses, balanced against the skill and ammunition in the hands of the cross-examiner. What has changed is the possibility of holding back important material to use to shake or unsettle a witness.

Proceedings are commenced by a Statement of Case which can be used as evidence provided it is verified by a statement of truth.[111] This consists of a signature at the bottom of the document stating "I believe that the facts stated in this [document being verified] are true". After commencement, the court has case management control over the proceedings. This will include directions for service of witness statements.[112] There is no necessary requirement that such statements are to be exchanged simultaneously, but this will be the usual direction. This is to ensure that one party does not doctor his statement to deal with something in the other party's statement. It does, however, mean that the witness may not deal with issues raised by the other party.

The service of witness statements does not obviate the need to call the witness. If the witness attends and gives evidence the witness statement will normally stand as the evidence in chief.[113] The court may give permission for the witness to amplify the statement or to give evidence in chief about new matters raised by the other side, but this is by no means automatic. It is, therefore, essential that the witness statement contains all the facts relied on. **2.29**

Careful proofing of witnesses has always been an essential part of case preparation. It ensures that the witness has addressed his or her mind to the matters which have to be resolved and that counsel presenting the case has a fair idea of what the witness has to say. The need to serve witness statements has, however, rendered this even more important. The temptation is to dress up the witness's words in legal language or to include tendentious propositions. In general, however, the most effective statements are those which stick most closely to the witness's own words.[114] Such statements are also more likely to stand up to cross-examination. It is also important to omit opinion from the statement served. Where it contains hearsay this should say so and identify the source of the information.[115] The exact form of witness statements is set out in the Practice Direction.[116]

If a witness statement is served, but the witness does not attend to give evidence the court may give leave for the statement to be adduced as **2.30**

---

[111] CPR PD 32.
[112] CPR r.32.4.
[113] CPR r.32.5.
[114] CPR PD 32 para.18.1.
[115] CPR PD 32 para.18.2.
[116] CPR PD 32 para.19.

hearsay evidence. If this is permitted the absence of the witness to be cross-examined will, of course, have a significant effect on the weight which the court will attach to it. If the party serving the statement does not seek to rely on it as hearsay evidence the other side may put it in for this purpose. Once the statement has been put in evidence, it becomes a public document and is open to inspection.[117]

If a party has a witness whom he believes will assist, but who refuses to sign a witness statement, the court can give leave to serve a witness summary instead.[118] This should identify the name and address of the witness and set out the evidence which he or she is expected to give.

This summary is based on the standard rules. There is provision for specialist protocols, but no such protocol has, as yet, been produced for boundary or other property disputes.

2.31 It must be remembered that these rules are purely procedural. The witness statements do not become evidence until the witness has been called and has verified his or her statement.[119] Until that has been done, the witness statement is of no probative value, although it can be used by the other side in cross-examination as a prior inconsistent statement or as hearsay evidence.[120]

The risk inherent in the new procedure is that a witness will express not his or her own recollections, but the evidence that the party and his advisers want the witness to say. In practice, however, it soon becomes apparent in cross-examination if the witness statement differs from what the witness wants to say. What it has removed is the tedious sight of a nervous witness trying to recollect things which in another place he would remember well and drifting off into irrelevancies.

Whether to disclose evidence before proceedings are commenced or before the order for exchange of witness statements takes effect is a matter of tactics. Early disclosure may often aid settlement and an early letter setting out the facts succinctly, though in theory self-serving, in practice adds authority to the testimony and demonstrates that it is not a recent invention (or at least that it has not been invented since the letter).

2.32 For various reasons a witness may not be available to give evidence at court. He or she may have died, may be overseas, may be too sick to attend, or dragging a witness unwillingly to court may seem an unnecessarily heavy-handed way of dealing with essentially uncontested evidence. In these circumstances there are several options available.

---

[117] CPR r.32.13.
[118] CPR r.32.9.
[119] CPR r.32.5.
[120] CPR r.32.5.

In such situations the traditional method of giving written evidence is by affidavit. An order for evidence to be given by affidavit can be made at or before the trial.[121] If an order is made that the evidence be given by affidavit the witness need not attend and cannot be cross-examined unless an order is made to this effect.

Although the rules make provision for evidence by affidavit, they **2.33** clearly contemplate that the more common method will be by treating the written statement as hearsay evidence under the Civil Evidence Act 1995.[122]

The need for separate notice of proposal to call hearsay evidence as required by the 1995 Act[123] has been considerably affected by the Civil Procedure Rules. Where a witness statement in the prescribed form is served, but the witness is not called, this service of the witness statement obviates the need for a separate notice, and the witness statement can be allowed in evidence.[124] Equally, if a witness statement is served which contains hearsay evidence, whether that witness is being called or not, the service of that statement is treated as a notice under s.2(1) of the 1995 Act. It is difficult to see, therefore, in which circumstances a separate hearsay evidence notice will be required.

Where the witness is not called, the other side can apply to the court for the witness to attend for cross-examination[125] within 14 days after the service of the notice of intention (or the witness statement). The court then has a discretion as to whether to make such an order. Whether such an order is made will depend on the potential importance of the evidence.

If, therefore, an application is made for the evidence of a witness to be given by affidavit, it is important for the other party to consider at that stage whether the evidence is accepted, or whether the application should either be opposed or be made on condition of attendance for cross-examination.

Reference has already been made to statutory declarations.[126] Although **2.34** these count as affidavits, the rules set out above apply only to affidavits made in the action and not to any affidavit or statutory declaration which may have been made for conveyancing purposes before the action was begun.

It has long been established that a photograph is real evidence,[127] but the position is not so clear in respect of tape recordings. It was made clear

---

[121] CPR r.32.15.
[122] CPR r.32.5(5)(b).
[123] Civil Evidence Act 1995 s.2(1).
[124] CPR r.32.5(5)(b).
[125] CPR r.33.4.
[126] See para.2.07.
[127] See para.2.11.

in the Civil Evidence Act 1968 (now repealed) that a tape recording is a document.[128] The 1995 Act defines a document as "anything in which information of any description is recorded",[129] which plainly includes a tape recording. However, in *Ventouris v Mountain (No.2)*[130] a conversation between George Ventouris and his cousin Apostoulos Ventouris was secretly recorded by George. It was held that what George said was admissible, as he had authorised it, but what his brother said was not admissible, because he was unaware of it. The Civil Evidence Act has since been amended, but the principle is still the same.

The position is complicated by the Human Rights Act 1998 and art.8 of the European Convention on Human Rights which provides, "Everyone has the right to respect for his private and family life, his home and his correspondence". By s.6 of the Human Rights Act, a court must act in a way that is compatible with this provision. As set out in para.2.12 above, a balance must be struck between the rights to respect for private life and the interests of a fair trial. However, recording what you say to another party to proceedings (which is not really a private conversation) may be seen as different from tapping into what you say to a friend which you believe to be private.

2.35   There may be situations, however, where the party wishing to adduce the evidence wants it to be given orally, but the witness is unable to attend the trial, either because he is too old or sick, or because he will be abroad at the time of the hearing, or for some similar reason. Essentially, these reasons overlap, with the reasons for not calling a witness under the hearsay evidence rules. Where a witness is important and going to contradict evidence to be adduced from the other side, it may be desirable either for the judge to see the witness, or at least for the witness's evidence to be tested by cross-examination. This may be as much in the interests of the party calling the witness as of the party seeking to contradict his testimony.

There is no absolute rule as to the place at which a trial can take place and it is open to the judge to decide to adjourn the trial to the bedside of a sick witness. By r.2.7 of the Civil Procedure Rules 1998 "the court may deal with a case at any place that it considers appropriate". The power has always been commonly used. Indeed, it has been known for a judge to insist that he and counsel be fully robed while attending such a hearing!

The Rules also provide for evidence to be given by video link "or by any other means".[131] Video link is more appropriate for witnesses who are

---

[128] Civil Evidence Act 1968 s.10(1)(c).
[129] Civil Evidence Act 1995 s.13.
[130] *Ventouris v Mountain (The Italia Express) (No.2)* [1992] 1 W.L.R. 887; [1992] 3 All E.R. 414.
[131] CPR r.32.3.

overseas than for those who are sick, since it usually requires attendance at a video suite. It may, however, be helpful where the witness is unable to travel long distances. A video link may also be less stressful to a sick witness than attendance at court. Courts are usually reluctant to allow evidence to be given by telephone, since it prevents the Judge or counsel from seeing the witness or ensuring that he is not being coached from the side-lines.

The more traditional method, however, is for the deposition of a **2.36** witness to be taken in advance of the trial on examination.[132] This is very useful where the witness may die or become even more feeble before the trial, or if the witness is going overseas. Usually such evidence is taken before examiners of the court, who are barristers or solicitors appointed for this purpose.[133] However, it can also be taken before the district judge or, in certain circumstances before the judge who will hear the case. It is not within the scope of this book to deal with such examinations in full, but essentially the witness is cross-examined, and the evidence given is recorded and put in the form of depositions to be used at the court hearing. Under the Rules of the Supreme Court, the examiner did not have power to exclude evidence, but could note any objections made and send a special report of the proceedings to the court. This practice is not contained in the Civil Procedure Rules 1998 and it is not clear whether it still applies.

Finally, it may be possible to avoid having to call a witness at all by using a notice to admit facts.[134] The disadvantage of this procedure is that if admissions are not made following such a notice, then the other party is not thereby deemed to admit the facts set out. However, if the other party does not admit the facts, the party serving the notice may be entitled to the costs of proving the facts even if he loses the case. This rule was expressed in absolute terms in the Rules of the Supreme Court, but does not seem to be replicated in the Civil Procedure Rules 1998. However, there is no reason to think that the principles have changed. The procedure, therefore, is of considerable use in dealing with matters which are not substantially in dispute, but will involve considerable expense to prove. An admission made following a Notice to Admit Facts is only binding against the party making it and for the purposes of the trial. In certain circumstances, a party may be allowed to resile from the admissions.[135]

---

[132] CPR r.34.8.
[133] CPR r.34.15.
[134] CPR r.32.18.
[135] *Bird v Birds Eye Wall's Ltd, The Times,* July 24, 1987; *Heggarty v Murray* [1993] 11 C.L. 446.

16. View

2.37   Part of the ritual of boundary disputes is the view, during which the judge inspects the property accompanied by the parties and their representatives. This was expressly provided for in the Rules of the Supreme Court, but is not expressly dealt with in the Civil Procedure Rules. Such a visit is "sensible and proper".[136] What the judge sees at the view is as much evidence as if it was produced in court as an exhibit. It is real evidence[137] and accordingly, as with an exhibit, can be used by the judge to supplement or test the testimony of the witnesses.[138] However, the opinions formed by the judge on the site visit cannot be used to override the evidence given in court.[139] The parties and their representatives are not allowed to give evidence at the view, but it is often essential for the particular features of the property to be pointed out to the judge. This must be done with considerable discretion, but can be an important part of the presentation of the case. It has, however, been held that it would be wrong for the court to make a finding based entirely on the view, without hearing oral evidence as well.[140] It would be wrong for the judge to have a view in the presence of one party but not the other,[141] but a private view in the absence of all parties is perfectly admissible.[142] In the context of a boundary dispute, however, a judge is unlikely to want to visit the site without the parties being present. Even if he does not need to go onto private land, he may well wish to ensure that he does not himself become embroiled in the problems that have given rise to the action.

The stage at which the view takes place is in the discretion of the judge. The question is always whether it is better for the judge to see the site before the evidence is given to make it easier for him to understand it, or whether it is better to wait until the evidence is given so as to ensure that he knows what to look for. Often the judge will prefer to see the site at the end of the opening, though views at the end of the evidence are also common.

An alternative which is at present rarely used is to make a video recording of the site. The court has an inherent jurisdiction to make an order permitting such video recording.[143]

A party is entitled to apply for inspection of the property before commencement of proceedings.[144]

---

[136] *Horrod v Finney* [1992] N.P.C. 144.
[137] per Denning L.J. in *Goold v Evans & Co* [1951] 2 T.L.R. 1189.
[138] *Buckingham v Daily News* [1956] 2 Q.B. 534; [1956] 3 W.L.R. 375.
[139] *Charles v Beach* [1993] N.P.C. 102.
[140] *London General Omnibus Co Ltd v Lavell* [1901] 1 Ch. 135.
[141] *Goold v Evans & Co* [1951] 2 T.L.R. 1189.
[142] *Salsbury v Woodland* [1970] 1 Q.B. 324; [1969] 3 W.L.R. 29.
[143] *Ash v Buxted Poultry, The Times*, November 29, 1989, QBD.
[144] CPR r.25.

Chapter Three
Rectification and Estoppel

1.   Rectification

Rectification is an equitable remedy which allows a contract or convey- **3.01**
ance to be corrected when it does not reflect the common intention of the
parties, or in some cases, where one party has made a unilateral mistake
about its terms or meaning. It applies, therefore, only after any questions
of construction have been resolved. It should be expressly pleaded, and
the proposed rectified words of the parcels should be included in the
claim. However, the court has in fact ordered rectification even though
there is no claim for rectification in the pleadings[1] and in view of the wide
powers to allow amendments to the pleadings, the reality is that a failure
to include a claim for rectification in the pleadings is more likely to result
in a reprimand for the representatives than in the client losing his case.

The remedy of rectification is a general one, and authorities from
outside the field of boundary disputes are relevant in establishing the
principles on which an order for rectification will be made.

The requirements for rectification were set out by the House of Lords in
Chartbrook Ltd v Persimmon Homes Ltd[2] where the principles set out by Peter
Gibson L.J. in *Swainland Builders Ltd v Freehold Properties Ltd*[3] were approved:

> "The parties must show that:
>
> (1)   the parties had a common intention, whether or not amounting
>   to an agreement, in respect of a particular matter in the
>   instrument to be rectified;
> (2)   there was an outward expression of accord;
> (3)   the intention continued at the time of the execution of the
>   instrument sought to be rectified;
> (4)   by mistake the instrument did not reflect that common
>   intention".

---

[1] *Butler v Mountview Estates* [1951] 2 K.B. 563; [1951] 1 All E.R. 693 at 700 per Danckwerts J.
[2] [2009] UKHL 38; [2009] 1 A.C. 1101.
[3] [2002] EWCA Civ 560 at [33] and [34].

The first requirement, therefore, is to show that there was indeed a common intention or consensus which was not reflected in the conveyance as actually produced. It used to be considered that for such common intention to be shown, it was necessary in effect to show an explicit oral agreement which did not correspond with the contract. However, *Joscelyne v Nissen*,[4] approving dicta of Harman L.J. in *Earl v Hector Whaling Ltd*[5] makes it clear that the doctrine also applies where the intention of the parties has never been expressed in common words. The question is therefore whether there was a common intention or consensus, and not necessarily whether there has been an oral agreement that differs from the conveyance as drawn.

3.02 It also allows rectification in cases where the parties made a mistake about what conveyancing steps were required to achieve their common objective.[6] The classic commercial authority of *Rose v Pym*[7] was distinguished in *Joscelyne v Nissen*[8] where it was made clear that insofar as *Rose v Pym* suggested that an antecedent concluded contract is necessary, it would be in conflict with other authorities.[9] It is a little difficult to reconcile the principle that where both parties intended to contract for feveroles, but actually contracted for horsebeans there can be no rectification, as decided in *Rose v Pym*, with the decision that where both parties intended to convey the beneficial interest, but in fact conveyed only a share in the management company, there could be rectification, as decided in *Joscelyne v Nissen*.[10] Insofar as there is a conflict, the wide interpretation is now accepted law. However, claims for rectification do not always succeed. In *Thomas v GT Pryce (Farms Ltd)*[11] everyone thought that the buildings were on Lot 2, not Lot 1, but the Particulars made clear reference to the OS number and made no reference to the buildings, so rectification was refused. *Re Butlin's Settlement Trusts*[12] makes it clear that rectification is not restricted to mistakes of fact, but applies equally to mistakes as to construction of documents, though not necessarily to mistakes as to more general principles of law.[13]

In *Munt v Beasley*[14] the need for an "outward expression of accord" was held not to be a strict legal requirement, but more a matter of evidence.

---

[4] [1970] 2 Q.B. 86; [1970] 2 W.L.R. 509.
[5] [1961] 1 Lloyd's Rep. 459 at 470.
[6] *Re Slocock's Will Trusts* [1979] 1 All E.R. 358.
[7] *Frederick E Rose (London) Ltd v William H Pim Junior & Co Ltd* [1953] 2 Q.B. 450; [1953] 3 W.L.R. 497.
[8] [1970] 2 Q.B. 86.
[9] *Crane v Hegeman Harris* [1971] 1 W.L.R. 1390; [1939] 1 All E.R. 662.
[10] *Joscelyne v Nissen* [1970] 2 Q.B. 86.
[11] [2005] EWCA Civ 1111.
[12] [1976] Ch. 251; [1976] 2 W.L.R. 547.
[13] *Chartbrook Ltd v Persimmon Homes* [2009] UKHL 38; [2009] 1 A.C. 1101.
[14] [2006] EWCA Civ 370.

Rectification is allowed in cases where the mistake is in the interpretation of the agreed words, as in *Chartbrook*[15] where the complex formula for deciding the price resulted, on one interpretation, in an outcome which was never intended, because the drafting of the agreement did not produce the intended effect. This was the case, even though one side gave evidence that they knew what the conveyance meant, even though it did not reflect the intention of the parties as shown in a previous letter.[16] Where there is a prior written agreement, this document must also be construed objectively even if the parties might hold different views about what it means.[17] The same applies to an oral consensus

Despite Peter Gibson L.J.'s reference to a common mistake the doctrine can still apply where the transaction which is to be rectified is unilateral, for example a voluntary settlement. In such a case, of course, unilateral mistake suffices.[18] Rectification can be ordered in respect of a unilateral transaction even if the effect is to benefit the settlor at the expense of the revenue.[19] Evidence that the settlor was acting under a mistake will, however, be treated with caution.[20] It would not apply, for example, where the settlor's advisers have subsequently discovered that another way of carrying out the transaction would be more advantageous from the point of view of taxation.[21]

In cases where the transaction is mutual, i.e. it involves two or more **3.03** parties, a unilateral mistake can only be rectified where the other party is to some extent at fault in standing by in the knowledge of that mistake. It does not apply, therefore, where one party is mistaken, but the other party does not know of his mistake.[22] There can be rectification where the other party is aware of the mistake and fails to point it out to the party making the mistake, even if the mistake was not caused by any action of his.[23] This decision may seem somewhat at odds with the principle of caveat emptor, but it can be explained in that particular case on the basis that the omission of a clause, which had been included in previous leases and was a common form clause, was so obviously a slip that the conduct was

---

[15] *Chartbrook Ltd v Persimmon Homes* [2009] UKHL 38; [2009] 1 A.C. 1101.
[16] In fact, the House of Lords interpreted the conveyance in a way which did not require rectification—see Ch. 2 above.
[17] Per Lord Hoffman in *Chartbrook Ltd v Persimmon Homes* at [59].
[18] *Re Butlin's Settlement Trusts (Rectification)* [1976] Ch. 251.
[19] *Re Colebrook's Conveyances* [1972] 1 W.L.R. 1397.
[20] *Whiteside v Whiteside* [1949] Ch. 448, approved by Court of Appeal [1950] Ch. 65.
[21] *Allnutt v Wilding* [2007] EWCA Civ 412.
[22] *Riverlate Properties Ltd v Paul* [1975] Ch. 133; [1974] 3 W.L.R. 564.
[23] *Thomas Bates & Son Ltd v Wyndham's (Lingerie) Ltd* [1981] 1 W.L.R. 505; [1981] 1 All E.R. 1077.

"such as to affect the conscience of the party who has suppressed the fact that he has recognised the presence of a mistake".[24]

The relevance of unconscionable conduct by the party who is not mistaken, even if it falls short of actual misrepresentation or even actual knowledge, as opposed to suspicion that the other party was mistaken, was emphasised by Stuart-Smith L.J. in *Commission for the New Towns v Cooper*.[25] To put it another way, "knowledge in this context includes 'shut-eye' knowledge".[26] There is, therefore, a wide measure of discretion in the court to decide what degree of silence justifies rectification and in less plain cases the court may refuse to grant rectification except where one party has done something to encourage the other party's mistake. Rectification for unilateral mistake will, or course, only be granted where the mistake is calculated to benefit the party keeping silent.

This line of authority seems somewhat at odds with the principles set out by Peter Gibson L.J. in *Swainland Builders Ltd v Freehold Properties Ltd*.[27] and in *Chartbrook Ltd v Persimmon Homes*[28] but none of those cases involved an allegation that a party had been misled and there was no suggestion that this line of authority was being questioned.

However, it must be remembered that the Court of Appeal upheld the rectification of the lease, despite absence of clear words of agreement, and the Court was not dealing with a unilateral mistake.

The standard of proof required for rectification has been the subject of various judicial descriptions. The latest is that of Peter Gibson L.J. in *Swainland Builders Ltd v Freehold Properties Ltd*[29] that the standard proof is the normal one of the "balance of probabilities". A previous description was "very clear and convincing proof",[30] though this is not some special principle of evidence, but just an expression of the caution required when witnesses seek to suggest that the words of a written document, which is presumed to represent their intentions at the time, ought to be altered because of their oral evidence, which may well be coloured by subsequent events. In *Chartbrook*[31] Lord Hoffman approved the words of Denning L.J. in *Rose v Pym*[32] that one should be able to "predicate with certainty what their contract was".

---

[24] At 515H per Buckley L.J.
[25] *Commission for the New Towns v Cooper (Great Britain) Ltd (formerly Coopind UK)* [1995] Ch. 259 at 280B.
[26] per Evans L.J. at 292E.
[27] [2002] EWCA Civ 560; [2002] 2 E.G.L.R. 71.
[28] *Chartbrook Ltd v Persimmon Homes* [2009] UKHL 38; [2009] 1 A.C. 1101.
[29] *Swainland Builders Ltd v Freehold Properties Ltd* EWCA Civ 560 at [34].
[30] *Re Butlin's Settlement Trusts (Rectification)* [1976] Ch. 251.
[31] *Chartbrook Ltd v Persimmon Homes* [2009] UKHL 38 at [63].
[32] *Frederick E Rose (London) Ltd v William H Pim Junior & Co Ltd* [1953] 2 Q.B.450.

As it is an equitable remedy, rectification is discretionary. It is not so clear, however, what this means in particular cases. It has long been established that an injunction, which is also an equitable remedy, may be refused because of the conduct of the successful party including his conduct during the course of the case.[33] There is no reported case where a similar course has been taken in a case of rectification. As rectification is a more technical remedy than an injunction and, above all, as the court does not have an alternative remedy available comparable to the remedy of damages in lieu of injunction or of specific performance, it seems that it will only be in exceptional cases that the remedy of rectification will be refused to a party because of the way he has conducted himself during the case (see *Williams v Staite*, a case on equitable licences, where the county court judge's decision that quite serious misconduct disqualified the defendants from asserting their equitable rights was overruled by the Court of Appeal).[34] In principle, however, there is no reason why the argument used to avoid an injunction should not also apply to rectification, and in boundary disputes it is not unusual to find that the parties have conducted themselves badly during the dispute. It is, perhaps, an argument which is more likely to succeed where the rectification claimed effects only a small change to the party's rights, than where the party disqualified from rectification would thereby lose property of substantial value.

Rectification, as an equitable remedy, is also subject to the other **3.04** equitable defences. The most important of these, in this context, are:

(a) that rectification is not possible against a bona fide purchaser for value of a legal estate without notice of the error; and

(b) laches and acquiescence.

It must be remembered, however, that the fact that the property has changed hands since the conveyance does not necessarily matter. In the first place, the claim can be raised by a successor of the original buyer. Secondly it can be raised against successors in title who are not purchasers, such as persons who have inherited the property and tenants. A mortgagee, however, is a purchaser and so a claim cannot be pursued against him if he is a bona fide purchaser without notice.[35] Finally the purchaser may have knowledge that the original conveyance was an error, in which case he has notice and the equitable defence does not apply.

There is no statutory limitation period restricting a claim for rectification. The time between the execution of the document to be rectified and

---

[33] *Armstrong v Sheppard & Short* [1959] 2 Q.B 384; [1959] 3 W.L.R. 84. See para.24.40 below.
[34] *Williams v Staite* [1979] Ch. 291; [1978] 2 W.L.R. 825.
[35] See Law of Property Act 1925 s.205(1)(xxi) and *Lloyds Bank v Bullock* [1896] 2 Ch. 192 at 197.

the commencement of proceedings is only relevant, therefore, in deciding whether the claim is barred by laches or acquiescence. The equitable doctrines of laches and acquiescence are closely linked and it may be that there is in reality no difference between them, though Patten L.J. disputed this in *Lester v Woodgate*.[36] Laches (which means delay) may be just one aspect of acquiescence. In any event whether they are two separate principles or two aspects of the same principle they are based on justice. It follows that time alone will not necessarily bar a claim for rectification, though it may have considerable evidential value in indicating that there has been acquiescence.

3.05   The defence of acquiescence to an equitable claim for rectification is not dissimilar to the defence of acquiescence as a bar to a legal right which can in turn give rise to proprietary estoppel.[37] They are, however, different sides of the coin. Proprietary estoppel in effect has become a claim in its own right, allowing a person who has entered on land and acted to his detriment to claim various rights including a conveyance of the land to him, whereas the defence of acquiescence is simply a defence to a remedy which is specifically discretionary. It must follow, therefore, that lesser delay and acts of acquiescence will suffice to bar a claim to rectification than those necessary to justify a claim to proprietary estoppel.

Nevertheless, as with proprietary estoppel, the defence of acquiescence depends on what acts the owner against whom rectification is claimed has done in the belief that he owned the land and the extent to which the person claiming, or his predecessor in title, has stood by and allowed him to act on the basis that the conveyance is correct.

Time can only be regarded as beginning to run from when the person accused of laches knows of the facts which justify a claim for rectification.[38] However, as proprietary estoppel apparently can arise even where the person standing by does not know of the true facts, it should follow that, in theory at least, the same applies to acquiescence and laches; that they can bar rectification, even where the party against whom rectification is claimed did not know of the facts on which the claim to rectification is based.

It is tempting to conclude that if the degree of acquiescence required to bar rectification is less than that required to found proprietary estoppel, then it is equivalent to the degree of acquiescence which will bar an injunction. It seems, however, that the acquiescence needed to bar rectification comes somewhere between the two, since it has to be enough to justify the plaintiff failing completely in his claim, but need not be enough for a party's purely legal (as opposed to merely equitable) rights to be completely defeated.

---

[36] [2010] EWCA Civ 199; [2010] 2 P. & C.R. 21.
[37] See para.3.10 below.
[38] *Beale v Kyte* [1907] 1 Ch. 564.

Rectification of a conveyance must be contrasted with rectification or **3.06** alteration of the register in respect of registered land, under s.65 of the Land Registration Act 2002, which is dealt with later.[39] Rectification of the register is a much wider remedy, since it is ordered where it is shown that land has been wrongly registered whether or not the registration is as a result of common mistake. However, it can also be used in circumstances where rectification of the conveyance would be ordered. The difference is that, whereas rectification of the conveyance is an equitable remedy, rectification of the register is a statutory remedy. As a result rectification of an error in the register caused by common mistake can be ordered even where this would affect the rights of a bona fide purchaser of the land without notice of the mistake.[40] It is, nevertheless, a discretionary remedy and, no doubt, in many cases the fact that the land in dispute is now held by a bona fide purchaser would be sufficient to persuade the court not to order rectification.

A right to rectification is capable of being an overriding interest for land registration purposes.[41] This only applies where the defendant is in occupation or in receipt of the rents and profits at the date of the document to be rectified. The right of the person in actual occupation to claim an overriding interest is subject to several exceptions—an interest of a person of whom inquiry was made before the disposition and who failed to disclose the right when he could reasonably have been expected to do so[42] and an interest which belongs to a person whose occupation would not have been obvious on a reasonably careful inspection of the land at the time of disposition and which the transferee does not have actual knowledge of at the time.[43]

Holaw (470) Ltd v Stockton Estates Ltd[44] is a good example of the correlation between the equitable remedy of rectification and rectification of the Land Register. It is clear that the court first has to decide whether there is in equity a right of rectification of the contract or transfer and then, if there is, whether this should result in rectification of the Register. It is only if the Register is rectified that the claimant obtains the advantage of the equitable rectification.

Quite apart from the equitable remedy of rectification it seems that an obvious mistake in a conveyance or other document can be corrected as part of the exercise of construction. This concept was reviewed in *KPMG*

---

[39] See Ch. 4.
[40] *Blacklocks v JB Developments* [1982] Ch. 183; [1981] 3 W.L.R. 554.
[41] Land Registration Act 2002 Schs 1 and 3 para.2.
   Holaw (470) Ltd v Stockton Estates Limited (2001) 81 P. & C.R. 29.
[42] Para.2(b) of Sch.3 to the Land Registration Act 2002 see *Davies v John Wood Property – Adjudicator* 2008/0528.
[43] Para.2(c) of Sch.3 to the Land Registration Act 2002.
[44] (2001) 81 P. & C.R. 29.

v Network Rail Infrastructure Ltd.[45] It is not easy to identify exactly where this concept fits between construction of the words and the equitable remedy of rectification. It seems that it applies where the actual words of the document contained a clerical error, but the reference to "the power to correct obvious errors in the written expression of the intention of the parties" has many similarities to the principle of rectification. This concept, therefore, must be approached with some caution and, perhaps, should be limited to clerical errors and obvious linguistic mistakes, where the wrong word is inserted.

2. Boundary agreements

3.07   At some stage after the conveyance has been completed a dispute may arise and the adjoining owners may get together to try to agree on the true boundary. Their agreement may take the form of a confirmatory conveyance, a Deed of Exchange, a written agreement, a formal oral agreement, or simply a chat over the garden fence.

Verbal agreements between adjoining owners as to the line of the boundary have received increased attention in recent years:

> "it would seem to me somewhat absurd, in a case where there is no verbal description of the land such as would serve to identify its boundary accurately and where the plan is imprecise . . . and where both vendor and purchasers were of the view . . . that the boundary was not clear and so proceeded to agree its exact position, if the court were then to shut its eyes to evidence of what they agreed was the true boundary".[46]

In *Neilson v Poole*[47] Megarry J. went further and indicated that such an oral agreement could itself be valid. This has now been authoritatively approved by the Court of Appeal in *Joyce v Rigolli*.[48] The decision of Megarry J. contains important guidance on this difficult topic.

If the variation in the boundary is contained in a deed there can be no difficulty. Its effect is simply to supersede the original conveyance and, in so far as it effects a change from the original conveyance, it operates as a fresh conveyance of land. Equally where the agreement is in writing it seems that few problems arise. As long ago as 1750, in the resolution of the battle between Mr Penn and Lord Baltimore to fix the boundaries between Pennsylvania and Maryland the Lord Chancellor stated:

[45] [2008] 1 P. & C.R. 187.
[46] per Peter Gibson L.J. in *Clarke v O'Keefe* (2000) 80 P. & C.R. 126 at 134.
[47] (1969) 20 P. & C.R. 909.
[48] [2004] EWCA Civ 79 followed in *Haycocks v Neville* [2007] EWCA Civ 78; [2007] 1 E.G.L.R. 78.

"An agreement between the parties relative to these boundaries, if proper in other respects to carry it into specific performance, is a matter of equity ... To say that such a settlement of boundaries amounts to an alienation is not the true idea of it; for if fairly made without collusion (which cannot be presumed) the boundaries so settled are to be presumed to be true and ancient limits."[49]

In *Joyce v Rigolli*[50] Arden L.J. dealt with the proposition that a boundary agreement requires writing since it is a contract for the disposition of land within s.2 of the Law of Property (Miscellaneous Provisions) Act 1989.

In some cases, an agreement between adjoining landowners is very clearly a disposition of land. There can be an agreement to exchange parcels of land for their mutual benefit. However, more frequently a boundary agreement is intended to resolve a dispute about where the exact line of the boundary is. The above quotation from *Penn v Lord Baltimore* puts the situation very clearly:

"A boundary agreement which is to identify the boundary rather than convey land does not require writing."[51]

This is so even where land may be conveyed under the 1989 Act. The problem is that if the agreement does not represent the true boundary then there is a contract to dispose of land, but the whole point of the agreement was to try to avoid having to go to court to establish the exact legal position. This approach is in accordance with authorities such as *Colchester BC v Smith*[52] and *Clarke v O'Keefe*[53] where every effort was made to validate boundary agreements.

The question also arises as to whether such agreements should be registered under the Land Charges Act 1972 as a contract to convey land. It would appear that the same logic applies. If it is a genuine attempt to resolve a dispute, it is not a contract to convey land, even if the true boundary prior to the agreement would have been different.

It seems clear that such an agreement, whether in writing or oral, is a **3.08** contract and as such can be avoided in the same way as any other contract. Thus it can be set aside for mistake or misrepresentation, or can be nullified by estoppel or set aside due to duress or undue influence. Equally it will only be valid if there is consideration on both sides. This will be the case where it is to resolve a dispute, but not where one owner

---

[49] *Penn v Lord Baltimore* 27 E.R. 1132; (1750) 1 Ves. Sen. 444 at 448.
[50] [2004] EWCA Civ 79.
[51] per Arden L.J. in *Joyce v Rigolli* [2004] EWCA Civ 79.
[52] [1992] Ch. 421; [1992] 2 W.L.R. 728.
[53] (2000) 80 P. & C.R. 126 at 134.

simply concedes a claim by the adjoining owner. Finally, it may be so informal that it cannot properly be regarded as an agreement which was intended to create legal relations.[54] A person engaged in a neighbourly chat over the fence might not expect his words to be construed as amounting to a boundary agreement.

3.09   Since *Joyce v Rigolli*[55] the courts have shown a considerable willingness to endorse comparatively informal agreements between neighbours rather than to pick out the meaning of a difficult conveyance. It is true that the principle does tend to give rise to evidential problems of the precise kind which the Statute of Frauds and now s.2 of the Law of Property (Miscellaneous Provisions Act 1989) were designed to avoid, e.g. where it is alleged that two adjoining owners, one now deceased, discussed and agreed on the boundary, it may be very difficult for the successor in title to the deceased owner to challenge evidence from his neighbour as to the terms of any such discussions. However, this may well be overridden by the feeling that an owner should not be allowed to override an agreement he has made or even one made by this pre-decessor.

3.   Estoppel

3.10   Even though the true boundary has been established in law and has not been varied by a boundary agreement, an owner may lose his right to the land by estoppel. This form of estoppel, usually called proprietary estoppel, is to be contrasted with the doctrine of adverse possession[56] by which a person can acquire title to the property by remaining in posses-sion for 12 years.[57] There is no specific time required for proprietary estoppel to arise, and accordingly if it is construed too widely there is a danger that the courts might create a kind of short-term adverse posses-sion (whereby a person who is not the owner of land in effect obtains title to it by using it as his own for a much shorter period than 12 years).

Since the last edition of this book the doctrine of proprietary estoppel has been analysed almost to the point of destruction, particularly in two House of Lords cases, *Cobbe v Yeoman's Row Management Ltd*[58] and *Thorner v Major*.[59] It is important to remember that, while proprietary estoppel does apply to boundary and easement disputes, it applies more often in cases where friends or relatives have done work on a property or where there has been a commercial relationship where an informal agreement

---

[54] See *Site Developments (Ferndown) v Curthbury Ltd* [2010] EWHC 10 (Ch); [2011] 2 W.L.R. 74.
[55] [2004] EWCA Civ 79.
[56] See Ch. 5.
[57] This is restricted in respect of registered land by ss.96-98 and Sch.6 to the Land Registration Act 2002.
[58] *Cobbe v Yeoman's Row Management Ltd* [2008] UKHL 55; [2008] 1 W.L.R. 1752.
[59] *Thorner v Major* [2009] UKHL 18; [2009] 1 W.L.R. 776.

has been reneged on. It is also important to note that these cases were not cases of acquiescence and standing by, but on people relying on perceived promises to their detriment.

The outcome of these cases is that there are three essential requirements for proprietary estoppel:

(a) a promise or assurance by one party;

(b) an act by the person claiming estoppel to his detriment in the belief that he owns or will own the land; and

(c) that it would be unconscionable to allow the other party to rely on his rights.[60]

(a)   A promise or assurance by one party

In *Thorner v Major*[61] Lord Walker qualified this requirement by saying, in relation to acquiescence:

"But if all proprietary estoppel cases (including cases of acquiescence or standing by) are to be analysed in the terms of assurance, reliance and detriment, then the landowner's conduct in standing by in silence serves as the element of assurance".[62]

It is, therefore, apparent that simply standing by can be construed as an assurance without any accompanying conduct or words.

There is a case for saying that the requirement of a representation or assurance is really only part of the third element of unconscionability. This would certainly simplify the mental exertions put into trying to fit the facts of many of these cases into this traditional requirement, but the courts have not been willing to go down that line.

It was said by Lord Scott in *Thorner v Major* that the assurance must be "clear and unequivocal" and that was the basis on which the claim lost in *Cobbe v Yeoman's Row Management Ltd.*[63] However, the reality is that the words used in *Thorner v Major* which led the old farmer to believe that he would inherit the farm were far from clear and unequivocal. It was the unconscionability of the outcome when his cousin died intestate which was key. Equally, in *Cobbe v Yeoman's Row Management Ltd* it was the fact that it was a commercial arrangement in which both sides knew that there was no binding contract to transfer the land

---

[60] *Shaw v Applegate* [1977] 1 W.L.R. 970; [1978] 1 All E.R. 123; *Taylor Fashions Ltd v Liverpool Victoria Trustees Co Ltd* [1982] Q.B. 133; [1981] 1 All E.R. 897; *Lim Teng Huan v Ang Swee Chuan* [1992] 1 W.L.R. 113; (1992) 64 P. & C.R. 233.

[61] [2009] UKHL 18; [2009] 1 W.L.R. 776.

[62] per Lord Walker at [55].

[63] *Cobbe v Yeoman's Row Management Ltd* [2008] UKHL 55; [2008] 1 W.L.R. 1752.

which rendered it not unconscionable when one party reneged on the understanding.

Although the promise is usually described in terms of a representation relied on by the claimant, it is often, in reality, an informal agreement for the transfer of land. It is, on the face of it, surprising that the point has never previously been raised that any such deal, if not in writing, falls foul of s.2 of the Law of Property (Miscellaneous Provisions) Act 1989 (and formerly of the Statute of Frauds). It is now fully established that proprietary estoppel is an exception to the requirement of the 1989 Act and it seems that this is on the basis of public policy.[64] Or possibly that it is also a constructive trust which is excluded from the Act.[65] A proprietary estoppel is not invalidated by not being registered under the Land Registration Act 2002 because it is based on actual occupation of the land and accordingly is usually an overriding interest.[66]

There is some suggestion that estoppel by acquiescence is a separate category of estoppel, known as estoppel by acquiescence rather than proprietary estoppel. It used to be thought that it could only apply where the person standing by was aware of his rights, but still omitted to enforce them.[67] "At the heart of acquiescence lies an encouragement or allowance of a party to believe something to his detriment".[68] It seems, however,[69] that this is just part of the general principle of unconscionability and that knowledge of the other party's rights is not necessary. The question is whether it is unconscionable to allow the strict rights to be enforced and not whether the person standing by has himself acted unconscionably.[70] The fact that the person standing by does not know his strict rights is nevertheless a relevant factor in assessing unconscionability.[71] Even for a party who knows his legal rights, there may be different degrees of standing by. A minor will not be bound by acquiescence unless he continues after he reaches majority[72] and the same would, no doubt, apply to an old or infirm person or a person living away from the land who just lets matters slide.

(b)   Act by party claiming estoppel

3.11   To justify a claim for proprietary estoppel in the context of boundary disputes the act must be of a permanent nature. The most obvious such

---

[64] *McGuane v Welch* [2008] EWCA Civ 785; [2008] 2 P. & C.R. 24.
[65] See Lord Scott's speech in *Cobbe v Yeoman's Row Management Ltd* [2008] 4 All E.R. 713.
[66] *Brocket Hall (Jersey) Ltd v Clague, The Times*, March 26, 1998.
[67] *Hopgood v Brown* [1955] 1 W.L.R. 213.
[68] per Aldous L.J. in *Jones v Stones* [1999] 1 W.L.R. 1739; (1999) 78 P. & C.R. 293 at 298.
[69] *Taylor Fashions Ltd v Liverpool Victoria Trustees Co Ltd* [1982] Q.B. 133.
[70] *Lim Teng Huan v Ang Swee Chuan Lim v Ang* [1992] 1 W.L.R. 113; (1992) 64 P. & C.R. 233.
[71] *Shaw v Applegate* [1977] 1 W.L.R. 970; [1978] 1 All E.R. 123.
[72] *Somersetshire Coal Canal Company v Harcourt* (1858) 2 De G. & J. 596.

act is building a permanent structure on the land,[73] but any substantial expenditure may be enough,[74] though where the expenditure is far less than the value of the land involved this will both affect the issue of whether it would be unconscionable to allow the other party to rely on his right and also the appropriate remedy which may fall short of allowing the party claiming to assert an absolute title to the land. This is more the case in boundary or easement disputes than in cases where people are claiming an inheritance[75] or a claim based on an inchoate contract.[76] Detriment is necessary, but is not a narrow or technical concept.

By contrast, acquiescence or proprietary estoppel must never be used as a substitute for adverse possession. The fact that someone has trespassed on his neighbour's land, for example by putting an oil tank or flower pots on his neighbour's wall, does not give him a right to the wall or to leave the items in position, unless the other party has encouraged him, or at least, allowed him to believe that he is entitled to do so.[77] It follows that acts of cultivation and user, such as dumping soil, of the type successfully relied on by the occupier as evidence of adverse possession in cases like *Treloar v Nute*[78] cannot give rise to an estoppel even where they are done with a false belief in ownership. Instead, the party trespassing has to wait long enough to mount a claim of adverse possession.

Normally such actions will be carried out on the land in dispute, but the doctrine does not only apply to boundaries and it seems clear that any irrevocable act can give rise to a sufficient detriment. Selling off part of the plaintiff's own property has been held sufficient to give rise to an easement by estoppel.[79] It can, however, only be in rare cases that acts on a party's own undisputed property can give rise to proprietary estoppel of the disputed land in boundary disputes since the sort of acts which could give rise to such a claim, such as erecting a building which is then denied access, can usually be dealt with by creating a right of way by estoppel.

(c)   Unconscionability

The third and crucial requirement is that the actions of the defendant **3.12** should be such that it is unconscionable to allow him to enforce his strict

---

[73] *Hopgood v Brown* [1955] 1 W.L.R. 213; *Inwards v Baker* [1965] 2 Q.B. 29.
[74] *Lester v Woodgate* [2010] EWCA Civ 199; [2010] 2 P. & C.R. 21.
[75] *Henry v Henry* [2010] UKPC 3; [2010] 1 All E.R. 988.
[76] *Cobbe v Yeoman's Row Management Ltd* [2008] UKHL 55; [2008] 1 W.L.R. 1752 where the claimant failed on the clarity of the agreement and not the nature of the detriment.
[77] *Jones v Stones* [1999] 1 W.L.R. 1739; (1999) 78 P. & C.R. 293 which contains a full explanation of the modern law of estoppel and acquiescence.
[78] *Treloar v Nute* [1976] 1 W.L.R. 1295; [1977] 1 All E.R. 230.
[79] *Crabb v Arun District Council* [1976] Ch. 179; [1975] 3 W.L.R. 847. See Ch.16.

legal rights. Even though estoppel by representation may have its origins in the common law and may be, in essence, a rule of evidence,[80] it has long been treated as an equitable principle,[81] giving the court discretion as to when to enforce it. The recent cases have moved further in the direction of giving the court hearing the case discretion to decide whether, on the facts of the particular case, it would be unconscionable to allow strict enforcement rather than controlling the doctrine by a number of specific requirements. It is, however, possible to extract from the cases elements which will be of significance in assessing what behaviour will be held to be unconscionable.

Where the act is done following a specific representation or assurance by the party estopped, then obviously the attempt to rely on strict rights is more likely to be treated as unconscionable even if the person making the representation is unaware that what he is saying does not represent the true position in law.[82] However, the wide approach of unconscionability allows the court to look into and balance out:

(1) the nature of the representation or assurance, e.g. whether it was made in a casual conversation or in detailed negotiations;

(2) the extent to which the person making the representation was at fault in making it (i.e. whether he knew it was untrue, or made it recklessly without caring whether it was true or false, or was negligent in failing to check the true position);

(3) the extent to which the representation persuaded the other party to act, or whether he might well have gone ahead anyway[83]; and

(4) the extent to which the other party acted to his detriment or would suffer loss should the defendant's strict rights be enforced. Putting up a fence on the disputed land which is comparatively easy to move may be a very different matter from building a garage.[84]

The second crucial element to render reliance on the representation unconscionable, of course, is that it was believed by the person to whom it was made and relied on by him. It is not necessary that the reliance be total—the party may have had other reasons for believing that the land was his—but there must be significant reliance and, as stated

---

[80] *Avon CC v Howlett* [1983] 1 W.L.R. 605; [1983] 1 All E.R. 1073.

[81] Or even a general principle, irrespective of its common law or equitable origins, see per Oliver L.J. in *Habib Bank Ltd v Habib Bank AG* [1981] 1 W.L.R. 1265 at 1285B.

[82] *Hopgood v Brown* [1955] 1 W.L.R. 213.

[83] *Jones v Stones* [1999] 1 W.L.R. 1739; [1999] 78 P. & C.R. 293 where this was the crucial element which caused the defendant to lose on appeal.

[84] *McGuane v Welch* [2008] EWCA Civ 785; [2008] 2 P. & C.R. 24.

above, the extent of the reliance will affect the exercise of the court's discretion.

Even if an estoppel is proved, the court has a discretion as to the **3.13** remedy. This discretion goes beyond the equitable discretion not to allow rectification in that it will not only be exercised where the claimant is in some way at fault. The court can choose what remedy is most appropriate to deal with the justice of the situation. In the context of a boundary dispute it may well not be appropriate for the claimant's action simply to be dismissed without any specific decision being given on the ownership of the land, though this is what seems to have happened in *Hopgood v Brown*.[85] In such circumstances it is open to the court to order a conveyance of the land in respect of which the estoppel arises[86] or to make whatever order seems appropriate, including an order that the party benefiting from the proprietary estoppel should pay compensation to the other party for the loss of his land.[87] The principle explained in *Jennings v Rice*[88] is of proportionality between expectation and detriment. The claimant expected the whole house, but what he actually did to help the deceased was worth much less than that. The judge decided to award a sum broadly representing the deceased's nursing costs, which were just less than half the value of the house.[89] This was upheld by the Court of Appeal. This seems broadly in line with the approach of the House of Lords to proprietary estoppel in relation to co-habiting couples in *Stack v Dowden*.[90]

On the other hand the court may take the view that the expenditure, though sufficient to give rise to an estoppel, should not give the claimant any permanent right to the land. In that case the court can provide that the land be subject to a constructive trust or equitable lien for repayment of the money spent.[91]

If estoppel is a purely equitable doctrine then an estoppel by representation or by acquiescence should not be binding on a bona fide purchaser for value without notice of the estoppel. This, however, was precisely one of the matters at issue in *Hopgood v Brown*[92] and the Court of Appeal clearly decided that an estoppel is as much binding on a successor in title, as against the original representor or the person acquiescing.[93]

---

[85] *Hopgood v Brown* [1955] 1 W.L.R. 213.
[86] *Pascoe v Turner* [1979] 1 W.L.R. 431; [1979] 2 All E.R. 945.
[87] *Lim Teng Huan v Ang Swee Chuan* [1992] 1 W.L.R. 113; (1992) 64 P. & C.R. 233.
[88] *Jennings v Rice* [2002] EWCA Civ 159; [2003] 1 P. & C.R. 8.
[89] See also *Henry v Henry* [2010] UKPC 3; [2010] 1 All E.R. 988.
[90] [2007] UKHL 17; [2007] 2 A.C. 432.
[91] *Re Sharpe Ex p. Trustee of the Bankrupt's Property* [1980] 1 W.L.R. 219; [1980] 1 All E.R. 198, cf. *Cobbe v Yeoman's Row Management Ltd* [2008] UKHL 55; [2008] 1 W.L.R. 1752, where a constructive trust was considered but rejected. And *Thorner v Major* [2009] UKHL 18; [2009] 1 W.L.R. 776 per Lord Scott at [20].
[92] *Hopgood v Brown* [1955] 1 W.L.R. 213.
[93] Now enshrined in Land Registration Act 2002 s.116.

If proprietary estoppel is an equitable remedy, it ought also to follow that it can be lost if the claimant is guilty of misconduct such as to disentitle him to pursue it, or is guilty even of acquiescence. This proposition was accepted obiter by the court in *Williams v Staite*.[94] However, Lord Denning M.R.[95] said this could only apply in "an extreme case" and would not apply on the facts of that case. It must be noted that the other members of the court, while deciding the case on other grounds, felt obiter that it would have applied in the particular circumstances of that case where the claimants had put unfair pressure on the other party, broken court undertakings and given false evidence. It is noticeable, however, that in *Armstrong v Sheppard & Short*,[96] the court, while refusing an injunction, did not exclude the claimant's rights altogether, even though there had been misconduct on the part of the claimant.

3.14   It is also possible for a claimant who has proved estoppel to be deprived of his right as a result of his own acquiescence when the true owner seeks to enforce his legal rights, either by taking proceedings or by direct action, but again it is much harder to prove this than to raise the acquiescence as a ground for refusing an injunction and awarding damages in lieu.[97]

Nevertheless it seems clear that normally a claimant who has proved estoppel will not be deprived of his rights by the kind of minor misconduct or acquiescence which is not uncommon in boundary disputes.

A claim of proprietary estoppel may be raised in an action and not only by way of defence. In practice, however, it is usually raised by the person in possession. In these circumstances the limitation period will be that limiting the other party's claim (12 years in the case of trespass to land). Therefore, the question of what limitation period applies in a claim for proprietary estoppel has not arisen in practice. It seems clear, however, that there is no specific limitation period and the general equitable principles of laches and acquiescence apply.

Apart from proprietary estoppel, there are other forms of estoppel which may impact on boundary disputes. Acts done in the belief that a boundary has been agreed can lead to an estoppel preventing the other party from asserting his claim.[98] If the parties act on an underlying assumption of fact or law, they may both be prevented from going back on it—this is "estoppel by convention".[99] A previous court case may give rise to res judicata or issue estoppel. However, such estoppels may well fall short of giving the claimant ownership of land he would not otherwise be entitled to.

---

[94] *Williams v Staite* [1979] Ch. 291; [1978] 2 W.L.R. 825; [1978] 2 All E.R. 928.

[95] *Williams v Staite* [1978] 2 All E.R. 928 at 932c.

[96] *Armstrong v Sheppard & Short* [1959] 2 Q.B. 384; [1959] 3 W.L.R. 84.

[97] *Shaw v Applegate* [1977] 1 W.L.R. 970; [1978] 1 All E.R. 123.

[98] *Chadwick v Abbotswood Properties* [2004] EWHC 1058 (Ch); [2005] 1 P. & C.R. 10.

[99] *Valentine v Allen* [2003] EWCA Civ 915.

Chapter Four
Boundaries of Registered Land

1. Introduction

Registration of land in England and Wales dates back as far as the Land **4.01** Registry Act 1862. By 1897,[1] the legislature had abandoned the idea of registering precise boundaries. Registration was voluntary until 1925.[2] Since then the Land Registry has been gradually increasing the area of the country and the types of transactions requiring compulsory registration. Over eighty years later this process is still not complete, but compulsory registration has been greatly extended. Since 1990 compulsory registration has applied to the whole country and since the Land Registration Act 1997 it applies not only to conveyances of freehold and long leasehold property, but also to assents, vesting deeds and first legal mortgages. The Land Registration Act 2002 extends leasehold registration to leases of more than seven years, though it still excludes assignments of mortgages and surrenders of leases.[3] Over 22½ million titles in England and Wales have now been registered, covering 73 per cent of the land area. The Land Registry clearly regards the exercise of registering all the titles in England and Wales as largely accomplished, since there is now no reference to completing this exercise in their strategic plan.

By s.13 there is power to make provision for the registration of the proprietor of appurtenant estates, including easements and profits appurtenant. Profits in gross along with rentcharges and franchises are now subject to voluntary registration.[4] By s.27(2)(d) the express grant of easements and profits has to be registered as a disposition on the title of the servient tenement. This is dealt with more fully in Chapter 12. Customary rights, franchises, public rights, the rights of people in actual occupation

---

[1] Land Transfer Act 1897.
[2] Land Registration Act 1925.
[3] Land Registration Act 2002 ss.4(2)(b), 4(4).
[4] Land Registration Act 2002 s.3(1).

and leases of less than seven years are still overriding interests,[5] but crucially easements and profits are not necessarily overriding interests on a disposition.[6]

The Land Registration Act 2002 repealed the Land Registration Act 1925 and subsequent legislation and represents a complete redrafting of land registration legislation. The Act does not change the essential principles that registered boundaries are normally general boundaries only,[7] but there is increasing use of the system for fixing boundaries contained in r.118 of the Land Registration Rules 2003, despite the Land Registry's strict requirements of accuracy before a determined boundary can be registered.

4.02   One of the central changes made by the Land Registration Act 2002 was supposed to be the introduction of electronic conveyancing. It is difficult to separate firm proposals from aspirations. However, the current position is that the Land Registration (Electronic Conveyancing) Rules 2008 have been revoked and it is proposed to introduce the Land Registration (Electronic Conveyancing) Rules 2011. The position, therefore, is that, while some operations can be carried out electronically, electronic conveyancing is not yet in existence and there is no firm date for implementation.

From the point of view of boundaries, the crucial decision was that made in 1897, that the register would show only general boundaries.[8] The French institution of the official boundary marker, checked by a government official, is still therefore a stranger to this country. Accordingly while the Land Registry may have concentrated the minds of conveyancers required to register their title and required them to ensure that the boundaries are clearly shown, it has had only a limited effect on boundary disputes. This, however, is beginning to change. The Land Registration Rules 2003 not only include the long-standing provision for applying for the determination of the exact line of a boundary,[9] but also a system for implementing it. This is dealt with at s.7 below.

Where the boundary has not been fixed, it is still necessary to go back to the effective conveyance by which the two properties were separated and to look at what has happened since and what can be seen on the ground. This may involve going back before the first registration. As the registration is only of the general boundary the fixing of the boundary

---

[5] Land Registration Act 2002 Sch.1, 3.
[6] Land Registration Act 2002 Sch.3 para.3.
[7] Land Registration Act 2002 s.60(1).
[8] Land Registration Act 2002 s.60.
[9] Land Registration Rules 2003 r.118.

does not involve a transfer of any land.[10] By s.11(2) of the Land Registration Act 2002 registration with absolute title means that the estate is vested in the proprietor, regardless of whether there is someone with a better title. The only way the person with a better title can regain it is by rectification. However, no such rectification is needed even where the boundary finally decided on is not the same as the boundary line shown on the registered plan. This is the difference between a "boundary dispute" and a "property dispute".[11] There are, however, significant differences between registered and unregistered land, particularly in respect of the remedies which are available. It is this area which is concentrated on in this chapter.

Where "T" marks are referred to in the deeds and shown on the deed plan they will be reproduced on the filed plan or referred to in the description. A "T" mark usually indicates the ownership of a boundary feature. A "T" mark shown on a plan, but not otherwise referred to in the deeds, will not usually be reproduced, but it may still be relevant in a boundary dispute. This is another example of the importance of pre-registration deeds.

2. The Register

(1) The Register of title

The Register of title of any piece of land may be kept in electronic or **4.03** paper form.[12] It may contain more than one registered estate if they are of the same kind and vested in the same proprietor.[13] When land is registered it is then possible to open a new register for any part of the land, while retaining the existing register for the remainder. The idea, therefore, is that any piece of land will only appear on one register at any one time.

(a) The property register

The property register is the key document. It contains: **4.04**

    (i)   a description of the registered estate which must refer to a plan based on the ordnance survey map and called "the title plan"[14];

---

[10] *Steward v Gallop* [2010] EWCA Civ 823; [2011] 1 P. & C.R. 17.

[11] *Strachey v Ranger* [2008] 2 P. & C.R. 154; *Steward v Gallop* [2010] EWCA Civ 823; [2011] 1 P. & C.R. 17

[12] Rule 2(1) of the Land Registration Rules 2003.

[13] Land Registration Rules 2003 r.3(1).

[14] Land Registration Rules 2003 r.5(1)(a) "except where otherwise permitted".

(ii) details of:

- Exclusion or inclusion of mines.
- "[E]asements, rights, privileges, benefiting the registered estate and other similar matters".[15] This is not further defined and it appears to enable the applicant to include any ancillary rights which he considers to be annexed to the estate rather than to the individual owner or licensee.
- Any information on copyhold enfranchisement.
- Anything else which is needed.

The property register is the starting point for any boundary issue. It shows the general boundaries of the title on the plan and also contains the crucial description of the property. If a boundary has been fixed, it will also show the exact boundary.

Under s.66 of the Land Registration Act 2002, any person has the right to inspect the register of title and to take copies of it. An official copy of any part of the register is admissible in evidence to the same extent as the original.[16]

(b)   The proprietorship register

4.05   This register, which is also open to public inspection, contains the name of the proprietor, his address for service, the class of title and any covenants, restrictions or notices.[17]

(c)   The charges register

4.06   This contains details of leases, charges, notices and other dealings which may affect priority. It contains the name and address or the proprietor of any registered charge.[18]

(2)   The Indices

(a)   Index of proprietors names[19]

4.07   Until every individual register is held in electronic form, the index need not contain the name of any corporate or joint proprietor of an estate.

---

[15] Land Registration Rules 2003 r.5(b)(iv).
[16] Land Registration Act 2002 s.67.
[17] Land Registration Rules 2003 r.8 as amended.
[18] Land Registration Rules 2003 r.9 as amended.
[19] Land Registration Rules 2003 r.11 as amended.

(b)   The index map

This enables a person to ascertain in respect of any piece of land on the **4.08**
map (based on the Ordnance Survey Map) whether it is registered and
whether there are any subsidiary registrations such as a pending application for first registration, an application for a caution against first registration, a registered rentcharge or profit à prendre in gross, or a caution
against first registration.[20]

(c)   Index of verbal descriptions

This contains the same information verbally, together with details of **4.09**
registered manors.

(d)   The Day List

This is a chronological register showing the date and time of all activity **4.10**
on the register, such as cautions, searches and alterations.[21]

(3)   Searches and Official Copies

The indices and registers are open to public inspection and copying.[22] **4.11**
This must be done on the official form CIT. If it is done in person, it must
be in the presence of a member of staff.

Land Certificates are no longer issued on registration. They have been
replaced by Official Copies.[23] The application must be in form OC1 and a
separate application must be made in respect of each registered title or
individual caution register.[24]

The change to an open register in 1988 led to considerable concern about
confidential information contained in the register. This is dealt with in the
Rules mainly by the concept of "exempt information". A person may apply
to the registrar to designate a relevant document as exempt information
document if he claims that the document contains "prejudicial information".[25] The Registrar must then designate the document accordingly, unless
he considers the application "groundless". This does not, however, necessarily prevent the document being disclosed. If a person wishes to inspect
an exempt information document, he can then challenge the proposition
that the information is "prejudicial" and the registrar has a discretion to
disclose the information by balancing the public interest on either side.

---

[20] Land Registration Act 2002 s.68, Land Registration Rules 2003 r.10.
[21] Land Registration Rules 2003 r.12.
[22] Land Registration Act 2002 s.66 and Land Registration Rules 2003 r.133.
[23] Land Registration Rules 2003 r.134.
[24] Land Registration Rules 2003 r.134(2), (3).
[25] Land Registration Rules 2003 r.136(1).

The 2008 Rules[26] introduce some further excepted documents— "an identity document",[27] "an investigation of crime document"[28] and "a network access agreement.[29]

3. Types of registration

(a) Introduction

4.12   In order to effect registration the person applying has to produce deeds or statutory declarations sufficient to prove the title applied for.[30] The requirement under the Land Registration Act 2002 is that,

> "a person may be registered with absolute title if the registrar is of the opinion that the person's title to the estate is such as a willing buyer could properly be advised by a competent professional adviser to accept."[31]

The Land Registration Rules 2003 flesh out the requirements on first registration. These are:

- "sufficient details", by plan or otherwise (subject to rule 25 and 26) so that the land can be identified clearly on the Ordnance Survey map;

- all deeds and documents relating to the file that are in the control of the applicant.

Rule 25 only deals with mines and minerals but r.26 deals with boundaries of "cellars flats, tunnels etc." It provides:

> "(1) Subject to paragraph (2), unless all of the land above and below the surface is included in an application for first registration the applicant must provide a plan of the surface on under or over which the land to be registered lies, and sufficient information to define the vertical and horizontal extent of the land."

The registration should include appurtenant easements, i.e. those benefiting the estate rather than those burdening it. Under the Land Registration

---

[26] Land Registration (Amendment) Rules 2008.
[27] Rule 133(6) & (7) as substituted.
[28] Rule 133(8) as substituted.
[29] Land Registration (Amendment) Rules 2008 para.1(4) of Sch.5.
[30] These may include deeds prior to the root of title (i.e. a valid conveyance or other deed more than 15 years old). The root of title is only a conveyancing practice. The Registrar may need to go back further to be sure that the title is absolute: ibid., r.20(I).
[31] Land Registration Act 2002 s.9(2).

Act 2002 existing legal easements and profits override first registration.[32] However, they only override registered dispositions if they are not within the actual knowledge of the person to whom the disposition is made and would not have been obvious on a reasonably careful inspection of the land.[33]

Rule 203[34] sets out the system for the retention and return of documents. The registrar may retain all or any of the documents and return the rest. The applicant for registration may request the return of any documents, either at the time of the application or for five years thereafter (with power for the registrar to extend the time).[35] The registrar must then return the documents, unless there is a dispute as to who should have them. The registrar can destroy the documents at the end of the five year period. The registered owner is not obliged to retain the returned deeds. However, if they are retained they will be discoverable documents and can be used in a claim for rectification of the register or for fixing a precise boundary.

(b) Effect of registration

The registration itself gives the registered proprietor an indefeasible **4.13** title to the land. "The estate is vested in the proprietor together with all the interests subsisting for the benefit of the estate."[36] The meaning of this apparently unequivocal phrase was considered by the Court of Appeal in *Baxter v Mannion*[37] when the Court had to deal with the position (foreseen in the previous Edition) where the true owner had simply failed to respond to a notice from the Registry within the time limit. In respect of an application for rectification the Court decided that this was a mistake in the register even though the proper procedure had been followed, simply because the person registered was not in adverse possession of the property and therefore could not properly be registered. It remains to be seen whether the understandable conclusion of this unfortunate (if foreseeable) case has other ramifications as to the absolute nature of the registration, particularly with regard to a bona fide purchaser for value of the estate or, indeed, a mortgagee.

Registration will be either of absolute, possessory or qualified freehold title or of an absolute, good, possessory or qualified leasehold title.

---

[32] Sch.1 para.3 to the Land Registration Act 2002.
[33] Land Registration Act 2002 Sch.3 para.3.
[34] Land Registration Rules 2003.
[35] Land Registration Rules 2003 r.204.
[36] Land Registration Act 2002 s.11(3).
[37] *Baxter v Mannion* [2011] EWCA Civ 120; [2011] 1 W.L.R. 1594.

(c)   Absolute freehold title

4.14   The vast majority of titles are title absolute. Registration of an absolute title is in itself sufficient to enable the owner to dispose of the property without further proof of title. Equally it entitles him to compensation should it be shown that someone else has a better right to the land, but such a title is subject to rectification and, accordingly, is not a bar to a boundary dispute.

If the registration is shown to have been made wrongly the question will then arise as to whether the register should be rectified or left alone and whether the registered proprietor or the true owner or either of them should be indemnified by the state.

(d)   Possessory freehold title

4.15   The difference between an absolute and a possessory title is that registration of a possessory title does not,

> "affect the enforcement of any estate, right or interest adverse to or in derogation from the proprietor's title subsisting at the time of registration or then capable of subsisting".[38]

It will, however, only be registered where the registrar is satisfied on the information before him that the registered proprietor has a good title to the land. A person who is simply in possession, but, for example, has not been in possession for 12 years, is not entitled to have his title registered as a possessory title, though in some circumstances such a title could be registered as a qualified title.

In terms of boundary disputes the fact that the title is only registered as possessory is a point in favour of the other party. Possessory title does not mean that the registered proprietor has a title based only on adverse possession. Where the title deeds have been lost, it may well be possible to obtain an absolute title by showing that they were lost, stolen or destroyed while in proper custody. However, where there are problems about how the deeds came to disappear or what they actually said, the applicant may be limited to a possessory title. It will, however, encourage a party who feels that he has a good paper title to believe that that paper title will not be challenged and that all he has to worry about is a claim of 12 years' adverse possession.

A possessory title is subject to rectification in the same way as an absolute title.

---

[38] Land Registration Act 2002 s.11(7).

(e)   Qualified freehold title

A qualified title is registered where title can only be established for a **4.16**
limited period or subject to certain reservations.[39] The qualification will
be in respect of any estate or interest arising before a specified date
or arising under a specified instrument. Such registrations are very
rare. They are most usually found where a possessory title is claimed
but cannot be made out for the full 12 years or where there has been
a breach of trust. Again though, discovering that the other claimant
to the disputed land has only a qualified title would undoubtedly
encourage a party in pursuing an allegation that his own paper title is
superior.

(f)   Absolute leasehold title

A new lease for more than seven years and a transfer of a lease with **4.17**
more than seven years to run must be registered.[40] For the purposes of
boundary disputes an absolute leasehold title is very similar to an absolute freehold title. It means that the registrar is satisfied that the registered
proprietor is entitled to a qualifying lease which has been granted by a
person entitled to an absolute freehold title.

Where the freeholder is already registered this creates no difficulty.
However, where the freehold is not registered the lessee cannot obtain an
absolute registration without proving, not only his own title from the
lessor, but also that of his lessor. Since he is not himself entitled to demand
proof of title from his lessor,[41] he can only obtain a leasehold title if the
freeholder co-operates.

(g)   Good leasehold title

Where the freehold land is not registered and the freeholder does not **4.18**
co-operate or the leaseholder does not bother to pursue him the title will
normally be registered with a good leasehold title.

The difference between good and absolute leasehold title is caused by
the usual and much criticised[42] covenants for quiet enjoyment which
pertain to nearly all leases, namely that the title is subject to any claim by
title paramount against the lessor.

For the purposes of a boundary dispute the significance of this is that
if the other party has a claim against the lessor the existence of a

---

[39] Land Registration Act 2002 s.9(4).
[40] Land Registration Act 2002 ss.4(1)(c) and 4(2)(b).
[41] Law of Property Act 1925 s.44.
[42] See e.g., *Woodfall on Landlord & Tenant* (London: Sweet & Maxwell), "However it is
framed, such a covenant may be safely entered into by the landlord who never had any
title whatever to the demised premises or any part thereof".

registration of good leasehold title in favour of the lessee will not affect his claim. This can create real problems for lessees, whether registered or not. A lessee is not entitled to challenge the lessor's title,[43] but if an adjoining owner claims ownership the lessee cannot rely on his own leasehold title and cannot join his lessor as third party because there will be no breach of the covenant of quiet enjoyment. If the lessor is not a party he can now be required to disclose his title under r.25.5 of the Civil Procedure Rules 1998.

(h) Possessory leasehold title

4.19   A person who is paying rent is a tenant and is not entitled to be registered unless he has a lease for seven years or more. A person who is not paying rent, even if he is holding over after a long lease, is in adverse possession and, at the end of the requisite period, becomes a freehold owner. Possessory leasehold title can, however, arise where the person in possession has gained a possessory title against the leaseholder, but not against the freeholder, e.g. where he has been in possession for 12 years without paying rent to the leaseholder, but where the leaseholder has been paying rent (usually ground rent) to the freeholder.[44] Such a registration prevents the documentary lessee from surrendering it to the lessor and thereby depriving the lessee with possessory title of his rights. Also it can apply where the lessee satisfies the registrar that he has a leasehold interest but has lost the deeds. Where the lessor has only a possessory title presumably the leasehold interest can be registered as a good leasehold title.

(i) Qualified leasehold title

4.20   A qualified title is theoretically possible for a leasehold interest as for a freehold, but in practice is very rare.

4.   Title documents

4.21   Since the commencement of the Land Registration Act 2002 the title documents held by an owner will consist of an Official Copy of the Register in respect of the land in question, together with the Transfer. In respect of earlier titles there will be a Land Certificate.

The proprietorship register is indefeasible and a party can therefore be sure that the registered proprietor is the person against whom any action should be brought. The cause of action by which boundary disputes are commenced, however, is trespass and in order to found a claim in

---

[43] Law of Property Act 1925 s.44.
[44] *Spectrum Investment Co v Holmes* [1981] 1 W.L.R. 221; [1981] 1 All E.R. 6.

trespass it is only necessary to prove a right to possession and not title. If, therefore, an action is commenced by a person in possession who is not the registered proprietor this does not prevent his claim succeeding,[45] though the fact that one or both parties are registered as proprietor of the land may affect the remedy.[46] Furthermore it is not necessarily sufficient simply to bring an action against the registered proprietor. The object of boundary proceedings is usually both to fix the boundary and to prevent incursions. Such incursions are as likely to be carried out by a person in possession of the land who is not the owner as by the actual registered proprietor. Indeed trespass in pursuance of a boundary claim may often be carried out by other occupiers such as a lodger or a relative of the owner, or indeed by persons who do not live there.

Normally a person conducting a boundary dispute is looking for a declaration as to his rights, an injunction to prevent or dispose of incursions and damages. These remedies are dealt with later,[47] but in dealing with registration it is important to remember that the parties to be joined in respect of these different issues may be different. Normally a declaration will be made against the registered proprietor and indeed the Court may refuse this remedy unless the registered proprietor is joined.[48] It is not necessary to join all persons who might seek to support the other party in his claim since an injunction will bind not only the actual parties to the injunction but all persons with notice of it. Nevertheless, where a person with no proprietorial claims has in fact been active in pursuing the claim, for example by building or destroying fences, this person should be joined and an injunction or damages can be ordered against him as much as against the true proprietor of the adjoining land.

In considering the effect of a Land Certificate or Official Copy it must **4.22** be remembered that:

- where the boundary is to be a general boundary only, title is registered without notice to adjoining owners;

- although a title is registered as absolute, the register can be rectified if a registration is proved to have been wrongly effected[49]; and

- most registrations show only the general boundaries.[50]

Where both the adjoining titles are registered it is unlikely that there will be a substantial dispute about ownership of large parcels of land

---

[45] *Chowood Ltd v Lyall* (No.2) [1930] 2 Ch. 156.
[46] See under Rectification and Indemnity paras 4.33–4.35 below.
[47] See Ch.24.
[48] *New York Insurance Co v Public Trustee* [1924] 2 Ch. 101 per Atkin L.J. at 122.
[49] See later at s.8 of this Chapter.
[50] Land Registration Act 2002 s.60.

since the Land Registry will not deliberately register the same land under two different freehold titles. It is still possible for an adjoining owner to claim ownership on the basis that land included in his title has been accidentally omitted from registration, but such claims are comparatively rare. The effect of the Land Registration Act 2002 on adverse possession is considered in Chapter Five below. While disputes about the ownership of the paper title to entire blocks of registered land are comparatively rare, as the registration is only of general boundaries there is plenty of scope for dispute about the exact line of the boundary.

4.23 The old definition of a general boundary contained in the 1925 Rules has not been repeated in the Land Registration Rules 2003. There is, therefore, no definition of a general boundary. However, it seems clear that the right to challenge the registered boundary is not restricted to the boundary features themselves, but can include the suggestion that the boundary line shown on the filed plan is not the true line, either because it contains kinks or curves or because it is simply in the wrong place. There is a distinction between a dispute of this kind, and a dispute as to the ownership of a parcel of land as a whole. It may be that sometimes it will be hard to decide which category the claim comes into. Is a claim amounting to half the defendant's land a dispute about the parcel of land or only about the precise boundary? This issue was considered in *Derbyshire CC v Fallon*[51] in terms of whether the dispute is a "boundary dispute" or a "property dispute". It is only if it is a property dispute that the title can be rectified or, indeed, that rectification can be refused. Otherwise the additional land is simply added to one title and taken from the other without any change to the Register itself. Because, in the absence of a fixed boundary,[52] only general boundaries are shown on the register, a plan annexed to the Transfer may be looked at in addition to the filed plan. If it shows the boundary as agreed and pegged out, the Transfer plan will take priority.[53] As stated above, "T" marks referred to in the deeds will be shown on the filed plan, but "T" marks" shown on the transfer or on earlier deeds will not be referred to. However, they may still have evidential value.

As registration of a general boundary is usually effected without notice to adjoining owners, where only one of the parcels of land is registered the case proceeds as if both were unregistered unless and until the question of rectification of the register arises. It is as easy for the adjoining owner to claim that the registration is wrong as it is for him to claim that the other party's conveyance is wrong. In such circumstances the title

---

[51] [2007] EWHC 1326 (Ch).
[52] Land Registration Rules 2003 r.118.
[53] *Lee v Barrey* [1957] Ch. 251; [1957] 2 W.L.R. 245.

deeds which preceded registration may be just as important as title deeds preceding the root of title may be in unregistered conveyancing cases.

5. Subsequent dealings

Once land is registered any further dealings are completed by executing **4.24** a Transfer and then registering the new proprietor. It is the registration, as opposed to the Transfer, which actually transfers the title.[54] Until registration the transfer has no effect against third parties.[55] Even a surrender of a leasehold interest has no effect unless it is effected by a transfer followed by closure of the registration.[56] The transferee can then obtain an Official Copy of the new Register and accompanying documents.[57]

The problems associated with the time gap between transfer of an existing estate or creation of an interest and registration of that transfer or interest were a significant factor in the proposal to introduce electronic conveyancing,[58] but the introduction of e-conveyancing has, in any event, been delayed.

Once the Transfer is registered, therefore, the Transfer document is not **4.25** strictly necessary or relevant for showing title. Nevertheless situations can and do arise where the Transfer has to be construed for the purposes of seeing whether the vendor is in breach of his covenants for title.[59] Thus it is a breach of the covenant for title to execute a Transfer referring to title numbers, but to include a plan which shows additional land not included in the filed plan.

It is submitted, however, that the construction of the Transfer, though relevant for the purposes of an action for damages for breach of the covenant for title, is not relevant for determining the extent of the registered land. In a boundary dispute, the registered owner can only rely, as against his neighbour, on the land shown as his in the filed plan. If he feels that the land shown on the filed plan as being his is less than that which should have been transferred under the Transfer, then he should claim rectification of the register as against the person from whom he bought the land. It therefore seems very unlikely that a Transfer can ever be of substantial aid to a party in a boundary dispute where the other party was not involved in that Transfer, if it conflicts with the property shown on the filed plan. The only circumstances in which it could be

[54] Land Registration Act 2002 s.29.
[55] Land Registration Act 2002 s.28.
[56] *Spectrum Investment Co v Holmes* [1981] 1 W.L.R. 221; [1981] 1 All E.R. 6.
[57] Land Registration Rules 2003 rr.134-135.
[58] Land Registration Act 2002 ss.91-95.
[59] *AJ Dunning & Sons (Shopfitters) Ltd v Sykes & Son (Poole) Ltd* [1987] Ch. 287; [1987] 2 W.L.R. 167.

relevant is where it supplies details of the precise boundary which do not conflict with the general boundaries shown on the filed plan.

Of course disputes can arise between a vendor of registered land who has retained adjoining land and the purchaser as to the boundaries between the retained and the transferred land. In these circumstances a new title number has to be created. The purchaser is then in the position of a first registered proprietor who wishes either to maintain or to challenge the boundary shown on the filed plan. If he maintains that the filed plan does not represent the land included in the Transfer then he may be able to obtain rectification of the register. Alternatively he can sue the vendor for breach of his covenant for title.

6. Control of the register

4.26   Where both properties are registered it has been seen that the effect of registration is largely evidential. If a person can prove a good title to the disputed land dating from before the registrations (and not lost by adverse possession), he will win whether or not he is the registered title holder. However, the remedy to which he is entitled may be either rectification or just an indemnity.[60]

It is, however, common for boundary disputes to arise at a time of change in ownership. In these circumstances a party may seek to strengthen his case by applying voluntarily for registration or may create difficulties for another party who is trying to register the land or to register himself as proprietor of an existing registered title following a transfer. The Land Registration Act 2002 contains various provisions that are designed to prevent land being wrongly registered or to prevent the wrong person from being registered as proprietor. Because of the restrictions on rectification, even where a party is shown to be the true owner of the land, it is important for a litigant or a prospective litigant to ensure, if possible, that the other party does not get himself registered as the proprietor of the disputed land.

(a)   Caution against first registration

4.27   It has already been observed that registration can be effected without notice to adjoining owners. It has also been observed that until recently boundaries have general boundaries[61] only, though, in future, they can be fixed under the Land Registry system for fixing boundaries.[62] Boundary disputes can affect parcels of land as well as precise boundaries and therefore if a party believes that land he claims to own is still unregistered but may well be the subject of a claim for registration by the other party he may

---

[60] See later para.4.33 et seq.
[61] Land Registration Act 2002 s.60.
[62] Land Registration Act 2002 s.60; Land Registration Rules 2003 r.118.

wish to enter a caution against first registration. Under the Land Registration Act 2002 the person entering the caution must claim to be "entitled to an interest affecting the qualifying estate". This would appear to be sufficient to include a claimant under a boundary or easement dispute, but s.15(3) excludes a caution "by virtue of ownership of a freehold estate in land" or a registrable leasehold estate. It may be that this excludes a claimant under a boundary dispute, but not to an easement claim. The Rules do not appear to clarify this. The object of the caution is to prevent registration of the land without notice being given to the cautioner.[63] The caution is effected by an application in Form CT1 which does not require any detail about the cautioner's interest in the land.[64] It is, therefore, a simple precaution to effect, though whether it is worth doing in any particular case is a matter of nice judgment. There is a specific obligation not to exercise the right to lodge a caution (or to apply for a notice or restriction) without reasonable cause.[65] The duty is owed to anyone who suffers damage in consequence of its breach.[66] It follows that unjustified use of the caution procedure could result in an action for breach of statutory duty.

If someone applies to register the land after the caution has been entered then the cautioner is given notice and allowed time (usually 14 days) in which to enter an objection.[67] Meanwhile, the caution is entered on the register of cautions against first registration.[68] The application for cancellation is made in Form CTT.[69] Under the new system, the Register can be altered by the Registrar or the court.[70] The issue can be referred by the Registrar to the adjudicator.[71] Now that the post of adjudicator is fully operational, the Registry is increasingly encouraging this method of resolving issues relating to cautions, which will include boundary disputes. However, the parties still have the option of going to court.

(b) Notices and restrictions

The Land Registration Act 2002 replaces cautions against dealing and **4.28** inhibitions with provisions for notices and restrictions.[72] Pending land actions count as "an interest affecting an estate or charge" and, therefore can be the subject of a notice or restriction[73]:

---

[63] Land Registration Act 2002 s.16(1).
[64] Land Registration Rules 2003 r.42.
[65] Land Registration Act 2002 s.77.
[66] ibid. s.77(2).
[67] Land Registration Rules 2003 r.53.
[68] Land Registration Act 2002 s.19; Land Registration Rules 2003 r.40.
[69] Land Registration Rules 2003 r.44. This must be in form UN1, Land Registration Rules 2003 r.83.
[70] Land Registration Act 2002 ss.20 and 21.
[71] ibid. ss.107-114.
[72] See *Guy v Pannone LLP* [2009] EWCA Civ 30 at [14].
[73] Land Registration Act 2002 s.87.

"The fact that an interest is the subject of a notice does not necessarily mean that the interest is valid, but does mean that the priority of the interest, if valid, is protected for the purposes of sections 29 and 30".[74]

Such an application can be for a unilateral notice.[75] A person affected by a notice, i.e. the registered proprietor of the estate or a person entitled to be so registered, or a person entitled to an unregistered overriding interest within Schs 1 or 3,[76] can then apply to cancel it and the applicant for the notice must then object to the cancellation.[77]

While a notice gives warning to a prospective purchaser of a possible claim, a restriction actually prevents the registered owner from registering any disposition.[78] This can be indefinite, for a fixed period or until a court order or some other event.[79] The Registrar has wide powers to make such an order[80] and the application can be made by anyone with a sufficient interest in the making of an entry. The purpose can be to protect a claim in relation to a registered estate or to secure that interests are not overreached.

4.29   It is clear that these are the two principal powers to be used by claimants under a boundary or easement dispute to protect their interests. However the specific statutory duty to act reasonably contained in s.77 of the Land Registration Act 2002 qualifies the use of these provisions, particularly of restrictions. A person who asserts an unreasonable claim and thereby causes the owner to lose a proposed sale may find himself liable to substantial damages. With regard to the similar provision in the 1925 Act relating to a caution against dealing it was suggested that this cannot be used against a person who believes he has a claim and acts on legal advice.[81]

Until there is a larger body of authority on how the 2002 Act and the 2003 Rules work in practice it is difficult to know how different this new system will be from the previous system of cautions against dealing together with the rarely used inhibitions.

4.30   A registered proprietor who finds, when he wishes to dispose of the property, that an adjoining owner has entered a notice[82] or restriction has a number of alternatives at his disposal.

---

[74] ibid. s.32(8).
[75] ibid. ss.34(2)(b) and 35. This must be in form UN1, Land Registration Rules 2003 r.83.
[76] ibid. s.37.
[77] Land Registration Rules 2003 rr.86 and 8.
[78] Land Registration Act 2002 s.40(1); Land Registration Rules 2003 rr.91-100.
[79] ibid. s.40(2) and (3).
[80] Land Registration Act 2002 s.42.
[81] per Templeman J. in *Clearbrook Property Holdings Ltd v Verrier* [1974] 1 W.L.R. 243; [1973] 3 All E.R. 614.
[82] Or, prior to the commencement of the Land Registration Act 2002, a caution against dealing.

The most direct and immediate course is to apply to the court for rectification of the Register by cancellation under r.86 or r.97 of the Land Registration Rules 2003. The robust approach used in unregistered land, where there is no remedy available for a person damaged by an incorrect registration of a pending action,[83] has been applied in respect of registered land.[84] In *Clearbrook Property Holdings Ltd v Verrier*,[85] Templeman J. took the ingenious course of vacating the register but inviting the plaintiff instead to apply for an interlocutory injunction restraining sale, which would, of course, be subject to an undertaking as to damages.

7. Fixed boundaries

The Land Registration Rules 2003 provide for a new system for **4.31** determining the exact line of a boundary. The old system was very rarely used. Consent applications for fixed boundaries are becoming more common, but parties are also availing themselves of the new adjudicator procedure to conduct litigation about the precise line of the boundary.[86]

Where there is a transfer of part of a registered estate in land, or the grant of a registrable leasehold interest, there is a common boundary and the registrar considers that there is sufficient information to determine the exact line of the boundary, he may register it without any application.[87]

Where boundary owners have agreed the exact line of the boundary or there has been a court order, one owner may apply for registration of the exact line, attaching a plan, an arguable case that this is the exact line and evidence that he can identify all the adjoining owners and an agreement in writing by the adjoining owner. There is then no need for the registrar to send out any notices.[88] If there is no such agreement, a notice is sent out and the adjoining owner has 20 days to respond.[89] The owner is defined as the proprietor of a registered estate or a person entitled to apply for registration of an unregistered legal estate.[90] The Registrar then decides whether the requirements in r.119(1) are met and, if so registers the boundary. It is only where there is an application and the adjoining owner objects that there is a need for a hearing.

The Land Registry Practice Guide No. 40, however, provides some discouragement to the fixing of boundaries since it requires that:

---

[83] *Heywood v BDC Properties (No.1)* [1963] 1 W.L.R. 975; *Rawlplug Co Ltd v Kamvale Properties Ltd* (1969) 20 P. & C.R. 32; (1968) 112 S.J. 723.
[84] See *Calgary & Edmonton Land Co v Dobinson* [1974] Ch. 102; [1974] 2 W.L.R. 143.
[85] *Clearbrook Property Holdings Ltd v Verrier* [1974] 1 W.L.R. 243.
[86] See *Derbyshire CC v Fallon* [2007] EWHC 1326 (Ch).
[87] Land Registration Rules 2003 r.122.
[88] Land Registration Rules 2003 r.119(2) and form DB.
[89] Rule 119(3) extendable on application, r.119(4).
[90] Rule 119(8)—or the Queen if it is demesne land.

"Measurements shown on the plan need to be both precise and accurate to 10mm and should be taken from at least two defined points on surrounding permanent features".

There are seven other specific requirements.[91] Very few County Court judgments would meet these exacting requirements.

The potential problem where part of a boundary has been determined and another part has not is dealt with by stating that the ends of the determined boundary in relation to the undetermined boundary are not treated as determined.[92]

4.32   When a court reaches a decision on a boundary dispute concerning unregistered land it is normal for the decision to be kept with the deeds. Indeed because of the tendency of county courts, in particular, to lose or even to destroy their orders after a period this may be the only way of ensuring that the decision is not lost, thereby opening the way to another boundary dispute on the same issue at a later date. This course cannot be taken in respect of registered land, since the only document of title is the Register itself. In theory the best way of ensuring that the fruits of a successful boundary claim are not lost is to ensure that the boundary is fixed under these rules. Where the Register is proved wrong it will either be rectified or the true owner will lose his rights for ever and have to make do with an indemnity,[93] but where the only result of the dispute is to fix a boundary which has been only general the fixing of a more precise line does not demonstrate a "mistake" on the register and there will be no rectification of the register. The best course in these circumstances is to apply under r.119(2)[94] for a fixed boundary, which can then be registered by the Registry without notice to the other party.

8.   Rectification or alteration of the register

4.33   The Land Registration Act 2002[95] provides for the court to make orders for alteration of the register for the purpose of:

(a)   correcting a mistake;

(b)   bringing the register up to date; or

(c)   giving effect to any estate, right or interest excepted from the effect of the registration.

---

[91] Land Registry, *Land Registry Practice Guide 40*, (London: Land Registry, October 2005), para.3.3.2.

[92] Land Registration Rules 2003 r.121.

[93] See s.9 of this Chapter.

[94] As substituted by the Land Registration (Amendment) Rules 2008.

[95] Land Registration Act 2002 para.2 of Sch.4.

The Court means either the High Court or the county court.[96] This is a private right and application can only be made by a person with locus standi. It does not, therefore, allow a third party, such as a Parish Council, which might be concerned about the registration to apply.[97] This decision has, however, been rejected by the adjudicator in *Burton v Walker*.[98]

The area which has given rise to controversy is alteration which involves "rectification". This is defined as meaning an alteration which:

(a)   involves the correction of a mistake; and

(b)   prejudicially affects the title of a registered proprietor.

It appears that it has now been established that the term "correcting a mistake" is wide. In *Barclay's Bank Plc v Guy*[99] it was acknowledged that it would apply if the registration was effected by the fraud of the person applying for registration, but not where a chargee had honestly registered a charge on the basis of that fraudulent registration. However, in *Baxter v Mannion*[100] the Court of Appeal went much further and decided that mistake is not limited to a mistake through some official error, or by fraudulent application. This case related to the registration of a possessory title when the true registered owner had had the opportunity to object, but had failed to do so. This was a very hard case, but the Court was clear that the "mistake" was simply that the person claiming a possessory title did not have one. None of the earlier cases were considered in that case.

The power of rectification does, however, only apply where the mistake affects the title of the registered proprietor. Boundary disputes concerning registered land can be divided into those disputes where the wrong person is shown as the proprietor of an entire parcel of land ("a property dispute") and those where the area of dispute comes with the uncertainties which arise where only general boundaries have been registered ("a boundary dispute"). Although any judgment on a boundary, however small the change, is likely to affect the ownership of some of the land, a change in the title which comes within the normal margins of the general boundaries rule means that the registered title can remain unchanged even if the registered owner loses some land he thought he had.

Where a judgment has been made on the precise line of the boundary it has always been common practice for a note to be placed on the register

---

[96]   Land Registration Act 2002 s.132(3)(a).
[97]   *Wells v Pilling Parish Council* [2008] EWHC 556 (Ch).
[98]   *Burton v Walker* 2007/1124 Adjudicator to HM Land Registry.
[99]   [2008] EWCA Civ 452, though it was asserted by the adjudicator in *Knights Construction Ltd v Roberto Mac Ltd* Ref 2009/1459 that the observations on the meaning of "correcting a mistake" are strictly obiter.
[100]   *Baxter v Mannion* [2011] EWCA Civ 120; [2011] 1 W.L.R. 1594.

referring to this. Although "Notes" are mentioned at various places in the Rules,[101] they are not referred to in the Act and their significance has never been judicially considered. It appears that their effect is to draw the attention of the parties to the matter therein contained, rather than to affect their rights. Therefore, if there is a note about the boundary, it may be necessary to go back to the Court's Judgment to identify its precise effect.

Now that the Rules have been changed[102] to allow the Registrar to register a fixed boundary following a court order, this would seem to be the correct course, since it can be done unilaterally.

Even if the true owner of the land is able to show that he is seeking to correct a mistake and that he has been prejudicially affected by it[103] the power of the court to order rectification of the register is also subject to the qualification that no such order should be made without the registered proprietor's consent unless the proprietor has "by fraud or lack of proper care caused or substantially contributed to the mistake"[104] or if, for any other reason, it would be unjust for the alteration not to be made.[105]

Once the requirement for rectification are met, the Court has an obligation to make the order unless there are exceptional circumstances which justify its not doing so.[106]

4.34 The Courts have, always[107] set their face against situations where the true owner of land is deprived of his ownership in favour of a person who has obtained registration without justification. The draftsmen of the 2002 Act may have intended a situation where the true owner would normally receive only financial compensation, but this is not the way the Act has been interpreted. In effect, the "neglect or lack of proper care" consists of registering the land when it did not belong to him. The exception is where there is an intervening party, who will be deprived of his or her rights if the true owner is given back the land. This is most notably a mortgagee. As the law stands a mortgagee, even one who has been duped into lending money to a fraudster[108] will retain his mortgage, even if the true owner gets his land back. The restriction on the right to rectification, however, is still there and, no doubt, the Court will be willing to refuse rectification where the justice of the case favours leaving the registered owner in place.

---

[101] e.g. rr.71 and 76.
[102] By the Land Registration (Amendment) Rules 2008.
[103] *Re 139 Deptford High Street, Ex p. British Transport Commission* [1951] Ch. 884.
[104] Land Registration Act 2002 Sch.4 para.3(2)(a).
[105] ibid. para.3(2)(b). See the decision of the Adjudicator in *Knights Construction v Roberto Mac Ltd* of February 9, 2011.
[106] Land Registration Act 2002 Sch.4 para.2(3).
[107] *Chowood Ltd v Lyall (No.2)* [1930] 1 Ch 426.
[108] *Barclays Bank Plc v Guy* [2008] EWCA Civ 452; *Guy v Barclays Bank Plc* [2010] EWCA Civ 1396; [2011] 1 W.L.R. 681.

The procedure following a court order for alteration (including rectification) is for the successful party to apply for alteration of the Register.[109] The Registrar is then under a duty to alter the register.[110]

9. Indemnity

The right to an indemnity is governed by Sch.8 to the Land Registration **4.35** Act 2002. It only applies to rectification of the register and not to other kinds of alteration. As such it applies to cases where there has been rectification, or where there would be rectification if the mistake was corrected, or other mistakes or defaults made by the registry.[111] There is no need to show that the Registry or anyone else is responsible for the mistake.

The right to an indemnity is lost if any of the loss is due, wholly or in part, to his own fraud, or if it is wholly the result of his own lack of proper care.[112] This, therefore, is lack of proper care by the claimant, as opposed to Sch.4 which refers to lack of proper care by the registered owner. If it partly due to lack of care it is reduced "to such extent as is fair".[113]

The provision does not apply to mines and minerals unless they are noted on the register.[114]

The Schedule contains provisions as to valuation, time limits[115] recovery of costs expended by agreement of the registrar and interest.[116]

Most issues as to indemnity are settled by agreement with the Land Registry. However, there is power to apply to the court which can resolve issues between the Registrar and the applicant.[117]

10. Adjudicator

The Land Registration Act 2002 created a new judicial post of **4.36** Adjudicator in order to provide a proper system for resolving disputes relating to Registered Land. The system was never intended to replace the courts as a forum for resolving boundary or property disputes, but it has provided a valuable alternative route to the extent that many boundary disputes coming before the courts are now appeals from the adjudicator. The Rules are contained in the Adjudicator to Her Majesty's Land Registry (Practice and Procedure) Rules 2003 ("the 2003 Rules") and the Adjudicator to Her Majesty's Land Registry (Practice and Procedure)

---

[109] Land Registration Rules 2003 r.127.
[110] Land Registration Act 2002 Sch.4 para.22.
[111] Land Registration Act 2002 Sch.8 para.1.
[112] ibid. para.5(1).
[113] ibid. para.5(2).
[114] ibid. para.3(1).
[115] Which is six years from the date the claimant knows or should have known of the claim, ibid. r.8.
[116] Land Registration Rules 2003 r.195.
[117] Land Registration Act 2002 Sch.8 para.7.

(Amendment) Rules 2008 ("the 2008 Rules"). The main hearing centre is in London,[118] but hearings are also held at various hearing centres throughout the country.

There are two separate ways in which a dispute may be brought before the Adjudicator. One is a direct reference from the Registrar under s.73(7) of the Land Registration Act 2002. This arises where there has been an application for a registration followed by an objection under s.73(1). If the matter cannot be resolved by agreement, the Registrar must refer it to the adjudicator. The adjudicator then has the option of referring the matter on to the court or dealing with it himself.

The second method is by direct application to the Adjudicator under the Act. This may be for rectification or alteration of the register under Sch.4, for the registration of a determined boundary under r.118 Land Registration Rules 2003 or to exercise the equitable jurisdiction of the Court to rectify or set aside a document.[119] He does not, however, have the power to grant an injunction. If an injunction is needed to enforce the judgment, the parties will have to go to the court.[120]

The law relating to the jurisdiction of the Adjudicator is still developing and was considered by Christopher Nugent QC in *Derbyshire CC v Fallon*.[121] From this it is clear that, where there is a reference under s.73(7) the adjudicator can resolve any property issues, including, for example, whether there is a valid title by virtue of adverse possession. The breadth of the adjudicator's powers and the extent of his discretion have been upheld by the Court of Appeal in *Chief Land Registrar v Silkstone & Tatnall*.[122]

Where there are complex issues, such as whether or not there is a resulting trust, the adjudicator has a discretion as to what issues he should decide. That discretion can only be challenged on appeal on the usual basis, namely that it is not a proper, judicial exercise of that discretion. However, the High Court has endorsed the principle that relevant issues should be decided by the Adjudicator unless the application forms part of other litigation in the High Court and that it is in accordance with the overriding objective that the issue before the adjudicator should be dealt with by the High Court.[123]

The Rules are essentially in line with the Civil Procedure Rules and the Rules used by a variety of tribunals. They allow for full case management

---

[118] 7th Floor, Victory House, 34 Kingsway, London, WC2B 6EX.
[119] Land Registration Act 2002 s.109(2); r.16 Adjudicator to Her Majesty's Land Registry (Practice and Procedure) Rules 2003 (SI 2003/2171).
[120] *Derbyshire CC v Fallon* [2007] EWHC 1326 (Ch), where the fact that a court would not have granted an injunction was the basis for refusing rectification in "exceptional circumstances".
[121] *Derbyshire CC v Fallon* [2007] EWHC 1326 (Ch).
[122] [2011] 2 P. & C.R. 258.
[123] *Jayasinghe v Liyanage* [2010] EWHC 265 (Ch); [2010] 1 W.L.R. 2106.

by the Adjudicator. Although hearings are to be the norm,[124] the adjudicator can dispose of cases without a hearing providing the parties do not object.[125] There is a new provision for summary disposal of either the whole proceedings or a particular issue in the proceedings where the adjudicator considers that the applicant or respondent has no real prospect of success.[126] The adjudicator can hold a site inspection, supported if necessary by an order for entry. There is no formal restriction on where hearings can be held. He has to give his reasons in writing.[127] There is no restriction on who can act as a representative.[128] The adjudicator has a discretion as to costs,[129] which, if appropriate, he can assess. The practice is for costs to follow the event as in the courts, but there are no court fees or hearing fees. There is a right of appeal to the Chancery Division of the High Court,[130] which, in turn, allows for a further appeal through the courts system to the Court of Appeal and the Supreme Court.

---

[124] Land Registration Rules 2003 r.33(1).
[125] ibid. r.343.
[126] Rule 32A inserted by the 2008 Rules.
[127] ibid. r.41.
[128] ibid. r.35.
[129] ibid r.42.
[130] There have already been several such appeals, e.g. *Hicks Developments Ltd v Chaplin* [2007] EWHC 141 (Ch).

Chapter Five
Adverse Possession

1. Introduction

Title to unregistered land can be shown by proving adverse possession **5.01** of the land in question for a period of 12 years (sometimes known as squatters' rights).[1] Twenty per cent of all land is still unregistered; so the old law still has some application.

The rationale behind this principle is much the same as the reason for limitation periods in all other kinds of action. It is undesirable, and ultimately unjust, for the courts to have to look back into history to trace the paper title where there is a person who is in long established possession of the land. As such it emanates from the strong emphasis of the common law on possession rather than ownership.

In respect of registered land, the same principle applied until the passing of the Land Registration Act 2002, the central provision of which is s.96(1):

> "No period of limitation under section 15 of the Limitation Act 1980 (time limits in relation to recovery of land) shall run against any person, other than a chargee."

Since 80 per cent of land in the jurisdiction is now registered, this represents a fundamental change in the approach to "squatter's rights".

The basis for this change comes from the Law Commission's strong attack on the principle in its application to registered land.[2] The development of the law of proprietary estoppel has allowed a person who deserves to get a title because of the unconscionable behaviour of the true owner to have the freehold conveyed to him. The more rigid principle of adverse possession can amount not to possession of right, but

---

[1] Limitation Act 1980 s.15(1).

[2] Law Commission, *Land Registration for the Twenty-First Century: A Conveyancing Revolution* (London: The Stationery Office, 2001) Law Com. No.271, pp.202 et seq.

"possession of wrong". "The deserving and the undeserving alike may be caught or spared by the operation of the Limitation Acts."[3]

5.02　In some common law countries with full registration of land the concept has been simply abolished. Despite the perception that it is a purloiner's charter, it does ensure, with unregistered land, that long forgotten disputes are not revived. In respect of registered land, however, the principle is much harder to justify since the person with a registered title is surely entitled to sit back and leave the property relying on his registration. Furthermore a distinction between registered and unregistered land can be justified in part as an encouragement to voluntary registration.

A further attack on the old system has come from the Human Rights Act 1998,[4] which protects the right to property and, in particular, the right not to have it expropriated without compensation. This issue came before the European Court of Human Rights in *JA Pye (Oxford) Ltd v United Kingdom*[5] which held that the UK legislation was a potential breach of the legislation, but that it addressed a legitimate aim in the public interest and, furthermore, that the legislation came within the margin of appreciation which is allowed to national legislatures. This judgment was approved by the Court of Appeal in *Ofulue v Bossert*[6] and was endorsed on appeal to the House of Lords.[7] Accordingly this attack on the entire concept of adverse possession as a means of obtaining ownership of property has failed.

The new system is set out below. Although it makes substantial changes it does not abolish all rights to adverse possession either in respect of registered or unregistered land. Indeed the transitional provisions[8] provide that a person who has obtained a title by adverse possession by the commencement of the Act in October 2003 is entitled to be registered as the owner without going through the new process. The fact is, however, that the principle of adverse possession has lost much of its sting.

While the judgment in *JA Pye (Oxford) Ltd v United Kingdom*[9] related to the old law, it applies *a fortiori* to the new provisions and there is no reason to think that the new system is in conflict with the Human Rights Act or the European Convention on Human Rights.

The criticism of the new system is that, in trying to meet perceived problems, such as estoppel, or the existence of an independent right, such as a bare trust, or mistake, it creates complications which will give rise to

---

[3] per Sedley J. in *Central London Commercial Estates Ltd v Kato Kagaku Ltd* [1998] 4 All E.R. 948; [1998] 3 E.G.L.R. 55.
[4] Article 1 of 1st Protocol, incorporated by Sch.1.
[5] *JA Pye (Oxford) Ltd v United Kingdom* (2007) 46 E.H.R.R. 1083.
[6] [2008] EWCA Civ 7; [2009] Ch 1.
[7] *Ofulue v Bossert* [2009] 3 All E.R. 93.
[8] Land Registration Act 2002 Sch.12 para.18.
[9] *JA Pye (Oxford) Ltd v United Kingdom* (2007) 46 E.H.R.R. 1083.

fresh litigation. This is borne out by the unstemmed flow of litigation coming before the Adjudicator. Furthermore any system which relies on the true owner objecting to another's claim will meet up with the problems of the true owner who is absent or incapable or just inefficient.

2. Principles

In *R. v Oxfordshire CC Ex p. Sunningwell Parish Council* [10] Lord Hoffman **5.03** has provided an authoritative analysis of the common-law principle of prescription in relation to private and public rights of way. Although he does not deal specifically with adverse possession, he makes clear that, in the common-law tradition, prescription is based on the true owner losing his rights by limitation rather than the other party taking rights by use.[11] This does not explain, however, how, as a matter of principle, adverse occupation, particularly against a registered owner, should give rise to ownership.

The potential injustice of the principles of adverse possession, particularly in the case of registered land, is succinctly summarised by Lord Bingham in *J A Pye (Oxford Ltd) Ltd v Graham*,[12] the latest House of Lords decision on this vexed subject:

> "They [the defendants] were not at fault. But the result of *Pye's* inaction was that they enjoyed the full use of the land without payment for 12 years. As if that were not gain enough, they are then rewarded by obtaining the title to this considerable area of valuable land without any obligation to compensate the former owner in any way at all. In the case of unregistered land, and in the days before registration became the norm, such a result could no doubt be justified as avoiding protracted uncertainty where the title to land lay. But where land is registered it is difficult to see any justification for a legal rule which compels such an apparently unjust result, and even harder to see why the party gaining the title should not be required to pay some compensation at least to the party losing it. It is reassuring that the Land Registration Act 2002 has addressed the risk that a registered owner may lose his title through inadvertence."

Despite this clear endorsement of the 2002 Act, there is still a lingering feeling that the squatter represents the underdog, taking advantage of the laxity of big business and that freehold tenure is only tenure from the Crown and not absolute ownership, with an implied obligation to look after and then make use of the land. In the vernacular— "use it or lose it!"

---

[10] [2000] 1 A.C. 335; [1999] 3 W.L.R. 160.
[11] "Usucapio" in Roman law.
[12] [2003] 1 A.C. 419 at [2].

5.04   The claim of a person to a possessory title, therefore, is based on the negative effect of the extinguishment of the rival title, coupled with the basic principle of English law that all that is needed to found a case in trespass is not ownership but possession or a right to possession. Although its juridical origin is fairly complex, once established, a title obtained by adverse possession is essentially just as good as a paper title and can be disposed of or inherited in exactly the same way.

Dispossession and discontinuance have been treated in the past as two quite separate issues.[13] However, in order to commence or defend an action, the party claiming a possessory title has to show either actual possession or a right to possession. It would be no defence to a person who had not been in possession for 12 years (either himself or through his predecessors) to show that the true owner had abandoned or discontinued his possession more than 12 years previously[14]:

> "We are clearly of opinion that the statute applies not to cases of want of actual possession by the plaintiff, but to cases where he has been out of, and another in, possession for the prescribed time."[15]

5.05   The difference between dispossession and discontinuance has been expressed in this way,

> "the one is where a person comes in and drives out the others from possession, the other case where the person in possession goes out and is followed into possession by other persons".[16]

However, this is somewhat unrealistic. What normally happens is that the true owner leaves land unoccupied or at least unused, without necessarily going out of possession and the squatter starts by making some use of the land, without the true owner being aware of what is happening and certainly without driving the true owner out. Then the squatter gradually increases his use of the land until he is in exclusive possession. It is submitted that the term "discontinuance" adds little to the definition and that what is really required is "dispossession" which usually will not involve any element of "driving out", but simply the process whereby the true owner loses possession to the squatter. This approach was endorsed by the House of Lords in *J A Pye Ltd v Graham*[17] and is now only of academic interest. The impact of this is explained at 5.14 below.

Paragraph 8(1) of Schedule[18] provides that:

---

[13] *Williams Bros Direct Supplies v Raftery* [1958] 1 Q.B. 159; [1957] 3 W.L.R. 931.

[14] Limitation Act 1980, Sch.1 para.8.

[15] *Buckinghamshire CC v Moran* [1990] Ch. 623; [1989] 3 W.L.R. 152.

[16] per Fry J., *Rains v Buxton* (1880) L.R. 14 Ch. D. 537, cited with approval in *Buckinghamshire CC v Moran* [1990] Ch. 623.

[17] *J A Pye (Oxford Ltd) Ltd v Graham* [2003] 1 A.C. 419.

[18] Limitation Act 1980.

"No right of action to recover land shall be treated as accruing unless the land is in the possession of some person in whose favour the period of limitation can run (referred to below in this paragraph as 'adverse possession')".

This paragraph contains the only references to "adverse" possession in the Act. Although the use of the word "adverse" was criticised by Lord Browne-Wilkinson in *J A Pye Ltd v Graham*,[19] the expression has been regularly used in the authorities and it is better to look at whether the party claiming a possessory title can show adverse possession for the relevant period, than to become bogged down in considering the nature of dispossession and discontinuance.

Once the title is extinguished the owner of the paper title is not entitled to claim damages for trespass or mesne profits for the period while the squatter was in adverse possession, but had not been there for 12 years.[20]

3. Land Registration Act 2002

The Land Registration Act 2002, which came into force on October 13, **5.06** 2003, does not change the concept of adverse possession in respect of registered land. It just makes it much more difficult for a person in adverse possession to obtain a title. The definition of adverse possession in the Act[21] relates back to the Limitation Act 1980. Therefore all the previous law relating to whether a person is in adverse possession, etc. continues to have effect where the 2002 Act applies.

The scheme of the Act is that a person who has been in adverse possession of land for 10 years may apply to the Registrar to be registered as proprietor.[22] He can also apply if he has been evicted after 10 years' adverse possession. He has six months to do so.[23] If he does not do so, he stands at risk of an action claiming possession. However, if he can show that on the day preceding the action he could have applied for registration that is a defence to a possession action.[24]

On receiving an application, the Registrar gives notice to all interested parties, in particular the registered owner. If anyone objects then the new procedure clicks in. If not the squatter is entitled to be registered as the new owner.[25] This is a crucial issue. What of the old, the absent or the negligent registered owner? The Rules provide no protection for such people. Unsurprisingly, this is an issue which the courts have had to address and they have done so by means of the power of rectification,

---

[19] [2003] 1 A.C. 419.
[20] *Mount Carmel Investments v Peter Thurlow* [1988] 1 W.L.R. 1078; [1988] 3 All E.R. 129.
[21] Land Registration Act 2002 Sch.6 para.11(1).
[22] ibid. Sch.6 para.1(1).
[23] ibid. Sch.6 para.1(2).
[24] Land Registration Act 2002 s.98(1).
[25] Land Registration Act 2002 para.4.

deciding, in short, that if a person who is not in adverse possession obtains registration because the true owner was distracted by personal difficulties and failed to object, then the Court can rectify the register accordingly.[26]

5.07   If the application for registration under the Act is contested the squatter will have to show that one of three conditions apply:

(1)   It would be unconscionable for him to be dispossessed because of an "equity by estoppel and, in the circumstances, he should be registered as the proprietor".[27] In effect this means that there is a proprietary estoppel which should result in a full registration.[28]

(2)   There is "some other reason" why he should be registered.[29]

(3)   There is a boundary dispute, the exact line has not been determined under s. 60 of the 2002 Act, that for at least 10 years of the 12 year period the squatter or his predecessor reasonably believed he was the owner and the estate had been registered in the past year.[30]

The squatter is not entitled to be registered if the registered owner is incapable either due to mental disability or physical impairment or an enemy or detained in enemy territory.

If a person makes an application and it is rejected the registered owner then has two years to evict him. If he has not either evicted the squatter or commenced proceedings against him during this period the squatter, having been in possession by this time for at least 12 years, has an absolute right to registration.[31]

Rules 187 to 194 Land Registration Rules 2003[32] give effect to the new provisions, but do not contain any further safeguards. It appears that there is still a risk of injustice if the registered owner either ignores the notice,[33] or, indeed, has not corrected an address for service left with the Registry.[34] The time limit for the owner of the paper title to make an application challenging a claim for adverse possession is the 65th business day after the date of issue of the notice.[35] This injustice can only be corrected by an application for rectification of the register,[36] which would be an expensive process and involve satisfying all the requirements for rectification.

---

[26] *Baxter v Mannion* [2011] EWCA Civ 120; [2011] 1 W.L.R. 1594.
[27] Land Registration Act 2002 Sch.6 para.5(2).
[28] See Ch. 3 above at 3.10.
[29] Land Registration Act 2002 Sch.6 para.5(3).
[30] ibid para.5(4) see *Lory v Harpserve* decision of Adjudicator 2008/1530.
[31] ibid. Sch.6 para.6.
[32] As amended by the Land Registration Amendment Rules 2005 and 2008.
[33] *Skipwith v Singh* decision of Adjudicator 2009/0850.
[34] See Land Registration Rules 2003 r.198.
[35] Land Registration Rules 2003 r.189.
[36] *Baxter v Mannion* [2011] EWCA Civ 120; [2011] 1 W.L.R. 1594.

4. Possession

The first element in adverse possession is to show actual possession **5.08** throughout the required period. Unlike the doctrine of proprietary estoppel,[37] the nature of possession does not depend on the amount of money spent on the land by the claimant. It depends rather on whether the nature of the acts carried out on the land shows clearly that possession is being asserted:

> "Factual possession signifies an appropriate degree of physical control. It must be a single and exclusive possession ... Thus an owner of land and a person intruding on that land without his consent cannot both be in possession of the land at the same time. The question what acts constitute a sufficient degree of exclusive physical control must depend on the circumstances, in particular the nature of the land and the manner in which land of that nature is commonly used or enjoyed."[38]

This passage was approved, but refined by Lord Browne-Wilkinson in *J A Pye (Oxford) Ltd v Graham*[39]:

> "To be pedantic, the problem could be avoided by saying there are two elements necessary for legal possession:
>
> 1. a sufficient degree of physical custody and control ("factual possession"). [This can be personal possession or by way of a licensee or lessee, providing he shows that he has himself authorised these acts and this is the basis on which the licensee or lessee has entered onto the land.[40]]
>
> 2. an intention to exercise such custody and control on one's own behalf and for one's own benefit ("intention to possess")."

The same applies where two squatters vie with each other for possession of land which neither owns. Neither will gain possessory rights.[41]

In *Treloar v Nute*[42] the acts carried out by the claimant were:

---

[37] See above para.3.10 et seq.
[38] per Slade L.J. in *Buckinghamshire CC v Moran* [1990] Ch. 623; [1989] 2 All E.R. 225 at 236b quoting his own judgment in *Powell v MacFarlane* (1979) 38 P. & C.R. 452 at 470.
[39] *JA Pye (Oxford) Ltd v Graham* [2003] 1 A.C. 419 at [40].
[40] *Roberts v Swangrove Estates Ltd* [2007] EWHC 513 (Ch), upheld on appeal sub nom. *Roberts v Crown Estate Commissioners* [2007] 2 P. & C.R. 17.
[41] *Marsden v Miller* (1992) 64 P. & C.R. 239; *Roberts v Swangrove Estates* [2007] EWHC 513 (Ch), upheld on appeal sub nom. *Roberts v Crown Estate Commissioners* [2007] 2 P. & C.R. 17.
[42] *Treloar v Nute* [1976] 1 W.L.R. 1295; [1977] 1 All E.R. 230.

- grazing cows on the land;

- taking spoil onto the land and partially filling up a gully;

- storing materials;

- riding motor-cycles on the land.

In 1963 the claimant erected a fence, but it was necessary to show possession before that date to justify the claim. The Court of Appeal assumed that the judge had held that these acts amounted to possession and said:

> "The particular acts found by the judge are, we think, rather on the borderline of what can properly be regarded as constituting possession."[43]

Nevertheless they held that in the particular circumstances of that case the acts did constitute possession, relying particularly on the placing of spoil which was a preliminary part of the operation of levelling the land for building. In *Buckinghamshire CC v Moran*[44] the crucial acts of possession consisted of securing "a complete enclosure of the plot" and changing the locks on the gate.

5.09　On the other side of the line, in *Wilson v Martin's Executors*,[45] the Court of Appeal overturned a decision that there was adverse possession when the squatter had repaired fences and cut trees for sale. Although this issue has used up considerable Court of Appeal time in recent years, it is not possible to lay down any specific rules as to what may or may not constitute possession:

> "The acts implying possession in one case may be wholly inadequate to prove it in another. The character and value of the property, the suitable and natural mode of using it, the course of conduct which the proprietor might reasonably be expected to follow with a due regard to his own interest-all these things, greatly varying as they must, under various conditions are to be taken into account in determining the sufficiency of a possession."[46]

Lord O'Hagan was talking about fisheries, but his statement has been regularly approved as setting out the law in respect of the possession of land.[47]

---

[43] Per Sir John Pennycuick at 233h.
[44] *Buckinghamshire CC v Moran* [1990] Ch. 623.
[45] [1993] 1 E.G.L.R. 178.
[46] *Lord Advocate v Lord Lovatt* (1879-1880) L.R. 5 App. Cas. 273 at 288.
[47] e.g. *Treloar v Nute* [1976] 1 W.L.R. 1295; [1977] 1 All E.R. 230 at 234a.

It is, however, possible to seek some guidelines from the cases. Many of them stress the need for exclusion of the true owner.[48] Fencing or any other form of enclosure[49] is the most obvious act of possession since it usually shows an intention to keep other people out.[50] However, it may depend on the nature and purpose of the fence. A fence built on part of the land to keep geese in is of far less significance than a fence round the boundary to keep people out.[51] A gate erected on your right of way and kept locked will not necessarily amount to adverse possession against the owner of the land over which the right of way runs, since you may just be intending to keep the public out,[52] but changing the lock on the gate is a significant indication of possession.[53] The fence or gate does not have to be substantial; it is enough to show that the intention is plain and overt.[54] The reverse situation may arise where the true owner builds a fence or plants a hedge within his land leaving a strip of land on the far side. This in itself does not show any abandonment of the land,[55] but where it is coupled with acts of cultivation by the owner on the other side it may contribute towards the conclusion that the true owner has been excluded.[56]

Building on the land, whether a house or some other structure, is also **5.10** a fairly clear assertion of possession.[57]

> "My neighbour must take actual possession of it, as, for instance, by cultivating the ground, building upon or paving it, or something of that kind."[58]

It was the levelling of the ground for building which was a major factor in *Treloar v Nute*.[59] A problem can arise, however, where only part of the land has been built upon. A building erected to assist the use of the whole land, such as a cowshed, will give an indication of possession of the whole land, though it will not necessarily be enough.[60] It is all a matter of degree.

Cultivation, too, can amount to possession.[61] On the other hand it can just indicate that the person wishes to make use of the land whilst the true

---

[48] *Marshall v Taylor* [1895] 1 Ch. 641; *Bligh v Martin* [1968] 1 W.L.R. 804; *Buckinghamshire CC v Moran* [1990] Ch. 623; [1990] Ch. 623; [1989] 3 W.L.R. 152.

[49] *Tower Hamlets LBC v Barrett* [2005] EWCA Civ 923; [2006] 1 P. & C.R. 9.

[50] See *Tower Hamlets LBC v Barrett* [2005] EWCA Civ 923.

[51] *Basildon DC v Charge* [1996] C.L.Y. 4929.

[52] *Littledale v Liverpool College* [1900] 1 Ch. 19.

[53] *Buckinghamshire CC v Moran* [1990] Ch. 623; [1989] 3 W.L.R. 152.

[54] *Purbrick v Hackney LBC* [2003] EWHC 1871 (Ch); [2004] 1 P. & C.R. 34.

[55] *Kynoch Ltd v Rowlands* [1912] 1 Ch. 527.

[56] *Marshall v Taylor* [1895] 1 Ch. 641; *Hounslow LBC v Minchinton* (1997) 74 P. & C.R. 221.

[57] *Tower Hamlets LBC v Barrett* [2005] EWCA Civ 923; [2006] 1 P. & C.R. 9, where building work on the land retained possession even after the fence was removed.

[58] *Kynoch Ltd v Rowlands* [1912] 1 Ch. 527.

[59] *Treloar v Nute* [1976] 1 W.L.R. 1295; [1977] 1 All E.R. 230.

[60] *Marshall v Taylor* [1895] 1 Ch. 641.

[61] *Bligh v Martin* [1968] 1 W.L.R. 804.

owner does not need it.[62] Indeed, it is submitted that this is the only extent to which the true owner's reasons for not requiring the land are relevant. A decision that even quite major acts of cultivation including cutting timber, fishing, growing rice and building a dam to show the boundary did not amount to possession has been upheld by the Privy Council,[63] and the need for "cogent and compelling evidence" was emphasised at first instance in *Basildon DC v Charge*.[64] On the other hand the Privy Council has also upheld a decision from Ceylon that taking grass might be sufficient.[65] It is even possible to assert adverse possession of a party wall by doing works on the whole of it, but this was in an unusual case where the adjoining owner had virtually abandoned it by diverting a public highway to the other side of it.[66]

Parking on land can be evidence of possession[67] but to amount to adverse possession it must be on quite a large scale and more or less continuous.[68] Fishing on the land is of doubtful significance, since it could be seen as purporting to exercise a profit à prendre over the land, rather than exclusive possession, but in appropriate circumstances it can be seen as an assertive act of possession.[69]

5.11   The adverse possession will normally only extend to the area of land actually occupied and it will be unusual for constructive possession of more land to be upheld.[70] As is explained below,[71] however, this does not mean that the person in possession has to make continual use of all of the land:

> "It is clearly settled that acts of possession done on parts of a tract of land to which possessory title is sought may be evidence of possession of the whole."[72]

Receiving sums from a third party or a fortiori from the true owner is capable of amounting to exercising rights of possession. This is in many

---

[62] *Williams Bros Direct Supplies v Raftery* [1958] 1 Q.B. 159.
[63] *West Bank Estates v Arthur* [1967] 1 A.C. 665; [1966] 3 W.L.R. 750.
[64] [1996] C.L.Y. 4929.
[65] *Umma v Appu* [1939] A.C. 136.
[66] *Prudential Assurance Co v Waterloo Real Estate Inc* [1999] 2 E.G.L.R. 85, a hard-fought case over an historic wall vital to two conflicting major property developments in Knightsbridge.
[67] *Williams v Usherwood* (1983) 45 P. & C.R. 235.
[68] *Pavledes v Ryesbridge Properties Ltd* (1989) 58 P. & C.R. 459; *Tennant v Adamczyk* [2005] EWCA Civ 1239; [2006] 1 P. & C.R. 28.
[69] *Roberts v Swangrove Estates Ltd* [2007] EWHC 513 (Ch) upheld on appeal sub nom. *Roberts v Crown Estate Commissioners* [2007] 2 P. & C.R. 17.
[70] *Glynn v Howell* [1909] 1 Ch. 666; *Davies v John Wood Property* decision of Adjudicator 2008/0528.
[71] See below para.5.18.
[72] *Higgs v Nassauvian* [1975] A.C. 464; [1975] 2 W.L.R. 72; [1975] 1 All E.R. 95 at101f; see *Roberts v Swangrove Estates Ltd* [2007] EWHC 513 (Ch) where the Scottish principle of "unum quid" was discussed.

ways a more specific assertion of possession than actual cultivation which could be interpreted as just taking advantage of the situation without seeking to assert any exclusive right.[73]

Equally it is perfectly possible for possession to be obtained or continued through an agent such as a building contractor,[74] or through any licensee or lessee providing that it is clear that the acts are done on the squatter's authority.[75]

The exclusiveness of the possession is not affected by the fact that other people are continuing to exercise ancillary rights to the property, such as rights of way.[76]

A person can be in exclusive possession of part of a building:

> "But if a claimant is to establish title by adverse possession to part only of a building, it is necessary that the pleadings should precisely define the part of the building claimed to have been in the possession of the claimant, and that there should be credible evidence that that part of the building was capable of being possessed by the claimant to the exclusion of others (apart from the claimant's licensees), and that the claimant did in fact enjoy such possession throughout the limitation period. A case of that sort might be relatively easy to plead and prove if the property in question was a self-contained residential flat in a purpose-built block. It might be much more difficult in a building which had slipped into informal multiple occupation with shared facilities."[77]

The nature of the possession may be affected by the intention of the **5.12** person asserting it, but, at the initial stage of asserting adverse possession, this does not depend on whether he believes that he has a right to do so or whether he knows he is trespassing:

> "It is the unequivocal nature of the conduct which matters and the clear intention to possess made plain to all the world".[78]

In the context of implied dedication of a highway and prescription in respect of private rights of way Lord Hoffman has emphasised that the

---

[73] *Bligh v Martin* [1968] 1 W.L.R. 804; [1968] 1 All E.R. 1157; *Hayward v Chaloner* [1968] 1 Q.B. 107; [1967] 3 W.L.R. 1068; *Fowley Marine (Emsworth) Ltd v Gafford* [1968] 2 Q.B. 618; [1968] 2 W.L.R. 842.

[74] *Lloyds Bank Plc v Rossett* [1989] Ch. 350; [1988] 3 W.L.R. 1301; reversed on other grounds [1991] 1 A.C. 107; [1990] 2 W.L.R. 867.

[75] *Roberts v Swangrove Estates* [2007] EWHC. 513 (Ch) upheld on appeal sub nom. *Roberts v Crown Estate Commissioners* [2007] 2 P. & C.R. 17.

[76] *Roberts v Swangrove Estates* [2007] EWHC 513 (Ch) upheld on appeal sub nom. *Roberts v Crown Estate Commissioners* [2007] 2 P. & C.R. 17.

[77] per Lord Walker in *Ramroop v Ishmael* [2010] UKPC 14 at [25].

[78] *Prudential Assurance Co v Waterloo Real Estate Inc* [1999] 2 E.G.L.R. 85.

essence of prescriptive rights is the extinguishment of the true owner's rights by time and that the requirement is open use and not an honest belief in the existence of the right.[79] It seems clear that a person deliberately trespassing and seeking to enter into possession of the land is in at least as strong a position as the person who innocently believes that he has a good title to the land.[80]

The position of a person who believes that he is simply using the land until the time comes when the true owner needs is more complex. It is not, however, necessary that the person in possession should assert ownership of the property. Thus "a person who wrongly believes he is a tenant can occupy property in such a way that he has possession",[81] just as much as a squatter. It is adverse possession that must be shown and expressed willingness to give up the plot at some time in the future is not inconsistent with possession.[82] "An admission of title is not inconsistent with the squatter being in possession in the meantime"[83] and simply admitting that you would have paid if asked is not fatal. On the other hand a person who never intends to assert any rights has been held not to be truly in possession.[84] Thus a claimant who believes that his occupation is with the permission of the paper owner has no intention to dispossess and therefore is not in possession.[85] This also applies to a person who starts out as a licensee and just carries on without intending to assert adverse possession.[86]

In respect of registered land, however, this principle applies only to the first stage of being able to assert adverse possession. When the squatter applies for registration under the Land Registration Act 2002 the position is reversed since he has to show that he reasonably believed that the land belonged to him.[87]

Equally the extent of user required to assert ownership will depend on the nature of the land.[88] Simply paying taxes on a large, wild and uncultivated area of British Columbia has been held to be sufficient.[89] Applying this principle to more prosaic circumstances, paying rates on a piece of waste land where you park your car would certainly be a significant element in asserting possession. However, it must not be forgotten that

---

[79] *R. v Oxfordshire CC Ex p. Sunningwell Parish Council* [2000] 1 A.C. 335; [1999] 3 W.L.R. 160.
[80] *Sava v SS Global Ltd* [2008] EWCA Civ 1308; *Leigh v Jack* (1879-80) L.R. 5 Ex. D. 264 per Cockburn C.J.
[81] per Arden L.J. in *Ofulue v Bossert* [2008] EWCA Civ 7; [2009] Ch 1 at [63].
[82] *Buckinghamshire CC v Moran* [1990] Ch. 623; [1989] 3 W.L.R. 152.
[83] per Lord Browne-Wilkinson in *J A Pye (Oxford) Ltd v Graham* [2002] UKHL 30; [2003] 1 A.C. 419.
[84] *Williams Bros Direct Supplies v Raftery* [1958] 1 Q.B. 159; [1957] 3 W.L.R. 931.
[85] *Clowes Developments (UK) Ltd v Walters* [2005] EWHC 669 (Ch); [2006] 1 P. & C.R. 1.
[86] *JA Pye (Oxford) Ltd v Graham, The Times,* February 13, 2001, CA overturned on other grounds [2003] 1 A.C. 419.
[87] Land Registration Act 2002 Sch.6 para.5(5)(c).
[88] *Roberts v Swangrove Estates Ltd* [2007] EWHC 513 (Ch), upheld on appeal sub nom. *Roberts v Crown Estate Commissioners* [2007] 2 P. & C.R. 17.
[89] *Kirby v Cowderoy* [1912] A.C. 599.

time only begins to run when a right of action arises. Thus it may be theoretically possible to obtain title to common land by adverse possession, but this would require showing that the possession was excluding the true owner, which would be very difficult while allowing the commoners to exercise their rights.[90]

Once possession has been established, it can only be ended within the 12-year period by the occupier vacating the property, by the occupier giving a written acknowledgment of title, by the true owner granting the occupier a tenancy or licence (even a unilateral licence,[91]) or by the true owner physically re-entering upon the land.[92] Claiming ownership, even if backed up by proceedings, does not terminate possession, though where proceedings continue to judgment, time runs back from the commencement of those proceedings.[93]

5. Adverse

The acts of possession must be adverse to the true owner. In *JA Pye* **5.13** *(Oxford) Ltd v Graham*[94] Lord Browne-Wilkinson explains how the term "adverse possession" came into the judicial vocabulary and disdains the term:

> "In my judgment much confusion and complication would be avoided if reference to adverse possession were to be avoided so far and possible and effect given to the clear words of the Acts. The question simply is whether the defendant squatter has dispossessed the paper owner by going into ordinary possession of the land for the requisite period without the consent of the owner."

It is, however, this question of "consent" or "permission" which is at the heart of references to the possession being "adverse", though perhaps it would be more accurate to say that such a person is not in possession at all.

The basic position is that a person who occupies land with the express or implied permission of the true owner cannot assert a right to possession even after 12 years.[95]

There has been substantial judicial consideration in recent times of what constitutes "implied permission". In *Colin Dawson Windows Ltd v King's Lynn and West Norfolk BC*[96] the fact that for part of the time negotiations

---

[90] *Mellstrom v Badgworth Land Co* decision of Adjudicator 2008/1498.
[91] See *BP Properties v Buckler* (1988) 55 P. & C.R. 337.
[92] *Markfield Investments Ltd v Evans* [2001] 1 W.L.R. 1321; [2001] 2 All E.R. 238.
[93] See also *Hounslow LBC v Minchinton* (1997) 74 P. & C.R. 221.
[94] *JA Pye (Oxford) Ltd v Graham* [2002] UKHL 30; [2003] 1 A.C. 419.
[95] *Hyde v Pearce* [1982] 1 W.L.R. 560; [1982] 1 All E.R. 1029.
[96] [2005] EWCA Civ 9; [2005] 2 P. & C.R. 19.

for purchase were continuing was held to amount to implied permission: "It is natural to draw an inference of permission when a person is in possession pending negotiations to buy". In *Batsford Estates v Taylor*[97] the conclusion was that a reasonable person would have appreciated that the user was with permission. The fact that a person believes he is in possession as of right, does not necessarily prevent his possession being permissive.[98] Furthermore, a person in possession under a contract to buy the land which is never completed is not in adverse possession even after the true owner has asked for the keys back and even though the time during which he could have obtained specific performance may well have expired.[99]

In the case of possession originally acquired by licence it may be difficult to decide the exact moment when occupation ceases to be by licence and becomes adverse. The clearest and most obvious way of rendering the possession adverse is a demand for possession by the true owner, whether that demand is in writing or oral. The position of a tenant who ceases paying his rent is dealt with below.[100]

The essential question, however, is not whether the true owner ever intended to relinquish possession, but whether the squatter has the *animus possidendi* (or intention to possess):

> ". . . the *animus possidendi* involves the intention, in one's own name and on one's own behalf, to exclude the world at large, including the owner with the paper title, if he be not himself the possessor, so far as is reasonably practicable and so far as the processes of law will allow".[101]

This intention is limited to an intention to exclude others for the time being. It does not matter if, for example, you only intend to assert possession until the true owner needs the land and recovers it. Furthermore the required intention is to possess and not to be in adverse possession. So if a person is in possession because he erroneously believes he owns the land the *animus possidendi* is still shown.[102] It is, indeed, a central tenet of the provisions of the Land Registration Act 2002 that a squatter is only entitled to be registered as owner if he has been in adverse possession of

---

[97] [2005] EWCA Civ 489; [2006] 2 P. & C.R. 5.
[98] *Hicks Developments Ltd v Chaplin* [2007] EW.HC 141 (Ch).
[99] *Sandhu v Farooqui* [2003] EWCA Civ 531; [2003] H.L.R. 55.
[100] See below para.5.15.
[101] per Slade J. in *Powell v MacFarlane* (1979) 38 P. & C.R. 452, approved (unsurprisingly) by Slade L.J. in *Buckinghamshire CC v Moran* [1990] Ch. 623; [1989] 2 All E.R. 225; see *Site Developments (Ferndown) Ltd v Cuthbury Ltd* [2010] EWHC 10 (Ch); [2011] 2 W.L.R. 74 where the claimant specifically asserted that his intention was to obtain adverse possession.
[102] *Prudential Assurance Co Ltd v Waterloo Real Estate* [1999] 2 E.G.L.R. 85; *Site Developments (Ferndown) Ltd v Cuthbury Ltd* [2010] EWHC 10 (Ch).

the land in the reasonable belief that he owns it.[103] Acts or omissions of the squatter may be relevant, either as indicating that he has no intention to occupy or as amounting to an estoppel. Indeed in respect of current law in relation to registered land, failing to respond to an enquiry can result in the burgeoning interest ceasing to be an overriding interest under Sch.1 to the Land Registration Act 2002.

There has been a divergence of judicial opinion, now resolved, on the **5.14** question of whether and to what extent it makes a difference that the true owner has to any degree abandoned the land. More often than not adverse possession is claimed in cases where the land has been forgotten about by the true owner or where it has been left vacant pending some future development. It has been suggested that in the latter case, where the land is development land not immediately required, acts of occupation by another occupier cannot give rise to adverse possession. This view emanates from *Leigh v Jack*[104] where Bramwell L.J. said:

> "Acts of users are not enough to take the soil out of the Plaintiff and her predecessor in title and to vest it in the Defendants. In order to defeat a title by dispossessing the former owner, acts must be done which are inconsistent with his enjoyment of the soil for the purposes for which he intended to use it; that is not the case here where the intention of the Plaintiff and her predecessors in title was not either to build upon or to cultivate the land, but to devote it at some future time to public purposes."

This approach was followed in subsequent cases,[105] but the position has now been clearly explained in *Buckinghamshire CC v Moran*[106]:

> "In circumstances where an owner has no present use for his land but has future plans for its use (for example by development or by dedication to the public as a highway), then the court will, on the facts, readily treat a trespasser, whose acts have not been inconsistent with such future plans, as having not manifested the requisite *animus possidendi* or alternatively, as not having acquired a sufficient degree of exclusive occupation to constitute possession".

This approach was followed by the House of Lords in *J A Pye (Oxford) Ltd v Graham*.[107] Thus in *Buckinghamshire CC v Moran* itself the County Council had no immediate use for the land, but intended to use it in the

---

[103] Land Registration Act 2002 Sch.6 para.5(4)(c).
[104] (1879-80) L.R. 5 Ex. D. 264.
[105] e.g. *Williams Bros Direct Supply v Raftery* [1958] 1 Q.B. 159; *Wallis's Cayton Bay Holiday Camp Ltd v Shell-Mex and BP Ltd* [1975] Q.B. 94; [1974] 3 W.L.R. 387.
[106] [1990] Ch. 623; [1989] 3 W.L.R. 152.
[107] [2002] UKHL 30; [2003] 1 A.C. 419.

future as a by-pass. It would have been open to the court to conclude that all the trespasser intended was to use the land for the time being and not to obtain possession as against the Council. It seems that the conclusive evidence was that the gate was locked and the Council officers were not allowed access through the gate, but only by climbing over the fence. Although the law is now clear there is still room for differences in interpretation of the facts. In *Buckinghamshire CC v Moran* itself there was ample room for the court to have decided on the facts that the squatter never really intended to dispossess the County Council, but the finding to the contrary was still upheld. Two subsequent Court of Appeal cases have returned to an approach where consideration is given to the knowledge and attitude of the true owner as colouring the actions and intentions of the squatter. In *Pulleyn v Hall Aggregates*[108] the Court of Appeal while re-asserting the law as stated in *Buckinghamshire CC v Moran* upheld a decision that use by the squatter, including accepting payments for parking from third parties did not amount to possession because the acts were in accordance with the true owner's purpose for the land. In *Stacey v Gardner*[109] the Court went further:

> "If the land is undeveloped and the stranger is aware that the owner has a purpose in mind for it in the future, a court is likely to require very clear evidence of factual possession and intention."

However, in *Prudential Assurance Co v Waterloo Real Estate Inc*[110] the Court of Appeal re-asserted the principle that it is the unequivocal nature of the conduct which counts, even where the true owner (of half the party wall) had no immediate use for it and, in *Roberts v Swangrove Estates*[111] Lindsay J. described the proposition that the intention of the true owner is relevant as "heretical and wrong".[112] Although the Land Registration Act 2002[113] fundamentally changes the position by restricting the right of the squatter to obtain a registered title, the process concentrates on the belief of the squatter and not the intentions of the registered owner. In *Sava v SS Global*[114] the Court of Appeal again concentrated on the acts of the squatter (who freely confessed that he was trying to obtain ownership by squatting) while not ignoring the act (as opposed to the intentions) of the true owner.

5.15   Where a person originally enters into possession as a lessee and then ceases to pay rent the question arises as to when, if at all, his possession becomes adverse so that time begins to run. If the lease is for a term of years

---

[108] *Pulleyn v Hall Aggregates (Thames Valley) Ltd* (1993) 65 P. & C.R. 276.
[109] [1994] C.L.Y. 568.
[110] [1999] 2 E.G.L.R. 85.
[111] [2007] EWHC 513 (Ch).
[112] [2007] EWHC 513 (Ch) at [53].
[113] Land Registration Act 2002 ss.96-98 and Sch.6.
[114] [2008] EWCA Civ 1308.

certain, time does not begin to run against the landlord until the term of years has expired, whether or not rent has been paid.[115] By para.7 of Sch.1 to the Limitation Act 1980, the right of action to recover land in the event of forfeiture or breach of condition accrues when the forfeiture occurs or the condition is broken. Most leases contain a right of re-entry on non-payment of rent which can be enforced by forfeiture, but time only begins to run against the landlord when he takes steps to enforce the forfeiture.[116]

If the tenancy is a periodic tenancy with a lease in writing, time runs from when the lease expires under the terms of the tenancy. However, where there is no lease in writing time begins to run from the expiry of the first period in which rent is not received. Subsequent receipt of rent revives the tenancy.[117] However, further payments of rent by the paper lessee after the 12 year period has run cannot revive the previous lease and dispossess the squatter.[118] Therefore time runs on the expiration of a fixed term lease or on non-payment of rent by an oral periodic tenant without any further acts asserting ownership or otherwise adverse to the landlord.

The corollary of this is that receipt of rent is sufficient to prevent time **5.16** from running against the true owner even where the lessee is not in actual possession. In these circumstances the squatter, after 12 years' possession, only gets the title of the lessee. To establish freehold title he has to retain possession for 12 years after the freehold owner's right of action against him accrues.[119]

This differs from the situation where occupation has originally been obtained under a licence or a tenancy at will[120] in which case time will not run as long as the occupation is with the owner's consent.

This, however, needs further explanation. Where the original occupation is under, for example, an annual grazing agreement, the position after the annual grazing agreement expires may be quite different. In *Topplan Estates Ltd v Townley*[121] after the death of the defendant's father, the owner showed no interest in grazing agreements, but the defendant carried on regardless. The Court of Appeal refused to accept that,

> "acts which would otherwise amount to factual possession during the relevant period can somehow be diluted or denatured by reference to the relations between the squatter and the true owner".[122]

---

[115] *Jessamine Investment Co v Schwarz* [1978] Q.B. 264; [1977] 2 W.L.R. 145.
[116] *Barratt v Richardson* [1930] 1 K.B. 686.
[117] Limitation Act 1980 Sch.1 para.5.
[118] *Nicholson v England* [1926] 2 K.B. 93.
[119] *Fairweather v St Marylebone Property Co* Ltd [1963] A.C. 510; [1962] 2 W.L.R. 1020. See also para.5.19 et seq., below.
[120] See *Ramnarace v Lutchman* [2001] UKPC 25; [2001] 1 W.L.R. 1651, per Lord Millett, where the English law is contrasted with that of Trinidad which retained the pre-1980 statutory provision.
[121] [2004] EWCA Civ 1369.
[122] [2004] EWCA Civ 1369 per Parker L.J. at [79].

Furthermore the principle is subject to the interaction of promissory estoppel. If the landlord has promised not to enforce the rent, then the continuing possession cannot be said to be adverse, despite the express provisions of the Limitation Act, and the occupant's rights are limited to those afforded by estoppel, in this case a right to remain for life free of charge.[123]

6.   Twelve years

5.17   The Limitation Act 1980 provides that no action shall be brought "after the expiration of 12 years from the date on which the right of action accrued to him".[124] The Land Registration Act 2002, which excludes this provision,[125] allows a person to apply to be registered,

> "if he has been in adverse possession of the estate for the period of ten years ending on the date of the application."

Under both provisions the date when the cause of action accrues is the date when the true owner is dispossessed. Under the Limitation Act, once 12 years have expired from that date the owner's title to the land is extinguished and cannot be revived. Under the 2002 Act, the true owner's title is only extinguished on registration of the new owner, but the cause of action still accrues to the true owner on the date of dispossession. Many of the cases in practice work on the understandable basis of going back 12 years from the date proceedings were commenced, but strictly this is not correct and could be misleading in a case where, for example, there was a resumption of possession by the true owner, or a payment of rent to him by the person in possession, more than 12 years after he was dispossessed, but before bringing his action. This point is also important in the cases, dealt with below,[126] where the lessee has purported to surrender his lease after the 12-year period has expired.

The loss of possession must be continuous, but it cannot be brought to an end by anything short of a resumption of possession or the commencement of an action. Writing letters or making verbal claims to the land is not sufficient.[127] Commencing an action is, however, in itself sufficient to stop time running further providing that the action is pursued. If the action is dismissed for want of prosecution time is treated as running throughout.[128] It is not necessary to apply for an interim injunction. Nevertheless, if the other party is in possession and is spending money

---

[123] *Smith v Lawson* (1998) 75 P. & C.R. 466; *Warren v Murray* [1894] 2 Q.B. 648.
[124] Limitation Act 1980 s.15(1).
[125] Land Registration Act 2002 s.96.
[126] See below para.5.19 et seq.
[127] *Mount Carmel Investments v Thurlow* [1988] 1 W.L.R. 1078; [1988] 3 All E.R. 129.
[128] *Markfield Investments Ltd v Evans* [2001] 1 W.L.R. 1321; [2001] 2 All E.R. 238.

on the property it is advisable to do so.[129] The extent to which the true owner is entitled to possession of land as of right or only subject to the equitable requirements necessary to obtain an injunction is dealt with later.[130] The Land Registration Act 2002 makes specific provision about this subject. Eviction of the squatter within the 10-year period prevents any application being made. Eviction without court order more than six months before the application also prevents an application being made,[131] as does bringing proceedings asserting a right to possession before an application for registration is made by the squatter.[132]

The adverse possession must be continuous. However, it does not **5.18** follow that the person in adverse possession must be continuously doing something on the land. Where a fence or some other structure is placed on the land there is no difficulty in showing continuity, but where acts of cultivation or grazing of animals are relied on the court will look at those acts by reference to the kind of use that an owner would make of the land:

> "Possession is a matter of fact depending on all the particular circumstances of a case. In very many cases possession cannot, in the nature of things, be continuous from day to day, and it is well established that possession may continue to subsist notwithstanding that there are intervals, and sometimes long intervals, between the acts of user."[133]

Therefore, if it is held, on the facts of a particular case, that regular cultivation of the land is sufficient evidence of possession, the fact that there is a gap between reaping one crop and sowing the next makes no difference.[134] Equally, where grazing the land is held sufficient, the fact that the land is left unused during the winter months when grazing is not possible will not interrupt the period of possession.[135] The circumstances in which and the extent to which such acts may amount to adverse possession are dealt with above.[136]

Once dispossession or discontinuance is shown, the period can only be interrupted either by commencing and pursuing an action to its conclusion[137] or actually resuming possession. Minor acts done on the land by the true owner will not suffice. Thus a person may come onto the land to

---

[129] Cf. *Bracewell v Appleby* [1975] Ch. 408 (easements) and *Shaw v Applegate* [1977] 1 W.L.R. 970 (restrictive covenants).
[130] See later under Remedies Ch. 24.
[131] Land Registration Act 2002 Sch.6 para.1(2)(a).
[132] ibid. Sch.6 para.1(3)(a).
[133] *Bligh v Martin* [1968] 1 W.L.R. 804; [1968] 1 All E.R. 1157 per Pennycuick J. at 1160G [1968] 1 W.L.R. 804.
[134] ibid. at 1160I.
[135] ibid.
[136] See above para.5.10.
[137] *Markfield Investments Ltd v Evans* [2001] 1 W.L.R. 1321; [2001] 2 All E.R. 238.

clip the boundary hedge just because he owns the hedge and not the land on the far side of it,[138] or because he has a duty to maintain it,[139] and using the land to graze heifers without realising that the land is yours will not amount to a resumption of possession by the true owner.[140]

When a property is acquired by compulsory purchase, but the previous owner remains in possession, time begins to run against the local authority from the date of the purchase.[141]

7. Lessees

5.19 In the simplest case a squatter appears and takes possession of freehold land belonging to another. The reality, however, is usually different. In most cases adverse possession is the result of encroachment by an adjoining occupier. The land encroached upon may be in the possession of a tenant or a licensee. The encroacher may himself be the tenant of an adjoining property or indeed the tenant of the freeholder on whose land he encroaches.

Where the squatter takes possession of land which is subject to a lease, his possession is, in the first instance, only adverse to that lessee.

> "No-one supposes that adverse possession against a lessee during his term is itself adverse possession against his landlord".[142]

The freeholder is, for all practical purposes, not in possession of his lease-hold land, and accordingly time does not run against him. If the lease expires, the landlord then gains a right to claim possession against the squatter and, if he fails to do so, time begins to run against him.

5.20 Where a squatter enters into possession of leasehold property and continues in possession for the full period of 12 years, without the lease having expired or been forfeited or surrendered, the next question is the nature of the title he obtains. Under the Land Registration Act 1925, if he applied for registration of a freehold title, the registration would be refused, but he might be allowed a possessory leasehold title.[143] The excluded lease-holder would forfeit his estate to that part of the land. Where the lease-holder had a registered title, but the squatter had not, the leaseholder held the lease of that part of the property on trust for the squatter and cannot surrender it to the freeholder.[144] However, the squatter's title was only leasehold and would expire at the end of the leasehold period.

[138] *Marshall v Taylor* [1895] 1 Ch. 641.
[139] *Norton v London & North Western Railway Co* (1879-80) L.R. 13 Ch. D. 268.
[140] *Bligh v Martin* [1968] 1 W.L.R. 804.
[141] *Rhondda Cynon Taff CBC v Watkins* [2003] EWCA Civ 129; [2003] 1 W.L.R. 1864.
[142] *Fairweather v St Marylebone Property Co Ltd* [1963] A.C. 510.
[143] *Spectrum Investment Co v Holmes* [1981] 1 W.L.R. 221; [1981] 1 All E.R. 6.
[144] *Central London Commercial Estates Ltd v Kato Kagaku Ltd* [1998] 4 All E.R. 948.

Under the Land Registration Act 2002, i.e. as from October 13, 2003, it depends on whether the leasehold is a registrable estate.[145] If it is, the squatter will be applying for leasehold registration. If not, the normal rules must apply and his possession is not adverse to the freehold owner.

By contrast, where the land is unregistered, the lessee's title is only **5.21** extinguished against the squatter and remains against the freeholder. Accordingly, the lessee can surrender the lease to the freeholder and the squatter's leasehold interest falls with it.[146] This situation is still far from clear or satisfactory. The authorities involve long leases at low rents where the adverse possession is only of a small part of the holding and do not deal with what obligations the squatter takes on. Does he have to pay rent? Does he have to keep to the covenants?

The other side of the coin is where the squatter is himself a lessee of adjoining land. The law on this subject has been authoritatively considered by the Court of Appeal in *Tower Hamlets LBC v Barrett*.[147] The court upheld the judgment of Pennycuick V-C in *Smirk v Lyndale Developments Ltd*[148] that there is a rebuttable presumption that the title of the lessees is acquired on behalf of their landlords provided that the relevant land is close to and occupied with the land demised under the tenancy. The leaseholders subsequently bought the reversion and the adverse possession continued.

It must be remembered, however, that the presumption is rebuttable. If **5.22** the lessee annexes a piece of land which is still kept quite separate from his own tenanted land, for example a piece of unused land on the other side of the road, or even an adjoining piece of land which he keeps separate from his own land, then the presumption does not apply and he is treated like any other squatter.

Where the encroachment is on the landlord's own land the question will be whether what the tenant does can be regarded as being adverse to the landlord's freehold. This is unlikely to be the case if the landlord is aware of it[149] or where the tenant has expressly claimed that it is part of his leasehold holding.[150]

8. Acknowledgment of title

An acknowledgment of title in writing made by the person in posses- **5.23** sion to the true owner within the limitation period[151] will stop time

---

[145] i.e. a lease of more than seven years, s.4(1)(c)(i).
[146] *Fairweather v St Marylebone Property Co Ltd* [1963] A.C. 510.
[147] *Tower Hamlets LBC v Barrett* [2005] EWCA Civ 923; [2006] 1 P. & C.R. 9.
[148] *Smirk v Lyndale Developments Ltd* [1974] 3 W.L.R. 91; [1974] 2 All E.R. 8.
[149] *Tabor v Godfrey* (1895) 64 L.J.Q.B. 245.
[150] *JF Perrott & Co v Cohen* [1951] 1 K.B. 705.
[151] See *Colchester BC v Smith* [1992] Ch. 421; [1992] 2 All E.R. 561 at 565g.

running against the true owner and the cause of action will accrue afresh from that date.[152]

To be effective an acknowledgment has to be in writing[153] and signed by the person making it.[154] It also has to be made to the true owner.[155] A document made to a third party such as an Inland Revenue affidavit sworn by an executor is not, therefore, sufficient.[156] The acknowledgment may be made to or by an agent providing that he is duly authorised.[157]

The nature of an acknowledgement of title was considered by the House of Lords in *Ofulue v Bossert*.[158] An acknowledgement, for example an admission in a pleading in previous proceedings, only amounts to an acknowledgement as at that moment in time. Time can begin to run again from then.

Where the acknowledgment is made by a person in possession it binds all other persons in possession during the ensuing period of limitation.[159] However, where it is made by a head landlord who is not in possession it has no effect.[160] The effect of there being a succession of persons in adverse possession is dealt with below.[161]

Where an acknowledgment is made after more than 12 years have passed, it may still be possible for the true owner to rely on it as a compromise agreement resolving a genuine dispute.[162] This was treated as being quite different from an acknowledgment of title under the 1980 Act. However, a "without prejudice" offer cannot be relied on as an acknowledgement.[163]

This acknowledgment need not be in a formal document. In *Lambeth LBC v Archangel*,[164] a passing reference to "Lambeth's property" was held to be a sufficient acknowledgment of the title of the council. The fact that an acknowledgement is made in a "without prejudice" letter is not fatal.[165]

9. Successive owners and occupiers

5.24   While the limitation period is running in favour of the squatter, the paper title may pass to another person either because of sale, death of the

---

[152] Limitation Act 1980 s.29.
[153] *Browne v Perry* [1991] 1 W.L.R. 1297; (1991) 135 S.J. 173.
[154] Limitation Act 1980 s.30(1).
[155] Limitation Act 1980 s.30(2)(b).
[156] *Bowring-Hanbury's Trustee v Bowring-Hanbury* [1943] Ch. 104.
[157] *Curwen v Milburn* (1889) L.R. 42 Ch. D. 424; *Lambeth LBC v Archangel* (2001) 33 H.L.R. 44; [2002] 1 P. & C.R. 18.
[158] [2009] UKHL 16; [2009] 1 A.C. 990.
[159] Limitation Act 1980 s.31(1).
[160] *Tower Hamlets LBC v Barrett* [2005] EWCA Civ 923.
[161] See below, para.5.24 et seq.
[162] *Colchester BC v Smith* [1992] Ch. 421; [1992] 2 W.L.R. 728.
[163] *Offulue v Bossert* [2009] UKHL 16; [2009] 1 A.C. 990.
[164] (2001) 33 H.L.R. 44; [2002] 1 P. & C.R. 18.
[165] *Tower Hamlets LBC v Barrett* [2005] EWCA Civ 923.

owner, expiry of a lease or change of trustees. Equally, beneficial interests in the paper title may cease or fall into possession.

The basic rule is that any such changes do not affect the running of time. There are, however, a number of situations set out below[166] where, for various reasons, the running of time is suspended because the owner or a person with a beneficial interest is under a disability or there is a beneficial interest which has not fallen into possession.

In the case of leases the situation is rather more complex and is explained more fully above.[167] If the squatter occupies leasehold land, he may well be asserting adverse possession against both the tenant and the landlord and therefore obtain a freehold title. However, if he is an existing tenant who encroaches onto the landlord's land, the encroachment may be subsumed into his own tenancy. In respect of a long lease at a ground rent, it has been accepted that the acts of adverse possession which dispossessed the lessee did not dispossess the freeholder. In these situations the squatter holds the land until the lease expires by effluxion of time. In respect of unregistered land, the paper lessee can still surrender the lease even after the 12-year period has expired and the squatter loses all his rights.[168] This is because the lessee's paper title is extinguished as against the squatter, but not as against the freeholder. However, in respect of a leasehold interest registered under the Land Registration Act 1925, the lessee held the registered title as trustee for the squatter and cannot validly surrender the lease without the squatter's permission.[169] This is no longer the position under the Land Registration Act 2002.[170]

Where a lessee who is in the process of annexing land on behalf of his landlord under the rule in *Smirk v Lyndale Developments*[171] buys the freehold, he continues his possession as freeholder, without there being a break in continuity.[172]

There may also be a succession of persons in adverse possession. This **5.25** is usually because they are occupying in the belief that they have a genuine right to the land and accordingly the successor believes he has bought or inherited the land from the previous squatter. However, the essence of the doctrine of adverse possession is that it is the true owner who loses his right of action and not any other person who gains it. Accordingly, the person in possession at the date when the 12 years

---

[166] See below para.5.27 et seq.
[167] See above para.5.19 et seq.
[168] *Fairweather v St Marylebone Property Co Ltd* [1963] A.C. 510.
[169] *Central London Commercial Estates Ltd v Kato Kagaku Ltd* [1998] 4 All E.R. 948.
[170] Land Registration Act 2002 para.9 of Sch.1.
[171] *Smirk v Lyndale Developments Ltd* [1974] 3 W.L.R. 91; [1974] 2 All E.R. 8, approved in *Tower Hamlets LBC v Barrett* [2005] EWCA Civ 923.
[172] *Tower Hamlets LBC v Barrett* [2005] EWCA Civ 923.

expires has a good title against the person with the paper title whether or not he can himself show continuity of possession for that period. He does not, therefore, lose his possessory title because he has "inherited" it from a previous squatter. It may, however, still be possible for the first squatter to claim possession from the subsequent squatter if he has in turn entered as or become a trespasser:

> "If squatter A is dispossessed by squatter B squatter A can recover possession from squatter B and he has 12 years to do so, time running from the dispossession."[173]

The situation may, however, then arise that squatter A abandons the property before he has obtained a possessory title, in which case he loses all rights to claim possession.

Where a squatter is in possession he is still subject to any existing easements or other incorporeal hereditaments which bound the previous owner. The reason for this is that his occupation is not adverse to these rights and, as long as the person in possession does not interfere with his rights, there is no reason why the owner of an easement should be concerned who is in possession of the servient tenement.

5.26 The position is much the same where the land is subject to restrictive covenants. A restrictive covenant is binding on persons other than the original covenantee in equity as being akin to a negative easement. As such it binds the squatter as much as the true owner and his successors in title, *Re Nisbett & Potts' Contract*.[174] The Court of Appeal, however, left open the position of a purchaser from the squatter who is not aware of the covenant and could not have become aware of it by using reasonable diligence. The argument is that if he buys from a person who has obtained a good possessory title he is a bona fide purchaser of a legal estate without notice and as such should not be bound by the covenant. It remains to be seen, however, whether this argument will prevail.

Under the Land Registration Act 2002, a squatter who is registered as owner takes free of any registered charges.[175] However, since he is in effect registered as successor to the previous registered owner, he is bound by easements and restrictive covenants in the same way as in respect of unregistered land.

---

[173] *Mount Carmel Investments v Thurlow* [1988] 1 W.L.R. 1078; [1988] 3 All E.R. 129 at 135h; (1989) 57 P. & C.R. 396 at 403 per Nichols L.J., followed in *Site Developments (Ferndown) Ltd v Cuthbury Ltd* [2010] EWHC 10 (Ch); [2011] 2 W.L.R. 74.

[174] *Re Nisbett & Potts' Contract* [1906] 1 Ch. 386.

[175] Registration of Land Act 2002 Sch.6 para.9(3).

10. Exceptions

(a) The Crown

Adverse possession can be claimed against the Crown, which includes **5.27**
the Duchy of Cornwall[176] and the Duchy of Lancaster,[177] in the same way
as against a normal owner except that the time is extended to 30 years,[178]
or 60 years in the case of foreshore.[179] Where a person obtains title from
the Crown but there is already someone in adverse possession, the 60
years keeps running but a fresh period of 12 years begins and the title is
extinguished when the first of these periods expires.[180] If the Crown buys
property the longer period clicks in. The reference to "first" in para.12 of
Sch.1 means "earlier".[181] Where rent, which should be paid to the Crown,
is paid to some other person this does not amount to adverse possession
against the Crown as it would in the case of an ordinary owner.[182] Where
the Crown erroneously grants a permit to a person to occupy land
belonging to another, the Crown is in adverse possession of that land for
the period of the permit, the adverse possession reverting to the occupier
when the permit expires.[183]

Under the Land Registration Act 2002 demesne land can be registered.
If this happens, the same periods apply except in the case of foreshore
where the 10 years becomes 60 years.[184]

The right to sue the Crown emanates from the Crown Proceedings Act
1947. Before that there was no right to sue the Crown at all, though a
special procedure by petition of right had developed. "The Crown" is
not defined in that Act nor is there any comprehensive definition of
Crown Lands. However, it is clear that the land belonging to the
Crown includes both the residual properties of the Crown, such as the
foreshore, and property which has become escheat to the Crown through
the death of the owner without heirs, land owned by government
departments, including the Forestry Commission, and the Crown Estates
which are the lands administered by the Crown Estates Commissioners
on behalf of the sovereign. It does not include the property of public
corporations, unless the statute expressly states that they act on behalf
of the Crown. There is no right to sue the sovereign personally since
she is the fountain of justice, but it does not seem that a claim of

---

[176] Limitation Act 1980 s.37(3)(c).
[177] ibid. s.37(3)(a).
[178] ibid. Sch.1 para.10.
[179] Limitation Act 1980 Sch.1 para.11(1).
[180] ibid. Sch.1 para.12.
[181] *Hill v Transport for London* [2006] 1 P. & C.R. 272.
[182] Limitation Act 1980 Sch.1 para.6(2).
[183] *Sze To Chung Keung v Kung Kwok Wai David* [1997] 1 W.L.R. 1232.
[184] Land Registration Act 2002 Sch.6 para.13.

adverse possession would ever be treated as being against the sovereign personally.

5.28 The palatinates of Durham and Chester have long been vested in the Crown and no special provisions were required to include them within the definition of the Crown in the Limitation Act 1980. The sovereign is automatically Duke of Lancaster and thereby entitled to the lands of the Duchy of Lancaster including the county palatine. Proceedings against Her Majesty in right of the Duchy of Lancaster count as Crown proceedings for the purposes of the Limitation Act.[185]

The Dukedom of Cornwall is anomalous in that it passes automatically to the eldest son of the sovereign. The Duchy estates are not Crown land, but they are treated as belonging to the Crown for the purposes of the Limitation Act 1980.[186] Despite doubts about the legality of the Charter of 1337 which created the Duchy (because it creates a mode of descent unknown to the common law), it has never been challenged.

(b)   Spiritual and eleemosynary corporations

5.29 The same thirty-year rule applies to spiritual or eleemosynary corporations sole as applies to the Crown.[187] Neither appears to have been defined in this context. Most land belonging to the Church of England is owned by a spiritual corporation whether a corporation sole or aggregate. A corporation sole is an individual who holds land personally solely by reason of his office. The most obvious example is the land vested in a vicar or rector by reason of his office, including glebe land.[188] The difference between this and freehold ownership is that his interest ceases when he gives up the office and the property then vests automatically in his successor.

The exception applies only to corporations sole and not to corporations aggregate. Ecclesiastical corporations aggregate include a dean and chapter and some hospitals. The normal rules apply to land held by these. Only Church of England land is held by corporations sole and aggregate in this way. Non-conformist and Roman Catholic property and the property of other sects and religions is normally held by charitable trustees and time runs in the normal way. Therefore, whether or not such land is held by charitable corporations, they are not corporations sole.

Eleemosynary corporations have also not been defined in the context of this Act. The meaning of "eleemosynary" has, however, been defined in the context of the Local Government Acts.[189] There, "eleemosynary charity" was defined as covering,

---

[185] Limitation Act 1980 s.37(3)(2).
[186] ibid. s.37(3)(c).
[187] Limitation Act 1980 Sch.1 para.10.
[188] For the meaning of "Lords Marcher Spiritual" see per Lewison J. in *Roberts v Crown Estate Commissioners* [2008] EWHC 1302 (Ch).
[189] *Re Armitage* [1972] Ch. 438; [1972] 1 All E.R. 708.

"all charities directed to the relief of individual distress, whether due to poverty, age, sickness or other similar individual afflictions".[190]

The adjective derives from the Greek word for "alms" and therefore covers anything which could be seen as relating to alms. Normally, however, such corporations are either corporations aggregate or incorporated under the Charities Act 1993 or the Companies Act 1985. The exception does not, therefore, include the wide range of charities which are comprised in eleemosynary corporations generally.

The Land Registration Act 2002 and the Land Registration Rules 2003 make no reference to spiritual and eleemosynary Corporations. It seems, therefore, that there are no special rules in relation to these. This is because the new provisions are perceived as improving the position of registered owners, of whom such corporations are among the more vulnerable to adverse possession claim.

(c)   Highways

A person cannot obtain ownership of an adopted road by adverse possession, even if he closes it off for the required period.[191] A person can obtain ownership by adverse possession of the sub-soil of the highway[192] but the public right to use the way still exists and cannot be extinguished by non-user or obstruction.[193] It follows, therefore, that a person who is in possession of a parcel of land over which a public highway runs can obtain title albeit subject to the right of way.[194]

(d)   Disability

The Land Registration Act 2002 provides that no one may apply for **5.30** registration on the basis of adverse possession if the registered proprietor is unable, because of mental disability, to make decisions about issues of the kind, or unable to communicate such decisions because of mental disability, or physical impairment. "Mental disability" is defined as

"a disability or disorder of the mind or brain, whether permanent or temporary, which results in an impairment or disturbance of mental functioning".[195]

---

[190] ibid. at 711g.
[191] *R. v The Land Registry Ex p. Smith* [2010] 2 P. & C.R. 384.
[192] ibid per Arden L.J at [38].
[193] See Ch. 7.
[194] *Haigh v West* [1893] 2 Q.B. 19; *Davies v John Wood Property* decision of Adjudicator 2008/0528.
[195] Land Registration Act 2002 Sch.6 para.8(3).

Unlike the Limitation Act 1980 the Land Registration Act 2002 makes no reference to "minors" or infants. However, the structure of the 2002 Act is to limit the operation of the Limitation Act 1980 in its application to registered land. It follows that if time does not run against an individual under the Limitation Act, then there is no need for an additional restriction under the 2002 Act.

The position under the Limitation Act 1980 is that time does not run against an infant or person who "lacks capacity" within the Mental Capacity Act 2005 to conduct legal proceedings.[196] The Mental Capacity Act 2005, for the first time, sets out a modern and comprehensive approach to mental capacity. The principal definition is at s.2

> "a person lacks capacity in relation to a matter if at the material time he is unable to make a decision for himself in relation to the matter because of an impairment of, or a disturbance in the functioning of, the mind or brain."

The Act makes clear that the incapacity may be permanent or temporary, but shall not be judged by the person's age or appearance or by people's "unjustified assumptions" about what he can do. Inability to make a decision applies where he is not able to understand or weigh the relevant information when it has been properly explained.

Where land is owned by a person under a disability the limitation period is six years from the date when he ceased to be under a disability[197] subject to an overall limitation of 30 years.[198] This does not, however, in itself prevent a person who is under a disability from bringing an action within the 30 year period if he wishes.

Where a person under a disability claims through someone against whom time has already begun to run he cannot then take advantage of the special provisions of the statute. "Claiming through" is widely defined,[199] but it does not include a person under a disability who has come into the property by reason of a special power of appointment.[200]

Minors (persons under the age of 18 years) cannot hold land in their own name.[201] Where a minor inherits land it will be held by trustees, usually the personal representatives, on his behalf. In such a case, time only runs against the trustees to the extent that it could also run against the beneficiaries. Accordingly where the beneficiary, or one of them, is a minor, there is in effect no adverse possession during the minority.

---

[196] Limitation Act 1980 s.38(2) as amended.
[197] Limitation Act 1980 s.28(1).
[198] ibid. s.28(4).
[199] Limitation Act 1980 s.38(5).
[200] Limitation Act 1980 s.38(6).
[201] Law of Property Act 1925 s.1(6).

There used to be a rule whereby time would run against an infant if his guardian or parent was in possession for him.[202] However, it does not appear that this rule has survived the 1925 legislation. Even where the trustee is also the minor's parent it seems that he will be regarded as being in possession as trustee and not as parent.

If a person under a disability dies while still under a disability and is succeeded by another person under a disability no further extension of time is allowed by reason of that second disability.[203] The limitation period, therefore, is either 12 years from the date when the cause of action arose or six years from the death, whichever is the later, unless the overall 30 year period has expired.

(e) Death

The death of the person entitled to the cause of action does not stop **5.31** time running. It might be thought that there might be a period before grant of probate or letters of administration during which there was no-one entitled to bring an action and accordingly that time would not run. Section 26 of the Limitation Act 1980, however, expressly provides that an administrator shall be treated as if there had been no interval of time between the death and the grant of the letters of administration. In the case of executors the title of the executor after probate automatically relates back to the date of the death. This means that if the adverse possession has started before the death then time runs during the period between death and Letters of Administration. However, if the squatter takes possession during the period between death and Letters of Administration time does not run because of the provisions of para.9 Sch.1 to the Limitation Act 1980, even though the land is, in theory, in the possession of the President of the Family Division.[204]

(f) Co-owners

The only form of co-ownership of land that can exist in law is a joint **5.32** tenancy. Joint tenants each have a right to possession of the whole of the property. Accordingly occupation by a joint tenant will not normally be adverse to the other joint tenant. However, where a person occupies the land and claims it as sole owner then the occupation can be adverse even though the person whose title is extinguished is a co-owner.[205]

---

[202] See e.g. *Re Hobbs* (1887) L.R. 36 Ch. D. 553.
[203] Limitation Act 1980 s.28(3).
[204] *Earnshaw v Hartley* [1999] EWCA Civ 1199.
[205] *Paradise Beach v Price-Robinson* [1968] A.C. 1072; [1968] 1 All E.R. 530; *Earnshaw v Hartley* [1999] EWCA Civ 1141.

(g)   Land held on trust

5.33   Much land is held by trustees on trust, including charitable trusts. Under the Trusts of Land and Appointment of Trustees Act 1996 trusts for sale and settlements are abolished and replaced by a single concept of "trusts for land". The effect is that trusts for sale are no longer treated as interests in money rather than land, but the old rules about strict settlements are abolished and no new settlements can be created.

Apart from leases, interests in remainder and reversion now exist only as equitable interests. For most conveyancing purposes the plan of the 1925 legislation was to draw a curtain over those equitable interests so that the only matter which a person dealing with the land had to concern himself with was the legal title. The position is different, however, where the person is claiming by virtue of adverse possession. In such circumstances it is necessary to look behind the legal title to the interests of the beneficiaries.

Where land is held on trusts for land, time runs against a beneficiary entitled in possession in the same way as if he was the legal owner.[206] However, where the beneficial interest of any person has not accrued, the title of the trustees is not extinguished and time only runs from when that beneficial interest does accrue.[207] In such circumstances the trustees retain the right to bring an action to recover the land even though 12 years have elapsed from the time when their cause of action accrued.[208]

The situation is very similar where there is a settlement created before the 1996 Act. The title of the tenant for life or the statutory owner is not extinguished as long as a beneficiary has a right of action and time does not run against the beneficiary until he is entitled in possession.[209]

5.34   It must be remembered that the effect of these provisions is to prevent the trustees' right of action from becoming barred. Accordingly, a person claiming adverse possession cannot succeed even against a beneficiary who would otherwise be barred, if there is another beneficiary preventing time from running against the trustees.

It is wise, therefore, to tread very warily in any case where the paper title is in the hands of trustees. However, in the very common case of land being held jointly and beneficially on the statutory trusts no particular problem arises since the beneficiaries will be entitled to possession and time will be running against them.

A beneficiary will not be treated as being in adverse possession of the land as against the trustees, tenant for life or any other beneficiary.[210]

---

[206] Limitation Act 1980 s.18(1).
[207] ibid. s.18(2).
[208] ibid. s.18(4). This principle is repeated in the Land Registration Act 2002 Sch.6 para.12.
[209] ibid. s.18(1), (2) & (4).
[210] Limitation Act 1980 Sch.1 para.9.

Therefore, a person in possession who also has an entitlement under an intestacy cannot claim to have obtained adverse possession against his co-beneficiaries, even though he takes possession before Letters of Administration are granted[211] and, strictly speaking, during the interval before Letters of Administration, he is not entitled under a trust for land.

(h)   Fraud or concealment and estoppel

Time will not run where the action is based upon the fraud of the **5.35** person in adverse possession or where any fact relevant to the right of action has been deliberately concealed by the person in adverse possession.

There is no significant difference in this context between concealment and fraud. Concealing the true position is just an example of fraud. However, just going onto the land and claiming ownership is not concealed fraud:

> "What is meant by concealed fraud? It does not mean the case of a party wrongfully entering into possession; it means a case of designed fraud, by which a party knowing to whom the right belongs conceals the circumstances giving that right and by means of that concealment enables himself to enter and hold."[212]

For example trying to pass off someone else's child as your heir, as was alleged in *Willis v Earl Howe*,[213] would be concealed fraud. Occupying a concealed cellar under your neighbour's property, whether or not you have dug it yourself, would not be fraud, unless you had set out to conceal this occupation.[214]

In order to affect the person in possession the concealment or fraud must have been carried out by himself or his agent, or by someone through whom the person in possession claims or his agent.[215]

The principle is therefore of limited application to boundary disputes. **5.36** In most cases the person occupying the land has simply taken possession of it, either under a claim of right which, though false, he genuinely believes in, or simply because the land seems to be there and unoccupied. However, cases do arise where the person in possession has involved himself in deliberate deception to try to prevent the true owner from

---

[211] *Earnshaw v Hartley* [1999] EWCA Civ 1199.
[212] per Kindersley V.C. in *Henry Petre v The Honourable Laura Maria Stafford Petre* (1853) 1 Drew. 371 at 397 quoted with approval in *Willis v Earl Howe* [1893] 2 Ch. 545.
[213] *Willis v Earl Howe* [1893] 2 Ch. 545 against Lady Sophia Curzon.
[214] *Rains v Buxton* (1880) L.R. 14 Ch. D. 537.
[215] Limitation Act 1980 s.32(1).

reclaiming the land and in such cases this exception may be of considerable use. Fraud in land transactions is by no means a rarity.[216]

It has also been stated obiter in *Wallis's Cayton Bay Holiday Camp Ltd v Shell-Mex and BP Ltd*[217] that the principles of estoppel can be used so as to preclude a squatter from enforcing his strict rights under the Limitation Act.[218] The Act, however, expressly provides that it precludes the true owner from bringing any action after the limitation period has expired and that once that has happened his title is extinguished. It is not, therefore, a question of the person in adverse possession exercising his rights, but of the true owner losing his. The courts have consistently refused to apply the principle of estoppel to other limitation periods, unless there is fraud. In particular, apart from this dictum it has never been held that there is any responsibility on the person in adverse possession to inform the true owner that the period of 12 years is about to elapse or even to reply to letters on this point.

It has, however, been held that an occupier can be estopped from asserting a title by adverse possession where, after the 12 years expired, he entered into a fresh tenancy agreement in which he expressly acknowledged that he had no title; *Colchester BC v Smith*.[219] This was in fact, a rather unusual case and it does not follow that acts within the limitation period which fall short of an acknowledgement of title will give rise to an estoppel.

(i) War

5.37   Limitation periods are not automatically suspended during time of war,[220] but there is an express statutory provision[221] that if the person with the paper title is an enemy or is detained in enemy territory the limitation period is extended until 12 months after the date when he ceased to be an enemy or to be detained in enemy territory.

This provision is repeated in the Land Registration Act 2002.[222]

---

[216] See *Guy v Barclay's Bank* [2008] EWCA Civ 452.
[217] [1975] Q.B. 94; [1974] 3 W.L.R. 387.
[218] *Wallis's Cayton Bay Holiday Camp Ltd v Shell-Mex and BP Ltd Wallis's* [1974] 3 All E.R. 575 at 580h per Lord Denning M.R.
[219] [1991] Ch. 448; [1991] 2 W.L.R. 540.
[220] *Bowring-Hanbury's Trustee v Bowring-Hanbury* [1943] Ch. 104.
[221] Limitation (Enemies and War Prisoners) Act 1945.
[222] Land Registration Act 2002 Sch.6 para.9(1).

Chapter Six
Party Structures

1. Introduction

If a person owns some land he may wish to mark the boundary with **6.01** his neighbour with a wall or fence. When he does so he will normally go as near as he can to the actual boundary to build his wall or fence, but will ensure that it remains on his land. The structure so built is a boundary wall or fence but, at Common Law it is not strictly a party wall. Where he wanted a ditch, either for drainage or to keep cattle in or to mark the edge of his land the theory was that he would dig the ditch and throw the earth into his side. The ditch is then not a party ditch.

Frequently, however, before selling building land, the estate owner has laid out his estate and then wishes to mark the boundaries on the ground by building a wall or fence. In so doing he may have no clear idea of whether he wants the legal boundary to run along the middle of that wall or fence or whether the wall or fence is to be owned solely by one or other of the adjoining owners or, when tenancies in common of land were possible, whether the boundary feature would be held in common between the adjoining owners. If, however, after the plots have been sold off, problems arise with the wall or fence, it may be necessary to decide who owns or is responsible for it.

The problem is even more acute where the estate consists of semi-detached or terraced houses. In such a case the boundary wall will not only be used to mark the legal boundary, it will be an essential part of the structure of both houses. In such circumstances it would be little consolation to the owner of one house to know that he owns half of the boundary wall if his adjoining owner allows his half to fall into disrepair and eventually to cause the whole wall to collapse.

Another possibility is that adjoining owners may together decide **6.02** that they wish to build a boundary wall or fence either along an undefined line or to replace an existing structure. Again they may or may not have a clear idea of how that new boundary feature is to be owned.

After the construction of the boundary wall one or other adjoining owner may add to the wall, or may pull it down in order to re-build it, or may construct his own building using the existing wall either for support or as an integral part of his construction.

Over the centuries the Common Law has developed the law of party walls to deal with these problems.

6.03   There is a tendency to refer to the law of "party walls" rather than party hedges or party fences although the same principles can apply to any structure. It seems, however, that a boundary hedge, even though the boundary runs through the middle of it will be treated simply as being divided in the middle without any clear rights of support. There does not appear to be a decided case where an adjoining owner has removed his half of the hedge and thereby damaged or removed the support of the other half. In *Jones v Price*[1] the question of the duty to repair a boundary hedge was treated as a matter of prescription without reference to the law of party structures.

Consideration has already been given to the ownership of boundary features.[2] Consideration will be given later[3] to the rights of support and duties of repair which can be created in such circumstances.

2.   The Party Wall etc. Act 1996

(a)   Objective

6.04   The problem with the common law in this respect is that it is strong on ownership, but weak on mutual obligations. This has meant that complex and technical issues arise as to what is or is not a party wall and, if so, how it is owned, but a person whose boundary wall is damaged by his neighbour may have no remedy and a neighbour who wishes to develop his own land may find his hands tied by restrictions on doing work to the party wall.

The Party Wall etc. Act 1996 was passed in an attempt to deal with the practical problems associated with boundary structures of all kinds. In essence it extends the London Building Acts to the whole of England and Wales (except the Temple in London) and was followed immediately by the repeal of the relevant London Building Act, together with the local Bristol Act whereby there was a presumption that a dividing wall is a party wall.[4]

---

[1] *Jones v Price* [1965] 2 Q.B. 618; [1965] 3 W.L.R. 296.
[2] See Ch. 2.
[3] See below Ch. 19—Support.
[4] Party Wall etc. Act 1996 (Repeal of Local Enactments) Order 1997 (SI 1997/671).

Although this Act has proved a welcome alternative to the rather esoteric world of party walls at common law, it may still be necessary, in certain circumstances, to decide who owns a boundary structure.[5]

(b) Definitions

The Party Wall etc. Act 1996[6] defines a party wall as:

"(a) a wall which forms part of a building and stands on lands of different owners to a greater extent than the projection of any artificially formed support on which the wall rests; and
(b) so much of a wall not being a wall referred to in paragraph (a) above as separates buildings belonging to different owners".

The first part of this definition is somewhat obscure but the second part makes it clear that the Act is dealing with any boundary wall, whatever its ownership, since a wall which separates buildings belonging to other owners may belong solely to one or the other.

The Act also takes the London Building Act definition of a "party fence wall":

"a wall (not being part of a building) which stands on lands of different owners and is used or constructed to be used for separating such adjoining lands, but does not include a wall constructed on the land of one owner the artificially formed support of which projects onto the land of another owner".

This definition, therefore, applies only to what is normally considered a party wall, namely a wall which straddles the boundary.

Finally the Act defines a "party structure" as:

"a party wall and also a floor partition or other structure separating buildings or parts of buildings approached solely by separate staircases or separate entrances' ".

In effect, the intention of the Act is to get away from issues concerning the ownership of boundary walls and to concentrate on issues concerning their repair or demolition and on the way in which work on adjoining property can affect the wall.

---

[5] The importance of whether a wall is a party structure or part of the property of one or other of the adjoining properties is illustrated by *Prudential Assurance v Waterloo Real Estate* [1999] 2 E.G.L.R. 85 where the viability of two rival development plans in Knightsbridge depended on the ownership of an eighteenth century wall on the boundary.
[6] Party Wall etc. Act 1996 s.20.

"'Owner" includes:

6.05   "(a) a person in receipt of, or entitled to receive, the whole or part of the rents or profits of land;

(b) a person in possession of land, otherwise than as a mortgage or as a tenant from year to year or for a lesser term or as a tenant at will;

(c) a purchaser of an interest in land under a contract for purchase or under an agreement for a lease, otherwise than under an agreement for a tenancy from year to year or for a lesser term."[7]

It should be noted that the Act refers throughout to the other owner as the "adjoining owner". There may be more than one such owner.[8]

(c) Process

(i) *New building*

6.06   At common law no owner has the right to build across his boundary. Even if he builds close to the boundary he runs the risk that he will not be able to obtain access to the far side of his structure.[9] The Party Wall etc. Act,[10] enables either owner to build on the line of the junction between the properties providing that there is no party wall (i.e. a wall between buildings) or other party structure in existence. An existing party fence wall does not preclude the exercise.

The owner wishing to build serves a notice.[11] If the adjoining owner consents the wall is built across the boundary and he may have to pay a proportion of the cost relating to the use made by him of the new wall.[12] It is then a common law party wall.

If, on the other hand, the other owner does not consent, the developing owner has to build on his own side of the boundary and at his own expense.[13] However, he gains the right for the 12 months after his notice expires to place the necessary footings and foundations below ground level. He then has to compensate the adjoining owner under the statutory system for any damage to his property caused by the building of the wall or the placing of the footings.

---

[7] Party Wall etc. Act 1996 s.20.
[8] Party Wall etc. Act 1996 s.20.
[9] See Access to Neighbouring Land Act 1992 below.
[10] Party Wall etc. Act 1996 s.2.
[11] Either under Party Wall etc. Act 1996 s.1(2) or (5).
[12] Party Wall etc. Act 1996 s.1(3)(b).
[13] Party Wall etc. Act 1996 s.1(4).

(ii)   Existing structures

Where there is an existing boundary wall on the boundary line, which **6.07** is either the external wall of a building or a party fence wall, the building owner has a range of powers under the Party Wall etc. Act[14] described in the margin as "repair etc, of party wall" which are intended to free the owner from some of the restrictions placed on him by party walls, while giving the neighbour a chance to object and to ensure that everything is done to minimise inconvenience.

It is interesting that the section refers to "building owner" even though the right accrues also to an existing party fence wall, which may divide land which has no building on it at all. However, in respect of the London Building Acts, it has been held that the right applies to a wall which survives after the building has been demolished.[15]

(d)   Permitted works

The rights are set out at s.2(2) of the Party Wall etc. Act 1996:

"(2) A building owner shall have the following rights:

   (a)   to underpin, thicken or raise a party structure, a party fence wall, or an external wall which belongs to the building owner and is built against a party structure or party fence wall;

   (b)   to make good, repair, or demolish and rebuild, a party structure or party fence wall in a case where such work is necessary on account of defect or want of repair of the structure or wall;

   (c)   to demolish a partition which separates buildings belonging to different owners but does not conform with statutory requirements and to build instead a party wall which does so conform;

   (d)   in the case of buildings connected by arches or structures over public ways or over passages belonging to other persons, to demolish the whole or part of such buildings, arches or structures which do not conform with statutory requirements and to rebuild them so that they do so conform;

   (e)   to demolish a party structure which is of insufficient strength or height for the purposes of any intended building of the building owner and to rebuild it of sufficient strength or height for the said purposes (including rebuilding to a lesser height or thickness where the rebuilt structure is of sufficient strength and height for the purposes of any adjoining owner);

---

[14] Party Wall etc. Act 1996 s.2.
[15] *Gyle-Thompson v Wall Street (Properties) Ltd* [1974] 1 W.L.R. 123; [1974] 1 All E.R. 295 at 299d per Brightman J.

(f) to cut into a party structure for any purpose (which may be or include the purpose of inserting a damp proof course);

(g) to cut away from a party wall, party fence wall, external wall or boundary wall any footing or any projecting chimney breast, jamb or flue, or other projection on or over the land of the building owner in order to erect, raise or underpin any such wall or for any other purpose;

(h) to cut away or demolish parts of any wall or building of an adjoining owner overhanging the land of the building owner or overhanging a party wall, to the extent that it is necessary to cut away or demolish the parts to enable a vertical wall to be erected or raised against the wall or building of the adjoining owner;

(j) to cut into the wall of an adjoining owner's building in order to insert a flashing or other weather-proofing of a wall erected against that wall;

(k) to execute any other necessary works incidental to the connection of a party structure with the premises adjoining it;

(l) to raise a party fence wall, or to raise such a wall for use as a party wall, and to demolish a party fence wall and rebuild it as a party fence wall or as a party wall;

(m) subject to the provisions of section 11(7), to reduce, or to demolish and rebuild, a party wall or party fence wall to:

    (i) a height of not less than two metres where the wall is not used by an adjoining owner to any greater extent than a boundary wall; or

    (ii) a height currently enclosed upon by the building of an adjoining owner;

(n) to expose a party wall or party structure hitherto enclosed subject to providing adequate weathering."

The 1996 Act largely follows the London Building Acts provisions[16] with some tidying up. However, the new provision gives a general power to underpin, thicken or raise any party structure[17] or any external wall belonging to the owner and to build against the party structure, for any reason. The right to demolish and rebuild, however, is restricted to cases where the wall is defective or in want of repair. There is also a new provision (reflecting previous case law[18]) allowing the owner to demolish and re-build or reduce the height of a party wall or party fence wall to two metres, if the adjoining owner does not use it to a greater height for any

[16] London Building Acts (Amendment) Act 1939 s.46(1).
[17] As defined in Party Walls etc. Act 1996 s.20.
[18] *Gyle-Thompson v Wall Street (Properties) Ltd* [1974] 1 W.L.R. 123; [1974] 1 All E.R. 295; *Reading v Barnard* (1827) Mood. & M. 71.

other purpose, or to the height currently enclosed upon by the adjoining building.

(e) Adjacent excavation and construction

Section 6 of the Party Wall etc. Act 1996 restricts the right of an owner **6.08** to excavate below foundation level within three metres of an adjoining owner's building or within six metres for deeper foundations.

(f) Detailed procedures

The Act makes a distinction between repairs, etc., under s.2 and new **6.09** building or excavation under ss.1 and 6. In the latter cases there is no provision for a counter-notice.

(i)   Under section 2—repairs, etc.

Before exercising any such right, the "building owner" must serve a **6.10** "party structure notice" on any adjoining owner. This must be served at least two months before the proposed work will begin. This notice should contain full particulars, at least sufficient to enable the recipient to frame his counter-notice.[19]

Service may be effected by delivering it to him, sending it to his usual or last known residence or place of business in the United Kingdom, or, for a body corporate, by post or in person to the secretary or clerk at the registered office. Alternatively it can be addressed to "the owner" and delivered to a person at the premises or fixed to a conspicuous part of the premises.[20] It should not be served on the adjoining owner's surveyor.[21]

The adjoining owner may then serve a counter-notice within one month beginning with the day on which the party structure notice is served (i.e. if notice is served on January 20 counter-notice must be served on February 19).

(ii)   New building and adjacent excavation and construction

Under ss.1 and 6 notice has to be given at least one month before the **6.11** building owner intends to start work. He then has to wait for one month further before commencing the work and must complete the projecting footings and foundations 12 months after he serves the notice.[22]

---

[19] *Hobbs Hart & Co v Grover* [1899] 1 Ch. 11.
[20] Party Wall etc. Act 1996 s.15(2).
[21] *Gyle-Thompson v Wall St. (Properties) Ltd* [1974] 1 W.L.R. 123; [1974] 1 All E.R. 295.
[22] Party Wall etc. Act 1996 s.1(6).

The building owner must then pay compensation for any damage caused to his property by the building of the wall and the placing of the footings. Any dispute about the amount of compensation is referred to a surveyor in the same way as with repairs.

The procedures in respect of adjacent excavation and construction are essentially the same.

(g) Compensation and expenses

6.12 The basic rule is that the building owner who wants the work done does it at his own expense[23] and compensates the adjoining owner for damage.[24] Furthermore he is under an obligation not to exercise any right under the Act in such a manner or at such time as to cause unnecessary inconvenience to any adjoining owner or occupier.[25] He must put up proper hoardings, shorings, fans or temporary construction. He cannot lay special foundations without consent.[26] He must comply with the statutory requirements and must follow the agreed plans, which he cannot deviate from without agreement.

There are, however, some situations where the adjoining owner must pay a proportion of the expense of the work. The principal such situations are:

(1) where the adjoining owner consents to the building of the wall straddling the boundary, the expenses are defrayed in proportion to the use made or to be made of the wall by the respective owners[27];

(2) underpinning, thickening or raising the wall under s.2(1)(a) or repairing or demolishing and replacing under s.2(1)(b) where a balance is struck based on their respective existing and potential use of the wall and the responsibility for the defect or want or repair concerned, if both make use of it[28];

(3) where a counter-notice requires works to be done for the adjoining owner's benefit;

(4) where the adjoining owner has requested work to be done.

---

[23] Party Wall etc. Act 1996 s.11(1).
[24] Party Wall etc. Act 1996 s.7(2).
[25] Party Wall etc. Act 1996 s.7(1).
[26] "[S]pecial foundations means foundations in which an assemblage of beams or rods is employed for the purpose of distributing any load," Party Wall etc. Act 1996 s.20.
[27] Party Wall etc. Act 1996 s.1(3).
[28] Party Wall etc. Act 1996 s.11(4).

A right to compensation under the Act is not a registrable interest and accordingly cannot be protected by a caution under the Land Registration Act 1925.[29] Presumably the same applies to a notice under the Land Registration Act 2002.

(h) Disputes

The object of the counter-notice is to enable the recipient to require the **6.13** building owner to carry out works to benefit his own land, such as putting in chimney flues, or to require special foundations to be deeper. The counter-notice has to specify the works and be accompanied by plans, sections and particulars. The counter-notice procedure only applies where the recipient of the notice actually wants the building owner to do some additional works. Where he simply dissents from the proposal he does not need to serve a counter-notice. Unless he expresses his consent in writing he is deemed not to agree and a difference arises.[30] Such differences are resolved by the appointment of surveyors, or, in the last resort, by a hearing before the county court. The procedure is that both parties should appoint surveyors. If they do not within 10 days of a written request the other party may make the appointment for him. The two surveyors if they wish can select a third surveyor to act as arbitrator, though he also has power to become involved in the negotiations. If the surveyors do not agree the third surveyor makes an award.

Once an award is made either party can appeal against that award to the county court within 14 days beginning with the day on which the award is made. There is no power to extend this period and time runs from when it can be presumed that the notice has been received.[31]

The differences these provisions deal with are not differences as to the advisability or reasonableness of the works as a whole. It seems that the building owner has an absolute right to execute the works even though they involve the removal of the party wall and, no doubt, considerable inconvenience to his neighbour, though any re-building has to be in a similar form, without, for example, involving new openings.[32]

Where the recipient wishes to challenge the validity of the party structure **6.14** notice he should do so by applying to the court for an injunction.[33] Equally if the award made by the surveyors exceeds their powers under the Act, the High Court has jurisdiction to grant an injunction despite the fact that s.10(16) of the Act states that the surveyor's award shall be conclusive

---

[29] *Observatory Hill Ltd v Camtel Investments SA* [1997] 1 E.G.L.R. 140.
[30] Party Wall etc. Act 1996 s.5.
[31] *Riley Gowler v National Heart Hospital Board of Governors* [1969] 3 All E.R. 1401.
[32] *Burlington Property Co Ltd v Odeon Theatres Ltd* [1939] 1 K.B. 633.
[33] *Sims v Estates Co* (1866) 14 L.T. 55.

subject to the right of appeal to the county court.[34] The conclusiveness of the award was upheld in *Rodrigues v Sokal*[35] where it was held that the surveyor's award against the developer was conclusive in respect of events both before and after the notice, subject only to the appeal to the county court.

A party structure notice is not effective unless the work to which it relates is begun within 12 months beginning with the day on which the notice was served has been served and is prosecuted with due diligence.[36] However, where there is a reference to surveyors this time limit does not apply.[37] In order to enable the owner who serves the notice to carry out the works if the adjoining owner does not co-operate, the Act contains power enabling him to enter the premises (by force if accompanied by a police officer) and to remove furniture and fittings.[38]

3. Interaction between the Party Wall etc. Act and the common law

6.15 This raises the issue of whether the common law concept of a party wall still exists. The interaction between the London Building Acts and the common law has been around for over 100 years and there is plenty of authority. There is also now some authority which specifically relates to the 1996 Act.[39] Unfortunately the comments in the case where this was most carefully considered, *Arena Properties v Europa 2000 Ltd*[40] are strictly obiter.

In *Selby v Whitbread & Co*[41] McCardie J. said:

> "The two sets of rights ... are quite inconsistent with one another. The plaintiffs' common law rights are subject to the defendants' statutory rights. A new set of respective obligations has been introduced. The common law was seen to be insufficient for the adjustment of modern complex conditions. Hence I think the Act ... is not an addition to but in substitution for the common law with respect to matters which fall within the Act. It is a governing and exhaustive code and the common law is by implication repealed."

Although this dictum was approved by the Court of Appeal in *Louis v Sadiq*[42] it was also substantially qualified. The analysis seems to be this.

---

[34] *Gyle-Thompson v Wall St. (Properties) Ltd* [1974] 1 W.L.R. 123; [1974] 1 All E.R. 295.
[35] [2008] EWHC 2005 (TCC).
[36] Party Wall etc. Act 1996 s.8.
[37] *Leadbetter v Marylebone Corp* [1905] 1 K.B. 661.
[38] London Building Acts (Amendment) Act 1939 s.53.
[39] *Rodrigues v Sokal* [2008] ECHR 2005 (TCC); *Jones & Lovegrove v Ruth* [2010] EWHC 1538 (TCC).
[40] [2003] EWCA Civ. 1943.
[41] [1917] 1 K.B. 736 at 752 cited with approval in *Louis v Sadiq* (1997) 74 P. & C.R. 325 at 332.
[42] (1997) 74 P. & C.R. 325.

The common law sets out the principles of ownership and rights of support and also the claims in trespass and nuisance that follow from that and, until such time as either party invokes the 1996 Act that right can be pursued. The same applies if an invalid notice is served. When a notice is served and the work is carried out in accordance with the award, then the claimant is limited to the compensation assessed by the surveyor and cannot pursue any claim in nuisance or any claim for consequential loss in respect of that work. The intermediate situation is where the defendant starts the work without authorisation and then serves a valid notice. This is what happened in *Upjohn v Seymour Estates*[43] and in *Louis and Louis v Sadiq*[44] itself. The outcome was that the claimant was entitled to damages for the losses suffered, including consequential loss, in respect of the damage caused to the claimant's house even though the works were subsequently completed under the London Building Acts. However, *Louis v Sadiq* was distinguished, at 1st Instance, in *Rodrigues v Sokal*[45] where the subsequent findings of the surveyor that there had been no damage to the party wall were held to be binding on the claimant. This case is difficult to reconcile with *Louis v Sadiq*, but it does indicate that, where the surveyor has carried out a full analysis of the operation of the works and has made findings of fact, the Courts will be reluctant to go over the whole ground again in respect of the period before the notice was served.

The difficulty which then arises comes from s.9 of the 1996 Act. Which provides:

"Nothing in this Act shall:

(a) authorise any interference with an easement of light or other easements in relation to a party wall; . . ."

One of the key easements is the easement of support. Any award which allows demolition of all or part of a party wall will inevitably involve interference with that right, temporarily at least. It seems clear, however, that at least in relation to the rights of support, which are essential to the concept of party walls, this section must be interpreted as meaning that the surveyor cannot make an order which removes part of the party wall, e.g. to turn it into an entrance, and that if he does so his order may be set aside.[46]

The position in relation to other easements is more complex. The easement in *Arena Property Service v Europa 2000 Ltd*[47] was a right to an air

---

[43] (1938) 54 T.L.R. 465.
[44] (1997) 74 P. & C.R. 325.
[45] [2008] EWHC 2005 (TCC).
[46] *Burlington Property Co Ltd v Odeon Theatres Ltd* [1939] 1 KB 633.
[47] [2003] EWCA Civ. 1943.

vent. It seems that the Court of Appeal was prepared to find that s.9 does not prevent the extinguishment of the common law rights.

The position therefore is that until a statutory notice is given, the common law rights exist and can be enforced. Once the award is made, the only option in respect of work done under the award, is to try to overturn the award. However, if the adjoining owner commits an actionable trespass or nuisance before the award, or actions of the adjoining owner go outside the award then a common law action would arise.

This means that the common law principles are less important than they used to be, since the usual reason for asserting rights under a party wall is that someone else is seeking to interfere with them. However, despite the Party Wall etc. Act 1996, the recent cases show that they may still arise in practice.

4. The common law

(a) Definitions

6.16 The meaning of party walls became caught up with the abolition of tenancies in common. It is probably no longer necessary to deal with the historic definitions. There has been no recent comprehensive consideration of common law party walls, but it is possible to distill from the definitions in the old cases some simple principles:

- The term "party wall" can be used to mean simply a boundary wall but in its stricter sense it means a wall which straddles the land of adjoining owners.

- Normally such a wall will be severed vertically between the two owners with mutual rights of support and user in favour of the other.

The cases from the past about whether a party wall can be altered or demolished have been overtaken by the Party Wall etc. Act 1996, which enables a person who carries out the correct procedures to do work on a party wall regardless of its strict ownership. It is, therefore, only where an adjoining owner carries out work without giving the appropriate notices that the common law has any relevance.

(b) Complex structures

6.17 It has already been seen that a boundary is three dimensional. It is therefore possible to own a space hanging or hovering over land in the ownership of another. For this reason the boundary between two properties cannot always be described on a map, however precise and accurate.

Frequently properties have rooms extending above their adjoining property or cellars running underneath. There is some discussion above about where the boundary lies in such circumstances.[48] However, there is no difference in principle between a vertical and a horizontal party structure. There is, therefore, no reason why a floor or ceiling dividing flats should not be a party structure, though the exact dividing line may not be half way, but will depend on the way the building is constructed.[49] This concept is acknowledged in the Party Wall etc. Act 1996, which refers to a "party structure" as including both a party wall and a structure "separating buildings or parts of buildings approached solely by separate staircases or separate entrances".[50]

Another complex situation concerns walls which are party walls for only part of their height. Where a party wall is extended by agreement between the adjoining owners there is no difficulty. The new structure is just a party wall on the same basis. But where there is a statutory presumption that a dividing wall is a party wall, then an additional structure built over that wall which benefits only one adjoining owner may belong solely to that owner[51] and

> "the mere fact that part of the external flank wall has become a party wall clearly does not result in that part of the external flank wall which is not a dividing wall between the properties becoming a party wall".[52]

However, it very much depends on the specific facts of each individual case and the circumstances may indicate that although the extension was built by only one of the adjoining owners for his own benefit, nevertheless it is treated as being an extension to the party wall.[53] Decisions on this subject concerning the London Building Acts now carry considerably more weight, since the Act has, in effect, been extended to the whole country, but it must still be remembered that the statutes contain their own special definitions which may differ from the common law principles in so far as they remain relevant.[54]

5. When is a boundary wall a party wall?

The question of whether or not a boundary wall or other structure is a **6.18** party wall in the strict sense will depend on the express terms of the

---

[48] See above para.2.25 et seq.
[49] *Sturge v Hackett* [1962] 1 W.L.R. 1257; [1962] 3 All E.R. 166; see para.2.26.
[50] Party Wall etc. Act 1996 s.20.
[51] *Weston v Arnold* (1872-73) L.R. 8 Ch. App. 1084.
[52] *Jones and Lovegrove v Ruth* [2010] EWHC 1538 (TCC).
[53] *Waddington v Naylor* (1889) 60 L.T. 480.
[54] *Drury v Army & Navy Auxiliary Cooperative Supply Ltd* [1896] 2 Q.B. 271 and *Matts v Hawkins* (1813) 5 Taunt. 20.

conveyance or other disposition, implication by statute, the outcome of any disputes resolution under the Party Wall Act[55] and implication from the presumed intention of the parties.

(a)   Express term

6.19   The conveyance or other disposition may specifically provide that a particular wall shall be a party wall or that all boundary walls shall be party walls. This is commonly the case where an estate is laid out in plots and conveyances of long leaseholds on flats almost invariably have detailed provisions as to the ownership of the various boundary structures, both vertical and horizontal. Neither the London Building Acts, nor the Party Wall etc. Act 1996 normally affect this kind of situation since the boundaries are usually constructed by the developer on his own land and the title is then divided as the plots are sold off.

The definition of party walls contained in the standard form conveyance in the fourth edition of the Encyclopedia of Forms and Precedents[56] made it quite clear that the wall is to be divided vertically and equally between the two adjoining owners with mutual rights of support, but the latest edition[57] has abandoned this definition in favour of a clause which expressly provides for mutual repairing obligations. There could, therefore, be no doubt about the effect of a conveyance of a party wall where the old precedent was used in the operative conveyance but where, as in the new precedent, the conveyance just states that the walls are to be party walls without defining what that is supposed to mean, the wall will be regarded as divided vertically as provided by s.38 of the Law of Property Act 1925, but, because of the wording of s.38 there could still be a difference between a party wall which is subject to the same rights and obligations as if it were held by tenants in common, and a wall which is simply divided vertically with mutual rights of support.

There is no special way of indicating party structures in the Land Registry. Neither the Land Registry Plan nor the plan annexed to the Land Certificate will have anything to indicate whether the boundary is a party structure. However, where party walls have been specifically dealt with in a pre-registration conveyance this fact will be included as a note on the register. "T" marks, however, are used to identify who owns the boundary feature, i.e. to indicate that the feature is not a party structure. They now have judicial recognition:

---

[55] Party Wall etc. Act 1996 s.20(12)(c). This is not intended for the resolution of legal disputes, but if there is a finding it will be binding on the parties.

[56] *Encyclopedia of Forms and Precedents*, 4th edn (London: Butterworths, 1985), Vol. 16, p. 411.

[57] *Encyclopedia of Forms and Precedents*, 5th edn (London: Butterworths, 1991), Vol.16(1), Form 6.

"In my view it is not possible to disregard the ordinary understanding of "T" marks. The natural implication is that they were
intended to represent existing boundary features and that those
features were to belong to Clock House".[58]

The Land Registry Practice with regard to "T" marks is now contained in
the Land Registry Practice Guide No.40. Essentially "T" marks referred to
in the conveyance are shown on the filed plan, but "T" marks just shown
on a plan, but not in the conveyance are ignored by the Registry.[59] Where
it is simpler to do so they are referred to "verbally" on the register. The
Practice as presently written refers to "T" marks indicating ownership, or
liability to maintain and repair, but Carnwath L.J.'s remarks seem clearer
and comprehensive.

A plan annexed to the conveyance may have "party wall" written on it **6.20**
even though there is no reference to party walls in the body of the conveyance. The extent to which plans which are for "identification only" can be
used to assess boundaries has been dealt with above.[60] As the approach
to such plans is now more liberal it seems likely that such a statement will
be accepted as an express indication of the intention of the parties and
that a reference to a party wall in the plan to the operative conveyance
will be enough to make it a party wall without any such reference elsewhere in the conveyance.

"H" marks straddling the land are sometimes used in conveyancing
plans to indicate party walls. They have not been given any judicial
approval. Nevertheless if evidence can be produced to suggest that this is
the effect of such a mark, there seems no reason why it should not be as
much an indication of the intention of the parties as are express references
to "party walls" on the plan. The "H" mark is the complement to the "T"
mark, which indicates ownership of the boundary.

The basic position regarding the easement of support is clear. As soon
as a wall becomes a party wall, properly so called, mutual rights of
support arise immediately and automatically, but these rights of support
are themselves no greater than the easement of support in respect of other
structures that can arise under the rule in *Wheeldon v Burrows*[61] or by
prescription. As is made clear later,[62] however, the right of support is very
limited and may amount to no more than a right to lean against another
structure without any obligation on the other party to maintain the

---

[58] per Carnwath L.J. in *Seeckts v Derwent* [2004] EWCA Civ 393 at [28].
[59] Because, in the opinion of the Land Registry they "have no special force or meaning in
law"— Practice Note 40 para.3.5.
[60] See above, Ch. 2.
[61] *Wheeldon v Burrows* (1879) L.R. 12 Ch. D. 31.
[62] See Ch. 19.

support,[63] keep the servient tenement in repair,[64] or to protect the dominant tenement from the weather.[65] Nevertheless, it seems clear that any right to abatement[66] or any other action is subsumed within the Party Wall etc. Act procedures.[67]

The problems highlighted in *Bradburn v Lindsay*[68] where the adjoining house was left unmaintained and rotting, should be resolved at least in part by the Party Wall etc. Act, since the owner of the adjoining property will have the right to carry out works on the dividing wall. However, this is not a complete answer, since the dry rot and other problems associated with the adjoining property would not necessarily be resolved by works on the dividing wall and, in any event, the owner affected might not have the funds to carry out the works. In such circumstances the law of negligence and nuisance will still be important.

(b)   Statutory implications

6.21   The Party Wall etc. Act 1996[69] has repealed the London Building Acts and, in effect, applied them to the whole of the country. It also repealed the Bristol Improvement Act 1847, which had also set out such a presumption. It seems clear, therefore, that there is no statutory presumption that a boundary wall is a party wall.

However, if any such presumption existed in the past it would apply to party walls erected before that date and nothing in subsequent legislation would change that. Not surprisingly many of the pre-1996 Act authorities concern properties in London,[70] however, and, until it was repealed by the London Building Acts (Amendment) Act 1939,[71] there was a statutory provision that:

> "In either of the following cases:
>
>   (a)   where a wall is after the commencement of this Act built as a party wall in any part; or

---

[63] *Jones v Pritchard* [1908] 1 Ch. 630.

[64] *Bond v Nottingham Corp* [1940] Ch. 429.

[65] *Phipps v Pears* [1925] Ch. 630. That is why the Encyclopedia of Forms & Precedents contains a Form giving mutual repairing covenants, *Encyclopedia of Forms and Precedents*, 5th edn (London: Butterworths, 1991), Vol.16(1), Form 6.

[66] See *Leakey v National Trust for Places of Historic Interest or Natural Beauty* [1980] Q.B. 485; [1980] 1 All E.R. 17.

[67] *Holbeck Hall Hotel Ltd v Scarborough BC* [2000] Q.B. 836; [2000] 2 W.L.R. 1396.

[68] [1983] 2 All E.R. 408 affirmed in *Holbeck Hall Hotel Ltd v Scarborough BC* [2000] Q.B. 836.

[69] With effect from July 1, 1997 by virtue of the Act together with the Party Wall etc. Act (Repeal of Local Enactments) Order 1997 (SI 1997/671).

[70] City of London and the Inner London Boroughs of Camden, Greenwich, Hackney, Hammersmith, Islington, Kensington & Chelsea, Lambeth, Lewisham, Southwark, Tower Hamlets, Wandsworth, Westminster. London Government Act 1963 s.43(1).

[71] The 3rd Sch. repealed London Building Act 1930 s.64 which had replaced London Building Act 1894 s.59.

(b) where a wall before or after the commencement of this Act
becomes after the commencement of this Act a party wall in
any part;

the wall shall be deemed a party wall for such part of its length as is
so used."

It may be that the draftsman of the 1939 Act considered this provision
tautologous but it seems more likely that he decided to remove from the
Act all provisions which could make people's rights to ownership of
party structures different in London from elsewhere.[72] The Party Wall etc.
Act 1996 also omits any presumption of a party wall.

Even if the presumption contained in the London Building Acts
survived the 1939 Act, it seems clear that since the commencement of the
Party Wall etc. Act 1996 there is now no presumption in London or
elsewhere. It is submitted that the situation is the same in respect of
walls built in London since 1939, but in respect of walls built in London
before 1939 and walls governed by the local Acts the presumption still
applies.

It is, however, clear that the importance of the actual ownership of a
boundary wall is considerably reduced because of the need to use the
statutory procedure whatever the ownership.

(c) By implication from the circumstances

In many of the old cases the question of whether a wall was a **6.22**
party wall was left to the jury and accordingly the precise facts necessary
to establish that a wall is a party wall, in the sense of being equally
divided with mutual rights of support, have not been very clearly
set out.

It has been said that the common use of a wall separating lands
belonging to different owners is prima facie evidence that the wall and
the land on which it stands belongs to the owners of those adjoining lands
in equal moieties as tenants in common.[73] It has been seen above that by
s.38(1) of the Law of Property Act 1925 this now means equally divided
with mutual rights of support:

"When the builder of two houses grants off one, it is more reasonable
to presume he grants the whole wall in undivided moieties, than that
he should leave to either party the power of cutting the wall in half.
That would be the case if the houses were built by one and the same

---

[72] See also the repeal in 1939 of London Building Act 1894 s.99 previously considered in
Mason v Fulham Corp [1910] 1 K.B. 631.
[73] *Cubitt v Porter* (1828) 8 B. & C. 257.

person. If two persons built at the same time, the probability is that they would take a conveyance of an undivided moiety of the ground on which the wall was to be erected, in order that the property might afterwards be kept in the same state."[74]

This inference from the facts, however, does not apply in all cases where adjoining owners both use the wall. For example, where someone builds a shed against the wall of an adjoining substantial house the inference is that the wall is not a party wall, but remains in the ownership of the owner of the substantial house. The person who builds the shed will not obtain rights of support until the shed has been there for 20 years.[75]

It follows that it may be necessary to analyse the time at which and the purpose for which the wall was originally constructed. It is submitted that what the authorities are dealing with are really inferences from the facts rather than legal presumptions. In some cases a careful analysis of the facts may show either that the wall was originally erected for the benefit of one of the adjoining owners only, or that it was clearly erected for their joint benefit either because both properties were then in common ownership or because the adjoining owners got together to build it. Where, however, the court is not able to reach any clear conclusion on the purpose for which the wall was built it seems that it will be regarded as a party wall providing that both parties use it. This is the extent of the presumption.

6.23   Where the wall divides two houses or buildings there may be no diffi-culty in concluding that both parties use it, but the position is less clear where the wall is a garden wall or even a garden fence or hedge. In such cases there is much less reason to presume that the wall or other structure was intended to be a party structure.

There is a difference in this regard between a wall, a fence and a hedge. A wall is inevitably of a certain thickness. Unless there is an indica-tion that it was originally constructed for the benefit of one of the adjoining owners (for example because it is tied in with a wall running off from it which belongs to that owner), it will usually be regarded as a party wall.

The word "fence" is used in other areas of the law for any structure which separates land. Thus, for example, "unfenced land" in the Animals Act 1971 means land which has nothing to stop animals escaping. A hedge or wall would be as good a fence in this context as a wooden paling fence. Nevertheless, in common parlance the word "fence" excludes walls, ditches and hedges. What is commonly called a fence is of compar-atively narrow width and will frequently be constructed by one owner

---

[74] per Bayley J. in *Wiltshire v Sidford* (1826) 1 Man. & Ry. 404 at 407.
[75] See below Ch. 19.

only in order to demarcate his boundary line. It may be possible to reach conclusions about the ownership of a fence from where the fence posts are. It is usual when constructing a boundary fence to have the fence posts on the inside. This would indicate that the whole fence belongs to the owner of the property on the fence post side and that the actual boundary is immediately beyond the far side of the fence.[76] However, where the fence is part of a building estate there is a greater likelihood that it is a party structure since it may well have been erected initially by the common owner or the builder simply to demarcate the boundary. As the ownership of the fence is of limited commercial significance there is little authority on this subject.

In respect of hedges it is unusual for any party structure obligations to **6.24** apply. Usually either the conveyance will indicate who owns the hedge, or the conveyance will be by reference to Ordnance Survey numbers, in which case the boundary will be the mid point of the hedge. If there is a ditch, the hedge and ditch presumption may apply, leaving the person who owns the ditch owning the hedge as well. And so in cases like these it does not necessarily follow that the hedge is a party hedge, since the mutual rights and obligations of support which may be important in the case of a wall do not apply in the case of a hedge. There does not seem to be any case where the owner of half a hedge has removed his half and thereby damaged or killed off the other half. In *Jones v Price*[77] the question of a duty to repair a hedge was in issue, but the question was decided purely on the grounds of prescription without reference to party structures. In that case the hedge was held by the Court of Appeal to be a boundary hedge divided equally between the adjoining owners. The implication from that case was that unless prescriptive rights have arisen to oblige either or both owners to keep the hedge in repair there are no mutual obligations on the respective owners. This does not mean, however, that a court would reach the same conclusion if the claim was in respect of a withdrawal of support or a specific grubbing out of half of the hedge as opposed to neglect as in *Jones v Price*.[78]

As indicated above, it may still be important to decide whether a **6.25** boundary feature is a "party wall" in accordance with the common law definition, or is in the sole ownership of one or other of the adjoining occupiers. However, the principal importance is to establish how it is to be maintained and to what extent the respective owners can demolish, reconstruct or alter it.

---

[76] *Howe v Hawkes* [2002] EWCA Civ 1138.
[77] [1965] 2 Q.B. 618; [1965] 3 W.L.R. 296.
[78] [1965] 2 Q.B. 618.

6. Access to Neighbouring Land Act 1992

6.26   The Access to Neighbouring Land Act 1992 has been partially superseded by the Party Wall etc. Act 1996. It is, however, of wider application.
The deliberately limited aim was to address the case of a landowner who
needs to repair his own property but cannot do so without access to that
of his neighbour.

The most obvious example of such a situation is where the owner of a
boundary wall needs access to repair it. Although the Party Wall etc. Act
1996 defines a party wall and a party fence wall to include a wall which
separates adjoining land, but is entirely on the land of one owner, both
definitions exclude a wall of a building which is solely on one party's
land and does not separate two buildings. It therefore excludes the
common case of a building built right up to the boundary wall, but
without any corresponding structure on the adjoining owner's side.

The only reported appellate case, *Dean v Walker*[79] accepts that the 1992 Act
can deal with party walls in the common law sense. However, as it preceded
the 1996 Act and involved property in Cumbria, far from London, it did not
deal with the interaction between the two Acts. Since s.8 of the 1996 Act
makes specific provision for rights of entry and since work cannot be done
on a party wall without notice being given under s.2, it seems likely that no
orders under the 1992 Act will be required in respect of statutory party walls
as defined by the 1996 Act (which includes common law party walls).

6.27   The Law Commission which recommended the passing of the Access
to Neighbouring Land Act 1992[80] specifically rejected both a general
right of access and the London Buildings Acts system incorporated into
the 1996 Act and plumped instead for orders obtained by application
to the county court.

In addition to the Party Wall etc. Act 1996, there is also a right to enter
and repair ancillary to an easement of support.[81] However, the Access to
Neighbouring Land Act 1992 deals with situations where a landowner
needs to repair any part of his own property. It includes cases where the
building owner has built close to the boundary, though it does not allow
an owner to obtain an order to enable him to carry out new building.
Furthermore it does not give him a right to repair the adjoining property.
It would not, therefore, deal with problems such as *Bradburn v Lindsey*,[82]
where the problem is not only failure to repair the party wall, but neglect
of the whole property. This remains a real problem for owners of properties adjoining derelict properties where damp and rot and even collapse

---

[79] (1997) 73 P. & C.R. 366.
[80] Law Com. No.151.
[81] *Ward v Kirkland* [1967] Ch. 194; [1966] 1 W.L.R. 601.
[82] [1983] 2 All E.R. 408.

of non-boundary walls are as great a danger as disrepair of the party wall. The desire for caution, coupled with the feeling that parties should be able to know in advance whether the order will be made, means that the procedure is complex. There was surely a strong case for a simple right to apply leaving the judge with a wide discretion?

A person who wishes to carry out work to "the dominant land" may **6.28** apply to the county court (or the High Court) for an access order to the "servient land" to carry out works to the dominant land. Any application must be made in the first place to the county court, but there is power to transfer to the High Court where the issues at stake justify this. The references to dominant and servient land originate from the law of easements, but there is no easement involved. It is simply a situation in which a court order may override the normal law of trespass.

The court makes the order if satisfied that the works are reasonably necessary for the preservation of the whole or any part of the dominant land and that they cannot be carried out (or would be substantially more difficult to carry out), without entry upon the servient land.[83] Even where the court is so satisfied there is a discretion to refuse an order where the respondent or any other person would suffer interference with, or disturbance of, his use or enjoyment of the servient land or the respondent or anyone else in occupation would suffer hardship to such a degree that it would be unreasonable to make an order.

The court has a general power to make an order for works reasonably necessary for the preservation of the whole or part of the dominant land, but there is an express provision that the following "basic preservation works" are to be regarded as reasonably necessary:

"(a) the maintenance, repair or renewal of any part of a building or other structure comprised in, or situate on, the dominant land;

(b) the clearance, repair or renewal of any drain, sewer, pipe or cable so comprised or situate;

(c) the treatment, cutting back, felling, removal or replacement of any hedge, tree, shrub or other growing thing which is so comprised and which is, or is in danger of becoming, damaged, diseased, dangerous, insecurely rooted or dead;

(d) the filling in, or clearance, of any ditch so comprised".[84]

However, even if the works are basic preservation works the court still has an overriding discretion to refuse an order on disturbance and hardship grounds.

[83] Access to Neighbouring Land Act 1992 s.1(2).
[84] Access to Neighbouring Land Act 1992 s.1(4).

6.29   The fact that the works incidentally involve some alteration or improvement, or an element of demolition does not matter. However, the word "incidentally" makes it clear that if the principal objective is demolition or improvement, the fact that there is some element of preservation works within s.1(4) may not be enough.

The Act also provides for Access Orders to give a right to inspection. The procedure to be adopted is contained in Practice Direction 56 para.11. The claimant must use the Pt 8 procedure which is really the successor to Originating Applications, involving a claim with written evidence attached and an Acknowledgment of Service. Where the defendant claims that there is substantial dispute of fact, he can object to the use of Pt 8 procedure.[85] On receipt of the Acknowledgment of Service or the time expiring the court gives directions for disposal of the claim.

The claim must set out details of both dominant and servient land, the work required, why entry is required (with plans), the names and addresses of the people who will carry out the work, the dates and details of insurance provisions.

The defendants are the owner and occupier of the servient land. It seems that r.8.2A may apply where the owner and occupier have not been identified. There is no other provision for dealing with this problem. However, this is increasingly rare as more and more land is registered and the Register is open.

6.30   The Act contains detailed provisions as to the terms and conditions of access orders. These are set out at s.2. They include the power to impose restrictions on the applicant and for payment of compensation by the applicant. The order may also provide for a payment of consideration for the privilege of entering the land, in effect a way-leave charge. However, this sum is not payable where the dominant land is residential land, as defined in s.1(7), though sums can still be ordered to be paid under s.1(4) to compensate the servient owner or other person affected for loss, damage, injury, loss of privacy of substantial inconvenience.

Where payment of a fee is ordered under s.1(7) it will be such as is "fair and reasonable" having regard to the financial advantage to the applicant and the degree of inconvenience to the respondent or any other person. The financial advantage is defined in s.2(6) as being either the increase in value of the land or the cost of carrying out the work in some other way, whichever is the greater. This financial advantage is, however, not the basis of the compensation, but only a matter which the court must have regard to in assessing compensation.

6.31   The effect of an access order is to require the respondent (so far as he has power to do so) to permit the applicant and his associates to do anything

---

[85] CPR r.8.8.

authorised. His associates are defined as anyone he may reasonably authorise in order to carry out the works. It also allows the applicant and his associates to enter the land without consent. The effect, therefore, is a dual one. If the respondent fails to comply with the order he is in breach of the Act. There is no specific provision for enforcement and, in particular, there is no criminal sanction, but the Act specifically provides for damages for failure to comply "without prejudice to any other remedy available".

It appears that the Act could also be enforced by injunction, with the resultant contempt of court if the injunction is not complied with. The Law Commission recommended that the order be directly enforceable by committal proceedings. The Act followed the draft Bill in this respect, but there is no reference to direct enforcement. As the order is not itself an injunction it is submitted that it cannot be directly enforced by contempt of court, but it is necessary first to obtain an injunction.

The Court in making its order can make provision for reimbursement of any expenses incurred by the respondent over and above those set out in s.2(3) and for the applicant to provide security for any sum that might become payable.

An access order is binding upon the respondent, his successors in title and any person with an estate or interest in the servient land or any part of it (including, of course, a tenant of the property).

One of the most serious problems faced by landowners is where the **6.32** ownership of the adjoining land is unknown. Some owners would take the robust view that, if they cannot find out the owner of the land, they are unlikely to be prevented from doing the work, but, in this case, there is the risk that the owner will appear and sue for trespass. The Act seeks to deal with this problem by Rules of Court. Unfortunately these Rules of Court have not yet been made though it may be that r.8.2A could be used. Section 4(4) renders void any agreement purporting to prevent a person applying for such an order.

Access orders can be registered under the Land Charges Act 1972 and the Land Registration Act 2002. Under the Land Charges Act they come under a new paragraph of "writs and orders"[86] and under the Land Registration Act 2002 they can be registered as a notice.[87] An application for an order can be registered as a pending action under both Acts. However, they do not count as an overriding interest of a person in actual possession of land.[88]

---

[86] Land Charges Act 1972 s.6(1)(d).
[87] Land Registration Act 2002 s.133 and Sch.11 para.26.
[88] Access to Neighbouring Land Act 1992 s.5(5).

Chapter Seven
Highways

1. Introduction

The vast majority of properties abut a highway. For the most part the **7.01** principles which determine the boundary between the property and the highway are much the same as those which determine the boundary with other adjoining properties. However, the crucial distinction is that a public highway is a public right of way and, as with private rights of way, someone or some corporate body has to own the sub-soil. Though the highway is sometimes described as the Queen's Highway, this refers to the right of all subjects to pass over it and not to any rights of ownership in the Crown. A "highway" is not the same as a "road". A person can be "using" a road for Road Traffic Act purposes, which is not a public highway[1] and a public footpath or bridleway is usually not a road.

The ownership of the sub-soil may be important, at least at common law, in deciding the ownership of pipes and drains under the highway; whether the adjoining owner may construct pipes and drains under the highway; whether he may excavate under it to build cellars, etc. and the right to mines under the highway, quite apart from what becomes of the sub-soil if the highway ceases to exist. Most of these aspects, are now covered by express provisions of the Highways Act 1980, but ownership of the subsoil can also be important in providing a locus standi for a claim for excessive user[2] or for showing that user has been without the owner's consent.[3]

The right of public access to open country contained in the Countryside and Rights of Way Act 2000[4] is quite separate from the public right to use the highway.

---

[1] *Price v DPP* [1990] R.T.R. 413.
[2] *Giles v County Building Constructors (Hertford), Ltd* (1971) 22 P. & C.R. 978.
[3] *Wild v Secretary of State for the Environment, Food & Rural Affairs* [2010] 1 P. & C.R. D65.
[4] See Ch. 11 s.8 below.

2. Proof of highway

(a) Creation by statute

7.02   Many highways have been created by statute. In recent years this has been effected by schemes under the Highways Act 1980 or its predecessors. In years gone by, highways were created under the Turnpike Acts or the Inclosure Acts. However, where there is an absence of use as a public highway, the court will look with considerable care at roads apparently created by Inclosure Acts, in particular looking to see whether the Commissioners have properly exercised their power to create public highways.[5]

(b) Express dedication

7.03   In modern times, highways are often created by express dedication, for example in a Memorandum of Agreement with the highway authority. The highway authority will then usually take on responsibility. However, it is the dedication itself which creates the highway and, as this is an overriding interest under Schs 1 and 3 to the Land Registration Act 2002,[6] it does not need to be registered to be valid. Although evidence of user by the public is helpful, the dedication can be accepted by the highway authority on behalf of the public by the deed itself,[7] provided that it creates an immediate dedication and not the intention of a dedication in the future.[8] As from May 2, 2006 no public right of way for mechanically propelled vehicles can be created unless the Deed expressly says so.[9]

(c) Adoption

7.04   Most highways are adopted, which means that they are maintainable at the public expense.[10] As such, they are shown on the highway authority's records though this may not be conclusive where the alleged highway has never really been used and has not in fact been maintained by the council.[11] Although there is no statutory or legal presumption that a road which has been maintained by the highway authority is a public highway, in fact once this is shown there will usually be no difficulty in satisfying

[5] *Buckland v Secretary of State for the Environment, Transport and the Regions* [2000] 1 W.L.R. 1949; [2000] 3 All E.R. 205.
[6] para.5 of both Schedules.
[7] *Secretary of State for the Environment, Transport and the Regions v Baylis* (2000) 80 P. & C.R. 324.
[8] *Overseas Investment Services Ltd v Simcobuild Construction Ltd* (1995) 70 P. & C.R. 322.
[9] Natural Environment and Rural Communities Act 2006 s.66.
[10] See below para.7.17 et seq.
[11] *Secretary of State for the Environment, Transport and the Regions v Baylis* (2000) 80 P. & C.R. 324, where it was held that there was in fact express dedication by deed.

the court that it is a public highway.[12] As regards ways which are not maintained at the public expense, inclusion in the definitive map is conclusive proof of a public highway at least for the kind of use shown on that map.[13] However, if a way is neither maintained at the public expense nor shown on the definitive map it is necessary to look at the user in relation to the actions of the landowner.

(d)   Presumption of dedication

Section 31 of the Highways Act 1980 (which originates from the Rights **7.05** of Way Act 1932, now repealed) provides:

"(1) Where a way over any land, other than a way of such a character that use of it by the public could not give rise at common law to any presumption of dedication, has been actually enjoyed by the public as of right and without interruption for a full period of 20 years, the way is to be deemed to have been dedicated as highway unless there is sufficient evidence that there was no intention during that period to dedicate it."

On the face of it this section applies to all public highways. However, in respect of dedication after May 2, 2006 the dedication is limited to use by non-mechanically propelled vehicles.[14] This is an important and substantial restriction on the creation of new highways by implied dedication. The interaction between this commencement date, the provisions of s.31(2) and the common law is considered below.[15]

The Act provides a specific safeguard for a landowner who does not object to or cannot stop the public using his way, but nevertheless wants to prevent a public right of way being created. He can erect and maintain a notice visible to persons using the way inconsistent with the dedication of the way as a highway and this will be sufficient, in the absence of proof of a contrary intention, to negative the intention to dedicate the way as a highway.[16] The landowner may do this even though he has let the land.[17] This is the origin of all the notices saying "Private Road" to be seen around the leafier estates[18] as well as the more formal notices referring specifically to the 1932 Act to be seen in city courtyards and passageways. However, if there is sufficient evidence to indicate that the highway had

---

[12] *Eyre v New Forest Highway Board* (1892) 56 J.P. 517 at 519.
[13] See below para.7.23 et seq.
[14] Natural Environment and Rural Communities Act 2006 s.66.
[15] At para.7.7.
[16] Highways Act 1980 s.31(3).
[17] ibid. s.31(4).
[18] Though this may not always be enough: *Secretary of State for the Environment v Beresford Trustees* [1996] C.L.Y. 5019.

already been dedicated before the notice was put up, the notice would be of no effect. An alternative method for public paths is provided by s.31(6) whereby a landowner may deposit a map and statement of all admitted rights of way and that no more have been dedicated on his land. This avoids dedication for 10 years at a time.[19]

(e)   Use "as of right"

7.06   The use has to be by the public openly and freely. It used to be thought that the reference in the Act to "as of right" meant that the public had to believe themselves to be exercising a public right to pass from one highway to another,[20] but the unreality of this has been acknowledged by the House of Lords in *R. v Oxfordshire CC Ex p. Sunningwell Parish Council*[21] where Lord Hoffman has explained that the user referred to in the Act is a form of prescription and that it means the same as with private rights of way. Therefore the fact that the user is "subjectively indifferent" to the existence of the right, does not prevent it from being user relevant to a public right of way.[22] Most of the recent cases about use "as of right" have related to commons and village or town greens and there are risks in applying the language used in those cases to highways. However, in *R. (on the application of Lewis) v Redcar and Cleveland BC*[23] the Supreme Court overturned an Inspector's decision that the fact that members of the public "deferred" to golfers who were using the golf course did not mean that they were not using the land "as of right". In short, it is appropriate to look at the attitude and "body language" of the members of the public using the way. This may also be relevant in assessing the attitude of the landowner in order to decide whether he is impliedly dedicating the way as a public right.

It is also not necessary for the way to pass from one highway to another. In towns there are many cul-de-sacs which are undoubtedly public highways and use for getting to somewhere where the public are entitled to go, e.g. a beauty spot, is just as valid as use to get to another public highway.[24] There is no rule of law that you cannot have a right of way to a cul-de-sac in the countryside.[25] If the landowner does not interfere with use as of right by a restricted class of people, for example seafaring men[26] or villagers,[27] this will still amount to public user, unless he gives them a specific licence.

---

[19] As extended by Countryside and Rights of Way Act 2000 Sch.3.
[20] *Hue v Whiteley* [1929] 1 Ch. 440.
[21] [2000] 1 A.C. 335; [1999] 3 W.L.R. 160.
[22] *R. v Oxfordshire CC Ex p. Sunningwell Parish Council* [2000] 1 A.C. 335; [1999] 3 W.L.R. 160.
[23] [2010] UKSC 11; [2010] 2 A.C. 70.
[24] *Roberts v Webster* 66 L.G.R. 298.
[25] *R. v Secretary of State for the Environment Ex p. Bagshaw* (1994) 68 P. & C.R. 402.
[26] *R. v Broke* (1859) 1 F. & F. 514.
[27] *Fairey v Southampton CC* [1956] 2 Q.B. 439; [1956] 2 All E.R. 843 at 846E per Denning L.J.

Use of a private cul-de-sac by the frontagers and their visitors does not indicate that they are using it as of right as a public highway, even where there is no "private road" sign.[28]

(f)   Permission

There is an important difference between public and private rights of   **7.07**
way in relation to "permission" or licence. A private right of way can only be granted by deed. Accordingly, permission or licence by the dominant owner prevents a prescriptive right arising. However, a public right of way can, it seems, be dedicated expressly or by implication. This (new?) principle was considered in *R. (on the application of Beresford) v Sunderland City Council*.[29] Like *R. v Oxfordshire CC Ex p. Sunningwell Parish Council*[30] this was a case about customary rights to a sports arena, but the House of Lords took the opportunity to deal with dedication of a highway:

> "An implied permission that sufficiently evidences an intention to dedicate creates the public right of way immediately. Twenty years' use by the public is not necessary. But twenty years' use "as of right" following a permission by a landowner that is indicative of an intention to dedicate will produce a deemed intention to dedicate unless the landowner can produce sufficient evidence that he had no such intention (see section 19(1) of the 1932 Act and section 31(1) of the 1980 Act)".[31]

This creates the anomaly that user without permission may give rise to a presumption of dedication, but user with permission may itself amount to an implied dedication. The immense factual problems which this creates in relation to highways were considered in the slightly earlier case of *Rowley v Secretary of State*[32] and, in particular, by Lord Scott in *R. (on the application of Beresford) v Sunderland City Council*.[33] Once it is accepted that there can be an implied permission to use a way which is intended to create a temporary licence rather than a dedication, this creates the problem of whether the acts or omission of the true owner are intended to give a licence, (which means that there is no implied dedication), or to amount to toleration of a person using the way as of right. Although permission is not a complete answer, the decision of the Inspector in *Rowland v Secretary of State* was set aside because he had failed to make

---

[28]   *Sinclair v Kearsley* [2010] EWCA Civ 112; [2010] 2 P. & C.R. DG10.
[29]   [2003] UKHL 60; [2004] 1 A.C. 889.
[30]   *R. v Oxfordshire CC Ex p. Sunningwell Parish Council* [2000] 1 A.C. 335; [1999] 3 W.L.R. 160.
[31]   per Lord Scott at [39].
[32]   [2003] 2 P. & C.R. 359.
[33]   [2003] UKHL 60; [2004] 1 A.C. 889 at 903[39]-[40].

proper findings of fact about the circumstances in which permission was given to individuals. The result is that where a way has been used in practice over the correct period, there may be considerable uncertainty about whether or not a public right of way has been created. This case also seems to indicate that the acts and omissions of the tenant can enure to the benefit or disadvantage of the landowner.

(g) Contrary intention

7.08 The wording from the Highways Act[34] is "unless there is sufficient evidence that there was no intention during that period to dedicate it". The meaning of that phrase has been authoritatively decided by the House of Lords in *R. v Sec of State Ex p. Godmanchester TC*[35] overruling the Court of Appeal. Having reviewed the authorities Lord Hoffmann comes down firmly on the side of an objective show of contrary intention.

> "I think that upon the true construction of s. 31(1), 'intention' means what the relevant audience, namely the user of the way, would reasonably have understood the landowner's intention to be".

The sections in the Act[36] making provision for the owner to put up a sign and, if this is pulled down, to deposit a statement with the appropriate council demonstrate that the objective of the Act is that the contrary intention should normally be demonstrated clearly to the public and not, for example, be contained in a letter to the County Planning Officer.
Thus:

> "A single act of interruption by the owner was of much more weight upon the question of intention than many acts of enjoyment",[37]

but the intention not to dedicate must be demonstrated by overt action.[38] The test is objective, i.e. whether there has been a continuous and plain assertion of a public right of way by virtue of public use. Evidence that the owner was merely tolerating the use and did not actually intend to dedicate is irrelevant in the absence of overt acts by the owner such as preventing people from using the way.[39]

---

[34] Highways Act 1980 s.31(1).
[35] [2008] 1 P. & C.R. 210.
[36] Highways Act 1980 s.31(3) to (6).
[37] per Parke B. in *Poole v Huskinson* (1843) 11 M. & W. 827, cited with approval in *R. v Secretary of State for the Environment Ex p. Cowell* [1993] J.P.L. 851 and *R. v Secretary of State for the Environment Ex p. Bagshaw* (1994) 68 P. & C.R. 402 at 408.
[38] *Jacques v Secretary of State*, Independent, June 8, 1994.
[39] *Cumbernauld and Kilsyth DC v Dollar Land* [1992] S.L.T. 1035; see also *R. (on the Application of Beresford) v Sunderland* [2002] 1 P. & C.R. 422 at [12] per Dyson L.J. where this issue is addressed in relation to commons.

"The court ought to be slow to find that a landowner's unexpressed intention not to dedicate is sufficient evidence for the purposes of section 31."[40]

This is in accordance with the origin of implied dedication in prescription and limitation rather than any true implied grant.[41]

(h) Common Law

The Act, however, expressly states that nothing in the section prevents **7.09** the dedication of a way being presumed or proved in any circumstances in which it might have been presumed or proved immediately before the commencement of the Act.[42] The common law rule is "once a highway always a highway"[43] and if it can be shown that a way is an ancient highway the fact that it has fallen into disuse, for example because another more convenient highway has been dedicated, does not cause it to cease to be a highway. So, in those circumstances there may be a public right of way at common law, even though the statutory requirement for user up to the date it is brought into question does not apply.

The common law provisions are, of course, subject to the provisions of s.66 Natural Environment and Rural Communities Act 2006. So no public right of way of mechanically propelled vehicles can now be created without express grant.[44]

(i) Length of use

The old authorities and, indeed, the Act make it clear that there is no **7.10** specific period of user which will give rise to a common law presumption of dedication. As little as 18 months user has been held to be sufficient in the case of a bridge over a railway which was clearly constructed for use by the public.[45] In modern conditions a short period of user may be sufficient to justify a presumption of dedication even if the road is not adopted, for example, where the road has been laid out as part of a building estate, particularly if it is a through route and no attempt is made to show that it is a private road. Where, however, the user was in the past and the way is no longer in use the courts will require evidence of a much longer period of use and may well be tempted to use the 20 year period as the period required at common law by analogy with the

---

[40] per Nicholls V.C. in *Ward & Ward v Durham CC* (1995) 70 P. &. C.R. 585 at 590.
[41] *R. v Oxfordshire CC Ex p. Sunningwell Parish Council* [2000] 1 A.C. 335.
[42] Highways Act 1980 s.31(9).
[43] See, e.g. *Eyre v New Forest Highway Board* (1892) 56 J.P. 517.
[44] Excluding electrically assisted pedal cycles.
[45] *North London Railway v St. Mary's Islington* (1872) 27 L.T. 672.

statute (and with the doctrine of lost modern grant that applies to private rights of way).[46]

It is necessary to relate these legal principles to the statutory prohibition of implied dedication in the case of mechanically propelled vehicles.[47] It would seem to follow that, in respect of any road laid out after 2006, there would be no presumption of dedication for vehicles, however obvious the intention unless it is a road

> "created by the construction, in exercise of powers conferred by virtue of any enactment, of a road intended to be used by such vehicles".[48]

It is also clear that there was no intention to exclude vehicles from public highways dedicated before 2006, whether expressly or by implication.

For the statutory presumption to arise the user has to be up to the time when the right of the public to use the way is brought into question. This does not mean the time when action is brought to prevent such user. As soon as the landowner seeks to prevent the public from using the way, time stops running. If the public then start using the way again this temporary stopping up is not an interruption destroying the public right, but simply a point in time which requires the person asserting the right to show 20 years' user before or after that date.[49] Therefore any period of 20 years' user will suffice providing that it is brought to an end by the owner seeking to stop the use.[50]

However, where the interruption or attempted interruption takes place after May 2, 2006 the person asserting the right of way would not be able to rely on any user since that date and therefore would not be able to show continuous user to the date of the action. However, it would seem that at Common Law the person asserting the right would be able to rely on any sufficient period prior to 2006, whether that period was 20 years or any shorter period held sufficient to demonstrate that the road had been dedicated by that date.

(j) Purpose of user

7.11   If a person is using a way as a means of getting somewhere else it clearly does not matter whether, when he reaches his destination, he is going to indulge in recreation or business. This, however, is not the same

---

[46] See below, Ch. 18.
[47] Natural Environment and Rural Communities Act 2006 s.66.
[48] Natural Environment and Rural Communities Act 2006 s.66(1)(b).
[49] *Fairey v Southampton CC* [1956] 2 Q.B. 439.
[50] See, e.g. *Chivers & Sons v Cambridge CC* [1957] 2 Q.B. 68; [1957] 1 All E.R. 882 at 885b.

thing as using the way itself for recreation such as picnicking or football. Where an area of land is used by the public for recreation, the case is usually based on the proposition that it is a town or village green[51] which has been used for more than 20 years since the Common Registration Act 1965. Even where this does not apply it may be possible to justify recreational use on the basis of an implied trust[52] or some other analogous right,[53] but the whole area will not normally be a public highway.

This problem was addressed by the Court of Appeal in *Dyfed County Council v Secretary of State for Wales*.[54] There, the distinction was made between "pure walking" which could give rise to a public right of way and other recreational activities such as picnicking or fishing in the same area. The argument put forward was that if there was no right to picnic on the land, then there could be no public right of way for gaining access to picnic, whereas walking was a legitimate use of the way itself which could give rise to a presumption of dedication, but the decision makes it clear that recreational walking can give rise to a public right of way even if it is purely recreational and not with the purpose of getting anywhere in particular.

The Act does not apply where the way is

"of such a character that use of it by the public could not give rise at common law to any presumption of dedication".[55]

It is not at all clear what this refers to. At common law it was once open to the owner to prove that the freehold owner could not have dedicated it (e.g. because he was not sui juris), but it is not easy to see what kind of way is of such a character that it could not be dedicated even though it has been used by the public for the requisite period.

(k) Interruption

An interruption in user once a highway has been created cannot cause **7.12** it to cease to be a highway though, under the Countryside and Rights of Way Act 2000, it may be relevant in considering whether to make a public path extinguishment order, in relation to footpaths and bridleways.[56] However, interruptions during the period of user which is being relied upon can affect the rights and it must be remembered that the period under the Highways Act 1980 is the 20 years prior to the right being challenged. Closing a way on one day every year is the main statutory method

---

[51] *R. (on the application of Lewis) v Redcar and Cleveland BC* [2010] UKSC 11; [2010] 2 A.C. 70.
[52] *Goodman v Saltash Corp* (1881-82) L.R. 7 App. Cas. 633.
[53] *R. v Doncaster MBC Ex p. Braim* (1989) 57 P. & C.R. 1.
[54] (1990) 59 P. & C.R. 275.
[55] Highways Act 1980 s.31(1).
[56] Highways Act 1980 s.118ZA as amended by Countryside and Rights of Way Act 2000 Sch.6.

of showing that there is no intention to dedicate,[57] though the Act also provides for lodging maps showing the admitted ways backed by a statutory declaration that no additional way has been dedicated. This method lasts six years, but creates only a rebuttable presumption.[58] However, more sporadic attempts to prevent a right from arising are also relevant. It seems that these are particularly relevant in relation to whether the user is *vi* ("with force"). In *R. (on the application of Lewis) v Redcar and Cleveland BC*[59] the Supreme Court, in relation to a town green, considered the relevance of the finding that the walkers and others enjoying recreation "deferred" to the golfers who were playing round the golf course. They did not consider this "politeness" [not to mention, no doubt, concern for their own safety] meant that the use was not as of right. A similar approach could be used to people using an alleged public highway. They would, no doubt, "defer" to the landowner's tractors or avoid the hay when it was growing. The difficulty is to decide at what point the user ceases to be continuous over the 20 year period. In relation to a town green, the taking of an annual hay crop (which causes the public to avoid the hay crop), does not affect continuity,[60] though it might well be different if this prevented the way being used at all during the hay season.

(l)   Extinguishing highway by statute

7.13   The Countryside and Rights of Way Act 2000, while primarily designed to increase access to the countryside, contains a procedure for public path extinguishment orders[61] and public path diversion orders.[62] Decisions will be made following a public inquiry conducted by specifically appointed inspectors. The alternative is for the landowner to seek to show that it never was a highway and should be removed from the definitive map. If an extinguishment order is made a landowner who is affected by the loss of this way may apply for compensation and the person applying for the extinguishment can be ordered to contribute to this.[63]

(m)   Diversion

7.14   There is no specific right to divert a public highway should the existing route be blocked either by the landowner or for some other reason, but

---

[57] ibid. s.31(3).
[58] ibid. s.31(5).
[59] [2010] UKSC 11.
[60] *R. (on the application of Lewis) v Redcar and Cleveland BC* [2010] UKSC 11 at [28] per Lord Walker.
[61] Highways Act 1980 s.118ZA as amended by Countryside and Rights of Way Act 2000 Sch.6.
[62] ibid.
[63] Highways Act 1980 ss.28 and 121(2).

there is a right to deviate temporarily if the way becomes "foundrous".[64] If the route of the way changes for any reason, the court may not find it difficult to imply an intention to dedicate the new route even where there has been less than 20 years' user.[65] A farmer has a limited statutory right to plough a field over which a footpath or bridleway passes but he must reinstate it within 14 days for the first disturbance for sowing and 24 hours for any subsequent disturbance, unless the highway authority allows an extension up to 28 days. He must then make it good to at least the minimum width which must then be indicated on the ground.[66] If he does so the path is temporarily diverted round the ploughed section.

Section 119Z of the Highways Act 1980[67] makes provision for an owner, lessee or occupier of land to apply for a public path diversion order "on the ground that in his interests it is expedient that the order should be made". This provision is intended to give local authorities a wide discretionary power to divert public paths. The council also has power to divert powers for special reasons, such as crime prevention,[68] paths across schools[69] and protecting sites of special scientific interest.[70]

A public highway should be over a defined route. There is no right to stray generally over open land unless the land is a town or village green.[71] This does not mean, however, that a public highway cannot be found where the route has varied or where not all members of the public using it take exactly the same route.[72] Equally, there may be ways in which a right of public resort can be enforced as a customary right or under an implied trust even though the right is not strictly a public highway.[73]

(n)   Disturbance

The Rights of Way Act 1990 significantly restricts the power of land-   **7.15** owners and other occupiers to interfere with public highways running over their land. This is done by amendment of the Highways Act 1980. No-one may so disturb the surface of a footpath, bridleway or un-made up road as to render it inconvenient for the exercise of the right.[74] This is

---

[64] ibid. at 518 per Wills J.
[65] *Boultwood v Paignton U.D.C.* (1928) 92 J.P. 98 though there was held to be no public highway in this case.
[66] Highways Act 1980 s.134 as substituted by the Rights of Way Act 1990.
[67] As amended by Countryside and Rights of Way Act 2000 Sch.6.
[68] Highways Act 1980 s.119B.
[69] ibid. s.119C.
[70] ibid. s.119D.
[71] *R. (on the application of Lewis) v Redcar and Cleveland BC* [2010] UKSC 11.
[72] *Eyre v New Forest Highway Board* (1892) 56 J.P. 517.
[73] See Ch. 10, *Goodman v Saltash Corporation* (1881-82) L.R. 7 App. Cas. 633; *R. v Doncaster MBC Ex p. Braim* (1989) 57 P. & C.R. 1, but see *Dyfed CC v Secretary of State for Wales* (1990) 59 P. & C.R. 275, above.
[74] Highways Act 1980 s.131A.

subject to the limited right of ploughing set out above[75] and the right to apply to the highway authority for authorisation.[76] Where crops are growing on the land the occupier has to ensure that the line of the highway is indicated and that the crops do not encroach onto the highway so as to make it inconvenient. It also provides that a footpath has a minimum width of one metre, a field edge path one and a half metres, a bridleway two metres and any other highway three metres.

The duty to enforce these provisions is placed on the highway authority and the sanctions are criminal. It seems unlikely that a member of the public will have a right of action against an occupier who fails to comply.

3.   Ownership of the sub-soil

(a)   Recent through roads

7.16   In the last hundred years or so a vast number of new through roads, by-passes, motorways, ring roads, etc. have been constructed and many existing roads have been widened or straightened taking in new land. These operations have been carried out on land acquired by compulsory purchase or by purchase by agreement from the landowners. The Highways Act 1980, ss.239 to 262 contain extensive and complex provisions setting out these powers and how they are to be exercised.

The boundary between such roads and the adjoining land is ascertained in exactly the same way as any other property boundaries. The land over which the road runs is owned by the body who bought it, usually the Crown, and any boundary disputes will be decided by construing the relevant conveyances[77] and by applying normal common law and equitable rules such as the principles of proprietary estoppel. Such roads, therefore, differ from adopted roads in that the actual land on which the road has been built is owned by the highway authority. Where the road has been adopted without purchase of the sub-soil the extent to which the sub-soil vests in the highway authority is much more limited.

(b)   Adopted roads

7.17   All roads maintainable at the public expense vest in the highway authority,[78] except trunk roads which vest in the Minister of Transport[79] and GLA roads which vest in the Greater London Authority.[80] Such vesting gives them full ownership in fee simple of the surface of the

[75] ibid. s.134.
[76] ibid. s.135.
[77] *Bexley LBC v Maison Maurice Ltd* [2006] EWHC 3192 (Ch).
[78] ibid. s.263.
[79] ibid. s.265.
[80] Highways Act 1980 ss.14A,14B,14C and 14D.

road,[81] sufficient, for example, to maintain an action of trespass against travellers who set up camp on the highway.[82] Roads maintainable at the public expense are usually described as "adopted roads", an expression used in the headings of the Act though not in the main body, and this expression will be used in this chapter. The drains in roads which vest in the highway authority also vest in the county.[83] The effect of this "vesting" is explained more fully below.

The vast majority of roads are adopted. The procedures for adoption of a road are now contained in the Highways Act 1980, but many highways were adopted under previous enactments and s.36(1) of the Act provides that any roads already maintainable at the public expense for the purposes of the Highways Act 1959 remain so maintainable. It is worth remembering, however, that just because a road is not adopted does not mean that it is not a public highway. The standard local inquiries only ask whether the lane is "maintainable at public expense". A purchaser who wishes to know whether it is a public highway may have to ask this in preliminary inquiries of the vendor.[84]

Where a new road is constructed by the highway authority it automatically becomes adopted.[85] Difficulties, however, can still arise as to the extent of the highway.[86]

In respect of estate roads the more common procedure is for the developer to build the road and for it then to be adopted by agreement under s.38 of the Highways Act 1980. The conveyance should make clear whether the estate road has been adopted under this section.

If for some reason there is no adoption by agreement, s.37 of the Act **7.18** makes provision for adoption by notice given by the developer. The council should then issue a certificate that the road has been dedicated by the developer. If they do so and the road is constructed in a satisfactory

---

[81] *Tithe Redemption Commission v Runcorn UDC* [1954] Ch. 383; [1954] 2 W.L.R. 518.

[82] *Wiltshire CC v Frazer* (1984) 47 P. & C.R. 69. The Criminal Justice and Public Order Act 1994 gives the police power to remove people trespassing on land where there are two or more people and the police officer reasonably believes they are there with the common intention of residing there providing that reasonable steps have been taken to ask them to leave and any of the people involved has caused damage to the land or to property on the land or used threatening, abusive or insulting words or behaviour towards the occupier or a member of his family or an employee or agent of his, or there are more than six vehicles (Criminal Justice and Public Order Act 1994 s.61). This section applies to footpaths, bridleways, byways open to all traffic, roads used as a public path and cycleways, but not to other highways. Presumably it was thought that existing powers were sufficient to deal with normal roads. In the separate provision in ss.77 and 78 giving local authorities power to remove campers from land, "land" is defined as "land in the open air" with no reference to highways. Therefore, it should apply to people camping on highways, since highways are land over which there is a public right of way.

[83] Highways Act 1980 s.264.

[84] See L.Gaz. June 21, 1989.

[85] *Hale v Norfolk CC* [2001] Ch. 717; [2001] 2 W.L.R. 1481.

[86] *Bexley LBC v Maison Maurice Ltd* [2006] EWHC 3192 (Ch).

manner, is kept in repair for 12 months and used as a highway during that period, then it automatically becomes an adopted road. If the council refuses to issue a certificate then the developer can appeal to the magistrates' court. Equally, if the council are not satisfied that it is of sufficient utility to justify its being adopted then they can apply to the magistrates' court for an order to that effect. Trunk roads are those so designated by the Minister.[87]

Highway authorities maintain a map of all their adopted roads. The maps are prepared pursuant to their duty under s.36(6) of the Highways Act 1980 to maintain a list of adopted roads. Such lists and maps are of considerable evidential value in deciding whether a particular road is or is not a public highway, though there is no statutory presumption that a road included in the list is a public highway.[88]

Footpaths and bridleways are highways in exactly the same way as roads and, as such, have always been maintainable at public expense, unless some individual has an obligation to repair them. This obligation now falls on the Highway Authority the exception being footpaths created after 1949 which they have not agreed to repair.

7.19   At common law there was no separate category of cycle track. A cycle has been held to be a vehicle[89] and it seems quite clear therefore that a bicycle is not entitled to use a footpath. It was argued in that case that a bicycle was really a form of iron horse, but this was rejected and accordingly it seems that at common law cyclists have no right to use bridleways either. However, by statute[90] a bicycle can be used on a bridleway, giving way to pedestrians and persons on horseback, providing that the bicycle is not a mechanically propelled vehicle. An "electrically assisted bicycle" is not a mechanically propelled vehicle.[91] A jury has been directed that a perambulator can be used on a footpath providing that it is of a size and weight not to inconvenience the public or cause damage to the way,[92] but this seems a very slight concession and even on that direction the jury could not agree! However, the Highways Act 1980 allowed for the construction of cycleways attached to adopted roads and the Cycle Tracks Act 1984 makes provision for orders to be made turning footpaths into cycle tracks. The cycle path then becomes a highway maintainable at the public expense.[93] The same rules about vesting and ownership therefore apply as in respect of any adopted road. The new category of "restricted

---

[87] Highways Act 1980 s.10.
[88] See *Secretary of State for the Environment, Transport and the Regions v Baylis and Bennett* (2000) 80 P. & C.R. 324.
[89] *Sheringham UDC v Hosley* (1904) 91 L.T. 225; (1904) 68 J.P. 395.
[90] Countryside Act 1968 s.30(1).
[91] Road Traffic Act 1988 s.189(1)(c).
[92] *R. v Matthias* (1861) 2 F. & F. 570.
[93] Cycle Tracks Act 1984 s.3(1).

byway" is dealt with below. Cycles are the principal form of "vehicles other than mechanically propelled vehicles" for which this category was intended. However, there are also dedicated cycleways created in connection with road schemes.

The provisions vesting highways in the highway authority or the Minister are, however, much more limited than might appear at first sight. The vesting provisions of the present Highways Act reflect those in earlier Acts. It has been held under previous statutes that all that is vested in the highway authority by virtue of the statutory provisions is the street itself, that is the metalled part, and not the whole of the sub-soil.

> "It is intelligible enough that Parliament should have vested the street qua street, and, indeed, so much of the actual soil of the street as might be necessary for the purpose of preserving and maintaining the street. But the provisions with respect to the sub-soil are totally different."[94]

Much of the litigation on this subject deals with problems which have been superseded by statutory provision at least in respect of adopted roads. The old authorities are, however, still relevant in determining the extent of the ownership vested in the highway authority (or the Minister in the case of trunk roads) by virtue of the vesting provisions, as opposed to roads where the whole subsoil has been acquired by compulsory purchase or private treaty.

The vesting is limited to the surface of the street and "such portion as **7.20** may be absolutely necessarily incidental to the repairing and proper management of the street".[95] It does, however, mean that the highway authority

> "actually become the owners of the street to this extent; they become the owners of so much of the air above and of the soil below as is necessary to the ordinary user of the street as a street and no more".[96]

This means that the highway authority has no rights over the mines and minerals lying under the road and the Highways Act specifically excludes such rights from the vesting provisions.[97]

The highway authority's ownership does extend far enough to enable it to sanction a tramway over the road[98] or the erection of a portico to first

---

[94] *Tunbridge Wells Corp v Baird* [1896] A.C. 434 at 438.
[95] *Municipal Council of Sydney v Young* [1898] A.C. 457. See *Commissioners for Land Tax for London v Central London Railway Co* [1913] A.C. 364.
[96] *Finchley Electric Light Co v Finchley Urban DC* [1903] 1 Ch. 437.
[97] Highways Act 1980 s.335.
[98] *Municipal Council of Sydney v Young* [1898] A.C. 457.

floor level over the road,[99] without the consent of the owner of the sub-soil. It does not, however, enable it simply by virtue of the vesting provisions to prevent the owner of the sub-soil passing telegraph wires over the road[100] or even building an office block over the road, providing that it is at sufficient height above the road not to interfere with the uses to which the road is being put.[101]

These restrictions on the definition of vesting have, however, been largely overtaken by express statutory powers. Thus, in respect of an adopted road no-one can, without the consent of the highway authority, erect a building,[102] or a bridge over a highway, or place any overhead beam, rail, pipe, cable or wire or other similar apparatus over, along or across a highway,[103] or erect scaffolding on or over the highway.[104] Any licence to erect a building over the highway must not authorise any interference with the convenience of persons using the highway, or affect the rights of owners of premises adjoining the highway or the rights of statutory undertakers or the operator of a telecommunications code system.[105]

7.21 The licence to build a bridge, under s.176, can be granted to any adjoining owner or occupier whether he owns the sub-soil or not. However, the restriction on erecting buildings over the highway in s.177 does not contain any express power and so, presumably, the right can only be exercised, even with the licence of the highway authority, if the person[106] exercising it also has the right to do so at common law. It was held under previous statutes that the vesting provisions vested in the highway authority the right to lease out the herbage[107] and also to cut down any trees planted within the highway, at least if they had been planted since the highway was dedicated.[108]

However, these decisions too have been largely superseded by s.96 of the Highways Act 1980 which gives express power to the highway authority to plant trees and shrubs and lay out grass verges, and s.142 which gives the highway authority the power to authorise adjoining owners and occupiers to plant and maintain trees and shrubs in the highway. This power can be exercised regardless of whether the adjoining owner or occupier owns the sub-soil.

---

[99] *Maharajah of Jaipur v Arjun Lal* [1937] 4 All E.R. 5.
[100] *Wandsworth Board of Works v United Telephone Co Ltd* (1883-84) L.R. 13 Q.B.D. 904.
[101] *Hemel Hempstead Development Corp v Hemel Hempstead BC* [1962] 1 W.L.R. 1158; [1962] 3 All E.R. 183.
[102] Highways Act 1980 s.177.
[103] ibid. s.178.
[104] ibid. s.169.
[105] Highways Act 1980 s.177(4).
[106] Highways Act 1980 s.329.
[107] *Coverdale v Charlton* (1878-79) L.R. 4 Q.B.D. 104.
[108] *Stillwell v New Windsor Corp* [1932] 2 Ch. 155.

Since the extent to which the sub-soil is vested in the highway authority is limited, it may still be necessary in some cases to decide who owns the part of the sub-soil which is not so vested.[109] In such cases the same principles apply as to unadopted highways.[110] It must be remembered, however, that special rules apply to estate roads[111] and that a body of law has grown up over roads originally dedicated under Enclosure Acts and awards (a not uncommon origin for minor roads).[112] To decide whether the sub-soil remains with the person who owned the land before the enclosure or whether it has passed to the adjoining owners may involve a detailed investigation of the specific Act or award, but essentially, despite some older indications to the contrary, the court will presume in the absence of evidence that the soil remains with the previous owner (usually the lord of the manor,[113]) that the soil has passed to the adjoining owners to the middle of the road.[114] This applies whether or not there is a specific reference in the deeds to "bounded by a road".[115] A highway can cease to be adopted by an order under s.47 of the Highways Act 1980, but this does not mean that it ceases to be a highway.

(c) Estate roads

In the past 150 years most new houses have been built on estates laid **7.22** out as building plots before sale. This process usually involves laying out new roads, which are then adopted by the highway authority and become public highways.

It has always been treated as settled law that there is a presumption that a conveyance of land abutting a highway passes the adjoining half of the highway. This presumption has, however, been explained in *Giles v County Building Construction (Hertford) Ltd*,[116] the leading modern case on this subject, as consisting of two presumptions.

"As I understand the law there are two presumptions relative to the ownership of the soil of a roadway. One presumption operates in certain circumstances when the conveyancing history of the land and road is unknown. This presumption supplies a fact of which there is no direct evidence, namely, the ownership of the road. The presumption is that the owner of the land abutting the road is also the owner

---

[109] *Commissioners for Land Tax for London v Central London Railway Co* [1913] A.C. 364.
[110] See below, para.7.34 et seq.
[111] See below, para.7.22.
[112] e.g. *Marton v Turnjer* [1997] C.L.Y. 4233.
[113] *Wild v Secretary of State* [2010] 1 P.& C.R. D65.
[114] *Haigh v West* [1893] 2 Q.B. 19; *Neaverson v Peterborough RDC* [1901] 1 Ch. 22; *R. v Hatfield Inhabitants* (1835) 4 Ad. & E. 156.
[115] *Collett v Culpin* [1996] C.L.Y. 5020, cf. the different rule in relation to riparian rights.
[116] (1971) 22 P. & C.R. 978.

of the adjoining section of the road up to the middle line. There is no room for this presumption when the conveyancing history of the land and the road is known from the time when they were in common ownership as in the case before me. In such a case there is, in certain circumstances, a totally different presumption which is more in the nature of a canon of construction that a conveyance of land includes half the adjacent roadway".[117]

"The conclusion which I draw from the authorities cited to me is that the second presumption, if it applies at all to a conveyance of a plot of land forming part of a building estate by a grantor who owns both land and road, is a presumption which readily yields to indications of a contrary intent".[118]

Before this authority it used to be thought that the presumption in either case was difficult to rebut and would not be rebutted by indications such as that the area of the land conveyed was not sufficient to include the highway, that the land was not described as bounded by the highway or the highway was not included in the land coloured on the plan. However, it now seems that the normal conveyance of a property abutting an estate road will not convey the sub-soil in half the highway which will remain the property of the developer. Equally it may be possible to show from the circumstances that the landowner on one side owns the whole of the sub-soil.[119] The presumption is, however, much stronger outside building estates.[120]

(d)   Highways on the definitive map

7.23   There is a definitive map of all "public paths". The categories, however, are quite complex.There are four specific categories of public paths—footpaths, bridleways, restricted byways and byways open to all traffic. The category of "road used as a public path" has been abolished. Any "roads used as a public path" on the definitive map, which have not been reclassified as byways open to all traffic are automatically reclassified as "restricted byways".[121]

(i)   Footpath

7.24   A footpath is limited to use on foot. It does not include pedal cycles which have been held to be vehicles.[122] As stated above a jury has been

---

[117] *Giles v County Building Construction (Hertford) Ltd* (1971) 22 P. & C.R. 978 per Brightman J. at 981.
[118] *Giles v County Building Construction (Hertford) Ltd* (1971) 22 P. & C.R. 978 at 986.
[119] *Baillie v Mackay* (1994) 25 G.W.D. 1516.
[120] *Collett v Culpin* [1996] C.L.Y. 5020.
[121] Countryside and Rights of Way Act 2000 s.47.
[122] *Sheringham UDC v Hosley* (1904) 91 L.T. 225; (1904) 68 J.P. 395.

directed that a perambulator can be used on a footpath providing that it is of a size and weight not to inconvenience the public or cause damage to the way.[123] The writer is not aware of any authority on roller-blades or skate boards.

(ii) Bridleway

A bridleway is specifically for riding or leading horses, though it also **7.25** incorporates use as a footpath. It can be used by a bicycle, providing that it is not mechanically propelled.[124] It does not, however, include a horse-drawn vehicle.

(iii) Restricted byway

A restricted byway involves the right of way on foot, on horseback or **7.26** leading a horse and "for vehicles other than mechanically propelled vehicles".[125] It therefore includes bicycles, electrically assisted bicycles, skateboards and roller-blades as well as a horse and cart.

(iv) Byway open to all traffic

The Countryside and Rights of Way Act 2000 sought to deal with the **7.27** mischief inadvertently created by this category which is a public right of way for "vehicular and all other kinds of traffic".[126] The effect is that green lanes, used in the past by horses and carts and then by the odd tractor, are legally open to all traffic which can negotiate them. Without the definitive map it would be difficult for a member of the public to know whether these green lanes are public highways or private accom-modation roads. Now that they are shown on the map, four-wheel drive vehicles and motor-cycles can use them as they wish for sport. These byways are usually unmetalled and as a result are unsuitable for such uses.[127] The 2000 Act prevents the automatic creation of any more such byways, but it does not remove those already classified and does not prevent a decision that a way initially registered as a restricted byway is in fact a byway open to all vehicles.[128]

---

[123] *R. v Matthias* (1861) F. & F. 570.
[124] Countryside Act 1968 s.30 as amended by Countryside and Rights of Way Act 2000 Sch.7 para.2.
[125] Countryside and Rights of Way Act 2000 s.48(4).
[126] Wildlife and Countryside Act 1981 s.56(1)(c).
[127] *Lasham Parish Meeting v Hampshire CC* (1993) 65 P. & C.R. 331.
[128] *R. v Secretary of State for the Environment Ex p. Riley* (1990) 59 P. & C.R. 1.

(v)   Cycleway

7.28   The Highways Act 1980 allows for the construction of cycleways attached to adopted roads and the Cycle Tracks Act 1984 makes provision for orders to be made turning footpaths into cycle tracks. However, since both a bridleway and a restricted byway allow use by bicycles, this seems the likeliest way forward, except for new dedicated cycleways.

(vi)   Cartway

7.29   There is no separate category of "cartway".[129] Evidence of user by horses and carts has been used as evidence of vehicular use to enable a way to be designated as a byway open to all traffic. However, under the new categorisation, a restricted byway can be used by a horse and cart. Council maps do refer to "CRF" or "cartroad footpath" and "CRB" or "Cartroad Bridleway", but this is just to show that it is a private track with public rights of way over it. These abbreviations are not used by the Ordnance Survey which uses "CT" for "cart track". A track with public rights for horses and carts will be a restricted byway.

(vii)   Driveway

7.30   The existence of specific rights for driving cattle is expressly reserved by the 2000 Act.[130]

The owner of the sub-soil has no obligation to maintain the way. Until the passing of the Countryside and Rights of Way Act 2000 obligations to maintain highways were sometimes imposed on adjoining owners by Inclosure Acts.[131] However, s.49(2) extinguishes all such obligations whether by tenure, enclosure or prescription.

The definitive map is conclusive evidence that all highways shown on it are highways at least to the extent indicated.[132] However, the absence of a road or path from the map is not conclusive evidence that it is not a highway and the fact that a highway is shown as a footpath or bridleway does not preclude evidence that there is a wider public highway.[133]

7.31   Although the Countryside and Rights of Way Act 2000 has created a new category of public path, known as a restricted byway, it has not altered the process of dedication. Section 48(6) expressly provides that the

---

[129] Though the expression is still used, e.g. *Chapman v Godnin Properties Ltd* [2005] EWCA Civ 941.
[130] Countryside and Rights of Way Act 2000 s.48(4).
[131] *Marlton v Turner* [1997] C.L.Y. 4233.
[132] *R. v Secretary of State for the Environment Ex p. Simms* [1991] 2 Q.B.354; [1990] 3 W.L.R. 1070.
[133] Wildlife and Countryside Act 1981 s.56(1).

fact that a way is registered as a restricted byway does not prevent someone from showing that it is in fact a right of way for mechanically propelled vehicles, though s.66 of the Natural Environment and Rural Communities Act 2006 prevents the creation of any new ways for mechanically propelled vehicles except by express grant. Furthermore, evidence of user in the past for carts and other horse-drawn vehicles will not be sufficient to prove that the way is for all vehicles including mechanically propelled vehicles.

The Countryside and Rights of Way Act 2000 maintains the existing process of review, but couples it with a parallel process of creation and extinguishment. It has been held that a change to a lower category on review does not prevent a person from claiming that in fact there is a wider right.[134]

The Act has, however, set out a cut-off date of 2025. If a way created before 1949 has not been put onto the definitive map by that date, it is extinguished.[135]

In addition the Act provides a new procedure for applying for the extinguishment of an existing public right of way. Under s.118 of the Highways Act 1980 the local authority could apply for an extinguishment or diversion order on the grounds that the way is not needed for public use. However, by s.118ZA and s.119ZA[136] the owner, lessee or occupier of land used for agriculture, forestry or the breeding or keeping of horses may apply for such an order and there are also other specialised bases for stopping up orders.[137] The Act sets up a complex procedure.

The corollary to this is the very limited provision for public path creation orders to enable the public to gain access to "access land" under Pt I of the Act.

The Highways Act provides that all roads maintained at public expense **7.32** are vested in the Highway Authority.[138] This applies to the vast majority of public paths. However, vesting applies only to the surface and does not mean that the highway authority owns the fee simple. If the way ceases to be a public highway or the highway is diverted then the vesting reverts to the original owner.

By s.49 of the Countryside and Rights of Way Act 2000 all restricted byways become highways maintainable at the public expense. As such they vest in the highway authority in the same way as any other adopted road. The existing rights to the sub-soil of adjoining or adjacent owners are replaced by a full right of way, including vehicular use "so far as is

---

[134] *R. v Secretary of State for the Environment Ex p. Riley* (1990) 59 P. & C.R. 1.
[135] Countryside and Rights of Way Act 2000 s.53.
[136] ibid.
[137] To prevent crime, for schools, for areas of special scientific interest, etc.
[138] Highways Act 1980 s.263(2)(a).

necessary for the reasonable enjoyment and occupation of the premises". However, in order to be entitled to this right the adjoining or adjacent owner has to show that he owned the sub-soil of the restricted byway.[139] The right does, however, extend to leaseholders who also held a lease of the sub-soil. The old law as to the ownership of the sub-soil therefore retains its importance. The same applies to byways open to all traffic created by the 1981 Act[140] and to footpaths and bridleways created under the 2000 Act. For other public paths the law is the same as for all highways.

(e) Bridges

7.33   Public highways frequently cross over bridges and have bridges crossing over them. Where a highway passes over a bridge or through a tunnel that bridge or tunnel is part of the highway for the purposes of the Highways Act 1980.[141] It follows that any bridge which forms part of an adopted road is maintainable by the highway authority and vests in them in accordance with the Act. Special rules apply to canals and railways which are not relevant for our purposes.

If a public highway which is not maintainable at public expense contains a bridge, the position is not so clear. The ownership of the bridge is not a matter which is dealt with in the Highways Act and so the provisions of s.328(2) do not apply. The first question will be to whom the sub-soil belongs. The Wildlife and Countryside Act 1981 makes no mention of bridges. If an unadopted highway runs over a bridge it would follow that the bridge belongs to the owner of the sub-soil. It does not follow, however, that he has any obligation to maintain it (except in so far as he could be held liable in nuisance if it became a danger to road users) unless it could be held to be a "structure" under s.146 of the Highways Act 1980.

(f) Unadopted highways

7.34   In respect of all ancient highways (as opposed to estate roads or new roads purchased under compulsory powers[142]) the presumption is that the soil of the highway belongs to the owner or owners of the land on either side. This is essentially a conveyancing presumption, namely that a conveyance of land adjoining the highway includes half the sub-soil of the highway[143] even if it is not referred to in the plan and the measurements would exclude it. If the owner of the whole of the sub-soil conveys

---

[139] Countryside and Rights of Way Act 2000 s.50(2).
[140] ibid., s.49.
[141] Highways Act 1980 s.328(2).
[142] See above paras 7.16 and 7.22 et seq.
[143] *Pardoe v Pennington* (1998) 75 P. & C.R. 264.

land adjoining the highway there is an assumption that the whole of the sub-soil is included, even if the plan appears to exclude the highway.[144] It is a valuable rule because it ensures that small pieces of land, which may be of limited value, are not left without an owner[145] and it is submitted that it can be relied on, even when there is no direct evidence of a conveyance of the adjoining land. It may be that if the presumption does not apply and neither adjoining owner can claim the sub-soil, then the sub-soil may be manorial waste and belong to the lord of the manor.[146]

If the highway constitutes the boundary between the two properties then the presumption is that this ownership is to the middle line, though as set out above this presumption is rebuttable.

It has been seen that in respect of adopted roads this right has been largely nullified by the vesting of the highway itself in the highway authority, and by statutory restrictions on what can be done on the highway without the licence of the highway authority. The right is, in any event, restricted by the common law obligation not to obstruct the highway or to cause a nuisance to highway users.

In practice such rights have mainly been asserted over adopted roads **7.35** and accordingly the contest has been between the highway authority claiming that the highway is vested in it and the adjoining owner claiming that it has no right to stop him doing what he wishes.

Looking at these cases from the other side, at the right of the owner of the sub-soil to do things on the highway, however, it has been accepted at common law that even within the area of the highway itself the owner may erect a building spanning the way providing that it does not cause a nuisance,[147] can put up telephone wires,[148] can build cellars or otherwise excavate under the highway and can let the herbage.[149]

The position of trees growing in the road is less clear. Quite apart from the express statutory provisions it seems clear that the highway authority can remove trees which are growing in the highway since they are an obstruction which the highway authority is entitled to clear, even if they are not causing a nuisance to anyone.[150] Doubt has, however, been expressed as to whether the same applies to trees which were already

---

[144] *Berridge v Ward* (1861) 10 C.B. (NS) 400 cited with approval in *Pardoe v Pennington* (1998) 75 P. & C.R. 264 at 269 and *Commission for the New Towns v JJ Gallagher Ltd* [2002] EWHC 2668 (Ch); [2003] 2 P. & C.R. 3.

[145] The presumption is a conveyancing presumption, *Commission for the New Towns v JJ Gallagher Ltd* [2002] EWHC 2668 (Ch); [2003] 2 P. & C.R. 3.

[146] *Wild v Sec. of State* [2010] 1 P. & C.R. D65.

[147] *Hemel Hempstead Development Corp v Hemel Hempstead BC* [1962] 1 W.L.R. 1158; [1962] 3 All E.R. 183.

[148] *Finchley Electric Co v Finchley Urban DC* [1903] 1 Ch. 436.

[149] *Coverdale v Charlton* (1878-79) L.R. 4 Q.B.D. 104.

[150] *Stillwell v New Windsor Corp* [1932] 2 Ch. 155; *Turner v Ringwood Highway Board* (1869-70) L.R. 9 Eq. 418.

there at the time of the dedication[151] and as to whether the cut wood is the property of the highway authority or the owner of the sub-soil.[152] The owner of the sub-soil may even extract minerals from under the road, but this does not give him the right to damage the road in the process.[153] It also seems implicit from *Giles v County Building Contractors (Hertford) Ltd*[154] that if the plaintiff had been found to be the owner of the sub-soil he would have had locus standi for claiming excessive user. The ownership of the sub-soil may also be relevant in deciding whether a person has locus standi in respect of a definitive map planning enquiry.[155]

It must be remembered, however, that the presumption of divided ownership is rebuttable.[156] Many public footpaths run along farm tracks. The track may run along the side of fields. Where the track leads to one particular farm or is shown on some previous conveyancing documents as belonging to a particular property, the presumption will be easily rebutted. Where there is a public highway adjacent to a parcel of land the first step is to see whether it is shown as part of the land conveyed. In the case of a track with a public highway open to all vehicles on it this will not usually be the case. The next step is to see whether it is included on any other conveyance. It may be that the parcel of land was part of a larger estate or farm. If the track was shown on a previous conveyancing document as forming part of the larger estate, but is not shown as being conveyed when the parcel of land involved was conveyed, it is likely that the ownership of the sub-soil will remain with the owner of the larger estate. Sometimes it is advisable, if the ownership of the way is of relevance, to seek to buy the sub-soil from the present owner of the estate who may just be a personal representative who believes that he has disposed of the whole. It is only where it proves impossible to find any conveyancing documents which show the ownership of the sub-soil that the presumption arises.

7.36 If the land ceases to be a highway because of an extinguishment or diversion order, the owner of the sub-soil becomes fully entitled whether the road was an adopted road or not. This is the only way in which highways can cease to be highways. At common law the rule is "once a highway always a highway".

Although the law governing public rights of navigation over inland waterways is similar in many ways to the law governing highways, the law as to public highways applies only to rights of way over land. The

---

[151] *Stillwell v New Windsor Corp* [1932] 2 Ch. 155.
[152] *Turner v Ringwood Highway Board* (1869-70) L.R. 9 Eq. 418.
[153] *Benfieldside Local Board v Consett Iron Co Ltd* (1877-78) L.R. 3 Ex. D. 54.
[154] (1971) 22 P. & C.R. 978.
[155] *Wild v Secretary of State* [2010] 1 P. & C.R. D65
[156] *Commission for the New Towns v JJ Gallagher Ltd* [2002] EWHC 2668 (Ch); [2003] 2 P. & C.R. 3.

provisions of the Highways Act 1980 which provide for dedication of a public highway from presumption of long user expressly provide that "land" includes "land covered by water",[157] but this refers only to fords and bridges over water and not to navigable waters themselves since in such cases the right is over the water and not over the land covered by the water.[158] The definition of a highway in the Act expressly excludes ferries and waterways.[159]

4.   Extent of the highway

The extent of the highway, whether it is vested in the highway authority **7.37** or is just land over which a public right of way exists, is not normally restricted to the metalled part, but includes the grass verges.

In deciding how far it extends, it is necessary to look at the history of the land. If fences or hedges have been erected to mark the edge of the highway it has been said that there is a rebuttable presumption that all the land between those fences or hedges is part of the highway,[160] but this presumption, if it exists at all, only applies where the likeliest explanation is that the hedge or fence was put up for this purpose.[161] The mere fact that a road has been designated as a new road and the landowner has been forced to set his house and fence back does not automatically mean that he has dedicated further land as a highway.[162] Where it is more likely that the fence or hedge was put in to enclose what had previously been an open area of land, there is no presumption.[163]

> "It is clear that the mere fact that a road runs between fences, which of course includes hedges, does not per se give rise to any presumption. It is necessary to decide the preliminary question whether those fences were put up by reference to the highway, that is to separate the adjoining closes from the highway or for some other reason. When that has been decided, then a rebuttable presumption of law arises, supplying any lack of evidence of dedication in fact, or inferred from user that the public right of passage, and, therefore, the highway, extends to the whole space between the fences and is not confined to such part as may have been made up.

---

[157] Highways Act 1980 s.31(11).
[158] *Attorney General Ex rel Yorkshire Derwent Trust Ltd v Brotherton* [1992] 1 A.C. 425; [1992] 1 All E.R. 230.
[159] Highways Act 1980 s.328(1).
[160] *Attorney General v Beynon* [1970] Ch. 1; [1969] 2 All E.R. 263.
[161] *Bexley LBC v Maison Maurice Ltd* [2006] EWHC 3192 (Ch).
[162] *Hale v Norfolk CC* [2001] Ch. 717; (2001) 82 P. & C.R. 26, followed in *Bexley LBC v Maison Maurice Ltd* [2006] EWHC 3192 (Ch).
[163] *Hinds and Diplock v Breconshire CC* [1938] 4 All E.R. 24.

161

It seems clear to me, however, as the principle has developed that one is to decide that preliminary question in the sense that fences do mark the limit of the highway unless there is something in the condition of the road or the circumstances to the contrary."[164]

However, while the general tenor of this judgment was approved, the idea that there is any presumption of law was rejected in *Hale v Norfolk CC*[165]:

"Whether it is right to infer, as a matter of fact in any particular case, that the landowner has fenced against a highway must depend, as Lord Russell of Killowen C.J. observed in *Neeld v Hendon Urban District Council*[166] on the nature of the district through which the road passes, the width of the margins, the regularity of the line of hedges, and the level of the land adjoining the road; and (I would add) anything else known about the circumstances in which the fence was erected."[167]

Instead, the courts will try to decide on the reality of the situation from the evidence, if that is possible. This may well involve a detailed consideration of the history of the site, possibly going back hundreds of years. If, however, this evidence is inconclusive the assumption that the highway extends over the whole space between the fences will usually apply, even if it is not strictly a presumption in law.

7.38   Where there is a ditch there is a presumption that the ditch is not part of the highway.[168] This presumption, however, is easily rebuttable. Again the question is—what was the purpose of the ditch? If it was put there to drain the adjoining land then it is not part of the highway. If it is there to drain the highway then it is part of the highway. If it is for both purposes then the presumption will normally apply and it will be held not to be part of the highway.

In the past there were substantial areas of roadside land which neither formed part of the highway itself nor were part of the adjoining land. These areas were part of the manorial waste and as such belonged to the lord of the manor. It was decided in *Re Britford Common*[169] that land can be waste of the manor even if no rights of common have been exercised over it. It can, therefore, be registered as common land. However, by s.1 of the Commons Registration Act 1965, all common land had to be registered and after the statutory period

---

[164] *Attorney General v Beynon* [1970] Ch. 1; [1969] 2 All E.R. 263 at267i per Goff J.
[165] [2001] Ch. 717; [2001] 2 W.L.R. 1481.
[166] *Neeld v Hendon Urban District Council* (1889) 81 L.T. 405.
[167] per Chadwick L.J.
[168] *Hanscombe v Bedfordshire CC* [1938] Ch. 944.
[169] [1977] 1 W.L.R. 39; [1977] 1 All E.R. 532.

"no land capable of being registered under this Act shall be deemed to be common land or a town or village green unless it is so registered".[170]

By section 22(1) of the Commons Registration Act 1965 "common land" means "(b) waste land of a manor not subject to rights of common and not part of a highway". It would appear to follow, therefore, that if land, including waste land beside a highway, is not registered under the 1965 Act it cannot be waste of the manor, even if it would be so regarded at common law. The only qualification of this is that new customary rights can have arisen in the years since the commencement of the 1965 Act, but it is hard to see how waste of the manor can come into this category.

The situation, therefore, is that if roadside waste has been registered under the 1965 Act either its ownership is set out in the rights register or the various presumptions set out in the Act apply, whether or not there are also rights of common over it. What is left unclear by the Act is what happens to any land which was manorial waste, but has not been registered. Since it is no longer manorial waste, it does not pass with the lordship of the manor, but who owns it? Does it belong to the lord of the manor in 1965 or his personal representatives? Or does it become vacant land open to anyone to claim? This problem was touched upon by Lord Templeman in *Hampshire CC v Milburn*[171] but has not yet been resolved.

In many towns and cities there are cellars under the streets often with **7.39** gratings or other openings onto the pavement. Such cellars and gratings will nearly always be under adopted roads the surface of which has vested in the highway authority.

At common law there is nothing to prevent the owner of the sub-soil of the highway constructing cellars under the street. This common law right, however, has been severely circumscribed by ss.179 and 180 of the Highways Act 1980 which prevent a person from constructing any part of a building or a vault, arch or cellar, or any opening to a cellar or vault, whether forming part of a building or not, under a street (which includes any highway, even a footpath)[172] without the consent of the highway authority. Furthermore the owner of any such vault, arch or cellar and of any opening to the street is under a statutory duty to keep it in good condition and repair. Although failure to do so is not a breach of statutory duty giving rise to a direct civil action by any person injured, failure to take reasonable steps to keep it in repair could amount to negligence or nuisance.[173]

---

[170] *Commons Registration Act 1965* s.1(2)(a).
[171] *Hampshire CC v Milburn* [1991] 1 A.C. 325 at 34A and in *Wild v Sec. of State* [2010] 1 P. & C.R. D65
[172] Highways Act 1980 s.329.
[173] *Scott v Green & Sons* [1969] 1 W.L.R. 301; [1969] 1 All E.R. 849; *MacFarlane v Gwalter* [1959] 2 Q.B. 332; [1958] 1 All E.R. 181.

5.   Evidence

7.40   Where, therefore, it is necessary for any reason to determine a boundary with a public highway there are a number of matters which have to be resolved.

(a)   Is it a public highway?

7.41   First it is necessary to determine whether or not there is a public highway.

MAPS

7.42   As has been seen above, there are several ways in which a highway can become a highway. Section 32 of the Highways Act 1980 expressly provides that a court or tribunal, before determining whether a way is a public highway, shall take into consideration any map, plan or history of the locality or other relevant document which is tendered in evidence, and shall give such weight thereto as the court or tribunal considers justified by the circumstances, including; the antiquity of the tendered document; the status of the person by whom and the purpose for which it was made or compiled; and the custody in which it has been kept and from which it is produced. It is not, therefore, usually necessary to make use of the provisions of the Civil Evidence Acts 1968 and 1995 in order to ensure that documents can be produced in evidence.

The first step is to discover whether the way is shown on the highway authority's map of adopted highways. This map is kept under the statutory duty contained in s.36(6) of the Highways Act 1980, though there is no statutory presumption that such roads are highways.[174]

If it is not shown on the map of adopted highways it may be shown as a footpath, bridleway, restricted byway or byway open to all traffic on the definitive map under the Wildlife and Countryside Act 1981 as amended. If it is on this map, that is conclusive evidence that it is a highway, to the extent shown on the map.[175] Omission from this map is not, however, conclusive that there is no highway. The Countryside and Rights of Way Act 2000 has created a cut-off date of January 1, 2026 for unregistered public rights of way. After that date any public rights in such ways will be extinguished.[176]

It is also necessary to look at the register kept under s.31A of the Highways Act 1980 to ensure that the landowner has not registered a statement under s.31(6) that he does not intend to dedicate it as a highway.

---

[174] *Secretary of State for the Environment, Transport and the Regions v Baylis* (2000) 80 P. & C.R. 324.
[175] Wildlife and Countryside Act 1981 s.56(1).
[176] Countryside and Rights of Way Act 2000 s.53, subject to the exceptions in s.53, currently not in force.

Ordnance Survey maps show public footpaths and public bridleways, but the indication of a track or road on the map is not an indication that it is dedicated to the public. Tithe maps may also be of use in showing the existence of tracks, but again the tithes commissioners were not strictly concerned with whether or not a way was public.

STATUTES

Many roads were originally set out under the Inclosure Acts and a **7.43** search of any such Act which relates to the land in dispute is therefore advisable. It has, however, been held that the Inclosure Act 1802 gave no power to create public footpaths, even though an award purported to do so.[177] Also many roads were created by Turnpike Acts and there is always the possibility that a highway so created has not subsequently found its way onto the local authority's map.

The obligations of maintenance imposed on adjoining owners under Inclosure Acts, as well as by tenure or prescription, has been abolished in respect of restricted byways by the Countryside and Rights of Way Act 2000.[178]

DEEDS

It is unusual to find any direct evidence of dedication in the historic **7.44** conveyancing documents, but a conveyance may refer to a highway either in the parcels or on the plan annexed. Where the highway is modern there may well be an express dedication. An agreement to dedicate a highway creates an overriding interest under s.70(1)(a) of the Land Registration Act 1925[179] and para.5 of Schs 1 and 3 to the Land Registration Act 2002.

Unlike water boundaries, the presumption does not depend on the deed expressing the land to be "bounded by" the way.[180]

WITNESSES

In the absence of documentary evidence a person seeking to show that **7.45** a highway is or is not a public highway must resort to producing evidence of public user, bearing in mind that a person may use a path by reference to a private right of way. Thus the milkman may deliver milk to a private house by way of a private drive. This would be no indication of public use.

---

[177] *R. v Secretary of State Ex p. Andrews* [1993] C.L.Y. 1625.
[178] Countryside and Rights of Way Act 2000 s.49(2).
[179] *Overseas Investment Services Ltd v Simcobuild Construction Ltd, The Times*, November 2, 1993.
[180] *Collett v Culpin* [1996] C.L.Y. 5020.

The subtle, but crucial distinction between implied permission and tolerance has been considered above. However, the nature of the evidence to be produced by the landowner and adjudicated upon by the Court was considered in *Rowley v Secretary of State*.[181] It is essential to decide whether or not users of the path were in fact turned back and if and when gates were locked. There can then be evidence from the owner who interfered with user as to what his intention was.

In this regard, the intention of the owner is more important than the intention of the user. The House of Lords in *R. v Oxfordshire CC Ex p. Sunningwell Parish Council*[182] has made it clear that it is unrealistic to try to look too carefully into the mind of the person using the way. He may be "subjectively indifferent" to whether he considers the way to be a public highway. The user "as a right" is free open user, without permission, in the same way as prescriptive user of a private right of way.

It is important to remember that once a way has become a public highway it will remain so permanently unless there is a formal stopping up or diversion order. It is not necessary, therefore for the evidence of use by the public to bring the case up to date, but only up to the date that it was stopped up.

(b)   Where is the boundary?

7.46   If it is once established that the highway is a public highway, evidence of its extent can be complex. It may be plain that the highway is bounded by hedges or fences which determine its extent, but it has been seen[183] that a hedge or fence does not necessarily indicate the extent of the highway. Equally the existence of a ditch does not necessarily mean that the highway cannot extend beyond it. It will be necessary to look into the history of the fence, hedge or ditch to see, if possible, when and why it was constructed.

For example, the fence may originally have been constructed to enclose open land for ornamental purposes, rather than to delineate the extent of the highway. Or the fence may have been erected by the highway contractors to establish the boundary of the adjoining owner's land rather than the extent of the highway, particularly if a strip is being retained as a "ransom strip" to prevent the adjoining owner from building a new entrance onto the highway.[184]

Frequently, however, the boundary will be a matter of factual inferences to be drawn in the absence of evidence.

---

[181] [2003] 2 P. & C.R. 359.
[182] [2000] 1 A.C. 335.
[183] See above para.7.37 et seq.
[184] *Bexley LBC v Maison Maurice Ltd* [2006] EWHC 3192 (Ch).

Evidence of use by members of the public, which may be important in deciding whether or not the highway is a public highway, is less important in deciding the extent of the highway. An adjoining owner may well have taken advantage of little used parts of the highway to park vehicles, etc. but this does not indicate that the highway is so limited.

Evidence of use by adjoining owners must be viewed with caution as it may well be pursuant to a private right of way.[185]

Finally it may be necessary to decide whether, whatever the extent of the highway, the soil under it or the airspace over it is retained by the adjoining owner and, if so, whether he owns the whole of it, or only his half.[186] Again this will be ascertained from the history of the road. If it is an ancient highway it is much more likely that the sub-soil will be held to belong to the adjoining owner than if the creation of the highway is known, for example, from the construction of a building estate, in which case any indication in the conveyances to the effect that the sub-soil of the highway is excluded will be sufficient to rebut any slight presumption there is in favour of the sub-soil having passed. If the sub-soil has not passed it will be retained by the estate developer.

---

[185] *Sinclair v Kearsley* [2010] EWCA Civ 112.
[186] *Commission for the New Towns v JJ Gallagher Ltd* [2002] EWHC 2668 (Ch); [2003] 2 P. & C.R. 3.

Chapter Eight
Water Boundaries

1.   Introduction

When a person becomes the freehold owner of real property, what he **8.01**
really obtains is the ownership of a three dimensional space. We have
seen that this space may not involve any actual land at all. It may be what
is known as a flying freehold or it may be entirely subterranean. The soil,
buildings and other property within the space normally belong to the
owner of the freehold. He can do what he likes with them, subject to:

- the considerable statutory restrictions on the use of land;

- the abstraction of soil and rock;

- common law obligations towards his neighbours based on the law
  of nuisance; and

- incorporeal hereditaments in respect of which his freehold is the
  servient tenement.

The reason for this jurisprudential discourse is that water is an exception to the principle that the owner of the land also owns what is on it. To
understand the law relating to water it is necessary to appreciate that all
substances found on land do not automatically belong to the person who
owns it. This applies particularly to two of the most important elements
of our planet—water and air.

The principle was well stated by Parke B. in *Embrey v Owen*,[1]

> "but flowing water is publici juris not in the sense that it is bonum
> vacans to which the first occupant may acquire an exclusive right,
> but that it is public and common in this sense only, that all may
> reasonably use it who have a right of access to it, but none can have
> any property in the water itself, except in the particular portion
> which he may choose to abstract from the stream and take into his

---

[1] *Embrey v Owen* (1851) 6 Ex 353 at 361,372.

possession and that during the time of his possession only . . . The same law will be found to be applicable to the corresponding rights to air and light. These are bestowed by Providence for the common benefit of man, and so long as the reasonable use by one man of this common property does not do actual and perceptible damage to the right of another to the similar use of it, no action will lie."

The trouble with water is that it does not stay in the same place. The water in a natural stream does not belong to anyone,[2] it is publici juris. The same applies to water percolating through the ground:

"It seems to my mind to be clear from the decision that no-one has at any time any property in water percolating below the surface of the earth, even when it is under his own land."[3]

Water, after it has been used for whatever purpose it is required, returns to being common property.[4]

8.02 It might appear, at first sight, that water in an artificial lake or pond, or a tank, or a canal was different. The intermediate state of water in a pond was referred to in *John White & Sons v J & M White*,[5]

". . . or turned it into a pond, so that the water enclosed within that pond should become, not *publici juris*, but water with somewhat of a proprietary right."

It must be remembered that this water too has come from natural sources and is subject to evaporation or leakage. If water leaks from a water tank onto the land of a neighbour, it would not be open to the owner of the water tank to ask for it back. A person's rights, therefore, even in water he has stored, fall short of full proprietary rights.

It is also very easy to fall into the trap of thinking of a river or stream as a thing, when it actually consists of a constantly changing volume of water. This flow is the main difference between a stream or river and, for example, an outcrop of rock.

It is apparent, therefore, that the common law's approach to water has been very different from its approach to land. What people obtain in relation to water is rights rather than ownership. Some of these rights are

---

[2] *Embrey v Owen* (1851) 6 Ex. 353; *Ballard v Tomlinson* (1885) L.R. 29 Ch. D. 115; *John White & Sons v J & M White* [1906] A.C. 72; *Attorney General Ex rel Yorkshire Derwent Trust Ltd v Brotherton* [1990] Ch. 136; [1989] 2 W.L.R. 938; [1989] 2 All E.R. 423 at 427f upheld by House of Lords [1992] 1 A.C. 425; [1991] 3 W.L.R. 1126.
[3] *Ballard v Tomlinson* (1885) L.R. 29 Ch. D. 115 per Brett M.R. at 120.
[4] *Embrey v Owen* (1851) 6 Ex. 353.
[5] *John White & Sons v J & M White* [1906] A.C. 72 at 80 per Earl of Halsbury.

easements, but others take the form of natural rights attached to land, akin to the natural right of support.[6] Although such rights are not strictly easements they fall more easily into the part of this work dealing with easements than into the present section.

The intention of this chapter, therefore is to deal with the effect of water **8.03** on boundaries and not the title to water or the easements and other rights relating to it. Rivers, tidal and non-tidal, streams, lakes, canals and the seashore are very common boundaries and the extent and line of the boundary will depend on which category the feature comes into. It is necessary therefore, to attempt some definitions.

In considering the private boundaries of land bounded by rivers, lakes and the sea it is worth remembering that many public boundaries, including county and parish boundaries, run along rivers and lakes and that most maritime municipal boundaries terminate at the sea. The fixing of public boundaries is in the hands of the Ordnance Survey and, while there is no absolute reason why private law should follow the practice of the Ordnance Survey surveyors,[7] it is obvious that very considerable assistance can be gained from this source.[8] Where, therefore, a boundary is shown on the relevant Ordnance Survey map it is likely that this can be accepted as the correct delineation of, for example, the centre line of a river, tidal or non-tidal, or the mean high or low tide level. If, however, a precise measurement is crucial, it must be remembered that these levels change over the years and the Ordnance Survey may not be up-to-date.

2. Rivers

(a) Non-tidal rivers

In respect of a non-tidal river the presumption is that the riparian **8.04** owners own the bed and the soil under it to the middle of the water. This is the case whether or not the property is expressed in the conveyance to be "bounded by" the river.

> "There is no logic or reason, in their lordships' opinion in distinguishing a case where property is described as bounded by water from one where the relevant map shows beyond doubt that a water boundary is intended."[9]

---

[6] See below, Ch. 21—Water Rights.

[7] per Lord Wilberforce in *Southern Centre of Theosophy Inc v South Australia* [1982] A.C. 706; [1982] 1 All E.R. 283 at 288f and see *Reece v Miller* (1881-82) L.R. 8 Q.B. 626.

[8] J. R. S. Booth, *Public Boundaries and Ordnance Survey 1840-1980*, (Ordnance Survey, 1980).

[9] per Lord Wilberforce in *Southern Centre of Theosophy Inc v South Australia* [1982] 1 All E.R. 283 at 288j; see also *Attorney General of Southern Nigeria v John Holt & Co (Liverpool) Ltd* [1915] A.C. 599.

This is, however, a rebuttable presumption.[10] If the title deeds indicate that the whole river bed is owned by one riparian owner this will override the presumption. Furthermore, title to the river bed can be obtained by adverse possession.[11]

First it is necessary to define what is meant by a non-tidal river. A river is a "natural watercourse running along a defined channel". The word "river" in common parlance indicates a fairly large watercourse, a smaller watercourse usually being called a stream, though there are many local descriptions such as beck, burn, brook, etc. The best legal description is a "natural watercourse". The presumption for all natural watercourses, therefore, is that the riparian owners own the bed and the soil to the middle of the water.

8.05 A natural watercourse will rise initially from a spring. As soon as it starts to run in a defined channel it becomes a watercourse.[12] "Defined" was defined in *Bleachers Association Ltd v Chapel en le Frith RDC*[13] as "a contracted and bounded channel", but it is clear from the earlier case of *Dudden v The Guardians of the Poor of the Clutton Union*[14] that the courts will consider a spring to become a stream very quickly. Obviously the exact point at which a marshy area becomes a stream is open to debate, but the principle is clear.[15]

It seems that an entirely underground stream running, for example, into a well is not a watercourse[16]:

> "If underground water flows in a defined channel into a well supplying a stream above ground, but the existence and course of that channel are not known and cannot be ascertained except by excavation, the lower riparian owners on the banks of the stream have no right of action for the abstraction of underground water"

but if once it emerges and becomes a stream it continues to be a watercourse even if it subsequently plunges back underground.[17] If, however, it simply disappears without ever re-emerging as a stream or river or dissipates itself over a field, it is still a watercourse for the section which runs above ground.[18] The size of streams and rivers varies greatly according to the seasons.

---

[10] *Micklethwait v Newlay Bridge Co* (1886) L.R. 33 Ch. D. 133 where the land was expressed to be "bounded by the river".
[11] *Maddera v Atkins* [1992] E.G.C.S. 82.
[12] *Dudden v The Guardians of the Poor of the Clutton Union* (1857) 1 Hurl. & N. 627.
[13] [1933] Ch. 356.
[14] (1857) 1 Hurl. & N. 627.
[15] See *Rugby Joint Board v Walters* [1967] Ch. 397; [1966] 3 W.L.R. 934.
[16] *Bradford Corp v Ferrand* [1902] 2 Ch. 655.
[17] *Dickinson v Grand Junction Canal Co* (1852) 7 Ex. 282.
[18] *Maxwell Willshire v Bromley R.D.C.* (1919) 82 J.P. 12.

"A river which naturally runs during a good part of the year does not cease to be a river merely because at times it is accustomed to become dry."[19]

A tidal river is defined later.[20]

The distinction between a natural and an artificial watercourse has **8.06** been more often considered in relation to riparian rights such as the right to draw water and the right to a reasonable flow,[21] than in relation to the actual boundary. Many artificial watercourses, however, simply represent a diversion or culverting of a natural stream. There is, therefore, a grey area between a totally natural stream or river and an entirely artificial watercourse. Furthermore, there may be situations in which the riparian owners of an artificial watercourse have the same rights as the riparian owners of a natural watercourse. Thus a stream which had been arched over and used as a sewer from time immemorial could still give rise to riparian rights.[22] On the other hand, the distinction is not so much one of age as the actual or presumed object of the diversion. It will be much more difficult to deduce that a riparian owner has the right to take water from an artificial watercourse where the diversion of the stream is for some "temporary" or specific purpose, for example a mill race, than a more permanent diversion of a stream to a new course for reasons such as flood prevention.[23]

The significance of the distinction between a natural and an artificial watercourse in relation to boundaries is that the presumption of ownership of half the bed and sub-soil does not apply to an artificial watercourse. It is not clear whether this presumption also applies to an artificial watercourse which is a permanent diversion of a natural stream. This problem is made more difficult by the fact that many of our rivers are the result of deliberate diversions and the construction of new courses in medieval times and many streams have been dug out so that they appear to be drainage ditches.

Although the mid-line is usually described as "*usque ad medium filum*", the actual flow of the stream is irrelevant. The mid-line is ascertained by taking the middle of the river in the sense of half way between the two banks at the normal level.[24] The Ordnance Survey take the normal winter level[25] and it seems clear that this is what was meant by the "normal

---

[19] *Stollmeyer v Trinidad Lake Petroleum Co* Ltd [1918] A.C. 485 per Lord Sumner at 491.
[20] See below, para.8.11 et seq.
[21] *Burrows v Lang* [1901] 2 Ch. 502.
[22] *Sutcliffe v Booth* (1863) 32 L.J.Q.B. 136.
[23] *Burrows v Lang* [1901] 2 Ch. 502.
[24] *Hindson v Ashby* [1896] 2 Ch. 1.
[25] J. R. S. Booth, *Public Boundaries and Ordnance Survey 1840-1980*, (Ordnance Survey, 1980), p. 431.

level" in *Hindson v Ashby*[26] because Lindley L.J. says at p.8: "The strip of land thus formed is dry in summer, but is under water in winter". He held that it was still part of the normal bed of the river. It seems likely therefore that the Ordnance Survey rule will also be observed by the courts. The reason for the use of the winter level is that this is the time when there is usually a good flow of water in the stream. If the summer levels were taken this could create distortions or leave exposed large areas of what everyone would describe as river bed.

8.07   There seems to be some judicial uncertainty as to whether an island in a river should be regarded as an entirely separate piece of land with two different rivers running around it, or whether the river should still be treated as a single large river, with the ownership of the island being split according to its proximity to the respective banks. In *Great Torrington Commons Conservators v Moore Stevens*[27] it was held at first instance that where there is an island the river is regarded as dividing into two parts. The ownership of the island is then regarded as a different question and the title of the riparian owner to the river bed only extends to the middle of the part of the river on his side. However, in Scotland in *Menzies v Breadalbane*[28] it was held that where there is a main and a minor channel the river can be looked at as a whole and the middle line taken as being between the two banks. The island should then be treated as part of the channel. The practice of the Ordnance Survey[29] is to treat the island as, in effect, part of the river, though where the island is close to one side with a minor channel running beside it, then the larger arm will be treated as the true river and not only will the whole of the island belong to the riparian owner, but the middle point of the river will be measured by bisecting the line from the bank of the island to the opposite bank. This differs from either of the principles set out above. The position, therefore, must be regarded as undecided.

It is clear, in any event, that the rules about islands refer only to proper islands which are permanent and above the level of the water at normal times. Shifting sand banks or other temporary islands are simply treated as being part of the river bed.[30] The Ordnance Survey only regard a feature as an island if it has vegetation above the normal flow line of the river.[31]

---

[26] [1896] 2 Ch. 1.
[27] [1904] 1 Ch. 347.
[28] (1901) 4 F. 59; (1901) 4 F. 55.
[29] J. R. S. Booth, *Public Boundaries and Ordnance Survey 1840-1980*, (Ordnance Survey, 1980), p. 322.
[30] *Earl of Zetland v Glover Incorporation of Perth* (1870-75) L.R. 2 Sc. 70.
[31] J. R. S. Booth, *Public Boundaries and Ordnance Survey 1840-1980*, (Ordnance Survey, 1980), p. 210.

Although there is a presumption of ownership of the river bed, this presumption can be rebutted. Normally the right of fishing the river goes with the river bed. Therefore, if the right of fishing is elsewhere, the presumption is reversed.[32] However, the fact that the river bed is not included either in the measurement of the property conveyed or in the plan does not necessarily rebut the presumption.[33] It is, therefore, a strong legal presumption which overrides the normal canons of construction.

The other special feature of water boundaries is that they tend not to be **8.08** constant. Land bounding rivers and the sea is always in a constant process of erosion or accretion. In relation to the seashore there is no doubt that a boundary running to the seashore takes the benefit of any accretions and suffers any erosions.[34] However, in *Hindson v Ashby*[35] the position in regard to rivers was regarded as undecided. Lindley L.J. said at p.13:

> "Passages were cited from Bracton, Britton, Fleta and Hale De Jure Maris and the Year Books to show that the doctrine of accretion does not apply where boundaries are well defined and known. This may be if the boundary of the waterside is a wall, or something so clear and visible that it is easy to see whether the accretions, as they become perceptible, are on one side of the boundary or the other. But I am not satisfied that the authorities referred to are applicable to cases of land having no boundary next flowing water except the water itself . . . But it is unnecessary to dwell now on this question. I leave it for reconsideration and decision when it shall arise."

It is perhaps surprising that Lindley L.J. should have been so doubtful in 1896 because previously in *Foster v Wright*[36] he held that where the riparian owner did not own the fishery he did not gain the fishery just because the river gradually crept onto what had been his land:

> "for if he [the owner of the fishery] was the owner of the old bed of the river, he has day by day and week by week become the owner of that which has gradually and imperceptibly become its present bed and the title so gradually and imperceptibly acquired cannot be defeated by proof that a portion of the bed now capable of identification was formerly land belonging to the defendant or his predecessors in title."[37]

[32] [1896] 2 Ch. 1 at 9, per Lindley L.J.
[33] *Hanbury v Jenkins* [1901] 2 Ch. 401.
[34] *Scratton v Brown* [1824-34] All E.R. Rep. 59; (1825) 4 B. & C. 485 and see later, para.8.24.
[35] *Hindson v Ashby* [1896] 2 Ch. 1.
[36] *Foster v Wright* (1878-79) L.R. 4 C.P.D. 438.
[37] *Foster v Wright* (1878-79) L.R. 4 C.P.D. 438 at 448.

Despite the remarks of Lindley L.J. in *Hindson v Ashby*,[38] it must now be accepted that the doctrine of accretion and erosion that applies to the seashore and tidal rivers also applies to non-tidal rivers. This view was expressly stated obiter by the Privy Council in *Thakurain Ritraj Koer v Thakurain Sarfaraz Koer*[39] and was taken as accepted law by A.L. Smith L.J. in *Hindson v Ashby*. More recently it was expressly accepted in respect of an inland and only partially tidal lake, in Scotland in *Stirling v Bartlett*[40] and in *Southern Theosophy v South Australia*.[41]

The latter case, however, was decided shortly after *Baxendale v Instow Parish Council*[42] where Megarry V.C. took a distinctly narrower view of the doctrine of accretion and erosion. *Baxendale v Instow PC* was distinguished in *Southern Centre of Theosophy Inc v South Australia* on the basis that "the applicability of the doctrine of accretion may be excluded by the use of clear words"[43] but in fact Megarry V.C. referred to the doctrine only as a "possible presumption"[44] and there was nothing in the terms of the conveyance in that case that could be considered "clear words". *Baxendale v Instow Parish Council* does, however, seem out of line with the other authorities. The limit of its authority is perhaps that it affirms that whether a conveyance of land bounding water or of the foreshore is subject to the doctrine of accretion and erosion is, in the end, a question of construction.

8.09   In cases where the doctrine does apply it applies only to gradual and imperceptible accretion and erosion. Where a river, whether tidal or not,[45] makes a sudden change of course, the riparian owner continues to own the bed to the middle of the old course of the river.[46] Equally, if the river is diverted onto his land he retains the ownership of the bed of the new course, though he does not thereby gain the fishery if it was owned by someone else.[47]

It is not enough that the accretion or erosion should be gradual. It must also be imperceptible. This does not mean that its results must be imperceptible over a period of time. Even quite large accretions or erosions can come within the doctrine,[48] but if you can actually see it happening, and

---

[38] *Hindson v Ashby* [1896] 2 Ch. 1.

[39] (1905) 21 T.L.R. 637.

[40] [1992] S.C. 523; [1993] S.L.T. 763.

[41] [1982] A.C. 706; [1982] 2 W.L.R. 544.

[42] [1982] Ch. 14; [1981] 2 All E.R. 620.

[43] per Lord Wilberforce at 289d.

[44] *Baxendale v Instow Parish Council* [1982] Ch. 14; [1981] 2 All E.R. 620 at 628f.

[45] *Thakurain Ritraj Koer v Thakurain Sarfaraz Koer* (1905) 21 T.L.R. 637.

[46] *Re Hull & Selby Railway* (1839) 5. M. & W. 327; *Stirling v Bartlett* [1993] S.L.T. 763.

[47] *Carlisle Corp v Graham* (1868-69) L.R. 4 Ex. 361.

[48] *Penang v Beng Hong Oon* [1972] A.C. 425; [1972] 2 W.L.R. 1; *R. v Yarborough* (1824) 3 B. & C. 91; *Nebraska v Iowa* 143 (1892) U.S. 359.

not just that it has happened, it seems that it is not accretion or erosion within this principle.[49]

There is some judicial uncertainty as to whether it matters that the accretion or erosion has been caused by the act of man. In *Hindson v Ashby*,[50] the Court of Appeal accepted that a gradual accretion caused by a weir upstream accrued to the property of the riparian owner. However, the Privy Council in *Attorney General of Southern Nigeria v John Holt & Co (Liverpool) Ltd*[51] held that where the seashore spread as a result of flood prevention works, the land reclaimed was the property of the Crown and not of the person who owned the land bounding the seashore. The problem was considered in detail in the Scottish case of *Stirling v Bartlett*.[52] The Outer House distinguished Holt's case as being limited to the proposition that a change brought about by work carried out by one proprietor alone would not bring about a change of ownership.[53] This case emphasised the problems caused by the changing nature of rivers, the precise cause of which is often difficult to identify, and re-affirmed the need to use common sense in deciding on the true line.

It is possible that acquiescence, in the form of inaction by the riparian **8.10** owner whose land is being eroded, may be relevant in deciding whether changes in the river effect changes to the boundary.[54]

The practice of the Ordnance Survey in respect of public boundaries is that alterations in the course of a river due to man-made changes or flooding are marked on any revision or new edition of the map, whereas what are seen as natural changes are simply effected by altering the map. Thus, if the alteration is gradual, a new edition or revision of the Ordnance Survey map will simply alter the alignment of the river and re-measure the centre to obtain the boundary. However, where the boundary has been altered by man-made changes or flooding the old boundary will be left intact and the symbol "def" for "defaced" will be put on the map. Where this involves a total change in the course of the river the original bed will be marked either by "COCS" ("centre of old course of stream" or, previously, "COCR" ("centre of old course of river") or "Tk S" ("track of stream") or, formerly, "Tk R" ("track of river"). Which of these two symbols is used depends on whether there is still water in the old course. If it is dry it is referred to as "track".[55] The distinction therefore is between

---

[49] *Southern Centre of Theosophy Inc v South Australia* [1982] A.C. 706; [1982] 1 All E.R. 283 at 290j.
[50] [1896] 2 Ch. 1.
[51] [1915] A.C. 599.
[52] [1993] S.L.T. 763.
[53] per Lord Coulsfield at 768I.
[54] *Marquis of Tweeddale v Kerr* (1822) 1 S. 397; *Stirling v Bartlett* [1993] S.L.T. 763 at 768E.
[55] J. R. S. Booth, *Public Boundaries and Ordnance Survey 1840-1980* (Ordnance Survey, 1980), p.431.

sudden traumatic changes and gradual changes rather than between natural and artificial changes.

Normally the doctrine of accretion and erosion applies to changes in the boundaries caused by the action of the water, whether flow or tide. However, it is not restricted to this and can apply equally to any natural cause such as sand blowing into the water.[56] On the other hand, it would probably not apply to the entirely artificial filling up of a river bed, for example by dumping rubbish.[57]

The Land Registration Act 2002 specifically provides that land gained by accretion does not need to be separately registered. The fact that a registered estate is shown on the register as having a particular boundary does not affect the operation of accretion or diluvion.[58] However, an agreement about the operation of accretion and diluvion has to be registered to be effective.[59]

(b)   Tidal rivers

8.11   Where the boundary of land runs up against a tidal river there is no presumption that the riparian owner owns half the bed. The presumption is that the bed of all tidal rivers including estuaries and creeks belongs to the Crown,[60] though it is held for the benefit of the subject so that the right of free navigation and anchorage will not be affected by a grant of a several fishery to a private individual or group, even if it is taken as including part of the riverbed.[61] The whole issue of ownership of river beds was considered in passing in *Crown Estate Commissioners v Roberts*[62] but, as it had already been decided[63] that, if the lordship of the manor had ever owned these they had returned to the Crown by adverse possession, the issue of whether they could be divested by the Crown was not finally decided.

Although there may be nice questions about what a person entitled to a several fishery may do in respect of the bed of a tidal river,[64] the significant point for the riparian owner is that if the river is tidal he is not entitled to the river bed or, more importantly, the fishery by reason of his riparian ownership. Accordingly, unless the riparian owner has obtained the bed of the river separately, his boundary is the edge of the river.

---

[56] *Southern Centre of Theosophy Inc v South Australia* [1982] A.C. 706; [1982] 1 All E.R. 283.

[57] ibid. at [1982] A.C. 706; [1982] 1 All E.R. 283 at 287a.

[58] Land Registration Act 2002 s.61(1).

[59] The procedure for registration is set out in Land Registration Rules 2003 r.123.

[60] *Lord Fitzhardinge v Purcell* [1908] 2 Ch. 139; *Crown Estate Commissioners v Roberts* [2008] EWHC 1302 (Ch); [2008] 2 P.& C.R. 15.

[61] *Gann v Free Fishers of Whitstable* (1865) 11 H.L.C. 192.

[62] [2008] EWHC 1302 (Ch); [2008] 2 P.& C.R. 15.

[63] *Roberts v Swangrove Estates* [2007] 2 P.& C.R. 287.

[64] See *Roberts v Swangrove Estates* [2007] EWHC 513 (Ch); [2007] 2 P. & C.R. 17 and *Crown Estate Commissioners v Roberts* [2008] EWHC 1302 (Ch); [2008] 2 P.& C.R. 15.

Essentially a river is tidal up to the point where the rise and fall at normal tides ceases. There is a distinction between the rise and fall of the tide and the ebb and flow. A river can still rise and fall above the point that there is a real ebb and flow or, indeed, where the water is salt.[65] The tidal river does not, however, extend so far as the point where in exceptional tides there may be some rise in the river level caused by the river water being held back by the incoming tide.[66]

In respect of the seashore, the boundary of land bounded by the sea is **8.12** the medium high water mark.[67] The line of both mean high and low tide are shown on the Ordnance Survey maps.[68] This is not irrefutable evidence. It is always possible that there is an inaccuracy in the measurement or, more importantly, the line may have been altered by accretion or erosion, but the line on the map is a good starting point. Ordinary high tide is the point of the medium high tide between the springs and the neaps, ascertained by taking the average of the medium tide during the year, being the point on the shore which is about four days in each week reached and covered by the tides.[69] The Scottish Law Commission has suggested that, in Scotland, legislation should incorporate the Ordnance Survey line as a rebuttable presumption, but this proposal has not yet been put into effect.

For parish boundaries, the boundary is the mean low tide. The method used by the Ordnance Survey is to take a half litre bottle, weighted with sand so that it is two-thirds submerged and to place it in the estuary. They then mark the point where it stops at the turn of the tide.[70] No doubt a similar method can be used to decide on the high tide on any particular day.

Tidal rivers can be divided into river bank, foreshore and river bed in the same way as the seashore, but there is no practical difference between the foreshore and the river bed. Both prima facie belong to the Crown.

There is no doubt in respect of tidal rivers that the boundary of the **8.13** riparian owners can vary according to the accretion and erosion of the

---

[65] *Attorney General Ex rel Yorkshire Derwent Trust Ltd v Brotherton* [1990] Ch. 136; [1989] 2 W.L.R. 938; (1990) 59 P. & C.R. 60 at 77 per Vinelott J. *West Riding of Yorkshire Rivers Board v Tadcaster RDC* (1907) 97 L.T. 436 approving *Calcraft v Guest* [1898] 1 Q.B. 759.

[66] *Reece v Miller* (1881-82) L.R. 8 Q.B.D. 626.

[67] *Penang v Beng Hong Oon* [1972] A.C. 425.

[68] A Report has been prepared on the Integrated Coastal Mapping Project (ICZMap), a joint project of the Ordnance Survey, the UK Hydrographical Office and the British Geological Survey. If this project is implemented it will provide more accurate and uniform data, including a full Mean High Water line and the mapping of the seashore between Mean Low Water and 10m depth.

[69] *Attorney General v Chambers* (1854) 4 De G.M. & G. 206.

[70] J. R. S. Booth, *Public Boundaries and Ordnance Survey 1840-1980* (Ordnance Survey, 1980), p.227.

river.[71] This matter is dealt with more fully above[72] under non-tidal rivers and also in respect of the foreshore[73] where the same principles apply.

3.   Artificial watercourse

8.14   Ancient rivers are obvious barriers to use to delineate boundaries. However, in respect of an artificial watercourse the assumption is that it was built by a person on his own land for his own purposes.

Nevertheless having been established it may well constitute a convenient and obvious boundary. As with rivers, most of the litigation involving riparian owners has been over rights to use the water rather than about the boundary. In respect of artificial watercourses, it has been established that any such rights emanate from grant or prescription or from implication from the circumstances in which it was constructed.[74] These rights will be dealt with later.[75]

In respect of boundaries, while it has been seen above[76] that there can be a thin dividing line between a natural and an artificial watercourse, once it is established that a watercourse is artificial the presumption that the riparian owner owns the bed up to the middle of the river does not apply.

Where, therefore, an artificial watercourse, such as a mill race, forms the boundary between two properties the question of which riparian owner owns the bed of the watercourse will depend on the usual rules of construction.

8.15   It may be that the ownership of the watercourse can be deduced from the description in the governing conveyance, or by the way it is shown in the relevant plan. However, if there is no other clear indication, help can be obtained from looking at the origin of the watercourse. If it is a mill race it is more likely to have been built by the owner of the mill. If it is a pond, some help may be obtained from the purpose for which it was built. If it is a ditch, it may be possible to deduce whose land it was intended to drain and if the drain has a hedge beside it the "hedge and ditch" rule may apply whereby the boundary is presumed to be on the far side of the hedge from the ditch.

However, it must be emphasised that these remarks can only be regarded as guides to construction. The actual decision in any case

---

[71] *Scratton v Brown* (1825) 4 B. & C. 485; *Brighton & Hove General Gas Co v Hove Bungalows Ltd* [1924] 1 Ch. 372.
[72] See above para.8.08 et seq.
[73] See below para.8.18.
[74] *Singh v Pattuck* (1878) 4 App. Cas. 121.
[75] See below under Water Rights.
[76] See above para.8.06 et seq.

concerning artificial watercourses will depend on the terms of the conveyances, the lie of the land, etc. just as with any other boundary.

Just because a watercourse is artificial does not free it from the effects of erosion and accretion. It has been held that the doctrine of accretion and erosion does not apply to "canals, lakes and ponds".[77] However, this decision was disapproved in *Southern Centre of Theosophy Inc v South Australia*,[78] where the doctrine was applied to an inland lake, and must not now be regarded as the law.

Although canals are simply a species of artificial watercourse, in practice they were all created by statute. Accordingly if land abuts a canal it is necessary to look at the private Act of Parliament whereby it was created. This will either vest the bed in the canal company (so that it will now be owned by the British Waterways Board)[79] or the Act will simply give the canal undertakers the right to construct the canal, in which case the ownership of the soil will remain with the original owners.[80]

4. Lakes

There are not very many natural freshwater lakes within the jurisdiction. Where they do exist they may simply be part of a river system and be treated as in effect part of the river. In any event the position of such lakes is much the same as that of a river. The soil does not belong to the Crown[81]:   **8.16**

> "Whether the rule that each adjoining proprietor, where there are several, is entitled *usque ad filum aquae* [sic] should apply to a lake is a different question. It does not seem very convenient that each proprietor of a few acres fronting Lough Neagh should have a piece of the soil of the lough many miles in length tacked onto his frontage."[82]

However, if it does not belong to the riparian owners it is difficult to see who else it would belong to in the absence of any specific conveyance.

The same doctrine of accretion and erosion applies to lakes as applies to running water.[83]

---

[77] *Trafford v Thrower* (1929) 45 T.L.R. 502. The case actually concerned the Norfolk Broads.
[78] [1982] A.C. 706; [1982] 1 All E.R. 283 at 287a.
[79] Transport Act 1962.
[80] *Mussett v Burch* (1876) 35 L.T. 486.
[81] *Bristow v Cormican* (1877-78) L.R. 3 App.Cas. 641.
[82] *Bristow v Cormican* (1877-78) L.R. 3 App. Cas. 641 per Lord Blackburn at 666.
[83] *Southern Centre of Theosophy Inc v South Australia* [1982] A.C. 706; [1982] 1 All E.R. 283.

5. The seashore

8.17   The seashore can be divided into three sections, the land above mean high water mark, the land between mean high water and mean low water and the sea bed beyond mean low water.

(a)   Land bounding the sea

8.18   A person who owns land bounding the sea is presumed to own it down to mean high water mark.[84] His position, therefore, is exactly the same as that of the owner of land bounding a tidal river, or indeed any tidal creek, inlet or arm of the sea.[85]

In England, as opposed to Scotland,[86] the relevant line is the mean high water mark. As stated above, this is the medium line between the spring and the neap high tides.[87] It is important to note that this can differ very widely from the beach as normally understood:

> "In my judgment, all that lies to the landward of high water mark and is in apparent continuity with the beach at high water will normally form part of the beach."[88]

In practical terms, therefore, a person owning land bounding the seashore will usually own the cliffs, the sand-dunes and often a substantial part of the beach, a fact which would surprise many holiday makers.

If the conveyance refers to the "seashore" or the "sea beach" as being the boundary this will be construed as being the beginning of the fore-shore, that is the line of the medium high tides and not "the beach" as defined above, which is more appropriate for less formal documents.[89] In *Mellor v Walmesley*[90] land described as "situate on the seashore" was held to have a fixed boundary and not to include any accretions, but this was because it was clear that there was a strip of land between the boundary and the medium high tide and the Court of Appeal by a majority construed the conveyance in the light of that fact. The decision, therefore, turned on its own particular facts.[91]

---

[84] *Penang v Beng Hong Oon* [1972] A.C. 425; *Attorney General v Chambers* (1854) 4 De G.M. & G. 206.

[85] See above para.8.11 et seq.

[86] *Musselburgh Real Estate Co v Musselburgh Provost* [1905] A.C. 491; *Tito v Waddell* [1977] Ch. 106; [1977] 3 All E.R. 129 at 264e and Scottish Law Commission, *Report on Law of the Foreshore and the Sea Bed* (Stationery Office Books, 2003), SE/2003/74.

[87] See above para.8.12.

[88] per Megarry V.C. in *Tito v Waddell* [1977] Ch. 106; [1977] 3 All E.R. 129 at 263b.

[89] *Penang v Beng Hong Oon* [1972] A.C. 425; [1971] 3 All E.R. 1163 at 1170.

[90] [1904] 2 Ch. 525; on appeal [1905] 2 Ch. 164.

[91] See per Lord Cross in *Penang v Beng Hong Oon* [1972] A.C. 425; [1971] 3 All E.R. 1163 at 1173.

(b)   Below mean low water

The seashore below mean low water mark is by no means useless. It **8.19**
can be a shellfish bed. Piers and jetties can be erected. Oil, natural gas and
minerals can be extracted.

The question of ownership, however, first involves consideration of
the sovereignty of the Crown, the jurisdiction of the English courts and
the concept of the high seas. In *R. v Keyn*[92] the question arose whether the
court had jurisdiction to consider a case of manslaughter which had
occurred within the three mile limit. The majority held that it could not:

> "The county extends to low-water mark where the 'high seas' begin;
> between high and low water mark the Courts of oyer and terminer
> had jurisdiction when the tide was out, the Court of the admiral
> when the tide was in. There appears to be no sufficient authority for
> saying that the high seas was ever considered to be within the
> realm."[93]

This may be seen, however, as the low water mark of the English courts'
assertion of jurisdiction and, by implication, sovereignty. In *Lord Advocate
v Wemyss*[94] Lord Watson said:

> "I see no reason to doubt that, by the law of Scotland, the *solum*
> underlying the water of the ocean, whether within the narrow seas,
> or from the coast outward to the three-mile limit, and also the
> minerals beneath it are vested in the Crown. Whether the Crown
> could make an effectual grant of that *solum* or of any part of it to a
> subject appears to me to be a question not unattended with doubt".

It will be noted that this dictum refers not only to sovereignty and jurisdiction, but also to ownership.

Before and since then Parliament has sought to assert jurisdiction over **8.20**
territorial waters (i.e. three nautical miles from the coast) and beyond, up
to the edge of the continental shelf by the Territorial Waters Jurisdiction
Act 1878 and the Continental Shelf Act 1964. Although the Territorial
Waters Jurisdiction Act 1878 deals with criminal jurisdiction it asserts in
the preamble that:

> "The rightful jurisdiction of Her Majesty, her heirs and successors,
> extends and has always extended over the open seas adjacent to the

---

[92] *R. v Keyn* (1876-77) L.R. 2 Ex. D. 63.
[93] per Phillimore J. in *R. v Keyn* (1876) L.R. 2 Ex. D. 63 at 67.
[94] [1900] A.C. 48 at 66.

coasts of the United Kingdom and of all other parts of Her Majesty's dominion to such a distance as is necessary for the defence and security of such dominions."

The Continental Shelf Act 1964, passed to give effect to provisions of the Geneva Convention of 1958, asserts rights over the seabed and sub-soil outside the territorial waters and states that they should be exercised by the Crown.

These assertions have always been in term of rights rather than ownership, though it has been submitted on behalf of the Crown and accepted by the courts that the rights asserted under the Continental Shelf Act 1964 include "sovereignty over territorial sea and the sea bed and subsoil thereof".[95] There seems little doubt, therefore, that for the purposes of English law the Crown has sovereignty over the seas, sea bed and sub-soil within the three-mile limit. The continental shelf is not, however, part of the United Kingdom or part of the European Union.[96]

The jurisdiction of the courts is for these purposes co-terminous with the sovereignty of the Crown. It was treated as trite law that everything within territorial waters was within the jurisdiction of the courts in *Earl of Lonsdale v Attorney General*[97] though the point was never argued since both parties wanted the matter decided by the English courts.

8.21   Strictly sovereignty and ownership are different and there is no clear English authority that the sea bed below low water mark, but within territorial waters, belongs to the Crown.[98] The nearest to such an assertion is the obiter remarks of Parker J. in *Lord Fitzhardinge v Purcell*[99] that:

"Clearly the bed of the sea, at any rate for some distance below low-water mark, and the beds of tidal navigable rivers, are prima facie vested in the Crown, and there seems no good reason why the ownership thereof by the Crown should not also, subject to the rights of the public, be a beneficial ownership."

This view was supported obiter by Winn L.J. in *Alfred F Beckett Ltd v Lyons*[100] where he said:

---

[95] *Earl of Lonsdale v Attorney General* [1982] 3 All E.R. 579 at 626b.
[96] *Addison v Denholm Ship Management (UK) Ltd* [1997] I.R.L.R. 389.
[97] *Earl of Lonsdale v Attorney General* [1982] 3 All E.R. 579 at 583b.
[98] Cf. *Lord Advocate v Wemyss* [1900] A.C. 48 at 66 for the law in Scotland. The Scottish Law Commission has recently stated that "while the Scottish courts have assumed that the Crown owns the sea bed beneath the sea adjacent to Scotland there is no authority expressly to this effect" and invited consideration on whether a statutory statement to this effect would be useful, SE/2003/74 at para 2.1.
[99] [1908] 2 Ch. 139 at 166.
[100] [1967] Ch. 449; [1967] 1 All E.R. 833 at 850H.

"It was, I gather, accepted by counsel in this appeal that the plaintiffs could not restrain anybody from coming in a boat from seaward and taking coal wherever it might be found below low tide mark. I desire only to comment that I think that it does not follow that the Crown might not be entitled to prevent this being done, either by asserting a proprietary right in the soil of the sea or possibly in Her Majesty's capacity as Lord High Admiral of England. It would be outside the proper scope of this judgment to consider the rights of the Crown in the sea adjoining the United Kingdom, and it suffices to say that there is considerable authority that, apart from the few special cases of express grant, the Crown has ever since the Conquest been the owner of the soil of the sea below low tide mark to a seaward extent which may be somewhat uncertain."

Certainly the Crown has granted rights to individuals over the sea bed and it seems now generally accepted that the Crown owns the sea bed and sub-soil within territorial waters in the same way as it owns the bed of tidal rivers, creeks, etc. below low water mark.[101] If such rights can be granted expressly there seems no reason why they should not also arise by prescription.[102] In *Crown Estate Commissioners v Roberts*[103] Lewison J., in the course of a very full and learned judgment, accepted without question that the title to the foreshore and seabed was always with the Crown.

To date, however, no attempt has ever been made by the Crown to divest itself of the freehold of any part of the sea bed or sub-soil in territorial waters[104] and perhaps the best approach is that individuals may obtain rights below low water mark, which may include rights in respect of the sea bed, but that these rights fall short of full ownership. This seems to be the position in respect of tidal rivers[105] and exactly the same principle applies to shellfisheries below mean low water level of ordinary tides on the foreshore: *Loose v Castleton*[106]; to illegal salmon fishing below low water mark[107]; and to the right to anchor and moor.[108] Furthermore, the same principle of limited ownership has been accepted by the House of Lords as representing the law of Scotland.[109]

[101] *Earl of Lonsdale v Attorney General* [1982] 3 All E.R. 579 at 583b. cf. *Attorney General of British Columbia v Attorney General of Canada* [1914] A.C. 153 at 174where Viscount Haldane L.C. specifically refused to accept such a principle.

[102] See Scottish Law Commission, *Report on Law of the Foreshore and the Sea Bed* (Stationery Office Books, 2003), SE/2003/74.

[103] [2008] EWHC 1302 (Ch); [2008] 2 P.& C.R. 15.

[104] The Charter of 1115 referred to in *Crown Estate Commissioners v Robert* [2008] 2 P.& C.R. 15 at [153] makes no express reference to the seabed. The argument was that it passed by implication to the Lord Marcher of Magor.

[105] *Gann v Free Fishers of Whitstable* (1865) 11 H.L. Cas 192.

[106] (1981) 41 P. & C.R. 19.

[107] *Ingram v Percival* [1969] 1 Q.B. 548; [1968] 3 All E.R. 657.

[108] *Attorney General v Wright* [1897] 2 Q.B. 318.

[109] *Lord Advocate v Wemyss* [1900] A.C. 48 at 66; see above.

8.22   What is clear is that owners of land abutting the seashore have no more rights than anyone else in respect of land below low water mark. If, therefore, an island appears below low water mark the owner of the coast line does not gain any rights over it.[110] Problems can also arise over off-shore islands. The strict idea that the realm, and therefore the jurisdiction of the courts, ends at the foreshore does not exclude islands from the jurisdiction of the courts. The question is simply whether the island forms part of the United Kingdom. If it does then the courts have jurisdiction over it. This principle was applied to Lundy Island in *Harman v Bolt*.[111] The same applies to islands which arise in the sea within territorial waters, *Secretary of State for India v Chelikani Rama Rao*[112] where the Privy Council asserted that any island which arises within territorial waters belongs to the Crown as a form of *maritima incrementa*.

(c) Foreshore

8.23   The foreshore is the land between medium high and low tides. It belongs to the Crown unless it has passed to an individual by grant or prescription.[113] It may be the subject of various rights and easements which will be dealt with separately.[114] Rule 31 of the Land Registration Rules 2003 (SI 2003/1417) sets out the procedure when land to be registered includes foreshore. Notice has to be served on the Crown Estates Commissioners.[115] They can then object if they think fit.

There is no reason why a squatter may not take adverse possession of the foreshore and the same rules apply as to any other land[116] but the acts required in order to exercise possession may be very different as Lord Watson said in *Lord Advocate v Lovat*[117]:

> "It is, in my opinion, practically impossible to lay down any precise rule in regard to the character and amount of possession necessary in order to give a riparian proprietor a prescriptive right to foreshore. Each case must depend on its own circumstances. The beneficial enjoyment of which the foreshore admits, consistently with the rights of navigators and of the general public, is an exceedingly variable quantity . . . In estimating the character and extent of his possession it must always be kept in view that possession of the foreshore, in its

---

[110] *Secretary of State for India v Chelikani Rama Rao* (1916) L.R. 43 Ind. App. 192.
[111] (1931) 47 T.L.R. 219.
[112] (1916) L.R. 43 Ind. App. 192 at 201.
[113] *Fowley Marine (Emsworth) Ltd v Gafford* [1968] 2 Q.B. 618.
[114] See Ch. 21.
[115] Together with, as appropriate, the Chancellor of the Duchy of Lancaster, the Duke of Cornwall or the Port of London Authority.
[116] *Roberts v Swangrove Estates* [2007] EWHC 513 (Ch); [2007] 2 P. & C.R. 17; upheld on appeal sub nom. *Roberts v Crown Estate Commissioners* [2008] 2 P.& C.R. 15.
[117] *Lord Advocate v Lovat* (1887) 12 App Cas 544 at 554.

natural state, can never be, in the strictest sense of the term, exclusive. The proprietor cannot exclude the public from it at any time; and it is practically impossible to prevent occasional encroachments on his right, because the cost of preventive measures would be altogether disproportionate to the value of the subject."

There is much authority on the meaning of the high water mark, as it marks the boundary between land owned by the riparian owner and the foreshore normally owned by the Crown. It is, however, rarely necessary to define what is meant by the low water mark. The low water mark will only be relevant as a boundary where the foreshore has been disposed of by the Crown and, in practice, the owner of the foreshore has not been concerned about the exact line. It had been assumed that the same principle of mean levels would apply as with the high water mark, but it has been now decided that this is not necessarily the case[118]:

"In our judgment there is no established rule of law that the low water mark is necessarily the line of median low water and the principle which identifies the landwards boundary of the foreshore at the line of the median high water depends upon factors which have no application at the seaward low water mark."

However, that case concerned the application of a bye-law. Accordingly there was no difficulty about the "low water mark" moving from day to day. If the low water mark is a boundary then (subject to erosion and accretion) it must be fixed and identifiable. It is submitted that, in so far as it is necessary for conveyancing purposes to identify a boundary between the foreshore and the sea-bed then the same principle of the mean low tide should be used.

It has been pointed out[119] that a freehold in the foreshore is a "moving **8.24** freehold", i.e. that it is subject to accretion and erosion. The same applies to land bounding the sea, but it is possible for the foreshore to move to such an extent that the land forming part of it can change completely.

Depending on the construction of the parcels there can be a conveyance by the Crown of land then forming part of the seashore, which is not subject to the doctrine of accretion and erosion and so can become simply land conveyed to the purchaser. Presumably any accretion then belongs to the Crown.[120] However, the general principles of accretion and erosion have been since re-affirmed[121] and it remains true that a grant of land

---

[118] *Anderson v Alnwick DC* [1993] 1 W.L.R. 1156; [1993] 3 All E.R. 613, per Evans L.J. at 620g.
[119] per Megarry V.C. in *Baxendale v Instow Parish Council* [1982] Ch. 14; [1981] 2 All E.R. 620 at 625f.
[120] *Baxendale v Instow Parish Council* [1982] Ch. 14; [1981] 2 All E.R. 620.
[121] *Southern Centre of Theosophy Ltd v South Australia* [1982] A.C. 706; [1982] 2 W.L.R. 544.

comprising the foreshore will normally be subject to accretion and erosion so that it consists of a movable band of land between the mean high and low water mark.

The law with regard to accretion and erosion has been dealt with above.[122] Apart from this and the rights which may be held by others, ownership of the foreshore is the same as ownership of any other land and can be conveyed and inherited in the same way. For this reason it is not proposed to repeat the principles on which the boundary of the foreshore is decided.

---

[122] See above para.8.08 et seq.

Chapter Nine
Mines

1. Introduction

The law of mining, mineral extraction and quarrying is a complex **9.01** subject which is outside the scope of this book. However, reservations of mines and minerals do impinge on boundaries and there are ancillary rights and obligations which go with ownership of mines and minerals as well as mining profits à prendre and other such rights, all of which are part of the law of easements and profits.

The principle that ownership of real property entitles a person to a three dimensional space is well illustrated by freeholds of mines. The principles behind ownership rights below the surface were authoritatively decided by the Supreme Court in *Bocardo SA v Star Energy UK Onshore Ltd.*[1]

The basic principle that the ownership of land involves ownership of the space from the centre of the earth to the sky[2] is of doubtful historical provenance and has been rejected in the USA[3] and doubted in Scotland, but:

> "In my opinion, the brocard[4] still has value in English law as encapsulating in simple language a proposition of law which has commanded general acceptance."

The practical significance of this is that the strata deep below the earth, but still accessible for mining or drilling, belong to the owner of the land. This does not mean, however, that the owner of the land owns all the minerals and other deposits buried under the land.

The freehold owner's prima facie ownership of the minerals is limited by Crown prerogative rights and by statute. Firstly all deposits of gold and silver belong to the Crown at common law.[5] Secondly all deposits of

---

[1] [2010] UKSC 35; [2011] 1 A.C. 380.
[2] "[U]sque at coelum et ad inferos".
[3] *US v Causby* [1946] USSC99.
[4] "[A]n elementary principle or maxim" Shorter Oxford Dictionary.
[5] *Case of Mines* (1567) 1 Plowd. 310 at336.

coal and petroleum have been vested in the Crown by statute[6] and Her Majesty has the exclusive right of searching and boring for and getting petroleum.[7] The Coal Industry Act 1994 has set up the Coal Authority which is a public corporation which owns all the interests of the British Coal Corporation in unworked coal and coal mines.[8] The Coal Authority then either disposes of the property by restructuring schemes or licenses it to approved operators. The holdings of the Coal Authority are not Crown property.[9]

This includes "the interests and rights of a freehold owner" of coal under the territorial sea adjacent to the United Kingdom, any extension of that territorial sea and any additional rights created by the Continental Shelf Act 1964, but no other interests outside Great Britain and the territorial sea.

The Coal Authority's Annual Report makes clear that it intends to retain ownership of the unworked coal in Britain and to operate its working by means of licences to private operators. The land disposed of has been non-operational land. Its continuing role also includes dealing with subsidence issues arising out of disused working. It also provides an information system for conveyancers.

The Petroleum Act 1998[10] vests in the Crown the exclusive right of searching and boring for and getting petroleum. It extends to petroleum "in its natural condition in strata in Great Britain or beneath the territorial seas adjacent to the United Kingdom".[11] Like the Continental Shelf Act 1964, it deals in terms of the right to extract petroleum rather than proprietary rights.

Petroleum includes any mineral oil, or relative hydrocarbon and natural gas existing in its natural condition in strata, but does not include coal or bituminous shales or other stratified deposits from which oil can be extracted by destructive distillation.[12] The dream of striking oil in your back garden, therefore, must remain a dream in Great Britain because anything you find will belong to the Crown. Since the ownership of minerals includes the right to take reasonable steps to extract them, finding oil in your back garden would be more of a nightmare than a dream.

---

[6] Coal Act 1938 s.3 (now repealed by the Statute Law (Repeal) Act 1973, but since the transfer has been effected, the repeal of the Act does not negate its effect); Coal Industry Nationalisation Act 1946 s.5 Sch.

[7] Not necessarily in person.

[8] Coal Industry Act 1994 s.7(3).

[9] Coal Industry Act 1994 s.1(5).

[10] Unlike its predecessor, the Petroleum Production Act 1998, see *Earl of Lonsdale v Attorney General* [1982] 1 W.L.R. 887; [1982] 3 All E.R. 579 at 626f. The dictum in that case about vesting of pre-existing petroleum rights is, it seems, superseded by the 1998 Act.

[11] Petroleum Act 1998 s.2(1).

[12] Petroleum Act 1998 s.1.

Bocardo SA v Star Energy UK Onshore Ltd[13] itself involved petroleum 1800 feet or more below the surface and accessed from adjoining land. The claimant owned the land but the respondents owned oil rights beneath it, which they had obtained on licence from the Crown. The Supreme Court held that the incursion into Bocardo Ltd's subterranean property amounted to trespass, but, since they did not own the petroleum, they were only entitled to damages from the loss suffered. While the High Court valued these at £621,180, the Court of Appeal and the Supreme Court reduced this to £1,000.

In effect this was compensation for the granting of a way-leave or on the basis of compulsory purchase. The claimant had not suffered any substantial loss of amenity and was not entitled to compensation on the "key" principle, i.e. that Star Energy owned the treasure, but Bocardo had the key to open it.

The soil of the bed of all channels, estuaries etc. is prima facie the property of the Crown.[14] It appears that the same applies to anything which is on or under the seabed of the territorial sea.[15]

The Energy Act 2004 makes specific provision for the creation of "Renewable Energy Zones" on areas outside the territorial sea in accordance with the UN Convention on the Law of the Sea.[16]

2. Extent of property conveyed

As long as the ownership of the land and the mines and minerals is **9.02** united in accordance with the normal principles set out above, no problems arise over mines and minerals. Boundary problems can, however, arise whenever there is a reservation or a grant or a lease of mines and minerals. While most of the problems involve the respective rights of the landowner and the miner, it may be necessary to decide where the boundary lies between the two parcels of land. It is important to remember, therefore, that a reservation or grant of mines (as opposed to merely mining rights) actually conveys a piece of freehold property in exactly the same way as any other conveyance. It is not merely a conveyance of an incorporeal hereditament.

Any grant of mines and minerals by a registered owner under the Land Registration Act 1925 has itself to be registered,[17] except for a coal mine. The Coal Industry Act 1994 amended s.70 of the Land Registration Act 1925 to provide that interests in coal or coal mines are an overriding interest. The same protection is contained in the Land Registration Act 2002 Sch.1.

---

[13] [2010] UKSC 35; [2011] 1 A.C. 380.
[14] See Ch.8 and *Crown Estate Commissioners v Roberts* [2008] EWHC 1302 (Ch); [2008] 2 P.& C.R. 15.
[15] See Continental Shelf Act 1964 s.1.
[16] Energy Act 2004 s.84.
[17] Land Registration Act 1925 s.18(1); Land Registration Rules 1925 rr.51 & 53.

Rule 32 of the Land Registration Rules 2003 requires the registrar to make a note on the register where he is satisfied that mines are included or excluded from the title. Where no such note has been entered and the registered owner considers that any mines or minerals are included in the registered land, he can apply for a note to be added on production of evidence that the mines and minerals were vested at first registration and have remained so thereafter.[18]

Where other mining rights have been disposed of before registration, the title to the surface property will still be registered with an absolute title and no indemnity is payable if it turns out that the mines and minerals have been disposed of separately, unless a note has been entered on the Register at the time of registration. If an owner of unregistered land, however, disposes of the mines and minerals below the surface that new interest still does not have to be registered.[19]

Mines registered before 1926 under previous legislation are not shown or noted on the Register.[20] The Land Registration Act 2002 contains protection for unregistered rights to mines created before 1898 and, where the land was registered between 1898 and 1925, mining rights created before registration.

9.03   The extent of the property conveyed is a question of construction. Normally mining reservations relate to the surface land conveyed. However, mining leases in particular may be by reference to faults, seams or veins. Such references give rise to considerable problems of construction, since the parties entering into the instrument may well not know what the line of the seam actually is. Usually references to seams, etc. will only be part of the description in the parcels and the courts will take a common-sense attitude, trying as far as possible to reflect the intention of the parties.[21]

The meaning in any particular instrument of the words "mines", "minerals" or "mines and minerals" has been the subject of much litigation over the past 150 years, reflecting the importance to landowners of the substances under their lands and the extent to which new substances have gained commercial importance.

In this regard there is a substantial difference between the expression "mines and minerals", frequently used in conveyances, and such words as "mines", "mining operations", etc. which are more commonly found in fiscal measures.

---

[18] Land Registration Rules 2003 r.71.
[19] Land Registration Act 2002 s.4(2).
[20] See Law Commission, *Land Registration in the Twenty-First Century: A Conveyancing Revolution* (HMSO, 2001), pp.107-108, Law Com. No.254, Cm.4027.
[21] *Davis v Shepherd* (1865-66) L.R. 1 Ch. App. 410.

Dealing first with "mines and minerals", it is not possible from these **9.04** authorities to reach a simple definition. Essentially two tests have emerged. Firstly there is the wide definition approved by the Court of Appeal in *O'Callaghan v Elliott*[22] in the context of the definition of a mining lease in the Landlord and Tenant Act 1927. In that case Lord Denning M.R. said:

> "The words 'mines and minerals' include every substance which can be got from underneath the surface of the earth for the purpose of profit."

This definition is sufficient, therefore, to include such things as sand and gravel, which were part of the ordinary soil of the land, as well as substances like natural gas, which 100 years ago would have been seen more as a hazard than an asset, and oil, whose value has only been fully realised in the past 100 years or so, though petroleum and natural gas now belong to the Crown.[23]

The removal of petroleum, as widely defined in the Petroleum Act 1998 has removed the most significant "minerals" from the equation, but there are numerous other materials which may be of value and it is still useful to look at the breadth of the definition.

The wide approach was rejected as the "primary or literal sense, which is always to be applied in the absence of a sufficiently clear contrary sense" by Slade J. in *Earl of Lonsdale v Attorney General*.[24] This case is the most recent authority on the subject and Slade J.'s conclusions were reached after a detailed and exhaustive review of the authorities.

The approach approved in *Earl of Lonsdale v Attorney General* is what is **9.05** described as the vernacular approach. This is that the phrase "mines and minerals" is not a definite term, but is one that is capable of bearing a wide variety of meanings derived either from direct evidence as to the vernacular meaning at the relevant time or by inference drawn by the court. The court must never overlook the commercial background and apparent commercial purpose of the transaction.[25]

As between these two cases *O'Callaghan v Elliott*[26] has the advantage of being a Court of Appeal decision. *Earl of Lonsdale v Attorney General* on the other hand is the more recent authority and purports to follow *O'Callaghan v Elliott*.

---

[22] [1966] 1 Q.B. 601; [1965] 3 W.L.R. 746.
[23] See above—Petroleum Act 1998.
[24] [1982] 1 W.L.R. 887; [1982] 3 All E.R. 579.
[25] per Slade J. at 609.
[26] *O'Callaghan v Elliott* [1966] 1 Q.B. 601.

The difficulty with Slade J.'s approach is a practical one. The case took 13 days to try[27] because he heard evidence from a series of experts about what the mining world, the commercial world and landowners would have considered to be minerals in 1880. His researches led to the conclusion that oil and natural gas would not have been included in mines and minerals at that time, especially in the particular circumstances of existing coal mines being granted. In the absence of such evidence the views of the relevant communities on any particular issue at any particular time would be very much a matter of guesswork.

It is submitted that the definition put forward by Lord Denning M.R. accords much more with common-sense. When an instrument is drawn up it is perfectly reasonable to suppose that the parties would have intended all commercially viable substances to be included, whether or not they were aware that such things as natural gas, which in 1880 they regarded as a nuisance, and oil would gain commercial importance in the future.

9.06 Where the word "mines" is used alone it is clear that it includes not only the underground tunnels and workings, but the unworked substances around them. However, "mines" on its own would not include substances which would be worked in other ways, such as oil and gas, which are worked by wells or shafts, or slate, which is normally quarried, even if in the particular instance it is being gained by underground working,[28] or gravel, the extraction of which may be neither mining nor quarrying.[29]

On the face of it Lord Denning's definition, though it refers to substances which can be got from under the surface, does not seem to restrict this to substances which can be got from underground working. In the Coal Industry Act 1994 "coal mine" includes "any space excavated underground for the purposes of coal-mining operations and any shaft or adit made for those purposes", "any space occupied by unworked coal" and "a coal quarry and opencast workings of coal". This definition could be extrapolated to other mines as appropriate. However, while mines and minerals (though not "mining" alone) can be wide enough to include sand and gravel or clay, it seems that it does not include stone and other substances which are quarried rather than being mined. The distinction between mining and quarrying is really a question of the substance involved. No-one has heard of a coal quarry or a stone mine. Therefore substances which are commonly extracted by underground workings are described as being mined even when that mining is open-cast.[30] This

---

[27] per Slade J. at 582e.
[28] *Jones v Cwmarthen Slate Co Ltd* (1879-80) L.R. 5 Ex. D. 93.
[29] *Mosley v George Wimpey* [1945] 1 All E.R. 674.
[30] ibid., *New South Wales Associated Blue Metal Quarries v Federal Commissioner of Taxation* (1956) 94 C.L.R. 509.

principle can be reconciled with *O'Callaghan v Elliott*[31] on the basis that whereas stone is always quarried, the extraction of sand and gravel would not, in ordinary parlance, be described as either mining or quarrying. Quarrying, therefore, imports something more than simply open cast working. In *Earl of Lonsdale v Attorney General* Slade J. said, dealing with the construction of the grant:

> "It was manifestly not intended to include substances which could only be worked by quarrying, drilling, boring or other work involving disturbance of the surface of the land."

Although he was dealing with a grant which was further restricted in that it did not allow injury to the surface of the land, it is clear that normally "mining" will not include quarrying. It does not even apply to all extraction of minerals that are usually mined. For example, getting minerals from a dump left over from ancient mining is not mining.[32]

As all petroleum (including natural gas as defined in the Act) belongs **9.07** to the Crown it is unlikely that the question of whether it is included in a mining lease or reservation will arise except in cases like *Earl of Lonsdale v Attorney General*[33] which deal with Crown grants of mining leases. However, oil or petroleum raises other problems since, unlike solid minerals, it is not found in particular strata from which it has to be extracted, but is in liquid or gas form and is seeking a way to the surface through impervious strata. It is not always possible, therefore, to define the boundaries of the land in which the oil lies.[34] In this respect it bears many similarities to water.

In *O'Callaghan v Elliott*[35] Lord Denning M.R. made clear that even his wide definition of "mines and minerals" could be restricted by the particular circumstances of the case. This is particularly the case where the minerals involved are the normal sub-soil of the land,[36] or where the circumstances of the grant indicate that limited types of mineral were included, for example, under the eiusdem generis rule.

3. Ancillary rights

Owning the mines and minerals beneath another person's property is **9.08** of no use unless you have the means of working them. This requires ancillary rights. Some of these are standard easements, such as a right of way

---

[31] [1966] 1 Q.B. 601.
[32] *Roger (Inspector of Taxes) v Longsdon* [1967] Ch. 93; [1966] 2 W.L.R. 861.
[33] [1982] 1 W.L.R. 887; [1982] 3 All E.R. 579.
[34] *Earl of Lonsdale v Attorney General* [1982] 1 W.L.R. 887; [1982] 3 All E.R. 579 at 614h.
[35] [1966] 1 Q.B. 601.
[36] *North British Railway Co v Budhill Coal and Sandstone Co* [1910] A.C. 116.

and a right of support from the land above. The mines themselves also owe easements of support to the land above. All this is in accordance with the law of easements.

Most mining operations are now carried out under statute, but the grant of mining rights in itself includes the right to get and carry away the deposits.[37] This includes a right to dig pits, drive shafts down and to make underground communications, but only in such a way as not to destroy the surface.

By s.51(3) of the Coal Industry Act 1994 a licensee's right in relation to any underground land is:

"(a) to enter upon, remove, execute works in, pass through or occupy that land; or

(b) to do any acts requisite or convenient for the carrying on of any coal-mining operations".

However, in respect of operations covered by the Petroleum Act 1998 ancillary rights are limited to those granted by the Mines (Working Facilities and Support) Act 1966. This applies to all minerals,[38] but only comes into operation if the person seeking the ancillary rights has been unable to reach agreement with the land-owner. In these circumstances he has the right to apply to the minister for ancillary rights, which will then be referred to the court which will decide how wide the rights will be and will assess compensation. No order can be made, however, in respect of any failure by the Coal Authority.

The amount of the compensation will be assessed under the *Ponte Guarde* principles, i.e. it will be based on what the land-owner is losing and not what the miner is gaining.[39] So if the mining operations are way below ground and the access is from adjoining land the amount of the compensation will be limited.

The rights granted under the 1966 Act are:

"(a) a right to let down the surface;

(b) a right of air-way, shaft-way or surface or underground wayleave, or other right for the purpose of access to [or conveyance of minerals or the] ventilation or drainage of the mines;

(c) a right to use and occupy the surface for the eretion of washeries, coke ovens, railways, by-product works or brick making or other works, or of dwellings for persons employed in connection

---

[37] See *Besley v John* [2003] EWCA Civ 1737, where this principle is extended to grazing rights.

[38] Mines (Working Facilities and Support) Act 1966 s.1.

[39] *Bocardo SA v Star Energy UK Onshore Ltd* [2010] UKSC 35; [2011] 1 A.C. 380.

with the working of the minerals or with any such works as aforesaid;

(d) a right to obtain a supply of water or other substances in connection with the working of minerals;

(e) a right to dispose of water or other liquid matter obtained from mines or any by-product works".[40]

This Act applies to petroleum licences.[41]

By contrast the Coal Industry Act 1994 contains its own free-standing set of rights and obligations. Thus by s.51(3) of the Coal Industry Act 1994 a licensee's right in relation to any underground land is:

"(a) to enter upon, remove, execute works in, pass through or occupy that land; or

(b) to do any acts requisite or convenient for the carrying on of any coal-mining operations".

It also includes its own compensation system based on the compulsory purchase acts.[42]

[40] Mines (Working Facilities and Support) Act 1966 s.2(1).
[41] Petroleum Act 1998 s.7.
[42] Sch.1B.

Part II:
Easements

Chapter Ten
The Nature of an Easement

1. History

The English word "easement" means something that makes life easier.[1] **10.01**
Thus Chaucer in The Reeve' s Tale:

> "For John, seyde he, als every moote I thryve,
> If that I may, yon wench wil I swyve,
> Some esement has lawe yshapen us;
> For, John, there is a lawe that says thus,
> That if a man in a point be agreved,
> That in another he sal be releved."

This seems closer to the principle of mutuality than the modern law of
easements, but it demonstrates the definition of easement set out above.

As appears from this quotation "easement" as a legal term has long
been known to the common law.[2] In Les Termes de la Ley[3] it was defined
thus:

> "Easement est un immunitie q. un vicine ad d'un autre, p. charter ou
> prescription sauns profit, come un voy ou un chanel p. son tre, or
> tiels semblables."[4]

This makes it clear that it consists of rights over neighbouring land, as
opposed to being a right in gross. However, no real attempt was made
to define the extent of the principles until the first edition of Gale on
Easements in 1839.

---

[1] From the Old French "aisement".
[2] The oldest reference in the Oxford English Dictionary is of 1463 where a will stated: "I
wille the seid Jenete terme of hyr lyff have esement of the kitchin to make hir mete and
esement of the well in the yard". This, however, looks very like an easement in gross.
[3] J, Rastell and W. Rastell, Les Termes de la Ley (London: Miles Fletcher and Robert Young,
1642).
[4] An easement is an immunity which a neighbour has from another, by deed or prescription without profit, such as a way or a channel through his land or suchlike.

Under the feudal system all land belonged to the Crown and so even freehold was only a form of tenure and not an absolute right. As a result there was no difficulty in conceiving limited rights attaching to land, ranging from copyhold, which came close to freehold ownership, to very limited incidents such as the incidents of petty serjeanty. As the law of inheritance developed it in turn placed various limitations on the rights of the owner or occupier of the land, so that he might have only a life interest or ownership restricted by entail or his fee simple might be subject to portions or annuities.

10.02   The property legislation culminating in the Law of Property Act 1925 and the Land Registration Act 1925 set out to reduce the estates in land to two, freehold and leasehold, and to ensure that minor rights in land existed only as trusts. As a result, in respect of registered land there must be one or more registered proprietors and in relation to unregistered land there must be a freehold owner, or not more than four people who hold the land as joint owners in law. However, it was clear to the draftsmen that the complexities of life required other minor rights in land and the legislation took no steps to alter the existing law of easements, which are still legal (as opposed to equitable) limitations on land. One of the few references to easements in the 1925 legislation is s.187(1) of the Law of Property Act 1925 which provides:

> "Where an easement right or privilege for a legal estate is created, it shall enure for the benefit of the land to which it is intended to be annexed."

Of course in the modern world even absolute freehold ownership of land is considerably circumscribed by the requirement that everything done on private land is subject to the general law, notably planning and anti-pollution restrictions, but the ownership of the land is also limited by other private obligations to individuals, such as land charges and restrictive covenants, as well as more recent concepts such as irrevocable licences.

Easements now are undoubtedly a separate category from other minor rights over land. While it is not easy to arrive upon a legal definition of an easement which covers all possibilities, it can be important to establish whether a right created either by grant or prescription is a true easement. Deciding whether or not a right is an easement may determine, for example, whether the benefit and burden of the right passes automatically on conveyance of the respective parcels of land. Furthermore, an easement passes automatically on a sale of the land; it can be exercised by a lessee; it cannot be sold separately. These and other results are dealt with in more detail later but they are mentioned here to emphasise that finding a satisfactory definition of "easement" is not a purely academic pursuit. Whether or not a particular right is an easement is of real practical importance.

The Law Commission has produced a Report on *Easements, Covenants and Profits à Prendre*[5] published on June 8, 2011 making substantial recommendations for changes to the law of Easements and Profits, though not as far reaching as the proposed changes to the law of covenants. The Report incorporates a Draft Law of Property Bill, which they hope to introduce to parliament as soon as parliamentary time can be found.

It is difficult to forecast when this is likely to be turned into legislation and, if it is, whether it will be in the same form as the draft Bill. There will, in any event, be a transitional period during which rights have already been obtained under the old law and also a period while cases commenced under the old law come before the courts.

The intention, therefore, is to refer to this Report where appropriate in the text, but to state the law as it stands.

The most dramatic proposal is to unify the three methods of obtaining an easement by prescription to produce a single statutory period of 20 years. This will mean an end of common law prescription with its quaint reference to 1189 as being the period of time immemorial and of the badly drafted Prescription Act 1832, together with the fiction of lost modern grant which was used to avoid its oddities.

The Report also recommends the abolition of the distinction between implied grant and implied reservation, so that it will cease to be necessary to distinguish which conveyance came first. There is also a helpful plan to allow people to grant easements over their own land, thereby allowing a developer to set up a system of easements before selling off the plots.

The Report takes the view that it is too difficult for easements to be determined by abandonment and proposes a specific presumption of abandonment on 20 years non-user. There is also an attempt to deal with the problems which have recently arisen as to termination of easements by merger and unity of title.

Another interesting proposal is that the Lands Tribunal should have the power to discharge or modify easements as well as covenants. This could provide a helpful safety valve in cases where easements are creating a substantial bar or hindrance to the reasonable use of land by the landowner.

In all there are 64 recommendations, more then 20 of which relate to easements and profits. The intention is to refer to these recommendations at the appropriate stage during the course of the text, but not to carry out a detailed analysis of the effectiveness or any prospective pit-falls of the proposed legislation.

Accordingly the law as stated is the law as it stands at the moment.

---

[5] Law Commission, *Making Land Work: Easements, Covenants and Profits à Prendre* (London: The Stationery Office, 2011) Law Com. No.327.

2. Definition of "easement"

10.03   An easement is a right benefiting land (or some other hereditament) exercisable over other land. As such it closely resembles the Roman Law concept of "servitude" (the Scottish equivalent) though the common law does not necessarily follow all the principles of servitudes (e.g. a *jus spatiandi* cannot exist as a servitude, but possibly can as an easement).[6] However, the two terms taken from the two jurisdictions neatly set out the two aspects of easements. The right "eases" the use of the one land and constitutes a restriction on the use of the other "serving" land.

Cheshire's Modern Real Property (approved in *Re Ellenborough Park*[7]) set out four requirements for the existence of an easement, namely:

(1)   there must be a dominant and a servient tenement;

(2)   an easement must "accommodate" the dominant tenement;

(3)   dominant and servient owners must be different persons;

(4)   a right cannot amount to an easement unless it is capable of forming the subject-matter of an easement.

Although these four requirements have been judicially approved, they do not add up to a very satisfactory definition. It is suggested that the essential elements of an easement are:

(1)   That it applies to land which is affected by it ("the servient tenement").

(2)   That it is annexed to other land which takes the benefit of it ("the dominant tenement").

(3)   That it is a right of a kind which, as a matter of common-sense and public policy, is capable of forming the subject-matter of an easement.

This suggested definition comprises all the elements of Cheshire's definition. The extent to which the easement must "accommodate" the land which benefits from it is dealt with below. The proposition that the dominant and servient owners must be different persons is, it is submitted, really a general land law principle, which is not peculiar to easements. However, the Law Commission[8] has drawn attention to problems created by the principle that you cannot create easements over your own land. In

---

[6] *Re Ellenborough Park* [1956] Ch. 131; [1955] 3 W.L.R. 892 and below para.10.24.

[7] *Re Ellenborough Park* [1956] Ch. 131.

[8] Law Commission, *Making Land Work: Easements, Covenants and Profits à Prendre* (London: The Stationery Office, 2011) Law Com. No.327.

drawing up building estates it would be helpful if the developer could set up the system of easements for the estate before selling the properties. For this reason they have suggested a specific statutory reversal of this rule to enable a landowner to grant express easements over his own land with a view to enabling him to sell the property with the benefit of the easement he has created.

Cheshire's fourth requirement (effectively the third requirement in the above definition) is also dealt with below.[9]

Easements are sometimes divided into positive and negative easements. The distinction is essentially that a positive easement involves the person exercising it coming onto his neighbour's land, whereas a negative easement is a benefit derived from the land which does not involve anyone going onto it. The two main examples of negative easements are rights of light and rights of support. It will be seen that both of these are to some extent anomalous. The distinction can sometimes be useful in analysing whether certain rights are capable of being easements and, particularly, when claims are made to easements of a new nature. However, once it is established that a right is an easement, it makes no difference to its enforcement whether it is positive or negative.

It is well established that any easement carries with it some ancillary rights. The principle has now been clearly formulated (at least in respect of express and implied grants) in *Moncrieff v Jamieson*,[10] which, although a case concerning a Scottish servitude, also states the English law.[11] A servitude [and therefore an easement] carries with it other rights which, although they would not qualify on their own as servitudes, are necessary if the dominant proprietor is to make reasonable and comfortable use of the property in favour of which it is granted.

The principle was set out in the context of a claim of a right to park as ancillary to a right of way and harks back to the principle set out in *Bulstrode v Lambert*[12] that a right to stop and unload is ancillary to a right of way.

These ancillary rights are dealt with more fully in relation to individual easements, but it is clear that they can be used as a means of dealing with some of the restrictions in easements, most notably the right to park, as in *Moncrieff v Jamieson*,[13] and the restriction on use of a way to give access to the dominant tenement itself, as in *National Trust v White*.[14]

Often such ancillary rights depend on the interpretation of the grant. However, in principle, they can also apply to prescriptive rights.

---

[9] See below para.10.19 et seq.
[10] *Moncrieff v Jamieson* [2007] UKHL 42; [2007] 1 W.L.R. 2620.
[11] per Lord Scott at [45].
[12] *Bulstrode v Lambert* [1953] 1 W.L.R. 1064.
[13] *Moncrieff v Jamieson* [2007] UKHL 42; [2007] 1 W.L.R. 2620.
[14] *National Trust for Places of Historic Interest or Natural Beauty v White* [1987] 1 W.L.R. 907.

3. The servient tenement

10.04   It is an essential element of an easement that it relates to property over or in respect of which it is exercised. This requirement does not cause problems because it would not occur to anyone to claim that a right which did not affect someone else's land was an easement. However, the requirement that the right claimed relates to property is nevertheless the main element which distinguishes an easement from a purely contractual right.

The property to which the easement relates and, in the case of positive easements, over which it physically runs, is known as the servient tenement, because it is "serving" the dominant tenement. There is, however, no need for the servient tenement to suffer any financial detriment as a result of the easement, though the absence of any burden on the servient tenement may encourage the court to refuse an injunction.[15]

While it is certainly of the essence of an easement that there should be a servient tenement, there are unlikely to be many instances where the question of the extent of the servient tenement arises. Any such question really relates to the extent of the easement itself rather than the extent of the servient tenement in respect of which it is exercised. If there is a right to spread coal dust, it is necessary to know how widely this right extends, but the dicta in *Woodman v Pwllbach Colliery*[16] which suggest that the servient tenement must be defined are really just emphasising how imprecise the grant was.

10.05   There could be questions as to whether a right of support affects only the immediate building or includes any buildings beyond, but in practice the problem has rarely arisen.

In short, the servient tenement is that part of the grantee's land which is affected by the easement. The requirement that there must be land affected by the easement is included in the definition of what constitutes an easement simply to ensure that contractual obligations owed by a landowner to his neighbour but unrelated to the land are not claimed as easements.

It is an essential characteristic of an easement that it does not place on the owner of the servient tenement any obligation to act. Such an obligation can only be imposed by a positive covenant, the burden of which will not pass with the land. As a result the owner of the servient tenement has, in principle, no obligation to maintain a right of way[17] or, as the law is generally understood, to keep in repair a building in respect of which there is an easement of support.[18]

---

[15] *Das v Linden Mews* [2002] EWCA Civ 590; [2003] 2 P. & C.R. 4.
[16] (1914) 111 L.T. 169, affirmed by the House of Lords sub nom. *Pwllbach Colliery Co Ltd v Wood* [1915] A.C. 634.
[17] See Ch. 19.
[18] See Ch. 20, where this proposition is doubted.

This feature of easements has caused particular problems with regard to fencing obligations,[19] because fencing obligations do place a positive burden on the servient tenement. For this reason they have been described as spurious easements.

Apart from the anomalous position of fencing easements, if a person wishes to place a positive burden on the owner or occupier of neighbouring land, he must do so by covenant which (as it is not a restrictive covenant) will not run with the land. Since the abolition of manorial incidents, therefore, it is impossible to burden land (as opposed to the landowner) with any positive obligations owed towards the neighbouring land.

4. The dominant tenement

The second requirement set out above, that it is annexed to other land **10.06** which takes the benefit of it, goes to the heart of the nature of an easement:

> "I think that it is an essential element of any easement that it is annexed to land and that no person can possess an easement otherwise than in respect of and in amplification of his enjoyment of some estate or interest in a piece of land."[20]

Even an easement giving a right to burial in the chancel only applies to persons dying in a particular house.[21]

Emanating from the analogy with the Roman Law concept of servitudes, the expression "dominant tenement" has long been used to describe the property benefiting from the easement, though the phrase now seems archaic, especially as "tenement" is not a phrase used elsewhere in land law and suggests in the layman's mind a run-down Glaswegian apartment. The principle, however, is important. Frequently rights may be granted to individuals or companies or claimed under prescriptive right which are not easements solely because of this requirement.

No doubt in earlier centuries there were uncertainties about the essential requirements for an easement. Indeed, as we shall see,[22] there are nineteenth century pronouncements which suggest the existence of a general law of prescription untrammelled by the restricting principles of easements. There has also been recent comparison between prescription in English law with *usucapio* in Roman Law.[23] But even if the need for a

---

[19] See Ch. 22.
[20] per Winn L.J. in Alfred F *Beckett Ltd v Lyons* [1967] Ch. 449; [1967] 1 All E.R. 833 at 852d.
[21] *Waring v Griffiths* (1758) 1 Burr 440.
[22] Ch. 15.
[23] *R. v Oxfordshire CC Ex p. Sunningwell Parish Council* [2000] 1 A.C. 335; [1999] 3 W.L.R. 160 considered more fully under Creation of Easements by Prescription.

dominant tenement was only fully accepted in the nineteenth century, the principle has been repeated frequently and universally since.[24]

10.07   The absolute requirement that an easement must have a dominant tenement does, however, raise the problem of how parties are supposed to express rights they wish to grant which are in gross. A profit à prendre can exist in gross, but there are other rights which parties might wish to grant, or indeed which have been exercised as of right for the prescriptive period, which cannot be defined as profits. A very common example is the right to park in a car park or even the right to use a particular way or the right to use a box at a racecourse. A person might well wish to purchase such a right unconnected with the ownership of land. Moreover timeshares have given rise to a whole body of law of their own, though since they give rise to exclusive rights of possession (albeit for only a limited part of the year) they form part of the law of lessor and lessee. There are also customary rights exercised over the centuries by the public at large or inhabitants of particular areas, together with village and town greens which have arisen by prescription since the cut-off date in the Commons Registration Act 1965.[25]

Generally the complexities of modern commercial practice give rise to a whole mass of rights which are not easements because they exist in gross. Rights relating to property which fall short of exclusive rights of possession and are not linked to other land in practice are undoubtedly granted by deed. The normal analysis would be that the rights thereby created are licences, but this might mean that they could not be freely traded and could be determined by the grantor even if to do so was a breach of contract. This creates problems which are not always foreseen by the laymen or lawyers involved in entering into such transactions.

This problem has arisen in two modern cases, in both of which the requirement of a dominant tenement could be seen as giving rise to an injustice. In *London and Blenheim Estates v Ladbroke Retail Parks*[26] there was an agreement giving the purchaser the right to add additional land, not then in his ownership, to the dominant tenement for a right to park. Although the right was registered it was held that it did not create an interest in land because of the uncertainty involved as to the identity of the dominant tenement.[27] As it was a pure contractual right, it did not bind the purchaser of the servient land.

[24] See the author's article in *The Conveyancer* Jan/Feb 2004 p.13.
[25] para.11.17 below.
[26] [1994] 1 W.L.R. 31; [1993] 4 All E.R. 157.
[27] In *Sainsbury's Supermarkets Ltd v Olympia Homes* [2005] EWHC 1235 (Ch); [2006] 1 P. & C.R. 17 a case relating to an option, *London and Blenheim Estates v Ladbroke Retail Parks* was distinguished specifically because the uncertainty was in respect of the dominant tenement.

Subsequently in *Voice v Bell*[28] the purchaser was granted a right of way which could only benefit land he hoped to purchase subsequently. Although, some years later, he did buy further land, there was no easement and no interest in land which could bind the purchaser of the servient tenement.

10.08 Another area where this problem has been the subject of litigation is in respect of public utilities. Water pipes, electricity cables, gas pipes, telephone wires and television cables all travel across the land of others. To a large extent the problems involved in ensuring that the rights of the supply companies are irrevocable are met by the various statutes relating to these rights, but problems may arise where the statute fails to cover the matter properly. Thus in *Re Salvin*[29] a water company had entered into deeds giving it a right to lay pipes over the servient tenement. Although the pipes were miles away from the reservoirs and other sources of the water the court held that the water company's land was the dominant tenement. The distinction between easements and way-leaves is considered below.[30]

The decision in *Re Salvin* has been criticised,[31] but there seems no real reason to question the decision on the facts. No doubt the pipes could be seen as being for the purpose of allowing the water to pass from the reservoir via various other pipes. It "eased" the reservoir because without outflow pipes it would be of no commercial use as a reservoir. This, it is submitted, is undoubtedly sufficient to found a valid easement. The extent to which an easement to be valid must "accommodate" the dominant tenement is dealt with below.

Prescriptive rights at common law, by statute and by virtue of the doctrine of lost modern grant can exist in respect of rights other than easements, such as fisheries, markets, mooring rights and public highways. In *R. v Oxfordshire CC Ex p. Sunningwell Parish Council.*[32] Lord Hoffman has addressed the concept of prescription specifically in relation to customary rights, which are considered below.[33] The wider concept of prescription is dealt with in Chapter 15.[34] In short he seeks to deal with prescription as a form of limitation of actions rather than by the implication of grant. Therefore the presumptions of lost modern grant in respect of private easements and dedication in respect of highways are imputed rather than implied. If a person is prevented from bringing an action in contract after six years this is based on the unfairness to the defendant of bringing it up

[28] (1994) 68 P. & C.R. 441.
[29] [1938] 2 All E.R. 498.
[30] See below para.11.13 et seq.
[31] Peter Brett, "The Dominant Estate" (1950) 14 Conv (N.S.) 264.
[32] [2000] 1 A.C. 335; [1999] 3 W.L.R. 160.
[33] Ch. 11.
[34] See the author's article in *The Conveyancer* Jan/Feb 2004 p.13.

after so long and not because the claimant is assumed to have forgotten about it. Much the same applies to prescriptive rights.

10.09 The failure to develop any general doctrine of prescription separate from the constraints of the law of easements has caused difficulties in respect of rights enjoyed by the public at large or by the inhabitants of a particular area by ancient custom.[35] Such rights do not slot easily into the law of easements or profits à prendre. Rights of common over common land have long been treated as a separate body of law. One of the objects of the Commons Registration Act 1965 was to establish a map of all commons and village and town greens. A village or town green is,

> "land on which either by specific statutory provision or customary right, or by continuous use for not less than 20 years, the inhabitants of the locality were entitled to pursue lawful sports and pastimes".

All such greens had to be registered by July 31, 1970, but it is now clear that new village or town greens can be created by 20 years user since 1970.[36] However there are many other rights which have been enjoyed by the public or the inhabitants of particular areas from time immemorial, but which are open to challenge from the owners of the land. There has long been a public perception that open, unfenced land should belong to the public, or at least be accessible to them. The concept of private ownership of land is not absolute. So-called land reform often means removing land from people who have a legitimate claim to it and giving it to others who may need it more. In English law all land is held on tenure from the Crown.[37] The foreshore is still largely Crown property treated as public, but most of the land where we like to wander freely is privately owned. This includes common land. However, our perception is still that that private ownership is not absolute. Places of natural beauty and historic interest are held on trust for the nation. This concept has now been given statutory form in the access rights enshrined in the Countryside and Rights of Way Act 2000.[38] The rights, which came into force on September 19, 2004, however, are still limited. The main way in which the common law has sought to address this perception is in the development of customary rights. These too are dealt with elsewhere.[39]

---

[35] See *R. (on the application of Beresford) v Sunderland City Council* [2003] UKHL 60; [2004] 1 A.C. 889, which involved a sports arena.

[36] *R. v Suffolk CC Ex p. Steed* (1999) 59 P. & C.R. 102; *Oxfordshire CC v Oxfordshire City Council* [2006] UKHL 25; [2006] 2 A.C. 674.

[37] See e.g. C. Harpum, *Megarry & Wade The Law of Real Property*, 6th edn (London: Sweet & Maxwell, 1999), p.12.

[38] Considered in Ch. 11.

[39] See Ch. 11.

It might be thought that, since there must be a dominant tenement, the **10.10** person to whom the easement is granted must be the owner of the dominant tenement at the time. However, it has been held at first instance in *Rymer v McIlroy*[40] that this is not the case and that an easement granted to a tenant from year to year, which would normally attach only to the leasehold interest, can be annexed to the freehold interest when purchased by the tenant. No real reason is given for this decision. At first sight it seems to be supported by a subsequent House of Lords decision in a Scottish case, *North British Railway v Park Yard Co*[41] However, there was no substantial analysis of this issue in the Scottish case and perhaps the reason for this is that the grant of the servitude, which in Scottish Law does not need to be by deed, was treated as a grant for the future, the equivalent in English Law of a contract to grant an easement, which, under Scottish Law, would not need a separate deed to turn it into an effective servitude.

It is submitted that the true position in English law is that an easement can only be granted to a person who owns the dominant tenement. This was clearly the approach in *London and Blenheim Estates v Ladbroke Retail Parks*[42] where no comment was made on *Rymer v McIlroy* because it was not cited. If he is a lessee the easement is restricted to his lease. If there is an agreement to grant an easement, this is simply an estate contract. Nevertheless, this view of the law is at odds with *Rymer v McIlroy* which is the only English decision specifically on the point.

5. Identifying the dominant tenement

Having postulated that there must be a dominant tenement it follows **10.11** that it must be possible to identify it. Identifying the dominant tenement presents different problems depending on whether the easement is created by deed or by prescription.

Where the easement is created by deed, whether expressly or by implication, the starting point is the deed or conveyance itself, whereas in the case of prescriptive rights there is no document from which the dominant tenement can be deduced.

Where the deed or conveyance makes clear the extent of the land to be benefited then the court has no option but to follow that definition. However, where there is no definition or where there is any ambiguity in the deed itself, the court will look at the extrinsic circumstances. Strictly the court is not entitled to receive evidence of what the parties meant by the terms in the deed,[43]or of pre-contractual negotiations,[44] but

---

[40] [1897] 1 Ch. 528.
[41] [1898] A.C. 643.
[42] [1994] 1 W.L.R. 31;[1993] 4 All E.R. 157.
[43] *Prenn v Simonds* [1971] 1 W.L.R. 1381.
[44] *Chartbrook Ltd v Persimmon Homes Ltd* [2010] 1 P & C.R.162.

evidence can be adduced not only of the surrounding facts, but also of what the parties' intentions were in relation to the land.[45] In effect, therefore, there are few restrictions on the extrinsic evidence which will be allowed. While it is undoubtedly true that the court cannot go behind an unambiguous definition of the dominant tenement in the grant, the courts will be vigilant to find ambiguities in a conveyance if a strict reading of the conveyance will produce an anomalous result. The question is what a reasonable person having all the background knowledge which would have been available to the parties would have understood them to be using the language in the deed to mean.[46] It is possible, however, that where the deed appears to contain a commonsense definition, the court might take a more restrictive view and refuse to admit complex evidence of extraneous circumstances and of the intentions of the parties.

10.12   In *Thorpe v Brumfitt* in 1873[47] the court accepted that a grant of a right of way contained in a deed which at the same time conveyed a small triangle of land was intended to be for the benefit of all the grantee's land and not just the small triangle. A similar approach was taken in *Callard v Beeney*[48] where a grant of a right of way "for the purpose of access from the point marked X on the plan to the field numbered 169" was construed as identifying only the point of access and not the dominant tenement. Accordingly the right could be us-ed for the benefit of the whole of the grantee's land and not just field 169. This approach was also followed in *Johnstone v Holdway*[49] where the dominant tenement was not mentioned at all in the deed creating the easement. This is a common conveyancing practice and the court not surprisingly held that the land to be benefited was the whole of the quarry owned by the grantee.

The principle was extended further in *The Shannon v Venner*[50] where the plaintiff had bought land and then bought further land together with a right of way. Evidence was admitted that the plaintiff's intention had always been to use the way for the whole of his land and accordingly that it was the whole of the land which was to be benefited. It followed on those facts that the dominant tenement was sufficiently identified, even though it was not actually owned at the time.[51]

As this is a matter of construction and not of rectification, the court does not have to find a common intention of the parties. If the grantor

---

[45] *The Shannon v Venner* [1965] Ch. 682; [1965] 2 W.L.R. 718
[46] *Chartbrook Ltd v Persimmon Homes* [2010] 1 P & C.R.162.
[47] (1872–73) L.R. 8 Ch. App. 650.
[48] [1930] 1 K.B. 353.
[49] [1963] 1 Q.B. 601.
[50] [1965] Ch. 682; [1965] 2 W.L.R. 718.
[51] See *London and Blenheim Estates v Ladbroke Retail Park* [1994] 1 W.L.R. 31; [1993] 4 All E.R. 157, where *The Shannon v Venner* [1965] Ch. 682 was not cited.

believes that the way is to benefit one piece of land, and the grantee believes that a larger piece is being benefited, the court will seek to make the best sense out of the transaction by looking at it objectively.

These authorities relate to the issue of the extent of the dominant tene- **10.13** ment at the time of the grant. The accepted principle has been that however loosely it is defined the extent of the dominant tenement is strictly limited to the land intended to be benefited at the time. Accordingly where the owner of the dominant tenement purchases further land adjacent to his existing land he cannot use a right of way granted for the benefit of the land he originally owned as a means of access to the new land, even if he gains access to the new land via his existing land.[52] This rule is known as the rule in *Harris v Flower*.[53] It applies even if the building is partly on the dominant land and partly on other land.[54] Equally if hay is taken off one field and stored in another field along a right of way annexed to the latter field, this is only permissible if the user is not colourable, that is, the storage is not just an excuse for using the field as a through route.[55]

Since these decisions a substantial body of law has built up involving **10.14** attempts to challenge or distinguish this rule. Unsurprisingly these relate more to property development than agricultural usage.

The doctrine was re-affirmed by the Court of Appeal in *Peacock v Custins*[56] and *Macepark v Sargeant*[57] and by the House of Lords (in relation to Scottish Law) in *Alvis v Harrison*.[58] However, there are also a number of cases where it has been distinguished, such as *Massey v Boulden*.[59]

The basis of these distinctions is that the use for the benefit of the other land is ancillary to the use for the dominant tenement. This means that there is no extension of the dominant tenement as such, but the user in respect of other land is treated as user for the benefit of the dominant tenement.

Thus in *National Trust v White*[60] the additional land was used as the car park for access to a National Trust property and in *Massey v Boulden*[61] the right of way was used for an enlarged house which had incorporated adjoining land. The same principle of including rights ancillary to the

---

[52] *Bracewell v Appleby* [1975] Ch. 408; [1975] 2 W.L.R. 282.
[53] (1905) 74 L.J. Ch. 127.
[54] *Harris v Flower & Sons* (1905) 74 L.J. Ch. 127.
[55] *Williams v James* (1866–67) L.R. 2 C.P. 577.
[56] [2002] 1 W.L.R. 1815; [2001] 2 All E.R. 827.
[57] [2003] EWHC 427 (Ch); [2003] 1 W.L.R. 2284.
[58] (1990) 62 P. & C.R. 10.
[59] [2002] EWCA Civ 1634; [2003] 1 W.L.R. 1792.
[60] *National Trust for Places of Historic Interest or Natural Beauty v White* [1987] 1 W.L.R. 907.
[61] [2002] EWCA Civ 1634; [2003] 1 W.L.R. 1792.

principal right of way was used to justify a right of parking on the way in *Moncrieff v Jamieson*.[62]

While this may give rise to uncertainty as to whether the use is really for the benefit of the adjoining land or ancillary to the dominant tenement, the principle is left intact, since the dominant tenement is not extended.

The only dictum challenging this is in *Graham v Philcox*[63] where May L.J. said that there is no "suggestion that the alteration of a dominant tenement to which a right of way may be appurtenant is sufficient to extinguish it". This dictum must be taken to relate to a user which remains the user of the dominant tenement, but includes ancillary user on behalf of other land as in *Massey v Boulden*.

10.15 While it is still the law that an owner of the dominant tenement cannot unilaterally increase its size, there is no reason why the servient owner should not extend the land benefited by means of a re-grant of the easement. Such a re-grant does not need to be express. Where there is a fresh lease or conveyance of the property which makes no reference to the right of way, the court will look under s.62 of the Law of Property Act 1925 to see what rights are appurtenant to the land granted. These will include not only rights which have actually been exercised by the owner but also rights exercised by his tenants under express rights of way. It seems clear that this is the true *ratio decidendi* of *Graham v Philcox*.[64] Furthermore if the new lease is of a larger tenement, the court may still interpret the fresh lease as including a fresh grant of the same rights as were previously exercised by the smaller tenement, thus in effect increasing the size of the dominant tenement.[65]

It has already been seen that the land to be benefited need not be adjacent to the servient tenement. This principle was set out in *Todrick v Western National*[66] and extended in *Re Salvin*.[67] On the facts of that case, the dominant tenement was held to be the whole of the undertaking of the water authority, a fairly indeterminate area of land an unspecified distance from the servient tenement. The only requirement, as will be seen later,[68] is that the easement should benefit the retained land and not be solely for the benefit of the land owner personally. To take an extreme example it would not be possible for a person to whom a right of way had

---

[62] [2007] UKHL 42; [2007] 1 W.L.R. 2620. Although this is a Scottish case on the law of servitude, it is a decision of the House of Lords and it seems that the laws of England and Scotland are the same on this issue—per Lord Scott at [45].

[63] [1984] Q.B. 747; [1984] 3 W.L.R. 150.

[64] [1984] Q.B. 747; [1984] 3 W.L.R. 150.

[65] *Wright v Macadam* [1949] 2 K.B. 744; see *Graham v Philcox* [1984] Q.B. 747; [1984] 2 All E.R. 643 at 648e per May L.J.

[66] [1934] Ch. 561.

[67] [1938] 2 All E.R. 498. See above para.10.08.

[68] See para.10.18 et seq.

been granted for his own recreation miles from his home to seek unilaterally to annex that right to his own property.

The identification of the dominant tenement will be dealt with further **10.16** in respect of individual easements and the importance of identifying the dominant tenement will vary according to the nature of the easement claimed. In the case of a right of light, which is created by prescription, the right itself largely defines the limit of the land to be benefited. But even in right of light cases, the issue of whether or not the amount of light has been reduced to below an acceptable level requires the court to decide what land has the benefit of the right. The right is,

> "an easement for the access of light to a building, not to a particular room within it; so that the extent of the right is not necessarily to be measured by the internal arrangements of the building".[69]

Thus when a building has been sub-divided and as a result the light from other sources has been reduced, this does not derogate from the dominant owner's right to a reasonable amount of light from the windows. Nevertheless, since a right to light is a right through a particular window, it is only in rare cases that the extent of the dominant tenement becomes relevant.

In the case of a right of support problems arise where there is an extension of the supported building. It seems that whether the existing easement continues or whether time begins to run for a new easement depends on the extent to which the burden of the servient land is increased.[70]

On the other hand, in the case of a right to extract water, for example, it may be crucial to know for the benefit of which land the right is to be exercised, since this may affect to some degree the amount of water extracted. The classic case of a right of way is referred to above.

In the normal case the dominant tenement is land, but it has been **10.17** realised for many centuries that other property rights can constitute a dominant tenement.[71] For example, a right of way can be annexed to a several fishery.[72] The rule does not depend on whether the right to be benefited is corporeal or incorporeal but on whether there is any incongruity in the union of the two. This principle has, however, very limited application in practice. It is never necessary to annex one easement to another since they must each be for the benefit of land to which they are respectively annexed. Thus a right to repair a property built on the edge

---

[69] per Millett J. in *Carr-Saunders v Dick McNeil Associates Ltd* [1986] 1 W.L.R. 922; [1986] 2 All E.R. 888 at 894a.
[70] *Ray v Fairway Motors* (1968) 20 P. & C.R. 261; see Ch. 19.
[71] See Coke on Littleton referred to in *Hanbury v Jenkins* [1901] 2 Ch. 401.
[72] *Hanbury v Jenkins* [1901] 2 Ch. 401, obiter.

of your land necessarily also involves a right of access, both of which benefit the property in need of repair.[73] This particular problem has been eased by the Access to Neighbouring Land Act 1992, which does not create rights of access as such, but only the right to obtain an access order from the Court. This leaves only profits à prendre and a few other anomalous rights, such as the several fishery referred to above, to which an easement can be attached. An attempt to annex a right to moor to a public right of navigation and a public right of way failed in *Sussex Investments v Jackson*.[74] This is another example of a commonly perceived and exercised "right" being shown to be without legal basis.

An easement cannot be annexed to a public right of way because a public right of way is not a hereditament either corporeal or incorporeal.[75] However, in the case of adopted roads, the land on which the public highway runs vests in the highway authority and when the highway is not adopted someone must own the sub-soil. An easement such as a right of drainage may, therefore, be annexed to the sub-soil rather than to the public right of way itself. If half the sub-soil is owned by the servient owner then it may well be that the other half is also being drained by the drain in question. Despite the fact that this was one of the reasons for the decision at first instance the problem does not seem to have been considered in the Court of Appeal in *Attorney General v Copeland* where it was simply assumed that an easement had arisen by lost modern grant.[76] The Countryside and Rights of Way Act 2000[77] contains an important

---

[73] See *Ward v Kirkland* [1967] Ch. 194.
[74] *Sussex Investments v Jackson The Times*, July 29, 1993.
[75] *Attorney General v Copeland* [1901] 2 K.B. 101, reversed on appeal on another point.
[76] *Attorney General v Copeland* [1902] 1 K.B. 690.
[77] Countryside and Rights of Way Act 2000 s.50 states that:

"(1) Restricted byway rights over any way by virtue of subsection (1) of section 48 are subject to any condition or limitation to which public rights of way over that way were subject immediately before the commencement of that section.
(2) Any owner or lessee of premises adjoining or adjacent to a relevant highway shall, so far as is necessary for the reasonable enjoyment and occupation of the premises, have a right of way for vehicular and all other kinds of traffic over the relevant highway.
(3) In subsection (2), in its application to the owner of any premises, 'relevant highway' means so much of any highway maintainable at the public expense by virtue of section 49(1) as was, immediately before it became so maintainable, owned by the person who then owned the premises.
(4) In subsection (2), in its application to the lessee of any premises, 'relevant highway' means so much of any highway maintainable at the public expense by virtue of section 49(1) as was, immediately before it became so maintainable, included in the lease on which the premises are held.
(5) In this section_
　　　'lease' and 'lessee' have the same meaning as in the 1980 Act;
　　　　'owner', in relation to any premises, means a person, other than a mortgagee not in possession, who is for the time being entitled to dispose of the fee simple of the premises, whether in possession or in reversion, and 'owned' shall be construed accordingly; and
　　　'premises' has the same meaning as in the 1980 Act."

provision for restricted byways, which are not open to vehicular traffic, granting a statutory right of way to adjoining owners who also owned the sub-soil before it became maintainable at public expense.

Uncertainty has been expressed as to whether an easement can be granted entitling the benefiting owner to cause a nuisance. Certainly an easement may allow the dominant owner to do something on the land of another which would otherwise constitute trespass. This is true of every positive easement. There seems no reason in principle why a right to create or continue a nuisance should not be conveyed in the same way. This has been accepted in general terms, at least by implication, in many cases, even though doubt has been expressed obiter about whether such a right could exist.[78] It is difficult to find a case where an easement to create or continue a nuisance has actually been upheld, but there are various dicta to this effect[79] and in other cases such rights have been claimed but rejected on other grounds.[80]

The principle appears to be that an easement can arise by express grant or prescription even if it gives rise to a nuisance, but that where there is an express grant which can be exercised without a nuisance it will be construed as excluding use which involves a nuisance.[81] Where the claim is by prescription and the previous use has not involved a nuisance, intensification of the use will not be permitted if it then becomes a nuisance.[82]

6. The easement must be for the benefit of the dominant tenement

It is submitted that this heading is all that is meant by the requirement **10.18** in Cheshire's definition that the easement must "accommodate" the dominant tenement. *Hill v Tupper*[83] has been cited as authority for the requirement contained in Cheshire's definition, but this case decided that an incident of the type claimed, namely an exclusive right to rent out pleasure boats, is not an easement at all. The right claimed therefore fell foul of the fourth element of Cheshire's definition. In fact the plaintiff did have land to be accommodated, and if the right had been capable of being an easement there seems no reason why the necessary dominant tenement could not have been found.

---

[78] *Woodman v Pwllbach Colliery* (1914) 111 L.T. 169 upheld on appeal [1915] A.C. 634.

[79] *Crump v Lambert* (1866–67) L.R. 3 Eq. 409; *Ball v Ray* (1872–73) L.R. 8 Ch. App. 467.

[80] *Baxendale v McMurray* (1866–67) L.R. 2 Ch. App. 790; *Woodman v Pwllbach Colliery* (1914) 111 L.T. 169;[1915] A.C. 634; *Liverpool Corp v H Coghill & Son Ltd* [1918] 1 Ch. 307.

[81] *Woodman v Pwllbach Colliery* (1914) 111 L.T. 169; [1915] A.C. 634.

[82] *Baxendale v McMurray* (1866–67) L.R. 2 Ch. App. 790; *Liverpool Corp v H Coghill & Son Ltd* [1918] 1 Ch. 307.

[83] [1863] 2 Hurl & C. 121.

The most significant case on this aspect is *Clapman v Edwards*[84] where it was held that a right included in an underlease to use the wall of the adjoining property for advertising was not sufficiently connected to the land contained in the underlease to amount to an easement. That decision, however, depended on the construction of the grant (which construction was crucial to the grantee's claim) that the right was not restricted to use in connection with the leasehold business, but could be let out to anyone he chose. On that construction the right claimed was, therefore, a right in gross.

It has been suggested that the easement must accommodate or be for the benefit of the land itself rather than the business conducted thereon. This argument is comprehensively disposed of in *Copeland v Greenhalf*[85] where the words of Fry J. in *Moody v Staples*[86] are quoted with approval. He pointed out,

> "that the house can only be used by an occupant and that the occupant only uses the house for the business which he pursues and therefore in some manner (direct or indirect) an easement is more or less connected with the mode in which the occupant of the house uses it".

It seems obvious that even if an easement is only of value to the owner of the land because of the business he carries on there, this does not prevent the right from being a valid easement which benefits or "accommodates" the land. The suggestion that commercial benefit is not enough originates from taking out of context a quotation from Buckley L.J. in *Attorney General v Horner (No.2)*[87] where he said that the right "may have been incident to his business but it cannot have been appurtenant to his land". However this dictum arose while he was dealing with an obscure argument that a right to a market was in some way appurtenant to the ownership of the sub-soil of adjoining highways, an argument that was rejected out of hand by the court.

7. The right must be capable of forming the subject-matter of an easement

10.19   Formulated in this way this requirement begs the question. A right which is capable of being an easement is an easement. One that is not capable of being an easement is not an easement. If, therefore, the other requirements of an easement are met, what characteristics of a right

[84] [1938] 2 All E.R. 507.
[85] [1952] Ch. 488.
[86] [1879] 12 Ch.D. 216.
[87] [1913] 2 Ch. 140.

render it incapable of forming the subject-matter of an easement? In this regard it is necessary to distinguish between rights acquired by grant and rights claimed by prescription. Although prescription is usually regarded as a form of implied or presumed grant, it has been seen above that in the past there was scope for the development of a generalised principle of prescription based on ancient usage rather than on the implied grant of an incident to ownership of land. If the idea of prescription as itself being capable of giving rise to rights which could not be created by grant (which was certainly canvassed in the nineteenth century cases) had been developed, then various kinds of ancient or customary rights exercised by groups of people or the public at large would be regarded as capable of arising by prescription. This would have slotted in well with the law on public highways and rights of navigation which could have developed along the same line. However, the opportunity to develop this concept has not been taken by the courts and rights exercised over a long period can only be enforced if it can be shown that they give rise to rights which could have been created by grant. This problem was addressed by Lord Hoffman in *R. v Oxfordshire CC Ex p. Sunningwell Parish Council*.[88] In dealing with public rights of way he pointed out that English law has no consistent theory of prescription. He suggested that, unlike Roman law usucapio or taking by use, the principle of prescription is based on the common law concept of possession and limitation of action. Therefore an easement by prescription comes not so much from the action of the user, but the inaction of the landowner. This analysis allows for the development of the idea that easements which could not be the subject-matter of a grant could nevertheless become rights by prescription because of the inaction of the landowner. However, the speech itself does not pursue the principle to this conclusion.

10.20 The problems caused by treating express grants of easements as the same thing as rights claimed by prescription are particularly apparent in the case of rights of light which are undoubtedly easements, but which are not usually created by express grant.

The judgment of Bramwell L.J. in *Bryant v Lefever*[89] set out below[90] explains the problem neatly. This point was taken up by Lord Denning M.R. in *Phipps v Pears*[91] in relation to a claim to a view:

> "Take this simple instance. Suppose you have a fine view from your house. You have enjoyed the view for many years. It adds greatly to the value of your house. But if your neighbour chooses to despoil it, by building up and blocking it, you have no redress."

[88] [2000] 1 A.C. 335.
[89] (1878–79) L.R. 4 C.P.D. 172.
[90] See para.11.01.
[91] [1965] 1 Q.B. 76; [1964] 2 W.L.R. 996.

The main reason given why there is no redress for such damage to the use and value of the property caused by the act of a neighbour is that really there would be little that the adjoining owner could do to prevent such a right being acquired. When your house with the view has been there for 19 years is he to erect a 30 foot screen to block your view just to demonstrate that no easement has been obtained?

The difficulty with this argument, as was acknowledged by Bramwell L.J., is that this may be as much true about rights which undoubtedly can be the subject of an easement, such as rights of support and rights of light, as it is of other advantages which have been held not to give rise to prescriptive rights.

The wide concept of maintaining natural support was endorsed in *Holbeck Hall Hotel v Scarborough BC*,[92] which put a partial obligation on the landowner to protect his land consisting of a cliff from falling into the sea and thereby exposing the nearby hotel. This Court of Appeal decision upheld *Bradburn v Lindsay*[93] and made clear that the law of nuisance can be used wherever the negligence of an occupier of land puts the adjoining occupier at risk. As set out above[94] the problem of protection from the weather has been substantially resolved by the Party Wall etc. Act 1996. This Act deals not only with party walls as traditionally defined, but with any boundary wall. The problem addressed in *Bradburn v Lindsay* and *Holbeck Hall v Scarborough BC*, however, goes further, dealing not only with dramatic risks like collapsing cliffs, but also with the destructive effect of a neighbouring derelict property, not only in relation to loss of support or even damp penetration, but also escape of dry rot. However, as stated, the method used is not the creation of a new negative easement, but the general law of private nuisance.

10.21 The problem usually arises with negative easements. "The law has been very chary of creating any new negative easements."[95] The two main negative easements are the right of light and the right of support. Superficially negative rights which have been accepted as easements such as a right to receive air through a defined channel, e.g. through a cellar vent,[96] and a right to receive a flow of water in an artificial stream,[97] both have positive elements since in each case there is a defined channel which the servient owner could block should he so wish.

The negative rights of light and support are of ancient origin and are difficult to fit in with the normal doctrines of easements. It would be better in some ways to treat them as remnants of the fledgling doctrine of

---

[92] [2000] Q.B. 836; [2000] 2 W.L.R. 1396.
[93] [1983] 2 All E.R. 408.
[94] Ch. 6.
[95] per Lord Denning M.R. in *Phipps v Pears* [1965] 1 Q.B. 76 at 83.
[96] *Bass v Gregory* (1890) L.R. 25 Q.B.D. 481.
[97] *Keewatin Power Co Ltd v Lake of the Woods Milling Co Ltd* [1930] A.C. 640.

prescription as creating rights sui generis which have a separate existence from easements, but there is no doubt on the authorities that they must both be regarded as true easements.

Not surprisingly various attempts have been made to set up new nega- **10.22** tive easements by analogy. In *Webb v Bird*[98] a claim was made to a right of passage of air to the plaintiff's windmill. A similar proposition was put forward in *Bryant v Lefever*[99] where the building of a higher house disrupted the plaintiff's chimneys and caused them to smoke, and also in *Harris v de Pina*.[100] Since these 19th century cases no attempt has been made to establish a right to the flow of air. The distinction in principle between the natural right to a free flow of air and a right to uninterrupted light is hard to understand. It would have been perfectly possible to formulate a rule whereby the dominant tenement was only entitled to a reasonable flow of air and whereby the erection and retention of a building such as a windmill could increase the burden on the adjoining land in much the same way as the duty not to block light is affected by the placing and size of the windows. The argument that a prescriptive right to a flow of air cannot arise because a flow of air cannot be blocked is of little substance, since, in a case of an easement of light, it is only in practice possible for the potential servient owner to prevent an easement arising by blocking the light through a particular window, if it actually abuts the servient tenement and, even then, the expense and inconvenience of erecting such a blockage could be considerable. There is nothing to stop a potential servient owner doing much the same to prevent an easement arising for a flow of air to chimneys, windmills and air-conditioning ducts. The basis on which the courts have rejected claims to such rights must, therefore, be the public policy of minimising the extent to which an owner's right to use land as he wishes is restricted by private rights and of leaving to the planning laws any protection from damage due to the disruption of air flow. The pollution of air, of course, is another matter since if it is severe enough it can give rise to a claim in nuisance whether or not the building or operation polluted has been in existence for a long period.

Just as there can be no easement entitling a person to a flow of air, equally an easement cannot arise giving a right of prospect. If a landowner wishes to reserve such a right expressly then it can only be by express covenant, which may be equally enforceable, but operates under different rules. The policy behind this is easier to understand and accept. A view or prospect is essentially subjective and to provide every long-standing householder with such a right would constitute a very severe

[98] (1863) 13 C.B. N.S. 841.
[99] (1878–79) L.R. 4 C.P.D. 172.
[100] (1886) 33 Ch. D. 238.

restraint on adjoining land, much greater than an obligation not to destroy the right of light or even a right to the free passage of air.

10.23   The natural right of drainage is considered in Ch. 21. Following *Green v Lord Somerleyton*[101] there is little difference between the natural obligation in negligence and any additional easement of drainage. On the face of it a natural right, such as the right to allow natural water to drain onto neighbouring land by force of gravity, should be superior to an easement to the same effect, since it does not require proof of land user and cannot be lost by interruption or abandonment. However, it seems that the natural right to drain your land does not bring with it a right to ensure that the lower land is able to receive it, by entering on that land to clear ditches. In *Palmer v Bowman*,[102] the Court of Appeal held that as the right to drain onto lower land by percolation was a natural right, it could not become an easement by lost modern grant.

The other negative right which has been put forward but rejected is a right to be protected from the weather. In *Phipps v Pears*[103] it was held that a right to be protected from the weather cannot arise by prescription. At first sight this decision seems obviously right. If I choose to build my house right beside my neighbour's house I can hardly complain if he chooses to pull down his house. The law has provided redress where removing the adjoining building actually removes my support, but if I have relied on my neighbour to provide protection from the weather as well as support the right to support is not extended to cover this further protection. This is part of the policy of not extending the categories of negative easements. However, *Rees v Skerrett*[104] accepted, for the first time, the right to "wind support", i.e. a right of support relating to the effects of the wind. This is really the logical extension of *Bradburn v Lindsay*[105] where the problem arose in particularly serious form in respect of a party wall. The court, without expressly finding that there was an easement to keep the property in repair nevertheless held that there was a breach of duty.

As set out above[106] the problem of protection from the weather has been substantially resolved by the Party Wall etc. Act 1996. This Act refers not only to party walls as traditionally defined but any wall on the boundary. It can be assumed that anyone with a building set back from the boundary cannot expect any right to be protected from the weather by his neighbour's land or buildings.

In deciding whether the right is capable of forming the subject-matter of an easement it is submitted that there is a distinction to be made

---

[101] [2003] EWCA Civ 198.
[102] [2000] 1 W.L.R. 842.
[103] [1965] 1 Q.B. 76.
[104] [2001] EWCA Civ 760; [2001] 1 W.L.R. 1541.
[105] [1983] 2 All E.R. 408; see Ch. 6.
[106] Ch. 6.

between rights created by express grant and prescriptive claims though this idea is rejected by Lord Scott in *Moncrieff v Jamieson*.[107] Where there is an express grant the very existence of the grant shows that the servient owner intended to create a right of some kind and all that the court has to do is to decide the nature of what was granted and whether or not it is enforceable. In such cases the court has to construe the grant to find out whether what was granted was intended to be an easement, or a covenant, or a licence, or whether it amounts, in effect to a conveyance of the land. If what was intended was an easement, the court must of course consider whether it is too vague and imprecise to form the subject matter of a grant, but in such cases will incline towards finding a valid grant rather than depriving the grantee of any benefit. A good example of a comparatively recent type of easement is the right to erect or connect to television or radio aerials.[108]

It is, of course, only if the right claimed meets the three basic require- **10.24** ments of an easement, in that it benefits land of the grantee, affects land of the grantor and is sufficiently certain, that the further question may arise of whether it is capable of forming the subject-matter of a grant. In the last resort the decision will be one of public policy, since it is public policy to restrict the extent to which land is encumbered by perpetual incidents, even if the grantor wishes it. This policy is in line with the policy of the Law of Property Act 1925 of restricting the extent to which land is encumbered with minor interests.

The classic exposition of the limits of what will be construed as creating an easement by express grant is *Re Ellenborough Park*[109] where the court considered whether a right to use a common garden could be the subject-matter of a grant. On the face of it, there seemed little difficulty. A right to wander freely seems little different from many other positive easements,[110] but the principles were somewhat clouded by the fact that a *"jus spatiandi"* or a right to wander at will, cannot form the subject of a Roman Law servitude. Furthermore Farwell J. had on more than one occasion said in terms that no such right can exist as an easement.

It is not entirely clear from the judgment of Lord Evershed M.R. whether he considered that a *jus spatiandi*, in the sense a right to wander at will, can exist, but that the right granted in *Re Ellenborough Park* was not such a right, or whether he accepted that such a right cannot exist. Initially in his judgment he is at pains to distinguish the right granted in that case from such a *jus spatiandi*, but subsequently in his

---

[107] [2007] UKHL 42; [2007] 1 W.L.R. 2620.
[108] See *The Encyclopaedia of Forms & Precedents*, 5th edn (London: Butterworths), Vol.13(1), paras 1631, 1632.
[109] *Re Ellenborough Park* [1956] Ch. 131.
[110] See, e.g. *Keith v Twentieth Century Club* (1904) 73 L.J. Ch. 545, where the existence of such a right went unchallenged.

critique of Farwell J.'s decisions he does not rule out the existence of such a right.

The decision nevertheless is an example of a case where it was obvious that both parties intended the grantees to have the benefit of the right granted and accordingly the court was prepared to find that such a right existed despite misgivings about the theoretical basis of the claim.

10.25   The situation is quite different in the case of prescriptive claims. Neuberger L.J. maintained in *McAdams Homes Ltd v Robinson*[111] that:

> "In my judgment, at least in the great majority of cases, there should be little difference in the principles applicable to the two types of cases ... It arises out of a set of facts which, pursuant to principles developed by the judges (albeit that prescription has in part been codified by the ill-drafted Prescription Act 1832) result in a deemed grant of an easement. In each case the existence, nature and extent of the deemed grant must depend on the circumstances existing at the date of the grant."

However, in reality the court has to be satisfied that it is right to infer or impute a right from the action of owners and occupiers of the dominant land. Where the claim comes within the accepted categories this may be simply a question of proving user, but the court will be much less inclined to find a prescriptive easement where the use comes into an unusual category.

While express claims in the nature of a *jus spatiandi* have been accepted, prescriptive claims to wander freely over land have not been upheld. Most prescriptive claims to use land for recreation have been presented as customary rights in the public at large or in the inhabitants of a particular area,[112] or as a right incidental to a town or village green or rights of common.[113] There can be no easement in such cases in the absence of a dominant tenement. There is no reason in theory why a right to wander over land should not be presented as being attached to a particular property. After all a right of way need not be over a defined path.[114] However, there is no reported case of a prescriptive easement to wander freely over neighbouring land and such a right would be very difficult to prove because its effect would be to prevent development of that land. In such circumstances the court would be reluctant to find that any such user was as of right rather than permissive.

---

[111] [2004] EWCA Civ 214; [2005] 1 P. & C.R. 30.
[112] *R. v Doncaster MBC Ex p. Braim* 85 L.G.R. 233; (1989) 57 P. & C.R. 1; see *R. (on the application of Beresford) v Sunderland City Council* [2003] UKHL 60; [2004] 1 A.C. 889.
[113] *ADM Milling v Tewksbury Town Council* [2011] EWHC 595 (Ch).
[114] *Wimbledon & Putney Commons Conservators v Dixon* (1875–76) 1 Ch. D. 362.

Another matter which has concerned the courts in deciding whether a **10.26** right, whether by grant or prescription, amounts to an easement, is whether it involves not just an incident, but actual occupation of the servient tenement by the plaintiff. Some fairly forlorn submissions have been made based on this principle. There could never have been much doubt that a right to use a lavatory, though, like a right of way, it involves temporary exclusive possession, is nevertheless capable of amounting to an easement.[115] Equally it seems tolerably obvious that a right to enter the servient owner's land to clean windows placed on the boundary is no more of a burden on the land than a right of way and certainly does not amount to joint occupation.[116] Even the proposition in *Re Ellenborough Park*[117] that a right to use a pleasure ground amounted to joint occupation seems pretty plainly wrong though it clearly exercised the minds of the Court of Appeal. While the right to use the pleasure grounds, like a right of way and many other easements, considerably restricts the uses to which the owner can put the servient tenement, it falls far short of occupation by the dominant owner.

There have, however, been more difficult cases. In *Copeland v Greenhalf*[118] the right to store and repair vehicles claimed by prescription "amounted practically to a claim to the beneficial user of the land".[119] Again in *Ward v Bruce*[120] the right to break up vessels and to maintain the silt level on what had been a dock was similarly too extensive a right to be the subject of an easement.

On the other hand, a right to use a coalshed, which must have excluded the servient owner totally, was upheld in *Wright v MacAdam*[121] and a prescriptive right to place chicken coops (though not boxes) on the servient tenement was upheld in *Smith v Gates*.[122] A right to put up illuminated signs was held to be capable of amounting to an easement in *William Hill (Southern) v Cabras*[123] even though it involved exclusive possession of the space where the sign was placed.

The most important easement to develop in recent years is the right to park. This issue was fully considered by the House of Lords in *Moncrieff v Jamieson*.[124] Although this was a Scottish case concerning servitudes, the English law was fully considered. The outcome of this case was that a right to park can be ancillary to a right of way. This involved consideration of whether a right to park can be a self-standing easement.

[115] *Miller v Emcer Homes* [1956] Ch. 304; [1956] 2 W.L.R. 267.
[116] *Ward v Kirkland* [1967] Ch. 194; [1966] 1 W.L.R. 601.
[117] [1956] Ch. 131.
[118] *Copeland v Greenhalf* [1952] Ch. 488.
[119] *Copeland v Greenhalf* [1952] Ch. 488 per Upjohn J.
[120] [1959] 2 Lloyd's Rep 472.
[121] [1949] 2 K.B. 744.
[122] [1952] 160 E.G. 512.
[123] [1987] 54 P. & C.R. 42.
[124] [2007] UKHL 42; [2007] 1 W.L.R. 2620.

"I can see no reason in principle, subject to a few qualifications, why any right of limited use of the land of a neighbour that is of its nature of benefit to the dominant land and its owners from time to time should not be capable of being created as a servitudal right *in rem* appurtenant to the dominant land ... An essential qualification of the above stated proposition, a qualification I would derive from the all important *civiliter* principle, is that the right must be such that a reasonable use thereof by the owner of the dominant land would not be inconsistent with the beneficial ownership of the servient owner."[125]

This wide statement, however, is qualified by two principles:

(1) the first is the *civiliter* principle, which is akin to the principle of excessive use. It means that the owner of the land must still be able to make use of the parking area, either for his own vehicles or any other use he might need to make of it e.g. getting access to services.

(2) the second the ouster principle, which is at the heart of the limitation discussed above. He concludes that,

"sole use for a limited purpose is not, in my opinion, inconsistent with the servient owner's retention of possession and control or inconsistent with the nature of an easement".

The issue therefore is not exclusiveness, but ouster.

The five speeches given in this case, show that the principles are difficult to apply in practice. A fixed space in a car park gives a greater level of ouster than a general right to park anywhere in the car park, or anywhere on a piece of open ground. On the other hand a general right to park, if over-used, could result in total ouster of the owner. Parking is, in essence, a kind of storage and storage only amounts to ouster when it effectively deprives the owner of possession of the land. It is, therefore, all a matter of degree.

One of the most important easements required by a property is the right to the benefit of service installations. In purchasing or leasing part of, for example, a tower block the purchaser or lessee needs the rights of passage or water, soil, gas, electricity and telephone. Water and drainage have been considered in many cases over the years,[126] but issues about gas, electricity and telephone have been considered more recently. Frequently these are obtained directly from the supplier, but in some cases the supply will be indirect.

[125] per Lord Scott at [47].
[126] See Ch. 21.

There is no real doubt that such an easement can be granted, but the problems created by this category are dealt with in *Duffy v Lamb*[127] and *Cardwell v Walker*.[128] The difficulty is that such services have to be paid for and can be cut off either by throwing a switch or by just failing to pay the bill and leaving it to the utility company to cut off the supply. The Court of Appeal decided, first, that the passage of electricity and telecommunications is essentially the same as the passage of water. If the current is there, the servient owner must not stop it, even by throwing a switch. It is the same as with a right to a flow of water or to allow effluent to pass. The servient owner does not have to keep the lines in repair or even to pay the bills, but he must not do anything positive to obstruct the passage. In *Cardwell v Walker*, Neuberger J. made it clear that the fact that the right was subject to payment did not prevent it from being an easement.

If such an easement can be granted by express grant, it would seem to follow that it could pass by prescription, for example where a landowner has had the benefit of a private electricity cable or telephone line passing through the land of a neighbour for more than 20 years, this could give rise to a prescriptive right not to have it removed.

The conclusion to be drawn from these cases, therefore, is that if it can **10.27** be shown that a right claimed amounts in effect to beneficial ownership of the servient tenement, this is certainly a valid basis for defeating an easement (though it may give rise to a claim to ownership by adverse possession).[129] This, however, is not to say that any easement which involves an element of exclusion from the land of the servient owner will be so defeated. It is all a matter of degree and impression and it will, in practice if not in principle, be much easier to prove the validity of an express right, even if it involves a degree of exclusive possession, than to show a similar right by prescription. The principle of *civiliter* or excessive user can ensure that a right which may amount to exclusive use while it is being exercised is not allowed to be extended to amount to ouster of the servient owner.

A right which amounts to a profit à prendre cannot also be an easement.[130] Therefore, a right cannot form the subject-matter of an easement if it involves removing part of the land (as in quarrying) or the produce of the land, such as fish or game. It seems that removing sea coal which is washed up on the seashore could only be a profit and not an easement.[131]

---

[127] [1998] 75 P. & C.R. 364.
[128] [2003] EWHC 3117 (Ch); [2004] 2 P. & C.R. 9.
[129] See Ch. 5.
[130] See later for profits à prendre and para.11.09 et seq. for the difference between easements and profits.
[131] *Alfred F Beckett Ltd v Lyons* [1967] Ch. 449.

8   An easement attaches to the land and not the owner

10.28   An easement is an incident to land and as such it is a right annexed to the land and not a personal right in the owner. The main consequences of this are: (a) that it can be exercised by anyone who is entitled to use the land (b) that it can be enforced by anyone in possession of the land and (c) that it cannot be alienated separately from the land.

(a)   Exercise of the easement

10.29   The principle that anyone who is entitled to use the land can exercise the easement applies mainly to positive easements. A negative easement, such as a right of support, is not exercised at all in any real sense.

The effect of this principle can be seen in its simplest form in a right of way. A freehold right of way can be exercised by the person in possession of the land, whether the freeholder himself or his tenant or licensee in occupation.[132] Furthermore it can usually be used by all lawful visitors to the property. Once the right of way is established, the identity of the persons using it is immaterial.[133] It is not open to the servient owner, therefore, to permit the owner to use the way but to seek to prevent the milkman delivering milk, or friends calling.

In the case of an express grant, there is no need for the deed to specify who can use the right at all. In the absence of any list of persons entitled to use or visit the way the right will be exercisable by anyone who is entitled to use the land that constitutes the dominant tenement and words such as "heirs and assigns and their servants customers and workmen and the tenants and occupiers" will be treated as illustrative rather than exhaustive.[134] Equally a prescriptive right is not restricted to the people who have actually used the way or other right. Once it is established it will extend to all persons entitled to occupy or visit the dominant tenement.

10.30   This principle is, however, subject to the terms of the grant itself. In *Keith v Twentieth Century Club*[135] the dominant owners owned several properties in a London square to which were annexed a right to use the communal gardens. The grant gave this right to the purchaser,

> "his heirs executors administrators and assigns and his and their lessees and sub-lessees or tenants (being occupiers for the time being of [Stanley Gardens]) and for his and their families and friends."

---

[132]   *Hammond v Prentice Brothers Ltd* [1920] 1 Ch. 201.
[133]   *Woodhouse & Co v Kirkland* [1970] 1 W.L.R. 1185; [1970] 2 All E.R. 587.
[134]   *Hammond v Prentice Brothers* [1920] 1 Ch. 201.
[135]   (1904) 73 L.J. Ch. 545.

It was held that this did not entitle the right to be exercised by the residents of a residential club for ladies established on the land. This decision, however, seems out of line with other decisions on the construction of express grants such as *Hammond v Prentice Brothers*[136] where a similar provision was held to be only illustrative and usually a very specific limitation on the terms of the grant will be required to restrict the persons who can exercise it.

Keith v Twentieth Century Club[137] illustrated the problems that can arise where the use actually made of the rights under the easement is beyond that contemplated at the time of the grant. On the face of it, the case was decided on the terms of the grant itself, but a similar result might have been arrived at on the basis of excessive user,[138] a principle which was not fully developed in 1904. It is, therefore, usually more appropriate to challenge the exercise of a right by claiming excessive user than by suggesting that the user is outside the terms of the grant.

The effect of these decisions on user is that, while the owner of the easement cannot alienate the easement itself (whether by sale or lease) separately from the land,[139] he can let or sub-let or licence out the land or part of it with the benefit of the easement. Thus a right to extract water could be sub-let with the land and then used for commercial extraction and a way could be licenced to a transport manager with a small part of the land, but a right to use an advertising hoarding, if it was held to be an easement, could not be let out to persons unconnected with the dominant tenement.[140]

Any problems created by the rule that the benefit of the easement can **10.31** be sub-let with part of the dominant tenement are effectively dealt with by a number of rules which are considered elsewhere. Firstly the right can only be exercised in conjunction with the land. Thus, as elaborated above, to use a way as an access to other separate land (even if the access is via the dominant tenement or part of it) is not permitted.[141] Equally, while extraction of water for use in a commercial operation on the dominant land would be permitted subject to the excessive user principles, extraction for the purpose of a commercial operation elsewhere, even if the water was carried across the dominant tenement, would not be permitted. In effect, therefore, the user has to be in connection with the use of the

---

[136] [1920] 1 Ch. 201.
[137] (1904) 73 L.J. Ch. 545.
[138] See later *Jelbert v Davis* [1968] 1 W.L.R. 589, but see *White v Grand Hotel Eastbourne* [1913] 1 Ch. 113.
[139] See below para.10.34.
[140] *Clapman v Edwards* [1938] 2 All E.R. 507.
[141] *Bracewell v Appleby* [1975] Ch. 408; *Peacock v Custins* [2002] 1 W.L.R. 1815; [2001] 2 All E.R. 827; *Macepark v Sargeant* [2003] EWHC 427 (Ch); [2003] 1 W.L.R. 2284 and *Massey v Boulden* [2003] 1 W.L.R. 1792.

dominant tenement or part of it. Furthermore, the use made of the ease-ment can be challenged as excessive in quantity even if the nature of the user comes within the terms of the grant.

As the right attaches to the land rather than the owner there is no reason why it should not be sub-divided between several owners of the dominant tenement. There is nothing to stop a right of way granted to the owner of a field being used by the purchasers of building plots when that field is sold off for building development, providing that the user is not held to be excessive.[142]

(b) Enforcement of the easement

10.32   This subject will be dealt with in more detail later. A person who is entitled to exercise an easement is not necessarily entitled to enforce it. If a way is blocked by the servient owner and this prevents me from visiting my friend I cannot sue, but my friend can do so.

An action enforcing an easement is an action in nuisance and actions in nuisance are brought by the person or persons in possession of the land. This has raised various questions. First, it is clear that the right extends to tenants, including weekly tenants[143] and tenants at will.[144] Secondly, it applies to licensees who are lawfully in possession. An occupier of a bedsitter, therefore, could sue to enforce a right to use the entrance way even if it was not owned by his landlord.

The law is not entirely clear where the plaintiff is certainly in posses-sion, but there is doubt about his title. It was held in *Foster v Warblington Urban District Council*[145] in relation to a claim in nuisance that the person in occupation of some oyster beds could sue in nuisance for damage by pollution regardless of his title. This principle was more recently affirmed in New Zealand in *Paxhaven Holdings v Attorney General*.[146] However, the position in the case of easements is not necessarily the same, because in order to claim an easement the plaintiff must show not only that he is in actual possession of the dominant tenement, but also that he is entitled to the easement. Since the easement is an incident of the title to the domi-nant tenement, it would appear that a person who has no right to occupy the dominant tenement would have no right to enforce the easement.

10.33   Thus, while it has not been decided, it seems on principle that it would be open to the owner of a servient tenement to challenge the exercise of an easement on the grounds that the claimant, or the person through

---

[142] *McAdam Homes Ltd v Robinson* [2004] EWCA Civ 214; [2005] 1 P. & C. R. 30.
[143] *Wright v MacAdam* [1949] 2 K.B. 744.
[144] *Burgess v Woodstock* [1955] 4 D.L.R. 615.
[145] [1906] 1 K.B. 648.
[146] [1974] 2 N.Z.L.R. 185.

whom the claimant claims a right to possession, had no title to the dominant tenement. This is not really raising a jus tertii since the owner of the servient tenement is entitled to his land and he is entitled to require the person claiming to show that he has a right to the easement he claims.

Where the owner of the dominant tenement is not in possession this does not prevent him from suing, since any obstruction or interference with the easement will affect his reversion. It is usual to try to ensure that the owner of the land is involved in any easement action; otherwise he will not be bound by the decision. Indeed the court may refuse to make a declaration in an action against a lessee or other occupier of the dominant tenement, unless the owner is also included in the action.

(c)   An easement cannot be alienated separately from the dominant tenement

It is axiomatic that, as the easement is an incident of the dominant tene- **10.34** ment, it cannot be separated from it to create an easement in gross.[147] If the right is not connected with the dominant tenement, then it is a contractual right that may well be assignable, but if this is the case then the law of contract and not the law of easements applies to it. In *Clapman v Edwards*[148] it was the owner of the servient tenement who claimed that the right to use the adjoining wall for advertising was an easement and therefore could not be let out to people unconnected with the dominant property. The court eventually decided that it was not an easement at all, but it was never doubted that if it was an easement it could not be alienated from the dominant tenement, and therefore could not be let out to other advertisers.

---

[147] *Ackroyd v Smith* (1850) 10 C.B. 164.
[148] [1938] 2 All E.R. 507.

Chapter Eleven
Easements and Other Rights

1. Easements and natural rights

Easements are rights attaching to property over and above those to **11.01** which an owner is entitled by virtue of his right of ownership or occupation, sometimes known as "natural rights". Interference with natural rights gives rise to an action in nuisance and it is more usual to look at such rights in terms of what conduct amounts to a breach than to define the rights themselves.

However, in *Bryant v Lefever*[1] Bramwell L.J., giving the judgment of himself and Brett L.J., sought to set out what they saw as natural rights:

"First, what is the right of the occupier of a house in relation to air independently of length of enjoyment? It is the same as that which land and its owner or occupier have: it is not greater because a house has been built: that puts no greater burden on adjoining owners. What then is the right of land and its owner or occupier? It is to have all the natural incidents and advantages, as nature would produce them; there is a right to all the light and air that would come, to all the rain that would fall, to all the wind that would blow; a right that the rain which would pass over the land should not be stopped and made to fall on it; a right that the heat from the sun should not be stopped and reflected on it; a right that the wind should not be checked, but should be able to escape freely; and if it were possible that these rights were interfered with by one having no right, no doubt action would lie. But those natural rights are subject to rights of adjoining owners, who, for the benefit of the community, must have rights in relation to the use and enjoyment of their property that qualify and interfere with those of their neighbours, rights to use property in the various ways in which property is commonly lawfully used. A hedge, a wall, a fruit tree, would each affect the land next to which it was planted or built. They would keep off some

[1] *Bryant v Lefever* (1878–79) L.R. 4 C.P.D. 172.

light, some air, some heat, some rain, when coming from one direction, and prevent the escape of air, of heat, of wind, of rain when coming from the other. But nobody could doubt that in such case no action would lie; nor will it in the case of a house being built and having such consequences."

This formulation is unusual in English law in that it seeks to set out the rights of a landowner or occupier. It is much more common to formulate the law in terms of the duties of adjoining owners. The right to enjoy the benefits of your land is a liberty which is of no concern to the courts until it is interfered with. This interference with the rights of the occupier of land gives rise to the tort of nuisance which is not part of the subject-matter of this book.

11.02   It is, however, instructive to look at these natural rights since the law of easements consists of additional rights or incidents grafted on to those natural rights in a particular case. Accordingly, if the action of the neighbour infringes the owner or occupier's natural rights there is no need for him to prove an easement.

Bramwell L.J. refers to the natural rights to light, air, heat, rainfall etc. However, interference with these natural rights will not necessarily give rise to a claim in nuisance. It has been seen that easements entitling the owner or occupier of land to the passage of air and the right to a prospect cannot arise by prescription. A fortiori, therefore, there is no such right in nuisance. Equally where an owner or occupier's light is interfered with, he will only have a claim if he can show an easement. Other rights, such as the right not to be unduly affected by noise or by airborne pollution, on the other hand, have always been accepted as giving rise to an action in nuisance even if long user of the land for the purposes affected by the pollution cannot be shown.

This distinction between the law of nuisance and the law of easements has most commonly arisen in respect of the right of support The natural right to support and the easement of support for buildings will be more fully dealt with later,[2] but the problems can be used to illustrate the distinction between natural rights and the additional incidents of ownership that are easements.

11.03   In *Leakey v National Trust*[3] the Court of Appeal, following and extending the Privy Council decision of *Goldman v Hargrave*,[4] went beyond the long-established concept of a natural right to support of land by neighbouring

---

[2] See Ch. 19.
[3] *Leakey v National Trust for Places of Historic Interest or Natural Beauty* [1980] Q.B. 485; [1980] 1 All E.R. 17.
[4] [1967] 1 A.C. 645; [1966] 3 W.L.R. 513.

land to formulate a general duty in relation to hazards occurring on neighbouring land:

> "Under English law there was both in principle and on authority a general duty imposed on occupiers in relation to hazards occurring on their land, whether the hazards were natural or man-made. A person on whose land a hazard naturally occurred, whether in the soil itself or in something on or growing on the land, and which encroached or threatened to encroach on another's land thereby causing or threatening to cause damage, was under a duty, if he knew or ought to have known of the risk of encroachment, to do what was reasonable in all the circumstances to prevent or minimise the risk of the known or foreseeable damage or injury to the other person or his property, and was liable in nuisance if he did not."[5]

That case concerned a natural mump or hill existing on the defendant's land part of which had fallen onto the plaintiff's land. Had the mump been man-made there would have been no difficulty. It would have constituted a nuisance, and damages and an injunction would have been granted regardless of how long any buildings on the neighbouring land had existed. But the mump was natural. Despite this, the court held that the defendants owed the plaintiff a duty to protect him from the risk that it would fall on his property.

In *Holbeck Hall v Scarborough BC*[6] the principle was extended further to loss of support by failing to maintain a nearby cliff. Since then the principle has been further extended beyond cases of support to encroaching tree roots, in *Delaware Mansions v Westminster City Council* [7]to obligations in respect of natural drainage in *Green v Somerleyton*[8] and to roof repairs in *Abbahall v Smee*.[9]

The relevance of these cases to the law of easements is that if a claim can be pursued in nuisance there is no need to seek to prove interference with an easement. On the other hand, as *Green v Somerleyton* shows, the duty of care owned by the upland owner can be overridden by an easement of drainage.

The distinction between natural rights and easements, therefore, is that a natural right is a right which attaches to the land without any express or implied act of the parties and without any need for prescription, whereas an easement is an artificial incident to land created either by an express or implied grant or reservation or by prescription. As is normal in

---

[5] *Leakey v National Trust for Places of Historic Interest or Natural Beauty* [1980] 1 All E.R. 17, headnote.
[6] [2000] Q.B. 836; [2000] 2 W.L.R. 1396.
[7] [2001] UKHL 55; [2002] 1 A.C. 321.
[8] [2003] EWCA Civ 198.
[9] [2002] EWCA Civ 1831; [2003] 1 W.L.R. 1472.

English law, these natural rights are more often expressed in terms of the duties owed by neighbours resulting in a cause of action in tort.

2. Easements and licences

11.04   It has been seen[10] that there are various requirements before a right can become an easement. However, landowners in practice regularly purport to grant minor rights to others over their land which do not amount to easements. This may be because the right is not for the benefit of other land, or that it is not a right which is capable of becoming an easement. Thus a right granted to another person to walk on land may not be an easement because that person does not own nearby land. Such rights are not without legal effect, but take effect as licences.

The existence of a licence prevents a prescriptive right from coming into existence, because if a use of land is exercised as a result of a licence granted by the owner of the land, the use is said to be "precario" i.e. precarious or subject to being withdrawn. There is a crucial difference between a licence, which prevents time running, and mere tolerance, which does not.[11]

A licence may be gratuitous or contractual. In the case of a contractual licence to occupy land it was held in *Greater London Council v Jenkins*[12] that,

> "when a contractual licence has been granted to a person who has been on the premises under a licence, he cannot be treated as a trespasser until a reasonable time after notice that the licence has been or will be withdrawn".[13]

It was suggested in *Minister of Health v Belotti*[14] that the notice determines the licence immediately, but does not become operative until a reasonable period has expired. This technical distinction, however, was only made to justify a decision that a notice which is too short is not void, but takes effect after a reasonable time.

11.05   It is not entirely easy to apply these principles to licences to exercise incidental rights, such as a licence to use a way or a licence to extract water or to park a car. It seems, however, that similar principles will apply. The result, therefore, is that the licensee must be given a reasonable time to re-organise things. If, for example, a licence had been granted to

---

[10] See above para.10.03 et seq.
[11] *R. (on the application of Beresford) v Sunderland City Council* [2003] UKHL 60; [2004] 1 A.C. 889, considered in Ch. 15 below.
[12] [1975] 1 W.L.R. 155; [1975] 1 All E.R. 354.
[13] *Greater London Council v Jenkins* [1975] 1 All E.R. 354 at 357b.
[14] [1944] 1 All E.R. 238.

enable a person to obtain access to his home by car, the court would not grant an injunction until he had had a reasonable time to make other arrangements. Until that time has passed, it seems that a person exercising the licence would not be a trespasser.[15]

It used to be said that a licence created only a contractual right and that accordingly it could be terminated even in breach of contract, subject, of course, to a claim in damages. However, this rule applies to temporary licences such as a seat in the theatre. Irrevocable licences and licences to occupy land which can only be terminated on notice certainly do exist. There are many cases where a licensee has been led to believe by the true owner that his licence to occupy property will not be revoked and has acted in reliance on that promise. Courts have refused to allow the true owner to recover the land and, indeed, have ordered the land to be conveyed to the licensee.[16] There is no reason why the same should not apply to licences falling short of a right to occupy, such as a right to park or a personal right to use a way. Inevitably a court is more likely to find a licence irrevocable when it is a licence to occupy a person's home, but there seems no logical reason why the same principle should not extend to any licence.[17]

Licences are commonly contained in covenants in leases. An example would be a covenant by the landlord in a lease of a flat forming part of a block of flats that the lessee should have a right to park in the communal car park. Such licences are irrevocable unless the lease is determined or forfeited.

Where the words "grant licence" are used in a deed this creates a licence and not an easement, even though the right granted has all the essential features of an easement and was expressed to be made on behalf of the grantors and their successors in title and to be for the benefit of the grantees and their successors in title. As a result of such careless use of words the right granted was not binding on successors in title of the grantors.[18]

3. Easements and covenants

Covenants and easements have always run in parallel, but their paths **11.06** have rarely converged. A covenant is strictly no more than a contract arising by deed (though, unlike a contract, it can be unilateral), but the use of covenants in relation to land has given rise to a large body of law whereby the benefit of covenants can be annexed to the land and the burden of covenants can pass in equity with the land.

---

[15] *Robson v Hallett* [1967] 2 Q.B. 939; [1967] 3 W.L.R. 28.

[16] See Ch. 3—Estoppel, para.3.10 et seq.

[17] *Evans v Cynon Valley BC*[1992] E.G. 3 (C.S.) where an irrevocable licence was found at first instance, but overturned on appeal.

[18] *IDC Group v Clark* (1993) 65 P. & C.R. 179.

While easements are expressed in terms of rights of the dominant tenement over adjoining land, covenants are expressed in terms of obligations imposed on the servient tenement. Since they must always be contained in a deed, whether expressly or by implication, such obligations cannot arise by prescription.

It has been seen that there are only a few negative easements, such as the right of support and the right of light, and that these normally arise by prescription. Such things as the right to a view and to a free passage of air have been rejected as prescriptive rights. However, a purchaser of land (or a vendor retaining neighbouring land) can protect such interests by means of a covenant. Thus a view can be protected by a covenant restricting building on the land sold or restricting the height of boundary walls and the support of a building may be protected by a covenant requiring that a retaining wall be maintained.

11.07 A covenant relating to land can only oblige the covenantor to act or refrain from acting on his own land. Furthermore as between freeholders only the burden of restrictive covenants can be transferred to successors in title. Nevertheless a covenant can give the covenantee a right to enter the covenantor's land. For example, the standard leasehold covenants include a right for the lessor to enter to inspect the premises. A lessor could covenant to allow the lessee joint use of the coal-shed, but granting an easement to use the coalshed would have the same effect.[19]

Where there is an overlap of this kind it is likely to be the form of the grant which decides whether the right is construed as a covenant or an easement. If the lease grants a right to a coal-shed it will be treated as an easement.[20] If the lease contains a covenant by the landlord to permit the lessee to use the coal-shed it will be construed as a covenant. Thus in *William Hill (Southern) Ltd v Cabras*[21] there were two illuminated signs maintained by the lessee on the lessor's property. It was held that the right to maintain the signs was an easement attaching to the leasehold property by virtue of the reference in the parcels to the premises "including the appurtenances thereto". It was therefore expressed as a right attached to the leasehold premises and was held to be an easement. But the lease could have contained a covenant by the landlord requiring him to permit the lessee to maintain the illuminated signs. If the lease had been drafted in this way, then the lessor would have been obliged to allow the lessee to keep them there and the lessee's right to go onto the lessor's property to maintain them would have been treated as a licence. Where such a right is construed as a covenant, the right of entry onto the covenantor's land is treated as a licence coupled with a grant which cannot, therefore, be revoked as long as the covenant exists.

---

[19] *Wright v MacAdam* [1949] 2 K.B. 744.
[20] *Wright v MacAdam* [1949] 2 K.B. 744.
[21] (1987) 54 P. & C.R. 42.

Covenants have been used to circumvent problems over perpetuities in **11.08** respect of easements. In *Sharpe v Durrant*[22] a right of way over a tramway which had not yet been built was void for perpetuity, but a corresponding covenant was held valid so that while the dominant owner did not have an easement to use the way, he was entitled to do so because the servient owner had covenanted not to stop him.

The law of covenants has gained a reputation for being arcane, but since *Federated Homes v Mill Lodge Properties*[23] the law has been simplified so that a restrictive covenant which touches and concerns the land will be annexed automatically to the land to be benefited unless a contrary intention is shown. It follows that a restrictive covenant follows the land in much the same way as an easement. The detailed law of covenants is, however, outside the scope of this book. Since easements and covenants have always been treated quite separately without any attempt at a synthesis it is inevitable that there are many detailed differences between the effect of a covenant and the effect of an easement, particularly in the way in which they are extinguished.

Covenants and easements come close together in respect of the anomalous easement of fencing.[24] Whilst fencing easements and fencing covenants may overlap, if the wording of the documents indicates that it is a covenant, then it is considered in accordance with the law of covenants.[25]

The Law Commission published a major Report on June 8, 2011.[26] In respect of covenants they have expressed considerable concerns about the state of the law of covenants, particularly in relation to positive covenants not running with the land and the technical difficulties in ensuring that the burden of restrictive covenants passes. They recommend the replacement of covenants with a new concept to be called "obligations" which would be an interest appurtenant to an estate in land analogous to an easement, thus bringing the law of easements and covenants closer together.

It remains to be seen whether their report is converted into legislation.

4. Easements and profits à prendre

Easements and profits à prendre are mutually exclusive; a right cannot **11.09** be both. There are various differences between easements and profits; for example an easement cannot exist in gross whereas a profit can. Equally there may also be restrictions on the extent to which a profit can be

---

[22] (1911) 55 S.J. 423.
[23] [1980] 1 W.L.R. 594; [1980] 1 All E.R. 371.
[24] See Ch. 22 below.
[25] *Sugarman v Porter* [2006] EWHC 331 (Ch); [2006] 2 P. & C.R. 14 at [46].
[26] Law Commission, *Making Land Work: Easements, Covenants and Profits à Prendre* (The Stationery Office, 2011), Law Com. No.327.

proved by custom,[27] whereas in appropriate circumstances an easement can arise by custom.[28] It may be important in some cases, therefore, to decide whether a right claimed is an easement or a profit.

The distinction between easements and profits has been authoritatively set out by the Court of Appeal in *Alfred F. Beckett Ltd v Lyons*[29] where Winn L.J., quoting Halsbury's Laws of England, stated that:

> "an easement only confers a right to utilise the servient tenement in a particular manner, or to prevent the commission of some act on that tenement, whereas a profit à prendre confers a right to take from the servient tenement some part of the soil of that tenement or minerals under it or some part of its natural produce, or the animals ferae naturae existing on it."

The most common examples of profits are rights of fishery, game rights and common rights of grazing. However, it can extend to mining rights and, as in *Alfred J. Beckett v Lyons* (though in that case the right was not proved), to collecting coal which has been washed up on the seashore.

11.10   It might be assumed that a right to extract water comes into the same category. However, because water is *publici juris* and does not actually belong to anybody,[30] extracting it is not a removal of part of the soil or its produce. A right to extract water is, therefore, an easement and not a profit.

Profits are something of an anachronism in a modern world of scarce resources and great demand, for such rights create considerable policing problems to prevent over-utilisation. The particular problems associated with profits are, however, dealt with later.[31]

5.   Easements and servitudes

11.11   To describe servitudes as the Scottish version of easements is the reverse of the truth. It would be truer to say that easements are the English version of servitudes. Servitudes originate in Roman law and Scottish law has followed and developed this concept. The English law of easements also owes much to the Roman law of servitudes and there are many similarities, but there are also many differences. Scottish cases on servitudes are only occasionally cited in English easement cases, but in *Moncrieff v Jamieson*[32] the House of Lords has not only carried out a

---

[27] per Winn L.J. in *Alfred F Beckett Ltd v Lyons* [1967] Ch. 449; [1967] 1 All E.R. 833 at 851D.
[28] *Egerton v Harding* [1975] Q.B. 62.
[29] [1967] Ch. 449; [1967] 1 All E.R. 833 at 851C.
[30] See para.8.01.
[31] Ch. 23—Profits à Prendre.
[32] [2007] UKHL 42; [2007] 1 W.L.R. 2620.

detailed analysis of the law of servitudes, but has also commented at length on their link with easements with extensive judgments from both Scottish and English law lords

It is useful, therefore to have some idea of the Scottish law and its differences from English law.

While easements are expressed in terms of incidents to property, servitudes are expressed in terms of obligations or burdens affecting land, though just as easements require land to be burdened and benefited, servitudes must attach to land to be benefited and cannot be alienated from it:

> " 'Servitude' is a burden on land or houses, imposed by agreement— express or implied—in favour of the owners of other tenements; whereby the owner of the burdened or 'servient' tenement and his heirs and singular successors in the subject, must submit to certain uses to be exercised by the owner of the other or 'dominant' tenement; or must suffer restraint in his own use or occupation of the property. Presupposing those extensions or restraints of the exclusive or absolute right of use which naturally proceed from the situation of coterminous properties, a servitude is a further limitation of that right in favour of the owner of another subject."[33]

There are, however, practical areas of difference. Scottish law makes no distinction between easements and profits. Servitudes can involve the right to remove substances from the land as in the servitude of pasturage and "fuel feel and divot", but servitudes are essentially restricted to uses that are "well-established and defined". As a result, therefore, sporting rights cannot be dissociated from any rights in the land themselves,[34] whereas salmon fishing rights can be granted separately from the land,[35] though such rights are not treated as servitudes.

By contrast, some obligations which would be regarded as covenants in England are treated as servitudes in Scotland. Thus an agreement not to build or to plant trees growing to more than a certain height is treated as a servitude whereas in England it would be a covenant. Furthermore there can be a servitude of "prospect" whereas no such easement is possible.[36]

One quite startling difference is that whereas in England negative **11.12** rights such as a right to light and a right to support are almost always obtained by prescription, only positive rights can be obtained by prescription in Scotland.

---

[33] Bell, Prin. para.979.
[34] D.Walker, *Principles of Scottish Private Law*, 4th edn (Oxford: Oxford University Press, 1989), p.36.
[35] D.Walker, *Principles of Scottish Private Law*, 4th edn (Oxford: Oxford University Press, 1989), p.36.
[36] *MacAlister v Wallace* [2003] S.C.L.R. 773.

It is clear, therefore, that the Scottish law of servitudes is a separate body of law from English easements, even though it is increasingly overlapping, and that it is dangerous to assume that authorities on servitudes can necessarily be applied in England.

The method by which servitudes are obtained by prescription is part of the law of limitation[37] and does not seem to be regarded as a means of obtaining ownership by *usucapio* as considered by Lord Hoffman in *R. v Oxfordshire CC Ex p. Sunningwell Parish Council.*[38] The law of servitudes in relation to rights of way has been recently reviewed in *Bell v Campbell*[39] and in respect of the right of parking in *Moncrieff v Jamieson.*[40]

Although servitudes are a civil law concept the word has been used in English statutes, for example in the Coal Act 1938, now repealed, where it was defined as:

> "'Servitude' means any liberty, privilege, easement, right or advantage annexed to any land and adversely affecting other land."

6.   Easements and way-leaves

11.13   It has been found necessary for statutory undertakers, whether nationalised or privatised, to have special powers to enter on private land to install services. These rights are created by statute and each of the statutes deals with the matter in a different way. Only in respect of electricity wires and oil pipe-lines are those described in the statute as way-leaves. The various forms by which these rights are created, varied and enforced are set out in Chapter 14.

The nature of these rights was considered by the Court of Appeal in *Newcastle-under-Lyme Corp v Wolstanton Ltd*[41] and by J. F. Garner, "Statutory Easements" (1956) 20 Conveyancer (NS) 208. The conclusion, in short, was that these rights were neither rights of ownership nor easements, but rights sui juris which amounted to exclusive rights of occupation.

There was no judicial or statutory definition of a way-leave until the Electricity Act 1989. The Electricity (Supply) Act 1919 did not actually refer to way-leaves in the body of the Act, though the term was used in the margin. The Land Powers (Defence) Act 1945 referred to way-leaves for pipe-lines without any definition.

"Way-leave" is not used in the other statutes creating comparable rights such as the Gas Act 1986, the Telecommunications Act 1984 and the

---

[37] Prescription and Limitation (Scotland) Act 1973.
[38] [2000] 1 A.C. 335 at 349D.
[39] [2004] Scot CS 14.
[40] [2007] UKHL 42; [2007] 1 W.L.R. 2620.
[41] [1947] Ch. 427.

Water Industry Act 1991. The rights referred to as way-leaves in the Electricity Act 1989 are rights which the electricity suppliers obtain under Sch.4 to the Electricity Act 1989. The 1989 Act defines "the necessary way-leave" as,

> "consent for the licence holder to install and keep installed the electric line on, under or over land and to have access to the land for the purpose of inspecting, maintaining, adjusting, repairing, altering, replacing or removing the line".

Whether the servient owner consents to the way-leave or it is ordered by the Secretary of State under the statutory power, compensation is payable which may be by lump sum or by periodic payments in the nature of rent.

Such rights were treated as being much the same as easements in *Central Electricity Generating Board v Jennaway*,[42] but there are many differences between these sui generis rights and true easements. Nevertheless, though creatures of statute they have been treated as sufficiently close to easements for ancillary rights to be implied by analogy with easements, in order to render the actual terms of the consent effective.

The term "way-leave" had been used for a long time before the creation **11.14** of a network of electricity supply and it is necessary to look at its meaning in cases where the right is granted by agreement and does not form part of any statutory framework.

It seems that it originates from the principle that if a person without your knowledge carries out commercial activities on your land which benefit him, he should be ordered to pay you the equivalent of rent, in addition to compensation for any damage you have actually suffered.[43]

Quite apart from this use of the term it has long been used to describe agreements reached between landowners and various undertakers, such as railway companies, whereby the undertaker, in return for the sale of the land over which the line ran, agreed to pay specific sums, either on the basis of a rent or on the basis of tonnage.[44] Similar systems were used in respect of mining rights.

In the only reported case where a way-leave created by agreement **11.15** has been considered by the courts, *North-Eastern Railway Co v Lord Hastings*,[45] the House of Lords dealt with the matter purely as a question of construction without considering the status of way-leaves. In that case

---

[42] [1959] 1 W.L.R. 937.
[43] *Whitwham v Westminster Brymbo Coal & Coke Co* [1896] 2 Ch. 538.
[44] *North Eastern Railway Co v Lord Hastings* [1900] A.C. 260.
[45] [1900] A.C. 260.

the landowner's predecessor in title had granted a 1,000 year lease of a way-leave to the railway company in return for a levy on all coal using the railway. This was construed to include coal which did not actually pass over the landowner's land.

This way-leave as so construed could not have been a valid easement, even if a rent for a leasehold easement is possible,[46] because the payment was unrelated to the servient tenement, there was no clear dominant tenement and the lease was not by deed. On the other hand it is difficult to see how the right could have been purely contractual, especially as it was not clear whether the right had been expressly assigned to the plaintiff. It seems likely, however, that the House of Lords were not seeking to create a new concept and that questions about the nature of the right were simply not considered.

It is submitted that where the term way-leave is used in some context other than that of rights created by statute it may either refer to an easement at a rent, which it seems must be by lease because a rent cannot be payable on a freehold easement[47] or, alternatively, can be a reference to a contractual agreement whereby one contracting party agrees to pay sums to the other in respect of the use of his land, such right being therefore either a contractual licence or just a contract to pay money.

There is no doubt that there is a gap in the common law in this regard. There is a clear commercial need for various undertakers to run pipes and wires which are not true easements because they do not in any real sense attach to adjoining land. The principles of contract and licence are not sufficient to cover the need for such rights to bind all persons with an interest in the servient land and their successors in title. However, no such concept has ever been formulated and the only conclusion that can be drawn is that the way-leaves created by statute are rights sui juris and that way-leaves created by agreement must be treated as either true easements or licences and not as a separate concept.

7. Easements and customary rights

11.16 Customary rights have become much more important in recent years. In the past they centred on agriculture and other foraging rights, such as fishing and gathering sea coal. However, now the emphasis is very much on leisure activities in traditional open spaces. As such the focus has moved away from the rights of common, attached to particular properties, to development of the law of town and village greens and of public highways. Under ss.193 and 194 of the Law of Property Act 1925 the public have rights of access over all town and village greens and all commons and manorial waste. So a limited common right, such as a right

---

[46] See below para.12.27 et seq.
[47] ibid.

of aftermath, can result in a much wider right of open access.[48] The access rights in the Countryside and Rights of Way Act 2000[49] provide new rights for the public to use open land for recreational purposes, but those rights are circumscribed by a statutory process and it seems likely that the law of customary rights will continue to develop.

These rights emanate from the concept of prescription, essentially the right of individuals, local inhabitants and the public at large to continue to do what they have always done. There is no general concept of prescription at common law. Prescriptive rights have to be fitted into specific categories. Easements can be created by grant or prescription, but they must be for the benefit of a dominant tenement. Public rights of way can be created by user, but they are over specific routes and have to be used to get from one place to another. Customary rights are rights based on long user by inhabitants of a particular locality or group of people. They are to be regarded as the local common law.[50] These three categories of prescriptive rights, however, fall far short of a general right for members of the public to roam over open land. However, people expect to be able to walk along the foreshore or over the mountains and this idea has resulted in the Countryside and Rights of Way Act 2000.[51]

In *R. v Oxfordshire CC Ex p. Sunningwell Parish Council*[52] the House of Lords has brought together these three categories of prescription. It is now clear that in each category what is required is long user that is open and uncontested. It does not matter whether the person exercising the right has any specific belief in the existence of the right, providing he does so in good faith. Indeed prescriptive rights are not based on any implied grant or dedication, nor on "taking by use" or usucapio, but on principles of limitation, that when people have exercised a right for a long time to the detriment of another's land, it is wrong that they should be prevented from doing so in the future.

The principal significance of customary rights has been in relation to the Commons Registration Act 1965 (now replaced by the Commons Act 2006), which is not part of the subject-matter of this book. The Law of Property Act 1922 abolished copyhold tenure, socage tenure and land held subject to custom and turned it into freehold. At the same time the customary rights enjoyed by copyholders were abolished except for commonable rights. The Commons Registration Act 1965 then required that all rights of common should be registered. The cut-off date for registration was 1970, but that does not prevent new rights coming into

---

[48] *ADM Milling Ltd v Tewkesbury Town Council* [2011] EWHC 595 (Ch).
[49] See below para.11.20.
[50] *Alfred F Beckett Ltd v Lyons* [1967] Ch. 449; [1967] 1 All E.R. 833 at 846G.
[51] See below para.11.20.
[52] *R. v Oxfordshire CC Ex p. Sunningwell Parish Council* [2000] 1 A.C. 335.

existence by 20 years user after the cut-off point.[53] Once common rights have been registered then the public right of access in s.193 Law of Property Act 1925 applies, but only if there are some true rights of common registered.[54]

11.17 Apart from rights of common, such as the right to graze sheep, the Commons Registration Act 1965 and the Commons Act 2006 deal with the registration of town or village greens, which is land "on which the inhabitants of any locality have a customary right to indulge in lawful sports and pastimes" or "on which the inhabitants of any locality have indulged in such sports and pastimes as of right for not less than 20 years". All customary rights properly so called had to be registered by 1970, but the Acts make clear that new greens can be created by user since the cut-off date. The passing of the separate 20 year period since the 1970 cut-off date has given rise to considerable litigation where local inhabitants and other members of the public are seeking to prevent the closing off of open space. As "pastimes" includes use for such purposes as walking, tobogganing and family games, there is considerable scope for this process, but the land must still have a significant link with a particular community.

As Pill L.J. remarked in *R v Suffolk CC Ex p. Steed*[55]:

> "It is no trivial matter for a landowner to have land, whether in public or private ownership, regarded as a town or village green."

Registration applications have been used by objectors opposed to developments on open ground. The wide approach in *R. v Oxfordshire CC Ex p. Sunningwell Parish Council*[56] has been challenged by Lord Scott in *R. (on the application of Beresford) v Sunderland City Council*[57] where he suggested that where open space is created by statutory powers, such as under the Local Government Acts, the local authority may be able to override customary rights where it considers it is in the public interest to do so. In *Oxfordshire CC v Oxford City Council*[58] in the Court of Appeal Carnwath L.J. took a consciously restrictive view of modern village greens, which had not originally been registered under the Commons Registration Act 1965. In that case the "green" was no more than an area of scrubland which had been used for "dog-walking, children's play and general informal recreation". Section 15 of the Commons Act 2006 seeks to deal

---

[53] *R. v Suffolk CC Ex p. Steed* (1998) 75 P. & C.R. 102, overruled on another point by *R. v Oxfordshire CC Ex p. Sunningwell Parish Council* [2000] 1 A.C. 335.
[54] *ADM Milling Ltd v Tewkesbury Town Council* [2011] EWHC 595 (Ch).
[55] (1998) 75 P. & C.R. 102.
[56] 2000] 1 A.C. 335.
[57] [2003] UKHL 60; [2004] 1 A.C. 889.
[58] [2005] EWCA Civ 175; [2006] Ch. 43.

with the Court of Appeal's interpretation of the Act by a graduated approach to situations where the use had been blocked by the owner before registration took place. It also[59] provides that permission does not prevent use being "as of right". In relation to registration of greens, this takes away much of the relevance of the discussions about the difference between permission and tolerance. Ironically many of the concerns which the 2006 Act was seeking to deal with were resolved by the House of Lords,[60] which held (perhaps unsurprisingly) that user need only be to the date of the application, but that the amendment to the 1965 Act (replicated in the 2006 Act) means that the use has to be up to the date of the application and not any period of 20 years chosen by the claimant.

The next question, therefore, is whether there are any other rights that have been exercised by the public or the inhabitants of a particular area from time immemorial, but which are open to challenge from the owners of the land on which they have been carried on.

Prescriptive rights of this nature which have been claimed as easements or customary rights include a right in the inhabitants of Saltash in Devon to fish,[61] a right to gather coal washed up on the seashore,[62] a right of public resort to the shores of a lake[63] the right to use Doncaster race-course for general recreation[64] and the right of the inhabitants of Washington, County Durham to use their open air arena.[65]

In 1882 the House of Lords held in *Goodman v Saltash Corporation*[66] that **11.18** the inhabitants of the area had a right to fish which was in the nature of a charitable trust. However, in *Alfred Beckett Ltd v Lyons*[67] the Court of Appeal considered a claim for a right to gather sea-coal from the beach. The plaintiffs alleged a right in the nature of a charitable trust based on *Goodman v Saltash Corporation*[68] and in the alternative a custom in favour of the inhabitants of the County Palatine of Lancaster. There were two difficulties in the way of the plaintiffs in proving customary rights.

Firstly, a profit à prendre cannot arise by custom and collecting sea-coal was held by the Court of Appeal to be a profit à prendre and, secondly, the evidence did not indicate that people were taking the coal under a right connected with the County Palatine.

---

[59] Commons Act 2006 s.15(7).
[60] *Oxfordshire CC v Oxford City Council* [2006] UKHL 25; [2006] 2 A.C. 674.
[61] *Goodman v Saltash Corp* (1881–82) L.R. 7 App. Cas. 633.
[62] *Alfred F Beckett Ltd v Lyons* [1967] Ch. 449.
[63] *Dyfed C.C. v Secretary of State for Wales* (1990) 59 P. & C.R. 275.
[64] *R. v Doncaster MBC Ex p. Braim* (1989) 57 P. & C.R. 1.
[65] *R. (on the application of Beresford) v Sunderland City Council* [2003] UKHL 60; [2004] 1 A.C. 889.
[66] (1881–82) L.R. 7 App. Cas. 633.
[67] [1967] Ch. 449.
[68] (1881–82) L.R. 7 App. Cas. 633.

"It would at least be necessary to show that the coal gatherers supposed themselves to be gathering coal in right of their inhabitancy of the county, and of this I see no sign."[69]

The case does, however, work on the basis that such customary rights do exist and can exist over land which is not common land and where there has been no copyhold enfranchisement. Customary mining rights were excluded from copyhold enfranchisement and the House of Lords in *Newcastle under Lyme Corp v Wolstanton Ltd*.[70] accepted the principle of customary rights, although it found that the custom claimed could not succeed because it was not reasonable.

In *Egerton v Harding*[71] the Court of Appeal again seems to have considered that a duty to fence could arise by custom even though it was over common land and was not, it seems, a registered right of common. In that case Scarman L.J. considered the cases about custom, but felt that the distinction between custom and prescription was rather academic. He was, nevertheless, prepared to accept that there could be a customary right in favour of a particular group of people, in that case the persons entitled to grazing rights on the common.

11.19   If there are circumstances in which a customary right in a particular group of people is liable to arise which is not covered by other rights, nor excluded by copyhold enfranchisement, nor by the need to register rights of common nor by the exclusion of profits à prendre from customary rights, such circumstances are very limited.

In *R. v Doncaster MBC Ex p. Braim*[72] the court proceeded on the basis of prescriptive rights based on an imputed trust rather than on the basis of a custom. This case concerned general recreational rights on Doncaster racecourse. The court decided that the public had used Doncaster Common for recreation from time immemorial, but as the right was in the public as a whole it was not contended that it was a customary right.[73] Another reason why it was not contended that it was a customary right seems to have been that if it was it would have had to be registered under the Commons Registration Act 1965.[74] In *Dyfed CC v Secretary of State for Wales*[75] what was being alleged was a public right of way and not a customary right of recreation.

In so far as customary rights can still be claimed they are subject therefore to certain restrictions:

[69] At 845A per Harman L.J.
[70] [1947] Ch. 427.
[71] [1975] Q.B. 62; [1974] 3 All E.R. 689.
[72] (1989) 57 P. & C.R. 1.
[73] ibid. at 9.
[74] ibid. at 8.
[75] (1990) 59 P. & C.R. 275.

- they must be exercisable predominantly[76] by a particular group of people and not by the inhabitants at large;

- they must be exercised as of right. This means the right has to be exercised openly. Being "subjectively indifferent" to the existence of a right does not affect the character of the user[77];

- They must have been exercised from time immemorial.[78] It is noted above that in respect of town and village greens there is a specific statutory provision of user for 20 years. This was the provision relied on in *R. v Oxfordshire CC Ex p. Sunningwell Parish Council*[79] It is still possible that the courts will extend the principle to any user for 20 years or more, but as the law stands at present it means that the exercise must be shown at all times within living memory. The proposition that it is a defence to show that it was not being exercised at any specific time after 1189 was not accepted in *L.N.W.R. v Fobbing Levels Sewers Commissioners*[80];

- They must either be registered under the Commons Registration Act 1965 (or Commons Act 2006) or not excluded under s.22(1)(a) or (b);

- they must not amount to a profit à prendre; and

- they must be reasonable.[81]

The manorial rights claimed in *Crown Estate Commissioners v Roberts*[82] come under a different category. Mr Roberts's claim was as "Lord Marcher of St David's", a lordship which he had purchased at auction and which was re-defined during the case. It has long been considered that these manorial rights, or, in this case, customary rights based on the need to control the marches of Wales, are of purely nominal value. However, the list of franchises claimed in that case—wreck, several fishery, treasure, estrays[83]—shows that many of these customary rights can still exist and could be of significant value. In the end he succeeded on a moiety of wreck and estrays, but the former could be of real value.

8. Access to open country

In the absence of any common law right to roam over open land, the **11.20** Countryside and Rights of Way Act 2000[84] has created a statutory right of

---

[76] *R. v Oxfordshire CC Ex p Sunningwell Parish Council* [2000] 1 A.C. 335.
[77] *R. v Oxfordshire CC Ex p. Sunningwell Parish Council* [2000] 1 A.C. 335.
[78] *Alfred F Beckett Ltd v Lyons* [1967] Ch. 449; [1967] 1 All E.R. 833.
[79] [2000] 1 A.C. 335.
[80] [1875] 75 L.T. 629 at 632.
[81] *Wolstanton v Newcastle-under-Lyme BC* [1940] 3 All E.R. 101.
[82] [2008] EWHC 1302 (Ch); [2008] 4 All E.R. 828.
[83] The right to stray sheep.
[84] In force from September 19, 2004.

access to "open country". This is defined as "land which is predominantly mountain, moor, heath or down". Unlike the comparable legislation in Scotland,[85] this does not include tidal waters. However, the access rights have now been extended to the "coastal margin" which in turn relates to the "coastal route" which is being set up under the Marine and Coastal Access Act 2009. The Access to the Countryside (Coastal Margin) (England) Order 2010[86] sets out the limits which include the path itself, 2 metres to either side of it, everything on the seaward side and "any foreshore, cliff, bank, barrier, dune beach or flat" to the landward side of it. The first section of new coastal margin land is planned to be around Weymouth in time for the 2012 Olympic Games.

The concept of the Act is based on the mapping process used for public highways. Substantial progress has been made and there are now 865,000 hectares of land subject to the open access process. However, it is not clear how much of this is land to which access was formerly denied. The right is not exercisable until a particular piece of land is shown on the map, which is subject to appeal and review. There will, no doubt, be considerable argument at the margins about what land should be included on the map and what is "excepted land", which includes land with buildings on it, parks and land which has been disturbed by ploughing or tree planting within the past year. In particular it does not include improved or semi-improved grassland. It can, however, include land which is fenced providing that it is mountain, moor, heath or down. The DETR (as it then was) believe that there are around 500,000 hectares of open countryside in England and Wales where access is not permitted.[87] The Act does not apply to land which is already open to the public as of right. It does, however, apply to land which is currently open on a voluntary basis.

The access is only for "open-air recreation".[88] It excludes use by vehicles, including bicycles, water craft or horse-riding and there will be controls on use by dogs. Other restrictions will be contained in by-laws.

One of the major concerns was that landowners should not become liable to keep their land tidy and free from risks for people exercising the right. This is done by the simple expedient of reducing the liability of occupiers of the land towards people exercising the right to that which they would owe to trespassers under the Occupiers' Liability Act 1957,[89] but further restricts it so that there can be no liability in respect of risks due to natural features or getting over gates, fences or walls.

---

[85] Land Reform (Scotland) Act 2003.
[86] Access to the Countryside (Coastal Margin)(England) Order 2010 (SI 2010/558).
[87] Explanatory Notes to the Countryside and Rights of Way Act 2000 para.7.
[88] Countryside and Rights of Way Act 2000 s.2.
[89] Countryside and Rights of Way Act 2000 s.13.

Chapter Twelve
Creation of Easements—
Express Grant

1. Introduction

Easements can be created in a number of ways which will be dealt with **12.01** separately:

    (a) by express grant;

    (b) by implied grant;

    (c) by statute;

    (d) by prescription;

    (e) in equity.

2. Creation by express grant

(a) Form of grant

At common law an easement can only be granted expressly by deed, **12.02** usually by express grant or reservation contained in a conveyance or transfer. Easements are also frequently contained in leases. However, separate deeds of easement can be executed.

The grant must make clear that it is granting an easement. A deed stating that the grantors "hereby grant their licence and consent" will create only a licence, which cannot pass as an interest in land, even though the grant is expressed to be for the grantor's successors in title.[1]

The normal form of grant is by the words "together with ... " in the parcels immediately after the description of the property. If there are a number of easements these will be set out in a separate schedule.

---

[1] *IDC Group v Clark* (1993) 65 P. & C.R. 179; see also *Sugarman v Porter* [2006] EWHC 331 (Ch); [2006] 2 P. & C.R. 14, where it was argued that a fencing covenant was really a fencing easement.

Although it is beyond doubt that these words can create an easement, they are also used where there is an existing easement annexed to the land sold which is then conveyed with the land. It follows, therefore, that a conveyance "together with" a particular easement will only be a grant of an easement if the vendor is the owner of the servient tenement at the time of the grant. If the vendor is not the owner of the servient tenement he may simply be expressing a belief that the easement already exists. It will be necessary, in that event, to look further back to the original conveyance by the common owner of both the servient and the dominant tenement. It is good conveyancing practice where an easement is believed to exist but is not expressly contained in any operative conveyance to say so expressly, for example by qualifying the reference to the easement by words such as "in so far as the same may subsist". However, this practice is not always followed and it cannot be assumed that a reference to an easement in a conveyance or other deed will be backed up by an earlier express grant.

12.03   If the earlier conveyance is found and makes no reference to the easement, then there is no express grant and the owner of the land will have to rely on an implied grant. The party claiming such an implication will, of course, be assisted by an express reference to the easement in a deed subsequent to the division of the dominant and servient tenements, but if it is once established that the easement was not granted expressly or by implication in the deed that split the properties, then no amount of references to it in subsequent conveyances can create an express easement where none existed before.

Where the dominant and servient tenement return to the same ownership an easement is extinguished.[2] If the common owner then disposes of part of the land again he may grant a similar easement. If he conveys the land "together with" the easement, which he sets out afresh, then this takes effect as a fresh grant. But what if instead he refers back to the previous grant? Is this intended as a fresh grant or is it simply intended to pass on the right previously granted in so far as it still subsists? This may depend on the precise wording of the conveyance, but it is likely that the court would take the common-sense view that the reference to the earlier deed is simply shorthand and the intention is to make a fresh grant of the same easement. Otherwise the effect would be that the purchaser did not obtain any rights at all since the previous easement was extinguished by merger and there would be no grant of a new easement.

Where an easement is being reserved by the vendor for the benefit of his retained land, the words "excepting and reserving . . . "are added to

---

[2] See later at para.17.16.

the parcels. Strictly, "excepting" refers to existing easements and "reserving" refers to the creation of new easements by grant by the purchaser to the vendor. However, these words (just like "together with") are sometimes used when there is an existing easement in favour of third parties which the vendor wishes to draw to the purchaser's attention. Therefore, while normally a reference to "excepting and reserving" will involve the creation of new easements, the conveyance may be so construed as to refer only to pre-existing easements.[3]

As stated above, a reservation in a conveyance or a lease is essentially **12.04** a grant by the purchaser or lessee to the vendor or lessor. Before 1926 it was necessary either for the purchaser to execute the conveyance as well as the vendor, or for the reservation to be by way of "use" under s.62 of the Conveyancing Act 1881.[4] However, since 1925 a reservation of a legal estate operates at law even if there is no execution of the conveyance by the grantee of the legal estate out of which the reservation is made, by virtue of s.65 of the Law of Property Act 1925. Strictly, however, it still operates as a re-grant.[5] For example in *Johnstone v Holdway*,[6] a sale was executed by two vendors, one of whom was a bare trustee and the other the equitable owner. The purchaser therefore obtained both the legal and beneficial title. There were reservations in favour of both the vendors. As the reservations operated as re-grants they could both obtain legal easements from the purchaser. If a reservation had just been something held back from the sale then the vendor of the equitable interest would only have obtained an equitable easement. As a reservation is really a re-grant, if it is ever necessary to construe an instrument contra proferentem, the purchaser, and not the vendor, will be treated as the *proferens*.[7] In the case of a lease executed before 1926 the correct procedure was for the lessee to execute the counterpart, thereby effecting the re-grant.

Therefore, where a claim to an easement by express grant depends on a reservation before 1926, whether in a conveyance or a lease, it is worth checking whether the purchaser executed the conveyance as well as the vendor or, in the case of leasehold land, whether the lessee executed a counterpart.

Absence of execution by the purchaser was not always fatal, however, even before 1926. Where there was a binding contract signed by both parties followed by a conveyance which was not executed by the purchaser, the vendor obtained an equitable easement, which was binding

---

[3] *Re Freehold Land in Dances Way etc.* [1962] Ch. 490; [1962] 2 W.L.R. 815.
[4] See *St Edmundsbury and Ipswich Diocesan Board of Finance v Clark (No. 2)* [1975] 1 W.L.R. 468; [1975] 1 All E.R. 772 at 780f.
[5] ibid.
[6] [1963] 1 Q.B. 601 at 612.
[7] See *St Edmundsbury and Ipswich Diocesan Board of Finance v Clark (No. 2)* [1975] 1 W.L.R. 468; [1975] 1 All E.R. 772 at 780f.

against a purchaser of the servient tenement with notice of the contract. Since that part of the contract had not been completed it did not merge in the conveyance.[8] The chances are that any such grant has been referred to in any subsequent dealings with the land and accordingly that such a grant will still be binding in equity even though the property has since changed hands. The position might, however, be different if the land is registered.[9]

12.05   Use of the words "subject to"' rather than "Excepting and reserving" suggests that the land is subject to existing easements and not that the purchaser is granting new easements to the vendor. "The wording is by common consent inappropriate for the reservation of a new right of way."[10] However, s.65(2) of the Law of Property Act 1925 expressly states that,

> "a conveyance of a legal estate expressed to be subject to another legal estate not in existence immediately before the date of the conveyance shall operate as a reservation unless a contrary intention appears".

Accordingly, if a conveyance states that it is subject to a right of way and there was no right of way in existence in favour of a third party at the time of the grant to which the parcels could be referring then it operates to create by reservation a right of way in favour of the vendor, even though the words "subject to" are not strictly appropriate for this purpose.[11]

Where the reservation is contained in a lease it must be remembered that it is only binding against the lessee and his successors in title and would not bind a subsequent purchaser of the freehold of the servient tenement.

Although easements are often created by grant or reservation contained in a conveyance or lease, it is quite common for an easement to be created by an express grant contained in a quite separate deed. It must be remembered that such an instrument can only create a legal easement if it is a deed. If it is just a contract, the easement can only take effect in equity. Furthermore, the express grant of an easement can only be made by the owner of the servient tenement in favour of the owner of the dominant tenement. If either is not the owner, but only has an equitable interest or a leasehold interest, the validity of the easement will be limited accordingly.[12] If the grantor does not own the land affected, or only owns part of it, then equally the grant has no or only limited effect. It is perfectly possible to

---

[8] *May v Belleville* [1905] 2 Ch. 605.
[9] See below para.12.07 et seq.
[10] per Sir John Pennycuick in *St Edmundsbury and Ipswich Diocesan Board of Finance v Clark (No. 2)* [1975] 1 W.L.R. 468; [1975] 1 All E.R. 772 at 780f.
[11] *Wiles v Banks* (1985) 50 P. & C.R. 80.
[12] See, however, *Rymer v McIlroy* [1897] 1 Ch. 528.

grant a right akin to an easement to an individual without there being any dominant tenement, but such right will only take effect as a licence and not an easement.[13] A grant expressed to be a licence will only take effect as a licence, even though it has all the characteristics of an easement.[14]

The grant of an easement will be for the same estate as the rest of the **12.06** parcels unless there is a specific statement to the contrary.[15] So in a conveyance in fee simple the easement will be in fee simple. In a lease it will be leasehold. If the grant is by a separate deed it will (since 1925) be presumed to be in fee simple, unless the estate of either the grantor or the grantee is limited. Before 1926 it was necessary to use the words "in fee simple"; otherwise the grant would be limited to the life of the grantee,[16] though in the absence of the words "fee simple" various other words were permitted by the Conveyancing Act 1881.

3. Registered land

Legal easements do not have to be registered as land charges under the **12.07** Land Charges Act 1972. The position with regard to registered land is more complex.

The Land Registration Act 1925 provided for all new easements created by a transfer for the benefit of the land transferred to be registered.[17] The requirement applies, therefore, only to the dominant land. If the servient land is unregistered, there is no compulsory registration.

However, in many circumstances an unregistered easement may still be an overriding interest. The Land Registration Act 2002 has considerably tightened this situation, but it only applies to new easements granted after the commencement of the Act on October 13, 2003. New easements created after this date can still be overriding interests in certain circumstances. The situation therefore is as follows:

(a) Express easements granted over registered land before October 13, 2003

Under the Land Registration Act 1925, where the easement was a **12.08** new easement created by the transfer for the benefit of the land transferred it had to be registered, whether the estate was registered in freehold or leasehold.[18] It might be thought that this peremptory requirement would be an end of the matter and that a new easement which was not registered would have no validity. That was not the case, however. A new

---

[13] See Chs 10 and 11 above.
[14] *IDC Group Ltd v Clark* (1993) 65 P. & C.R. 179.
[15] Law of Property Act 1925 s.60.
[16] Williams on *Vendor and Purchaser*, 3rd edn, p.610.
[17] Land Registration Act 1925 ss.18(1)(c), 19(2), 21(1)(d).
[18] Land Registration Act 1925 ss.18(1)(c), 19(2), 21(1)(d), and 22(d).

easement granted before the commencement of the Land Registration Act 2002 on October 13, 2003, which is not registered is an overriding interest within s.70(1) and takes effect as a minor interest,[19] which is liable to be overridden by the disposition of land for valuable consideration unless protected against purchasers by notices, cautions, restrictions and inhibitions.[20] The 2002 Act does not affect any such entitlement.

The 1925 Act also provided that a separate grant of an easement benefiting registered land must be registered. Where there is an easement created by reservation it had to be registered (somewhat anomalously) against the servient tenement.[21] The benefit of it could only be registered if the dominant tenement (i.e. the transferor's retained land) is registered land.[22]

Where the Transfer creates an easement over the vendor's retained land in favour of the land transferred, this will usually be done by adding "together with. . ." to the parcels.[23] Where this is a new grant the registrar only has to be satisfied that the vendor is indeed the owner of the servient tenement. In this event the easement will be added to the description of the property as registered and as such will be found in the Land Certificate.

12.09   Where the easement to be included in the Transfer is an existing easement appurtenant to the land transferred, the proprietor may register an appurtenant right on the register.[24] Once the easement is registered pursuant to this process, it confers an absolute, good leasehold, qualified or possessory title to the right according to the nature of the title to the land.[25] It is enough, therefore, to show that the easement has been registered and it is not open to the other party to seek to show that this has been done wrongly.

If the registrar's inquiries in response to the application did not make the position clear he could register it with such qualification as he deems advisable or he could merely enter notice of the fact that the proprietor claims it.[26] The entry is made as far as practicable by reference to any instrument creating the right or by setting out an extract from it.[27] Once it is registered it passes automatically to any subsequent registered proprietor subject to any express exception or reservation.[28]

---

[19] ibid. s.101.
[20] Cautions and inhibitions are abolished by the new Act, see Ch. 4.
[21] Land Registration Act 1925 ss.18(1)(d), 21(1)(c).
[22] Land Registration Rules 1925 r.257.
[23] See above para.12.03.
[24] Land Registration Rules 1925 r.252 repealed by the 2003 Rules, but not in respect of existing registrations.
[25] Land Registration Rules 1925 r.254(1); *Peachey v Lee* (1964) 192 E.G. 365.
[26] Land Registration Rules 1925 r.254(2).
[27] Land Registration Rules 1925 r.255.
[28] Land Registration Rules 1925 r.256.

The position, therefore, under the 1925 legislation is that if the benefit of an easement is shown without qualification in the Land Certificate or on the Register, that in itself is sufficient proof of the grant, because it will either be a new grant or the benefit of it will have been conferred on the registered proprietor by virtue of the registration. It does not, however, necessarily follow that it is a valid easement. The registration procedure is concerned with whether the proper formalities have been complied with. If the right granted is incapable of being an easement, for example because the dominant tenement is not definable, the fact of registration cannot turn an invalid grant into an effective one.[29]

As the registration of existing easements is optional, a purchaser under **12.10** a contract for the sale of land together with the benefit of existing easements is not entitled to insist that the vendor gets the easements registered as appurtenant to the land, though he can always do so himself after completion.[30]

The Registrar may have entered a note on the Register but, if for any reason an existing legal easement has not been noted on the register, this does not affect its validity.

The Land Registration Act 1925 made specific provision for reserva- **12.11** tions to be registered against the servient tenement's title where the reservation is a new creation.[31] Furthermore, reservations are re-grants of the easement by the transferee to the transferor.[32] Therefore where it is a new right created by the transfer it should also be registered against the transferor's title if the transferor's land is registered.

Where the reservation is merely an exception of an existing easement it seems that it does not need to be registered though it can be entered as a notice against the land.[33]

The whole question of equitable easements is dealt with separately,[34] but it is clear that equitable easements cannot be registered in the property register under s.18 or s.21 of the Land Registration Act 1925. Rule 252 of the Land Registration Rules 1925 made it clear that the only appurtenant rights that could be entered on the register are those "capable of subsisting as a legal estate". The extent to which overriding interests,

---

[29] *London and Blenheim Estates Ltd v Ladbroke Retail Parks Ltd* [1994] 1 W.L.R. 31; [1993] 4 All E.R. 157.
[30] *Re Evans's Contract* [1970] 1 W.L.R. 583; [1970] 1 All E.R. 1236.
[31] Land Registration Act 1925 s.18(1)(d).
[32] *St Edmundsbury and Ipswich Diocesan Board of Finance v Clark (No.2)* [1975] 1 W.L.R. 468; [1975] 1 All E.R. 772.
[33] Land Registration Rules 1925 r.253(2).
[34] See later Ch. 16.

as defined by s.70 of the Land Registration Act 1925, exclude equitable easements[35] is open to doubt and will be considered separately.[36]

(b)   Express easements over registered land granted after the commencement of the Land Registration Act 2002

12.12   By s.27(2)(d) of the Land Registration Act 2002 the express grant or reservation of an easement over registered land must itself be registered. This is the same as the position under the Land Registration Act 1925, but there is a difference in the effect of a failure to register.

The crucial difference is in whether such a grant or reservation is an overriding interest, even if it is not registered. For this it is necessary to divide express grants or reservations of easements into three different categories.

1)   In respect of easements granted or reserved before October 13, 2003 (the commencement date of the 2002 Act) such easements remain overriding interests, even if they are over registered land and should have been registered under the provisions of the Land Registration Act 1925.

2)   In respect of easements granted or reserved after October 13, 2003, the transitional provisions provide that they remained overriding interests until October 13, 2006.

3)   After October 13, 2006 any new legal easement only operates as a overriding interest if:

— it is within the actual knowledge of the person to whom the disposition is made; or
— it would have been obvious on a reasonably careful inspection of the land over which the easement of profit is exercisable; or
— it has been exercised during the year before the disposition.

It appears that the effect of this for the future is that failure to register the express grant of an easement or profit puts its effectiveness at risk, but does not render it totally void. The effect, therefore, is a tightening of the screw on unregistered incorporeal hereditaments, but not to bring them totally within the registration framework.

As the 2002 Act leaves the structure in place, it seems that the previous authorities concerning the 1925 Act will normally still apply to newly granted easements.

---

[35] Land Registration Act 1925 s.70(1)(a) "not being equitable easements".
[36] See below 16.05 et seq, per Cross J. *Postel v Slough Estates* [1969] Ch. 495; [1968] 3 All E.R. 257 at 262H; per Scott J. *Celsteel Ltd v Alton House Holdings Ltd* [1985] 1 W.L.R. 204; [1982] 2 All E.R. 562 overruled on other grounds [1986] 1 W.L.R. 512; [1986] 1 All E.R. 608.

Existing express easement and implied easements, including those granted under s.62 Law of Property Act 1925, do not need to be registered and remain overriding interests. However, by r.73A of the Land Registration Rules 2003[37] the owner of a registered estate has an option to register any legal easement or profit granted over an unregistered estate or any legal easement which has been acquired otherwise than by express grant or reservation i.e by implied grant under s.62, under the rule in *Wheeldon v Burrows*, or by prescription. In a transfer of part of registered land the easement or profit will then be registered on the dominant and servient titles.

4. Competent grantors and grantees

Generally speaking anyone who can convey or lease land can grant an **12.13** easement. Thus an absolute owner can grant an easement in fee simple or for a leasehold term. A lessee can grant an easement limited to his term.

Other limited owners can grant easements in fee simple. Trustees of land have all the powers of an absolute owner[38] and can create easements in the same way as they can dispose of land and are subject to the same restrictions. No new strict settlements can be created after January 1, 1997 and ecclesiastical trusts cease to be settled land, but existing settlements continue.[39] By s.49(1)(a) of the Settled Land Act 1925, on a sale or other disposition or dealing under the powers of the Act, any easement, right or privilege of any kind may be reserved or granted over or in relation to the settled land or any part thereof or other land, including the land disposed of. An existing easement can be sold under s.38. Section 49(1)(a), however, was new in 1925 and the position is less clear where a tenant for life purported to grant a right of way before 1926. It was held in 1861 (before an express statutory power relating to minerals and timber was added in 1862) that a reservation of minerals was not possible on a sale under an express power of sale of settled land.[40] However, in *Re Brotherton's Estate*[41] it was held that an existing easement could be sold to the owners of the servient tenement by virtue of the earlier Settled Land Acts. These Acts, however, applied only to existing easements and not to the grant of new easements.

There is a similar situation where a mortgagee sells. By s.101(2)(ii)(a) of the Law of Property Act 1925, a mortgagee exercising his power of sale can grant or reserve any easements. This section replaced s.4 of the Conveyancing Act 1911. Before that in 1900, however, Byrne J. declined to decide whether there could be a grant of a new easement over land

---

[37] As amended by the Land Registration (Amendment) Rules 2008.
[38] Trusts of Land and Appointment of Trustees Act 1996 s.6.
[39] ibid.
[40] *Buckley v Howell* (1861) 29 Beav. 546.
[41] (1908) 77 L.J. Ch. 373.

retained by the mortgagee, though he did hold that rights under an implied grant could pass.[42]

12.14   Fortunately it will only rarely be necessary to consider the validity of express grants by tenants for life or mortgagees made before the statutory powers were created.

Since 1842 an incumbent of a benefice has had a limited power to grant or take easements, either without payment or at a rent. The power is now enshrined in s.9 of the Church Property (Miscellaneous Provisions) Measure 1960. This power, however, does not include a right to grant easements over the church and churchyard, which requires a faculty.[43] It refers only to the benefice which is,

> "the vicarage or rectory itself and the glebe and other land which is vested in the incumbent for his own benefit qua incumbent".

It also excludes, therefore, any land which has come into the hands of the vicar for any other purpose.[44] There was doubt whether such a power existed before 1960, but any such doubts were resolved (at least about the position since 1858) by *Oakley v Boston*[45] where the Court of Appeal held that such powers were enshrined in the Ecclesiastical Leasing Act 1858.

The situation is somewhat different with consecrated land. In such a case the incumbent of the parish has a right to grant a licence, including an indefinite licence, but not an easement. This is a further reason why the doctrine of lost modern grant cannot apply to consecrated land. In such a case it is necessary to apply to the consistory court for a faculty.[46]

12.15   Commoners, since they only have limited rights over the common, have no right to grant easements over it.[47] Any such grant should be made by the owner of the land itself.

Corporations, being artificial persons, can only act in accordance with their powers. Therefore, a grant of an easement which was outside the objects of a company would be ultra vires. In practice this has arisen in respect of corporations created by statute, which tend to have much more limited objects. Even in such a case, however, the courts have taken a wide view of a corporation's powers so as to allow it to grant rights of way either public or private, even if the grant does little to further its objects.[48]

---

[42] *Born v Turner* [1900] 2 Ch. 211.
[43] *Hamble Parish Council v Haggard* [1992] 1 W.L.R. 122; [1992] 4 All E.R. 147.
[44] ibid.
[45] *Oakley v Boston* [1976] Q.B. 270; [1975] 3 W.L.R. 478.
[46] *Re St. Martin Le Grand, York* [1990] Fam 63; [1989] 2 All E.R. 711.
[47] *Paine & Co Ltd v St. Neots Gas & Coke Co* [1939] 3 All E.R. 812.
[48] *Re Gouty and Manchester Sheffield & Lincolnshire Railway* [1896] 2 Q.B. 437, B.T.C. v *Westmorland County Council* [1958] A.C. 126.

The situation where either the grantor or the grantee is a leaseholder was considered by the Court of Appeal in *Wall v Collins*[49] in relation to an implied grant under s.62 Law of Property Act 1925. The Court accepted the basic proposition, contained in the previous edition of this book that "a person cannot grant an easement for an estate greater than that which he holds in the property". However, the merger of the leasehold in the freehold estate in the servient tenement does not affect the continuing validity of the original grant, "at least for the period of the original lease":

> "This seems right as a matter of common sense. The owner of a servient tenement should not be able to escape the burden of an easement by dealings to which those interested in the dominant tenement are not parties".[50]

In that case the original lease was for 999 years and, accordingly, the question of what happens when the original lease would have expired did not arise.

In relation to the dominant tenement, the position is essentially the same:

> "It follows, in my view, that the merger of the lease into a larger interest in the dominant tenement is not in itself fatal to the continued existence of the easement for the period for which it was granted."

The important rationale for this is that the right does not "attach" to the leasehold interest, but to the dominant tenement as a whole.

There is, of course, a distinction between the evidence required to show the grant of an easement under s.62, which is not directly related to the occupation of the servient tenement up to that date, and the effect of an implied grant under s.62 which is then attached to the instrument. Accordingly, it must follow that the implied grant is of a leasehold easement and not a freehold one. The difficulty then arises if the leaseholder then obtains the freehold of the dominant land. His leasehold interest then becomes of no significance and merges with the freehold, but what of any appurtenant rights attached to the leasehold and not the freehold? These rights may be express or implied and they may be against persons other than the freeholder. It would be wrong if they were lost and it would be equally wrong if they could be unilaterally converted into freehold rights. It is for this reason that there can, it seems, be no such thing as a leasehold prescriptive right.[51]

The judgment of the Court of Appeal makes it clear, therefore, that where the leasehold title merges in the freehold title, incorporeal

---

[49] [2007] EWCA Civ 444; [2007] Ch. 390
[50] per Carnwath L.J. at [18].
[51] See Ch. 15 at 15.26.

hereditaments appurtenant to the leasehold title remain a leasehold rights for the full term of the lease. Similar problems have been encountered in relation to adverse possession by a lessee of adjoining property.[52]

This issue was considered, without reference to *Wall v Collins* in *BOH v Easter Power Networks*[53] where it was made clear that a lease does not necessarily merge with the freehold in equity when the leaseholder buys the freehold and that, therefore, the ancillary rights of access may remain in force. This was a case involving, in effect, a ransom strip at Wembley Stadium.

5. Construction of the grant

12.16 The principles governing the construction of the parcels of a conveyance have been considered above with regard to boundaries.[54] The grant or reservation of an easement forms part of the parcels and should be construed in exactly the same way. Thus the parcels clause of the operative conveyance should be construed in its own terms, but if there is ambiguity it is possible to look at extrinsic evidence. Where an easement is created by a separate deed and not as part of a conveyance then the subject-matter of the easement itself forms the parcels of the deed and the same principles of construction apply.

For the most part the way in which grants of particular easements have been construed will be considered under the headings of the different types of easement. However, it may be helpful to set out some general points. In respect of grants of easements, two recent authorities[55] have relied heavily on the general principles of interpretation set out by Lord Hoffman in *Investors Compensation Scheme Ltd v West Bromwich Building Society*[56] and re-asserted by the House of Lords in *Chartbrook Ltd v Persimmon Homes Ltd.*[57]

12.17 "Almost all the old intellectual baggage of "legal" interpretation has been discarded. The principles may be summarised as follows.

(1) Interpretation is the ascertainment of the meaning which the document would convey to a reasonable person having all the background knowledge which would reasonably have been

---

[52] Ch. 5 at para.5.19.

[53] [2011] EWCA Civ 19.

[54] See Chs 1 and 2.

[55] *Mobil Oil Co Ltd v Birmingham City Council* [2001] EWCA Civ 1608; [2002] 2 P. & C.R. 14 per Aldous L.J. at [24] and *Partridge v Lawrence* [2003] EWCA Civ 1121; [2004] 1 P. & C.R. 14 at [28].

[56] *Investors Compensation Scheme Ltd v West Bromwich Building Society* [1998] 1 W.L.R. 896 at 912F.

[57] *Chartbrook Ltd v Persimmon Homes Ltd* [2009] UKHL 38; [2009] 1 A.C. 1101.

available to the parties in the situation in which they were at the time of the contract.

(2) The background was famously referred to by Lord Wilberforce as the "matrix of fact", but this phrase is, if anything, an understated description of what the background may include. Subject to the requirement that it should have been reasonably available to the parties and to the exception to be mentioned next, it includes absolutely anything which would have affected the way in which the language of the document would have been understood by a reasonable man.

(3) The law excludes from the admissible background the previous negotiations of the parties[58] and their declaration of subjective intent. They are admissible only in an action for rectification. The law makes this distinction for reasons of practical policy and, in this respect only, legal interpretation differs from the way we would interpret utterances in ordinary life. The boundaries of this exception are in some respects unclear. But this is not the occasion to explore them.

(4) The meaning which a document (or any other utterance) would convey is not the same thing as the meaning of its words. The meaning of words is a matter of dictionaries and grammars; the meaning of a document is what the parties using those words against the relevant background would reasonably have been understood to mean. The background may not merely enable the reasonable man to choose between the possible meanings of words which are ambiguous but even (as occasionally happens in ordinary life) to conclude that the parties must for whatever reason, have used the wrong words or syntax; see *Mannai Investment Co Ltd v Eagle Star Life Assurance.*[59]

(5) The "rule" that words should be given their "natural and ordinary meaning" reflects the common sense proposition that we do not easily accept that people have made linguistic mistakes, particularly in formal documents. On the other hand, if one would nevertheless conclude from the background that something must have gone wrong with the language, the law does not require judges to attribute to the parties an intention which they plainly could not have had."[60]

---

[58] This was the specific issue in *Chartbrook Ltd v Persimmon Homes Ltd* [2009] UKHL 38, where the principle was re-asserted, while qualifying it by allowing such evidence to be called as background.

[59] [1997] A.C. 749.

[60] This principle was re-asserted and applied in *Chartbrook Ltd v Persimmon Homes Ltd* [2009] UKHL 38.

12.18   There are many other summaries of the modern approach, including, in particular, the judgment of the Court of Appeal in *St Edmundsbury and Ipswich Diocesan Board of Finance v Clark (No.2).*[61] This broad approach encourages parties to seek to adduce evidence about the background to documents. In some cases this may elucidate; in others it may add to the confusion.

> "At a distance of over a century from the creation of the right, the safer and more sensible course is to put trust in the firm anchor of what is recorded and known rather than to set out on an uncharted sea of speculation about all the possible circumstances surrounding the way in 1898."[62]

This approach was followed in *White v Richards*[63] where an unlimited right of way was construed as being restricted to vehicles up to eight feet wide and 10 tons laden weight because of the physical characteristics of the way.

It used to be said that the grant of an easement should be construed contra proferentem, i.e. against the grantor. This in itself is a slightly odd concept since it is the grantee and not the grantor who gets the benefit from the easement. It is nevertheless a long accepted principle, but its significance has been eroded by *St Edmundsbury and Ipswich Diocesan Board of Finance v Clark (No.2)*[64] where Sir John Pennycuick[65] made it clear that:

> "this presumption can only come into play if the court finds itself unable on the material before it to reach a sure conclusion on the construction of a reservation. The presumption is not itself a factor to be taken into account in reaching the conclusion."

The reference to a "reservation" is because of the facts of that case and the same principles apply to a grant. In the light of this dictum it seems that the presumption can usually be ignored.

12.19   Easements, whether by grant or reservation (or indeed by implication or prescription), have always been construed, as far as possible, in such a way as to render them effective. Accordingly:

> "the grant of an easement is prima facie also the grant of such ancillary rights as are reasonably necessary to its exercise or enjoyment".[66]

---

[61] [1975]1 W.L.R. 468.
[62] per Mummery L.J. in *Wikinson v Farmer* [2010] EWCA Civ 1148 at [35].
[63] (1994) 68 P. & C.R. 105.
[64] [1975] 1 W.L.R. 468; [1975] 1 All E.R. 772.
[65] *St Edmundsbury and Ipswich Diocesan Board of Finance v Clark (No.2)* 1 All E.R. 772 at 780b.
[66] per Parker J. in *Jones v Pritchard* [1908] 1 Ch. 630 at 638.

The effect of this principle will be considered further in relation to the various different easements, but it has been applied in respect of most easements. Thus a grant of a right of way will be construed as allowing vehicles to stop to load and unload,[67] including swinging up the doors,[68] though not swinging them out beyond the width of the way. A right of way of a specified width may allow a certain amount of leeway to get round corners,[69] though this leeway will be limited to only a foot or so. Importantly the House of Lords has decided in *Moncrieff v Jamieson*[70] that a right of way can include an ancillary right of parking where that is the only practical way of exercising the vehicular right as a means of access to a private house.

An express grant of a right of way only for purposes in connection with the use authorised by a restrictive covenant allows for the extension of the use if the restrictive covenant is modified by the Lands Tribunal.[71] Furthermore the owner of the servient tenement has an ancillary right to repair or improve the road to enable it to be used for access to housing as well as agricultural use.[72]

The principle has been particularly strongly operated to allow repairs to pipes and watercourses.[73] If a person has a right of drainage or to take water through pipes he has the right to go onto the land to carry out repairs, even if this means some disruption for the servient owner.

The same principle applies to a right of support. While the servient **12.20** owner may be under no obligation to keep the supporting building in repair, the dominant owner can, in theory at least, enter the premises to carry out repairs to protect his own building.[74] However, the difficulties involved in actually exercising any such rights were referred to in relation to abating a nuisance by Megaw L.J. in *Leakey v National Trust for Places of Historic Interest or Natural Beauty*.[75] The problem is approached in a different way in the Access to Neighbouring Land Act 1992 which allows an adjoining owner to apply to the court for an access order.

Other examples are the right to water sheep ancillary to a right of grazing[76] and the right to erect towers to support an electricity way-leave.[77]

---

[67] *Bulstrode v Lambert* [1953] 1 W.L.R. 1064.
[68] *VT Engineering Ltd v Richard Barland & Co* (1968) 19 P. & C.R. 890.
[69] ibid.
[70] *Moncrieff v Jamieson* [2007] UKHL 42; [2007] 1 W.L.R. 2620. Although this is a case about Scottish servitudes the speeches from the English law lords make it clear that it applies equally to England.
[71] *Hotchkin v McDonald* [2004] EWCA Civ 519; [2005] 1 P. & C.R. 7.
[72] *Newcomen v Coulson* (1877) L.R. 5 Ch. D. 133.
[73] *Jones v Pritchard* [1908] 1 Ch. 630 at 638.
[74] See below in Ch. 24 at para.24.60 and *Bond v Nottingham Corp* [1940] Ch. 429 at 439 sub nom. *Bond v Norman* [1940] 2 All E.R. 12.
[75] [1980] Q.B. 485; [1980] 2 W.L.R. 65.
[76] *White v Taylor (No. 3)* [1969] 1 Ch. 160; [1968] 2 W.L.R. 1402.
[77] *Central Electricity Generating Board v Jennaway v Jennaway* [1959] 1 W.L.R. 937.

These rights are usually referred to as ancillary easements. However, in many cases an ancillary easement is no more than a right to prevent the servient owner from doing things which interfere with the effective exercise of the easement.

6.   Future easements

12.21   Usually an easement is to take effect immediately. Even if the building which is to benefit from the right has not been built at the time of the grant the right is an immediate one. However, it may be desired to grant a right to use facilities which themselves have not yet been constructed or defined or even purchased. Thus the purchaser of a house might want rights of way over estate roads the routes of which have not yet been decided, or a right of drainage might be required through whatever drains are constructed in the future.

In these circumstances it is not uncommon to grant a right, for example, to use the sewers and drains "now passing or hereafter to pass" under a road or "when and so soon as the same shall have been made".[78]

It is well established that such future easements can be validly granted and that such interests are subject to the rule against perpetuities.[79] This latter principle has been authoritatively considered by the Court of Appeal in *Shrewsbury v Adam*,[80] which demonstrates the problems which can arise when, as so often happens, plans change. Ms Adam's aim was to obtain vehicular access to her land by way of a garage on an access road to a small estate of houses which had not been built at the time she bought her property. The conveyance was construed as including an immediate right of way, but one which could only be exercised once the relevant part of the road had been constructed. However, this conveyance was executed more than 21 years previously and, even under the "wait and see" rule, the right had expired under the rule against perpetuities.

12.22   There are, however, various ways round this problem. A right granted for the future may be interpreted simply as a personal contract,[81] or as a covenant not to prevent the person with the benefit of the right from crossing the land.[82] Alternatively the right may be construed not as a future right at all, but as an immediate right which has not yet been

---

[78] *Nickerson v Barroughclough* [1981] Ch. 426; [1981] 2 All E.R. 369 at 374f.
[79] *Shrewsbury v Adam* [2005] EWCA Civ 1006; [2006] 1 P. & C.R. 27; *Dunn v Blackdown Properties* [1961] Ch. 433; *Newham v Lawson* (1971) 22 P. & C.R. 852; *Nickerson v Barroughclough* [1981] 2 All E.R. 369 at 374h per Brightman L.J.
[80] [2005] EWCA Civ 1006.
[81] *South Eastern Railway Co v Associated Portland Cement Manufacturers* [1910] 1 Ch. 12.
[82] *Sharpe v Durrant* (1911) 55 S.J. 423.

exercised, such as a right to construct and use a tunnel,[83] or it may be treated as a contract to grant an easement valid in equity.[84]

Before *Dunn v Blackdown Properties* in 1961[85] the application of the rule **12.23** against perpetuities to easements was by no means clear and was sometimes ignored.[86] In the Law of Property Act 1925 there is at s.162(1), "for removing doubts", a list of easements to which the rule against perpetuities does not apply. These include:

> "(d) to any grant, exception or reservation of any right of entry on, or user of, the surface of land or of any easements, rights or privileges over or under land for the purpose of:
>
> (i) winning, working, inspecting, measuring, converting, manufacturing, carrying away, and disposing of mines or minerals;
> (ii) inspecting, grubbing up, felling and carrying away timber and other trees, and the tops and lops thereof;
> (iii) executing repairs, alterations, or additions to any adjoining land, or the buildings and erections thereon;
> (iv) constructing, laying down, altering, repairing, renewing, cleansing and maintaining sewers, watercourses, cess-pools, gutters, drains, water-pipes, gas-pipes, electric wires or cables or other like works."

The section applies to easements granted before and after the passing of the Act and the draftsmen clearly considered that it represented the preexisting law. However, in *Dunn v Blackdown Properties Ltd*[87] Stamp J. construed para.(iv) narrowly to mean only rights additional to a grant which is not itself void for perpetuity.

7. Payment for easements

An easement can be a very valuable right. It may enhance the value of **12.24** the dominant tenement and reduce the value of the servient tenement. Where a freehold easement is purchased with freehold land it is not usual to pay any separate sum for the value of the easement. Its value is simply included in the purchase price. Equally, when an easement is annexed to leasehold land the value of the easement will be reflected in the rent and any premium paid.

---

[83] *South Eastern Railway Co v Associated Portland Cement Manufacturers* [1910] 1 Ch. 12.
[84] See below Ch. 16. See also *London and Blenheim Estates Ltd v Ladbroke Retail Parks* [1994] 1 W.L.R. 31, [1993] 4 All E.R. 157.
[85] [1961] Ch. 433.
[86] See, e.g. *Ardley v Guardians of Poor of St. Pancras* (1870) 39 L.J. Ch. 871.
[87] *Dunn v Blackdown Properties* [1961] Ch. 433.

Where a freehold easement is granted separately from a conveyance of the dominant tenement then payment may or may not be required. It has been said that there can be no rent for an easement.[88] However, it is not unusual for an easement to be granted for the benefit of leasehold land by way of a charge of rent which may be payable to the landlord or to the owner of the adjoining land over which the easement runs.[89]

There seems no reason in principle why rent should not be charged in this way. The authority cited for the proposition that there can be no rent for an easement is Coke on Littleton and *Capel v Buszard*,[90] where it was decided that there could be no distress upon boats exercising an easement attached to a lease. This case, however, does not lay down a clear general principle and it seems strange that it should be impossible for a landowner to grant a lease of an easement with payments of periodic rent.

12.25   What is not permitted is an obligation to pay rent or other periodic sums attached to a freehold easement. The situation is precisely the same with all freehold land. Unless the owner has executed a freehold rentcharge, he cannot charge the owner for his possession of the land or for his use of the easements annexed to it. Indeed payment of a nominal sum is sometimes used as a way of showing that a right in the nature of an easement is being exercised by licence only or that the right is a leasehold one terminable in the same way as any other leasehold.[91]

8.   Covenants to repair

12.26   The existence of an easement probably does not give rise to any general obligation on either the dominant or the servient owner to repair.[92] The granting of an easement does, however, mean that the owner of the servient tenement must do nothing to interfere with the existing supply. This applies not only to a water supply,[93] but also to an electricity supply.[94] There is a narrow distinction between positive action cutting off a water or electricity supply and inaction, such as informing the electricity supply company that the owner of the servient tenement no longer intends to pay for the supply. A dominant owner who uses the right excessively may be sued for excessive user and if, for

---

[88] *Gale on the Law of Easements*, 17th edn (London: Sweet & Maxwell, 2002), p.57.
[89] See *Encyclopedia of Forms & Precedents*, 4th edn (London: Butterworths), Vol. 7, p.677. This precedent is not included in the 5th edition.
[90] *Capel v Buszard, Assignees of Jones, Bankrupts* (1829) 6 Bing. 150.
[91] See *Wiles v Banks* (1985) 50 P. & C.R. 80.
[92] See below para.18.24 et seq. as to rights of way and para.19.10 et seq. as to Easements of Support.
[93] *Rance v Elvin* (1985) 50 P. & C.R. 9.
[94] *Duffy v Lamb* (1998) 75 P. & C.R. 364.

example, water escapes from a pipe so as to amount to a trespass the dominant owner is liable,[95] not because of any obligation to repair, but because he is not exercising his rights in accordance with the terms of the grant.

In *Transco v Stockport MBC*[96] Lord Scott set out the position succinctly:

"Entitlement to the easement [of support to a gas main] carries with it the subsidiary right of the dominant owner to carry out any necessary repairs to the servient land. A deliberate act by the servient owner damaging the servient land and thereby interfering with the enjoyment of the easement would be actionable in nuisance. In principle I can see no reason why a servient owner should not owe a duty of care to the dominant owner not to damage the servient land so as to interfere with the enjoyment of the easement. But it would, it seems to me, be contrary to principle to hold a servient owner liable to the dominant owner for damage to the servient land, or for any other interference with the easement, caused neither by a negligent act nor by an intentional act of the servient owner."

It follows that damage caused by ordinary wear and tear does not give rise to an automatic obligation to repair. As a result it is normal practice to include in a grant of an easement, such as a right of way or a right of water supply or drainage, a covenant by the dominant owner to pay a reasonable proportion of the cost of keeping the way, pipe or watercourse in repair. In the case of a water supply this does not include an obligation to pay a proportion of the water charges incurred as a result.[97]

Normally the repairing covenant is in favour of the owner of the servient tenement and accordingly the benefit passes in accordance with the principles in *Federated Homes v Mill Lodge Properties*.[98] Covenants of this kind can be regarded as touching and concerning the land.[99]

What is more difficult is where the owner of the dominant tenement, **12.27** on whom the burden of complying with the covenant should lie, is no longer the original covenantor. Such a covenant is not a restrictive covenant and accordingly the burden does not run with the land. The successor in title of the original covenantor cannot, therefore, be sued directly for his part of the cost of repair. The problem has been largely solved by *Halsall v Brizell*,[100] where it was decided that a person whose predecessor had covenanted to pay a fair proportion of the costs of

---

[95] *Jones v Pritchard* [1908] 1 Ch. 630.
[96] [2003] UKHL 61; [2004] 2 A.C. 1 at 31A.
[97] *Rance v Elvin* (1985) 50 P. & C.R. 9.
[98] [1980] 1 W.L.R. 594; [1980] 1 All E.R. 371.
[99] *Smith v River Douglas Catchment Board* [1949] 2 K.B. 500.
[100] [1957] Ch. 169.

repair will simply not be allowed to use the road unless he does so. This decision has been followed without question since. It does, however, leave the problem of the dominant owner who no longer wishes to use the easement and is accordingly unwilling to pay his share of the cost of repair.

In *Rance v Elvin*[101] the Court of Appeal went further than *Halsall v Brizell* and stated obiter, in a case where the dominant tenement had a right to a water supply, that the owner of the dominant tenement would be under an obligation in quasi-contract to pay a fair proportion of the actual charges incurred by the servient owner in charges through a water meter. This was in a case where there was no covenant to pay these water charges. It still, however, does not cover the person who does not wish to use the way, pipe or other easement and uses this as an excuse for not paying his share. It seems that there is no way that such a person can be obliged to meet his share of the cost of repair.

12.28   Occasionally, the servient owner has to covenant to maintain the subject-matter of the easement. This has happened, for example, in the case of a railway company anxious to obtain the land for the railway and willing to agree to provide and maintain accommodation ways. It has been held in Eire that in such a case the benefit of the covenant can pass with the ownership of the easement.[102] It has been held in England in *Grant v Edmondson* that a covenant to pay a rentcharge does not run with the rentcharge.[103]

However, that case involves an obscure point of the law of succession and there seems little reason to doubt that the benefit of a covenant to repair by the servient owner will pass with the easement and the land to which it is annexed. This seems consistent with *Smith v River Douglas Catchment Board*.[104] The same problem would arise, however, where the original covenantor has disposed of the property and in that case the solution used in *Halsall v Brizell*[105] would be ineffective to force a servient owner to pay since he would not wish to use the easement himself.

The position, therefore, is that the courts have run into difficulties in enforcing obligations to make payments in respect of easements, but where such payments are simply reimbursement for costs actually expended by the servient owner as a result of the dominant owner's use of the benefit of the easement, a way is usually found to ensure that the dominant owner pays.

---

[101] (1985) 50 P. & C.R. 9.
[102] *Gaw v Coras Iompair Eireann* [1953] I.R. 232.
[103] [1931] 1 Ch. 1.
[104] [1949] 2 K.B. 500.
[105] [1957] Ch. 169.

Chapter Thirteen
Creation of Easements—
Implied Grant

1. Introduction

Where there is a conveyance or other instrument passing land or an **13.01** interest in land, easements pertaining to that land or interest in land can pass or be created by implication, even though they are not expressly mentioned in the instrument. It has been seen[1] that, where a conveyance or other instrument contains an express grant of an easement, as a matter of construction additional rights may be included as ancillary rights beyond those actually mentioned, but this Chapter deals with the implied grant of easements which are not mentioned at all in the conveyance of other instruments.

In deciding whether a grant or reservation should be implied in any particular case, the central issue is the intention of the parties, deduced either from evidence from the people who entered into the deed or imputed from all the circumstances.

The primary way in which implied rights are granted is by virtue of the statutory implication contained in s.62 of the Law of Property Act 1925, but where, for any reason the statute cannot be used, the Courts will look broadly and in considerable detail at the circumstances surrounding the deed into which the grant or reservation is to be implied.

The modern law on this latter issue is set out in *Stafford v Lee*[2] and goes back to *Pwllbach Colliery Co Ltd v Woodman*,[3] but it used to be regarded as being of limited application. It has since been reinforced and extended in *Mobil Oil Co v Birmingham City Council*,[4] and *Shrewsbury v Adam*.[5]

Rights can also be created by implied grant under the rule in *Wheeldon v Burrows*[6] and by application of the principles of non-derogation from

---

[1] See para.12.19 et seq.
[2] (1993) 65 P. & C. R. 172.
[3] [1915] A.C. 634.
[4] [2002] 2 P. & C.R. 14.
[5] [2005] EWCA Civ 1006; [2006] 1 P. & C.R. 27.
[6] (1879) L.R. 12 Ch. D. 31.

grant. Where these doctrines are applicable, courts still apply them,[7] but it may be possible to deduce an overriding principle as set out above of which the rule in *Wheeldon v Burrows* is an example and the principle of non-derogation from grant is a justification.

Despite this observation the correct approach is still to look at the application of the various doctrines in sequence, though, in relation to the rule in *Wheeldon v Burrows*, it may be that some of the more technical approaches in the older cases are overridden by the wider principle of following the intention of the parties. The Law Commission Report, *Making Land Work: Easements, Covenants and Profits à Prendre*,[8] issued on June 8, 2011, makes some quite far reaching proposals for the reform of implied grants and reservations of easements. As stated above, there is no clear time-table for this reform, nor any certainty that it will take place.

The main proposed changes are:

- A provision that reservations of easements should be implied in the same circumstances as grants.

- The abolition of grants implied from the intention of the parties and under the rule in *Wheeldon v Burrows* with a single statutory basis for implication.[9] This would make a grant of an estate in land include "any easement over land retained by the grantor that is necessary for the reasonable use of the land which is the subject-matter of the grant" having regard to five specific factors. This is intended broadly to replicate the existing law, but it remains to be seen whether, in fact, it would reduce substantially the circumstances in which a grant would be implied. It is specifically and deliberately different from the test which applies to an implied term in a contract, including that which would be implied in a contract for the sale of land.

- The amendment of s.62 of the Law of Property Act 1925 to exclude precarious rights or advantages being, in effect, created by the Act or to convert a rights form leasehold to freehold. This, again, if put into effect would substantially reduce the scope of s.62 by excluding "advantages" which had been used by the dominant land when it was in common ownership, but were not actual easements.

---

[7] e.g. *P & S Platt Ltd v Crouch* [2003] EWCA Civ 1110; [2004] 1 P. & C.R. 18 (derogation from grant) and *McAdams Homes v Robinson* [2004] EWCA Civ 214; [2005] 1 P. & C.R. 30.

[8] Law Commission, *Making Land Work: Easements, Covenants and Profits à Prendre* (London: The Stationery Office, 2011), Law Com. No.327.

[9] Set out in cl. 20 of the draft Law of Property Bill, included in the Report.

2. Section 62 of the Law of Property Act 1925

Section 62(1) of the Law of Property Act 1925 provides: **13.02**

"A conveyance of land shall be deemed to include and shall by virtue of this Act operate to convey with the land, all buildings, erections, fixtures, commons, hedges, ditches, fences, ways, waters, watercourses, liberties, privileges, easements, rights and advantages whatsoever, appertaining or reputed to appertain to the land, or any part thereof, or, at the time of the conveyance, demised, occupied, or enjoyed with, or reputed or known as part or parcel of or appurtenant to the land or any part thereof."

Section 62(2) provides:

"A conveyance of land, having houses or other buildings thereon, shall be deemed to include and shall by virtue of this Act operate to convey with the land, houses or other buildings, all outhouses, erections, fixtures, cellars, areas, courts, courtyards, cisterns, sewers, gutters, drains, ways, passages, lights, water-courses, liberties, privileges, easements, rights, and advantages whatsoever, appertaining or reputed to appertain to the land, houses or other buildings conveyed, or any of them, or any part thereof."

Section 62(3) contains a similar provision for a conveyance of a manor.[10] The section applies to conveyances made after December 31, 1881 (when the Conveyancing Act 1881 came into effect). By s.205(1)(ii) "conveyance" includes a mortgage, charge, lease, assent, vesting declaration, vesting instrument, disclaimer, release and every other assurance of property or an interest therein by any instrument, except a will. It applies, therefore, to virtually any instrument which transfers or creates a legal estate in freehold or leasehold land. By virtue of s.52(2)(d) and s.54(2) of the Law of Property Act 1925 a "conveyance" under s.62 includes a lease which can be created effectively under hand, though it does not apply to an oral tenancy, which cannot be described as having been created by an "instrument".[11] Equally it does not apply to an agreement for a lease, even though express equitable easements can be created by an agreement for a lease.[12] The principle applies to enfranchisement under the Leasehold Enfranchisement Act 1997.[13] For simplicity, the terms "conveyance" and "vendor" and "purchaser" are used in this Chapter to include all of the

---

[10] *Crown Estate Commissioners v Roberts* [2008] EWHC 1302 (Ch); [2008] 4 All E.R. 828.
[11] *Rye v Rye* [1962] A.C. 496; [1962] 2 W.L.R. 361.
[12] *Borman v Griffith* [1930] 1 Ch. 493.
[13] *Kent v Kavanagh* [2006] EWCA Civ 162; [2007] Ch. 1.

instruments which come within the section and accordingly all the different kinds of transferor and transferee.

The section is framed in very wide terms. Initially it was regarded simply as shorthand to avoid inclusion of a long clause setting out what was included in the conveyance. Since then the authorities show two divergent approaches. In some cases s.62 is construed widely as including all rights which a purchaser might expect to be granted on the conveyance. In other cases it is regarded primarily as a conveyancing device, not intended to create new rights but simply to ensure that existing rights are passed to the new owner. In recent years the wider approach has become more and more generally accepted. It seems that it is the latter interpretation which is favoured by the Law Commission.[14]

13.03   These "easements, rights and advantages" can be divided into two kinds. First there are pre-existing legal easements in respect of which the land sold was the dominant tenement and where the servient tenement belongs to a third party. Although the word "profits" is not included in the mass of different terms in the section, it has been held that s.62 applies equally to profits.[15]

Such pre-existing legal easements could not exist over any land retained by the vendor since the dominant and servient tenements would be in common ownership and an owner, as the law stands, cannot have a legal easement over his own land. However, the vendor may also have existing easements over the other land which are not expressly referred to in the conveyance.

Where the vendor does not retain land there is no difficulty. Whatever easements he had pass to the purchaser and it is simply a question of deciding what pre-existing easements there were. However, in many cases the vendor does retain adjoining land. Even in respect of pre-existing easements over other land in the ownership of a third party it has been seen that there may be occasions when it is difficult to identify the dominant tenement. This problem has been dealt with above.[16] When the ownership of the grantee's land is split it may be more difficult to ascertain whether the dominant tenement is the land sold, the land retained, or both. There may, therefore, be a dispute as to whether the easement being exercised before the conveyance is for the benefit of the land disposed of and therefore passes to the purchaser, or is solely for the benefit of the vendor's retained land and therefore remains with the vendor, or can be exercised by both vendor and purchaser.

13.04   If once it is established that the land disposed of formed part of the dominant tenement of the pre-existing easement, then the benefit of the easement

---

[14] Law Commission, *Making Land Work: Easements, Covenants and Profits à Prendre* (London: The Stationery Office, 2011), Law Com. No.327.

[15] *White v Williams* [1922] 1 K.B. 727.

[16] See above para.10.06 et seq.

passes automatically to the new owner, even though the vendor may himself retain the same right in respect of all or part of his own land. To take the most obvious example, a farmer has a right of way for all purposes to his field. He obtains planning permission and sets out the field as a building estate. Even if, by some mischance, he omits to refer to the right of way when he sells the individual plots, the benefit of the right of way will pass to each of the purchasers, all of whom will be able to use the way. This was exactly what happened in *P & S Platt Ltd v Crouch*.[17] A hotel, house and bungalow had been operated together, with moorings being used in conjunction with both. The hotel was sold with an option to buy the house and bungalow, but the option was never exercised and the house and bungalow were sold separately. The access to the moorings was over the frontage of the house and bungalow. No mention was made of the moorings in the conveyance because everyone assumed that the option would be exercised. The Court of Appeal upheld the judge's decision that the right of access to moorings passed by implication with the hotel, even though it caused considerable inconvenience to the owners of the house and bungalow.

The problems with regard to pre-existing legal easements over other land, therefore, involve deciding whether the land conveyed forms part of the dominant tenement and, if it does, deciding whether the user by the purchaser, coupled with the continuing user by the vendor amount to excessive user.[18]

Most of the problems which specifically focus on s.62 concern "quasi-easements" or, in the terms of the section, "advantages" appertaining to the land conveyed and exercisable over the vendor's retained land. Frequently, although the land conveyed and the land retained by the vendor were previously in common ownership, they were not, at the time of the sale, in common occupation. The land sold may have been occupied by lessees. The former lessee may, indeed, be the purchaser. The chances are that any express easement referred to in the lease will be repeated in the conveyance, but these may be omitted or the lessee may have been exercising rights in the nature of easements without any express grant. Alternatively the land may have been occupied by a licensee, such as a relative of the vendor. **13.05**

It is in respect of these quasi-easements or "advantages" that there has been some divergence of judicial opinion. As long ago as 1897, it was held by the Court of Appeal in *Broomfield v Williams*[19] that when the vendor sold land with a building on it and retained adjoining open land, the general words included "all lights enjoyed with the house" so as to prevent the vendor from building beside it in such a way as to interfere with his right

---

[17] [2003] EWCA Civ 1110; [2004] 1 P. & C.R. 18.
[18] See Ch.18 and *Graham v Philcox* [1984] Q.B. 747; [1984] 2 All E.R. 643.
[19] [1897] 1 Ch. 602.

of light. This was followed in *International Tea Stores Co v Hobbs*[20] where it was held that by s.62 a conveyance will pass all ways actually used by the lessee at the date of the conveyance of the freehold to the lessee.

This, however, was not the universal view. The law was finally decided in favour of the wider view that such quasi-easements can be conveyed under s.62 in *Wright v MacAdam*[21] where Jenkins L.J. said:

> "First, the section is not confined to rights which, as a matter of law, were so annexed or appurtenant to the property conveyed at the time of the conveyance as to make them actually enforceable legal rights. Thus, on the severance of a piece of land in common ownership, the quasi-easements de facto enjoyed in respect of it by one part of the land over another will pass although, of course, as a matter of law, no man can have a right appendant or appurtenant to one part of his property exercisable by him over the other part of his property."[22]

Even since this decision views have been expressed to the contrary. In *White v Taylor (No.2)*[23] Buckley J. suggested obiter that sheep grazing rights could not pass under s.62 because the rights could not be appurtenant, because the two parcels were in common ownership at the time of the sale, though as Russell J. said in *Hansford v Jago*[24]

> "But from as long as the fourth year of Philip and Mary (*Hill v Grange*) the word 'appurtenances' has easily admitted of a secondary meaning and as equivalent in that case to usually occupied."[25]

Despite Buckley J.'s remarks, it is now clearly established by *Wright v MacAdam*[26] that rights which were not true easements at the time of the sale (because the two parcels of land were in common ownership) can pass under s.62. If, therefore, the right actually exercised by the tenant of the property conveyed is clearly in the nature of an easement, for example a right of way or a right of drainage, then there will be no difficulty. There will be an implied grant of the right exercised to the purchaser, unless a contrary intention appears from the conveyance.

13.06 However, even where the two parcels of land are not in common occupation there may be advantages of a much less clear-cut nature exercised by the occupant of the land subsequently conveyed. The vendor and the

---

[20] [1903] 2 Ch. 165.
[21] [1949] 2 K.B. 744.
[22] *Wright v MacAdam* [1949] 2 K.B. 744 at 748.
[23] [1969] Ch. 150; [1967] 3 All E.R. 349.
[24] [1921] 1 Ch. 322 at 331.
[25] See *William Hill (Southern) Ltd v Cabras Ltd* (1987) 54 P. & C.R. 42.
[26] [1949] 2 K.B. 744.

occupant may be friends or relatives. The vendor may allow the occupant to use a short cut through his garden or to share his woodshed.

It might be thought that such advantages could only become the subject of an implied grant if they were exercised without permission. However, that is not the case.[27] This appears odd at first sight, but it must be remembered that this "advantage" has not, up to the date of the conveyance which separates the land from common ownership, been a true easement at all:

> "The right, in order to pass, need not be one which the owner or occupier for the time being of the land had what might be described as a permanent title. A right enjoyed merely by permission is enough".[28]

This situation arose in *Ward v Kirkland*,[29] where the rector conveyed land to the plaintiff's predecessor in title together with the right to use a yard. In conjunction with the use of the yard it was necessary from time to time to enter onto the rector's retained land to carry out repairs to a wall. This had in fact been done without consent in the past, but Ungoed Thomas J. held that it could be the subject-matter of an implied grant under s.62 whether it was by consent or not:

> "Nevertheless on its wording section 62 would apply to an advantage enjoyed by a common owner for one of his two properties over the other of his two properties as distinct from his enjoyment of that advantage merely as owner of that other property in as much as it would be unrealistic to consider whether he gave himself permission; and this tends to indicate that what the section looks at is not permission in any form at all but actual practice."

It is clear from this decision that "section 62 does not require that the advantage should be a continuous and apparent easement".[30]

This decision followed *International Tea Stores Co v Hobbs*[31] where the way had been used by permission and was locked at night and *Wright v MacAdam*[32] where a coal shed was used by the lessee with the landlord's permission.

On the other hand, it cannot be any privilege granted to the previous **13.07** occupant of the property conveyed which becomes the subject of an

---

[27] *Hair v Gillman* (2000) 80 P. & C.R. 108.
[28] per Jenkins L.J. in *Wright v MacAdam* [1949] 2 K.B. 744 at 748.
[29] [1967] Ch. 194; [1966] 1 W.L.R. 601.
[30] ibid. at 229G.
[31] [1903] 2 Ch. 165.
[32] [1949] 2 K.B. 744.

implied grant. The vendor may have allowed his relative to make all sorts of use of the other parts of his property which he never intended to pass on to the purchaser of the freehold as easements.

This problem was addressed in *Green v Ashco Horticulturist Ltd.*[33] In that case the plaintiff had been the lessee for many years. During this time he had frequently used a back way into his shop which went over the lessor's property. He had done so with the consent and permission of the lessor, but this was not fatal to his claim. It was held that there were two circumstances in which, even though there had been long user, there would be no implied grant:

> "In the first place the section can only operate if the kind of user relied on could have been the subject of a grant of a legal right, and secondly, the section will not operate if at the time of the conveyance or lease in question it was or should have been apparent to the grantee or lessee that the enjoyment which he claims to have been converted into a right by the section was only temporary."

In that particular case the use had gone on for so long that the court held that it was not obvious that it was temporary, but because it was only "as and when convenient to the landlord" it could not have been the subject matter of a grant, for you cannot have a grant of a right of way as and when convenient to the grantor. However, it was held in *Bartlett v Tottenham*[34] that a watercourse caused by a tank which overflowed was only a temporary right and accordingly did not pass with the land, even though the tank had been overflowing continuously for many years so that it produced a regular flow of water through the stream. The court held that it was obvious from the fact that the water came from an over-flowing tank that one day the person who owned the tank might cover it over and prevent the overflow.

In *Crow v Wood*,[35] F had bought land from a common vendor with a right to stray sheep on the moor owned by the vendor, but subject to a duty to keep his fences up. It was held that with that sale went a right to have other walls adjoining the moor kept up so that when his sheep strayed onto the farm of another farmer who had bought on the same terms from the common vendor he had a defence to cattle trespass. It was rather a specialised case, but it seems that it fits in with the principles set out above, although the right claimed was a right in the nature of an easement rather than a normal easement.

---

[33] [1966] 1 W.L.R. 889; [1966] 2 All E.R. 232.
[34] [1932] 1 Ch. 114.
[35] [1971] 1 Q.B. 77; [1970] 3 All E.R. 425.

The position is even more difficult where the property sold and the **13.08** property retained have previously been in the same occupation. In *Broomfield v Williams*,[36] a right of light case, the fact that the two properties had formerly been in common ownership and occupation did not prevent the easement passing under s.62. However, in *Sovmots Investments v Secretary of State for the Environment*[37] Lord Wilberforce stated:

> "Whatever the owner does, he does as owner and, until a separation occurs, of ownership or at least of occupation, the condition for the existence of rights etc. does not exist".

It is possible to argue that this was obiter and that the law on s.62 had not been properly argued. However, since then this principle has been reiterated in *Squarey v Harris-Smith*[38] and in *Payne v Inwood*.[39] In the latter case, the argument that Lord Wilberforce's dictum in *Sovmots Investments v Secretary of State for the Environment*[40] should be ignored was met head on and the Court of Appeal distinguished *Broomfield v Williams*[41] stating that this case,

> "is . . . to be confined to cases dealing with such advantages as light to buildings. It is an exception to the general rule stated by Sargant J.[42] and accepted by Lord Wilberforce and Lord Edmund-Davies".[43]

In all of these cases the exclusion of s.62 is justifiable on the basis that the user was not specifically for the benefit of the proposed dominant tenement. Thus in *Payne v Inwood*[44] the appeal was also allowed on the basis that a wrong inference had been drawn on the facts that the gate between the two back gardens was to facilitate crossing the back garden, rather than visiting the house next door. Nevertheless, despite the very short period of common ownership, Roch L.J. was keen to emphasise that the decision on the law was to follow *Sovmots* and to distinguish *Broomfield v Williams*.

In *Nickerson v Barroughclough*[45] it was suggested that a conveyance **13.09** could include an implied grant in favour of other land previously purchased by the purchaser, but the Court of Appeal held that,

---

[36] [1897] 1 Ch. 602.
[37] [1979] A.C. 144 at 169B.
[38] (1987) 42 P. & C.R. 118.
[39] (1997) 74 P. & C.R. 42.
[40] [1979] A.C. 144.
[41] [1897] 1 Ch. 602.
[42] In *Long v Gowlett* [1923] 2 Ch. 177.
[43] per Roch L.J. at 51.
[44] *Payne v Inwood* (1997) 74 P. & C.R. 42.
[45] *Nickerson v Barroughclough* [1981] Ch. 426; [1981] 2 All E.R. 369.

"what section 62 does not, I think, do is to make a piece of land which is not the subject-matter of the grant the dominant tenement in relation to an easement deemed to have been granted by the conveyance".[46]

In *Graham v Philcox*[47] on the other hand, it was held that where a transferor of land is the same person as the owner of an adjoining servient tenement over which part of the land transferred enjoys a right of way, then s.62 enlarges that right in the sense that it thereafter enures for the benefit of the whole of the land transferred. *Nickerson v Barroughclough* was not cited in *Graham v Philcox*, but there is a difference between the two cases, in that it would have been open to the vendor in *Graham v Philcox*, as owner of the adjoining land, to have made an express grant of the right claimed without referring expressly to the servient land, whereas this would not have been possible in *Nickerson v Barroughclough* without referring expressly to the proposed dominant tenement.

It was held in *MRA Engineering Ltd v Trimster Co Ltd*[48] that s.62 cannot create easements over other land which the vendor could not have created by express grant at the time of the conveyance because he had already disposed of that land free of such easements. This means, therefore, that when an incumbent of a benefice sells the rectory he cannot by implication grant a right of way over the churchyard because he has no power to deal with the churchyard without a faculty and this could not be implied.[49]

13.10   In *Green v Ashco Horticulturist Ltd*[50] the claim was rejected on the grounds that it could not have been the subject-matter of a grant, as was the claim to a supply of hot water in *Regis Property Co Ltd v Redman*,[51] but it is not entirely clear that this is a sufficient reason for rejecting a claim under s.62. In *Goldberg v Edwards*[52] a personal right was held to pass under the general words and in *Crow v Wood*[53] a right to have land fenced, which is arguably not a true easement, was held to pass under s.62.[54] The words of s.62 are certainly wide enough to cover rights which are not capable of amounting to easements, but it seems illogical that a right which is not capable of being the subject matter of a grant could pass by implication and this was conceded in *P&S Platt Ltd v Crouch*.[55]

The position is far from clear, but from these authorities it is possible to formulate some tentative rules. To be the subject of an implied grant:

---

[46] *Nickerson v Barroughclough* [1981] Ch. 426; [1981] 2 All E.R. 369 Per Brightman L.J. at 382a.
[47] [1984] 1 Q.B. 747; [1984] 3 W.L.R. 150.
[48] (1988) 56 P. & C.R. 1.
[49] *Re St Clement's, Leigh on Sea* [1988] 1 W.L.R. 720.
[50] [1966] 1 W.L.R. 889; [1966] 2 All E.R. 232.
[51] [1956] 2 Q.B. 612; [1956] 3 W.L.R. 95.
[52] [1950] Ch. 247.
[53] [1971] 1 Q.B. 77; [1970] 3 W.L.R. 516.
[54] See Ch. 21.
[55] [2003] EWCA Civ 1110; [2004] 1 P. & C.R. 18.

- the right claimed must have been actually exercised prior to the conveyance, whether or not by permission. The court looks at what was happening at the time of the conveyance and for a reasonable time before[56];

- it must have been exercised in circumstances where it was not and should not have been apparent that the exercise was only temporary;

- it must be capable of being the subject matter of a grant of a legal easement;

- it must have been exercised for the benefit of the land conveyed and not just as common owner of the two properties;

- it must have been capable of being granted expressly by the instrument into which it is being implied without adding new parties or making any express reference to other land;

- the two properties must have been in separate ownership or occupation.

In relation to rights of light, it might be thought that the mere existence of the building at the time of the grant would not be enough to imply a grant of a right of light. However, in *Lyme Valley Squash Club Ltd v Newcastle under Lyme BC*[57] it was held, following *Broomfield v Williams*,[58] that,

> "the conveyance to the club prima facie carried an easement of light to its windows similar to the right which was being de facto enjoyed at the time of the conveyance".[59]

Section 62(4) provides that the section applies if and as far as a contrary **13.11** intention is not expressed in the conveyance and has effect subject to the terms of the conveyance and to the provision therein contained. This section has, however, been strictly construed. The mere fact that the conveyance contains a grant of a right of way over the same route which is much narrower than that previously enjoyed, has been held not to amount to a contrary intention.[60] Equally a reference in the conveyance to "gardens, outbuildings and appurtenances" even if "appurtenances" did not refer to quasi-easements would not prevent such quasi-easements

---

[56] *Green v Ashco Horticulturist Ltd* [1966] 1 W.L.R. 889 at 898G per Cross J.
[57] [1985] 2 All E.R. 405.
[58] [1897] 1 Ch. 602.
[59] *Lyme Valley Squash Club Ltd v Newcastle under Lyme BC* [1985] 2 All E.R. 405 per Judge Blackett Ord V.C. at 412b.
[60] *Gregg v Richards* [1926] Ch. 521.

passing under the general words[61] and a reference in the plan to "building land" adjoining the property sold did not controvert the grant by implication of a right of light.[62] However, where the section creates an injustice, for example where there is an option of re-purchase and the effect would be to give the original vendor additional benefits over those he had at the time of the original sale,[63] a contrary intention was inferred from the circumstances. This suggests that a less strict approach to contrary intention may be emerging.

Section 62(1) and 62(2) both contain the words "or reputed to appertain". While these words have been considered on occasion,[64] it is not clear whether they add anything. They do counter any suggestion that easements granted under s.62 must have been "continuous and apparent" before the grant, but it seems that really they are inserted to make it clear that the section applies to quasi-easements as well as pre-existing legal easements.

3.   The rule in *Wheeldon v Burrows*

13.12   Before s.62 of the Law of Property Act 1925 and its predecessor, s.6 of the Conveyancing Act 1881, the courts had already developed a principle of implied grant. This developed from the more general principle of non-derogation from grant based in turn on the general moral principle that a person should not be allowed to make a grant with one hand and effectively take it away with the other.

The principle was succinctly set out in *Wheeldon v Burrows*[65] and has come to be known as the rule in *Wheeldon v Burrows*, though it is worth remembering that Thesiger L.J. was only setting out what he believed to be the law at the time and that his words should not be treated as if they were the words of a statute. In recent times, the principles of implication from the intention of the parties and implication from the circumstances have, to a considerable degree, extended or even superseded the rule in *Wheeldon v Burrows*. Nevertheless, tribunals still deal with this principle where it is applicable before moving on to alternative approaches.[66]

What Thesiger L.J. said in *Wheeldon v Burrows*[67] was:

> "The first of these rules is, that on the grant by the owner of a tenement of part of that tenement as it is then used and enjoyed, there

---

[61] *Hansford v Jago* [1921] 1 Ch. 322.

[62] *Broomfield v Williams* [1897] 1 Ch. 602.

[63] *Selby DC v Samuel Smith Old Brewery* (Tadcaster) (2000) 80 P. & C.R. 466.
   See e.g. in *White v Taylor (No.2)* [1969] 1 Ch. 150; [1967] 3 All E.R. 349.

[64] e.g. in *White v Taylor (No.2)* [1969] 1 Ch. 150.

[65] (1876) L.R. 12 Ch.D. 31.

[66] e.g. *McAdams Homes Ltd v Robinson* [2004] EWCA Civ 214; [2005] 1 P. & C.R. 30.

[67] (1876) L.R. 12 Ch. D. 31 at 49.

will pass to the grantee all those continuous and apparent easements (by which, of course, I mean quasi-easements), or, in other words, all those easements which are necessary to the reasonable enjoyment of the property granted, and which have been and are at the time of the grant used by the owners of the entirety for the benefit of the part granted."

The rights which pass under the rule in *Wheeldon v Burrows* are signifi- **13.13** cantly more limited than those that pass under s.62 and accordingly it is only in circumstances where s.62 does not or may not apply that it is necessary to consider in any depth whether a grant can be implied at common law.[68] One such example is an agreement for a lease. Such an agreement does not count as a conveyance for the purposes of s.62, but nevertheless rights pass by implication in equity under the rule in *Wheeldon v Burrows*.[69]

The reference in Thesiger L.J.'s statement to "quasi-easements" is to make the point, which has been made above with regard to s.62, that rights which are de facto exercised in respect of one property over other property in the same ownership, whether by the occupier of both properties or by a tenant or separate occupier of the part sold off, are not true easements since no one can have an easement over his own property.

The first limitation contained in Thesiger L.J.'s judgment is the requirement that the rights must be "continuous and apparent". *Wheeldon v Burrows*[70] concerned lights and the lights of a building are bound to be continuous and apparent, but a problem arises in respect of rights which are exercised intermittently. A right exercised as and when necessary to repair the side wall of a house, while exercised perfectly openly, will not be continuous and apparent, because it leaves no mark on the ground to show it has been exercised.[71] It is not, however, necessary that the user should be literally continuous. A metalled path or even a worn track will be sufficient.[72] It seems that even a gate at either side of the servient tenement or some other such obvious sign of a way will be sufficient.[73] A gate in itself, however, may not be sufficient to indicate a way. A gate in the garden wall may just indicate that the two adjoining occupiers used to visit each other.[74]

---

[68] In *Millman v Ellis* (1996) 71 P. & C.R. 158 the Court chose to deal first with the rule in *Wheeldon v Burrows* and to make no finding on s.62 of the Law of Property Act 1925. It is not clear what the "difficult issues" which would have arisen under s.62 were.

[69] *Borman v Griffith* [1930] 1 Ch. 493.

[70] *Wheeldon v Burrows* (1879) L.R. 12 Ch. D. 31.

[71] *Ward v Kirkland* [1967] Ch. 194; [1966] 1 W.L.R. 601.

[72] *Hansford v Jago* [1921] 1 Ch. 322.

[73] *Donnelly v Adams* [1905] 1 I.R. 154.

[74] *Payne v Inwood* (1997) 74 P. & C.R. 42.

13.14   The position at the actual moment of the conveyance is not crucial.

> "One must look at a reasonable period of time before the conveyance was made to see if there was any apparent or regular use."[75]

In respect of rights of way, the emphasis has been on the importance of the way being "apparent" even if use has not been continuous, but in respect of water rights, which are almost always continuous, it has been held that a water supply from a well on the vendor's property passed by implication, even though it was so hidden that the owner of the servient tenement was not aware of it,[76] and in *McAdams Homes Ltd v Robinson*[77] Neuberger L.J. stated that "drainage is within the category of 'continuous and apparent easements".[78] This demonstrates the willingness of the courts to expand the concept as necessary to do justice between the parties.

Thesiger L.J.'s judgment seems to indicate that "continuous and apparent" and "necessary to the enjoyment of the part granted" are synonymous, but they plainly are not:

> "Secondly the doctrine in *Wheeldon v Burrows* can only be prayed in aid where the easement claimed, in addition to being continuous and apparent, is necessary for the reasonable enjoyment of the dominant tenement. That is in fact a debatable proposition, for it is arguable that the continuity and apparency of and the necessity for the easement are alternative and not cumulative requirements."[79]

Despite this recent comparatively statement, over the years there have been many references to the word "necessary" which treat it as a further requirement. Maugham J. in *Borman v Griffith*[80] spoke of a road which "is necessary for the reasonable enjoyment of the property", and the Court of Appeal in *Goldberg v Edwards*[81] approved this with the gloss of its being necessary for the reasonable and convenient use of the property.

It is certainly true that easements have been held to pass under the rule in *Wheeldon v Burrows* which could not in any real sense be said to be necessary. Thus in *Watts v Kelson*[82] it was held that a watercourse through a drain and pipes passed with the conveyance. Mellish L.J. said that "we think it proved that no other supply of water equally convenient or

---

[75] per Megarry J. in *Costagliola v English* (1969) 210 E.G. 1425.
[76] *Schwann v Cotton* [1916] 2 Ch. 459.
[77] [2004] EWCA Civ 214; [2005] 1 P. & C.R. 30.
[78] *McAdams Homes Ltd v Robinson* [2004] EWCA Civ 214; [2005] 1 P. & C.R. 30 at [8].
[79] per Oliver L.J. in *Squarey v Harris Smith* (1981) 42 P. & C.R. 118 at 124.
[80] [1930] 1 Ch. 493.
[81] [1950] Ch. 247.
[82] (1870–71) L.R. 6 Ch. App. 166.

equally pure could have been obtained".[83] In *Millman v Ellis*[84] the Court of Appeal construed "necessary" widely, particularly where the way could not otherwise be used safely. The fact that the alternative route is unsafe is an important factor in deciding whether the implication of a right of way is "necessary".

Nevertheless, *Goldberg v Edwards*[85] made it clear that it is not every **13.15** continuous and apparent easement that will pass. In that case there were alternative ways of getting to the property, one through the house and one via a back passageway. It was held that a right through the house did not pass by implication because it was not "necessary". This was also the approach taken in *Wheeler v J J Saunders Ltd*[86] where there were two means of access and no reference to one of them in the conveyance. The Court of Appeal held that as the one means of access was perfectly suitable, it was not necessary to imply a right of way over the other. Staughton L.J. said:

"Even to a novice in the law of easements it seems clear that the class of easements implied in favour of a grantee is wider than easements of necessity. The question is, how much wider?"[87]

Perhaps the most obvious such case is *Burrows v Lang*,[88] where a farm was sold off. The farm had benefited from a subsidiary watercourse which ran from a mill stream. Though the watercourse was continuous and apparent, it was held that it did not pass because it was obvious that it would be expensive to maintain the mill race and, since the benefit was limited, it would not be reasonable to imply an obligation to continue such a supply.

In all of these cases the rule in *Wheeldon v Burrows* has been treated as a **13.16** clear statement of the law. However, an alternative approach is to suggest that the rule in *Wheeldon v Burrows* is not a rule at all, but just a statement of the obvious proposition that some rights are intended to pass when a property is conveyed and that others are not, and that all that is necessary is to look at the conveyance and the surrounding circumstances and see what must have been intended.

This is the principle set out by Lord Parker in *Pwllbach Colliery v Woodman*,[89] quoted and dealt with more fully below.[90] However, it is clear

---

[83] *Watts v Kelson* (1870–71) L.R. 6 Ch. App. 166 at 175.
[84] (1996) 71 P. & C.R. 158.
[85] [1950] Ch. 247.
[86] [1996] Ch. 19; [1995] 3 W.L.R. 466; [1995] 2 All E.R. 697.
[87] *Wheeler v J J Saunders Ltd* [1996] Ch. 19; [1995] 3 W.L.R. 466; [1995] 2 All E.R. 697 at 702a.
[88] [1901] 2 Ch. 502.
[89] [1915] A.C. 634 at 646.
[90] See below paras 13.26 et seq.

that in *Ward v Kirkland*[91] for example, the right to inspect and repair the wall would have been implied if one simply looked at the circumstances. In none of the cases where reference has been made to "common intention" or implication from the circumstances has it ever been suggested that the judgment expressed by Thesiger L.J. in *Wheeldon v Burrows*[92] is wrong, but it now appears that the argument has moved on and the courts will not allow themselves to be restricted by decisions made in some of the older cases, if the result will create an injustice.

As with s.62, if a contrary intention appears either from the conveyance or from the surrounding circumstances, easements which would otherwise be implied under the rule will not pass by implication. However, the fact that there is an express grant of a more restricted right is not in itself sufficient to amount to a contrary intention.[93]

4. Implied reservation

13.17   The one major limitation of s.62 of the Law of Property Act 1925 is that it does not apply to reservations. The same applies to the rule in *Wheeldon v Burrows*:

> "The second proposition is that, if the grantor intends to reserve any right over the tenement granted, it is his duty to reserve it expressly in the grant."[94]

It is true that there is a certain logic to the proposition that while a purchaser can reasonably expect to get all that goes with what he has purchased, it is reasonable to expect the vendor to set out precisely what rights he wishes to retain over the property he is disposing of. Otherwise he is derogating from his grant.[95]

In practice, however, the distinction between grant and reservation frequently creates an anomaly. It is often a matter of chance which of two plots of land is disposed of first. If the vendor of two plots of land has not really thought about the respective easements created over the two properties the one disposed of first gets all the easements which can be implied under s.62 and under the rule in *Wheeldon v Burrows* while the purchaser of the second plot can obtain only such rights as the vendor has reserved over the first plot.

It follows that one of the things to discover when considering whether an easement claimed by a party has passed by implication is whether the

---

[91] [1967] Ch. 194.
[92] (1876) L.R. 12 Ch. D. 31.
[93] *Millman v Ellis* (1996) 71 P. & C.R. 158.
[94] *Wheeldon v Burrows* (1876) L.R. 12 Ch. D. 31 per Thesiger L.J. at 49.
[95] *Adealon International Corp Proprietary Ltd v Merton LBC* [2006] EWHC 1075 (Ch); 2 P. & C. R. DG13.

predecessor in title of the alleged dominant tenement bought the property from the common owner before or after the predecessor in title of the alleged servient tenement.

The situation may arise, however, where the purchaser of one plot of land was the first to contract, but the purchaser of the other plot of land was the first to complete the purchase. In this situation, the rights implied in favour of the person who was first to contract will be those implied on a grant. It follows that reservations will be implied into the first conveyance to be completed of all rights which have been granted in equity by the earlier contract to sell the other land.[96]

There are, however, exceptions to the second rule in *Wheeldon v Burrows* **13.18** set out above. These exceptions were considered by the Court of Appeal in *Re Webb's Lease*.[97] There Jenkins L.J.[98] said:

> "As to the law applicable to the case, it is not disputed that as a general rule a grantor, whether by way of conveyance or lease of part of a hereditament in his ownership, cannot claim any easement over the part retained unless it is expressly reserved out of the grant . . . There are, however, certain exceptions to the general rule. Two well-established exceptions relate to easements of necessity and mutual easements, such as rights of support between adjacent buildings. It is however recognised in the authorities that these two specific exceptions do not exhaust the list, which is, indeed, incapable of exhaustive statement as the circumstances of any particular case may be such as to raise a necessary inference that the common intention of the parties must have been to reserve some easement to the grantor or such as to preclude the grantee from denying the right consistently with good faith, and there appears to be no doubt that where circumstances such as these are clearly established, the court will imply the appropriate reservation."

The requirement that an easement should be expressly reserved does not mean that the terms of the reservation should be construed any more strictly than any other conveyance. For example the omission of express reference to a right of common does not prevent the Court from construing a general reservation as being intended to include such a right.[99]

Perhaps the reality is that the fact that the claimant is claiming an implied reservation is only one part of the attempt to discover or impute the true

---

[96] *Beddington v Atlee* (1887) L.R. 35 Ch. D. 317, approved in *White v Taylor* (No.2) [1969] 1 Ch. 150; [1967] 3 All E.R. 349.
[97] [1951] Ch. 808; [1951] 2 All E.R. 131.
[98] *Re Webb's Lease* [1951] Ch. 808; [1951] 2 All E.R. 131 at 141E.
[99] *Hall v Moore* [2009] EWCA Civ 201.

intention of the parties. The principle of non-derogation from grant, below, is at the centre of what the parties intend, or are presumed to intend. However, matters such as whether the reservation was a mere technicality and whether the vendor really needed to have a right of way will be taken into account in trying to assess the true intention of the parties.

(a) Necessity

13.19 It has always been considered that the reservation of an easement by necessary implication is different from the principle whereby a way of necessity is implied in the case of a conveyance of land-locked land. This is dealt with below.[100] However, in *Adealon International Property Ltd v Merton LBC*[101] Kirkham J., having reviewed the authorities, decided the case on the intention of the parties.

It is easier to find examples of what has not been considered necessary than examples of what has. *Wheeldon v Burrows*[102] itself involved a right of light for a workshop retained for a month when the adjoining land was sold and then itself disposed of. It was held that there was no implied reservation of a right of light for the windows in the workshop which overlooked the land sold. In *Kwiatkowski v Cox*[103] it was held that there was no implied reservation of a right of access for inspecting and maintaining a flank wall, and in *Hatfield v Moss*[104] it was held that there was no implied reservation in favour of the landlord of the rest of the building of a right to go into the roof space above the top flat. Equally in *Aldridge v Wright*[105] there was no implied reservation of a right of way through the garden of the land conveyed.

It is clear that an implied reservation will apply where the land retained is otherwise land-locked in the same way as a grant of a way of necessity.[106] Equally, it seems that a right of access for maintenance of overhanging eaves and the opening of windows can be impliedly reserved, as can the right to use the drains.[107]

Although the necessity referred to in the second rule in *Wheeldon v Burrows* is less stringent than that required for a way of necessity, it is narrower than the "necessity" for the reasonable and convenient enjoyment of the property required for the implied grant of continuous and apparent easements under the first rule in *Wheeldon v Burrows*.

---

[100] See para.13.32 et seq.
[101] [2006] EWHC 1075 (Ch); [2006] 2 P. & C.R. DG13.
[102] *Wheeldon v Burrows* (1879) L.R. 12 Ch. D. 31.
[103] (1969) 213 E.G. 34.
[104] [1988] 2 E.G. 58 (C.S.).
[105] [1929] 2 K.B. 117.
[106] *Antigua v Boxwill* (1969) 15 W.I.R. 56.
[107] *Williams v Usherwood* (1983) 45 P. & C.R. 235.

(b) Other exceptions

Various attempts have been made to set out the other exceptions to the **13.20** rule that reservations are not implied. Jenkins L.J. in *Re Webb's Lease*[108] singled out "mutual easements such as rights of support between adjacent buildings." This would seem to be a reference to *Jones v Pritchard*,[109] where on the sale of a house with a party wall with the vendor's retained property all necessary easements were held to be granted and reserved.

The exception has also been applied in the right of light cases. In the normal way, a right of light to existing windows, even though newly built, will pass under the rule in *Wheeldon v Burrows*; see *Lyme Valley Squash Club Ltd v Newcastle under Lyme BC*[110] (though the argument in that case was actually founded on non-derogation from grant), and *Broomfield v Williams*.[111] However, where the retained land has been set out for building so that it is obvious that if the buildings intended to be built on the retained land are built there is bound to be a diminution of light, then the implied easement which passes is restricted to that extent.[112]

In short, "an implied reservation is very different from an implied grant, and the burden of proving an intended reservation is a heavy one",[113] but it is not insuperable.[114]

(c) Leases of adjoining land

There is a particular problem where before the conveyance or lease the **13.21** vendor or lessor has leased adjoining land with the benefit of easements over the land disposed of. If the rule in *Wheeldon v Burrows* was applied strictly to this situation, such easements would not be reserved by implication and accordingly the rights would cease to exist unless the vendor had expressly reserved them. The only remedy of the lessee of the other land would be a claim for breach of covenant against his landlord.

That, however, is not the position. Where land is conveyed or leased and there is an existing lease of adjoining land which has the benefit of implied easements, there is an implied reservation of the easements in favour of the adjoining land.[115]

This may seem an obvious principle, but this exception to the second rule in *Wheeldon v Burrows* goes further because where there is an existing quasi-easement in favour of land which is subject to a lease at the time of

---

[108] [1951] Ch. 808.
[109] [1908] 1 Ch. 630.
[110] [1985] 2 All E.R. 405.
[111] [1897] 1 Ch. 602.
[112] *Birmingham, Dudley and District Banking Co v Ross* (1888) L.R. 38 Ch. D. 295; *Godwin v Schweppes Ltd* [1902] 1 Ch. 926.
[113] *Rysaffe Trustee Co v Ataghan Ltd* [2006] EWHC 2324(Ch) at [124].
[114] See *Hall v Moore* [2009] EWCA Civ 201.
[115] *Thomas v Owen* (1888) L.R. 20 Q.B.D. 225.

a freehold conveyance of the servient tenement, there is an implied reservation not only of that leasehold easement, but of a freehold easement as well. The owner of the land is then able to sell the retained land with the benefit of a full easement.[116]

Where the dominant tenement is subject to a periodic tenancy at the time of the sale, it seems, however, that there is no implied reservation of continuous and apparent easements in favour of the freehold reversion, but the sale is nevertheless subject to an implied reservation of such easements during the existing periodic tenancy and any statutory continuance of it.[117]

(d) Simultaneous transactions

13.22   Where a common vendor disposes of two plots of land at the same time, both conveyances are treated as grants within the first rule in *Wheeldon v Burrows*.[118] Simultaneous disposals may occur on sale, or winding up an estate,[119] or on disposals by gift.[120]

Where there is a sale the relevant date is the date of the contract and not the conveyance:

> "The implied grant of easements in those cases arises only, in my judgment, where both conveyances are the result of contracts deemed to be contemporaneous and so are deemed to be themselves contemporaneous parts of one transaction".[121]

The rationale of this is that if the contracts are exchanged simultaneously, then equitable easements arise immediately and such equitable easements are converted into legal easements and reservations on the respective conveyances even if the actual conveyances are not simultaneous.[122]

13.23   It is not clear how much leeway will be allowed on simultaneous transactions. Certainly a delay of a month was held to prevent the transactions being simultaneous.[123]

The principle is based on the doctrine of non-derogation from grant[124] and there would not seem to be any difference in principle between a

---

[116] *Westwood v Heywood* [1921] 2 Ch. 130.
[117] *Re Flanigan and McGarvey and Thompson's Contract* [1945] N.I.L.R. 32.
[118] *Allen v Taylor* (1880–81) L.R. 16 Ch.D. 355; *White v Taylor* (No.3) [1969] 1 Ch. 160; [1968] 1 All E.R. 1015 at 1026.
[119] *Allen v Taylor* (1880–81) L.R. 16 Ch. D. 355.
[120] *Phillips v Low* [1892] 1 Ch. 47 at 51.
[121] per Fry L.J. in *Russell v Watts* (1884) L.R. 25 Ch. D. 559; overruled on the facts by H.L.(1885) 10 App. Cas. 590.
[122] *White v Taylor* (No.3) [1969] 1 Ch. 160; [1968] 1 All E.R. 1015.
[123] *Wheeldon v Burrows* (1879) L.R. 12 Ch. D. 31.
[124] *Russell v Watts* (1884–85) L.R. 25 Ch. D. 559 and see below para.13.25.

building scheme where there is a single estate plan but which results in successive contracts and a building scheme where all the plots are sold in the same auction. Nevertheless *Wheeldon v Burrows*[125] is authority for the proposition that, whatever may have been contemplated by the vendor, a close temporal link is needed.

There has been no clear decision on the effects of simultaneous transactions on the implied grant under s.62 of the Law of Property Act 1925. Since s.62 applies only to grants, it is not possible for a right to be reserved under s.62. However, there seems no reason why the common law principle that simultaneous transactions are both treated as grants should not also be applied to the statutory implication under s.62.

5. Non-derogation from grant

The principle of non-derogation from grant is a general rule applying **13.24** to all conveyances and leases and is not restricted to easements. In its most general form it is a rule that a person disposing of property should not do anything to render that disposal nugatory. As such it is a rule of common honesty.

The rule in *Wheeldon v Burrows*[126] was specifically based on the principle. In addition, s.62 of the Law of Property Act 1925 has now been interpreted in such a way as to cover most situations where non-derogation from grant could arise. In *Ward v Kirkland*[127] Ungoed-Thomas J., having decided that the easement claimed did not pass under the first rule in *Wheeldon v Burrows*, went on to consider the principle of non-derogation from grant, but having observed that it usually operates to restrict the vendor in acts he does on his own land, suggested that "this may no longer be a very important consideration in view of the operation nowadays of general words".

The central importance of the doctrine to the whole concept of implied grant of easements was emphasised in *Saeed v Plustrade*.[128] It seems, in reality, that the two rules in *Wheeldon v Burrows* and s.62 of the Law of Property Act 1925 and the general principle that a grant is implied from the intention of the parties and the circumstances are all part of the proposition that a vendor or lessor should not derogate from his grant.

Although the doctrine undoubtedly applies to freehold conveyances, at **13.25** least to the extent of the two rules in *Wheeldon v Burrows*, its main use has been in respect of leases where it is closely linked to the covenant for quiet

---

[125] *Wheeldon v Burrows* (1879) L.R. 12 Ch. D. 31.
[126] See above, para.13.12 et seq.
[127] *Ward v Kirkland* [1967] Ch. 194; [1966] 1 All E.R. 609 at 617.
[128] [2001] EWCA Civ 2011; [2002] 2 P. & C.R. 19.

enjoyment.[129] It must be remembered that between lessor and lessee there is a continuing relationship, involving, inter alia, payment of rent by the lessee and the implied covenant of quiet enjoyment by the lessor. Furthermore, leases frequently make it clear what is the purpose for which the lease is granted and what uses are permitted. In such circumstances it is not difficult to imply as against the landlord an obligation not to do anything to frustrate those purposes. One example is *Wong v Beaumont Property Trust*,[130] a leasehold case. The implied grant was described as an easement. Although the case was argued on the basis of implication from the circumstances, it is submitted that the decision could equally well have been based on non-derogation from grant.

It is difficult to find cases of freehold grants where the doctrine has been applied except under the rules in *Wheeldon v Burrows*. One such case is *Cable v Bryant*[131] where Neville J. specifically held that the principle was not based on implied covenant, but on legal implication. The problem in that case was that the servient tenement was on lease at the time of the sale. Nevertheless it was held that there was in effect an easement created against the freeholder under the principle of non-derogation from grant.

The basis of the principle was considered in *Saeed v Plustrade*[132] (which involved a 99-year lease) and the authorities were considered. The judgment of the Court of Appeal was that the principle of non-derogation of grant is a general principle which includes all dealings (including the sale of a car.[133]) It follows that it applies as strongly to a sale of land (where there is no implied covenant of quiet enjoyment) as to a lease.

The principle is also applied to *profits à prendre*.[134]

6. Implication from the intention of parties

13.26 This principle, sometimes called "intended easements",[135] emanates from the dictum of Lord Parker in *Pwllbach Colliery v Woodman*[136]:

> "The law will readily imply the grant or reservation of such easements as may be necessary to give effect to the common intention of the parties to a grant of real property, with reference to the manner or purposes in and for which the land granted or some land retained by the grantor is to be used."

---

[129] *Browne v Flower* [1911] 1 Ch. 219.
[130] [1965] 1 Q.B. 173; [1964] 2 W.L.R. 1325.
[131] [1908] 1 Ch. 259.
[132] [2001] EWCA Civ 2011; [2002] 2 P. & C.R. 19.
[133] *British Leyland Motor Corp Ltd v Armstrong Patents Co Ltd* [1986] A.C. 577; [1986] 2 W.L.R. 400.
[134] *Peech v Best* [1931] 1 K.B. 1.
[135] per Nourse L.J. in *Stafford v Lee* (1993) 65 P. & C.R. 172 at 175.
[136] [1915] A.C. 634 at 646.

However, Lord Parker then qualified this by saying:

"But it is essential for this purpose that the parties should intend that the subject of the grant or the land retained by the grantor should be used in some definite and particular manner. It is not enough that the subject of the grant or the land retained should be intended to be used in a manner which may or may not involve this definite and particular use".

Most of the older cases on this, including *Pwllbach* itself, concerned leases where the purpose for which the land granted or retained was to be used was expressly set out in the lease. Thus in *Wong v Beaumont Property Trust Ltd*[137] a grant of an easement was implied in a lease to allow a restaurateur lessee to install an air vent which was essential to comply with the food hygiene regulations. Such an easement could not have been implied under the rule in *Wheeldon v Burrows* because it was not usual and apparent at the date of the lease. Equally it could not have been implied under s.62 of the Law of Property Act 1925 because it did not pertain to the property at the time of the grant. Nevertheless the Court of Appeal implied the term because it was necessary to enable the lessee to use the property in the manner specifically contemplated by the lease.

In *Stafford v Lee*[138] the Court of Appeal made clear that the principle also applies to freehold conveyances. On the face of it a freehold conveyance does not specify the use to which the land is to be put. However, Nourse L.J. stated in relation to "intended easements",[139] "the parties must intend that the subject of the grant shall be used in some definite and particular manner".

This passage was quoted with approval in *Mobil Oil v Birmingham CC*[140] and again in *Shrewsbury v Allen*.[141] However, he also said:

"The ... class of cases in which easements may impliedly be created depends not upon the terms of the grant itself, but upon the circumstances under which the grant was made. The law will readily imply the grant or reservation of such easements as may be necessary to give effect to the common intention of the parties to a grant of real property, with reference to the manner or purposes in and for which the land granted or some other land retained by the grantor is to be used."[142]

---

[137] [1965] 1 Q.B. 173.
[138] (1993) 65 P. & C.R. 172.
[139] *Stafford v Lee* (1993) 65 P. & C.R. 172 at 175.
[140] [2001] EWCA Civ 1608; [2002] 2 P. & C.R. 14 at [32].
[141] [2006] 1 P. & C.R. 474 at [25].
[142] per Nourse L.J. in *Stafford v Lee* [(1993) 65 P. & C.R. 172 at 175; approved in *Mobil Oil Co Ltd v Birmingham CC* [2001] EWCA Civ 1608; [2002] 2 P. & C.R. 14 at [32].

13.27   This led to the latest statement of principle by Neuberger L.J. in *Shrewsbury v Allen*:

> "In my judgment, therefore, the resolution of the issue raised on the present appeal turns on the proper analysis of the common intention of the parties, as gathered from the terms of the conveyance, the position on the ground and the communications passing between the parties before the execution of the conveyance, which would include the provisions of the contract."

Thus, in *Stafford v Lee* woodland was conveyed "having a frontage to Marley Drive" but no right of way over Marley Drive was granted. The plan showed the land with two houses on it, but there was no other indication of the purpose for which the land was sold and no planning permission had been granted. The Court of Appeal upheld H.H. Judge Willcock's decision that the intention of the parties could be deduced from the presence of this plan and that there was an implied grant of a right of way for vehicular access for the purposes of the dwelling houses which were to be built.

There are, however, limitations to the principle of intended easements. Firstly they are implied more readily in favour of a grantee than a grantor. But also there must be true clarity in the intention of the parties.[143]

It is difficult to be sure of the extent of application of this principle. There are many cases where it is difficult to ascertain the intention of the parties or where the parties have no clear common intention. Furthermore, these cases all involve situations where the parties to the deed are still the owners. What about the situation where a purchaser buys a property without knowledge of the intended easement? These easements are not equitable easements, subject to the rights of a bona fide purchaser without notice.

In *Mobil Oil Co v Birmingham CC* Aldous L.J. divides implied grants of easements, in effect, into four categories:

> "(1)   rights implied by s.62 of the Law of Property Act 1925 (these are not specifically mentioned because *Pwllbach Colliery* preceded the Act);
>
> (2)   rights implied under the rule in *Wheeldon v Burrows*;
>
> (3)   rights which are necessary for the enjoyment of some other right expressly granted; and
>
> (4)   intended easements, based on the principle in *Stafford v Lee*.

---

[143]   *Shrewsbury v Allen* [2006] 1 P. & C.R. 474.

There is, of course, a difference between the implication of terms in contracts, which may be informal and which only bind the parties to the contracts and not usually their successors in title, and conveyances, which are formal documents in respect of which the parties can properly be expected to have set out all the rights and obligations and on the basis of which mortgagees lend large sums of money. It is reasonable to suggest that it should be more difficult to create permanent incidents to the ownership of land without expressly referring to them than to imply a term in a contract.

7. Way of necessity

It is established that a way of necessity is created by implication and **13.28** not as a matter of public policy; *Nickerson v Barroughclough*.[144] In reaching this conclusion the Court of Appeal overruled the view of Megarry V.C. at first instance,[145] a view which goes back several hundred years.[146]

The implication of a way of necessity is different from the reservation of an easement by necessity, referred to above.[147] The principle is that where a parcel of land is conveyed there is implied by necessity a right of access to that land over the land retained. The same applies in reverse where a parcel of land is conveyed leaving retained land land-locked.

The extent to which there is a general principle by which easements can be implied from the circumstances has been discussed above.[148] It may be that *Nickerson v Barroughclough*[149] brings the doctrine of ways of necessity into that broader principle.[150] However, ways of necessity date back to medieval times and they have always been regarded as a special case.

It is only rarely that the issue of way of necessity arises, because in most cases there is either an express or an implied right of way to enable the owner to gain access to his property from his own land or from the public highway. Either there will be an existing path (either apparent or appurtenant to the land), or possibly, the grant or reservation of a right of way can be implied from the circumstances. However, circumstances do occasionally arise where there is no existing path and the purchaser has failed to obtain an express grant, perhaps because he thinks he can use some other way by permission,[151] or mistakenly believes that he has some other right.

---

[144] [1981] Ch. 426; [1981] 2 All E.R. 369; followed in *Manjang v Drammeh* (1990) 61 P. & C.R. 194.

[145] *Nickerson v Barroughclough* [1980] Ch. 325; [1979] 3 All E.R. 312.

[146] *Packer v Welsted* (1657) 2 Sid. 39.

[147] See above, para.13.19.

[148] See above, paras 13.29 et seq.

[149] *Nickerson v Barroughclough* [1981] Ch. 426; [1981] 2 All E.R. 369.

[150] See *Adealon International Corp Proprietary Ltd v Merton LBC* [2006] EWHC 1075 (Ch); 2 P. & C.R. DG13.

[151] *Barry v Hasseldine* [1952] Ch. 835.

13.29   Usually it makes little difference whether the rationale of a way of necessity is that it is implied from the presumed intention of the parties or that it emanates from the public policy that land should not be left "fresh and unoccupied".[152] However, in *Nickerson v Barroughclough*[153] the distinction was crucial because the conveyance had been so framed as expressly to exclude an implication of a right of way until the anticipated way became a made up road (which never happened). It is now clear, therefore, that, whatever the effect on the land of its becoming land-locked, a way of necessity cannot be implied or imputed if it overrides the clear provisions of the conveyance.

The principle of a way of necessity is pleaded often but rarely success-fully. It is important to note that there can only be a way of necessity over land which has previously been in common ownership with the proposed dominant tenement.[154] It is not possible to buy a land-locked piece of land and then claim a right of way over adjoining land, though where this has happened the courts have been reluctant to grant an injunction if it means that the land is effectively cut off: *Bracewell v Appleby*.[155] It does not, however, matter that the land-locked property is not entirely surrounded by the other property. It is enough that it has no right of access to the public highway, unless a way of necessity is implied.[156]

13.30   Because it must arise out of a grant, it does not arise in circumstances where land is obtained otherwise than by grant, for example by adverse possession[157] or, presumably, by compulsory purchase.[158]

The principle is restricted to cases where there is absolute necessity. The fact that the existing access to the highway is inconvenient, as in *Titchmarsh v Royston Water Co*,[159] or over water[160] does not give rise to a way of necessity. In *Titchmarsh* the only alternative route was onto a public highway which ran in a deep cutting some 20 feet below. The posi-tion might well be different, however, if planning permission was unob-tainable to make a fresh access onto the highway at that point.

The extent of the right implied is that which is necessary at the time of the implied grant or reservation. Therefore, if the use of the property changes after the property is acquired, the right of way will be restricted

---

[152] *Packer v Welsted* (1657) 2 Sid. 39.
[153] [1981] Ch. 426; [1981] 2 All E.R. 369.
[154] *Manjang v Drammeh* (1991) 61 P. & C.R. 194.
[155] [1975] Ch. 408; [1975] 1 All E.R. 993.
[156] *Barry v Hasseldine* [1952] Ch. 835.
[157] *Wilkes v Greenway* (1890) 6 T.L.R. 449.
[158] See *Sovmots Investments Ltd v Secretary of State* [1979] A.C. 144; [1977] 2 All E.R. 385 but cf. *Serff v Acton Local Board* (1886) L.R. 31 Ch. D. 679 which was not referred to in *Sovmots*.
[159] (1899) 81 L.T. 673, followed in *Adealon International Corp Proprietary Ltd v Merton LBC* [2006] EWHC 1075 (Ch); 2 P. & C.R. DG13.
[160] *Manjang v Drammeh* (1991) 61 P. & C.R. 194.

to that use which was necessary at the time of the grant.[161] In the case of a lease, it is a way "suitable to the business for which the lease was made".[162] It has been suggested that the only way of necessity that can be implied is a right on foot,[163] but in *Adealon International Property Co v Merton LBC*[164] the Judge would have implied a wider right had he been convinced that any right was necessary. It is not clear, therefore, whether in the case of an ordinary private house the way implied would now include a vehicular right of way.

In so far as there is a separate concept of "way of necessity" which is **13.31** not just part of the general law of implied grant and reservation, it is submitted that the principle does not apply to any other kind of easement. For example, the right of necessity over a ventilation duct in *Wong v Beaumont Property Trust*[165] was decided on the basis of implication from the intention of the parties where the lease was for a specific purpose. Nevertheless, in *Midland Railway v Miles*[166] the Court considered a claim to a right to work minerals by necessity on the basis that it could give rise to an easement of necessity.

The doctrine usually only applies where there is no obvious route. In these circumstances the question has arisen as to what the route should be. In *Osborn v Wise*[167] it was held that the way is to the nearest public highway by the shortest line. It is, however, for the servient owner to select a convenient route.[168] If the dominant owner considers it unsuitable, it is open to him to object.[169] Presumably if the parties cannot agree, the matter will be referred back to the court.

---

[161] *London Corp v Riggs* (1879–80) L.R. 13 Ch. D. 798.
[162] *Gaylord v Moffatt* (1868) 4 Ch. App. 133.
[163] *Osborn v Wise* (1837) 7 Car. & P. 761.
[164] [2006] EWHC 1075 (Ch); 2 P. & C.R. DG13.
[165] [1965] 1 Q.B. 173.
[166] (1886) 33 Ch. D. 632.
[167] (1837) 7 Car. & P. 761.
[168] *Bolton v Bolton* (1879) L.R. 11 Ch. D. 968; *St Edmundsbury and Ipswich Diocesan Board of Finance v Clark (No.2)* [1975] 1 W.L.R. 468; [1975] 1 All E.R. 772 at 783g.
[169] *Packer v Welsted* (1657) 2 Sid. 39.

Chapter Fourteen
Creation of Easements— By Statute

1. Introduction

Easements created by statute come in two distinct categories. Firstly, **14.01** there are easements created in the course of compulsory purchase of land. A body purchasing land under statutory power may need additional rights over adjoining land in order to carry out the purpose for which the land is being purchased. This category gives rise to no conceptual problems. The rights created are easements in the normal sense of the word.[1] They are incidents annexed to the land purchased and thereafter they pass to successors in title to the land purchased and bind successors in title to the land in respect of which the right is created in the same way as easements created by deed.

The other category is much more difficult. Statutory undertakers, whether public or private, need to install pipes, cables and wires on private land. The various enabling statutes give powers to enter such land to install these pipes, cables and wires and give further powers to repair and replace them. The terms in which these powers are granted are many and various, but what these statutes do not make clear is the nature of the right obtained by the statutory undertakers. They are not purchasers of the piece of land or air over which the pipe, cable or wire passes. If they were, they would be entitled to dispose of the freehold to whoever they wished and would be subject to requirements like the need to register title under the Land Registration Act 2002. On the other hand the rights are not easements in the normal sense of the word because there is not, in any real sense, a dominant tenement. True, it was held in *Re Salvin*[2] that a right to lay pipes created by agreement could be a valid easement as benefiting the other property of the water company, but there is certainly no indication in the statutes that the intention is that the rights will annex to any particular land.

---

[1] *Newcomen v Coulson* (1877) L.R. 5 Ch. D. 133 at 144 per James L.J.
[2] *Re Salvin* [1938] 2 All E.R. 498.

14.02   This problem was considered by the Court of Appeal in *Newcastle under Lyme Corp v Wolstanton Ltd*.[3] The conclusion reached by the Court of Appeal was that:

> "They have by force of the statute the exclusive right to occupy for the purposes of their statutory undertaking the space in the soil taken by the pipes . . . but that exclusive right of occupation, which continues so long as the corporation carry on their undertaking, does not depend upon or involve the vesting in the plaintiff corporation of any legal or equitable estate in the land."[4]

If the exercise of these powers creates no legal or equitable estate in the land, what is the nature of the right created?

> "The only remaining explanation, it is submitted, is that the rights given by the statute are sui generis, fit in with no known other jurisprudential concept and amount to an exclusive right to occupy the space or cavity occupied by the actual pipes themselves."[5]

Section 50 of the Countryside and Rights of Way Act 2000 has created a new category of easements created by statute which does not fit neatly into either of the above categories. This is considered below in s.3.

2.   Easements created by compulsory purchase

14.03   In the field of compulsory purchase there is a distinction between new easements created by statute and existing easements acquired under statutory power. The various statutes which provide for compulsory purchase of land usually define land in such a way as to include easements. Existing easements can, therefore, pass under s.62 of the Law of Property Act 1925, even if they are not specifically mentioned in the compulsory purchase order. However, if, for some reason, such an easement cannot be implied under s.62 (for example, because it has never actually been exercised and accordingly does not appertain to the land at the time of the grant) it cannot be held to pass either under the rule in *Wheeldon v Burrows* or as being necessary to put into effect the common intention of the parties, because on a compulsory sale there is no common intention and there can be no requirement that a person forced to sell against his will should not derogate from his grant. A compulsory purchase order, therefore, passes only such easements as exist as actual

---

[3] [1947] Ch. 427; [1947] 1 All E.R. 218.

[4] *Newcastle under Lyme Corp v Wolstanton Ltd* [1947] Ch. 427; [1947] 1 All E.R. 218 per Morton L.J., at 456, quoting Evershed J. at first instance.

[5] J. F. Garner, "Statutory Easements" (1956) 20 Conv. (N.S.) 208, 213.

easements or as advantages under s.62. Unless there is any specific power in the legislation there is no implied right to create new easements which did not exist before the sale, *Sovmots Investments Ltd v Secretary of State for the Environment*.[6]

The key distinction between a compulsory purchase order and a normal conveyance, therefore, is that with compulsory purchase there is no common intention of the parties or requirement of good faith on the unwilling transferor's part from which a grant of new easements could be implied.

The Land Clauses Consolidation Act 1845 was the main general act **14.04** under which compulsory purchase orders were made. The Act makes no provision for the creation of new rights and, in view of *Sovmots Investments Ltd v Secretary of State for the Environment*,[7] it must follow that no new rights can be created by any compulsory purchase order under this Act. The Act does not in fact make any express reference to ancillary rights at all. Section 3, which defined "lands", says it extends to "messuages, lands, tenements and hereditaments of any tenure". The House of Lords has in the past suggested that this description does not permit the purchaser to take an easement in the normal sense but only to acquire land subject to an easement which can then be extinguished subject to the payment of compensation. Thus, if the acquirer wished to acquire land which was subject to an existing right of way, the compulsory purchase order could extinguish the right of way,[8] but would not permit the conveyance to include the benefit of existing easements over other land. However, the statutory form of conveyance in Sch.A conveys the land "together with all ways, rights and appurtenances thereto belonging". Furthermore, as from 1881 all conveyances executed under the Act would include the terms implied by s.62 of the Law of Property Act 1925. Accordingly, by virtue of *Wright v MacAdam*[9] the conveyance includes "advantages" or quasi-easements where the purchase is of only part of the land owned by the person from whom the land is compulsorily acquired, at least where the land acquired was previously in separate occupation.

The Defence of the Realm (Acquisition of Land) Act 1916 extended the definition of land to "any easement or right over or in relation to land".[10] This makes it clear that existing easements can be acquired, but leaves open the question of quasi-easements. However, s.6 of the Defence of the

---

[6] [1979] A.C. 144; [1977] 2 All E.R. 385.
[7] [1979] A.C. 144; [1977] 2 All E.R. 385.
[8] *Great Western Railway Co v Swindon and Cheltenham Extension Railway Co* (1883–84) L.R. 9 App. Cas. 787 at 800.
[9] [1949] 2 K.B. 744.
[10] Defence of the Realm (Acquisition of Land) Act 1916 s.12.

Realm (Acquisition of Land) Act 1920 amends the 1916 Act by making it clear that,

> "the exercise or enjoyment of any easement or right over or in relation to land shall be deemed to be possession of that easement or right".

This would appear to cover quasi-easements but in any event these can still pass under s.62 of the Law of Property Act 1925. What is clear, however, is that this statute does not permit the creation of new rights which are not existing quasi-easements or advantages within s.62 of the Law of Property Act 1925 over adjoining land.

14.05   The Requisitioned Land and War Works Act 1945 makes specific provision in s.36 for the creation of new rights referring to the "creation by grant to him . . . of the easement or right". This would seem sufficient to allow for the creation of any easement required to carry out the intended purpose.

Following the decision at first instance in *Sovmots Investments Ltd v Secretary of State for the Environment*, finally upheld by the House of Lords,[11] the Local Government (Miscellaneous Provisions) Act 1976 gave to a local authority the power "to purchase compulsorily for that purpose such new rights over the land as are specified in the order".[12] The Act is not, however, retrospective and accordingly does not apply to any compulsory purchase orders made before its commencement on February 14, 1977.

The Acquisition of Land Act 1981, which is the primary Act by which the government, local authorities and various other bodies obtain land by compulsory purchase, does not contain any provision for creating new rights, though it does contain in Sch.3 a procedure to adopt where a statute which incorporates the 1981 Act does make this provision. Since the *Sovmots* decision it has become the norm for specific Acts which contain compulsory purchase provisions to make specific reference to new rights.

14.06   The position, therefore, is that if an easement is claimed in a case where the servient tenement has been obtained by compulsory purchase it is necessary first to decide whether the easement passed to the body obtaining the land by implication under s.62 of the Law of Property Act 1925. If it did not, it would not pass by necessary implication from the intention of the parties. Even if there was specific reference to the

---

[11] [1979] A.C. 144; [1977] 2 All E.R. 385.
[12] Local Government (Miscellaneous Provisions) Act 1976 s.13.

easement it could be challenged as ultra vires unless the statute contained a specific power to create new rights. This is only likely to be the case if the Act under which the order was made was passed since 1976.

Although *Sovmots Investments Ltd v Secretary of State for the Environment*[13] lays down that there can be no easement implied by implication from common intention, an authority buying land does gain a natural right of support and also an easement of support for all buildings contemplated when the land was conveyed.[14] *Jary v Barnsley Corporation*, however, was not referred to in *Sovmots* and, at least as far as an implied grant of a right of support for proposed buildings is concerned, the decision must be open to some doubt.

3.   Countryside and Rights of Way Act 2000

As explained in Chapter 7,[15] where a public highway passes over **14.07** private land the sub-soil will be retained by the landowner. Where, as in most cases, the way is maintainable at public expense, the way will vest in the highway authority.[16] However, this vesting applies only to the surface of the way. The sub-soil remains in the ownership of the land-owner. Accordingly the owner of the land can use the way for his own purposes providing that he does not obstruct the highway. The most obvious example is a public footpath which may be used for grazing by the landowner.

In addition to creating a right of public access (which, being a public right does not come within the ambit of this book) the Countryside and Rights of Way Act 2000 also alters the "road used as a public path", which was open to all traffic and changed it to a "restricted byway"[17] giving only a right of way on foot, on horseback or leading a horse and for vehicles other than mechanically propelled vehicles.[18] As a supple-mentary provision the Act also provides that all restricted byways which are converted from roads used as a public path become highways main-tainable at the public expense and therefore vested in the highway authority.

The effect of this on the landowner would be that he could no longer use the way for agricultural or other mechanically propelled vehicles either as a public right of way or as a use of his own land. Equally he would not be able to claim a prescriptive right of way, since any user in the past would have been of his own land. Accordingly by s.50(2):

---

[13] [1979] A.C. 144.
[14] [1907] 2 Ch. 600.
[15] See para.7.34.
[16] Highways Act 1980 s.263(1).
[17] Countryside and Rights of Way Act 2000 s.47.
[18] ibid. s.48(3).

"Any owner or lessee of premises adjoining or adjacent to a relevant highway shall, so far as is necessary for the reasonable enjoyment and occupation of the premises, have a right of way for vehicular and all other kinds of traffic over the relevant highway."

However, this does not mean that all adjoining or adjacent owners and occupiers have a private right of way over the path, because the definition of "relevant highway" is restricted to so much of the highway as was (before it became vested in the highway authority) "owned by the person who then owned the premises". There is an equivalent provision for leasehold land.[19]

What this appears to mean is that an adjoining or adjacent landowner who has never owned the sub-soil loses the right to use the way and, on the face of it, an adjoining owner who owns half the sub-soil (on the *ad medium filum* principle) has a right to use half the way. It is hard to believe that this is a correct interpretation of the section. The Act came into force on May 2, 2006.[20]

4. Rights created in favour of statutory undertakers or licence holders

(a) Electricity

14.08 In Sch.4 to the Electricity Act 1989 the rights granted by the Act to the licence holder are described as way-leaves. This is the only statutory reference to this term, the nature of which is discussed above.[21] The licence holder is the company responsible for supplying electricity to an area under the new privatised system.

The procedure is that the licence holder gives notice to the owner of the land who may then give the necessary way-leave. It is clear, therefore, that if permission is granted it will be a licence and not an easement. Quite apart from any other considerations, such as the need to define the dominant tenement, etc. a true easement would have to be by deed. If the owner does not grant the way-leave, or if he decides to terminate it, the licence holder can apply to the Secretary of State who may grant a way-leave which "shall continue in force for such period as may be specified in the way-leave" and which binds any person who is at any time the owner or occupier of the land.[22]

When a way-leave is granted the owner of the land is entitled to compensation which may be by lump sum or by periodical payments or

---

[19] ibid. s.50(4).
[20] The Countryside and Rights of Way Act 2000 (Commencement No.11 and Savings) Order 2006 (SI 2006/1172).
[21] See above para.11–13 et seq.
[22] See *British Waterways Board v London Power Networks Plc* [2002] EWHC 2417 (Ch); [2003] 1 All E.R. 187.

by a mixture of the two. The practice in the past has been for very small periodical way-leave payments to be made. However, if specific loss can be shown a much larger sum can be awarded.[23]

The Electricity Act 1989 replaces the Electricity (Supply) Act 1919 which made provision for installing lines on private land and s.11 of the Electricity (Supply) Act 1922 which allowed for the continuance of wayleaves originally entered into by consent when the owner or occupier brings them to an end.

In *Central Electricity Generating Board v Jennaway*[24] it was held at first **14.09** instance that it was possible to imply into any way-leave order any additional rights necessary in order to put the intention into effect. Therefore when an order was made for a way-leave and the route could only be used by erecting pylons, the wayleave order included, by implication, a right to erect pylons. This decision was in the line of authorities starting with *Re Dudley Corporation*.[25] These authorities were not cited in *Sovmots Investments Ltd v Secretary of State for the Environment*[26] which decided that an easement cannot be implied into a compulsory purchase order unless it constitutes an existing advantage under s.62 of the Law of Property Act 1925, but it seems likely that *Central Electricity Generating Board v Jennaway*[27] is still correctly decided, despite the decision in *Sovmots*. One possible distinction is that between true easements implied by the common intention of the parties and way-leaves, which are not true easements at all, implied by necessary implication from the terms of the statute.

If a private person or company required to use a person's land for the purposes of his or their business, the landowner would want some recompense in the form of rent, not only for the inconvenience and disruption caused and any loss in the value of the land caused by having wires or cables under or over a part of the land he might wish to use in future, but also for the benefit gained by the other business through the advantage obtained. For example, if a landowner was asked to grant a licence to allow a neighbour to go across his land as access to a caravan site, he would consider, in assessing what rent to charge, not only the detriment to himself but also the extra profit the adjoining owner would get by using the route. This would be the basis on which any private way-leave would be granted. However, the compensation for statutory undertakers, whether public or private, has always been restricted to the loss suffered by the landowner. In this respect the term "way-leave" is misleading.

---

[23] *Welford v EDF Energy Networks (LPN) Plc* [2007] EWCA Civ 293; [2007] 2 P. & C.R. 15.
[24] [1959] 1 W.L.R. 937.
[25] (1881–82) L.R. 8 Q.B.D. 86.
[26] [1979] A.C. 144.
[27] [1959] 1 W.L.R. 937.

14.10   In *Duffy v Lamb*[28] the Court of Appeal grappled for the first time with the concept of an easement of electricity, rather than a way-leave. Generally electricity supply companies provide a supply to their main meter and charge the customer. If their cables pass over the land of a third party they will obtain the necessary way-leaves. This leaves the problem of dealing with the supply of electricity where the ultimate consumer is the owner of adjoining property. This is by no means an obscure problem. The supply from the main meter to, for example, owners of other units in a tower block, is frequently by sub-meters.

The problem, which applies also to gas, telephone wires and, indeed, water is that there is a distinction between a right to a supply of electricity and a right to the free passage of electricity. This point was considered in *Rance v Elvin*[29] in respect of a piped water supply[30] and *Duffy v Lamb* decided that the situation was the same for electricity and other services.

The distinction is made between ensuring a supply and not obstructing an existing supply. The owner of the property is obliged to pay for all electricity passing through the main meter and then has to recover from the owner or occupier of the other units payment for the electricity he consumes. It might be thought that, since he had no obligation to ensure a supply, throwing the switch on the meter would not be a breach of the obligation not to obstruct the supply, since there was no damage to the cable. The decision, however, was to the contrary. By throwing the switch the dominant owner had obstructed the existing supply. This means that where there is an express easement of passage the dominant owner does not have the right to cut off the supply, either of electricity or water, if the servient owner refuses to pay. It seems that the servient owner can fail to pay his bill, resulting in the supply being cut off by the electricity supplier, but he cannot switch off the supply to the dominant tenement.

What this decision reflects is the central place of these essential services in the practical use of the property. It seems clear that the servient owner has the right to recover electricity charges paid by him in respect of the dominant tenement from the dominant owner, but he cannot cut off the supply. The distinction between an easement in these terms and an easement giving a right to a supply is that if the servient owner decides to stop taking electricity from the supplier completely, then the dominant owner has no redress.

---

[28] (1998) 75 P. & C.R. 364.
[29] (1985) 50 P. & C.R. 9.
[30] See Ch. 7.

(b) Gas

The Gas Act 1986 contains no power for British Gas[31] or National Grid **14.11** Plc (who trade as Transco), or any public gas transporter to lay gas pipes on private land. Indeed para.3(1) of Sch.3 makes it clear that nothing in para.1, which allows them to open up streets, etc.,

> "empowers a public gas supplier to lay down or place any pipe or other works into, through or against any building, or in any land not dedicated to the public use".

The only exception, in para.2(2), is to provide gas supplies to a house abutting a street which has been laid out but not dedicated to the public use. This provision is substantially narrower than Sch.4 to the Gas Act 1972 which it repealed. The earlier Act allowed the Gas Corporation to enter property for the purpose of replacing repairing or altering any pipe lawfully placed on such land.

If Transco wish to obtain rights over private land they have to obtain compulsory purchase orders under Sch.3. Although this Schedule specifically allows for the creation of new rights, this provision can only be used to obtain or create rights, known to the law. The right would, therefore, have to be an easement annexed to a dominant tenement or a licence and not one of the anomalous rights created by other statutes.

A gas pipe is entitled to subjacent support. It has been held in a number of cases that the legislature, in giving the right to install pipes, must have intended that they should be supported by the subjacent land and therefore that the statutory undertaker has a right of support.[32] It seems likely that this principle still survives despite *Sovmots Investments Ltd v Secretary of State for the Environment*.[33] However, this implication was expressly countered in respect of mines by s.4 of the Public Health Act 1875 (Support of Sewers) Amendment Act 1883 which applies to gas pipes as well as sewers built after that date.[34] Nevertheless it was accepted without argument in *Transco v Stockport MBC*.[35]

(c) Telephones

The provisions for enabling telephone operators to execute works **14.12** on private land or to keep telecommunications apparatus installed on,

---

[31] The British Gas Corporation (Dissolution) Order 1990 (SI 1990/147). Gas Act 1986 s.9 as amended by the Gas Act 1995 s.10(i), Sch.3 para.3. Following a series of changes National Grid Plc ("Transco"') is the current operator.

[32] *Normanton Gas Co v Pope & Pearson* (1883) 52 L.J.Q.B. 629; *Re Dudley Corp* (1881–82) L.R. 8 Q.B.D. 86; *Transco Plc v Stockport MBC* [2003] UKHL 61; [2004] 2 A.C. 1.

[33] [1979] A.C. 144.

[34] *Newcastle under Lyme Corp v Wolstanton Ltd* [1947] Ch. 427.

[35] [2003] UKHL 61; [2004] 2 A.C. 1.

under or over private land or to enter land to inspect apparatus are contained in Sch.2 to the Telecommunications Act 1984, known as the Telecommunications Code. This works on the basis of obtaining consent from the occupier of the land.

What the operator seeks to obtain is the agreement in writing of the occupier for the time being of any land to execute works in connection with the installation, maintenance, adjustment, repair or alteration of telecommunications apparatus, to keep the installations installed and to enter the land to inspect them.[36]

The owner or lessee of the land is only bound by the agreement if he is himself the occupier, or if he has agreed to be bound by it in writing.

Where the owner is bound by the agreement it also binds everyone who for the time being owns an interest in the land, even if the interest has been created after the written agreement was entered into. The way this is achieved is by the statute providing that where there is a written consent which binds the owner or lessee, all persons for the time being having an interest are deemed to have given their consent.[37]

The rights set out above can only be exercised according to the terms (whether as to payment or otherwise) subject to which they are conferred. Accordingly, any person who is bound by the agreement by virtue of the deeming provisions is also entitled to the benefit of the terms.

14.13 If the necessary consents cannot be obtained the operator serves notice on the person against whom the right is sought and, if he still does not agree, goes to the county court which has power to confer the proposed right providing either that he can be properly compensated by compensation or that the benefit to the persons who will get the telephones outweighs the disadvantage to the owner of the land.[38]

If such an order is made by the court it will be on such terms and conditions as appear to the court appropriate for ensuring that the least possible loss and damage is caused by the exercise of the right in respect of which the order is made to persons who occupy, own interests in, or are from time to time on the land in question.

The compensation will be such sum, valued on the date of the court order, as is fair and reasonable as between willing parties. The compulsory purchase principles do not apply. The figure is likely to be rough and ready but the best method is to look at what has been paid by agreement in the past.[39] It will usually be an annual sum.

This procedure of obtaining agreement or applying to the court only applies to apparatus. Providing it does not interfere with access, the

---

[36] Telecommunications Act 1984 Sch.2 para.2(1).
[37] ibid. Sch.2 paras 2(3) and (4).
[38] ibid. Sch.2 para.5.
[39] *Mercury Communications Ltd v London and India Dock Investment Ltd* (1995) 69 P. & C.R. 135.

operator has the right to fly lines over adjacent or nearby land providing that they are three metres above the ground and two metres from any building. This, however, applies only to lines and not posts.[40] The operator also has the power, on notice, to carry out tree lopping in respect of trees overhanging streets.[41]

The appropriate compensation has been recently considered by the Court of Appeal in *Geo Networks v Bridgewater Canal Co Ltd.*[42] in relation to ducts under "linear obstacles", in this case a canal. The Court refused to order any compensation over and above the agreed rent for adding a fibre optic cable to the duct. This case was slightly different from the norm, since the Court decided that the provision for ducts was a special case and anyway the duct was already there, but it emphasised that the compensation would be limited to the inconvenience caused to the occupier and not to any assessment of the value to the statutory undertaker of the additional right.

If an owner or occupier wishes to carry out an improvement to the land **14.14** he can apply for an alteration of the apparatus.[43]

The deeming provisions of the 1984 Act are new. If apparatus has been installed without the necessary consents, either because no agreement has been reached or because a successor in title is not bound by a pre-1984 agreement, the occupier, owner or lessee may require the operator to remove the apparatus and restore the land to its condition before this was done.[44] However, there is a detailed procedure to go through before the apparatus can be removed,[45] including a court order, and the court has power to confer temporary rights on the operator for securing the service pending proceedings.[46]

The Act specifically provides that the rights created by these agreements are not subject to the provision of any enactment requiring the registration of interests in, charges on, or other obligations affecting the land.[47]

The Telecommunications Act 1984 therefore creates a different and far more complex structure and procedure from that which pertains in respect of other statutory undertakers. In other cases the Acts themselves give the undertakers powers which they can exercise subject to various constraints. These are statutory powers and, as set out above, the rights over the land created thereby are sui generis exclusive licences. The

---

[40] Telecommunications Act 1984 Sch.2 para.10.
[41] ibid. Sch.2 para.19.
[42] [2010] EWHC 548 (Ch); [2010] 1 W.L.R. 2576.
[43] Telecommunications Act 1984 Sch.2 para.20.
[44] ibid. Sch.2 para.4(2).
[45] ibid. Sch.2 para.21.
[46] ibid. Sch.2 para.6(2).
[47] ibid. Sch.2 para.2(7).

Telecommunications Act 1984, on the other hand, works on the basis of written agreements. But for the provisions of the Act such agreements would be licence agreements which, if entered into by the occupier, would not bind the owner; which would not bind successors in title; would be determinable on notice, and, possibly, would be registrable as estate contracts or other land charges. The Act seeks to avoid all these pitfalls by specific deeming provisions. It seems likely that the result is now the same as for other utilities, but the route taken is somewhat different.

(d) Oil pipe-lines

14.15 The Land Powers (Defence) Act 1958 provides for the compulsory purchase of land for oil pipe-lines,[48] though it makes no specific provision for the creation of new rights.

On the other hand it makes specific provision for wayleave orders including laying an oil pipe-line, the installation or construction of such minor works accessory to an oil pipe-line whether laid under that wayleave order or otherwise as may be so specified and to use the pipe line or works for any purpose appearing to the Minister to be expedient and not to be inconsistent with the purposes for which the order was made.

This is the only specific provision in the statutes allowing the statutory undertaker to use the pipe, cable or wire he has laid. As with electricity wires the right is described as a way-leave. It is apparent that it is not a normal easement since it does not relate to any dominant tenement. On the other hand the restriction to uses consistent with the purposes for which the order was made makes it clear that the statutory undertaker does not become the owner of the space through which the pipe-line runs. The right, therefore, is the anomalous sui generis right referred to above. Way-leaves created under the Act are local land charges and registrable as such.[49] Compensation is payable to people disadvantaged by the pipe line.[50]

Offshore and submarine pipelines are dealt with in the Petroleum Act 1998.

(e) Water and sewage

14.16 Section 159 of the Water Industry Act 1991 gives a water undertaker or a sewerage undertaker limited powers to lay a pipe over private land, to keep it there, to inspect, maintain, adjust, repair or alter it and to carry out works for securing that the water is not polluted or contaminated.[51]

---

[48] Land Powers (Defence) Act 1958 s.14.
[49] ibid. s.17.
[50] ibid. s.18.
[51] For the meaning of "sewer" see *Bromley LBC v Morritt* [2000] E.H.L.R. 24; (2000) 79 P. & C.R. 536.

The major difference between this Act and the other Acts giving powers to statutory undertakers is that the powers can be exercised by the privatised undertakers on notice and there does not seem to be any provision for challenge by the landowner or occupier except to apply to the court for an injunction if the operation has been carried out without the required notice. The notice must be "reasonable", which is three months for a new pipe and 42 days for altering an existing pipe. By contrast in the Electricity Act 1989 there has to be an order made by the Secretary of State before land can be entered and a telecommunications operator has to get an order from the county court dispensing with consent.

The restriction on this power contained in s.159(2) is that a water undertaker can only enter the land if there is already a service pipe there or if it has to install a water main in accordance with its statutory duty to supply water to the owner or occupier of any building under s.41.

Where this power is exercised compensation is payable both for distur- **14.17** bance and loss of value of the land, but not for the rental value of the facility.[52] Assessment of compensation is referred to an arbitrator.[53]

Section 179 of the Water Industry Act 1991 specifically provides that every relevant pipe and every sewage disposal works shall vest in the undertaker who laid or constructed it. It is submitted that, despite s.189(4) which includes tunnels and conduits in the definition of pipes, the provision refers to the pipes themselves rather than the space into which they are placed and accordingly that the right to use the pipe is the same kind of sui generis exclusive licence as was considered in *Newcastle under Lyme Corp v Wolstanton Ltd*.[54] The word "vest" reflects the provision in s.263 of the Highways Act 1980 that adopted roads vest in the highway authority. That has been held to amount to actual ownership albeit only of that part which is necessary to the ordinary users of the street,[55] but there has been no comparable decision in respect of water pipes.

Water pipes, like gas pipes, are entitled to subjacent support.[56] The absolute right of a developer to connect to the public sewer at the place of their choosing was upheld by the Supreme Court in *Barratt Homes v Dwr Cymru Cyfyngedig (Welsh Water)*.[57]

---

[52] s.180 and Sch.12.
[53] para.1 of Sch.12.
[54] [1947] Ch. 427.
[55] *Finchley Electric Light Co v Finchley Urban DC* [1903] 1 Ch. 437; see Ch. 8—Highways.
[56] See above para.14.11, and see also Ch.19—Support.
[57] [2009] UKSC 13; [2010] 1 P. & C.R. 25

5. Railway accommodation works

14.18   Most of our railways were built by private companies under powers contained in private Acts of Parliament. Those Acts which were passed after 1845 nearly all incorporated the Railways Clauses Consolidation Act 1845. Earlier Acts contained similar though not identical provisions, but the Act does not apply to subsequent alterations to railways originally constructed under earlier Acts.[58]

The 1845 Act contained at s.68 an obligation on the railway company to,

> "maintain the following works for the accommodation of the owners and occupiers of the lands adjoining the railway sufficient to deal with the interruptions to the use of the land and to convey water away as clearly as before",

provided that it was open to an adjoining landowner to accept compensation for loss of any such right rather than to require the railway company to construct the accommodation works.

The provision in s.68 of the Act is in the form of a statutory duty and accordingly where the railway company built accommodation works it was not necessary for it also to grant an easement to the adjoining owner. The fact that the works were constructed pursuant to the statutory duty gave the adjoining owners and occupiers the right to use the facility constructed. However, inevitably in practice it was common for the conveyance of land by the landowner to set out also rights reserved in favour of his adjoining land. These express reservations may either be normal easements and construed as such, as in *South Eastern Railway Co v Cooper*[59] and *British Railways Board v Glass*,[60] or may refer specifically to accommodation works in which case they are construed as easements created under the statute, as in *TRH Sampson Associates Ltd v British Railways Board*.[61]

14.19   Where the rights reserved are construed as normal easements the construction of such easements has been generous in favour of the adjoining landowner, in accordance with the general way in which express grants have been construed. Thus in *British Railways Board v Glass*[62] the grant was to and from "Cowleaze" and for "all manner of cattle", but nevertheless the Court of Appeal construed it as being a grant

---

[58] *Short v British Railways Board* [1974] 1 W.L.R. 781; [1974] 3 All E.R. 28.
[59] [1924] 1 Ch. 211.
[60] [1965] Ch. 538; [1964] 3 W.L.R. 913.
[61] [1983] 1 W.L.R. 170; [1983] 1 All E.R. 257.
[62] [1965] Ch. 538.

to and from all parts of the retained land and for all purposes, enabling the dominant owner to use the level crossing for the purposes of a caravan site on his retained land.

There are, however, a number of cases where the rights have either never been set out in a conveyance[63] or, though expressly set out, are clearly intended to be accommodation ways only. In *British Railways Board v Glass*[64] Lord Denning M.R. dissented on the construction of the conveyance, but his judgment nevertheless is a clear exposition of the nature of accommodation works and of the rights thereby created and, in this respect, is in agreement with the views expressed by the majority:

> "In the year 1847 the Wilts, Somerset and Weymouth Railway Company determined to construct a railway line from Bath to Westbury and Weymouth. They had to acquire land compulsorily for the purpose. They had power to do so under the Railway Clauses Consolidation Act 1845, which was incorporated into their private Act. That Act contained elaborate provisions as to what was to happen when the railway ran through a man's land and severed one portion of his land from the other. The railway company were to ensure that he could get across, as he did before, from one part of his land to the other. They were to construct bridges and arches, or allow him to cross at level crossings, as the case might require. These works were to be done 'for the accommodation of the owners and occupiers of land adjoining the railway'. They have ever since been called 'accommodation works'. The rights of the owners and occupiers over these works are very different from their rights over public rights of way. The owners and occupiers were entitled to have their access to and fro restored to them—so as to make good the severance—according to the use which they then made of their land, or any use that might reasonably then be anticipated; but not for any greatly increased use which no one could anticipate".

The extent of the rights to which the adjoining landowner and occupier is entitled have been the subject of a good deal of litigation. The first problem concerns the purposes for which the way can be used. A general grant of a right of way in a deed will be for all purposes for which the owner or occupier of the dominant tenement wishes to use it then or in the future, subject to restrictions on excessive user. However, an accommodation way is more limited.

In *Great Northern Railway Co v M'Alister*[65] the rights were defined as **14.20** follows:

---

[63] As in *Taff Vale Railway v Canning* [1909] 2 Ch. 48.
[64] [1965] Ch. 538.
[65] [1897] 1 I.R. 587.

"The owner of the adjoining lands was entitled, when the railway was made, to a convenient passage over the railway sufficient to make good, so far as possible, any interruption which the construction of the railway caused by severance in the working of his farm, including, I should say, any alteration or extension of that working which could or ought to have been contemplated by the parties when the accommodation works were made and accepted":

This statement has been accepted as a true statement of the law in *Great Western Railway Co v Talbot*[66] and by Lord Denning M.R. in *British Railways Board v Glass*.[67] However, in *TRH Sampson Associates Ltd v British Railways Board*[68] it was held that the accommodation works could be used for a purpose not contemplated at the time, providing the change of user did not impose an added burden on the railway company. This decision followed the actual declaration in *Great Western Railway v Talbot*,[69] that:

"The defendant is not entitled to use the level crossing for the purpose of conveying goods and traffic so as substantially to increase the burden of the easement by altering or enlarging its character, nature or extent as enjoyed at or previous to March 13, 1868 . . .".

In this respect there is a considerable difference between a level crossing, where every time it is used there is a burden on the railway to take care for the safety of the user, and a bridge or archway where the only concern of the railway company is any additional cost of repair. Despite the approval of the dictum from *Great Northern Railway v M'Alister* set out above, it seems clear that a person entitled to use an accommodation way will not lose that right simply because there is a change in his business. In those cases where it has been held that the right has been lost, e.g. *Taff Vale Railway v Canning*[70] there were very significant changes in the kind of user being made of the way.

14.21   The second problem concerns extinguishment. An easement created inter partes continues until it is extinguished by express or implied release and it might be thought that an accommodation way and the repairing obligations attached to it would continue until it was released by all relevant parties or rescinded by Act of Parliament. However, it has

---

[66] [1902] 2 Ch. 759.
[67] [1965] Ch. 538.
[68] [1983] 1 W.L.R. 170; [1983] 1 All E.R. 257.
[69] *Great Western Railway Co (GWR) v Talbot* [1902] 2 Ch. 759 at 767.
[70] [1909] 2 Ch. 48 and *Great Western Railway Co (GWR) v Talbot* [1902] 2 Ch. 759.

been held in *R. Walker and Son v British Railways Board*[71] that the duty ceases if the purpose of the particular accommodation work becomes extinct, though the fact that the railway has closed down and the railway lines have been removed does not mean that the purpose is extinct. *R. Walker and Son v British Railways Board*[72] was a fencing case and one can see in certain circumstances that the need to fence could become obsolete. However, it is very difficult to see in what circumstances a right to use an accommodation bridge, archway or crossing could become extinct except in a case where the use of the land by the landowner has changed so as to make the accommodation way unnecessary, for example where he sells off the land on the other side without giving the purchaser a right of way over his own land, *Midland Railway v Gribble*.[73] The object of the duty was to provide ways which replaced the pre-existing ways, which in most cases would not have been actual easements since they would be between two parts of the same parcel of land. The fact that the railway closes down does not render the ways unimportant. It may be possible for a bridge over a railway to be replaced by a road across the path of the old track, but the need for the way still remains.

The obligation contained in s.68 of the Railways Clauses Consolidation Act 1845 is owed to "the owners and occupiers of lands adjoining the railway". Where accommodation ways are provided, therefore, they may be used for the owner or occupier for the time being of adjoining land. There is little difficulty in identifying what is an accommodation way since it will have been expressly constructed as such. However, where the adjoining landowner has accepted compensation in lieu of a right of way, this does not bind an occupier who has an estate at the time, but it does bind the owner and his successors in title and so it would bind any lessee under a lease entered into after the compensation payment.[74]

Although the duty is expressed to be owed to "owners and occupiers" **14.22** there is little doubt that it applies also to "those authorised by them".[75] It would seem that anyone who would be treated as exercising a right of way created by grant would also be treated as "authorised" by the adjoining owner or occupier. Thus a delivery driver, or a friend visiting would be entitled to use the way even if he had no previous authorisation. What was decided in *Greenhalgh v British Railways Board*[76] was that a person using the way as a member of the public, even though doing so lawfully, is not entitled to sue for breach of statutory duty if the railway

[71] [1984] 1 W.L.R. 805; [1984] 2 All E.R. 249.
[72] ibid.
[73] [1895] 2 Ch. 827.
[74] *Tudor v Great Western Railway* [1948] 1 K.B. 465.
[75] per Lord Denning M.R. in *Greenhalgh v British Railways Board* [1969] 2 Q.B. 286; [1969] 2 W.L.R. 892; [1969] 2 All E.R. 114 at 119.
[76] [1969] 2 Q.B. 286; [1969] 2 All E.R. 114.

company fails to keep the accommodation work in repair. The obligation contained in s.68, although akin to an easement created by statute, is in some ways much wider than an easement because it carries with it the obligation not only to make but also "at all times thereafter maintain" the works. This distinguishes the railway company's obligation from a normal easement in respect of which there is no obligation to maintain the way. It would be interesting to speculate what view the Court of Appeal would have taken in *British Railways Board v Glass*[77] if the complaint had been of the Board's failure to maintain the crossing, which, it would appear, would not have been actionable at the suit of the dominant owner on the court's construction of the deeds.

6. Grant by Enclosure Award

14.23   During the nineteenth century large areas of common land were enclosed and allotted to private owners. Inevitably this resulted in changes to the network of public highways. Accordingly the General Enclosures Act 1801,[78] since repealed but still relevant to awards made at the time, gave the Commission power to stop up public highways and

> "to set out and appoint such private roads, ways, bridleways, foot-ways, ditches, drains, watercourses in, upon and through or by the sides of the allotments to be made . . . as they shall think requisite . . . and the same shall be made, and at all times for ever thereafter be supported and kept in repair, by and at the expense of the owners and proprietors for the time being of the land and grounds directed to be divided and inclosed, in such shares and proportions as the . . . commissioners shall in and by his or their award order and direct."

There were various private Enclosure Acts which incorporated this clause. It involved the creation of a right of way by statute and, therefore, there was no need for the servient owner to be a party. Most of the private ways created by these Acts have been subsumed into the general convey-ancing process whereby the benefit and burden of easements attaching to land are referred to in conveyances without reference to their origin. However, the existence of the grant can be crucial where the dominant owner has not used the way, or has not used it sufficiently to prove prescription.[79]

The existence of an award is also relevant where there is an issue over repair. In the absence of express terms in the grant there is no obligation on either the dominant or the servient owner to maintain the way or other

---

[77] [1965] Ch. 538.
[78] Correctly called the Inclosure Clauses Consolidation Act 1801 41 Geo. 3 Ch. 109.
[79] *Smith v Muller* [2008] EWCA Civ.1425; *Benn v Hardinge* (1993) 66 P. & C.R. 246.

easement, but the enclosure award may place this obligation on the owner benefiting from it. Where the obligation to repair is of a way which has become a restricted byway under s.48 of the Countryside and Rights of Way Act 2000 it automatically ceases on the byway becoming maintainable at the public expense.[80]

The dominant tenement is identified by looking at the circumstances and the time of the award and, in particular, the terms of the award itself.

---

[80] Countryside and Rights of Way Act 2000 s.49(2).

Chapter Fifteen
Creation of Easements—
By Prescription

1. Introduction

For as long as easements have existed, it has been possible to obtain an **15.01** easement without a grant, express or implied, by virtue of the doctrine of prescription.

Lord Hoffmann said in his "magisterial"[1] judgment in *R. v Oxfordshire CC Ex p. Sunningwell Parish Council*[2]:

> "Any legal system must have rules of prescription which prevent the disturbance of long-established de facto possession".

The Law Commission, in its recent report *Making Land Work: Easements, Covenants and Profits á Prendre*[3] considered the possibility of abolitioning the whole concept, but, in the end, decided against it.

Lord Hoffmann, having unequivocally asserted the principle, subjected the law of prescription to the most searching analysis for a century. Having referred to Roman law he states:

> "English law, on the other hand, has never had a consistent theory of prescription. It did not treat long enjoyment as being a method of acquiring title. Instead it approached the question from the other end by treating the lapse of time as either barring the remedy of the former owner or giving rise to a presumption that he had done an act which conferred a lawful title upon the person in de facto possession or enjoyment."

---

[1] per Lord Walker in *R. (on the application of Beresford) v Sunderland City Council* [2003] UKHL 60; [2004] 1 A.C. 889 at [71].
[2] [2000] 1 A.C. 335; [1999] 3 W.L.R. 160.
[3] Law Commission, *Making Land Work: Easements, Covenants and Profits á Prendre* (London: The Stationery Office, 2011), Law Com. No.327.

By using this principle he brings together the law of prescription in easements, which must be "as of right"', with the similar principle in public rights of way and customary rights over village and town greens. In this he emphasises that it is the quality of the user, as it would appear, for example, to the owner of the land, which is essential, not the subjective belief of the person making use of the way:

> "To require an enquiry into the subjective state of mind of the users of the road would be contrary to the whole English theory of prescription, which, as I hope I have demonstrated, depends upon evidence of acquiescence by the landowner giving rise to an inference or presumption of a prior grant or dedication. For this purpose, the actual state of mind of the road user is plainly irrelevant."

The difficulty with this analysis is that a fiction is not a presumption. A fiction of a lost modern grant cannot be overturned by evidence that no such grant has been made nor can the fiction of acquiescence be overturned by evidence that the true owner was personally unaware of the user, for example because he was abroad.

15.02   In *Dalton v Angus*[4] most of the judicial minds of the time were asked to consider whether a right of support could arise by prescription. This prompted various comments on the nature of prescriptive rights including the suggestion, set out above, that all such rights are based on acquiescence. However, the statement by Fry J.[5] that,

> "the whole law of prescription and the whole law which governs the presumption or inference of a grant or covenant rest upon acquiescence"

was only part of the advice given by the judges to the House of Lords.

In the House of Lords itself, this view was rejected by Lord Blackburn who, in a long and learned dissertation on the subject referring back, like Lord Hoffman, to the Roman Law of *usucapio*, held that the doctrine was based on expedience.

It is submitted that this is in many ways a more compelling basis for the doctrine than acquiescence. Indeed, Lord Hoffman largely acknowledged this in his assertion that:

> "in a claim under the Act [the Prescription Act 1832] what mattered was the quality of enjoyment during the 20 year period. The essential

---

[4] (1880–81) L.R. 6 App. Cas. 740.
[5] *Dalton v Angus* (1880–81) L.R. 6 App. Cas. 740 at 773.

factor was the quality of the user and not either the belief of the person making use of the way or the knowledge or attitude of the owner."

His reference to acquiescence was, essentially, to make clear that prescription is not *usucapio*, the taking or ownership by user, but a more empirical principle. Therefore, it is not a reference to the kind of acquiescence which gives rise to equitable estoppel or to an interruption under s.4 of the Prescription Act 1832, but solely to a failure to take proceedings to stop the person continuing the user. Indeed the concept of acquiescence does not sit easily with the fact that permissive user cannot give rise to a prescriptive right.

The problem is that there is a very fine line between "permission" to use a way, which prevents time running, and "tolerance" which allows time to run. This point was addressed by Lord Walker in *R. (on the application of Beresford) v Sunderland City Council*[6] referring in particular to *Cumbernauld & Kilsyth DC v Dollar Land (Cumbernauld) Ltd*[7] and *Mills v Silver*[8] where Dillon L.J. said:

> "The topic of tolerance has bulked fairly large in recent decisions of this court dealing with claims to prescriptive rights . . . If passages in successive judgments are taken on their own out of context and added together, it would be easy to say, as, with all respect, it seems to me that the judge did in the present case, that there is an established principle of law that no prescriptive right can be acquired if the use by the dominant owner of the servient tenement in the particular manner for the appropriate number of years has been tolerated without objection by the servient owner. But there cannot be any such principle of law, because it is, with rights of way, fundamentally inconsistent with the whole notion of acquisition of rights by prescription. It is difficult to see how, if there is such a principle, there would ever be a prescriptive right of way."

However, Dillon L.J.'s attempted *reductio ad absurdum*, raises the possibility that, perhaps, indeed, there is no place for rights to be obtained by prescription in the absence of acquiescence. But why do we need it?[9] There are many international Conventions and Agreements which set out

---

[6] [2003] UKHL 60; [2004] 1 A.C. 889 at [70] et seq.
[7] [1992] S.C. 357.
[8] [1991] Ch. 271.
[9] For further consideration of this issue see C. Sara, "Prescription—What is it for?" (2004) *Conveyancer* (Jan-Feb 2004), p.13.

fundamental human rights.[10] Of these the European Convention on Human Rights is incorporated in our statute law[11]:

> "Every natural or legal person is entitled to the peaceful enjoyment of his possessions. No one shall be deprived of his possessions except in the public interest and subject to the conditions provided for by law and the general principles of international law".[12]

There is no derogation there for prescriptive rights. Now that the basis of adverse possession has been changed to focus more on whether the original owner is at fault[13] the spotlight passes to ancillary rights. It is not necessarily enough to say that they have always existed in English Law, though it may be enough to say that they are enshrined in statute.[14]

The creation of easements by prescription must be differentiated from the creation of easements by estoppel. Easements can arise from estoppel by acquiescence in circumstances where no prescriptive right could arise because there has been an insufficient period of user. On the other hand there are many cases where time runs when there has been no actual acquiescence either because the owner of the servient tenement has no actual knowledge of the user, or where both parties were acting in the mistaken belief that the right being exercised had in fact been granted by express grant.[15] This will be discussed further below.[16]

As the law stands, there are three ways in which easements can be obtained by prescription: (1) under the Prescription Act 1832; (2) by virtue of the doctrine of lost modern grant; or (3) at common law. Historically, the principle started with prescription at common law, which required user throughout living memory. Unfortunately this got stuck with the idea that living memory ran back to 1189. The courts then developed the doctrine of lost modern grant involving the fiction that if the easement had been used for a long time then it must be because someone had made a grant by deed which had been lost. Then in 1832 Parliament stepped in with the Prescription Act 1832

---

[10] e.g. Charter of Fundamental Rights of the European Union (2000/C 364/01)— Art.17:
"1. Everyone has the right to own, use, dispose of and bequeath his or her lawfully acquired possessions. No one may be deprived of his or her possessions, except in the public interest and in the cases and under the conditions provided for by law, subject to fair compensation being paid in good time for their loss. The use of property may be regulated by law in so far as is necessary for the general interest."

[11] Sch.1 of the Human Rights Act 1998—First Protocol, art.1.

[12] For further consideration of this issue see C. Sara, "Prescription—What is it for?" (2004) *Conveyancer* (Jan-Feb 2004), p.13.

[13] See Ch.5 and the Land Registration Act 2002.

[14] i.e. Prescription Act 1832.

[15] *Bridle v Ruby* [1989] Q.B. 169; [1988] 3 W.L.R. 191.; *Bosomworth v Faber* (1995) 69 P. & C.R. 288.

[16] See para.15.26 et seq.

"with the view to putting an end to the scandal on the administration of justice which arose from forcing the conscience of juries to find that there had been a lost grant when the presumption was known to be a mere fiction".[17]

For a long time this was the usual method of pursuing a prescriptive claim, but the doctrine of lost modern grant survived and in recent years has been used increasingly to circumvent the various problems and restrictions which have arisen in respect of statutory prescription. Apparently, since the abolition of juries in such cases, the judges' consciences have not been troubled by the exercise of this fiction.

The normal practice in pleading prescriptive claims is to claim prescription under the Prescription Act 1832, under the doctrine of lost modern grant and at common law, all in the alternative. Unless, on the facts, one of these three is clearly excluded this is the sensible course. As a result, in many cases the courts have been considering claims under all three principles and sometimes have not made it clear which heading the case is being decided under. The requirements relating to the actual exercise of the right claimed are essentially the same for each of the three different kinds of prescription and will be dealt with later.[18] In pleading lost modern grant strictly the plea should set out a date or a period during which the grant alleged could have been made.[19]   **15.03**

In *Tehidy Minerals v Norman*[20] Buckley L.J. bemoaned the co-existence of these three separate methods of prescribing and hoped for legislation, but the legislature's last major incursion into this field remains the 1832 Act. The Law Commission Report[21] proposes that these three principles be merged into a single method of proving prescription, but unless and until that report is translated into legislation,[22] the courts must act on the basis of the existing law.

2.   Prescription Act 1832

Section 2 of the Prescription Act 1832 (as amended) provides: **15.04**

"No claim which may be lawfully made at the common law, by custom, prescription, or grant, to any way or other easement, or to any watercourse, or the use of any water, to be enjoyed or derived

---

[17] per Lord Blackburn in *Dalton v Angus* (1880–81) L.R. 6 App. Cas. 740 at 799.
[18] See below para.15.15 et seq.
[19] *Tremayne v English Clays Lovering Pochin & Co* [1972] 1 W.L.R. 657; [1972] 2 All E.R. 234.
[20] [1971] 2 Q.B. 528; [1971] 2 All E.R. 475.
[21] Law Commission, *Making Land Work: Easements, Covenants and Profits á Prendre* (London: The Stationery Office, 2011), Law Com. No.327.
[22] See the draft Bill, included in the report at p.185.

upon, over, or from any land or water of our said Lord the King, or being parcel of the Duchy of Lancaster or of the Duchy of Cornwall, or being the property of any ecclesiastical or lay person, or body corporate, when such way or other matter as herein last before mentioned shall have been actually enjoyed by any person claiming right thereto without interruption for the full period of 20 years, shall be defeated or destroyed by showing only that such way or other matter was first enjoyed at any time prior to such period of 20 years, but nevertheless such claim may be defeated in any other way by which the same is now liable to be defeated; and where such way or other matter as herein last before mentioned shall have been so enjoyed as aforesaid for the full period of 40 years, the right thereto shall be deemed absolute and indefeasible, unless it shall appear that the same was enjoyed by some consent or agreement expressly given or made for that purpose by deed or writing".

This section refers to "any way or other easement" and there seems, as a matter of construction, no reason why it should not apply to any easement except for an easement of light which is dealt with separately. However, there is doubt about the extent to which the Act applies to other negative easements, notably easements of support. In *Dalton v Angus*[23] the issue was exhaustively considered at first instance, by the Court of Appeal and twice by the House of Lords with the help of advice from seven other High Court judges. As might be expected this produced a variety of opinions. The House of Lords decided that an easement of support could arise from long user, but there was some unwillingness to decide whether it arose under the Prescription Act 1832 or solely under the doctrine of lost modern grant. It was, however, the clear view of Lord Selborne L.C.[24] that the easement could arise under s.2 of the Prescription Act 1832. Since that time it has not proved necessary to decide this issue which is largely academic since the doctrine of lost modern grant provides perfectly adequate protection. However, as it is now universally accepted that a right of support is a true easement, there seems no reason why it should not be covered by the Prescription Act 1832.

Section 3 of the Prescription Act 1832 (as amended) makes similar provisions for rights of light:

"When the access and use of light to and for any dwelling, house, workshop, or other building shall have been actually enjoyed therewith for the full period of 20 years without interruption, the right thereto shall be deemed absolute and indefeasible, any local usage or custom to the contrary notwithstanding, unless it shall appear that

[23] (1877–87) L.R. 3 Q.B.D. 85.
[24] *Dalton v Angus* (1877–87) L.R. 3 Q.B.D. 85 at 798.

the same was enjoyed by some consent or agreement expressly made or given for that purpose by deed or writing".

For the most part the provisions of s.3 are similar to those of s.2, but there are significant differences: (1) there is no reference to the Crown and so the Act does not bind the Crown[25]; (2) there is no reference to "claiming right thereto". This is not an accidental omission. There is a difference between the way in which a positive easement, such as a right of way or a watercourse, is exercised and the way in which a right of light is exercised. While a person claiming a way has actually to use it, a right of light is gained simply by erecting your building and enjoying the light. There is, therefore, no opportunity to exercise the easement "as of right"[26]; (3) it expressly states that rights of light shall be "absolute and indefeasible". This is relevant in relation to s.7[27] which stops time running against a person under a disability; and (4) the "consent or agreement" has to be by deed or writing.

(a) The 20 year period

The basic period for which the easement must be exercised is 20 years **15.05** up to the date that the action is brought. This is expressly provided for in s.4 of the Act. It has proved to be a very considerable problem for claimants and has resulted in increased use of the doctrine of lost modern grant, where all that is required is 20 years' user at any time providing that the easement is not subsequently extinguished by express or implied release.[28]

Both ss.2 and 3 refer to claims being enjoyed "without interruption". This does not relate to the regularity or extent of the user, which will be dealt with below, but is a technical term. "Interruption" in this context means an actual obstruction of the way or other easement which prevents it from being used, whether that obstruction is made by the servient owner or some third party. Failure to use the easement for a year does not amount to an interruption, though it may be relevant in deciding whether the easement has been enjoyed for the relevant period.

An interruption does not prevent time running unless it is for a period of one year; s.4 of the Prescription Act 1832.[29] Successive obstructions of the exercise of the easement for periods of less than a year may be relevant in deciding whether the user is as of right, but this is a different

---

[25] *Perry v Eames* [1891] 1 Ch. 658; *Wheaton v Maple & Co.* [1893] 3 Ch. 48.
[26] See *RHJ Ltd v FT Patten (Holdings) Ltd* [2008] EWCA Civ 151; [2008] Ch. 341 per Lloyd L.J. at [2].
[27] See below para.15.08.
[28] *Tehidy Minerals v Norman* [1971] 2 Q.B. 528; [1971] 2 All E.R. 475.
[29] See *Bridle v Ruby* [1989] Q.B. 169; [1988] 3 W.L.R. 191 where this was the reason why a claim under the Prescription Act 1832 failed.

question from whether there has been an interruption within s.4. If there has been an interruption for a year within the 20 year period before the proceedings, then the claim under the Prescription Act 1832 fails.

15.06   It is not enough for there to be an actual obstruction of use of the right. The interruption has to be "submitted to or acquiesced in". This is a question of fact for the judge. The matter was considered by the Court of Appeal in *Dance v Triplow*.[30] In that case there was an established right of light which was interfered with by an extension completed in November 1980. Proceedings for damages for that obstruction were commenced in August 1984. The period was divided into two parts. Between 1980 and 1982 Mr Dance complained bitterly and consistently. Short of taking proceedings he could not have done more to make his views known. Then in 1982 he put the matter in the hands of his solicitors and nothing happened for two years. The Court of Appeal, overruling the County Court Judge, held that the latter period, while it could not be called "acquiescence" did amount to "submitting to ... " the interruption and accordingly that his right of light was lost.

This case followed *Davies v du Paver*[31] where the last challenge was just over a year before the action was brought. Even though nothing had happened for just over a year it was held that the last protest lasted for long enough to bring it into the one year period. Thus though the principles were the same the result was different. Equally, being refused the right to exercise the right for a year is not enough if the person refused makes clear he did not acquiesce or submit to the interruption; *Ward v Kirkland*.[32] There is therefore a difference between user "as of right" for the purpose of time running, and an interruption being submitted to. In *Newnham v Willison*[33] the user was contentious and therefore not as of right. However, even if the user remains contentious for more than a year, it does not become an interruption of an already existing easement, either created by express grant or lost modern grant.[34] This distinction was crucial in *Smith v Brudenell-Bruce*.[35]

It seems that if a person becomes aware that a prospective easement is being exercised without a grant and the exercise has continued for a period approaching 20 years, he can obstruct the use of the right, but if this obstruction is challenged, his only option is to bring proceedings which will then stop time running.

15.07   The combined effect of ss.2 and 4 of the Prescription Act 1832 has been held to allow a prescriptive easement to arise after use for over 19 years

[30] (1992) 64 P. & C.R. 1.
[31] [1953] 1 Q.B. 184.
[32] [1967] Ch. 194; [1966] 1 All E.R. 609 at 620.
[33] (1988) 56 P. & C.R. 8.
[34] *Dance v Triplow* (1992) 64 P. & C.R. 1.
[35] [2002] 2 P. & C.R. 4.

followed by interruption for a further period of less than a year making up to 20 years in all; *Flight v Thomas*.[36] "I always thought it was a strange decision" said Eve J., who was counsel in the case, in *Eaton v The Swansea Waterworks Co*,[37] but it has not been challenged since.[38]

The period of 20 years is the period,

> "next before some suit or action wherein the claim or matter to which such period may relate shall have been or shall be brought into question".

Such a suit can be brought by either party and, if an interruption is not acquiesced in, may be the only option available to the servient owner. The party seeking to challenge the prescriptive right does not have to stop it being used when he commences his action. Very often there will be an attempt to obtain an interim injunction to prevent the use continuing, but this will be decided on the principles set out in *American Cyanamid v Ethicon*[39] which might well favour the party who has been exercising the right for a long time. However, time still relates back to the commencement of proceedings whether or not such an interim injunction has been applied for, though it may affect the remedy granted if it is finally shown that there is no prescriptive right; *Bracewell v Appleby*.[40]

An attempt was made in *Reilly v Orange*[41] to suggest that the commencement of proceedings was just an interruption, so that use for 19 years plus, followed by proceedings, was sufficient. Not surprisingly this proposition was rejected.

What may be worth remembering in advising clients, however, if a way or other right exercised for a period of just less than 20 years is obstructed, is that it could be in the interests of the dominant owner to wait until nearly a year after the obstruction before commencing proceedings, since a period of less than a year between obstruction and the commencement of proceedings is an interruption which does not prevent time from running within s.4.

By s.7 of the Prescription Act 1832, time does not run where: **15.08**

> "any person otherwise capable of resisting any claim to any of the matters before mentioned shall have been or shall be an infant, idiot, non compos mentis, feme covert, or tenant for life, except only in

---

[36] 8 E.R. 91; (1841) 8 Cl. & F. 231.
[37] (1851) 17 Q.B. 267 at 272.
[38] *Reilly v Orange* [1955] 2 Q.B. 112; [1955] 1 W.L.R. 616.
[39] *American Cyanamid Co v Ethicon (No.1)* [1975] A.C. 396, [1975] 1 All E.R. 504.
[40] [1975] Ch. 408, [1975] 2 W.L.R. 282 and see under Remedies —Ch. 24.
[41] [1955] 2 Q.B. 112.

cases where the right or claim is hereby declared to be absolute and indefeasible".

The rationale of this provision (which also applied to lost modern grant) was that there was no-one in a position to make objection to or acquiesce in the user.[42] However, since 1925, the land of an infant (or minor) is held on trust either under a settlement or a trust for sale,[43] and, since 1996, as a trust of land.[44] Equally, a tenant for life has a fee simple on the trusts of the settlement. In such circumstances there is no more reason why time should be suspended during such periods than where the property is held on trust for sale or as a trust of land. Where the fee simple is vested in a trustee, whether on a trust for sale or trust of land or as trustee for a minor, he is the person capable of resisting the claim or acquiescing in the user. The section refers to a "tenant for life", and a tenancy for life no longer exists as a legal estate. Nevertheless it has been argued that s.12 of the Law of Property Act 1925, which provides that nothing in that part of the Act affects the operation of any statute or of the general law with reference to the acquisition of easements, ensures that time still does not run when the person solely entitled is under a disability. Surprisingly, this point does not seem to have been tested.

The same principle, that there must be someone against whom time can run, means that unity of ownership at any time within the 20 years period prevents a prescriptive claim being made.[45] There is a difference between unity of ownership and unity of possession. Since a prescriptive easement is freehold it follows as a matter of law that unity of ownership brings it to an end. However, in relation to unity of possession this affects the question of whether any user during this period is as of right. It was held in *Hulbert v Dale*[46] that unity of possession prevents time running under the Prescription Act 1832, but not under the doctrine of lost modern grant. Where there has been unity of ownership it is necessary to rely on implied grant or reservation.

(b) The 40 year period

15.09   The 40-year period exists more in theory than in practice. The Act provides that where the way or other matter has been:

"enjoyed as aforesaid for the full period of 40 years, the right thereto shall be deemed absolute and indefeasible, unless it shall appear that

---

[42] *Roberts & Lovell v James* (1903) 89 L.T. 282.
[43] Law of Property Act 1925 ss.1(6) and 19.
[44] Trusts of Land and Appointment of Trustees Act 1996.
[45] *Pugh v Savage* [1970] 2 Q.B. 373; [1970] 2 All E.R. 353 at 357h per Cross L.J.
[46] [1909] 2 Ch. 570.

the same was enjoyed by some consent or agreement expressly given or made for that purpose by deed or writing".

In theory this allows a prescriptive right to arise after 40 years in three situations where it would not arise after 20 years' user. Firstly, as the right becomes "absolute and indefeasible", s.7, which prevents time running against a person under a disability or against a tenant for life, does not apply to the 40 year period. Secondly, s.8 makes special provision for extension of the 40 year period. Thirdly, a right exercised by previous oral permission for 40 years can nevertheless be pursued. This last is a very difficult concept, because the easement has to be enjoyed "as aforesaid" which means "by any person claiming right thereto". How can a person who is exercising a right by permission, albeit oral, be exercising it "claiming right thereto"'?

This was the basis of *Gardner v Hodgson's Kingston Brewery*[47] where the House of Lords held that no prescriptive easement was proved after 40 years' user during which time a regular rental payment had been made. Although there was no written permission, the user could not have been as of right if payments were being made.

This decision was followed in turn by Goff J. in *Healey v Hawkins*.[48] In that case he made the distinction between a prior oral permission given before the period started and continuing oral permissions given from time to time during the 40 year period. The view he expressed was that the 40 year period only applied where oral permission was given more than 40 years previously and had not since been renewed. Apart from this rare situation a person with 40 years' user is no better off than a person with 20 years' user.

Another possible use for the 40 year period was considered in *Housden v Conservators of Wimbledon and Putney Commons*[49] where it was suggested that the "absolute and indefeasible" nature of the 40 year period meant that a grant which would otherwise be ultra vires because it was made in breach of the terms of a Private Act of Parliament would nevertheless be valid after 40 years. However, after a full consideration, the Court of Appeal rejected that proposition.

The effect of s.8 of the Prescription Act 1832, has never been authorita- **15.10** tively decided. It provided for an extension of the 40 year period to exclude periods when the servient tenement has been under a tenancy for more than three years or a term of life. In such a case the servient owner can require proof of 40 years' user excluding the tenancy, providing that

---

[47] [1903] A.C. 229.
[48] [1968] 1 W.L.R. 1967; [1968] 3 All E.R. 836 at 841G.
[49] [2008] EWCA Civ 200; [2008] 1 W.L.R. 1172.

the claim is within three years of the termination of the tenancy. Thereafter he cannot rely on the tenancy at all.

It has been seen that the existence of a tenancy of the proposed servient tenement is not necessarily fatal to a claim under the 20 year period and so the exclusion of the three or more year lease is of little significance. Equally by s.7, a time during which the proposed servient tenement is in the possession of a tenant for life is excluded for both periods. The reference to a "term of life" therefore must be to a normal leasehold term determinable with lives of the type which takes effect as a term of 90 years terminable on death under s.149(6) of the Law of Property Act 1925.[50]

It seems, therefore, that s.8 has been overtaken by the construction put upon s.2 which means that, at least for the purposes of the 20 year period, time can run during a tenancy. This is why there are no modern cases on the section.

In case a concatenation of events should result in s.8 becoming of significance in any particular case, it is worth noting that the section refers to "any such way or other convenient watercourse or use of water". There is no general reference to easements. The most likely explanation is that "convenient" is a misprint for "easement", but it is not certain whether the courts would be prepared to construe a statute in a way contrary to its express terms.[51]

3.   Lost modern grant

15.11   The popularity of the doctrine of lost modern grant in the past 40 years or so as a way of getting round the problems created by the Prescription Act 1832 really dates from the decision of the Court of Appeal in *Tehidy Minerals Ltd v Norman*.[52] There, Buckley L.J. considered in full the complex case of *Dalton v Angus*.[53] His conclusion was:

> "In our judgment *Angus & Co. v Dalton*[54] decides that, where there has been upwards of 20 years' uninterrupted enjoyment of an easement, such enjoyment having the necessary qualities to fulfil the requirements of prescription, then unless, for some reason such as incapacity on the part of the person or persons who might at some time before the commencement of the 20 year period have made a grant, the existence of such a grant is impossible, the law will adopt a legal fiction that such a grant was made, in spite of any direct evidence that no such grant was in fact made. If this legal fiction is

---

[50] *Laird v Briggs* (1881–82) L.R. 19 Ch. D. 22.
[51] ibid.
[52] [1971] 2 Q.B. 528; [1971] 2 All E.R. 475.
[53] (1877–78) L.R. 3 Q.B.D. 85.
[54] (1877–78) L.R. 3 Q.B.D. 85.

not to be displaced by direct evidence that no grant was made, it would be strange if it could be displaced by circumstantial evidence leading to the same conclusion, and in our judgment it must follow that circumstantial evidence tending to negative the existence of a grant (other than evidence establishing impossibility) should not be permitted to displace the fiction."[55]

It is crucial to understand that the doctrine is not a rebuttable presumption but a fiction. Although fictions had an important part to play in the development of the common law (notably in the action of ejectment) this is more or less the only survivor and it is not surprising that it has been referred to as a presumption. It does not, therefore, matter that there is irrefutable proof that there was no such grant. The fiction still applies. As such it is akin to various irrebuttable presumptions created by statute.

The great advantage that the doctrine has over prescription under the **15.12** Prescription Act 1832 is that user does not have to continue up to the commencement of proceedings.[56] Accordingly any period of 20 years' user at any time is sufficient to give rise to an easement. Once this easement has come into existence it can, of course, be extinguished in all the ways in which any other easement can be extinguished. Accordingly evidence of user for 20 years in the distant past followed by long non-user would normally mean that any easement created by lost modern grant had since been extinguished by implied release (though not if the land had been requisitioned).[57] It is not, therefore, a charter for digging up long-forgotten easements.

Nevertheless there are many cases where user has ceased for a period of several years and has then resumed, or where there has been non-user for a few years before the action is brought. In such circumstances the doctrine has proved invaluable.

Although it is a fiction, Buckley L.J. in *Tehidy Minerals Ltd v Norman*[58] makes it clear that the court has to identify a date for the presumed grant when it could have been made. If consents are necessary for the grant, for example by the ecclesiastical commissioners, such consents can be presumed, but only if the persons giving the fictional consent had actual or implied knowledge of the user.[59] If, for example, no such consents could have been given, because there was no power to grant a right of way for secular purposes over consecrated ground, then no grant can be

---

[55] *Tehidy Minerals Ltd v Norman* [1971] 2 Q.B. 528; [1971] 2 All E.R. 475 at 491d.
[56] *Tehidy Minerals v Norman* [1971] 2 Q.B. 528; *Oakley v Boston* [1976] Q.B. 270; [1975] 3 All E.R. 405 at 407g; *Smith v Brudenell-Bruce* [2002] 2 P. & C.R. 4.
[57] *Tehidy Minerals v Norman* [1971] 2 Q.B. 528.
[58] ibid.
[59] *Oakley v Boston* [1976] Q.B. 270; [1975] 3 All E.R. 405.

presumed.[60] Equally, if the right is not capable of existing as an easement, then it cannot be obtained under the doctrine of lost modern grant.[61] The same applies where a grant would be ultra vires, for example, because it is forbidden by the provisions of an Inclosure Act.[62]

4. Prescription at common law

15.13 The principle of prescriptive rights based on long user has been accepted as part of the common law from the earliest times. The period required was user from time immemorial or, in other words, user "during the time whereof the memory of man runneth not to the contrary".[63] Unfortunately this time was fixed by the Statute of Westminster 1275 at A.D. 1189. This period of 86 years was, no doubt, reasonable at the time, but it has ever since been held that user from time immemorial means user since 1189.

There is, however, some amelioration in this rule:

"When the existence of a way is spoken to over a period extending as far back as living memory goes, and there is nothing to show that there must have been a time when it did not exist, a case of prescription at common law is made out, and there is no need to have recourse to the artificial doctrine of a modern lost grant".[64]

The circumstances are few and far between where the evidence shows use of an easement as far back as living memory goes, but there is no valid claim under the doctrine of lost modern grant or prescription under the Prescription Act 1832. As a result, there are few modern cases on prescription at common law.[65]

15.14 However, in RPC *Holdings v Rogers*[66] Harman J. found that there was a right of way at common law for agricultural purposes over a way which was shown to have existed as far back as living memory goes:

"It was insisted at the Bar on the plaintiffs' behalf that it is not competent for the court to come to such a conclusion [of prescription at common law] unless concrete evidence is adduced proving user of the way for some continuous period of 20 years, and it was said that

---

[60] *Re St Martin Le Grand, York* [1990] Fam. 63; [1989] 3 W.L.R. 1207.
[61] *Palmer v Bowman* [2000] 1 W.L.R. 842.
[62] *Smith v Muller* [2008] EWCA Civ 1425.
[63] Co.Litt. 114b.
[64] per Harman J. in *RPC Holdings v Rogers* [1953] 1 All E.R. 1029 at 1031H.
[65] See *Tehidy Minerals v Norman* [1971] 2 Q.B. 528; [1971] 2 All E.R. 475 at 484g where common law prescription and lost modern grant were both proved in respect of some of the farms.
[66] [1953] 1 All E.R. 1029.

if the period to which the witnesses spoke be compared and tabulated, it will be found that no continuous period of 20 years is covered. This consideration might be relevant when considering the doctrine of lost grant, but it seems to me to have nothing to do with claims to prescription at common law where the court is asked to infer an immemorial user from evidence going back as far as living memory will run. Whether the memories in question cover continuous or discontinuous periods is beside the point."[67]

There is, therefore, a possible use for common law prescription where the evidence, while it goes back a long time, does not include a single continuous period of 20 years. Equally the principle can be used where there are problems concerning the capacity of the servient owner, which would defeat prescription under the Prescription Act 1832 or under the doctrine of lost modern grant. Even at common law, however, unity of ownership (as opposed to unity of possession) at any time must put an end to a prescriptive claim.

5.   The proposed unified system

The Law Commission[68] has recommended a unified system of prescription, doing away with the arcane division between the Prescription Act, lost modern grant and common law prescription. If this is translated into Statute in accordance with cl.16 of the draft Bill, "qualifying use of land for a continuous period of 20 years has effect to create an easement in relation to that use".

The draft Bill directly provides that:

"The existing law of prescription ceases to have effect in relation to use on or after the date on which this section comes into force".

If this is implemented (and parliamentary time has not yet been found for it) it seems to follow that the whole body of law on easements by prescription is abolished. The idea is to replace this body of law with a statutory code based on the meaning of "qualifying use". There are some transitional provisions, but they are only short-term.

Any new law is subject to the law of unintended consequences and it is not intended to carry out a detailed analysis of what is, at present, only a proposal. However, it appears that the intention is, not only to require any future prescriptive easement to be created under the new system, but also to require any person claiming a prescriptive right to rely on the new

[67] *RPC Holdings v Rogers* [1953] 1 All E.R. 1029 at 1031H–1032SA.
[68] Law Commission, *Making Land Work: Easements, Covenants and Profits á Prendre* (London: The Stationery Office, 2011), Law Com. No.327.

system even if he is able to claim that, for example, a right came into existence either under the principle of lost modern grant or at common law before the new Bill came into force.

Nevertheless, the requirements for "qualifying use" follow closely the existing requirements for prescriptive use and it may be that the courts will seek to interpret the new provisions in the light of the existing body of case law.

6. The enjoyment required

15.15   The Prescription Act 1832 requires that the easement "shall have been actually enjoyed by any person claiming the right thereto". The requirements for lost modern grant and common law prescription are essentially the same. From this statutory provision seven elements can be distilled:

(a) continuity;

(b) openness;

(c) absence of force;

(d) enjoyment "by the person claiming right thereto";

(e) actual or imputed knowledge of the servient owner;

(f) absence of permission; and

(g) legality.

These elements will be considered separately. Each of them is addressed in the Draft Law of Property Bill recommended by the Law Commission.

(a) Continuity

15.16   There is no requirement in the existing law that an easement must be continuously exercised throughout the requisite period. The word "continuous" is included in the draft Bill, without further definition and there is no reason to think that there is any intention to change this aspect of the law. Many easements, such as rights of way, cannot by their nature be exercised continuously. With some easements there is a visible manifestation of the enjoyment. A right of drainage, for example, is often manifested by a pipe. However, a drainage pipe may not be used all the time and even with a water pipe the supply may be cut off for a short or longer time. A right of way may or may not be manifested by a visible path or a gate. In respect of other easements, such as support and light, it is the building itself which enjoys the right, but even here problems can arise if there is a change in the size of the building or the positioning of the windows or the internal divisions of the building.

A break in continuity of user due to requisition of the servient tenement within the 20 year period before the action was brought is fatal to a claim under the Prescription Act 1832 even though the dominant owners had no choice in the matter.[69]

The particular problems involved with different easements will be dealt with in the sections dealing with those specific easements, but even in dealing with the problem generally it is helpful to consider the main easements separately.

(i) Rights of way

Use of a right of way is by its nature discontinuous. The regularity of **15.17** user which is required for a prescriptive claim is a question of fact.[70] The basis on which the court should decide was set out by Lindley L.J. in *Hollins v Verney*[71]:

> "no actual user can be sufficient to satisfy the statute unless during the whole of the statutory term (whether acts of user be proved in each year or not) the user is enough at any rate to carry to the mind of a reasonable person who is in possession of the servient tenement, the fact that a continuous right to enjoyment is being asserted and ought to be resisted if such right is not recognised, and if resistance to it is intended".

In *White v Taylor (No.2)*[72] Buckley J., in dealing with a prescriptive claim to a profit à prendre for grazing said:

> "the user must be shown to have been of such a character, degree and frequency as to indicate an assertion by the claimant of a continuous right, and a right of the measure of the right claimed".

This statement was approved by the Court of Appeal in *Ironside & Crabb and Crabb v Cook, Cook & Barefoot*.[73]

There are two main elements in these definitions. Firstly, the degree of user will depend on the purposes for which it is exercised and, secondly, it will be relevant to see to what extent the servient owner ought to have been aware of it. This latter element impinges on the requirement of actual or imputed knowledge of the prospective servient owner, dealt with below.[74] However, *Ironside & Crabb and Crabb v Cook, Cook & Barefoot*

---

[69] *Tehidy Minerals v Norman* [1971] 2 Q.B. 528.
[70] *Hollins v Verney* (1883–84) L.R. 13 Q.B.D. 304.
[71] (1883–84) L.R. 13 Q.B.D. 304 at 315.
[72] [1969] 1 Ch. 150; [1967] 3 All E.R. 349.
[73] (1981) 41 P. & C.R. 326.
[74] See below para.15.26.

brought home the fact that continuity and implied knowledge are not just aspects of the same requirement. In that case the user was on a very small scale from 1952 to 1960. However, the Court of Appeal held that it would have been sufficient but for the fact that there was nothing in the circumstances of the case which would have put the servient owner on notice that such a right of way was being asserted. In the particular circumstances of that case, this was because the use was of a small strip of land, adjoining an admitted right of way, which was on the far side of the servient owner's hedge.

15.18   Given that continuity is a question of fact, an analysis of the cases is of limited importance, but two modern cases provide some illustration of what will be sufficient. In *Diment v NH Foot Ltd*[75] the way was used on six to 10 occasions a year for agricultural purposes. Pennycuick V.C. had no doubt that this was sufficient. *Healey v Hawkins*[76] provides a fairly typical example of the sort of situation which is met in practice. The way was a driveway leading to a house. It was used by permission until 1938 when it was used regularly by the owner. It was, however, used very little during the war, due to petrol rationing. Then (it is not clear exactly when) the husband died and his widow did not have a car, but the son used the drive when visiting until 1961. Tenants then used the drive until 1966 when the house was unoccupied until the action was commenced. Despite these variations in user Goff J. held that the user was sufficiently continuous from 1938. One thing which these two cases illustrate is that the court will take into account the circumstances of the dominant owner or occupier at the time in considering what degree of user is sufficient. If there is a drive and the owner does not have a car then it will be sufficient to show that the drive is used by visitors or by deliverymen. If, on the other hand, he does have a car but does not use the drive, this may tend to suggest that there is no user as of right. They also demonstrate that the courts have taken a fairly generous approach to continuity, providing the evidence shows that the way was used as and when needed for the requisite period.

15.19   By contrast, an example of a case where the use was held to be too intermittent to satisfy the statute is *Hollins v Verney*,[77] where the way was used for removing wood which was only cut every few years. The Court of Appeal felt that so discontinuous a use could not amount to uninterrupted enjoyment, though Lindley L.J. suggested[78] that use at least once every year for the full period would have been enough. Again in

---

[75] [1974] 1 W.L.R. 1427; [1974] 2 All E.R. 785.
[76] [1968] 1 W.L.R. 1967.
[77] (1883–84) L.R. 13 Q.B.D. 304.
[78] *Hollins v Verney* (1883–84) L.R. 13 Q.B.D. 304 at 305.

Goldsmith v Burrow Construction[79] the fact that a gate was kept locked for substantial periods of less than a year rendered the use insufficiently continuous, though the decision was that these breaks in user in turn rendered the use of the way precarious.

A right of way can only exist over a defined path and normally it will be necessary to show that there is continuous use of the same path over the period of 20 years. However, in *Davis v Whitby*[80] it was held that an agreed variation in the route did not prevent time running. It seems to have been accepted that this agreement did not amount to a permission to use the varied way, but was an agreement relating to what was taken to be a valid right of way.

(ii) Water

Problems over continuity arise less commonly in cases of water rights. **15.20** Rights of drainage will usually be along a pipe or defined channel and will be used regularly, though if it is used only intermittently this may affect continuity.[81] Rights to a supply of water will also usually be continuous though even here there may be difficulties where the flow is variable or where the extraction rate varies.

> "It would be very dangerous to hold that a party should lose his right in consequence of such an interruption; if such were the rule the accident of a dry season or other causes over which the party could have no control might deprive him of a right established by the longest course of enjoyment."[82]

This statement, however, was said to go too far in *Hollins v Verney*[83] where the earlier authorities are reviewed. If the claim is to prescription under the Act or by lost modern grant there has to be enjoyment for the full period.

As far as extraction is concerned the courts are prepared to accept that the volume of extraction will vary over the years providing that a sufficiently clear pattern can be discovered.[84]

(iii) Light

Problems of continuity arise in respect of light where the building **15.21** benefiting from the light has changed. A change in the internal

---

[79] *The Times*, July 31, 1987.
[80] [1974] Ch. 186; [1974] 1 All E.R. 806.
[81] *Liverpool Corp V H Coghill & Son Ltd* [1918] 1 Ch. 307.
[82] per Tindall C.J. in *Hall v Swift* (1838) 4 Bing N.C. 381.
[83] (1883–84) L.R. 13 Q.B.D. 304.
[84] *Cargill v Gotts* [1981] 1 W.L.R. 441; [1981] 1 All E.R. 682.

arrangement of the building is not relevant because the easement is of access of light to the building and not to particular rooms.[85] Equally, the building does not actually have to be occupied; the light is enjoyed by the building even if there is no-one inside to take advantage of it.[86] Even keeping the shutters closed will not prevent time from running, but if a window is completely boarded up for a whole year then it cannot be said that the light is being enjoyed during this period and the continuity is broken.

The enjoyment depends on the light rather than the windows. As light travels in straight lines it is possible to identify the shafts of light being enjoyed. Therefore if you rebuild and bring the building forward you may still be using some of the same light.[87]

The question of enjoyment of rights of light will be dealt with more fully later.[88]

(iv) Support

15.22   Support of one building by another or by the adjoining ground is of its nature continuous. However, there is always a possibility that there will be alterations of the dominant tenement. Clearly if a building is demolished and a different building built in a different location leaning on a different part of the servient owner's property this would amount to a break in continuity.

However, the requirement of continuity goes a little further:

> "It might well be that if, in any case, it were proved that there had been a change at some time within the period of 20 years before action brought in the construction of the dominant tenement of such a kind as to throw a substantially greater weight upon the servient tenement, then in such a case an easement for the support of the changed building could not be maintained."[89]

If there is demolition followed by reconstruction it will be a question of fact whether the support has been sufficiently continuous. Providing that the new building is built promptly following the demolition of the previous one it seems likely that the court would take the view that there was sufficient continuity. Such demolition would not be an interruption under s.4 of the Prescription Act 1832 because it would not be caused by the act of the servient owner.

---

[85] *Carr-Saunders v Dick McNeil Associates* [1986] 1 W.L.R. 922; [1986] 2 All E.R. 888; *Price v Hilditch* [1930] 1 Ch. 500.
[86] *Smith v Baxter* [1900] 2 Ch. 138.
[87] *Andrews v Waite* [1907] 2 Ch. 500.
[88] See Ch. 20—Rights of Light.
[89] per Bennett J. in *Lloyd's Bank Ltd v Dalton* [1942] Ch. 466.

(b) Openness

In order that the easement be enjoyed by a person "claiming right thereto" **15.23** it must be exercised openly and not secretly—the word used in the draft Bill is "stealth".[90] For the most part this requirement equates with the actual or imputed knowledge of the servient owner, which is dealt with below. However, the need for openness is a separate element in the enjoyment of the easement. The owner of land may know that small boys living next door secretly sneak through his fence and use it as a short cut to the road. This does not mean that they are using the way "claiming a right thereto".

Usually if the exercise is secret the servient owner will not know of it or have the means of knowing of it, but the courts are less inclined to be generous towards a user which is carried out secretly and at night than towards a use which, though perfectly open, in fact escapes the attention of the servient owner. This was what happened in *Liverpool Corp v Coghill*[91] where the noxious effluent was discharged intermittently and often at night. Even there, however, the use, though secret in one sense was not "surreptitious or actively concealed from" the servient owners.

(c) Absence of force

The requirement of absence of force[92] is not so clear-cut as the require- **15.24** ment of openness. A person is unlikely to exercise a valid right secretly, but a person openly exercising what he believes to be his rights may meet with forcible resistance. It is by no means uncommon to find that an easement is exercised quite openly for the bulk of the relevant period, but that at some stage (often shortly before proceedings are commenced) the person over whose lands it is being exercised takes steps to try to stop the exercise of what the other person believes to be his rights.

Where the person seeking to exercise the right protests at being stopped there will be no interruption in his exercise of the right even if the obstruction lasts for more than a year.[93] On the other hand if he refuses to accept the obstruction and continues to use the easement by force it could be said that the user is no longer as of right.[94]

It is submitted that the distinction is this. If the exercise over the 20 year period has been consistently resisted then no easement will arise. If there is an interruption for a year which is submitted to or acquiesced in then that is an end of the matter at least under the Prescription Act 1832, but if over the period the easement has sometimes been exercised openly and

---

[90] Clause 17(2)(b).
[91] *Liverpool Corp v H Coghill & Son Ltd* [1918] 1 Ch. 307.
[92] Clause 17(1)(b) of the draft Bill—Law Com. No.397, p.195.
[93] *Davies v du Paver* [1953] 1 Q.B. 184.
[94] *Newnham v Willison* (1988) 56 P. & C.R. 8.

as of right and has sometimes been exercised after resistance or people have been turned away the court will look at the overall picture to decide whether the exercise as a whole has been without force.

The courts will be wary of finding that the exercise of the easement has been interrupted by a resisted obstruction in the period immediately before the action when the parties are preparing themselves for the fray, though in fact *Newnham v Willison*[95] was a case where the obstruction was erected shortly before the action was commenced.

Furthermore, in *Smith v Brudenell-Bruce*[96] Pumfrey J. sought to make a clear distinction between an interruption, which has to be submitted to by the person seeking to exercise the right and which causes the termination of an existing right obtained by lost modern grant and user which is contentious and therefore not "as of right". Such user, he decided, prevents a claim under the Prescription Act 1832, since the use has ceased to be as of right and become, in effect, forcible. In so doing he followed *Newnham v Willison*,[97] where the distinction between forcible use and interruption was not made clear, and indeed extended the principle where there was no attempt to obstruct the way forcibly, but only objections to his use. As a result he held that there was no right of way under the Prescription Act 1832, but that there was a right by lost modern grant because there had been twenty years' user before it became contentious.

(d) Enjoyment by the person claiming the right

15.25   Prescriptive easements can only exist in favour of the freehold owner of land. There is, it seems, no such thing as a leasehold prescriptive right.

> "Of course a tenant cannot by user gain a prescriptive right of way for himself as tenant but by user over land of a stranger he can gain a prescriptive right of way in fee for his landlord which he can use while he is tenant and which his landlord can grant to a subsequent tenant."[98]

This approach to user applies not only to tenants, but to any other lawful occupier of land. Equally, the user does not have to be by the owner or tenant personally providing that it is for the benefit of the dominant tenement. This is a question of fact. Any user which would constitute exercise of an existing easement[99] can be given in evidence as showing enjoyment as of right for the purposes of proving an easement by prescription. A

---

[95] (1988) 56 P. & C.R. 8.
[96] [2002] 2 P. & C.R. 4.
[97] (1988) 56 P. & C.R. 8.
[98] per Cross L.J. in *Pugh v Savage* [1970] 2 Q.B. 373; [1970] 2 All E.R. 353 at 356g.
[99] See above para.10–29.

tenant cannot obtain an easement by prescription against his own land-lord or another tenant of his landlord.[100]

(e) Knowledge of the servient owner

There is no doubt that the extent to which the servient owner knows or could or should have known of the user is relevant to the issue of whether it is being exercised by a person claiming a right thereto. On the other hand, it is only part of the general principle that the exercise should be as of right. It is logical that a right based on user without interruption can only be valid if it could have been interrupted by the servient owner. If the owner against whom the claim is made did not know about the exercise of the right, then he could not have prevented it. But this is only part of the story.

15.26

If prescription were based purely on acquiescence it would be neces-sary to show that the servient owner knew of the exercise of the right and did not object. However, it has been seen that prescriptive rights are based on expedience rather than on true acquiescence and it has never been clearly suggested that the servient owner has to have actual knowl-edge of the exercise of the right claimed.

The principle which has been accepted in all the cases was set out in *Union Lighterage v London Graving Dock*[101]:

> "On principle it appears to me that a prescriptive right to an ease-ment over a man's land should only be acquired when the enjoyment has been open—that is to say of such a character that an ordinary owner of the land, diligent in the protection of his interests, would have or must be taken to have a reasonable opportunity of being aware of that enjoyment".

That was a case of rights of support where the ties making use of the support were hidden underground. It was held that there was no basis for saying that the plaintiffs ought to have knowledge of these ties attributed to them or were put on enquiry as to their existence. No owner of the land could be expected to be aware of support gained from such a secret underground source.

The proposition quoted above relates essentially to the quality and nature of the user and not to the actual knowledge or ignorance of the servient owner. It says that use must be "open" and by way of illustration

15.27

---

[100] *Wheaton v Maple* [1893] 3 Ch. 48; *Bosomworth v Faber* (1995) 69 P. & C.R. 288 at 292 where it was held that this does not apply to a lease for 2,000 years which the lessee had a right to convert into a freehold by virtue of s.65 of the Conveyancing Act 1881 and s.153 of the Law of Property Act 1925.

[101] [1902] 2 Ch. 557 at 570.

refers not to the actual owner of the land, but to an "ordinary owner of the land". While the actual knowledge or ignorance of the owner must help the court in deciding what the ordinary diligent owner would know, this quotation does not suggest that there is any need to look into any special reasons (such as illness or absence abroad) why the servient owner should be ignorant.

However, it is hard to overlook the number of modern cases where prescription has been considered in terms of actual or constructive knowledge. This is a particular problem where the servient tenement is in the possession of a tenant. In such circumstances the owner has less reason to check up on what is happening and, indeed, may have no right to enter the land in order to stop it happening.

The leading case on prescriptive rights against a landlord is *Pugh v Savage*,[102] which was considered in *Williams v Sandy Lane (Chester) Ltd*[103] and upheld in *Llewellyn (deceased) v Lorey*.[104] In essence the question is not whether there was a tenancy, but whether the necessary circumstances exist for the freehold owner to be bound by the prescriptive user.

In *Williams* Chadwick L.J. set out the principles:

"• Where the grant of the tenancy of the servient land predates the user by or on behalf of the owner of the dominant land, the question is whether the freehold owner could take steps to stop the user.

• If the owner could prevent the user, did he know about it? The fact that he was out of possession when the user began may be sufficient to prevent knowledge being imputed.

• If the owner was in possession before the user began, but subsequently granted a tenancy, the question is whether he knew of it, or should have known. If he knew when it began, then he could take steps to stop it even after the tenancy.

• If the owner was not in possession when the user began, the question is the same, namely whether he should have known and could have stopped it."

In that case the landlord was the Local Council. Their lease expressly forbade the tenant from allowing user which would result in an easement. In breach of that covenant he continued to allow the user. But that did not prevent time running. There was no evidence that the Council actually knew about the owner. It was sufficient that they should have known if they had inspected.

[102] [1970] 2 Q.B. 373; [1970] 2 All E.R. 353.
[103] [2006] EWCA Civ 1738.
[104] [2011] EWCA Civ 37.

It seems clear, in the light of *Williams* that *Pugh v Savage*[105] was not setting out any rule of law about when time could run against a landlord. A landlord has a right of entry onto property and can (as happened in *Williams*) include a covenant by the tenant not to permit such user, which they can then enforce.

In truth this issue is part of the overall tension in the principle of prescription, namely that it is not a form of estoppel, but is often described as being based on acquiescence, which is very like estoppel.

These two cases[106] do, however, illustrate the relevance of a tenancy of the servient tenement since the claim is against the owner and it must be shown that the user binds the owner and not just the tenant.

The principle applicable to all cases, and not just those involving a landlord, is that there is a presumption from open user that the servient owner knew of the easement. This presumption can only be rebutted by the servient owner showing not only that he did not in fact know of the user, but also that such knowledge should not be imputed. The knowledge will be imputed in circumstances where, as a diligent owner, he could have discovered the user. The difference between actual and imputed knowledge is particularly important in easements such as support and drainage where an owner in possession would not necessarily be aware of what is happening unless he took some positive steps to find out. In *Lloyds Bank Ltd v Dalton*[107] it was held that a servient owner is expected or required to take positive steps to check up on his boundaries and simply stating that he did not know of the support will not be a defence.

Where a consent would be required for any imputed lost grant then the court will not presume knowledge by the person required to give the consent, e.g. the ecclesiastical commissioners.[108]

Where there is actual knowledge of the user the fact that the servient owner is under the mistaken belief that it is being exercised under an express grant does not prevent time from running.[109] This emphasises the difference between prescription and acquiescence. The servient owner can hardly be said to be acquiescing in the creation of the right if he is under the mistaken belief that the right exists already, but, as prescription concentrates on the openness of the user rather than on the mind of the servient owner, it is plain that the user is nevertheless as of right. It does not matter that the person exercising the right is under the same mistaken belief unless the belief would give him only a limited right, such as a leasehold easement.

[105] [1970] 2 Q.B. 373.
[106] Approved in *Llewellyn (deceased) v Lorey* [2011] EWCA Civ 37.
[107] [1942] Ch. 466.
[108] *Oakley v Boston* [1976] Q.B. 270.
[109] *Bridle v Ruby* [1990] Fam 63; [1988] 3 All E.R. 64; *Bosomworth v Faber* (1995) 69 P. & C.R. 288.

(f) Permission

15.28   The exercise of rights subsequently claimed as easements by prescription often begins with someone asking and being given permission. The use then continues for many years until someone claims that it is a right.

Such user is initially by way of licence. In such circumstances it could be said that the person is exercising a right of sorts but, at least where the user is for less than 40 years,[110] the use is not as of right, because it is not in purported exercise of a freehold right.

Where there is an annual payment[111] or where the permission is for a specific period there is little difficulty. The exercise is clearly by way of licence and not under a claim of right.

However, where permission is granted at the beginning on an open-ended basis the user continues to be permissive indefinitely until there is a change in the character of the user which causes it to cease to be permissive. In *Healey v Hawkins*[112] this change occurred when the user ceased to be in wet weather, at which times the user sought and obtained permission from time to time, and changed to regular use.

The exact point at which user which was originally permissive becomes as of right is a question of degree. A formal licence (even if oral) which is expressly open-ended is less likely to develop into user as of right than a casual oral permission. However, where user starts by permission and continues for a long period without any change in its character, it may be held that it remained permissive, especially when others, who were not claiming as of right, also used the way by permission.[113] Equally, a change of the ownership of either property may affect the extent to which the character of the user changes, but even a successor to the person originally given the permission can still be held to be exercising the right under the permission.[114]

Difficulties can also arise where the servient owner gives permission for the dominant owner or his visitors or tenants to continue to exercise a right which has been exercised as of right before. Permission may be given, even though it has not been sought. If permission is sought and obtained by the dominant owner within the relevant period then it cannot be said that his user thereafter is as of right. However, the servient owner cannot render user permissive simply by giving permission to someone who is claiming to exercise the easement as of right.

Permission is not the same as toleration. Where there has been no actual permission the exercise of the right will be sufficient. But even in

---

[110] See above, para.15–09.

[111] See *Gardner v Hodgson's Kingston Brewery Co Ltd* [1903] A.C. 229.

[112] [1968] 1 W.L.R. 1967.

[113] *Jones v Price* (1992) 64 P. & C.R. 404 —not the same Mr Jones and Mr Price who were arguing over hedges in Montgomeryshire in 1965.

[114] *Gaved v Martyn* (1865) 19 C.B. N.S. 732.

such circumstances the court will look at the user to see whether it can be seen as being under claim of right. Where it is casual in its nature the proper interpretation may be that it is being exercised as a result of toleration by the owners,[115] but where it has been used regularly the fact that the servient owner tolerated it because he did not object to limited exercise of the way does not stop time from running.[116] Such toleration is, indeed, close to the "acquiescence on which the whole concept of prescription is supposed to be based".[117]

It seems that it may be possible to stop time running in favour of a person who has been using a way for less than 20 years by putting up a sign saying that anyone using a way does so by permission.[118]

(g) Legality

After a period of uncertainty, the relationship between prescription and **15.29** illegality has been made clear again in *Bakewell Management Ltd v Brandwood*.[119]

In order that an easement can be exercised as of right, it must be something that the dominant owner can do lawfully. The acts on which prescription is based are usually tortious, because they involve trespass, but that is very different from acts which are illegal and in breach of statute.

However, there are acts which would cease to be illegal if they were done pursuant to a breach. As a result, the problem confronted in *Hanning v Top Deck Travel Group Ltd*[120] and *Massey v Boulden*, which were both overruled, does not arise. The use of a private drive over a common becomes legal if the freehold owner has granted a right of way. If it can have been granted, then, under the fiction of lost modern grant, it becomes lawful. As a result, the attempted solution to this apparent problem, provided by the Vehicular Access Across Common and Other Land (England) Regulations 2002 is no longer needed. There are various statutes restricting vehicular use of land. Section 193 of the Law of Property Act 1925 makes it illegal for people to drive on urban commons without permission from the trustees. As a result, 20 years' use by commercial vehicles of the way do not create a prescriptive right.[121]

It does not, however, follow that all illegal acts could have been put right by a grant or permission from the freeholder. Thus letting herbage

---

[115] *Alfred F Beckett Ltd v Lyons* [1967] Ch. 449; *Ironside & Crabb and Crabb v Cook, Cook & Barefoot* (1981) 41 P. & C.R. 326.
[116] *Mills v Silver* [1991] Ch. 271; [1991] Fam. 271.
[117] *R. v Oxfordshire CC Ex p. Sunningwell Parish Council* [2000] 1 A.C. 335.
[118] *Rafique v Trustees of Walton Estate* (1993) 65 P. & C.R. 356.
[119] [2004] UKHL 14; [2004] 2 A.C. 519; [2004] 2 W.L.R. 955.
[120] (1994) 68 P. & C.R. 14.
[121] *Hanning v Top Deck Travel Group Ltd* (1994) 68 P. & C.R. 14.

in breach of Enclosure Acts,[122] extracting water without a licence, as in *Cargill v Gotts*,[123] or discharging noxious fluids into a stream[124] have all been held not to give rise to prescriptive rights, and the House of Lords in *Bakewell Management v Brandwood* made it clear that *Cargill v Gotts* was not overruled. However, use which is in breach of planning permission does not count as being illegal until an enforcement order is made[125] and user which could have been in breach of a fencing obligation contained in an Enclosure Act is not in itself illegal.[126]

---

[122] *Neaverson v Peterborough Rural DC* [1902] 1 Ch. 557.
[123] [1981] 1 W.L.R. 441; [1981] 1 All E.R. 682.
[124] *Liverpool Corp v H Coghill & Son Ltd* [1918] 1 Ch. 307.
[125] *Batchelor v Marlow* [2001] R.T.R. 12; [2001] 1 E.G.L.R. 119, overturned on different grounds [2001] EWCA Civ 1051; (2001) 82 P. & C.R. 36.
[126] *Smith v Muller* [2008] EWCA Civ. 1425.

Chapter Sixteen
Equitable Easements

1.   Introduction

Equity affects easements in much the same way as it affects other inter- **16.01**
ests in land. If a person has an equitable interest in land then he has an
equitable interest in any easements which appertain to that land. Thus a
contract to buy land makes the purchaser the equitable owner of the land
and of any easements that go with it.[1] His right to exercise the easement
will depend upon his rights in respect of the land itself. If he has a right
of possession or of occupation then he will be entitled to exercise the easement like any other occupier. If his right is a future right then his right to
exercise the easement will only arise when his right to the land falls into
possession. Equally a mortgagee, whether legal or equitable, has the same
rights in respect of the easements appertaining to the land as he has over
the land itself. The mortgagee's easement is a right separate from and
independent of that which existed in the mortgagor, so that if the mortgagor releases his easement the mortgagee's easement can still exist,
though it comes to an end when the mortgage is redeemed.[2]

2.   Contract to grant an easement

A legal easement can only be created for an interest equivalent to an **16.02**
estate in fee simple absolute in possession or a term of years absolute.[3]
Such an interest can only be created by deed (though it may be implied in
a deed) except in the case of leases for three years or less which can be
created by parol. Accordingly any limited right in an easement can only
arise, if at all, in equity. Prescriptive rights can only be freehold.[4]

A person who owns land may enter into an agreement with his neighbour to grant him an easement over his land. By s.2(1) of the Law of
Property (Miscellaneous Provisions) Act 1989:

---

[1] *White v Taylor* (No. 2) [1969] 1 Ch. 150; [1968] 1 All E.R. 1015 at 1025.
[2] *Poulton v Moore* [1915] 1 K.B. 400.
[3] Law of Property Act 1925 s.1(2).
[4] *Bosomworth v Faber* (1995) 69 P. & C.R. 288; above para.15.25.

"A contract for the sale or other disposition of an interest in land can only be made in writing and only by incorporating all the terms which the parties have expressly agreed in one document or, where contracts are exchanged, in each."

The terms may be incorporated in a document either by being set out in it, or by reference to some other document.[5] The document (or documents exchanged) must be signed. A letter and a plan are separate documents and so a signature on a plan alone is not enough.[6] As the reference to an "interest in land" is the same as in s.40 of the Law of Property Act 1925 which it supersedes, it is clear that easements are interests in land and therefore that this section applies to contracts to grant an easement.[7]

The effect of this section is to abolish the law of part performance. Contracts to grant easements must be in writing. The effect of the 1989 Act is to bring about "a remarkably different regime from that which obtained hitherto".[8] An oral contract is void and not just unenforceable and only one document is allowed, except where contracts are exchanged, and all the terms must be contained in the document. As a result a contract for the grant or reservation of an easement cannot now be varied orally even if the variation is of a single term.[9] However, Morritt L.J. suggests that, while the original contract may not have been varied, a contract to vary the original contract might not be a contract for the sale of land and might not need to be in writing at all. Presumably the party seeking to resile from that oral agreement could then be forced (by specific performance) to execute a valid written variation of the contract. This comment was obiter because the plaintiff had to rely on the original contract and not a contract to vary.

16.03   It seems that a contract to grant an easement for the benefit of land not then owned by the proposed grantee can be an estate contract creating an interest in land, but this can only be the case where the prospective dominant tenement is identified with certainty to enable a purchaser of the servient tenement to know how much of a burden he is taking on.[10] It is not sufficiently certain if all that is known is the maximum limit of the land to be benefited.[11]

---

[5] Law of Property (Miscellaneous Provisions) Act 1989 s.2(2).
[6] *Firstpost Homes Ltd v Johnson* [1995] 1 W.L.R. 1567; [1995] 4 All E.R. 355.
[7] *Ives v High* [1967] 2 Q.B. 379; [1967] 1 All E.R. 504.
[8] per Peter Gibson L.J. in *Firstpost Homes v Johnson* [1995] 1 W.L.R. 1567 at 1571.
[9] *McCausland v Duncan Lawrie Ltd* [1997] 1 W.L.R. 38; (1997) 74 P. & C.R. 343.
[10] *London and Blenheim Estates Ltd v Ladbroke Retail Parks Ltd* [1994] 1 W.L.R. 31; [1993] 4 All E.R. 157.
[11] *Voice v Bell* (1994) 68 P. & C.R. 441.

It seems that a purported grant takes effect as a contract for the sale of land.[12] It follows that an oral grant of a right of way is invalid under the Law of Property (Miscellaneous Provisions) Act 1989.

By s.2 of the Land Charges Act 1972 an equitable easement is registrable under Class D(iii). There is no doubt that an agreement to grant an easement is an equitable easement for this purpose and accordingly is only valid if registered (assuming the contract was made on or after January 1, 1926).[13]

3. Other equitable easements

An equitable easement is defined for the purposes of the Land Charges Act 1972 as: "an easement, right or privilege over or affecting land created or arising on or after January 1, 1926 and being merely an equitable interest". **16.04**

> "It has always been rather a mystery what equitable easements are. Contracts to create easements can just as well be registered as estate contracts. What else is left? In fact nearly 2,000 equitable easements were registered in 1954 and one may wonder whether licensing agreements and other uncertain quantities are finding a home here. It would be more satisfactory to close the class, for it is just as objectionable on the score of vagueness as that of general equitable charges."[14]

It has been suggested that the definition, by including a "right or privilege" in addition to an easement, is intending to cover rights which are not capable of amounting to legal easements, but which nevertheless should be treated as some kind of equitable interest in land which can be binding on a purchaser of the land affected providing they are registered. This view, however, was rejected by the Court of Appeal in *ER Ives Investment Ltd v High*[15] where Lord Denning M.R. approved an article by Mr C. V. Davidge in the Law Quarterly Review.[16] He referred to s.4(1) of the Law of Property Act 1925 which provides,

> "an equitable interest in land shall only be capable of being validly created in any case in which an equivalent equitable interest in

---

[12] *Magrath v Parkside Hotels Ltd* [2011] EWHC 143 (Ch), though this point was expressly left open in *London and Blenheim Estates Ltd v Ladbroke Retail Parks Ltd* [1994] 1 W.L.R. 31; [1993] 4 All E.R. 157.

[13] *Huckvale v Aegean Hotels Ltd* (1989) 58 P & C.R. 163.

[14] H. W. R. Wade, "Land Charges Registration Reviewed" [1956] C.L.J. 216, 225.

[15] [1967] 2 Q.B. 379; [1967] 2 W.L.R. 789.

[16] C. V. Davidge, "Equitable Easements" (1937) 53 L.Q.R. 259.

property real or personal could have been validly created before such commencement".

Lord Denning M.R. went further and stated:

"An 'equitable interest' is a proprietary interest in land such as would before 1926 have been recognised as capable of being conveyed or created at law, but which since 1926 only takes effect as an equitable interest. An instance of such a proprietary interest is a profit à prendre for life."

This approach was followed by the Court of Appeal in *London and Blenheim Estates v Ladbroke Retail Parks*.[17]

16.05   Despite the large number of equitable easements registered, the narrow interpretation favoured in *ER Ives Investment Ltd v High*[18] does not in practice seem to have caused many problems. The true explanation of the large number of registrations may be that there are frequent cases where conveyancers wish to get matters on the register which they know are not properly registrable so that, binding or not, they are in fact drawn to the attention of prospective purchasers. Despite Professor Wade's strictures the opportunity to abolish Class D(iii) was not taken in 1972, when a new Land Charges Act was passed.

As a result of this narrow approach to the definition of equitable easements a right to requisition land[19] and a right to demolish a mill "at the end or sooner determination of the term"[20] have been held not to be equitable easements.

In *Poster v Slough Estates*[21] Cross J., while accepting the authority of the Court of Appeal and accepting the reasonableness of the interpretation, expressed concern about the effect on registered land. The sort of interest which is not capable of becoming a legal easement is also not an overriding interest. The result may be that "there is no way of making it bind a purchaser". However, it is acknowledged that there are numerous rights, notably licences, which have some of the characteristics of interests in land, but which must normally be treated as purely contractual rights and not binding on a purchaser.

16.06   An attempt was made in *Celsteel Ltd v Alton House Holdings*,[22] followed and approved by the Court of Appeal in *Sommer v Sweet*[23] to deal with this

---

[17] [1994] 1 W.L.R. 31; [1993] 4 All E.R. 157.
[18] [1967] 2 Q.B. 379; [1967] 2 W.L.R. 789.
[19] *Lewisham BC v Maloney* [1948] 1 K.B. 50.
[20] *Poster v Slough Estates* [1969] 1 Ch. 495; [1968] 1 W.L.R. 1515
[21] [1969] 1 Ch. 495.
[22] *Celsteel Ltd v Alton House Holdings (No.1)* [1985] 1 W.L.R. 204.
[23] [2005] EWCA Civ 227.

problem by using r.258 Land Registration Rules 1925 which was interpreted as meaning that equitable interests were overriding interests, and
therefore not registrable. However, r.258 is not repeated in the Land
Registration Rules 2003, which follow the Land Registration Act 2002 in
referring to a "legal easement or profit". In any event, this interpretation
is difficult to square with the express provisions of s.70(1)(a) of the 1925
Act, which specifically excludes equitable easements from overriding
interests.

It seems clear, therefore, that the Land Registration Act 2002 excludes
equitable easements from the registration provisions of the Act leaving
contracts to grant an easement registrable under the Land Charges Act
and any other equitable easements to be subject to the usual rules of
equity. It may, however, be possible to enter a notice under s.32 of the Land
Registration Act 2002, providing that it is not excluded under s.33(a)(i). So
equitable interests are not overriding interests. Schedule 3 refers only to a
"legal easement or profit à prendre". The reference in para.2 to:

> "An interest belonging at the time of the disposition to a person in
> actual occupation, so far as relating to land of which he is in actual
> occupation"

is intended to exclude an equitable easement, which will relate to other
land.

4. Estoppel

Easements can be created in equity by estoppel or acquiescence. This is **16.07**
really part of the general law by which rights of ownership can be created
by proprietary estoppel.[24] Such rights are not equitable easements as
defined in the Land Charges Act 1972[25] and therefore do not need to be
registered. They are, however, binding on purchasers with notice of their
existence.

The classic case of an easement created by estoppel is *Crabb v Arun
District Council*.[26] In that case the plaintiff and the defendants agreed in
principle that the plaintiff should have a right of access to their road and
they erected gates at the access point proposed. There was, however, no
final binding agreement. In the belief that he had or would be granted a
right of access the plaintiff sold off part of his land so as to render the rest
of it landlocked. It was held that an easement had been created in equity.
The question of registration did not arise because the defendant was the
person who had made the promise and not a successor in title.

---

[24] See Ch. 3.
[25] *ER Ives Investment Ltd v High* [1967] 2 Q.B. 379; [1967] 1 All E.R. 504.
[26] [1976] Ch. 179; [1975] 3 W.L.R. 847.

These facts were held to fit the requirements of proprietary estoppel. The conduct of the respondents in agreeing in principle to grant the right and then erecting the gates to enable it to be exercised led Mr Crabb to believe that he should have the right of access without more ado. In reliance on this belief he acted to his detriment by selling off the other land without reserving a right of way. In such circumstances it would be inequitable and unconscionable to allow the defendants to withdraw the right. However, had the original agreement been completed Mr Crabb would have been asked to pay something and it would have been open to the court to require him to do so as a condition of finding in his favour had he not suffered loss by reason of the Council's high-handed action in blocking it off.

16.08 In *ER Ives Investment Ltd v High*[27] there was a concluded agreement to grant a right of access. The agreement was evidenced by writing and, as the law then stood,[28] could have been enforced by an order for specific performance, but it was not. Instead, on the strength of the agreement the plaintiff built his house in such a way that the only sensible access to it was across the yard. Despite the absence of a legal easement it was held that he had a right of access in equity by acquiescence. Furthermore this equitable right bound a purchaser from the person who in turn had bought from the person who originally entered into the agreement. Both purchasers had notice of it. Lord Denning M.R. considered that "the right of the defendant to cross this yard was not a right such as could ever have been created or conveyed at law"[29] and was therefore not registrable. However, both the other judges, Danckwerts and Winn L.JJ. held that while the right under the agreement was an equitable easement and therefore void due to non-registration, the right which arose by acquiescence was not a right which was capable of registration as an equitable easement and accordingly was binding on a purchaser who had notice of it. Whatever the strict logic of this finding (since the right is certainly equitable and the effect is that an easement is created), it is the only way in which the doctrine of proprietary estoppel could work in practice for easements since it operates almost exclusively in cases where there have been informal agreements or arrangements of the kind which are unlikely to be registered. Although it seems to be accepted that easements by estoppel exist, the difficulty about registration has not yet been resolved. In respect of proprietary estoppel of land, such interests are overriding interests because the claimant is in actual occupation of the land. However, this does not apply to easements, where the person exercising the right is

---

[27] [1967] 2 Q.B. 379; [1967] 1 All E.R. 504.
[28] See Law of Property (Miscellaneous Provisions) Act 1989 s.2, considered above.
[29] *ER Ives Investment Ltd v High* [1967] 2 Q.B. 379; [1967] 1 All E.R. 504 at 508G.

not in actual occupation. The rationale used in *Sommer v Sweet*[30] does not apply because of the Land Registration Rules 2003. We are left, therefore, with the view expressed in *ER Ives Investment Ltd v High*[31] that an easement by estoppel is not an equitable easement.

While an easement created by estoppel is not an equitable easement for the purposes of registration, it is equitable and accordingly does not bind a bona fide purchaser for value of a legal estate in the servient tenement without notice of the easement.[32] There is, however, little authority on what would constitute notice. In *ER Ives Investment Ltd v High*[33] the existence of a garage which could only be approached by way of the yard amounted to notice. In *Ward v Kirkland*[34] the right claimed by equitable estoppel was specifically referred to in the conveyance to the defendant. In *Sommer v Sweet* it seems clear that the defendant was a bona fide purchaser without notice, but the problem was solved by making use of the superseded r.258.

There is, therefore, still an element of uncertainty about the situation where the servient tenement has changed hands since the representation or other act relied on as creating the estoppel.

---

[30] [2005] EWCA Civ 227.
[31] [1967] 2 Q.B. 379 approved in *Sommer v Sweet*.
[32] *Prinsep v Belgravian Estate Ltd* [1896] W.N. 39.
[33] [1967] 2 Q.B. 379.
[34] [1967] Ch. 194.

Chapter Seventeen
Termination of Easements

1. Introduction

Once an easement is created it becomes an incident of an estate in land. **17.01** Thereafter it continues until it is released expressly or by implication, or until there is unity of estate between the dominant and the servient tenement or, in the case of leasehold land, the leasehold estate comes to an end. It seems that where the leasehold estate merges in the freehold estate, because the leaseholder purchases the reversion, an easement over granted to the leaseholder over other land does not necessarily terminate.[1] An easement may also be extinguished by statute. There is, therefore, no need to refer to the existence of an easement when the land is conveyed.[2] Providing that the land conveyed forms part of the dominant tenement, the easement can be split between a number of owners and leaseholders. On the creation of a new leasehold estate, any existing easements relating to the land demised pass to the lessee under s.62 of the Law of Property Act 1925. An existing easement passes to the lessee even on an oral tenancy.[3]

Although an easement obtained by prescription is just as valid and enforceable as an easement created by deed, there is a technical difference which normally prevents a prescriptive right under statutory prescription from being released. An easement created by deed or under the doctrine of lost modern grant exists until released or extinguished in the ways set out above. However, a right can only be claimed under the Prescription Act 1832 if there has been user up to the date that the action was brought.

> "Each of the respective periods of years hereinbefore mentioned shall be deemed and taken to be the period next before some suit or action wherein the claim or matter to which such period may relate shall have been or shall be brought into question" (s.4 of the Prescription Act 1832).

[1] *Wall v Collins* [2007] EWCA Civ 444; [2007] Ch. 390.
[2] *Re Yateley Common* [1977] 1 W.L.R. 840; [1977] 1 All E.R. 505 at 512f.
[3] *Skull v Glenister* (1864) 16 C.B. N.S. 81.

This applies both to claims under s.2 and s.3 of the Act. The right only crystallises when the action is brought, and therefore the question of release does not arise. An easement obtained by lost modern grant, on the other hand, comes into existence after 20 years' user without any need for a decision of the court. It then continues to exist unless or until it is released whether expressly or by implication. The question of release of an easement claimed under the Prescription Act 1832 therefore only arises after an action has been brought and a declaration has been made that the right exists. Once this has happened the easement continues until it is released.

The Law Commission Report—*Making Land Work: Easements, Covenants and Profits à Prendre*[4]—has expressed a number of concerns about the termination of easements, in particular the uncertainty about the circumstances in which easements can be terminated by abandonment and the controversy, referred to below, about when a leasehold easement ceases on merger. The draft Bill attached to the Report contains a presumption of abandonment on non-user for any period of 20 years[5] and a new provision, amending the Land Registration Act 2002 so that easements are not automatically extinguished on unity of ownership and possession of the dominant and servient land. There is also a provision for the landlord to elect for the easement to continue on merger or surrender and for the tenant, on a technical surrender prior to a new lease, to elect to retain an easement for a new lease. As stated elsewhere, this is at present only a draft Bill, which does not yet have parliamentary time allotted to it.

While the main controversy has been about merger, the proposal to make it easier for a way to be abandoned is contrary to views expressed by many judges over the years and perhaps forgets that, particularly with an express grant, a person who has no use for the way, may nevertheless wish to hold onto it for the future because he feels that it may enhance the value of his property on the open market.

2.   Express release

17.02   An easement can only be expressly released at law by deed. However, equity applies to an agreement to release an easement in the same way as it applies to an agreement to grant an easement.[6] Thus an agreement to release an easement can be specifically enforced[7] providing that it is in writing and conforms to the statutory requirements.[8]

---

[4] Law Commission, *Making Land Work: Easements, Covenants and Profits à Prendre* (London: The Stationery Office, 2011), Law Com. No.327.
[5] Draft Bill Cl.27.
[6] See above para.16.02 et seq.
[7] *Waterlow v Bacon* (1866) L.R. 2 Eq. 514.
[8] Law of Property (Miscellaneous Provisions) Act 1989 s.2.

Equally the principles of estoppel and acquiescence apply to the release of an easement in the same way as to the grant of an easement.[9] There is considerable similarity between termination of an easement by estoppel and termination by abandonment, but they are not identical, see *Costagliola v English*.[10]

One of the difficulties faced by a servient owner seeking a release is to ensure that the person purporting to grant the release has full power to do so. The terms of an express grant of an easement often do not define the extent of the dominant tenement and if the right is obtained by implication or by lost modern grant there may be no simple way of identifying the dominant tenement. A person who purchases any part of the dominant tenement may obtain the benefit of the easement. The way in which the extent of the dominant tenement can be identified and the way in which an easement is divided when the dominant tenement is severed are dealt with above.[11] Perhaps the most common example is the private estate roads on a building estate. If access to the estate is over a private right of way, each of the purchasers of the building plots will have his own separate right of way which cannot be released by the developer. A servient owner seeking release of an easement, for example to change the route of the way to facilitate further development, must, therefore, make sure that all the dominant owners are joined.

A similar problem may arise where there are persons with lesser interests in the property and therefore in the easement. A tenant for life has a right to release an easement if there is a dispute about its validity, s.58(1) of the Settled Land Act 1925.[12] Even if there is no such dispute, by s.58(2) he can release an easement with the consent in writing of the trustees of the settlement.

On the other hand a servient owner negotiating the release of an easement with a dominant owner whose property is mortgaged should ensure that the mortgagee approves[13] and if the dominant tenement is held by joint owners on trusts of land or trust for sale both owners should join in the deed. Trustees of land under the Trusts of Land and Appointment of Trustees Act 1996 have the same powers as an absolute owner.[14] Accordingly they have the power to release easements, just as trustees for sale and trustees of a settlement before them.[15] **17.03**

[9] See below para.17.13 et seq.
[10] (1969) 210 E.G. 1425, see below para.17.13.
[11] See Nature of Easements—Ch. 10.
[12] Although no new strict settlements can be created by virtue of the Trusts of Land and Appointment of Trustees Act 1996, existing settlements are not abolished and will be here to irritate us for many years to come.
[13] *Poulton v Moore* [1915] 1 K.B. 400.
[14] Trusts of Land and Appointment of Trustees Act 1996 s.6.
[15] Law of Property Act 1925 ss.28 and 205(ix), now repealed.

If a lessor has granted a lease of his property with the benefit of an existing easement, it is not open to him to release the easement so that the lessee's rights come to an end.[16] On the other hand a person having a lesser right to use the easement, for example because he is in possession as a licensee, presumably has no right to complain if the owner releases the easement.

3. Implied release

17.04   An easement obtained by grant or reservation, whether express or implied or under the doctrine of lost modern grant, can be lost by abandonment caused by the act or omission of the dominant owner coupled with an intention to abandon the right:

> "To establish abandonment of an easement the conduct of the dominant owner must, in our judgment, have been such as to make it clear that he had at the relevant time a firm intention that neither he nor any successor in title of his should thereafter make use of the easement. Abandonment is not, we think, to be lightly inferred. Owners of property do not normally wish to divest themselves of it unless it is to their advantage to do so, notwithstanding that they may have no present use of it".[17]

The principle does not apply to a right claimed by prescription under the Prescription Act 1832 since any such right, whether claimed under s.2 or s.3, has to be exercised right up to the date of the commencement of the action. Since it is normal to plead a claim under both the Prescription Act and the doctrine of lost modern grant together as alternatives, there is bound to be some blurring of the lines between the need to prove continuity and evidence which amounts to abandonment. However, one of the main reasons for pleading lost modern grant is where there is evidence showing 20 years' user which has then come to an end at some period before the action was commenced. In such circumstances the court will have to decide not whether there has been continuous user up to the date of the action but whether the period during which the alleged easement has not been exercised amounts to abandonment.

In theory there is no difference between the acts or omissions which amount to abandonment of an easement obtained by express grant and one obtained by lost modern grant, but there is inevitably a tendency for the courts to be more reluctant to find abandonment of a right which is

---

[16] See *Richardson v Graham* [1908] 1 K.B. 39 where this proposition is implicit.
[17] per Cumming Bruce L.J. in *Gotobed v Pridmore* (1970) 115 S.J. 78, cited with approval in *Williams v Usherwood* (1983) 45 P. & C.R. 235 and *Benn v Hardinge* (1993) 66 P. & C.R. 246.

clearly set out in the deeds than one which has been established by long user.

It has long been established that mere non-user is not in itself sufficient to amount to abandonment,[18] even if the non-user has continued for 175 years.[19] It may however, call for an explanation:

"The authorities upon the subject of abandonment have decided that a mere suspension of the exercise of a right is not sufficient to prove an intention to abandon it. But a long continued suspension may render it necessary for the person claiming to show that some indication was given during the period that he ceased to use the right of his intention to preserve it".[20]

The requirement that the person not using the easement should give an indication of his intention to preserve it is not absolute. What is required is an explanation. For example, if the owner of a property has a right of way for vehicles and does not own a car, this may be a sufficient explanation of why the way has not been used, even if this has gone on for a very long time,[21] or even just that the dominant owner has been happy to use other routes to his land.[22]

The longer the period of non-user, the easier it is to find abandonment. In *Howton v Hawkins*[23] Cross J. held that after the property had been enclosed for 40 years the person claiming the easement could not now object even if neither he nor any agent of his knew what had been done, but this now seems out of line with the more recent cases.

Apart from non-user, specific acts which negate the existence of an **17.05** easement can amount to abandonment. Giving licence to the servient owner to erect something permanent which blocks the right will amount to abandonment:

"If I, having an easement of light, permit another to come and build a wall up against my window, so as to extinguish the easement, if the wall is built and completed, that may well be the end of it and I cannot complain of the infringement of my ancient light or require the wall to be taken down."[24]

---

[18] *Re Yateley Common* [1977] 1 W.L.R. 840.
[19] *Benn v Hardinge* (1993) 66 P. & C.R. 246.
[20] per Lord Chelmsford L.C. in *Crossley & Sons Ltd v Lightowler* (1866–67) L.R. 2 Ch. App. 478 at 482.
[21] *Obadia v Morris* (1974) 232 E.G. 333.
[22] *Benn v Hardinge* (1993) 66 P. & C.R. 246.
[23] (1966) 110 S.J. 547.
[24] per Lord Evershed M.R., *Armstrong v Sheppard & Short* [1959] 2 Q.B. 384 at 399.

Equally, entering into a licence agreement for a new tank and line of pipes amounts to abandonment of a previous right to a water supply.[25] On the other hand agreeing to pay for the use of the easement on a temporary basis will not necessarily amount to abandonment.[26] An easement can be abandoned in part, but the court will be slow to infer that acquiescence in a temporary obstruction amounts to abandonment rather than good-neighbourliness.[27]

Whether or not there has been abandonment is a question of fact.[28] The authorities, therefore provide only limited assistance. The principles set out above apply to all easements, but the problems which have been encountered differ somewhat between the different easements and it is helpful to look at the decisions which have been taken in respect of the different kinds of easement.

The Law Commission Report[29] has criticised the limited circumstances in which an easement is treated as abandoned and has suggested a statutory rebuttable presumption that non-use for 20 years amounts to abandonment.[30]

(a)   Way

17.06   A right of way is, by its very nature, not exercised continuously and it has been seen that very occasional use of the way is sufficient for proving continuity for the purposes of prescription. A fortiori, therefore, once a right of way is established, whether by express or implied grant or by lost modern grant, very clear indications are required to show that it has been abandoned.

Thus in *Gotobed v Pridmore*[31] Buckley L.J. said:

> "the ploughing of the plaintiff's land was not in the least inconsistent with an intention to retain the right of way. The cultivation of the lane had been mostly during the Second World War when an objection to such use might have been unpatriotic. The fence around the lane was of an unsubstantial kind and a failure to object to it would be slight ground for inferring any intention to abandon. The failure to maintain the earth bridge across the dyke and the maintenance of the fence on the plaintiff's land were not proper matters from which to

---

[25] *Bosomworth v Faber* (1995) 69 P. & C.R. 288.

[26] *Tehidy Minerals v Norman* [1971] 2 Q.B. 528; [1971] 2 W.L.R. 711.

[27] *Snell and Prideaux Ltd v Dutton Mirrors Ltd* [1994] E.G. 78 (C.S.).

[28] *Crossley & Sons Ltd v Lightowler* (1866–67) L.R. 2 Ch. App. 478; *Treweeke v 36, Wolseley Rd, Pty. Ltd* (1973) 1 A.L.R. 104.

[29] Law Commission, *Making Land Work: Easements, Covenants and Profits à Prendre* (London: The Stationery Office, 2011), Law Com. No.327.

[30] Clause 27 of the Draft Law of Property Bill.

[31] (1970) 115 S.J. 78 approved in *Williams v Usherwood* (1983) 45 P. & C.R. 235.

infer a resolution to abandon. The court was impressed by the ease with which the physical state of affairs could have been altered so as to restore the use of the right of way."

Equally in *Costagliola v English*[32] the way was blocked for vehicular traffic for eleven and a half years, but this was not held to amount to abandonment. In *Mann v Eayrs (RC)*[33] when a new way was provided on requisition, this did not mean that the old way was abandoned so that it could not be revived on derequisition.

The most recent and perhaps the most extreme case where non-user did not amount to abandonment is *Benn v Hardinge*[34] where the Court of Appeal reviewed the earlier authorities. In that case a right of way along a track and through a gate was granted by an Enclosure Award in 1818. There was no evidence that it had been used since, but equally there was no evidence of abandonment as such. The track was still there and the dominant owner had the right to use it.

On the other hand where the way is altered by agreement both the original and the new way are treated as one for the purposes of assessing how long they have been used.[35] It follows that in these circumstances the old way would be treated as having been abandoned from the date when the new way begins to be used.

Another case where a way was held to have been abandoned is *Williams* **17.07** *v Usherwood*[36] where

"Mrs. Whitehouse's acquiescence in the building of the wall behind the house and Mr. Whitehouse's nailing up of the gate when the temporary need to use it had long ended are facts that confirm beyond a peradventure an abandonment that had taken place 15 years earlier",

and in *Swan v Sinclair*[37] a grant of a right of way was held to have been abandoned when no attempt had been made to knock down the garden walls and form the way for 50 years. However in that case there were fresh obstructions erected after the grant of the right of way and the court re-affirmed the principle that non-user alone did not amount to abandonment. There was, furthermore, a strong dissenting judgment by Pollock M.R.

The court will, therefore, look both at any period of non-user and at any acts by the dominant owner or by the servient owner and accepted by the

---

[32] (1969) 210 E.G. 1425.
[33] (1973) 231 E.G. 843.
[34] (1993) 66 P. & C.R. 246.
[35] *Davis v Whitby* [1974] Ch. 186; [1974] 1 All E.R. 806.
[36] (1983) 45 P. & C.R. 235 at 257.
[37] [1925] A.C. 227.

dominant owner. It will then look at the reasons for non-user, the reasons for any actions by the dominant owner and the reasons why the acts of the servient owner have been accepted and decide, looking at all these facts, whether an intention to abandon can be inferred. It is, however, clear that abandonment will not be lightly inferred and that acquiescence in a temporary obstruction may be regarded as good-neighbourliness rather than abandonment.

There have also been problems where the use of the way has increased or changed. In so far as the use of the way has increased, it is hard to see that this can indicate an intention to abandon rather than the reverse.[38] Equally, a change either in the manner in which the way is used or in the dominant tenement does not indicate an intention to abandon unless the easement itself is seen as being for a particular purpose.[39] For this reason this aspect is considered below[40] as extinguishment due to a change in the character of the tenement rather than implied release.

(b)   Light

17.08   Although a right of light is a continuous easement, there is no difference in the general principles. The particular problem with regard to rights of light, however, is that where new windows are opened it is difficult for a servient owner to prevent rights being obtained in respect of those new windows without blocking off the light to the ancient windows. Where there has been an alteration of the windows, it is also difficult to analyse how much of the light is "ancient" and how much of it is recent and therefore can legitimately be stopped up. These problems have given rise to a good deal of litigation which has been dealt with empirically and without undue theorisation.

It has long been established that, as with other easements, the existence of the Prescription Act 1832 (which has a separate section for rights of light) does not prevent rights being obtained by lost modern grant.[41] This means that once an easement has been established by lost modern grant, it is not abandoned simply by demolishing the building even if the building owner would thereby lose any right to claim under the Prescription Act 1832. This applies even if the land is to be sold as an empty site, providing that the intention is to re-build taking advantage of the existing rights of light.[42]

Equally, altering a building or demolishing it and re-building does not mean that the rights are being abandoned.[43] The right is to the light and

---

[38] *Graham v Philcox* [1984] Q.B. 747; [1984] 2 All E.R. 643.
[39] *Huckvale v Aegean Hotels Ltd* (1989) 58 P. & C.R. 163.
[40] See below para.17.14.
[41] *Tapling v Jones* (1865) 20 C.B. N.S. 166.
[42] *Ecclesiastical Commissioners for England v Kino* (1880) L.R. 14 Ch. D. 213.
[43] *Greenwood v Hornsey* (1886) L.R. 33 Ch. D. 471.

not to the use of the window, so that altering the plane of the window does not affect the right providing that the same light goes through.[44] If, on the other hand, the dominant owner reduces the size of his windows, he cannot complain that a new building built by a neighbour reduces the light in his new building below an acceptable level, if it would have been adequate if he had not altered his windows.[45]

The reverse problem is where the dominant owner increases his **17.09** windows:

> "It would be contrary to the principles of law relating to easements that the burden of the servient tenement should be increased or varied from time to time at the will of the owner of the dominant tenement".[46]

This was a case primarily about the principle that there is only interference with a right of light when the quantity of light is reduced below an acceptable level. In practice the problem has been dealt with by considering these two aspects together, namely the amount of light which was available before alteration and the extent to which the offending building reduces that light to an unacceptable level. What happens, therefore, where there has been a comparatively recent change in the windows in the dominant tenement is that the court looks at the effect which the offending building would have had on the original building. It seems, however, that it is possible for the changes in the dominant tenement to be so fundamental that any easement of light is lost.

(c) Support

The position with regard to rights of support is very similar to that of a **17.10** right of light. Where the dominant owner has substantially increased the burden on the servient tenement since the right was established, the court has to consider whether that additional burden is such as to destroy the right which has been obtained. Again the problem is that it is very difficult to distinguish the extent to which any collapse would have happened anyway or is caused by the additional weight.[47] It is submitted that the real issue is whether the collapse would have occurred even if there had been no additional burden, rather than whether the right of support is lost altogether as a result of the additional burden.[48]

---

[44] *Scott v Pape* (1886) L.R. 31 Ch. D. 554.
[45] *WH Bailey & Son Ltd v Holborn & Frascati Ltd* [1914] 1 Ch. 598.
[46] per Lord Davey in *Colls v Home & Colonial Stores* [1904] A.C. 179.
[47] *Ray v Fairway Motors (Barnstable)* (1969) 20 P. & C.R. 261.
[48] See *Lloyds Bank Ltd v Dalton* [1942] Ch. 466.

(d)   Water

17.11   The classic case on implied release, *Luttrell's Case*[49] is about a water-course. This establishes that an alteration in the purpose for which the watercourse is used does not mean that the right is lost. Thus demolishing fulling mills and replacing them with corn mills does not lead to the loss of the right to the watercourse. The same applies where cattle sheds are replaced with cottages, providing that the increase in the burden is not excessive.[50] On the other hand in *Crossley v Lightowler*[51] it was held that a right to foul up a stream can be lost by enlarging the use, though in that case the right had anyway not been used for 20 years. More recently in *Bosomworth v Faber*[52] it was held that a right to a water supply was abandoned by entering into a licence to construct a new tank and line of pipes and in *McAdam Homes v Robinson*[53] it was held that the replacement of a bakery by two dwelling-houses (just) amounted to a radical change in the character of the site leading to a "suspension or loss" of the easement.[54]

(e)   Other easements

17.12   The same principles apply to all other easements. Thus a right to estovers and turbary is not lost by demolishing the house to which it was attached and building a new one.[55]

4.   Acquiescence and estoppel

17.13   It is obvious that the principles on which the court will find that the easement has been abandoned are very similar to those in which there will be a finding of acquiescence or estoppel. In *Costagliola v English*[56] the case had been pleaded as estoppel and it was argued that this was the same as abandonment. Megarry J. held that estoppel and abandonment were similar but not identical, but that in that case there was neither estoppel nor abandonment.

The application of the law of acquiescence, laches and estoppel to the enforcement of easements has been considered in *Lester v Woodgate*.[57] The principle is essentially the same as that relating to the creation of an easement by estoppel, but in reverse. Usually a person is claiming rights over

---

[49] (1601) 4 Co. Rep. 86.
[50] *Watts v Kelson* (1870–71) L.R. 6 Ch. App. 166.
[51] *Crossley & Sons Ltd v Lightowler* (1866–67) L.R. 2 Ch. App. 478.
[52] (1995) 69 P. & C.R. 288.
[53] [2004] EWCA Civ 214; [2005] 1 P. & C.R. 30.
[54] See below at 17.14.
[55] *Attorney General v Reynolds* [1911] 2 K.B. 888.
[56] (1969) 210 E.G. 1425.
[57] [2010] EWCA Civ 199; [2010] 2 P. & C.R. 21.

a property by proprietary estoppel, but the same principles can result in a dominant owner losing his easement by reason of his conduct or acquiescence.

The case concerned a way which had been rendered unusable by the dominant owner improving his parking space on his own land. The servient owner then built a house across the way in the belief that the way would not be enforced. The case was decided on the basis of estoppel rather than abandonment by implied release.

The distinction between an estoppel which only prevents the owner of the dominant tenement from exercising his equitable rights and an estoppel, akin to proprietary estoppel, which results in his losing his easement altogether is a matter of degree. In *Lester v Woodgate*[58] there was very little direct encouragement to the servient owner to carry on with the work, but the servient owner had, nevertheless, carried out substantial works without objection and in the belief that it would not be enforced. That was enough for a finding that the right of way had been lost entirely. A less serious case might have only meant that the dominant owner lost his right to an injunction. It followed that the actions of the servient owner in blocking the way did not amount to a nuisance and could not result in damages.

The Court took the opportunity to deal with the equitable defence of laches, which cannot give rise to substantive rights, but can result in the loss of a right to an injunction.

5. Change in character of the dominant tenement

A person may lose the right to enforce an easement because of radical **17.14** changes in his own land. These changes may result in suspension or loss of the easement, *McAdams Homes v Robinson*.[59] However, it is easy to blur the distinction between a change in the character of the dominant tenement which is sufficient to prevent the owner from using the easement unless and until the change is reversed and a change which will actually terminate the easement. In *McAdams Homes v Robinson* there was an implied or prescriptive right to an easement of drainage. The Court of Appeal upheld the judgment that the replacement of an existing bakery with two dwelling-houses both of which used the drainage system was enough to lead to the "suspension or loss" of the easement. It was not necessary to decide whether the right was terminated or suspended because the claim was for damages only.

The case was decided solely as an issue as to whether there was excessive user under the principles set out in *Jelbert v Davies*.[60] However, in

---

[58] *Lester v Woodgate* [2010] EWCA Civ 199; [2010] 2 P. & C.R. 21.
[59] [2005] 1 P. & C.R. 520.
[60] *Jelbert v Davies* [1968] 1 W.L.R. 589.

earlier cases[61] the proposition that an easement could be terminated by a change in the character of the neighbourhood had been challenged.

This proposition was rejected, certainly as far as discontinuous easements are concerned, in *Graham v Philcox*[62] where May L.J. said:

> "However I doubt whether any excessive user, at least of a discontinuous easement, in whatever respect the user may be excessive will ever of itself bring an end or indeed suspend such an easement ... The owner of the servient tenement on which, *ex hypothesi*, the excessive burden is placed is entitled to have that excessive user restrained. Provided that the owner of the dominant tenement subsequently reverts to lawful use of the easement, his prior excessive use of it is then irrelevant."[63]

Where the purpose for which the easement was originally required no longer applies, this does not extinguish the easement. It is only where the dominant tenement in effect ceases to exist that the easement may be extinguished.

> "For the purposes of this appeal it is unnecessary to decide whether an easement which accommodated the dominant tenement at the date of the grant, but which thereafter ceases to accommodate it, is extinguished by operation of law, notwithstanding the continued existence of the dominant tenement. Although the proposition is novel and unsupported by any authority which has been cited to use it could not be said that there might not be a case whose facts would attract its operation ... I would think it very surprising if facts which are not sufficient to support an abandonment of the right could, on the other hand, be sufficient to support an extinguishment of them".[64]

Before *McAdams Homes v Robinson*, the only authority for the proposition that an easement may be extinguished by a change in the character of the dominant tenement is the old case of *National Guaranteed Manure Co Ltd v Donald*.[65] That was a case where an easement was granted to supply water for a canal. When the canal was replaced by a railway, it was held that the easement disappeared with it. This case was considered in *Huckvale v Aegean Hotels*, where it was distinguished on the ground that the dominant tenement had ceased to exist by being converted into something entirely different.

---

[61] Not referred to in the judgment, including a judgment of Nourse L.J. who was part of the court in *McAdams Homes v Robinson*.

[62] [1984] Q.B. 747; [1984] 2 All E.R. 643.

[63] *Graham v Philcox* [1984] Q.B. 747; [1984] 2 All E.R. 643 at 649.

[64] per Nourse L.J. in *Huckvale v Aegean Hotels Ltd* (1989) 58 P. & C.R. 163 at 170.

[65] (1859) 4 H. & N. 8.

Although the issue is not directly addressed in *McAdams Homes v Robinson*, it now seems that Courts, faced with a change in the character of the neighbourhood, will treat the case as excessive user and make appropriate orders, including, if necessary, a permanent injunction preventing use of the easement. Where the change is effectively irreversible this will amount, in effect, to a termination of the easement. This was what happened in *Ashdale Land & Property Co v Maioriello*.[66] Nevertheless, the earlier cases have not been overruled.

The Law Commission Report[67] states that, although this point was dealt with in the Consultation Paper, they have decided not to make any recommendations.

6.   Unity of ownership

It may seem common sense that a person cannot grant an easement to **17.15** himself. If he uses one part of his land to get to another part, or runs a watercourse over part of his land for the benefit of his mill he has no need to make any grant. However, s.72(3) of the Law of Property Act 1925 expressly provides that, after 1925, a person may convey land to or vest land in himself and "land" includes incorporeal hereditaments.[68]

There are two situations in which the extent to which a person can have an easement over his own land can arise.

The first such situation is where the dominant and the servient tenements have previously been in common ownership. On severance it is likely that the existing quasi-easements or advantages will pass to the new owner by implication or under s.62 of the Law of Property Act 1925.[69] However, it may be that an easement certainly existed in the past, prior to unification, either by express grant, implied grant or lost modern grant, but has not been exercised even as a quasi-easement or advantage during the period of common ownership. In those circumstances it may be necessary to consider whether the previous easement is revived on the severance of the two properties or whether it is gone forever.

The principle that unity of ownership extinguishes an easement was **17.16** affirmed in *Payne v Inwood*.[70] It is an absolute principle and applies even if the unity of ownership is only for a week. The Law Commission[71] has considered this and suggests an amendment of the law to reverse this

---

[66] [2010] EWHC 3296 (Ch), citing dicta from *Cawkwell v Russell* (1856) 26 L.J. Ex. 34.
[67] Law Commission, *Making Land Work: Easements, Covenants and Profits á Prendre* (London: The Stationery Office, 2011), Law Com. No.327.
[68] Law of Property Act 1925 s.205(1)(ix).
[69] See para.13.04 et seq. and *Wright v MacAdam* [1949] 2 K.B. 744.
[70] (1997) 74 P. & C.R. 42 at 48, per Roch L.J.
[71] Law Commission, *Making Land Work: Easements, Covenants and Profits á Prendre* (London: The Stationery Office, 2011), Law Com. No.327.

principle in respect of registered land where both plots of land are registered unless someone applies to extinguish it. This is partly to prevent anomalies where the easement remains registered because the Land Registry has not picked up that the two plots of land are both owned by the same person.

Given that the law on unity of seisin remains unless and until it is amended by statute, it is, necessary to link this principle in with an implied grant under s.62 of the Law of Property Act 1925. It has been seen that where part of a property is sold and the part retained has previously been in different occupation, an implied easement may arise under s.62 or, indeed, under the rule in *Wheeldon v Burrows*.[72] Therefore, if there is an existing easement followed by unity of ownership, but not unity of occupation between the dominant and servient owners, the express easement extinguished by the unity of ownership may be revived on disposal as an implied grant under s.62. An old case[73] decided that this did not apply to a way of necessity, but this case could probably be construed in modern terms as an implied reservation of a way on sale.

The position also becomes complicated when tenancies are involved. There seems to be a distinction here between the circumstances in which time may run and the circumstances in which an existing easement may be extinguished. It has been held that an easement cannot be obtained by prescription by one tenant over another tenant of the same landlord,[74] but if an easement has been obtained, whether by grant or lost modern grant, it is not lost if the servient tenant buys the freehold of the dominant tenant's land; *Richardson v Graham*.[75] The rationale of *Richardson v Graham*, however, was that,

> "unity of seisin does not prevent the acquirement of a prescriptive right to light by one tenant against another tenant of the same landlord".[76]

This is inconsistent with *Kilgour v Geddes*[77] which (though only reported four years before) was not cited. It is clearly established that *Kilgour v Geddes* represents the modern law on acquiring prescriptive rights[78] and there must, therefore, be some doubt as to whether *Richardson v Graham* was correctly decided. In *Wall v Collins*[79] the Court of Appeal upheld the principle set out above, without referring to *Richardson v Graham*. The

---

[72] (1879) L.R. 12 Ch. D. 31.
[73] *Buckley v Coles* (1814) 5 Taunt. 311.
[74] *Kilgour v Geddes* [1904] 1 K.B. 457, approved in *Simmons v Dobson* [1991] 1 W.L.R. 720; [1991] 4 All E.R. 25 and *Bosomworth v Faber* (1995) 69 P. & C.R. 288.
[75] [1908] 1 K.B. 39.
[76] per Buckley L.J. at 44.
[77] [1904] 1 K.B. 457.
[78] *Simmons v Dobson* [1991] 1 W.L.R. 720; [1991] 4 All E.R. 25; *Bosomworth v Faber* (1995) 69 P. & C.R. 288.
[79] [2007] EWCA Civ 444; [2007] Ch. 390.

basis of the judgment was that the enjoyment of an easement is based on the nature of the dominant title rather than the estate for which the claimant holds it. Whatever the rationale, it made sense in that case, where the leaseholder had a 999 year lease and had bought the freehold and the right was claimed under s.62 of the Law of Property Act 1925.

The decision in *Wall v Collins*[80] however, has given rise to considerable controversy. In essence, the question is whether the grant of the easement is attached to the land, or appurtenant to the lease. A grant of an easement to a leaseholder is intended to be for the duration of the lease. If the lease comes to an end for any reason, the leaseholder loses not only his leasehold interest, but everything that goes with it. In *Wall v Collins* the leaseholder purchased the freehold estate and there was no dispute that the intention was that the freehold and leasehold estates should be merged.[81]

However, the problem arises not when the lease is forfeited, but when it is either surrendered and re-granted or the leaseholder obtains the freehold. In the words of Carnwarth L.J.:

"As a matter of common sense, it is difficult to see why a lessee should be worse off, so far as concerns an easement annexed to the land, merely because he has acquired a larger interest in the dominant tenement".[82]

Despite the clear terms of the decision, the law must still be seen as being uncertain, with the possibility of that judgment being regarded as being on its own particular facts. This means that it will only apply where the circumstances indicate that the easement was indeed granted for the benefit of the dominant tenement and not simply for the benefit of the leasehold interest. This will be the case where there is a virtual freehold, such as a 999 year lease, but may not be the case with a shorter lease.

The Law Commission[83] has discussed this issue at length and proposed a reversion to the law as understood before *Wall v Collins*, but giving the leaseholder on merger of surrender a statutory option to elect to retain the benefit of the easement by means of an amendment of the Land Registration Act 2002.

The other problem is where, though he may be owner in fee simple of **17.17** both, he holds one parcel of land as tenant for life or trustee. The purpose of s.72(3) of the Law of Property Act 1925 was to allow a tenant for life to convey land to himself. Equally, before 1926 the tenant for life would not

---

[80] *Wall v Collins* [2007] EWCA Civ 444; [2007] Ch. 390.
[81] See s.184 of the Law of Property Act 1925 and *BOH Ltd v Eastern Power Networks Plc* [2011] EWCA Civ 19.
[82] *Wall v Collins* [2007] EWCA Civ 444; [2007] Ch. 390 at [18].
[83] Law Commission, *Making Land Work: Easements, Covenants and Profits á Prendre*, Law Com. No.327 at p.74–82.

be the freehold owner of the land. It is submitted that whenever the legal owner is in a fiduciary position in respect of one parcel of land and in a different position with regard to the other, whether beneficial owner or subject to different trusts, the unity of ownership does not cause the easement to cease to exist[84] even if he is in possession of both. Indeed, in some circumstances it might be important for accounting purposes to know whether a right, such as a right of extract water, was being exercised by the owner as beneficial owner of the one parcel or as trustee of the other.

7. Termination by statute

17.18   Just as easements can be created by statute,[85] they can also be extinguished by statute. This usually arises in connection with developments which involve the compulsory acquisition of land. In modern times the normal way of acquiring land compulsorily has been by compulsory purchase orders made under statute, though there has been a recent return to the use of private Acts of Parliament.

Requisitioning of land is not the same as compulsory purchase. It does not involve the acquisition of any estate or interest in the land, but only possession of it. Accordingly, easements over land which was requisitioned during the War are not extinguished. Equally, non-user during this period will not amount to evidence of abandonment, *Re Yateley Common*.[86]

Whether a compulsory purchase order needs to specify the easements which it extinguishes depends on the statute under which it is made. There is no provision for automatic extinguishment of easements in the Land Clauses Consolidation Act 1845 nor in the Acquisition of Land Act 1981. There are, however, other Acts which provide that all private rights of way are automatically extinguished, with a right to compensation. These include the Town and Country Planning Act 1990[87] and the Housing Act 1985.[88] There is, however, a difference between these two Acts since the Town and Country Planning Act 1990 refers only to rights of way and rights in respect of apparatus whereas the Housing Act 1985 refers to "all other rights or easements in or relating to the land".

17.19   Other Acts take a middle course, making express provision for extinguishing easements, but only those specified in the order. These include the Requisitioned Land and War Works Act 1948[89] and the New Towns

---

[84] *Ecclesiastical Commissioners for England v Kino* (1880) L.R. 14 Ch. D. 213.
[85] See Ch. 14.
[86] [1977] 1 W.L.R. 840; [1977] 1 All E.R. 505.
[87] Town and Country Planning Act 1990 s.236.
[88] Housing Act 1985 s.295.
[89] Requisitioned Land and War Works Act 1948 s.4.

Act 1981.[90] They also make special provision for the extinguishment of statutory rights in the nature of easements.[91]

Accordingly, if an easement is claimed over land which has been the subject of compulsory acquisition, the only course is to look at the actual Act under which the acquisition was made to see whether the right was extinguished by it.

In addition to these four modern Acts, specific statutes have been stopping up easements and public highways for centuries. This has happened through Inclosure Acts,[92] Turnpike Acts, Canal Acts and Railway Acts. The effect of such provisions has been to extinguish the rights once and for all without prospect of revival should the Act be repealed,[93] and the same applies to extinguishment under more modern statutes and compulsory purchase orders.

Where the Act referred to all ways over land compulsorily acquired **17.20** being extinguished, this did not extinguish easements over land bought by agreement, even though there would have been a compulsory purchase order if the parties had not reached agreement.[94] This problem would arise for example where compulsory purchase has been considered under the Town and Country Planning Act 1990, but the sale has eventually gone through by agreement.

Another difficulty is the distinction between public and private rights. Where the Act referred to "all rights of way in over or affecting the footways numbered ..." being extinguished, the Act was construed as referring only to public rights of way.[95] The main reason why this Act was construed in this way was that no provision was made for compensation for the extinguishment. This was appropriate for a public way, but not for a private one in respect of which the owner would expect compensation. The Acquisition of Land Act 1981 contains specific provision for extinguishing footpaths and bridleways.[96]

Problems can also arise where the Act or compulsory purchase order does not specifically refer to the extinguishment of the easement, but it was clearly the intention of the developer that this easement should be extinguished. Where an Act provides specifically for the creation of an incorporeal right, such as a market or a right to take tolls, this can bring an end to a pre-existing prescriptive right which it was intended to replace, even though the Act does not refer specifically to this prior right

---

[90] New Towns Act 1981 s.19.
[91] See above para.14.08 et seq.
[92] See *Benn v Hardinge* (1993) 66 P. & C.R. 234 at 249.
[93] *Gwynne v Drewitt* [1894] 2 Ch. 616.
[94] *1 Great Central Railway Co v Balby with Hexthorpe Urban DC* [1912] 2 Ch. 110.
[95] *Wells v London Tilbury and Southend Railway Co* (1877) L.R. 5 Ch. D. 126.
[96] Land Act 1981 s.32.

being extinguished[97] so that when the Act expires the prescriptive right does not revive.[98]

17.21   The position is more difficult where the extinguishment of an easement is necessary for the object of the Act or order to be put into effect. In *Yarmouth Corp v Simmons*[99] a private Act allowed the construction of a pier. The plaintiff alleged that there was a public right of way which would have prevented the pier from being used and would therefore have frustrated the object for which the Act was passed. It was held that if the public right of way ever existed (which the court doubted) it was extinguished by implication by the Act. However, in *Sovmots Investments Ltd v Secretary of State for the Environment*[100] the House of Lords held that the creation of easements cannot be implied from the intention of a compulsory purchase order, even though such easements were necessary for the object of the order to be put into effect. It would be open to the court to take a similar view about the extinguishment of easements by implication where the continuance of the easement would frustrate the object of a statute or compulsory purchase order, especially where there is no provision for compensation.

However, in *Jones v Cleanthi*[101] it was held that an order to render the premises fit for habitation which included erecting a wall which obstructed the access was treated as extinguishing the easement although it did not say so. This is the most recent decision, albeit First Instance, and probably represents the current law.

It is possible that an easement might be terminated by implied release because of the acts or omissions of the dominant owner when dealing with the developer under the compulsory purchase order or private Act.[102] This, however, is not strictly termination by statute but a form of implied release.

Where there is no reference to extinguishment of an easement in the Act or compulsory purchase order it is necessary to consider the effect if in practice an easement is stopped up. It might be assumed that if the developer does not purchase the easement, (which after all is an incorporeal hereditament and counts as "land") then the easement would continue to exist and could be enforced by injunction. Surprisingly there is little modern authority on this, and much of the authority that exists is concerned with the distinction between a notice to treat and injurious affection as different methods of assessing compensation on compulsory purchase. It seems, however, that where a compulsory purchase order or

---

[97] *Manchester Corp v Lyons* (1882) L.R. 22 Ch. D. 287.
[98] *New Windsor Corp v Taylor* [1899] A.C. 41.
[99] (1878–79) L.R. 10 Ch. D. 518.
[100] [1979] A.C. 144; [1977] 2 All E.R. 385.
[101] [2005] EWHC 2646 (QB); [2006] 1 All E.R. 1029.
[102] *Turner v Crush* (1878–79) L.R. 4 App. Cas. 221.

a statute allows something to be done and this interferes with an easement, this is not trespass or nuisance even though the Act does not extinguish the easement and the developer has not compulsorily purchased it; *Thicknesse v Lancaster Canal Co*,[103] *Wigram v Fry*[104] (right of light), *Bush v Trowbridge Waterworks*.[105] However, this does not seem consistent with *London School Board v Smith*,[106] where the court held that an interim injunction to prevent the owner of a right of way exercising it "must go", i.e. it seems, must be continued. Furthermore, if the law is indeed that the owner of an easement cannot enforce it if it frustrates the object of the compulsory purchase order or the statute, but can only claim compensation for injurious affection, then this would seem to remove much of the importance of the issue of whether or not the easement has been extinguished by the Act.

---

[103] (1838) 4 M. & W. 472.
[104] (1878) 36 Ch. D. 57.
[105] *Bush v Trowbridge Waterworks Co* (1874–75) L.R. 10 Ch. App. 459, cf. *Long Eaton Recreation Co v Midland Railway Co* [1902] 2 K.B. 574 (breach of restrictive covenants); *Manchester Sheffield and Lincolnshire Railway Co v Anderson* [1898] 2 Ch. 394 covenant for quiet enjoyment.
[106] [1895] W.N. 37.

Chapter Eighteen
Rights of Way and Parking

1. Nature of right of way

A private right of way is an easement permitting people to pass to and **18.01**
fro over another person's land from one point to another for the benefit
of land belonging to the person entitled to the right of way.

The nature and characteristics of easements are discussed in Chapter Ten
and it is not proposed to repeat that discussion, except in so far as it has
particular application to rights of way. Accordingly, such matters as the
identification of the dominant and the servient tenement, the distinction
between freehold and leasehold rights, the persons entitled to use the way
and the ways in which a right of way can be created are not discussed in
this chapter.

As a private right of way is a common law easement there is no precise
definition of what is meant by "land". Certainly a right of way can be
over an artificial structure such as a staircase. It seems clear that a right of
way may be over any part of the property of another whether natural
or artificial and whether on the ground or up in the air. The question of
the physical extent of the way discussed below normally concerns the
width of the way, but its height can also come into question. A right
of way may be of limited or unlimited height. In *Bulstrode v Lambert*[1]
the physical way was restricted at the time of the grant both by a gate
restricting its width and by an overhead bar restricting its height, but it
was held that, when the bar was removed, the right of way granted was
sufficient to allow vehicles taller than the bar to pass through. There is
no doubt however, that, for example, a right of way along a covered
passageway is limited to the height of the ceiling. In short the same rules
of construction apply to the height of the way as apply to width as set out
below.

A right of way is essentially a right over land rather than water. It was **18.02**
held in *Attorney General Ex rel Yorkshire Derwent Trust Ltd v Brotherton*[2] that

[1] [1953] 1 W.L.R. 1064.
[2] [1992] A.C. 425; [1991] 3 W.L.R. 1126.

375

a navigable river cannot be a public highway because a waterway is not a "way over or upon any land" within s.1(1)(a) of the Rights of Way Act 1932 even though land expressly includes "land covered by water".[3] This is because, while the bed under the water may be "land", the way is over the water and not over the river-bed.[4] Although *Attorney General Ex rel Yorkshire Derwent Trust Ltd v Brotherton*[5] only relates to public rights of way, the same principles must apply to private rights of way. As with public rights of way it seems clear that a private right of way does not cease to be a right of way because it becomes flooded, nor if it involves fording a stream or using a bridge.

What is more uncertain is what would happen if a person used a waterway as a means of access to his property. Thus a person might have a house on an island on a lake or use a boat to cross a river or artificial watercourse to get to his property. Is there any reason why such a right should not give rise to an easement? The Prescription Act 1832 refers expressly to the "use of any water" as a right which can be obtained by prescription. There seems no reason why this should not include using water as a means of access, even if this is strictly not a right of way. Equally there is no reason why the doctrine of lost modern grant should not apply to a right of passage across water as much as to a right of way over land. There is, however, no authority specifically on these points.

18.03   The essence of a right of way is that it is a right of passage. As such it differs from a right to wander, sometimes called a *"ius spatiendi"*. There has been much controversy about the extent to which a right to wander can be granted by express grant,[6] and whether a right to enjoy a common for the purposes of recreation can give rise to an easement or a right in the nature of an easement.[7]

It was held in *Dyfed CC v Secretary of State for Wales*[8] that there is a distinction to be drawn between "pure walking", albeit of a recreational nature, and use of a way "as an incident of the fishing, swimming, sunbathing, picnicking, etc".[9] Pure walking is capable of being sufficient user for dedication of a public highway to be presumed, "whether or not such walking was itself purely recreational as opposed to walking for business purposes", but use for purposes incidental to other recreational uses could not give rise to a presumption of dedication.

---

[3] Highways Act 1980 s.31(11).
[4] See *Thames Heliport Plc v Tower Hamlets LBC* (1997) 74 P. & C.R. 164 at 168, a planning case.
[5] [1992] A.C. 425; [1991] 3 W.L.R. 1126.
[6] *Re Ellenborough Park* [1956] Ch. 131; see Ch. 10.
[7] *R. v Doncaster MBC Ex p. Braim* (1989) 57 P. & C.R. 1.
[8] (1990) 59 P. & C.R. 275.
[9] per Browne-Wilkinson V.C. at 279.

This decision, however, concerned a public right of way. A private right of way has to be from one point to another. Accordingly it seems that a private right of "pure walking" would not be a right of way and would amount to a *"ius spatiendi"* or right to wander.[10] A right of way cannot, therefore, strictly be used for recreation, whether for such activities as football or picnicking, or even for an evening stroll which is not aimed at reaching the other end of the right of way. Usually, however, it does not matter what the person using the way intends to do when he gets to the dominant tenement.[11]

It is sometimes said that a right of way must have a *terminus a quo* and a *terminus ad quem*, i.e. that it must lead from one fixed point to another. Usually one of these fixed points will be a public highway and the other will be the dominant tenement. There is no requirement, however, that the way must lead directly to the dominant land. There is nothing to stop a person obtaining a right of way over one parcel of land for the purpose of gaining access to his own land over intervening land.[12] Even though the right of way must be directly or indirectly a means of access to the dominant land, it can be exercised by driving over the right of way and then parking on the intervening land before proceeding to the dominant land on foot; *National Trust for Places of Historic Interest or Natural Beauty v White*.[13] The dominant owner may not, however, use the way as a means of access to other land owned by him which is not part of the dominant tenement.[14]

As it is a right of passage, it does not normally include a right to park. **18.04** The extent to which a right to park can exist as a separate easement is considered below.[15] Frequently, where there is a vehicular access the dominant owner does not have anywhere on his own land where vehicles can stop to unload. It has been accepted, therefore, that a right of way includes a right to stop for sufficient time to load or unload, *Bulstrode v Lambert*[16] approved by the Court of Appeal in *McIlraith v Grady*.[17] Although both these cases were of express grant there is no reason to doubt that a similar right can be obtained by prescription.

The existence of a right to park as an ancillary right to an express right of way has now been considered by the House of Lords in *Moncrieff v Jamieson*.[18] Although this was a Scottish case, there is no doubt that it also

---

[10] See Ch. 10.

[11] See below para.18.19.

[12] *Pugh v Savage* [1970] 2 Q.B. 373; [1970] 2 All E.R. 353; *Todrick v Western National Omnibus Co Ltd* [1934] Ch. 561.

[13] [1987] 1 W.L.R. 907.

[14] *Bracewell v Appleby* [1975] Ch. 408; [1975] 2 W.L.R. 282; *Das v Linden Mews Ltd* [2002] EWCA Civ 590 where *National Trust for Places of Historic Interest or Natural Beauty v White* [1987] 1 W.L.R. 907 was distinguished and the limitations of the decision were explained.

[15] See below para.18.22 et seq.

[16] [1953] 1 W.L.R. 1064.

[17] [1968] 1 Q.B. 468; [1967] 3 W.L.R. 1331.

[18] [2007] UKHL 42; [2007] 1 W.L.R. 2620.

applies to England and there is specific consideration of the English authorities. The House of Lords upheld the general principle:

> "It is not in dispute that an express grant of a vehicular right of way does not necessarily, or even usually, carry with it the right to park vehicles on the servient land".[19]

It was an unusual case in that the right of way was such that it was of no use as a vehicular right of way without a right to park, because there was nowhere on the dominant tenement where parking was possible and there was nowhere else to park within walking distance of the property. The House of Lords held that the implication was that it included a right to park as an ancillary right, providing that this did not interfere with the use of the property by the owner of the servient tenement.

The existence of a separate right to park as an easement by grant or prescription is considered below. Before the Court could decide that the right to park was ancillary to the right of way, they had to decide whether a right to park was capable of existing as a separate easement or servitude. They decided that it could and, therefore, could, in appropriate circumstances, be annexed to a right of way as an ancillary right, even though there was no reference to parking in the grant.

Although the right is of free passage, it does not follow that the way must be free of all obstructions. It is perfectly in order for there to be a gate on the right of way: *Pettey v Parsons*.[20] In that case the servient owner was required to keep the gate open at all times during business hours and to keep it unlocked at all times. In *Guest Estates v Milner*[21] it was held that locking a gate would be an obstruction even if a key was supplied. However, the headnote in *Johnstone v Holdway*[22] indicates that putting a chain across an entrance with a combination lock would not be a substantial interference if the combination number was supplied (though this is not clear from the judgment which leaves the parties to come to terms on how the way will be available to the dominant owner, but not to the public). In relation to the outer door of a block of flats an automatic lock was held not to be an obstruction providing that the postman could gain access.[23] A servient owner may be entitled to insist that a right of way created by express grant or reservation is locked at night for security reasons, even if this interferes with an altered use of the dominant tenement as a music-hall.[24]

---

[19] per Lord Scot at [46].
[20] [1914] 2 Ch. 653.
[21] (1911) 28 T.L.R. 59.
[22] [1963] 1 Q.B. 601.
[23] *Dawes v Adela Estates* (1970) 216 E.G. 1405.
[24] *Collins v Slade* (1874) 23 W.R. 199.

What the authorities amount to is that the degree of obstruction and interference that will be acceptable depends on the nature of the way and what it is used for. The kind of gate which would be acceptable at the entrance to a field through which an agricultural way runs would not necessarily be acceptable at the entrance to a private road leading to a housing estate. It is one thing to lock the outer front door on a block of flats, but another to lock an ordinary field gate.

A private right of way must be distinguished from a public right of way **18.05** or public highway. Such rights are discussed in relation to boundaries in Chapter Eight, but the full consideration of public highways is a specialist subject which is outside the ambit of this book.

> "It is clear law that there may be a private right of way and a public right of way existing along a road at the same time".[25]

Where there is a public highway open to all traffic over a way, a private right of way does not give the dominant owner any additional rights beyond those available to any member of the public, but frequently public footpaths, restricted byways, and bridleways run along tracks over which there is a private right of way for vehicles. Furthermore, a public highway may be extinguished by a stopping up order, in which case the private right of way may revive.[26] It seems that if the claim is of a prescriptive right of way, this can only be proved by showing sufficient user during a period before the public right of way is created, since user by a neighbouring owner of a public highway cannot be shown to be under a private right if he is entitled to use it as a member of the public.

There are many cases where the evidence available to the plaintiff is consistent either with a public highway or a private right of way. In such cases the pleadings often contain alternative allegations of a public right of way and a private right of way. There are many similarities in the evidence required, the distinction often being whether the way is being used to the particular purposes of the alleged dominant land or whether it is being used as a through route. The two concepts are nevertheless distinct.

2. Physical extent of the way

Where there is an express grant, the physical extent of the right of way **18.06** is essentially a matter of construction. In construing the grant the court

---

[25] per Denning L.J. in *Walsh v Oates* [1953] 1 Q.B. 578; [1953] 1 All E.R. 963 at 965H.
[26] *Walsh v Oates* [1953] 1 Q.B. 578; [1953] 1 All E.R. 963.

will take note both of the words of the grant and the physical extent of the way at the date of the grant.[27]

The usual way of expressing the extent of a right of way in a grant is either by defining the width or by referring to a plan. If the width of the way is defined in the grant, it will be very difficult for either owner to suggest that it is incorrect, even if the path which exists on the ground is narrower or wider.[28] The only course available will be to seek to rectify the deed of grant. A grant may also define the height of the way.[29] However, if there is any ambiguity or uncertainty the court will be quick to look at the circumstances of the grant and the physical extent of the way at the time of the grant.

Even where the grant is by reference to a plan, the courts have in the past been prepared to treat the right of way as covering the whole of the land coloured on the plan even if there are indications that no such comprehensive right was intended. However, more recently a more restrictive approach has been followed.[30]

One problem which has arisen is where there is a gate or other restriction of the way which in practice restricts the use of the rest of the way. If there is a narrow gate, a wider path beyond may still be useful, e.g. for turning round or passing, but only for people or vehicles that can actually get through the gate. In *Bulstrode v Lambert*[31] there was a grant over a way "with or without vehicles". At the time of the grant there was a gateway with an overhead bar which restricted the size of vehicles using part of the way to handcarts. However, when this was removed by the servient owner the court held that the dominant owner was entitled to use the way for vehicles which could not have used it at the time of the grant. What is not clear, however, is whether the dominant owner would have been entitled to insist on the removal of the bar.

18.07   In *Keefe v Amor*[32] the Court of Appeal went further and upheld a decision that when a gateway suitable only for pedestrians was widened by the servient owner, this allowed the person entitled to the right of way to use it for vehicles even though the gateway had been there at the time of grant and the grant did not specify that the way was "with or without vehicles". The right of way was over "the land . . . coloured brown", and accordingly included the site of the gateway:

---

[27] *St Edmundsbury and Ipswich Diocesan Board of Finance v Clark (No.2)* [1975] 1 W.L.R. 468; [1975] 1 All E.R. 772; *Soper v Leeman-Hawley* [1992] N.P.C. 95; *White v Richards* [1993] R.T.R. 318; (1994) 68 P. & C.R. 105.

[28] *West v Sharp* (2000) 79 P. & C.R. 327.

[29] See above para.18.01.

[30] e.g. *St Edmundsbury and Ipswich Diocesan Board of Finance v Clark (No.2)* [1975] 1 W.L.R. 468; [1975] 1 All E.R. 772; *White v Richards* [1993] R.T.R. 318; (1994) 68 P. & C.R. 105.

[31] *Bulstrode v Lambert* [1953] 1 W.L.R. 1064.

[32] [1965] 1 Q.B. 334; [1964] 3 W.L.R. 183.

"If the true conclusion is that the right granted embraces potentially the whole of the strip, the fact that the physical characteristics of the site (for example the existence of walls) make the exercise of the right at the time of the grant impossible over any but a limited route will not contradict or limit the scope of the grant".[33]

One cannot help wondering, however, whether the court would have been more reluctant to order the removal of the wall in either of these cases, had the servient owner not himself widened the opening for his own purposes.

The Court of Appeal in *St Edmundsbury and Ipswich Diocesan Board of Finance v Clark (No.2)*[34] took a rather different view and held that the words of the grant must be construed in the light of the physical characteristics of the way at the time of the grant. They held on facts which are not so very different from *Keefe v Amor* that a right of way "coloured red" on the plan was restricted by the existence of a gate which was there at the time of the grant. The court found no difficulty in distinguishing *Keefe v Amor* on its facts without making any specific comments on the rationale of that decision.

This more restrictive approach was also taken in *White v Richards*[35] where the Court of Appeal upheld the judge's concentration on the actual width of the way at the time of the grant, which means that wider, more modern vehicles were unable to use it. This was despite the fact that the way itself was not bounded by any particular strip of land, so that wider vehicles could in practice travel over the servient tenement. This is, however, a matter of construction and, for example, the extent of the coloured area in the plan will not necessarily limit the right of way if the physical extent of the track is plainly greater.[36] The conclusion in *West v Sharp*[37] (where only *Keefe v Amor*[38] was cited) was that the way included the whole of the area coloured brown on the plan, but the distinction was that the grant was for development and it might well have been contemplated that the way would be extended from that in existence at the time of the grant.

It appears from these somewhat contrasting cases, therefore, that the **18.08** extent to which the physical characteristics of the way at the time of the grant will affect the construction of the grant itself will depend on the particular facts of the case and on the precise terms of the grant, but that the physical nature of the way at the time of the grant is a crucial factor.

---

[33] per Russell L.J. at 520I.
[34] [1975] 1 W.L.R. 468; [1975] 1 All E.R. 772.
[35] [1993] R.T.R. 318; (1994) 68 P. & C.R. 105.
[36] *Wright Davies v Marler* [1995] 10 C.L.Y. 812.
[37] (2000) 79 P. & C.R. 327.
[38] *Keefe v Amor* [1965] 1 Q.B. 334.

"In order to ascertain the intention of the parties, the words [of the grant] had to be interpreted in context of the surrounding circumstances. The surrounding circumstances that the court is entitled to look at include, but are not limited to, the physical extent of the way."[39]

Where the way is claimed by prescription, the actual width of the way at various times becomes more important. Clearly if there is an obstruction preventing vehicular user of the way during a significant part of the prescription period, the right obtained will be limited accordingly. It is, however, important to remember that an obstruction of a right of way is only actionable if it affects the convenient use of the way for the purposes for which it is then required.[40]

One difficulty which tends to arise is that vehicles have over the years become larger. A way which is 12 feet wide may not in practice have been used by vehicles more than six feet wide until recently. In such situations the courts tend to take a common-sense approach. User for vehicular access for the prescription period has usually been enough to prove a right of way for the full width even though the full width has not in practice been used for the full 20 years. However, the more restrictive approach apparent in respect of express grants[41] may also be reflected in a tendency to require fuller evidence of use of the full width throughout the period. The fact that the way can only be used safely if the way is extended by implication beyond what is set out in the conveyance will encourage the court to imply an extension of the way.[42]

18.09 Normally a right of way will be over a defined path, but this is not necessarily the case. An implied grant of a right of way has been found where there was a gate at either end of a garden with no obvious track between[43] and in *Wimbledon and Putney Commons Conservators v Dixon*[44] a prescriptive claim succeeded even though a number of different tracks had been used:

"If from one terminus to another, say from the gate here to the end of a road 200 yards off persons have found their way from time immemorial across a common, although sometimes going by one track and sometimes by another, I am not prepared to say that a right of road across the common from one terminus to the other may not be

[39] per Morritt L.J. in *Mills v Blackwell* (1999) 78 P. & C.R. D43.
[40] *Simpson v Fergus* (2000) 79 P. & C.R. 398; *B&Q Plc v Liverpool & Lancashire Properties* (2001) 81 P. & C.R. 20, where an injunction was not granted.
[41] *White v Richards* [1993] R.T.R. 318; (1994) 68 P. & C.R. 105.
[42] *Millman v Ellis* (1996) 71 P. & C.R. 158.
[43] *Donnelly v Adams* [1905] 1 I.R. 154.
[44] (1875–76) L.R. 1 Ch. D. 362.

validly claimed and may not be as good as a right of way over any formed road . . .".[45]

As long as the user is as of right and amounts to an exercise of a right of passage across the land, the absence of any precise path is not fatal. In *Davis v Whitby*[46] a way was used for 15 years along one path and then, with the agreement of the owner, changed to another path for a further 18 years. The Court of Appeal upheld a prescriptive claim of 20 years continuous use. Despite this agreement it was held that the user did not become precarious. If the servient owner had denied the dominant owner's right to use the way, but then given permission to use another path then there would have been no user as of right over the whole period, but it seems that what actually happened was that the servient owner, before the 20 years period had expired, was nevertheless acknowledging the dominant owner's right to the way and simply offering a more convenient alternative route. The courts will, however, be reluctant to accept a right of way over a wide tract of land which would have the effect of blighting that land permanently from any kind of development.

If there is a right of way along a particular path and the servient owner, **18.10** or indeed anyone else, blocks it up, the dominant owner has a right of action in nuisance. However, it is established that where the obstruction is by the servient owner, the dominant owner has an alternative which is to deviate across some other part of the servient owner's land.[47] This does not give rise to a substituted right of way or mean that the original right of way has ceased to exist. The right to deviate will be protected by the court as long as the obstruction exists, but this does not prevent the owner of the servient tenement from substituting any other convenient mode of access.[48]

The right to deviate only arises where the obstruction is created by the servient owner or with his connivance. It does not apply if the way becomes impassable for some other reason.[49] In particular, there is no right to alter the route of an express right of way even though it is obviously beneficial to all concerned. However, a similar effect can be obtained by refusing an injunction and giving a declaration that there is no right of injunction to the servient owner to prevent the dominant owners using the varied way.[50] If a way is obstructed when land is requisitioned and an alternative route is offered, the original right of way is

---

[45] per James L.J. at 368. See also *Barba v Gas and Fuel Corp* of Victoria (1977) 51 A.L.J.R. 219.
[46] [1974] Ch. 186; [1974] 2 W.L.R. 333.
[47] *Stacey v Sherrin* (1913) 29 T.L.R. 555.
[48] *Selby v Nettleford* (1873) 9 Ch. App. 111 at 115 per Lord Selborne L.C.
[49] *Ballard v Harrison* (1815) 4 M. & S. 387.
[50] *Greenwich Healthcare NHS Trust v London & Quadrant Housing Trust* [1998] 1 W.L.R. 1749; [1998] 3 All E.R. 437.

only suspended, but the deviation does not count as exercise of the right of deviation.[51]

A right of way may be a right to pass and re-pass between two points or it may include a right to obtain access to the way at any point along its length. The problem only arises where the way runs alongside the dominant property. In such circumstances the dominant owner may wish to open a new gate onto the way. This issue has been the subject of much litigation. The latest analysis is that of Patten J. in *Perlman v Rayden*.[52] This relies primarily on two Court of Appeal cases, *Charles v Beach*[53] and *Mills v Blackwell*.[54] From these cases the following principles can be found:

- There is no overriding rule. It is all a matter of construction of the grant.[55]

- Where the words of the grant are apt to accommodate an easement at every point, the Court looks at the features in existence at the time of the grant to see whether they indicate that there was no right to open an access at any particular point.[56]

In *Charles v Beach* it was held that the existence of a flower bed was not enough to prevent an access being made at that point. However, in *Mills v Blackwell*, Morritt L.J. said:

"It would be absurd to conclude that Mr. Blackwell was entitled to demolish the wall so that access and egress might be obtained from any point along the strip."

These authorities largely supersede earlier authorities on this issue.[57]

3. The use of the right of way

18.11   The use made of the right of way can be conveniently divided into three categories (1) the type of use (2) the purpose of the use and (3) the quantity of use. This distinction was referred to in *Dewan v Lewis*,[58] which makes clear that there is "no rigid distinction between type or mode of use and its purpose of extent". Whether or not this categorisation is useful, there is certainly considerable elision between these three

---

[51] *Mann v Eayrs (RC)* (1973) 231 E.G. 843.
[52] [2004] EWHC 2192 (Ch).
[53] [1993] E.G. 124 (C.S.).
[54] (1999) 78 P. & C.R. D43.
[55] *Pettey v Parsons* [1914] 2 Ch 653.
[56] See Waite L.J. in *Charles v Beach*.
[57] e.g *South Metropolitan Cemetery Company v Eden* (1855) 16 C.B. 42; *Cooke v Ingram* (1893) 68 L.T. 671; *Sketchley v Berger* (1893) 69 L.T. 754.
[58] [2010] EWCA Civ 1382.

categories. It must be remembered that disputes about the use of a way arise because the servient owner admits that there is a right of way but objects to the way in which it is being used. This is almost always because there has been some change in the use of the dominant land leading to a user of the way which he finds objectionable. Really the servient owner is not so much concerned with the purpose for which the way is being used, as with the way in which the changed use is affecting him. This may take the form of a change in the type of use (e.g. from mainly pedestrian to mainly vehicular, or even from normal agricultural use to a use for driving cattle (which may be considerably more intrusive in a residential area)),[59] a change in the purpose of use (e.g. from agricultural to commercial), or a change in the quantity of use (e.g. from an occasional vehicle to a regular stream of vehicles), or it may be a mixture of all three or a change in the size and weight of the vehicles using the way.[60]

This point is illustrated by comparing two cases. In *RPC Holdings Ltd v Rogers*[61] the defendant proved a prescriptive right of way over a track which had been used for agricultural purposes. He had, however, bought the field to set up a caravan site. It was held that the right of way was for agricultural purposes only, so that he could not use it for the purposes of the caravan site. Strictly this would apply as much to one or two caravans as to the 60 or 70 he contemplated.

In *Jelbert v Davis*[62] the problem was almost identical except that there was an express right of way "at all times and for all purposes". At the time of the grant it was used for agricultural purposes. The plaintiff bought the dominant tenement and turned it into a caravan site. The court could not hold that the right of way did not cover use for this purpose since the grant was expressly for all purposes, but nevertheless it was held that the use was excessive and that the plaintiff was not entitled to use the right of way to an extent which exceeded that which was contemplated at the time of the grant. The plaintiff, therefore, (unlike the plaintiff in *RPC Holdings v Rogers*[63]) could have used the way for a small number of caravans, which would have been no more onerous than the agricultural user contemplated, but not for the 200 or so units he intended.

In deciding both the type and the purpose of the way there is a substan- **18.12** tial difference between rights of way obtained by express grant and rights of way obtained by prescription or implied grant. There is no jurisprudential logic to this distinction, since prescriptive rights can be obtained by the fiction of lost modern grant and accordingly the mythical grant

---

[59] *Dewan v Lewis* [2010] EWCA Civ 1382.
[60] *White v Richards* [1993] R.T.R. 318; (1994) 68 P. & C.R. 105.
[61] [1953] 1 All E.R. 1029.
[62] [1968] 1 W.L.R. 589; [1968] 1 All E.R. 1182.
[63] [1953] 1 All E.R. 1029.

would presumably have been in much the same terms as an express grant. The difference, however, is that an express grant has to be construed in its terms, whereas other forms of grant can only be deduced from the actual user made. The way in which an express grant should be construed was considered in *St Edmundsbury and Ipswich Diocesan Board of Finance v Clark (No.2)*[64] both as to the physical extent of the way[65] and the uses to which it could be put. There a distinction was made between words of grant which were wholly unambiguous and other more general words. Express grants of rights of way frequently contain the words "for all purposes". This is unambiguous and means that any use which is within the capacity of the way and which is not excessive is permitted, unless other words in the grant can be construed as words of limitation.[66] However, it is just as common for the grant to be of a right of way over a particular way without specifying the purposes for which it could be used. The Court of Appeal held that the conveyance should be construed according to its ordinary words, without any presumption in favour or against the grantee, but that the construction should be in the light of the surrounding circumstances at the time. The net result was that a reservation of a right of way "over the land coloured red" was held to be restricted as to the extent of the way to a narrow gateway and to give rise only to a right of way on foot because vehicles (or at least four-wheeled vehicles) could not get through the gateway.

A grant may contain less obvious words of limitation. Thus a grant through a covered passage "as used by her tenant Edward Collinson" who was a fishmonger was construed as limiting it to use as a rear entrance for deliveries and not for customers, so that when the premises became a pub and was used by customers of the pub for various undesirable purposes, the user was held to be outside that permitted.[67]

Grants of rights of way usually refer to the width of the way itself. However, in making a declaration about the manner in which the way can lawfully be used it is perfectly proper for the judge to put limits on the axle width and weight of the vehicles using the way.[68] This is quite separate from the question of excessive user. A way may be suitable only for vehicles of a limited width and weight and there be an overlap between use by unauthorised vehicles and excessive use by vehicles, both authorised and unauthorised. A fixed weight and width limit may be a convenient way of dealing with this problem, by drawing the line between acceptable and excessive use.

---

[64] [1975] 1 W.L.R. 468; [1975] 1 All E.R. 772.
[65] See above para.18.07.
[66] *Greatorex v Newman* [2008] EWCA Civ 1318.
[67] *Greatorex v Newman* [2008] EWCA Civ 1318.
[68] *White v Richards* [1993] R.T.R. 318; (1994) 68 P. & C.R. 105.

(1)   Types of way

It is no longer possible to divide rights of way simply into the three **18.13** types of use identified by Coke namely footway, horseway and vehicular way. The complexity of modern life requires the courts to consider passage on foot, with pushchairs or perambulators,[69] in wheelchairs,[70] carrying hearses,[71] pushing or pulling trolleys,[72] riding or pushing bicycles[73] or motor-cycles, riding or leading horses, driving cattle, pulling caravans, driving cars, lorries, buses[74] or agricultural vehicles quite apart from the different purposes set out below. Nevertheless Coke's three categories still provide a convenient starting point for looking at the different types of way.

(a)   Footway

A footpath is defined in the Wildlife and Countryside Act 1981[75] as "a **18.14** highway over which the public have a right of way on foot only . . .". That definition, however, applies only to public footpaths. Any way which is too narrow for four-wheeled vehicles is likely to be described either in a conveyance or by the persons using it as a footpath. In respect of private rights of way there is not very much authority on the extent to which the dominant owner is allowed to use the way for other purposes than walking.

If the way is expressed to be "for all purposes" then, even if the way is the width of a footway, the dominant owner will be entitled to use it with any vehicles which can in practice use the way. This would include bicycles and motorcycles. In *St Edmundsbury and Ipswich Diocesan Board of Finance v Clark (No.2)*[76] there was a grant of a "right of way" without any qualification of the purposes of user. Since the way was too narrow for four-wheeled vehicles the judge held that it was a right of way "for pedestrians only, and not for vehicles".[77] The way had in fact been used for carrying hearses and Megarry J. at first instance obviously considered that to be pedestrian use. This is because carrying anything normally carried on foot counts as user on foot,[78] though hearses are now often

---

[69] *R. v Matthias* (1861) 2 F. & F. 570.
[70] *Carlson v Cochinov* [1948] 2 W.W.R. 273.
[71] *St Edmundsbury and Ipswich Diocesan Board of Finance v Clark (No.2)* [1975] 1 W.L.R. 468; [1975] 1 All E.R. 772.
[72] *Re St Martin Le Grand, York* [1990] Fam 63; [1989] 2 All E.R. 711 at 720j.
[73] *Sheringham U.D.C. v Hosley* (1904) 68 J.P. 395.
[74] *Todrick v Western National Omnibus Co Ltd* [1934] Ch. 561.
[75] Wildlife and Countryside Act 1981 s.66(1).
[76] [1975] 1 W.L.R. 468; [1975] 1 All E.R. 772.
[77] *St Edmundsbury and Ipswich Diocesan Board of Finance v Clark (No.2)* [1973] 3 All E.R. 903 at 929g.
[78] *Austin v Scottish Widows Assurance* (1881) 8 L.R.Ir.197.

manoeuvred on trolleys. The issue in *St Edmundsbury v Clark (No.2)*, however was whether the way should be widened to accommodate four-wheeled vehicles and not what use of the unwidened way was permissible. Bicycles have been held to be vehicles,[79] and motor cycles certainly are. Would the decision in *St Edmundsbury and Ipswich Diocesan Board of Finance v Clark (No.2)* that there was no right to vehicular use have been the same if the plaintiffs had only been claiming the right to cycle along the existing way or to use it for motor-cycles instead of asking that it be widened? The surrounding circumstances considered by the Court of Appeal in that case were essentially the width of the way through the gate, which in fact was obviously adequate for bicycles and motorcycles. It may be, however, that where the issue is about use by cyclists or motor-cyclists the court would look more carefully at the adaptability of the way for the purposes claimed. A metalled path might be suitable for motor-cycles, a hardcore path for bicycles, but a way across a back garden for use only on foot.

18.15   While bicycles and motorcycles are undoubtedly vehicles (though the extent to which they can be used on footpaths may be in doubt) the position is even less clear in respect of other ways in which a dominant owner may wish to use a footway. As stated above, loads may be carried on foot. A jury has been directed that a perambulator can be used on a public footpath providing that it is of a size and weight not to damage the way; *R. v Matthias*.[80] On the other hand it has been held in Canada that, for other purposes, a wheelchair is a vehicle, and that vehicles include anything driven by muscular power whether human or animal.[81] It seems likely that the approach used in *R. v Matthias*[82] would be used for a private right of way even where the grant was "on foot only". However, such things as wheelbarrows and handcarts and even wheelchairs might well be excluded by a grant on foot only, but not by an unqualified grant of a right of way over a narrow way. For example in *Keefe v Amor*[83] the plaintiffs' allegation (not eventually accepted) was that:

> "it is only a footway, or, perhaps, alternatively, that if it does extend to vehicles then such vehicles must be limited to those that can pass through a gap approximately four and a half feet wide".[84]

[79] *Sheringham UDC v Hosley* (1904) 68 J.P. 395; *Hansford v London Express Newspapers* (1928) 44 T.L.R. 349.
[80] *R. v Matthias* (1861) 2 F. & F. 570, see Ch.7.
[81] *Carlson v Cochinov* [1948] W.W.R. 273.
[82] *R. v Matthias* (1861) 2 F. & F. 570.
[83] *Keefe v Amor* [1965] 1 Q.B. 334; [1964] 2 All E.R. 517.
[84] per Russell L.J. at 518I.

In deciding the types of user permitted in respect of a way obtained by prescription, there will be more emphasis on the manner in which the way has actually been used rather than on the physical extent of the way. In *Re St Martin le Grand*[85] the right claimed was "a right of way on foot with laden or unladen trolleys". This was treated as a pedestrian way quite separate from a vehicular way though it is hard to see why trolleys are not vehicles. However, that user had continued for "very many years". Would it have been different if there had been long user on foot, but less than 20 years user with trolleys?

It is not easy to set out any clear simple rules and the issues have not really been addressed in the authorities. It is submitted that there are certain kinds of user that are associated with a footpath. These include pushing prams, wheeling bicycles, wheeling wheelbarrows, pushing two wheeled trolleys, etc. Such user would be allowed once a pedestrian right of way was proved and would be included even if the conveyance expressly restricted the way to "on foot only". Other uses to which a path too narrow for normal vehicular access could be put would not be included in a grant of a right "on foot only", but could be included in a more general grant and could be proved by prescription if there had been 20 years of such user. This would include riding bicycles and motor cycles, pushing handcarts and larger trolleys, etc. Each case, however, will depend on its own facts including the precise nature of the way and the contemplation of the parties at the time of the grant.

(b) Bridleway or driftway

Coke's second category was "horseway" though he makes it clear that **18.16** this also could comprise a driftway, which is a way for driving cattle. In fact, of course, a way which is used for horses will not necessarily also be used or usable for driving cattle.[86] "Horseways" are still referred to in the authorities[87] and reflect not only Coke's categorisation but also the second category of public right of way known as bridleways, defined in the Wildlife and Countryside Act 1981[88] as

"a right of way on foot and a right of way on horseback or leading a horse, with or without a right to drive animals of any description along the highway".

---

[85] [1990] Fam 63; [1989] 2 All E.R. 711.
[86] See *Dewan v Lewis* [2010] EWCA Civ 1382, where agricultural use was found not to include driving cattle.
[87] See e.g. *Hart v Bowmer* [1937] 1 All E.R. 797. See also Countryside and Rights of Way Act 2000 s.48(4)(b).
[88] Wildlife and Countryside Act 1981 s.66(1).

This Act applies only to public highways and not to private rights of way, but it makes it clear that there are two kinds of bridleways, those which include driftways and those which exclude them.

Driftways have been superseded in practice, except in some old deeds, by ways limited to use for agricultural purposes, though this latter concept also has a long pedigree. No doubt in the eighteenth century a farmer who used a field for grazing would not need access to it with farm machinery. Now, any way used for driving animals would be used for farm machinery as well. There are, however, express grants, such as that in *British Railways Board v Glass*[89] which refer to use "with or without cattle". The effect of such a grant is to impose an additional burden on the land and does not imply that the way is limited to agricultural use. There is no necessary reason why a grant of a cartway should include the right to drive cattle.[90]

There is, of course, a distinction between the exercise of construing a direct grant and the judgment of the court on the extent of a prescriptive right. In *Dewan v Lewis*[91] (where these authorities were considered) the principal evidence was of use for normal agricultural purposes and not for driving cattle. The declaration was of "a right of way at all times for agricultural purposes with or without animals and with or without vehicles". There was little evidence of driving cattle and the Court of Appeal amended the declaration so that it specifically excluded driving cattle. Although this case specifically rejected the existence of different categories, in practice it emphasised that some agricultural uses are more disruptive than others and that it was necessary to look at the facts of each individual case.

Now that horse-riding is largely a leisure pursuit, user on horseback is a separate use from agricultural use and would not normally entitle the dominant owner to drive cattle along the way or, a fortiori, to use it for vehicles, whether with two or four wheels and whether mechanically propelled or pulled by hand or by horses.

(c)   With vehicles

18.17   The third and most important category of use is with vehicles. User with horse-drawn carts is vehicular use and accordingly can create a prescriptive right to use a way for motor vehicles even though the way has not been used for motor vehicles for the full period.[92] A grant of a "wagon or cart road" does not entitle the owner to lay down a

[89] [1965] Ch. 538; [1964] 3 All E.R. 418.
[90] *Ballard v Dyson* (1808) 1 Taunt. 279.
[91] [2010] EWCA Civ 1382.
[92] *Lock v Abercester Ltd* [1939] Ch. 861.

railroad.[93] As stated above, bicycles are vehicles[94] and so, it seems, is anything driven by mechanical or muscular power whether human or animal.[95]

A grant of a right of way "with or without motor vehicles" includes a right to ride or lead horses, but does not necessarily include a right to drive cattle.[96]

As explained above, an express grant of a right of way will be construed as allowing vehicular use unless there is any express restriction or unless the way, or part of it, is so narrow that only pedestrian user can have been contemplated. However, for a prescriptive right of way it is necessary to show actual vehicular use if the way is not to be restricted to pedestrian use, even if the way is physically capable of accommodating vehicular use.

Subject to restrictions on excessive user and restrictions on the purpose **18.18** of the user, a vehicular right of way normally permits user for any vehicles that can conveniently use the way. There is no distinction between cars, lorries and tractors. All are treated as motor vehicles, and if the vehicles used become larger they are still allowed to use the way if the way can accommodate them.[97]

In respect of public rights of way the Countryside and Rights of Way Act 2000[98] introduces the concept of a restricted byway which is open to people on foot, on horseback and leading a horse and "vehicles other than mechanically propelled vehicles". This is not currently a separate category of private way. While user by a horse and cart in the past would undoubtedly be seen as vehicular use which could be part of long user for vehicles, user in recent years solely by bicycles or other non mechanically propelled vehicles might well be seen as not giving rise to a prescriptive right of way for all purposes.

(2)   Purposes for which way may be used

A right of way may be limited not only in physical extent and in the **18.19** type of use which may be made of it, but also in the purposes for which it may be used. There are close analogies between the principles governing cases on the physical extent of the way and on the purposes for which the way may be used. However, there are differences which justify looking at this aspect separately.

---

[93] *Arbitration between Bidder and North Staffordshire Railway Co* (1878–79) L.R. 4 Q.B.D. 412.
[94] *Hansford v London Express Newspapers* (1928) 44 T.L.R. 349; *White v Richards* (1994) 68 P. & C.R. 105 at 114 per Nourse L.J.
[95] *Carlson v Cochinov* [1948] 2 W.W.R. 273.
[96] *White v Richards* (1994) 68 P. & C.R. 105, following *Ballard v Dyson* (1808) 1 Taunt. 279.
[97] *Woodhouse & Co v Kirkland* [1970] 1 W.L.R. 1185; [1970] 2 All E.R. 587.
[98] In force from May 2, 2006.

As with the physical extent and the types of use permitted, there is a difference between express grants and rights obtained by prescription. A grant of a right of way may be expressly for all purposes. The basic rule as set out in *Robinson v Bailey*[99] is that a right of way will be for all purposes for which the way can be conveniently enjoyed unless there is something in the words of the grant or the surrounding circumstances which indicate that it is to be more restrictively construed. The mere fact that the way leads to a residence or to allotments does not mean that the parties contemplate at the time of the grant that this will be the only user of the way for ever, even if the grant expressly refers to the house or the allotments.[100] Even a grant of a right of way "as at present enjoyed" has been held to apply to the types of user, i.e. "on foot, with horses and with vehicles" and not to the fact that the user was agricultural only.[101] Equally a grant of a way "with or without horses, carts and agricultural machines and implements" was construed not as restricting the use to agricultural purposes, but as allowing use with motor lorries to extract sand and gravel.[102] This generous approach to restrictive wording in grants of rights of way was reflected in *Hotchkin v McDonald*[103] where a grant of a right of way for all purposes in connection with the use of the Manor House authorised by the covenant was construed as including a further use authorised by a variation of the covenant granted by the Lands Tribunal. However, in *Greatorex v Newman*,[104] the words "as used by the tenant Edward Collinson" were held to be words of limitation which meant that, as it was a rear access used by him only for deliveries to his fishmongers, it was not to be used by customers of the public house for other less desirable purposes.

In general, certainly in respect of express grants, courts have been keen to enable valuable rights of way to be used for modern purposes even though, in theory, the grant is to be construed in the light of the circumstances pertaining at the time of the grant and not those pertaining at the time of the claim.[105] However, if the new use has become unduly onerous, it is still possible to construe such grants are words of limitation.[106]

The courts have been much more willing to restrict user to the purposes for which the way has in practice been used where the claim is based on

---

[99] [1948] 2 All E.R. 791.
[100] *Finch v Great Western Railway Co* (1879–80) L.R. 5 Ex. D. 254; *Milner's Safe Co Ltd v Great Northern and City Railway* [1907] 1 Ch. 208; *White v Grand Hotel Eastbourne* [1913] 1 Ch. 113.
[101] *Hurt v Bowmer* [1937] 1 All E.R. 797.
[102] *Kain v Norfolk* [1949] Ch. 163.
[103] [2004] EWCA Civ 519; [2005] 1 P. & C.R. 7.
[104] [2008] EWCA Civ 1318.
[105] *Investors Compensation Scheme Ltd v West Bromwich Building Society* [1998] 1 W.L.R. 896 HL.
[106] *Greatorex v Newman* [2008] EWCA Civ 1318.

prescription. This approach comes from *Wimbledon and Putney Commons Conservators v Dixon*[107] where James L.J. said at page 368:

"you cannot from evidence of user of a privilege connected with the enjoyment of property in its original state, infer a right to use it into whatsoever form and for whatever purpose that property may be changed . . .".

This view was confirmed by *RPC Holdings Ltd v Rogers*[108] and *Dewan v Lewis*.[109] If user is for agricultural or residential purposes this will not be sufficient to justify use for commercial purposes. If a way is used for agricultural vehicles, this does not mean it can be used for driving cattle. The principles which apply to prescriptive rights also apply to rights of way created by implied grant or reservation.[110]

The authorities have not sought to lay down specific categories of **18.20** purposes, but distinctions have clearly emerged from the authorities between agricultural, commercial and residential purposes and it seems that these are the three main categories. A variation in the kind of commerce for which the use is made will not affect the right even if it is prescriptive. The courts are, however, increasingly making a clear distinction between agricultural use and commercial use. This applies where the claim is prescriptive, where use for commerce for less than 20 years meant that the prescriptive way was only for agriculture,[111] and in an express grant for agricultural use when there was a change of use to storing wood.[112]

Once the physical extent of the way has been established, then that in itself may create some restrictions on the purposes for which it can be used. Thus in *Todrick v Western National Omnibus Co Ltd*[113] the way could not be used for buses because the clearance on either side was too small. However, the same kind of physical restriction would apply to other characteristics of the way. In *Todrick v Great Western Omnibus Co Ltd* a further problem was the fact that the way passed along a road with a retaining wall and it was doubtful whether the wall would be strong enough to hold up the road under the additional strain of the buses.[114] Farwell J. held that the use proposed was "not such use as is proper in my judgment

---

[107] (1875) 1 Ch. D. 362.
[108] [1953] 1 All E.R. 1029.
[109] [2010] EWCA Civ 1382.
[110] *Milner's Safe Co Ltd v Great Northern and City Railway Co* [1907] 1 Ch. 208.
[111] *Loder v Gaden* (1999) 78 P. & C.R. 223.
[112] *Jobson v Record* (1998) 75 P. & C.R. 375 where the Court of Appeal took a limited view of the meaning of "agricultural" use, holding that, though it includes forestry, it does not include storing wood which is cut elsewhere.
[113] [1934] Ch. 190.
[114] *Todrick v Western National Omnibus Co Ltd* [1934] Ch. 190 at 207 per Farwell J.

for a way of this kind".[115] Thus a way over a bridge would be limited to loads within the physical capacity of the bridge. An unmetalled way might be unsuitable for heavy vehicles which would damage it. Such physical limitations however, do not affect the purposes for which the way can be used within those limitations. While the way in *Todrick v Western National Omnibus Co Ltd*[116] could not be used for buses, it could be used by the bus company for other business purposes which were within the way's physical capacity.

The purposes for which the way can be used must relate to the dominant tenement. The way in which the dominant tenement is defined is considered above.[117] The Court of Appeal in *Peacock v Custins*[118] has authoritatively considered the vexed question of whether a right of way can be used for access to one piece of land when the true purpose of the use is for the benefit of other land. As is made clear there, a way can only be used for the purposes of the dominant tenement. However, in some circumstances it may not be outside the scope of the grant to use the way to access the dominant land and then go off the dominant land for an incidental or ancillary activity,[119] but where the essential purpose of using the way is to cultivate some other land, which is not the dominant land, this use can be prevented even if it does not add significantly to the burden upon the servient land.[120] Using the way for access to the dominant land for the purpose of works may, it seems, be permitted even if the object of the works is to clear out a drain to benefit other land.[121] It is, therefore, not possible to buy a small parcel of land with a right of way attached to it and then seek to use the way as a means of access to other land you own, whether adjacent to the servient tenement or not.

(3) Excessive user

18.21 Before *Jelbert v Davis*[122] the law as it was understood was that, providing you are entitled to use the way by vehicles and providing that you are using the way for a purpose permitted by the grant or prescription, and providing the use of the way is not such as to cause physical damage to

---

[115] *Todrick v Western National Omnibus Co Ltd* [1934] Ch. 190 at 207.

[116] [1934] Ch. 190.

[117] See Nature of Easements—Ch.10.

[118] [2002] 1 W.L.R. 1815; (2001) 81 P. & C.R. 34, where the authorities are reviewed.

[119] See *Macepark (Whittlebury) v Sargeant (No.2)* [2003] EWHC 427 (Ch); [2003] 1 W.L.R. 2284; [2003] 2 P. & C.R. 12 where, in the end, it was held that the user (as a means of access to Silverstone Motor Racing Circuit) would not be merely ancillary to the primary use as a hotel, as it was not only for hotel guests.

[120] See *Wilkins v Lewis* [2005] EWHC 1710 (Ch).

[121] *Britel Developments (Thatcham) Ltd v Nightfreight (Great Britain) Ltd* [1998] 4 All E.R. 432, this was an interlocutory motion and no final decision was given.

[122] [1968] 1 W.L.R. 589; [1968] 1 All E.R. 1182.

it, you may use the way as often as you like and with whatever vehicles you like. Thus in *Kain v Norfolk*[123] use changed from agricultural use to convoys of six to eight three-ton motor lorries, but no excessive user was found. In *British Railways Board v Glass*[124] a prescriptive use was proved for caravans. The fact that the number of caravans using the site had greatly increased did not render the user excessive. However, in *Jelbert v Davis* Lord Denning M.R. put forward for the first time the proposition that:

"no one of those entitled to the right of way must use it to an extent which is beyond anything which was contemplated at the time of the grant".

This was another caravan case and allowed the court to prevent an excessive use of the way even though the grant was expressly for all purposes. In *Woodhouse v Kirkland*[125] Plowman J. said[126]:

"It is unnecessary to consider whether an increase in use, if very great, can ever of itself amount to excessive user because that case is not this case".

However, though *Jelbert v Davis* was cited to him he did not refer to it in the judgment. Apart from this, *Jelbert v Davis* has not been doubted and the principle has proved a very effective way of controlling abuses of rights of way by and on behalf of dominant owners. The effect of any such excessive user is to give to the servient owner a right of action. Thus it has been stated that excessive user does not in any way suspend the easement:

"However, I doubt whether any excessive user, at least of a discontinuous easement, in whatever respect the user may be excessive, will ever of itself bring to an end or indeed suspend such an easement . . . The owner of the servient tenement on which, *ex hypothesi*, the excessive burden is placed is entitled to have that excessive user restrained. The fact that a court may grant an appropriate injunction or make a declaration to this end does not in my judgment either extinguish or suspend the easement. Provided that the owner of the dominant tenement subsequently reverts to lawful use of the easement, his prior excessive use of it is then irrelevant."[127]

---

[123] [1949] Ch. 163.
[124] [1965] Ch. 538.
[125] [1970] 1 W.L.R. 1185; [1970] 2 All E.R. 587.
[126] *Woodhouse & Co v Kirkland Ltd* [1970] 1 W.L.R. 1185; [1970] 2 All E.R. 587 at 592a.
[127] per May L.J. in *Graham v Philcox* [1984] Q.B. 74; [1984] 2 All E.R. 643 at 649b.

More recently, however, it has been held that there may be a right to obstruct a way where there is substantial use beyond the terms of the grant, even though the effect is to prevent use for the permitted purposes and that this may be backed up by an injunction.[128] It is hard to see how this decision is consistent with the above quotation, which suggests that May L.J may have gone too far.

There are therefore three questions to be asked:

(1) is the use being made of the way of the type permitted by the grant? This will not not be the case if the change represents "a radical change in the character" or a "change in the identity of the site"[129];

(2) is it for a purpose permitted by the grant?[130]; and

(3) is the quantity of use of the extent contemplated by the grant and, if not, will the use of the site as redeveloped result in a substantial increase or alteration in the burden on the servient land?[131]

It is possible to describe use which is not for a permitted purpose as excessive user,[132] but as set out above this is really a different concept. What was new about *Jelbert v Davies*[133] was that user which was certainly within the terms of the grant was held to be unlawful, not because it was for the wrong purpose, or by the wrong means of transport, but because it was too frequent, but *McAdams Homes v Robinson*[134] tends to merge this concept in with the construction of the grant.

(4) Parking

18.22   It is important to distinguish between the right to stop as an incident to a right of way and the existence of a separate easement of parking.

A right of way has always been essentially a right of passage and it was not until *Bulstrode v Lambert*[135] that it was established that stopping on a right of way for the purposes of unloading could be a legitimate incident of a right of way. However, whether the dominant owner is entitled to stop and unload on the way depends on the circumstances. Where a right of way is granted which leads to a forecourt suitable for parking then the

---

[128] *Ashdale Land & Property Co Ltd v Maioriello* [2010] EWHC 3296 (Ch).
[129] *McAdams Homes Ltd v Robinson* [2004] EWCA Civ 214; [2005] 1 P. & C.R. 30.
[130] As considered in *Hotchkin v McDonald* [2004] EWCA Civ 519; [2005] 1 P. & C.R. 7.
[131] *McAdams Homes Ltd v Robinson* [2004] EWCA Civ 214; [2005] 1 P. & C.R. 30.
[132] *Jobson v Record* (1998) 75 P. & C.R. 375.
[133] [1968] 1 W.L.R. 589, [1968] 1 All E.R. 1182.
[134] [2004] EWCA Civ 214; [2005] 1 P. & C.R. 30.
[135] [1953] 1 W.L.R. 1064.

right of way does not imply a right to unload from the access way.[136] Equally, a right of way into a large unloading area does not include a right to wait on the right of way outside the area, just because of a policy of only allowing one lorry into the unloading area at a time.[137]

All these cases concerned commercial rights of way. The position in relation to domestic ways is open to question. Clearly stopping to unload on the way is permitted, as long as it does not substantially interfere with the use of others, but if this moves into parking on the way then different considerations apply.

Whether a right to park vehicles either on a roadway, or in a car park or in a designated parking space is capable of subsisting as an easement has long been subject to debate. Historically this was because parking only became an issue with the spread of the motor car in the twentieth century. No one would claim a right to park a horse and cart overnight on a right of way!

This issue has now been considered in detail and resolved by the House of Lords in *Moncrieff v Jamieson*.[138] This was a Scottish case, about servitudes, and the leading judgment, by Lord Hope, set out the Scottish authorities. However, Lord Scott and Lord Neuberger both gave substantive judgments and Lord Scott expressly stated[139]that:

"there seems to me no difference relevant to any issue that arises in this case between the common law in England and Wales relating to easement and the common law in Scotland relating to servitudes".

Under the heading "the right to park as a servitude" Lord Scott said:

"I can see no reason in principle, subject to a few qualifications[140] why any right of limited use of land of a neighbour that is of its nature of benefit to the dominant land and its owners from time to time should be capable of being created as a servitudal right *in rem* appertenant to the dominant land."

The qualifications he makes to that general statement are that a right which amounts to ownership or possession of the land is not an easement and that a right which requires substantial positive action by the owner of the servient tenement (e.g. a swimming pool) may be excluded.

He deals with the two principal objections to the right to park, namely "where to park" and "deprivation of ownership".

---

[136] *London and Suburban Land and Building Co (Holdings) Ltd v Carey* (1991) 62 P. & C.R. 480.
[137] *B&Q Plc v Liverpool & Lancashire Properties* (2001) 81 P. & C.R. 20.
[138] [2007] UKHL 42; [2007] 1 W.L.R. 2620.
[139] *Moncrieff v Jamieson* [2007] UKHL 42; [2007] 1 W.L.R. 2620 at [45].
[140] He refers specifically to the right to use a swimming pool, which depends on the servient owner keeping it filled with clean healthy water.

The latter has always been the strongest argument against an easement of parking and he rejects the proposition, put forward in *Batchelor v Marlow*[141] that

> "there would no use that could be made by an owner of land over which he had granted parking rights. He can use the land for parking his own vehicles, he can build under or over it."

It is all, he says a matter of *"civiliter"* which is, in essence, the principle of excessive user.

> "But it is the servient owner, not the respondents, who is in possession and control of the pink land and entitled to remain so. The respondents are entitled to do nothing with the pink land other than park vehicles on it, while the appellants are entitled to do what they like with the pink land provided they do not interfere with the respondent's right to park two cars there. For the reason I have given I regard the 'ouster' principles as inapplicable to this case"[142]

Both Lord Scott and Lord Neuberger[143] state that *Batchelor v Marlow*[144] was "probably wrongly decided" but both decline to overrule it. The reason for not doing so is that they accepted that in some circumstances a right to park might be so extensive as to amount to "ouster" of the servient owner.

The acceptance in principle of a right to park as an independent easement, as well as a right ancillary to a right of way, does not deal with all the issues relating to parking. Lord Scott was quite clear that:

> "There is no difference between the characteristics of an easement that can be acquired by grant and the characteristics of an easement that can be acquired by prescription".[145]

However, as stated in the previous section, there are different problems. An express grant has to be construed and will depend to a substantial extent on the wording of the grant. A prescriptive right arises from use and therefore is dependent on the nature and extent of the use. The most common circumstances in which a prescriptive right to park may arise is where a person has parked his vehicle on land adjoining his property belonging to another. This right is not an exclusive right. The dominant

---

[141] [2001] EWCA Civ 1051; [2003] 1 W.L.R. 764.
[142] *Moncrieff v Jamieson* [2007] UKHL 42; [2007] 1 W.L.R. 2620 per Lord Scott at [60].
[143] *Moncrieff v Jamieson* [2007] UKHL 42; [2007] 1 W.L.R. 2620 at [143].
[144] [2001] EWCA Civ 1051; [2003] 1 W.L.R. 764.
[145] *Moncrieff v Jamieson* [2007] UKHL 42; [2007] 1 W.L.R. 2620 at [59].

tenement may also make use of the same land for parking. It may or may not be on the same plot of land.

> "In my opinion where there is a block of flats and the tenants in general regularly park their cars within the curtilege of the block, the liberty, privilege, easement, right or advantage of being allowed to do this will rapidly become regarded as being something which appertains or is reputed to appertain to each of the flats in the black and as being reputed to be appurtenant to each of those flats."[146]

In those circumstances, the flat-owner will have to take his chance with other flat-owners for the available spaces. What is made clear by Lord Scott is that the extent of the use will be monitored and, if necessary can be controlled by injunction.

It may be that this is not the last word on the issue, but it is submitted that it does fit in with what a lay-man would expect, namely that, if he is granted a right to park on the land of his neighbour, then this is a right which would pass to his purchaser and that, if he parked on a patch of land for 20 years without permission, he would gain a prescriptive right which would also pass with his property.

(5) Repairing obligations

In the absence of a covenant or other agreement, or a provision in the **18.23** statute creating a statutory easement, there is no obligation either on the dominant or the servient owner to maintain a right of way. In this regard the position is much the same as with a right of support or a right to a watercourse. However, quite apart from any specific obligation, the dominant and servient owners have common law rights of action against each other. If the servient owner interferes with the dominant owner's right of way, the dominant owner has a cause of action for disturbance. Thus if the servient owner digs up the right of way and obstructs it, the dominant owner can sue. The dominant owner's cause of action is in nuisance and the general principles of nuisance also apply where the servient owner does something on the way which is not intended to obstruct it but which eventually does interfere with the dominant owner's use of the way. This was the case in *Saint v Jenner*[147] where the servient owner put down ramps in order to slow the use of the right of way. This in itself was not an obstruction, but as time went on potholes formed beside the ramps caused by vehicles as they went over the ramps. The Court of Appeal agreed that the servient owner was entitled to put and keep the ramps there on his undertaking to keep them in repair. If he had

[146] per Megarry V.C. in *Newman v Jones*. As case under s.62 of the Law of Property Act 1925.
[147] [1973] Ch. 275; [1973] 1 All E.R. 127.

not given the undertaking he would have had to remove them. The liability of the dominant owner is comparable. It is up to him to make the way in the first place[148] and thereafter he is under an obligation not to do anything which amounts to trespass. The most obvious situation (though it relates to water rights and not rights of way) is where the dominant owner has a watercourse or a right to install a water pipe. If he builds a watercourse with water control measures he is under an obligation not to allow them to get into a dangerous state.[149] Equally if he installs a pipe, he must not let it spring a leak.[150]

While the dominant owner is not normally under an obligation to carry out repairs, he may do so if he wishes. He may even improve the way providing that he does not prevent the servient owner from using it as he wishes.[151]

18.24   These rules do not, however, provide a complete solution to the practical problems that arise in respect of rights of way. Very often a way is used by both the dominant and the servient owner and there may be other people with a similar easement. If the way deteriorates by natural decay, the position seems clear. It is up to whoever wants it repaired to repair it. But what if the way is damaged by the user of the dominant or the servient owner? In an extreme case the dominant owner may be found guilty of excessive user.[152] *Saint v Jenner*[153] is a case where the servient owner actually put something on the road, but it seems on principle that use of the road which actually damages it could be seen as nuisance.

The more usual situation, however, is where the damage to the way is caused, not by natural decay or excessive user, but by normal use, whether by the dominant owner alone or by the dominant and the servient owner. In such a case neither party may wish to accept the full expense of repair. This is particularly true of ways shared by several dominant owners. The large number of neglected and potholed tracks leading to well-maintained houses is testimony to the fact that the law on this matter is not entirely satisfactory.

In such situations the law appears to be that whoever is responsible for the deterioration of the way cannot be forced to carry out repairs unless his user can be held to be "excessive".

18.25   The obvious answer to the problem is for there to be an agreement when the easement is granted about who shall pay to maintain it. Such

---

[148] *Ingram v Moorcroft* (1863) 33 Beav 49.
[149] *RH Buckley & Sons Ltd v N Buckley & Sons* [1898] 2 Q.B. 608.
[150] *Jones v Pritchard* [1908] 1 Ch. 630.
[151] *Todrick v Western National Omnibus Co Ltd* [1934] Ch. 561.
[152] *Jelbert v Davis* [1968] 1 W.L.R. 589.
[153] [1973] Ch. 275; [1973] 1 All E.R. 127.

agreements are commonly made, but this situation has not proved satisfactory either.[154]

A covenant to maintain a way or to pay a share of the cost of maintenance is a positive covenant. If it is a leasehold covenant it is enforceable providing there is privity of estate.[155] Where the use of stairs, lifts etc. is necessary for the tenants occupying dwellings in an office block, such an obligation can be implied as a matter of necessity, *Liverpool City Council v Irwin*.[156]

However, most rights of way are freehold, and a covenant to keep the road in repair or to contribute to its upkeep cannot be directly enforced against a successor in title of the original covenantor because it is a positive covenant and not a restrictive covenant.[157] It may also offend against the rule against perpetuities.[158]

Fortunately, in respect of rights of way, a way was found round this problem by Upjohn J. in *Halsall v Brizell*.[159] "It is an ancient law[160] that a man cannot take benefit under a deed without subscribing to the obligation thereunder". Accordingly if the dominant owner has covenanted to pay all or a proportion of the cost, he is not allowed to use the way unless he pays it.

This has in general proved a satisfactory solution to the problem, but it must be remembered that it only applies where there is an actual covenant to pay[161] and that it does not work if the dominant owner (or one of several obliged to pay a proportion of the cost) decides that he does not want to use the way.

It is also ineffective in those cases where the servient owner has agreed **18.26** to maintain the lane. Since he does not need to rely on an easement to exercise his right to use his own land it would seem that he could not be forced to carry out his obligations unless he is the original covenantor. This most commonly happens where the servient owner agrees to maintain the way and the dominant owners agree to contribute. The servient owner may not wish to embark on the expense of maintenance work unless he is assured that all the dominant owners will pay, and a single dominant owner will then find it difficult to enforce the covenant. Of course if the dominant owners are united they can carry out the repairs together for their own benefit, but one dominant owner of many may be

---

[154] See *Crane Properties LLP v Hundalani* [2006] EWHC 2066 (Ch) and, in relation to enforcement, Ch.12, s.8.
[155] *Miller v Hancock* [1893] 2 Q.B. 177; *Dunster v Hollis* [1918] 2 K.B. 795.
[156] [1977] A.C. 239; [1976] 2 All E.R. 39.
[157] *Austerberry v Oldham Corp* (1885) L.R. 29 Ch. D. 750.
[158] *Halsall v Brizell* [1957] Ch. 169.
[159] [1957] Ch. 169.
[160] See the quotation from Chaucer at para.10.01 above.
[161] *Four Oaks Estate Ltd v Hadley* (1986) 83 L.S.Gaz. 2326.

reluctant to embark on the full expense from which his neighbours will then benefit free of charge.

As in several other areas of the law of easements, it may be that there is scope for dealing with this problem under the tort of nuisance. In *Green v Lord Somerleyton*[162] the Court of Appeal, in relation to an easement of drainage, affirmed in strong terms the obligation of neighbours towards each other. It may be that to use a way without accepting responsibility for its repair could be treated as nuisance.

The principle that there is no obligation on either the dominant or the servient owner to repair has also given rise to a quite different problem. If a person using the right of way is injured because of its bad repair he will look for someone to sue.

The law in respect of injuries both on public and private rights of way was authoritatively reviewed by the House of Lords in *McGeown v Northern Ireland Housing Executive*[163] approving *Greenhalgh v British Railways Board*.[164] It was held that a person using a right of way, whether public or private, is using that right of way as of right and accordingly is not the visitor of the owner of the sub-soil, who cannot stop him even if he wishes.

> "Rights of way pass over many different types of terrain, and it would place an impossible burden upon landowners if they not only had to submit to the passage over them of anyone who might choose to exercise them but also were under a duty to maintain them in safe condition".[165]

Lord Browne-Wilkinson, while agreeing with the decision in that case, expressed concern about the factual situation. The roads and paths had been laid out by the owner of the sub-soil. Someone ought to be responsible for keeping them up and he expressly reserved his position on whether the owner of the soil could owe a duty of care to an invitee, as opposed to a licensee, using the public way.

It has also been suggested obiter that the dominant owner might possibly be the occupier for the purposes of the Act.[166] There is common sense to this approach since a person using a private right of way is doing so in order to visit the dominant owner, but it is difficult to see how the owner of an incorporeal hereditament can be an "occupier of premises" within s.1 of the Act. As the case concerned a public right of way, the position of the dominant owner was not dealt with in *McGeown v Northern Ireland Executive*.[167]

---

[162] [2003] EWCA Civ 198.
[163] [1995] 1 A.C. 233; [1994] 3 W.L.R. 187.
[164] [1969] 2 Q.B. 286.
[165] per Lord Keith in *McGeown v Northern Ireland Housing Executive* [1995] 1 A.C. 233; (1995) 70 P. & C.R. 10 at 15.
[166] *Holden v White* [1982] Q.B. 679; [1982] 2 All E.R. 328 at 333d per Oliver L.J.
[167] [1995] 1 A.C. 233; [1994] 3 W.L.R. 187.

The wider problems caused by the fact that positive covenants do not run with the land has been addressed by the Law Commission in *Making Land Work: Easements, Covenants and Profits à Prendre*.[168] They propose replacing covenants with a new legal interest in land called a "land obligation". The Report contains a draft Law of Property Bill, but this does not yet have parliamentary time set aside for it.

---

[168] Law Commission, *Making Land Work: Easements, Covenants and Profits à Prendre* (London: Stationery Office, 2011), Law Com. No.327.

Chapter Nineteen
Support

1. Natural rights of support

An easement of support is supplementary to the common law rights of **19.01** any owner or occupier of land. A parcel of land, even if it is undeveloped, cannot exist in isolation. It is supported laterally by neighbouring land so that excavation of the neighbouring land may result in the land and the buildings erected on it slipping into the hole.

There are many ways in which what happens on neighbouring land can affect the use of a person's land. This is the very basis of the common law of private nuisance. Specifically, damage to neighbouring land can take various forms including subsidence. Equally, damage due to withdrawal of support from the neighbouring land can be caused by acts of nature occurring on the neighbouring land. A natural landslide does not respect legal boundaries. Not only will the spoil from above fall upon the land below, but also the slide of the land below will cause the removal of the support of the land above.

The distinction has often been drawn in the past between damage **19.02** caused by nature and damage caused by the positive action of the owner or occupier of the land. The Court of Appeal has now authoritatively stated the current law in *Holbeck Hall Hotel Ltd v Scarborough BC*.[1] In that case a claimant's hotel was perched precariously close to an eroding cliff. The defendants owned the land between the hotel and the edge of the cliff. The claimant alleged that they had done insufficient to protect the cliff or to reduce the erosion. The Court of Appeal held that they owed a duty of care towards the neighbouring owner to prevent danger to his property, but that danger was limited to reasonable steps to counter patent risks.

This makes it clear that the law relating to withdrawal of the natural right of support from adjoining land is part of the general law of nuisance. The principle of *Sedleigh-Denfield v O'Callaghan*[2] is that when you know or

---

[1] [2000] Q.B. 836, [2000] 2 All E.R. 705.
[2] [1940] A.C. 880.

ought to have known of the possibility of something encroaching from your land onto your neighbour's, you have a duty to do what you reasonably can to prevent it. *Holbeck Hall Hotel Ltd v Scarborough BC* extends this principle not only to the risk of noxious substances escaping, or even something natural escaping, such as the potentially falling tump in *Leakey v National Trust for Places of Historic Interest or Natural Beauty,*[3] but also to the loss of support of the adjoining land.

This is an important development of the law and links in with cases such as *Home Home Brewery Co v Davis and Co*[4] and *Bradburn v Lindsay*[5] to establish a general principle that acts or omissions committed on your own land which result in damage to your neighbour's land can give rise to an action in nuisance, whether the damage is due to natural causes or not. The principle has been applied and extended in a series of recent cases, *LE Jones (Insurance Brokers) Ltd v Portsmouth City Council*[6] in respect of tree roots, *Green v Lord Somerleyton*[7] in respect of drainage of land, *Abbahall v Smee*[8] in respect of roof repairs and in *Rees v Skerrett,*[9] protection from the weather, where Lloyd J. said:

"The duty found to exist in *Leakey* is to do that which is reasonable in all the circumstances to prevent or minimise the known risk of damage to the neighbouring property".

This has caused a revolution in considering cases which would formerly have been decided against the claimant, on the basis that there was no easement of support or no breach of the obligations. Mummery L.J. acknowledged this in *Abbahall v Smee* where he said[10]:

"Time was when the claim would have been thought to be concluded against Abbahall by the observations in this court of Greene MR in *Bond v Norman, Bond v Nottingham Corp*[11] and of Lord Denning MR in *Phipps v Pears.*[12] Nowadays, however, matters have been transformed by the developments in the law of nuisance and negligence heralded by the decision of the Judicial Committee of the Privy Council in *Goldman v Hargrave*[13]—developments subsequently adopted and elucidated in the decisions of this court in *Leakey v National Trust for*

---

[3] [1980] Q.B. 485; [1980] 2 W.L.R. 65.
[4] [1987] Q.B. 339; [1987] 1 All E.R. 637.
[5] [1983] 2 All E.R. 408.
[6] [2002] EWCA Civ 1723; [2003] 1 W.L.R. 427.
[7] [2003] EWCA Civ 198.
[8] [2002] EWCA Civ 1831; [2003] 1 W.L.R. 1472.
[9] [2001] EWCA Civ 760; [2001] 1 W.L.R. 1541.
[10] *Abbahall Ltd v Smee* [2002] EWCA Civ 1831; [2003] 1 W.L.R. 1472 at [9].
[11] *Bond v Nottingham Corp* [1940] Ch. 429.
[12] *Phipps v Pears* [1965] 1 Q.B. 76; [1964] 2 W.L.R. 996.
[13] [1967] 1 A.C. 645; [1966] 3 W.L.R. 513.

Places of Historic Interest or Natural Beauty,[14] *Holbeck Hall Hotel Ltd v Scarborough BC,*[15] *Bybrook Barn Garden Centre Ltd v Kent CC*[16] and *Rees v Skerrett".*[17]

There are, however, limitations to this principle. The duty is a "measured duty of care".[18] Examples were given by Megaw L.J. in *Leakey v National Trust for Places of Historic Interest or Natural Beauty*[19]:

> "Take, by way of example, the hypothetical instance which I gave earlier: the landowner through whose land a stream flows. In rainy weather, it is known the stream may flood and the flood may spread to the land of neighbours. If the risk is one which can readily be over-come or lessened—for example by reasonable steps on the part of the landowner to keep the stream free from blockage by flotsam or silt carried down, he will be in breach of duty if he does nothing or does too little. But if the only remedy is substantial and expensive works, then it might well be that the landowner would have discharged his duty by saying to his neighbours, who also know of the risk and who have asked him to do something about it, "You have my permission to come on to my land and to do agreed works at your expense"; or, it may be, "on the basis of a fair sharing of expense."

This was the precise situation faced in *Lambert v Barratt Homes*[20] where Barratt Homes were primarily responsible for the flooding, but it came in part from land belonging to Rochdale MBC. The Court of Appeal over-turned the liability of Rochdale MBC and left the whole liability on Barratt Homes.

Essentially, where the actions of a neighbouring owner cause a with- **19.03** drawal of support and subsidence the problem is simply one of causation, but difficulties have arisen due to the old case of *Popplewell v Hodkinson.*[21] On the face of it, it did not seem a very alarming decision. The plaintiff built some cottages on land "of a wet and spongy character" with limited foundations. His neighbours were building a church and needed to dig deeper foundations. To do this they pumped out a lot of water. It was

---

[14] [1980] Q.B. 485; [1980] 2 W.L.R. 65.
[15] [2000] Q.B. 836; [2000] 2 W.L.R. 1396.
[16] [2001] L.G.R. 239, involving an overflowing culvert in a highway.
[17] [2001] EWCA Civ 760; [2001] 1 W.L.R. 1541.
[18] *Goldman v Hargrave* [1967] 1 A.C. 645; [1966] 3 W.L.R. 513.
[19] *Leakey v National Trust for Places of Historic Interest or Natural Beauty* [1980] Q.B. 485 at [20].
[20] [2010] EWCA Civ 681.
[21] (1868–69) L.R. 4 Ex. 248.

decided that there is nothing to stop a person drawing water on his own land "if for any reason it becomes necessary or convenient to do so".

This principle emanates from the rule that no-one owns water and that a person does not have a right to a flow of water which is not through a defined channel.[22] However, the difficulties inherent in the concept became clear in *Jordeson v Sutton Southcoates and Drypool Gas Co.*[23] In excavating the foundation of a new building the builders came across a layer of "running silt". Understandably they pumped this out, but this had the effect of causing subsidence on adjoining land. The neighbour's claim succeeded. As Lindley M.R. said,[24] "Two conflicting rights have to be reconciled-namely the right to support and the right to pump water". The Court decided that pumping out running silt amounted to pumping out wet silt rather than pumping out water with silt in it and was therefore able to distinguish *Popplewell v Hodkinson*. The truth is, of course, that no land is solely supported by water and that there is no real distinction between removal of support caused by pumping out water and removal of support caused by pumping out liquid minerals.

19.04   *Popplewell v Hodkinson*[25] has been more distinguished than followed but it was followed in *Langbrook Properties v Surrey CC.*[26] On the other hand, in *Lotus Ltd v British Soda*[27] it was held that pumping out brine which caused subsidence was actionable. *Popplewell v Hodkinson* was distinguished and to some extent doubted. *Lotus Ltd v British Soda Co Ltd* is to be contrasted with *Salt Union Ltd v Brunner Mond and Co,*[28] which is not a subsidence case, where the owner of a salt mine sought to claim nuisance against the person who was abstracting brine from his mines. The distinction between the two is that, whereas any person may extract water (including brine) from his land and thereby deprive the adjoining owner of a water supply on which he relies, he may not do so if the result is that adjoining land and buildings subside.

It is submitted that there is no logic to the distinction between subsidence caused by the extraction of water and subsidence caused by the extraction of brine, running silt, oozing asphalt[29] or any other substance. The law of nuisance is always a balance between the right of a landowner to exploit his land and the right of his neighbour not to be disturbed. Where the disturbance consists of actions which cause subsidence, the balance favours the neighbour whatever the nature of the action

---

[22] *Palmer v Bowman* [2000] 1 W.L.R. 842.
[23] [1899] 2 Ch. 217.
[24] *Jordeson v Sutton Southcoates and Drypool Gas Co* [1899] 2 Ch. 217 at 232.
[25] (1868–69) L.R. 4 Ex. 248.
[26] [1970] 1 W.L.R. 161; [1969] 3 All E.R. 1424.
[27] [1972] Ch. 123; [1971] 2 W.L.R. 7.
[28] *Salt Union Ltd v Brunner Mond and Co* [1906] 2 K.B. 822.
[29] See *Trinidad Asphalt Co v Ambard* (1899) A.C. 594.

complained of. It applies, therefore, even to a case where the subsidence is caused by the shrinkage of clay due to evaporation caused by the removal of an adjoining building, *Brace v South East Regional Housing Association*.[30] In that case *Popplewell v Hodkinson* was again distinguished and treated without enthusiasm. It seems that the new approach culminating in *Holbeck Hall v Scarborough BC*[31] means that whatever the cause of the withdrawal of support, the courts will be keen to ensure that no one's land is damaged by the acts or omissions of his neighbour.

The natural right of support applies not only to adjoining land, but also to subjacent land. The surface land, therefore, has a natural right of support from the minerals below,[32] just as an upstairs flat has a right of support from the flat below.[33] However, where there is a licence to mine coal under the Coal Industry Act 1994, s.38 removes the natural right of support and anyone suffering loss as a result of subsidence has to seek redress under the Coal Mining Subsidence Act 1991.[34]

The cause of action only arises when actual subsidence is caused. Accordingly a landowner is not entitled to take action on his own land to avoid the consequences of possible subsidence caused by excavation on neighbouring land.[35] The Court of Appeal acknowledged that this was a difficult problem, since an adjoining owner cannot be expected to wait around while his property is at risk of collapse, but equally an owner who fears subsidence cannot spend large sums on speculative work and then charge his neighbour for it. The correct procedure is to bring proceedings for a quia timet injunction which may, in appropriate circumstances, give rise to a mandatory injunction requiring the neighbour either to fill in the excavation or to provide adequate shoring.[36]

2. Easement of support

It is rare that the landowner is primarily concerned about damage **19.05** to his land itself. More often he is concerned about damage to the buildings erected on his land. It has always been accepted that the right of action for the withdrawal of the natural right of support applies as much to withdrawal of support from buildings as to the land on which they stand.[37]

---

[30] (1984) 270 E.G. 1286.
[31] *Holbeck Hall Hotel Ltd v Scarborough BC* [2000] Q.B. 836, [2000] 2 All E.R. 705.
[32] *Davis v Treharne* (1880–81) L.R. 6 App. Cas. 460.
[33] *Dalton v Angus* (1880–81) L.R. 6 App. Cas. 740.
[34] See *McAreavey v Coal Authority* (2000) 80 P. & C.R. 41 decided under the 1957 Act.
[35] *Midland Bank Plc v Bardgrove Property Services Ltd* (1993) 65 P. & C.R. 153.
[36] *Redland v Morris* [1970] A.C. 652; [1969] 2 All E.R. 576.
[37] e.g. the prospective damage to the hotel in *Holbeck Hall Hotel Ltd v Scarborough BC* [2000] Q.B. 836; [2000] 2 All E.R. 705.

However, by constructing buildings on his land a landowner may be putting an additional burden on the adjoining land. The excavation carried out by the adjoining owner might have been completely harmless if there had been no buildings on the land affected, but because of the additional burden placed by the existing buildings, the excavation causes subsidence.[38]

If there is no easement of support, the adjoining owner, subject to the principles of nuisance set out above, is under no obligation to ensure that a building erected on the neighbouring land does not fall down.[39] However, even in the absence of an easement of support, the person carrying out the works must be careful to interfere as little as possible with the stability of the adjoining building, though he need not take any active steps such as shoring up. In New Zealand, however, it has been held that an independent contractor who removes support from a building which does not have an easement of support nevertheless owes a duty of care to the adjoining owner,[40] and this has since been extended to a general duty of care owed towards the owner of the neighbouring building (whether the work is being done by an independent contractor or by the landowner himself).[41]

19.06   Unsurprisingly the modern cases of *Leakey v National Trust for Places of Historic Interest or Natural Beauty*[42] and *Holbeck Hall Hotel Ltd v Scarborough BC*[43] do not deal with the law relating to easements of support. However, the developing principle that the owner of land owes a duty towards his neighbour indicates that the view adopted in New Zealand might well be accepted in England. If an adjoining owner owes a duty of care not to damage, by act or omission the land and buildings of his neighbour, the importance of an easement of support is correspondingly reduced. Nevertheless, there is a case for saying that a building that leans on a neighbour's building is asking for trouble and, until an easement has been established, deserves little legal protection. In *Dalton v Angus*,[44] after exhaustive argument, the House of Lords decided in favour of the concept of an easement of support which arises after a new or altered building has been in position for 20 years.

There has been much discussion about the nature of the right that arises. Lord Denning M.R. explained the principles very clearly in *Phipps v Pears*[45]:

---

[38] *Ray v Fairway Motors* (1969) 20 P. & C.R. 261.
[39] *Southwark & Vauxhall Water Co v Wandsworth District Board of Works* [1898] 2 Ch. 603.
[40] *Keegan v Young* [1963] N.Z.L.R. 720.
[41] *Bognuda v Upton & Shearer* [1972] N.Z.L.R. 741.
[42] [1980] Q.B. 485.
[43] [2000] Q.B. 836; [2000] 2 All E.R. 705.
[44] (1880–81) L.R. 6 App. Cas. 740.
[45] [1965] 1 Q.B. 76 quoted in *Rees v Skerrett* [2001] EWCA Civ 760 at [19].

"There are two kinds of easement known to the law: positive easements, such as a right of way, which give the owner of land a right himself to do something on or to his neighbour's land: and negative easements which give him a right to stop his neighbour doing something on his (the neighbour's) land. The right of support does not fit neatly into either category. It seems in some way to partake of the nature of a positive easement rather than a negative easement. The one building, by its weight, exerts a thrust, not only downwards but sideways on to the adjoining building or the adjoining land, and is thus doing something to the neighbour's land, exerting thrust on it: see *Dalton v Angus*."

Phipps v Pears rejected the concept of a right of protection from the weather but in *Rees v Skerrett*[46] the Court of Appeal re-assessed the nature of the right by accepting a further kind of easement of support which it called "wind support":

"Whereas, weight pressures operate on the structure continuously, being kept in equilibrium by the adjoining structure, the pressure from the effects of the weather is something to which, while the adjoining structure is in place, the dominant tenement is just not exposed."[47]

It may be that the development of the right of natural support has reduced the necessity for developing the principle of an easement of support, but it is clear from this case that it can still be valuable in cases where the property has indeed been supported by an adjoining or subjacent property for the 20 year period.

For the most part, the problem arises where a building has been constructed which leans against an adjoining building[48] although the easement also applies to a right of support of buildings by the adjoining land. The most obvious example of the problem is the terraced or semi-detached house. Quite apart from the existence of party walls[49] (now covered by the Party Walls etc. Act 1996), the stability of the houses themselves will depend on the presence and structural soundness of the house next door. Remove that support and the whole structure (and not just party walls) will be affected. This is all the more the case for subjacent support, where a flat or flying freehold is in practice totally supported by the property below.

---

[46] [2001] EWCA Civ 760; [2001] 1 W.L.R. 1541.
[47] per Lloyd J. at [33].
[48] *Lemaitre v Davis* (1881–82) L.R. 19 Ch. D. 281.
[49] See Ch. 6.

3.   Creation of easement of support

19.07   An easement of support can be created in the same ways as any other easement. It is common form now for a sale of a flat to contain a grant of rights of support though these are usually in rather general terms, for example:

> "the right of subjacent and lateral support and protection from [the Grantor's Land], including any party walls or structures, to support, uphold and maintain the buildings on [the Grantee's Land]."[50]

Such rights are not, however, so often spelt out in the case of terraced houses, especially older ones.

It is important to remember that such an express grant of a right of support is subject to the same limitations as a prescriptive right. It does not, therefore, automatically include a right to protection from the weather and it does not place any obligation upon the servient owner to keep the premises in repair.

This problem was faced head-on in *Abbahall v Smee*[51] which involved a freehold flat. The Court of Appeal bypassed any question of an easement of support. In the words of Mummery L.J.:

> "The law of easements may provide Abbahall with no remedy but the modern law of nuisance and negligence does."[52]

The problem related to the roof and the Court concluded that:

> "In a case such as this, where the roof serves equally to protect both the claimant's premises and the defendant's premises, common sense, common justice and reasonableness as between neighbours surely all suggest that those who are to take the benefit of the works ought also to shoulder the burden of paying for them."[53]

In *Abbahall v Smee* there were no covenants. In the case of a block of flats, the need for the adjoining property to be kept in repair is covered by the lessor's covenant to keep the common parts in repair and to enforce the repairing covenants by the other flat-owners. It would appear that this creates a local law for the premises, so that the specific provisions

---

[50] *Encyclopedia of Forms & Precedents*, 5th edn (London: Butterworths, 1991), Vol.13(1), para.1798, Form 200.
[51] [2002] EWCA Civ 1831; [2003] 1 W.L.R. 1472.
[52] At [19].
[53] per Mummery L.J. at [38].

of the covenant may override the more general "common justice" of the tort of nuisance.

Where there is such a covenant, the problem is still a real one. If an adjoining flat is allowed to fall into disrepair, this may allow damp to penetrate into other flats and, in the end, could involve a withdrawal of the support to the flat and resulting structural damage. To have to enforce this right by means of an action against the landlord for failing to enforce the lessee's covenants to him is unwieldy and can involve problems where the landlord is unknown, or is for some reason unwilling or unable to act. This is a problem which would be solved if the right of support involved a positive duty to keep in repair. There seems no reason why the recent law on a general duty of care should not extend to leasehold flats where there are existing covenants enforceable by the landlord.

Where a flat is conveyed freehold, the burden of the covenant to repair does not pass with the land and has to be included in a Deed of Covenant. One of the objects of the new commonhold system[54] is to ensure that the unit-holders have control of the whole building through the commonhold association, which is a company registered by guarantee, and can therefore enforce the covenants. The situation where there is an easement of support but no binding covenant to repair is considered below.[55]

In the absence of express grant, rights of support may be created by **19.08** implied grant or reservation. They will pass under s.62 of the Law of Property Act 1925 or under the Rule in *Wheeldon v Burrows*,[56] providing that the support exists at the time of the conveyance. Reservations, as opposed to grants, of easements of support are not usually implied, but a reservation of support will be implied where the rights are mutual[57] or where they are "necessary", but this will not be so in all cases where there is an existing de facto support, *Union Lighterage Co v London Graving Dock*.[58]

Where the building requiring the support is constructed after the conveyance or lease, the owner is thrown back on non-derogation from grant in the case of a lease and the uncertain concept of an easement implied from the circumstances in the case of a freehold conveyance.[59]

In the absence of express or implied grant, the easement must be obtained by prescription either under the Prescription Act 1832 or under

---

[54] Commonhold and Leasehold Reform Act 2002, in force from July 14, 2004—Commonhold and Leasehold Reform Act 2002 (Commencement No.4) Order 2004 (SI 2004/1832).

[55] See para.19.10.

[56] [1879] L.R. 12 Ch. D. 31.

[57] *Re Webbs Lease* [1951] Ch. 808; [1951] 2 All E.R. 131 at 141F per Jenkins L.J.; *Jones v Pritchard* [1908] 1 Ch. 630.

[58] [1902] 2 Ch. 557.

[59] See above paras 13.25–13.31.

the doctrine of lost modern grant.[60] In either case it is necessary for the support to have continued openly for a period of 20 years or more.

There is obviously a possibility that an adjoining building will be supported by the building next door for many years without the potential servient owner ever being aware of what is happening. This problem was addressed in *Lloyds Bank Ltd v Dalton*[61] where it was held, following *Lemaitre v Davis*,[62] that a reasonable owner would have been aware of the likelihood that the dominant building was being supported, even though it could not be seen from the servient tenement or the road. The decision was, however, based on the lie of the land and the way in which the plaintiffs' yard had been built. It leaves open the possibility that in an appropriate case an easement of support might be held not to have arisen because the servient owner could not be expected to realise that there was a building receiving support.

19.09   The easement must also be exercised "as of right". So where there were deeds passing between the dominant and servient owners which virtually amounted to an admission that there was no easement, the presence of the building cannot be said to have been exercising an easement as of right, *Tone v Preston*.[63]

One of the problems that arise is where buildings are altered. Adding to an existing structure can increase the load on the supporting building, so that a withdrawal of support, which would have made no difference to the building originally, then causes the altered building to fall.

This problem was considered in *Dalton v Angus*,[64] where the court held that the prescriptive right arose where the building was newly built or altered so as to increase the lateral pressure. Therefore, where there has been a significant increase in the support required, the 20 year period starts again. When this happens, however, do the existing rights of support disappear completely, or do they continue to exist until subsumed in the greater right at the end of the period of 20 years from the date of the alterations? In *Ray v Fairway Motors*[65] there was a wall which had a prescriptive right of support from the soil of the neighbouring land. Within the 20 year period prior to the action a shed was built using the existing wall as one of its sides. Excavations caused damage to the wall, which would still have been damaged if the shed had never been there. It was held that there was interference with the right of support. Russell L.J. said:

---

[60] *Dalton v Angus* (1880–81) L.R. 6 App. Cas. 740.
[61] [1942] Ch. 466.
[62] (1881–82) L.R. 19 Ch. D. 281.
[63] (1883) L.R. 24 Ch. D. 739.
[64] *Dalton v Angus* (1880–81) L.R. 6 App. Cas. 740.
[65] (1969) 20 P. & C.R. 261.

"As to the easement, where the structure in respect of which the easement of support had been acquired remained in position and all that happened was the leaning on it of an additional structure, the easement was not to be considered released or extinguished unless the additional support required would (if claimable in law) impose a substantial additional restriction on the use to which the servient tenement could be put or upon legitimate activities thereon."

This quotation implies that where (as was not the case in *Ray v Fairway Motors*)[66] there is a substantially increased burden, the existing easement simply comes to an end, and the court will not attempt the theoretical exercise of deciding whether the structure would have suffered the same damage had there been no alterations.

4.   Repair

It has been stated many times that an easement of support does not **19.10** include an obligation upon the servient owner to keep the supporting building in repair.[67] It must be remembered that in most cases the dominant owner has not paid anything for the privilege of being supported by his neighbour's building, and accordingly it was considered unreasonable to require the servient owner to do anything positive to protect his neighbour's property.

This rule, however, brings its own problems. The owner of a terraced house, or a flat, is at the mercy of his neighbours. Neglect of the neighbouring property can cause a mass of problems, including not only loss of support from the adjoining building falling down, but also such problems as penetrating damp and dry rot.

With regard to boundary walls the problem has been addressed by the Party Wall etc. Act 1996, which provides a comprehensive system for dealing with development or repair of boundary walls. It follows the London Building Acts (now repealed) in applying the same principles to all walls which are on the line of the junction between the adjoining properties.[68] The effect of this Act is that an owner who suffers damage or potential damage as a result of disrepair of a boundary wall is best advised to seek to deal with it by taking positive steps to repair and seeking compensation from the adjoining owner. This is dealt with fully in Chapter Six.

The alternative solution, which applies to all aspects of adjoining property is to bring an action in nuisance. In *Holbeck Hall Hotel Ltd v Scarborough BC*,[69] the Court of Appeal developed the law relating to escape of

---

[66] (1969) 20 P. & C.R. 261.
[67] *Jones v Pritchard* [1908] 1 Ch. 630; *Bond v Nottingham Corp* [1940] Ch. 429.
[68] Party Wall etc. Act 1996 ss.1 & 20.
[69] [2000] Q.B. 836; [2000] 2 All E.R. 705.

"noxious substances" and the duty of care in *Sedleigh-Denfield v O'Callaghan*[70] together with *Home Brewery v Davis and Co*[71] to develop a general principle that acts or omissions committed on your own land which result in damage to your neighbour's land, can amount to nuisance.[72]

The court made a distinction between patent and latent defects. If the defect was known, or presumed known, and the danger to the claimant's land was reasonably foreseeable, there is an actionable nuisance. If the defect is latent there is a duty if the defect was discoverable on reasonable investigation. However, the duty is a measured duty depending on factors including the ease and expense of abatement, the ability of the defendant to achieve it and the extent of the foreseen damage.

The principle was applied to roof repairs within a block of freehold flats in *Abbahall v Smee*,[73] but if it applies to subjacent freehold properties it must apply equally to adjacent properties regardless of whether the problem is lack of support, damage by wind and weather or infestation by dry rot.

This is wide enough to cover most problems which arise on neighbouring land. It is, of course, a less reliable method than using the Party Wall etc. Act 1996, since it is necessary to prove negligence, but it can be used in cases where the cause of the problem is not a boundary wall.

19.11   The Access to Neighbouring Land Act 1992 has become largely redundant. A person with a right of support is now entitled to apply for an access order to enable him to go onto the servient tenement, but only for the purpose of carrying out repairs to his own property. It does not resolve the problem where the servient tenement itself has fallen into disrepair.

---

[70] [1940] A.C. 880.
[71] [1987] Q.B. 339; [1987] 1 All E.R. 637.
[72] See above para.19.02.
[73] [2002] EWCA Civ 1831; [2003] 1 W.L.R. 1472.

Chapter Twenty
Light

1. Meaning of the right of light

Every owner of land has the right or liberty to make use of the light **20.01** which comes onto his property. Like air or water it does not belong to anyone:

> "Light, like air, is the common property of all, or, to speak more accurately, it is the common right of all to enjoy it, but it is the exclusive property of none".[1]

On the other hand at common law everyone has a right or liberty to build on his land and this may affect the access of light to adjoining properties. Open land is lit mainly from direct light coming from above, but windows are usually vertical and if they are near the adjoining property much of the light coming into them comes from that property. The construction of a high building on adjoining land can have a drastic effect.

A person who buys a house expects that the windows in the house will not be blocked off by the erection of a large building next door. On the other hand, there is no reason why a landowner should be able to blight adjoining land by erecting a building with windows overlooking his neighbour and then claiming that his light should not be diminished. There are, therefore, competing rights and expectations which the courts have to resolve.

Despite Lord Halsbury's reference to a common right for all to enjoy light, there is no natural right of light which is automatically incidental to the ownership or occupation of land in the way that there is a natural right of support of land by adjoining land. It has been long established, for example in *Potts v Smith*,[2] that, in the absence of an easement, it is not a nuisance to obstruct your neighbour's light and, furthermore, that it is not automatically a breach of the implied covenant of quiet enjoyment for

[1] per Earl of Halsbury in *Colls v Home & Colonial Stores Ltd* [1904] A.C. 179 at 182.
[2] (1868) L.R. 6 Eq. 311.

a lessor to lease adjoining land in such a way that it obstructs the right of light.

20.02   Whilst there is no automatic common law right not to have the light coming onto the property diminished, the fact is that over the centuries people have constructed buildings close to their boundary in such a way that the windows depend on light coming from the adjoining property, and expect that such light will continue. So the courts developed the concept of an easement of light, which gives the owner or occupier of the land a right to access of light over his neighbour's land to specific existing windows or other apertures. Where this easement derives from prescription it is sometimes known as "ancient lights". It is significant that the right is to "ancient lights", meaning ancient windows, and not to ancient light.

20.03   An easement of light therefore applies to buildings and not to land in general. It applies to all buildings including greenhouses[3] and covered timber yards.[4] The Prescription Act 1832 refers to "any dwelling house, workshop or other building". It has been suggested that "other building" should be construed eiusdem generis with "dwelling house or workshop" and, in *Clifford v Holt*,[5] it was accepted that "building" does not include everything built. However, there seems no reason why the Act should not apply to any edifice which has windows or other apertures, at least if it has a roof.[6] Even if the Prescription Act were restrictively construed so as to exclude some buildings, the doctrine of lost modern grant is not restricted by the statutory definition and would apply to any such erection.

The rule that the easement applies only to buildings, as opposed to open space, does not seem to have caused many problems in practice. However, it means, for example, that if a person's garden is affected by a new building, the garden's owner has no right of action, even if a patio loses its sunshine or the vegetable patch loses its direct sunlight.

The easement does not apply to a right of prospect. However much a person cherishes his view and however long he enjoys it, he cannot stop a building which blocks off the view, unless it affects the access of light to his windows.

The right is to a shaft or cone of light which can be interrupted at any point by a window. Accordingly, if you brought the window forward and upwards it would still be receiving the same light, *Scott v Pape*[7]:

---

[3] *Allen v Greenwood* [1980] Ch. 119; [1979] 1 All E.R. 819.
[4] *Harris v de Pinna* (1886) L.R. 33 Ch. D. 238.
[5] [1899] 1 Ch. 698.
[6] See *Collis v Laugher* [1894] 3 Ch. 659.
[7] (1886) L.R. 31 Ch. D. 554.

"The access and use of light depends upon the number of pencils of light which come directly or by refraction into that window."[8]

Scott v Pape[9] was decided before Colls v Home & Colonial Stores Ltd,[10] which emphasises more the extent to which light has been diminished, rather than the amount that is left. Nevertheless in Andrews v Waite,[11] the idea that the right depends on the identity of the light rather than of the window was held not to have been affected by Colls v Home & Colonial Stores Ltd.[12]

The right to light is through an opening and not, for example, to an open-sided timber yard where sometimes the timber is stacked too high to obtain any light and at other times is open.[13] Equally no easement of light arises through a door which is normally kept closed,[14] or a blocked window,[15] although it does apply to a glazed door.[16]

The sun does not only produce light. It also produces heat and "other energising properties"[17] together with infra red and ultra violet rays. It was acknowledged in Allen v Greenwood,[18] contrary to views previously expressed,[19] that an easement can be obtained not just to light, but to the rays of the sun. This means that the right can involve a right to direct sunlight.

20.04 The light coming through a window consists of both direct and reflected light. Both of these will contribute to the impression of lightness of the room as will the internal decoration. The problem is that an adjoining owner cannot be required to keep a particular surface on the walls and the servient owner may decide to change the decoration of his internal walls. It was said in Dent v Auction Mart Co[20] that an adjoining owner cannot be required to keep glazed tiles on his building, but the problem goes much deeper than that. A nearby building with light coloured rendering may reflect a great deal more light than a building built of dark red brick. For this reason the expert approach has been to concentrate on direct daylight and "the sky factor" rather than the amount of light perceived by an ordinary person on an ordinary day or

---

[8] per Cotton L.J. at 568.
[9] (1886) L.R. 31 Ch. D. 554.
[10] [1904] A.C. 179.
[11] [1907] 2 Ch. 500.
[12] Colls v Home & Colonial Stores Ltd [1904] A.C. 179.
[13] Harris v de Pinna (1886) L.R. 33 Ch. D. 238.
[14] Levet v Gas, Light & Coke Co [1919] 1 Ch. 24.
[15] Tamares (Vincent Square) Ltd v Fairpoint Properties (Vincent Square) Ltd [2006] EWHC 3589 (Ch); [2007] 1 W.L.R. 2148.
[16] Carr-Saunders v Dick McNeil Associates Ltd [1986] 1 W.L.R. 922.
[17] per Goff L.J. in Allen v Greenwood [1980] Ch. 119; [1979] 1 All E.R. 819 at 827e.
[18] [1980] Ch. 119; [1979] 1 All E.R. 819.
[19] See B. Anstey, M. Chavasse, Right to Light: Easement of Light (Estates Gazette Ltd, 1963).
[20] (1866) L.R. 2 Eq. 238.

even the level of light shown by a light meter. There is no appellate authority for this approach, although it was approved by Upjohn J. at first instance in *Cory v City of London Real Property Co*,[21] but it has been accepted in practice by the courts[22] with the reservation that, while the expert evidence is helpful, it cannot be allowed to become a rigid formula.[23] In *Smith v Evangelization Society*[24] there is some discussion about the difference between vertical and horizontal light.

It must be remembered, furthermore, that there can be a right to an exceptional amount of light.[25] The issue turns, in the end, on the effect that the new building has on the neighbour's ability to use his building and not on the nature of the light obstructed.

A right of light is said to be a negative easement. This means that it does not allow the dominant owner to do anything on the servient tenement. It just restricts what the dominant owner can do on his land.

2.   Creation of easement of light

20.05   Like other easements, rights of light can be created by express or implied grant or reservation or by prescription.

(a)   Express grant

20.06   It is not standard conveyancing procedure to make express grants of rights of light, even when the conveyance is of a new building which depends on light from land retained by the vendor. In a building estate, the usual method of protecting the light to the proposed buildings has been to include covenants restricting the buildings and other erections that can be constructed on the adjoining land.[26] There are, however, precedents for granting express rights of light, both generally and in respect of specific windows, in the Encyclopaedia of Form and Precedents[27] and express grants of a right of light are increasingly common, particularly in office or commercial developments.[28] Despite some doubts expressed in the past[29] it seems clear that such express grants are valid. Overlying the common law, there is, of course, the whole structure of planning law

---

[21] Unreported, 1954
[22] See *Regan v Paul Properties* [2006] EWHC 1941 (Ch).
[23] See *Carr-Saunders v Dick McNeil Associates Ltd* [1986] 1 W.L.R. 922; [1986] 2 All E.R. 888.
[24] *Smith v Evangelization Society* (Inc) Trust [1933] Ch. 515.
[25] *Allen v Greenwood* [1980] Ch. 119; [1979] 1 All E.R. 819 see below p.360.
[26] *Potts v Smith* (1868) L.R. 6 Eq. 311.
[27] *Encyclopaedia of Form and Precedents*, 5th edn (London: Butterworths, 1991), Vol.13(1) paras 1670–4 including a right to enter premises to paint a wall white.
[28] *Frogmore Developments v Shirayama Shokusan Co* [2000] 1 E.G.L.R. 121 where an express grant of a right of light was construed in favour of the dominant owner and not restricted by the fact that the parties contemplated development on the site (the old London County Hall) at the time of the lease.
[29] See, e.g. *Hall v Lichfield Brewery Co* (1880) 49 L.J. Ch. 655.

which will normally be used to prevent buildings being erected which block off a neighbour's light and may also protect the neighbour's view. Restrictive covenants can also be used to restrict buildings which would be likely to affect the light when adjoining land is sold.

(b)   Implied grant or reservation

An easement of light can be obtained by implied grant or reservation **20.07** either under the rule in *Wheeldon v Burrows* or under s.62 of the Law of Property Act 1925. It was held in *Birmingham, Dudley and District Banking Co v Ross*[30] that an easement of light is not created simply by selling someone a property with buildings on it which have existing windows. The rationale of that decision was that s.62 applied to easements which were already appurtenant to the property and did not create new easements.

Since this decision it has been settled that s.62 applies to "quasi-easements de facto enjoyed in respect of it by one part of the land over another",[31] at least where the two parcels of land are in different occupation.[32] Accordingly in *Lyme Valley Squash Club v Newcastle under Lyme Borough Council*[33] it was held that the conveyance included by implication under s.62 an easement of light to the windows similar to the right which was being de facto enjoyed at the time of the conveyance, even though the windows had not been there for 20 years. This approach was followed in *Midtown Ltd v City of London Real Property Co Ltd*.[34]

Birmingham, Dudley and District Banking Co v Ross[35] was distinguished in *Lyme Valley Squash Club v Newcastle under Lyme Borough Council*[36] on the grounds that:

> "it was known to the owner of the windows in that case that the land on the other side of the passage would be developed".

However, in *Broomfield v Williams*[37] it was held that the sale of land included all lights de facto enjoyed with the house even though it had not been there 20 years and the adjoining land retained was described as "building land". The basis of that decision was that while the purchasers knew that the adjoining land was building land, they had no reason to

---

[30] *Birmingham, Dudley and District Banking Co v Ross* (1888) L.R. 38 Ch. D. 295 followed in *Godwin v Schweppes* [1902] 1 Ch. 926.
[31] per Jenkins L.J. in *Wright v MacAdam* [1949] 2 K.B. 744 at 748; see above para.13.04 et seq.
[32] *Payne v Inwood* (1997) 74 P. & C.R. 42.
[33] [1985] 2 All E.R. 405.
[34] [2005] EWHC 33 (Ch).
[35] (1888) L.R. 38 Ch. D. 295.
[36] [1985] 2 All E.R. 405.
[37] [1897] 1 Ch. 602.

believe that the buildings to be constructed on it would affect their own light.

Broomfield v Williams was a case where the two parcels of land were in the same ownership and occupation. This was treated as a special rule applying only to rights of light in *Sovmots Investments Ltd Developments v Secretary of State for the Environment*[38] and *Payne v Inwood*[39] but there is no obvious reason why different considerations should apply between rights of light and other easements. In *Frogmore Developments v Shirayama Shokusan*[40] it was made clear that the fact that development is contemplated will not override an express grant of a right of light and air.

The present law is not entirely clear, especially as *Lyme Valley Squash Club v Newcastle under Lyme Borough Council*[41] is a first instance decision. It seems likely that where there is a conveyance or lease of an existing building or where the vendor or lessor himself retains an existing building, there will be an implied grant or reservation of an easement of light in respect of all existing windows (unless it is made clear in the conveyancing documents that the intention is that such rights should not pass, or unless implied rights are expressly excluded by the terms of the instrument). This view of the law fits in with the modern interpretation of s.62 generally.

20.08   Where the building is yet to be constructed at the time of the conveyance the problem, as with all easements, is the extent to which an easement can be implied from the circumstances; even though it cannot be said to be appurtenant to the land or "usual and apparent" at the date of the conveyance. This problem is dealt with in respect of all easements in Chapter 13 and the same considerations apply to easements of light and to any other easement. The other possibility is that there might be a claim that the easement is granted under the doctrine of non-derogation from grant.[42]

The reverse problem arises where the conveyance seeks to exclude easements. This has to be considered on the basis that it amounts to consent or agreement under s.3 of the Prescription Act 1832 and is considered below.[43]

(c)   Non-derogation from grant

20.09   It is often difficult to distinguish between the principles of implied grant and non-derogation from grant.[44] *Lyme Valley Squash Club v Newcastle*

---

[38] [1979] A.C. 144; [1977] 2 All E.R. 385 at 398a per Lord Edmund-Davies.
[39] *Payne v Inwood* (1997) 74 P. & C.R. 42.
[40] *Frogmore Developments Ltd v Shirayama Shokusan* Co [2000] 1 E.G.L.R. 121.
[41] [1985] 2 All E.R. 405.
[42] See below para.20.09.
[43] See below para.20.11.
[44] See above para.13.25.

under Lyme Borough Council[45] was decided primarily on the basis of non-derogation from grant, but the court found that there was also an implied grant under s.62 of the Law of Property Act 1925. It does not seem that there is any significant additional right coming from non-derogation from grant, which is not equally covered by an implied grant under s.62 of the Law of Property Act 1925 except perhaps where the building has not been constructed at the time of the lease or conveyance.

Non-derogation from grant tends to apply most significantly in leasehold cases where the purpose for which the lease is made is more likely to appear on the face of the lease. In *Potts v Smith*[46] it was held that there was no breach of the covenant for quiet enjoyment when a wall was erected by a neighbouring leaseholder obstructing a window less than 20 years old, but that decision was before the Law of Property Act 1925 or the Conveyancing Act 1881. It may be that if this case came before the courts today it would be held that there was an implied grant of a right of light under s.62. It is also possible that such an action on the lessor's land could be treated as a derogation from grant.

(d)   Prescription

The Prescription Act 1832 has a specific section dealing with rights of **20.10** light:

> "Section 3 ... When the access and use of light to and for any dwelling house, workshop, or other building shall have been actually enjoyed therewith for the full period of 20 years without interruption, the right thereto shall be deemed absolute and indefeasible, any local usage or custom to the contrary notwithstanding, unless it shall appear that the same was enjoyed by some consent or agreement expressly made or given for that purpose by deed or writing."

Unlike other sections of the Prescription Act, this section does not apply to the Crown.

Although the section seems to suggest that once the right has been exercised for 20 years, it becomes an indefeasible right which can only be lost by express or implied release, it was held in *Colls v Home & Colonial Stores Ltd*[47] that this was subject to s.4 which requires that any period shall be deemed and taken to be the period next before some suit or action. Accordingly, the right is inchoate until there is an action and it is then necessary to show 20 years continuous use in the period immediately

[45] [1985] 2 All E.R. 405.
[46] (1869) L.R. 6 Eq. 311.
[47] [1904] A.C. 179.

before. The only importance of the reference to "absolute and indefeasible" is that time is not interrupted when the servient tenement is owned by a person under a disability.

An easement of light can also be obtained after 20 years under the doctrine of lost modern grant. The requirement of 20 years user up to the date of the action does not apply to lost modern grant. Usually, allowing the construction of a building which obstructs the light without objection would in itself amount to an implied release unless the action is brought promptly. Lost modern grant is, however, relevant, for example, in cases where an exceptional amount of light is used for 20 years but then this special use ceases at some time before the action is brought or if there has been a discontinuance of user (as opposed to an obstruction) which falls short of an implied release.

There is a special custom of the City of London that rights of light cannot be obtained by prescription. This was overridden by s.3 of the Prescription Act 1832 which specifically states "any local usage or custom to the contrary notwithstanding", but if, for any reason, the section cannot be relied on, the alternative of lost modern grant or common law prescription does not apply within the very limited area comprising the City of London.

It is accepted that user by a lessee accrues to the benefit of the freehold owner.[48] The problems presented by this principle were addressed but not resolved in *Midtown v City of London Property Co.*[49] There were two separate actions. The freehold title was with *Midtown* and created no problems, but it appeared that the leasehold title had been under a number of different leases. It is asserted above[50] that a prescriptive easement can only exist in favour of a freehold owner, but *RHJ Ltd v FT Patten (Holdings) Ltd*[51] decided that this does not apply to rights of light because s.3 of the Prescription Act 1832 does not refer to "any person claiming a right thereto".

20.11   The section has a specific proviso that time does not run if the user is by consent or agreement by deed or in writing. This is needed because the section makes no reference to "claiming right thereto" as set out in s.2.[52] Equally, for lost modern grant the user must be as of right and not precarious. This provision has been considered in two recent cases which reached different conclusions on their respective facts. In *RHJ v FT Patten (Holdings) Ltd*[53] the Court of Appeal upheld the finding that a clause in a

---

[48] See para.15.25 above.
[49] [2005] EWHC 33 (Ch).
[50] See para.15.25 above.
[51] [2008] EWCA Civ 151; [2008] Ch. 341 upholding the judgment of Lewison J. [2007] 4 All E.R. 744.
[52] [2008] EWCA Civ 151 per Lloyd L.J. at [2]. See also 15.04 above.
[53] [2008] EWCA Civ 151 upholding [2007] 4 All E.R. 744

lease which expressly excluded the grant of any rights or easements by implication, coupled with a reservation that gave the landlord "the full free right to erect build . . ." on any land adjoining to property amounted to such "consent or agreement" even though there was no express reference to such building being free from easements on light. However, in *Salvage Wharf Ltd v G&S Brough Ltd*[54] a differently constituted Court of Appeal distinguished that case and found that an agreement not to object to a project, which might have interfered with their rights of light did not amount to abandonment of any existing rights or to consent to further potential infringements in the future.

These cases demonstrate the difficulties of construction of clauses which are intended to permit either a specific development or future development, but may not necessarily be intended to allow total carte blanche to the servient owner to override all rights of light.

For the easement to arise it is not necessary to show that the dominant owner has "used" the light. It does not matter, therefore, that the building is unoccupied for any part of the 20 year period.[55] The position is, however, more complicated where the window has actually been blocked off for any part of the 20 year period. Just as with rights of way there is no need for the way to be in constant use, so also with rights of light there is nothing to stop the dominant owner drawing his curtains even during daylight or closing the shutters. Providing the shutters are movable and are opened from time to time there is sufficient continuity to give rise to a prescriptive right.[56]

Actually boarding the window up may, however, cause time to stop running.[57] This goes beyond ceasing to use the aperture and would indicate to a potential servient owner that the dominant owner was no longer seeking to establish a right. Indeed it would be somewhat absurd to erect a hoarding blocking off a window in order to prevent an easement from arising if the window was already boarded up.

The most common problem arises where a building is demolished and a new building re-erected. This is not an interruption within the Act. It is only an interruption if there is an adverse obstruction.[58] The question is whether the removal of the building is such as to indicate discontinuance of the user. This will depend on the length of time during which the site is left unoccupied, but the fact that there has been no building with windows on the site for more than a year is not enough to prevent time running. Non-user which is insufficient for abandonment may, nevertheless, prevent a right from being acquired in the first place. This is a

---

[54] [2009] EWCA Civ 21; [2010] Ch. 11.
[55] *Cooper v Straker* (1889) L.R. 40 Ch. D. 21.
[56] ibid.
[57] *Smith v Baxter* [1900] 2 Ch. 138.
[58] ibid.

situation in which the distinction between lost modern grant and a claim under the Prescription Act 1832 could arise.

3. Interruption

20.12 By section 4 of the Prescription Act 1832:

> "... no act or other matter shall be deemed to be an interruption within the meaning of the statute unless the same shall have been or shall be submitted to or acquiesced in for one year after the party interrupted shall have had or shall have notice thereof".

This is the general provision about interruption,[59] which applies equally to rights of light. The most obvious way of interrupting a right of light is to build a building which interferes with the right. Issuing proceedings within the one year period may well be sufficient to prevent the interruption being submitted to or acquiesced in, but in *Dance v Triplow*[60] the Court of Appeal dealt with the situation where the servient owner objected strongly to the new building, but did not commence his action for four years. The Court emphasised the distinction been "acquiesced" and "submitted to". A person acquiesces if he is satisfied to allow the interruption, but he submits to it where he does nothing about it, even though he is not acquiescing.

It was obvious from his conduct that Mr Dance did not acquiesce in the building. He objected to planning permission, applied for a reduction in rates and, in 1982, placed the matter in the hands of his solicitors. During this period between 1980 and 1982, the Court of Appeal accepted that he had not acquiesced or submitted to the interruption of his right of light, but his total inaction between 1982 and 1984 was held to be sufficient to amount to submitting to an interruption of his right and therefore to prevent him from pursuing his claim, even though he did nothing to suggest that he had changed his mind about the obstruction. Where there has been an interruption of a right of light for one year before the action is brought the onus of proof is on the plaintiff to show that he has not submitted to or acquiesced in it.

20.13 This is the situation where there is an existing easement of light which is then interrupted by an obstruction. The reverse situation is where a person opens up a window in his own land, either by building a new building with windows or by opening up a window in an adjoining building. The neighbour has no private law right to stop him doing so. The traditional method was to put something up to obstruct the window.

---

[59] See para.15.05 et seq.
[60] (1992) 64 P. & C.R. 1.

This however is an expensive business and is likely to cause great ill-feeling. Accordingly, the Rights of Light Act 1959 was passed which entitles a servient owner to register a notice of objection to an ancient light rather than actually to obstruct it.

The procedure under the Act is to give notice of the proposed application to all persons who, in the circumstances existing at the time when the certificate is issued, appear to the Lands Tribunal to be persons likely to be affected by the registration of a notice in pursuance of the application.[61] There is a procedure for temporary registration in cases of urgency.[62] When the notice has been served the Lands Tribunal issues a certificate. Application is then made to the local authority for registration as a local land charge.[63]

The application must be in the prescribed form,[64] must identify the servient land and the dominant building,[65] and state that the registration of a notice in pursuance of the application is intended to be equivalent to the obstruction of the access of light to the dominant building across the servient land which would be caused by the erection in such position on the servient land as may be specified in the application, of an opaque structure of such dimension (including, if the application so states, unlimited height) as may be so specified.[66]

The effect of registration, as per the application, is that the access of **20.14** light to the building is treated as having been obstructed to the same extent, and with the like consequences as if an opaque structure of the dimensions specified had been erected in the position specified in the application by the person who made it on the date of the registration, and had remained there during the period for which the notice has effect and had been removed at the end of that period.[67]

The notice has effect for one year, unless it is cancelled before the end of that period. An emergency notice is for a specific period and expires at the end of that period unless renewed. The one year is defined as "beginning with the date of registration", so that a registration on April 1 expires on March 31 following and not on April 1 following.[68] If the servient owner considers that he has an existing easement of light which would be infringed by the fictional opaque structure he can apply to have it removed,[69] but if this is challenged by the registering owner the person

---

[61] Rights of Light Act 1959 s.2(3)(a).
[62] ibid. s.2(3)(b).
[63] ibid. s.2(4)(a).
[64] Local Land Charges Rules 1977 (SI 1977/985).
[65] Rights of Light Act 1959 s.2(2)(a).
[66] Rights of Light Act 1959 s.2(2)(b).
[67] ibid. s.3(1).
[68] See *Trow v Ind Coope* [1967] 2 Q.B. 899.
[69] Local Land Charges Rules 1977 r.10. See *Salvage Wharf v G&S Brough Ltd* [2009] EWCA Civ 21; [2010] Ch. 11.

claiming the easement has to bring an action in the courts for a declaration and cancellation or variation of the registration.[70]

The rule which allows a prescriptive easement to arise after 19 years' user followed by an obstruction for less than a year making 20 years in all[71] is dealt with by s.3(4) which provides:

> "Where, at any time during the period for which a notice registered under the last preceding section has effect, the circumstances are such that, if the access of light to the dominant building had been enjoyed continuously from a date one year earlier than the date on which the enjoyment thereof in fact began, a person would have had a right of action in any court by virtue of the last preceding subsection in respect of the registration, that person shall have the like right of action in that court by virtue of this subsection in respect of the registration of the notice."

Although the registration is only effective for one year it remains on the register for 21 years[72] since it is only when 21 years has passed since the registration that a dominant owner can allege that a fresh easement has arisen.

20.15 The effect of a registration under the Act, therefore, is not to create a permanent fictional obstruction, but only an obstruction sufficient to create a statutory interruption under the Prescription Act 1832. No-one has yet attempted to argue that since the notice is for one year commencing with the date of registration it is not "submitted to or acquiesced in for one year after the party interrupted shall have had notice thereof" but only for 364 days thereafter. Assuming, however, that the Act is effective, the effect is that time starts running again from the expiry of the one year period.

The Act applies to Crown land, but does not apply to Scotland or Northern Ireland.

4. Infringement of easement of light

(1) The Principle

20.16 The House of Lords decided in *Colls v Home & Colonial Stores Ltd*[73] that there is only a right of action in respect of diminution of light where the loss of light is such as to render the occupation of the house

---

[70] Rights of Light Act 1959 s.3(5).
[71] See *Flight v Thomas* (1840) 11 Ad. & El. 688.
[72] Local Land Charges Rules 1977 r.10.
[73] [1904] A.C. 179.

uncomfortable according to the ordinary notions of mankind and (in the case of business premises) to prevent the plaintiff from carrying on his business as beneficially as before:

> "In order to give a right of action, and sustain the issue, there must be a substantial privation of light, sufficient to render the occupation of the house uncomfortable, and to prevent the plaintiff from carrying on his accustomed business [that of grocer] on the premises as beneficially as he had formerly done" per Lord Macnaghten[74] quoting Best C.J. in *Back v Stacey*.[75]

This decision resolved a conflict which had previously existed between those who maintained that the easement was a right not to have the existing light substantially diminished, and those who maintained that the right was not to have the light reduced below an acceptable level. Decisions before *Colls v Home & Colonial Stores Ltd* particularly those such as *Scott v Pape*[76] which concentrated on the extent to which the light was diminished must be looked at with some suspicion.

What the court has to decide in a claim of infringement of a right of light, therefore, is whether the light has been reduced below an acceptable level. It is this question of fact which is the most common issue in right of light cases. Although it is an issue of fact it nevertheless involves a number of points of law.

(2)   The Evidence

The evidence on the basis of which the court will decide whether the **20.17** level of light has been reduced below an acceptable level comes from (a) lay witnesses (b) expert evidence and (c) the view carried out by the judge. Each of these kinds of evidence has a place in the decision making process.

(a)   LAY WITNESSES

In every case there will be a claimant who either considers that his light **20.18** has been affected, or fears that it will be if the proposed development is built. Where the building has been completed the court will take considerable note of the evidence of people who have had actual experience of using the building before and after the obstruction. Strictly the court is only concerned with the state of the light after the alleged infringement,

---

[74] ibid.
[75] (1826) 2 Car. & P. 465.
[76] (1886) L.R. 31 Ch. D. 554.

but despite the principles set out in *Colls v Home & Colonial Stores Ltd*[77] it is the practice to call evidence about the situation before the alleged infringement and inevitably the court is influenced by whether the allegation is of a slight deterioration of an already rather dark room or a change from a very light room to one that is barely acceptable, although it is also true that "in a room that is ill-lit every bit of light is precious".[78]

Although lay evidence is admissible it creates considerable difficulties. Firstly, of course, if the proceedings are *quia timet* the lay witness cannot experience the change until it has taken place. In *Carr-Saunders v Dick McNeil Associates*[79] Millett J.[80] concentrated on expert evidence in preference to the evidence of laymen, though because of further changes since the issue arose he could not see for himself:

> "To a considerable extent, particularly on the question of liability, I discount the evidence of the lay witnesses . . . their evidence is necessarily subjective, and the recollection of laymen of the amount of light formerly enjoyed is notoriously unreliable. Thirdly, the layman is incapable of distinguishing between direct and reflected light. Fourthly, the loss of privacy, the worsening of the view (from a wall surmounted by a sloping roof to a single expanse of brickwork) and the optical illusion that the two buildings have become closer all combine in the witnesses' minds with the loss of light to form a single, confused impression of a greatly deteriorating working environment which it is extremely difficult and perhaps impossible to attribute accurately to its different components".

This rather dismissive approach to lay evidence is, however, by no means universal and in many cases judges have preferred the evidence of ordinary people's impressions to complex calculations by experts.

(b) EXPERT EVIDENCE

20.19   Expert evidence began to be used in light cases around the turn of the century. However, in the 1920's a great deal of work was done on the subject by Mr. Waldram culminating in the deliberations of the International Commission on Illumination in Cambridge in 1932. The way this is worked out can be found in J. Swarbrick, *Easements of Light (A synopsis of modern practice and a brief explanation of simplified methods of measuring daylight and assessing compensation)*.[81]

---

[77] [1904] A.C. 179.
[78] per H.H. Judge Cooke in *Deakins v Hookings* [1994] 14 E.G. 133.
[79] [1986] 1 W.L.R. 922; [1986] 2 All E.R. 888 at 893a.
[80] *Carr-Saunders v Dick McNeil Associates* [1986] 1 W.L.R. 922; [1986] 2 All E.R. 888 at 891b.
[81] (London: Batsford, 1938).

The essence of the principle is that the easement is a right to direct light passing through the window and not to reflected light. The method therefore involves assessing the amount of direct daylight entering the room by geometric calculations based on the "sky factor". The expert will then produce contour plans showing the amount of light reaching different parts of the rooms. The principle is that the amount of light required to be adequate on an overcast day equates to 0.2 per cent of the available sky. This approach, first used in *Price v Hilditch*[82] has been largely accepted in the more recent authorities.[83] The only alternatives to this method are to rely on general impressions or to use light meters, but the amount of light coming into a room will vary enormously according to the time of year, the time of day and the weather and, furthermore, the human eye has great powers of adjustment to good and bad light and different people require substantially different amounts of light for normal purposes.

The problem with the method, of course, is that it excludes reflected light. There is no clear authority on the extent to which reflected light can be taken into consideration. Light from other windows can be taken into account, or even "borrowed" light through the glazed door of another building,[84] but it also makes a great deal of difference to the light coming into a room whether the buildings around are covered with, for example, light rendering or dark brick. It has been pointed out that the adjoining owners cannot be required to maintain their buildings in the existing state and not, for example, to change the colour of the rendering.[85] A clause attempting to deal with this can be found in the Encyclopedia of Forms & Precedents.[86] In *Deakins v Hookings*[87] the Judge, while accepting that he had to consider "what light is there now?" still refused to consider light reflected from a wall painted white.

While the general method of calculation has been largely accepted **20.20** the courts have been unwilling to accept anything in the nature of fixed standards and have rejected the concept that whether there has been an infringement can be decided by applying specific formulae. Mr. Waldram developed the "grumble factor" which he regarded as applying if less than half the room was adequately lit, which meant one lumen of light. Although this "half the room" or 50/50 principle is not a rule of law,[88]

---

[82] [1930] 1 Ch 500.
[83] See e.g. *Regan v Paul Properties* [2006] EWHC 1941 (Ch).
[84] *Deakins v Hookings* [1994] 14 E.G. 133.
[85] See *Dent v Auction Mart Co* (1866) L.R. 2 Eq. 238; *Deakins v Hookings* [1994] 14 E.G. 133.
[86] *Encyclopedia of Form and Precedents*, 5th edn (London: Butterworths, 1991), Vol.13(1), para.1674.
[87] [1994] 14 E.G. 133.
[88] *Carr-Saunders v Dick McNeil Associates* [1986] 2 All E.R. 888.

"it is a very useful guide which will apply to the majority of cases concerning infringements of rights to light, especially where the dominant tenement is a dwelling house and the room in question is a living-room, but it need not be followed in extraordinary circumstances", *Regan v Paul Properties*.[89]

The alternative argument which concentrated on whether the offices were still "marketable" was rejected.

The modern view was well summed up in *Ough v King*:

"I think the notions of mankind on the subject of light have changed and are changing. Possibly it is connected with improvement in electric light; because the standard of artificial light has gone up, the standard of natural lighting has gone up too. I do not think that ordinary people would accept now for a living room and office on the outskirts of a town like Gravesend, the daylight standard which was accepted 12 years ago for an office in the City of London."[90]

The trend in the more modern cases, therefore, has been to require a higher basic standard of lighting which, in turn, is more restrictive of development which affects a neighbour's light and to regard the 50/50 rule as at best a minimum standard.[91] It was suggested in *Midtown Ltd v City of London Real Property Co*[92] that in many offices the lights are on all the time, the preference being for a constant level of lighting rather than the inconvenient variations of sun, cloud and rain and, therefore, that a lesser level of lighting should be accepted. However, this argument was rejected by the court, not least because if artificial light is taken into account, there could never be an infringement of the right of light, and the same approach was followed in *Regan v Paul Properties*.[93] Even where the Court accepts that the natural light has fallen below an acceptable level, the automatic use of electric light may affect the Court's decision on whether to grant an injunction, or the measure of damages.

Before *Colls v Home & Colonial Stores Ltd*[94] a rule of thumb had grown up that there should be an angle of 45 degrees from the window. However, this method is clearly inadequate. The amount of light depends on things like the size of the building, how far away it is and the size and height of

---

[89] [2006] EWHC 1941 (Ch) at [39], appealed on remedy issues [2006] 3 W.L.R. 1131.
[90] Judge Glazebrook quoted with approval by Lord Denning M.R. in *Ough v King* [1967] 1 W.L.R. 1547; [1967] 3 All E.R. 859 at 61F.
[91] See *Deakins v Hookings* [1994] 14 E.G. 133.
[92] [2005] EWHC 33 (Ch).
[93] [2006] EWHC 1941 (Ch) appealed on another point [2006] 3 W.L.R. 1131.
[94] [1904] A.C. 179.

the window. It was rightly rejected in *Colls v Home & Colonial Stores* and no longer carries any weight.

The procedure with regard to experts' reports is now governed by r.35 of the Civil Procedure Rules 1998 which lays heavy emphasis on the duty of experts towards the court and the need to restrict expert evidence to that which is really necessary.

(c) VIEW

In *Ough v King* the Court of Appeal emphasised the importance of the judge visiting the site for a view. However, Lord Denning M.R. added[95]:   **20.21**

"I would not myself denigrate the value of expert evidence. All I can say is that a view can be a most helpful addition".

The balance between impression and expert evidence will vary in different cases. No doubt in most cases the decision will depend to a considerable extent on the impression gained by the judge at the time of the view and may even be influenced by his impression of who is being unreasonable, but the judge's view will be on one particular day and much may depend on the weather. Furthermore if the obstruction has taken place, the judge cannot see what the property was like before and, more importantly, if the action is proceeding on a quia timet basis he will not be able to see what the effect of the proposed development will be.

(3) Basis of Assessment

The Court of Appeal in *Ough v King*[96] accepted the proposition that it was permissible to consider the neighbourhood despite Russell J.'s remark[97] that "the human eye requires as much light for comfortable reading in Darlington Street, Wolverhampton, as in Mayfair".   **20.22**

It is, perhaps, more a question of looking at the nature of the neighbourhood to see whether it is generally hemmed in by tall buildings than to consider whether it is a prosperous or a deprived neighbourhood. Indeed in *Fishenden v Higgs and Hill*[98] it was argued that the standards of light to be expected in Mayfair were actually rather low and in *Midtown Ltd v City of London Real Property Co*,[99] it was pointed out that in most modern offices the lights are kept on all the time so as to provide a constant level of lighting, regardless of the conditions outside, but the Court still upheld

---

[95] *Ough v King* [1967] 1 W.L.R. 1547; [1967] 3 All E.R. 859 at 861E.
[96] [1967] 1 W.L.R. 1547; [1967] 3 All E.R. 859.
[97] In *Hortons Estate Ltd v James Beattie Ltd* [1927] 1 Ch. 75 following *Ambler v Gordon* [1905] 1 K.B. 417.
[98] (1935) 153 L.T. 128.
[99] [2005] EWHC 33 (Ch).

the principle that a right to natural light is important. The standard of light required depends on the nature of the building and the purposes for which it is normally adapted, *Allen v Greenwood*.[100] This means that if the building is a greenhouse the light required is that normally needed for a greenhouse and not the light needed for reading. It is not, however, very easy to say how widely this principle can be applied. Clearly a greenhouse is a building designed for a special use. The same may be true of a photographic or artist's studio, but there is no clear indication as to whether the light required for an office is more or less than that required for a private house, or whether the light required for a factory is more or less than that required for a shop.

Allen v Greenwood is, however, also authority for the important proposition that an easement can be obtained for an exceptional right of light for a particular purpose, if the dominant owner can show that he has made use of this exceptional light for the full period of 20 years to the knowledge of the servient owners. In *Allen v Greenwood* the exceptional light was required for a greenhouse, which was obvious to the adjoining property. Goff L.J. acknowledged that,

> "where the operation which needs special light is carried on indoors it may be very difficult in fact to prove sufficiently precise knowledge",[101]

but there must be many cases where a business needing exceptional light is being openly carried on.

(4) Changes in the dominant tenement

20.23   The right relates to the light passing through window openings and not to the light to the building itself or any part of it. One of the weaknesses of the 50/50 rule is that the internal arrangement of a building may change. It was established in *Carr-Saunders v Dick McNeil Associates*[102] that changes in the internal arrangements of a building are perfectly foreseeable. Accordingly, if the effect is to reduce the light coming through a window to such a level that the rooms lit by that window are changed from poorly but adequately lit rooms to "dark and gloomy cells",[103] it does not matter that those rooms have not been there for 20 years and that the effect on the previous open plan area would have been much less significant. This decision was reached in the face of various decisions,

---

[100] [1980] Ch. 119; [1979] 1 All E.R. 819.
[101] *Allen v Greenwood* [1980] Ch. 119; [1979] 1 All E.R. 819 at 826e.
[102] [1986] 1 W.L.R. 922; [1986] 2 All E.R. 888 at 893a.
[103] *Carr-Saunders v Dick McNeil Associates Ltd* [1986] 1 W.L.R. 922; [1986] 2 All E.R. 888 at 892e.

such as *Smith v Evangelization Society*[104] that the dominant owner cannot, by altering his property increase the burden placed on the servient property. These cases were distinguished on the basis that the sub-division did not actually increase the burden since the parts blocked off by the sub-division did not use the light from the affected windows anyway. Whether a change has significantly affected the burden is very much a question of fact and degree in each case.

There are also indications in *Allen v Greenwood*[105] that the right depends on the nature of the building and the purposes for which it is normally adapted, though the point being made was that a greenhouse usually requires an exceptional amount of light. However, Millett J. made it clear in *Carr-Saunders v Dick McNeil Associates*[106] that:

> "The court must, therefore, take into account not only the present use, but also other potential uses to which the dominant owner may reasonably be expected to put the premises in the future".

The principle set out in *Colls v Home & Colonial Stores Ltd*[107] is more **20.24** difficult to apply where the windows which are affected are not the only windows in the building, or where the windows themselves and not just the internal arrangement have been altered during the 20 year period.

It is clearly established that in deciding whether the light has been reduced below an acceptable standard the court should consider all the circumstances including light which comes from other sources, *Smith v Evangelization Society*.[108] The situation, however, is not so clear where the additional light comes from a window which itself does not have a prescriptive right to light. *In Smith v Evangelization Society*[109] the plaintiffs had blocked up two skylights and another window at some stage within the 20 year period. Lord Harmsworth M.R. considered that light from any other source should be considered and that it makes no difference whether the other light is an ancient light. However, both the other judges in the Court of Appeal, Lawrence and Romer L.JJ., considered that the light from the window and skylight was not precarious and was not light which the plaintiff could have been deprived of except by his own action. It is likely where there is a dispute about ancient lights that any other windows have been there for 20 years and usually a skylight will get most of its light from above and is not susceptible to obstruction. It is submitted that, despite the dicta of Lord Harmsworth M.R. in *Smith v Evangelization Society*, that case is not binding authority for the proposition that windows

[104] *Smith v Evangelization Society (Inc) Trust* [1933] Ch. 515.
[105] [1980] Ch. 119.
[106] [1986] 1 W.L.R. 922; [1986] 2 All E.R. 888 at 894e.
[107] [1904] A.C. 179.
[108] *Smith v Evangelization Society (Inc) Trust* [1933] Ch. 515.
[109] ibid.

without an easement of light should be taken into consideration when considering a claim to an infringement.

Even when there is light from other windows which have an easement of light it must be remembered that not every reduction in the amount of light coming through those windows will amount to an actionable infringement. Therefore, it is not necessarily enough to say that even if the window in question is blocked off there will be adequate light from other sources, since the servient owner on the other side might also wish to reduce the amount of light coming through the other window. It seems that the correct approach is to decide whether, if the light from the other window was reduced to the same extent as is proposed to the window in issue the light would still be sufficient.[110]

20.25   Where the windows themselves have been altered, added to or removed within the 20 year period the court looks to find windows, or alternatively, shafts of light that have been used for the 20 year period. It is possible, therefore, to demolish one building and erect another further forward with higher windows so that the light comes in through the same plane, without affecting the continuity of use.[111] If there is a new window partially replacing the old one or an old window opening has been blocked off the court then tries to carry out an assessment of what effect the infringement would have had had the light been as it was. This, however, raises difficult problems.

Where the new windows are in much the same place as the old ones, or where the light going into them is much the same, the problem is not too difficult, but in *News of the World Ltd v Allen Fairhead & Sons Ltd*[112] windows had been replaced so that only a small amount of the light which went through the old windows was coming through the new ones. It was held that if the dominant tenement is rebuilt in such a way that the area of coincidence between an old and new window is much smaller than the old window the court cannot be asked to treat the rest of the new window as blocked up.

The position therefore is (1) the court will take into account light from other sources providing the dominant owner has a right to that light; (2) the court will not normally take into account light from other precarious sources; (3) the dominant owner will not be allowed to increase the burden on the defendants by reducing the size of his windows so that more light has to come through what is left to keep the level of lighting acceptable.

---

[110]   *Sheffield Masonic Hall Co Ltd v Sheffield Corp* [1932] 2 Ch. 17.
[111]   *Scott v Pape* (1886) L.R. 31 Ch. D. 554.
[112]   [1931] 2 Ch. 402.

Chapter Twenty One
Water Rights

1. Introduction

Chapter Eight has already dealt with water boundaries and has divided **21.01** waters into tidal and non-tidal rivers, artificial watercourses, lakes and the sea. It deals with whether the riparian owners own the river bed and where the boundary is to be drawn. This chapter deals with the rights that people have over the waters themselves. Such rights can be divided into (1) riparian rights, (2) easements and (3) several rights and profits.[1] Under the Countryside and Rights of Way Act 2000 public access rights are extended to the coastal margin including the foreshore and this process has now begun.[2]

2. Riparian rights

A person who owns land bounding a natural watercourse has various **21.02** riparian rights regardless of whether he also owns the bed of the watercourse.[3]

The rights were thus described by Lord Templeman in *Tate & Lyle Industries Ltd v Greater London Council*[4]:

> "As riparian owners Tate and Lyle are entitled to access to the water in contact with their frontage, and to have the water flow to them in its natural state in flow, quality and quantity so that they may take water for ordinary purposes in connection with their riparian tenement including the use of water power".

In addition, riparian owners have a right not to have their banks eroded by changes made upstream.

---

[1] See Ch. 23.
[2] Countryside and Rights of Way Act 2000 s.3, see para.11.20 above.
[3] *Lyon v Fishmonger's Co* (1875–76) L.R. 1 App. Cas. 662.
[4] [1983] 2 A.C. 509; [1983] 2 W.L.R. 649.

(1)   The right to a flow of water and to extract water

21.03   The right to a flow of water set out in Lord Templeman's judgment above applies only to running water. If, for example, a person gathers water which had formerly seeped into the river from land drains and percolating water from boggy land and holds it in a reservoir he is entitled to use that water for his own purposes because it has never become flowing water, *Rugby Joint Water Board v Walters*.[5] If the water in that case had started as a spring and then gone into a small watercourse it would immediately have become flowing water, but as it did not form itself into a watercourse above the reservoir it was held not to be a flowing stream. On the other hand, forming a mill pond from a natural watercourse does not entitle the owner to treat it as still water and use it in breach of the rights of the lower riparian owners.[6] The point at which water becomes a stream is dealt with in Chapter Eight.

Lord Templeman's summary of the nature of the right raises several questions including the meaning of "bounding" a watercourse, the degree to which the watercourse must be natural and the extent of the right obtained.

(a)   THE EXTENT OF THE RIGHT

21.04   There is a patent inconsistency between the right of a riparian owner to abstract water and the right of the riparian owner below him to an undiminished flow:

> "It would normally be as impossible for a riparian owner to [abstract water and then return it all to the stream] as it would have been for Shylock to cut his pound of flesh without shedding one drop of blood".[7]

This problem was considered initially by the common law, but has been further constrained by statute.

The common-law right to abstract water has been divided into three different categories as set out by Lord Macnaghten in *McCartney v Londonderry & Lough Swilly Railway Co Ltd*[8]:

> "There are, as it seems to me, three ways in which a person whose lands are intersected or bounded by a running stream may use the water to which the situation of his property gives him access. He may

---

[5] [1967] Ch. 397; [1966] 3 W.L.R. 934.
[6] *John White & Sons v J&M White* [1906] A.C. 72.
[7] per Buckley J. in *Rugby Joint Water Board v Walters* [1967] Ch. 397; [1966] 3 All E.R. 497 at 504G.
[8] [1904] A.C. 301 at 306.

use it for ordinary or primary purposes, for domestic purposes, and the wants of his cattle. He may use it also for some other purposes—sometimes called extraordinary or secondary purposes—provided those purposes are connected with or incident to his land, and provided that certain conditions are complied with. Then he may possibly take advantage of his position to use the water for purposes foreign to or unconnected with his riparian tenement. His rights in the first two cases are not quite the same. In the third case he has no right at all."

Later Lord Macnaghten, setting out the common law position said[9]:

"In the ordinary or primary use of flowing water a person dwelling on the banks of a stream is under no restriction. In the exercise of his ordinary rights he may exhaust the water altogether. No lower proprietor can complain of that. In the exercise of rights extraordinary but permissible, the limit of which has never been accurately defined and probably is incapable of accurate definition, a riparian owner is under considerable restrictions. The use must be reasonable. The purposes for which the water is taken must be connected with his tenement, and he is bound to restore the water which he takes and uses for those purposes substantially undiminished in volume and unaltered in character."

Presumably any consumption which seriously affected the flow of a substantial river would count as an extraordinary use,[10] but it could well happen that domestic use could consume a large part of the flow of a small stream. There are, indeed, many private water supplies which draw water from a spring. Usually these are so designed that the water is drawn before it ever has the chance to become a stream, but the same principle applies, namely that the person owning the spring may use all of it for his domestic purposes. No doubt before the water supply was installed the water from the spring ran off as a stream.

Although the principle that the riparian owner can take as much of the **21.05** stream as he wishes for domestic purposes has been long stated and accepted there must still be doubt about what would happen if a domestic user in practice diverted a considerable volume of water for his own purposes thereby leaving an ancient stream dry or seriously reduced. It seems likely that if it had a significant effect on the stream it would be regarded as an extraordinary use.[11]

---

[9] *McCartney v Londonderry & Lough Swilly Railway Co* [1904] A.C. 301 at 307.
[10] As in *Rugby Joint Water Board v Walters* [1967] Ch. 397; [1966] 3 W.L.R. 934.
[11] See *Sampson v Hoddinott* (1857) 1 C.B.N.S. 590.

Once it is established that the user is extraordinary the use is subject to severe restrictions:

"In the exercise of rights extraordinary but permissible, the limit of which has never been accurately defined and probably is incapable of accurate definition, a riparian owner is under considerable restrictions. The use must be reasonable. The purpose for which the water is taken must be connected with the tenement, and he is bound to restore the water which he takes and uses for those purposes substantially undiminished in volume and unaltered in character".[12]

The obligation to return the water unaltered in character means that the upper riparian owner cannot extract water and then replace it with an equivalent volume of water from another source, such as water pumped out of a mine. The right is to the natural water.[13]

(b)   STATUTORY CONTROL

21.06   In addition to his obligation to the lower riparian owners, the upper riparian owner's rights are restricted by the statutory requirements of the Water Resources Act 1991.

Section 24 of the Water Resources Act 1991 provides that:

"no person shall:

(a)   abstract water from any source of supply; or

(b)   cause or permit any other person so to abstract any water, except in pursuance of a licence under this Chapter granted by the [Environment Agency] and in accordance with the provisions of that licence."

Section 27[14] qualifies this with an exception allowing the abstraction of small quantities of water. A small quantity is defined as a quantity of water not exceeding 20 cubic metres in 24 hours, or, where there is a continuous operation or a series of operation, an aggregate of 20 cubic metres in all. The Secretary of State has power to give a licence for further extraction on a local or limited basis on application from the Agency. The Secretary of State can also vary these quantities by Statutory Instrument, either generally or in specific areas or types of

---

[12]   per Lord Macnaghten in *McCartney v Londonderry & Lough Swilly Railway Co* [1904] A.C. 301 at 307.

[13]   *John Young & Co v Bankier Distillery Co* [1893] A.C. 691.

[14]   As amended by s.6 of the Water Act 2003.

waterway. The Act no longer makes any requirement as to the purpose of the abstraction.

The impact of the statutory control on common law rights was considered in *Cargill v Gotts*.[15] Any user which exceeds the licenced limit is illegal, even if it would have been permitted at common law. The user, therefore, cannot amount to a prescriptive user for the purpose of obtaining an easement to extract water, but user before the statutory control came into effect, if shown for the necessary period, can give rise to an easement by virtue of the doctrine of lost modern grant.

The converse situation is where the upper riparian owner has obtained **21.07** a licence, but the lower riparian owner complains that his riparian rights are being affected by the operations. In this case the licence overrides the common law right of the other riparian owners.[16] However, if the water authority has issued a licence to an upper riparian owner which affects the rights of the lower riparian owner to exercise his rights (being rights for which he has either got a licence or does not need one because of the low consumption) then he may be able to get compensation from the water authority, unless the lower riparian owner has consented to the licence.

Work may be carried out under other statutes which impinge on the riparian owner's rights. For example the highway authority may carry out work to bridges or may culvert a stream. As long as they are doing what they are authorised to do by statute they will be entitled to carry out the works even if they affect riparian rights, but if they should stray beyond what is strictly necessary there may be a breach of riparian rights.[17]

(c) LOWER RIPARIAN OWNER'S RIGHT

It must be remembered that the real question, in the case of the exercise **21.08** of riparian rights, is not whether the person removing the water has a right to do so, but whether the downstream riparian owner has a remedy. It is arguable therefore that the so-called riparian rights are no more than the general right of a person to do on his own land anything which will not affect the owner of other land. If the law went along this road then all that would be necessary would be to look at the claimant to see firstly whether he is a riparian owner and secondly whether his rights have been affected. It would not then matter whether the defendant was exercising riparian rights or not.

Although this approach makes a lot of sense, the fact is that the authorities have proceeded on the basis that the right to draw water is a specific

---

[15] [1981] 1 W.L.R. 441; [1981] 1 All E.R. 682.
[16] Water Resources Act 1991 s.48(2).
[17] *Provender Millers Ltd v Southampton City Council* [1939] 4 All E.R. 157.

right. In the leading case of *Swindon Waterworks Co Ltd v Wiltshire and Berkshire Canal Navigation Co*[18] Lord Cairns set out the rights of the upper riparian owner. In that case the waterworks which supplied Swindon from the river was the upper riparian owner. The Canal Company themselves wanted to supply water to Swindon and they bought up a disused mill downsteam of the waterworks and used this as the basis for claiming an injunction. Although the damage to the canal company as owner of the disused mill was negligible the House of Lords held that as the waterworks maintained that they had a right to use the water the canal company were entitled to an injunction to stop them since if they carried on for 20 years they would get a prescriptive right. Essentially the point was that the waterworks did affect the flow and accordingly if the mill were to be re-opened it would be affected.

This approach has been followed ever since. Thus in *McCartney v Londonderry and Lough Swilly Railway*[19] the railway company were seeking a declaration that they were entitled as riparian owners to use the water for their railway. Accordingly there was no need for the defendants to show damage. The claim failed on the basis that the riparian owner is not entitled to divert water and consume it for purposes unconnected with the tenement. The absence of any immediate damage to the lower riparian owner did not matter. The high point of this approach may be seen at *Attwood v Llay Main Collieries Ltd*[20] where it was held that an injunction would be granted without proof of damage or of the risk of a prescriptive right being produced.

21.09 The lower riparian owner will only have a right of action if his own riparian rights are materially affected, but if the flow is materially reduced he is entitled to a remedy even if he has not in fact exercised his rights in the past by making use of the water.

Lower riparian owners have not, however, always succeeded. In *Kensit v Great Eastern Railway*[21] the plaintiff failed on the basis that there was no actual or prospective damage and in *Sandwich v Great Northern Railway*[22] the lower riparian owner failed even though there was both actual and prospective damage. This case however, was specifically not followed by Buckley J. in *Rugby Joint Water Board v Walters*.[23]

This concentration on rights to do things (sometimes called "liberties") as opposed rights of action (or "claim rights") is unusual in English law. If the only question was whether the lower riparian owner's flow of water had been materially interfered with, then it would only be

---

[18] (1874–75) L.R. 7 H.L. 697.
[19] [1904] A.C. 301.
[20] [1926] Ch. 444.
[21] (1884) L.R. 27 Ch. D. 122.
[22] (1878–79) L.R. 10 Ch. D. 707.
[23] [1967] Ch. 397; [1966] 3 W.L.R. 934.

necessary to define the extent of the riparian ownership in relation to the lower owner.

(2) Right of access and mooring

A riparian owner is entitled to access to the river. This right applies **21.10** to all rivers, whether tidal or non-tidal and whether navigable or not.[24] It also applies to lakes[25] and to properties bounding the foreshore.[26] It applies whether or not the riparian owner owns the bed of the river.[27]

Where the river is navigable the riparian owner has the right to moor his boat in the river (providing that he does not interfere with the public right of navigation) and then get access to the bank by whatever means is appropriate whether by small boat, by wading or by spreading a plank across. Equally if there happens to be a jetty attached to his river bank he can use it free of charge.[28]

A right of mooring can also arise as an easement, either by express or implied grant or by prescription, providing that there is a dominant tenement, such as adjoining land.[29]

The public right of navigation does not include an ancillary right to moor other than temporarily in the course of navigation.[30] Thus a public right of navigation does not include a right to tie up a houseboat on the bank.[31]

> "But when this right of navigation is connected with an exclusive access to and from a particular wharf it assumes a different character. It ceases to be a right held in common with the rest of the public, for other members of the public have no access to or from the river in connection with the land and it becomes a form of enjoyment of the land and of the river in connection with the land the disturbance of which may be indicated in damages by an action, or restrained by an injunction."[32]

This does not mean, however, that a riparian owner has a right to build a jetty on the river bed. To do so without owning the river bed would be trespass, but if the riparian owner does build a jetty this will only give the

---

[24] *Montreal v Harbour Commissioners of Montreal* [1926] A.C. 299.
[25] *Marshall v Ulleswater Steam Navigation Co* (1871–72) L.R. 7 Q.B. 166.
[26] *Attorney General of the Straits Settlement v Wemyss* (1888) L.R. 13 App. Cas. 192.
[27] *Lyon v Fishmongers Co* (1875–76) L.R. 1 App. Cas. 662.
[28] *Marshall v Ulleswater Steam Navigation Co* (1871–72) L.R. 7 Q.B. 166.
[29] *P&S Platt Ltd v Crouch* [2003] EWCA Civ 1110; [2004] 1 P. & C.R. 18.
[30] *Moore v British Waterways Board* Unreported March 12, 2009 CD; Earl *Iveagh v Martin* [1961] 1 Q.B. 232; [1960] 3 W.L.R. 210.
[31] *Sussex Investments v Jackson* [1993] E.G. 152 (C.S.).
[32] per Lord Cairns L.C. in *Lyon v Fishmongers Co* (1875–76) L.R. 1 App. Cas. 662 at 671.

lower riparian owner a right of action if he can show that his right to a flow of water has been affected.[33] The fact that the upper jetty causes silting up of the river will not be actionable as breach of riparian rights, but as a breach of the common right of navigation.

Mooring a boat on a tidal river, particularly where it sits on the river-bed at low tide, can also amount to an exclusive right of possession giving rise, in due course, to adverse possession.[34]

What this riparian right does mean, however, is that if, without specific statutory authority entitling the undertaker to obstruct the riparian rights, something is built on the shore which restricts the right of access the riparian owner has a right of action.[35]

(3)   Other rights

21.11   The cases have largely concerned either the right of the upper riparian owner to extract water or the right of access to the shore, but in *Tate & Lyle Industries Ltd v Greater London Council*[36] an attempt was made to extend the right of the lower riparian owner to an undiminished flow to claim also a right not to have the direction of the flow interfered with by jetties which had caused silting up of the river bed. This attempt failed because the riparian owner could not complain about a decrease in the depth of water when the only effect of that decrease was to obstruct the public right of navigation. His correct course was to complain in nuisance of obstruction of his exercise of his navigation rights.

The erection of jetties and walls can, however, affect lower riparian rights. In addition to his right not to have his flow of water diminished the lower riparian owner also has a right not to have his bank eroded by injurious obstructions of the river.[37]

A riparian owner has a right to raise up embankments to prevent his land from being flooded even if this damages lower riparian owners. However, if a wall is erected by a riparian owner this does not render him liable in negligence to someone who depends on that wall if he fails to repair it,[38] though this claim might now be brought as a claim in nuisance under the principles in *Leakey v National Trust for Places of Historic Interest or Natural Beauty*.[39] It is rather surprising that erecting embankments should be regarded as a right which is worthy of note. One would have

---

[33] *Tate & Lyle Industries Ltd v Greater London Council* [1983] 2 A.C. 509; [1983] 2 W.L.R. 649.

[34] *Port of London Authority v Ashmore* [2010] EWCA Civ 30; [2010] 1 All E.R. 1139.

[35] *Montreal v Harbour Commissioners of Montreal* [1926] A.C. 299.

[36] [1983] 2 A.C. 509; [1983] 2 W.L.R. 649.

[37] *Bickett v Morris* (1866–69) L.R. 1 Sc. 47, approved in *Tate & Lyle Industries Ltd v Greater London Council* [1983] 2 A.C. 509; [1983] 1 All E.R. 1159 at 1167.

[38] *Thomas & Evans Ltd v Mid-Rhondda Cooperative Society Ltd* [1941] 1 K.B. 381.

[39] [1980] Q.B. 485; [1980] 2 W.L.R. 65;

thought that a riparian owner could do what he liked on his own land and would not need any specific right to build embankments, but the right to build embankments is sometimes expressed in terms of a right "provided that he does not thereby occasion injury to the lands of others"[40] and it seems that in truth it is a restriction on the freedom of the riparian owner to do what he likes on his own land.

(4) Extent of riparian ownership

As stated above, the rights connected with riparian ownership do not **21.12** depend on ownership of the bed of the river.[41] All that is necessary is that the ownership should be up to the bank. It has been said that this means that the property should be in daily contact with the river, though not necessarily all day,[42] but the upper point of the foreshore is mean high tide level, which will not be reached by the tide every day and there can be no doubt that a person entitled to land bounded by the foreshore is entitled to riparian rights even though the sea does not reach his land every day. Where the water level sinks due to the action of upper riparian owners the riparian owner remains a riparian owner and is entitled to go across the exposed bed to gain access to the water even though he does not own the river bed.[43]

Riparian rights are specifically incidents of the ownership of the land[44] comparable to the natural right of support of land by adjoining land. As such they cannot be alienated separately from the river bank. Thus it was held in *Ormerod v Todmorden*[45] that the riparian owner cannot confer on anyone who is not a riparian owner any right to use the water of the stream, and that any user by someone who is not a riparian proprietor is wrongful if it sensibly affects the flow of the water. Such an agreement is not, however, illegal and so the contract between the riparian owner and the third party still stands. Furthermore this is an old case and in *P&S Platt Ltd v Crouch*[46] the Court of Appeal dealt with the issue of moorings used in conjunction with a hotel and bungalows on the basis of s.62 of the Law of Property Act 1925 and actual enjoyment by the respective properties, rather than contiguity.

The fact that a sea wall or river bank has been constructed by statutory authority on the riparian owner's land does not automatically mean that the riparian owner's ownership is excluded.[47] The right, however, attaches

---

[40] See Editorial Note *Thomas & Evans v Mid-Rhondda Cooperative Society Ltd* [1941] 1 K.B. 381.
[41] *Lyon v Fishmongers Co* (1875–76) L.R. 1 App. Cas. 662.
[42] *North Shore Railway v Pion* (1889) L.R. 14 App. Cas. 612.
[43] *Hindson v Ashby* [1896] 2 Ch. 1.
[44] *Stockport Waterworks v Potter* (1864) 3 Hurl. & C. 300.
[45] *Ormerod v Todmorden Joint Stock Mill Co Ltd (No.2)* (1882–83) L.R. 11 Q.B.D. 155.
[46] [2003] EWCA Civ 1110; [2004] 1 P. & C.R. 18.
[47] *Port of London Authority v Canvey Island Commissioners* [1932] 1 Ch. 446.

to the bank and not to any temporary structures, such as jetties built on the bed of the river.[48]

21.13   As riparian rights, whether to a flow of water or to access, are limited to the purposes of the riparian land, the question arises as to how much of the land owned by the riparian owner can be regarded as riparian land. It was pointed out in *Attwood v Llay Main Collieries Ltd*[49] that it could be suggested that Paddington Station has riparian rights because it is connected to the Thames by a thin strip of land, to wit the railway line:

> "The question whether a particular piece of land sustains the character of a riparian tenement or not is a question of fact and must be decided according to the special circumstances."[50]

It was held in that case that a narrow strip of waterfront did not entitle the colliery to use water from the river for the purposes of the colliery since the whole colliery could not be regarded as bounded by the river.

This case concerned the extent of riparian ownership required to entitle an upper riparian owner to extract the water, but similar principles must apply to the lower riparian owner who is making the complaint.[51]

(5)   Artificial watercourses

21.14   The problems of defining natural and artificial watercourses are dealt with in Chapter Eight.

While a natural watercourse can be seen as something that existed in antiquity before property rights were defined, an artificial watercourse must have been constructed by someone and the respective rights of the riparian owners would have been defined then or when they ceased to be in common ownership.

The position, therefore, is that strictly there are no riparian rights in artificial watercourses.[52] However, riparian rights may be inferred from the actual use of the watercourse and, in respect of canals and navigations, such rights may be granted by the statute setting it up.[53] With an ancient artificial watercourse with no evidence of how or why it was constructed the court may be happy to imply riparian rights,[54] whereas it may be implied that there are no riparian rights in a mill race which

---

[48] *Tate & Lyle Industries Ltd v Greater London Council* [1983] 2 A.C. 509; [1983] 2 W.L.R. 649.
[49] [1926] Ch. 444.
[50] *Attwood v Llay Main Collieries Ltd* [1926] Ch. 444 per Lawrence J. at 450.
[51] Cf. *Swindon Waterworks v Wiltshire & Berkshire Canal Navigation Co* (1874–75) L.R. 7 H.L. 697.
[52] *Singh v Pattuk* (1878–79) L.R. 4 App. Cas. 121.
[53] *Moore v British Waterways Board* Unreported, March 12, 2009 CD.
[54] *Baily & Co v Clark Son & Morland* [1902] 1 Ch. 649.

can be assumed to have been built by the mill owner for his own purposes.[55]

3. Water easements

There is no special rule about easements relating to water, nor is there **21.15** any special thread which joins all the various kinds of rights involving the use of water that may become incident to land. There are, however, some special considerations about the different kinds of water easements which merit separate consideration.

There are no accepted categories of water easement. For convenience the various easements will be divided into (1) the right to use a pipe, (2) the right to receive water from a watercourse, (3) the right of drainage, (4) the right to a mooring and (5) the right of eavesdrop. These categories are, however, set out for convenience only. The only real distinction between the different kinds of water easements is whether what is claimed is a right to receive or make use of water or, on the other hand, a right to discharge it. Water easements can be created by express or implied grant or reservation or by prescription in the same way as any other easement and are subject to the same requirements of dominant and servient tenement, etc. which are set out in general above in respect of easements. It is, therefore, not proposed to repeat the general principles and to relate them specifically to water easements. Many of the cases referred to in the general sections do involve water rights.

(1) The right to use a pipe

Most people obtain their water from the public water supply and **21.16** discharge their sewage into the public sewer. However, in many cases the water main or the sewer can only be reached by passing over the land of another. In such cases there is a need for a right of some kind to enable a pipe to be installed and maintained on the land and then for the pipe to be used. This pipe will not usually be the property of the water company. The rights of statutory undertakers are considered above.[56] Although the right to run or receive water or sewage by means of a pipe running across another's land is a very common right,[57] it tends to be given little prominence in the conveyancing process and often it is only when something goes wrong that people discover the route that these pipes have taken.

It was pointed out in *Taylor v St Helens Corp*[58] that a grant of a "watercourse" may mean any of three things:

---

[55] *Burrows v Lang* [1901] 2 Ch. 502.
[56] See above Ch.14.
[57] e.g. *McAdams Homes Ltd v Robinson* [2004] EWCA Civ 214; [2005] 1 P. & C.R. 30 where there was no express grant.
[58] (1877) L.R. 6 Ch. D. 264.

"It may mean the easement or the right of the running of water, it may mean the channel, pipe or drain which contains the water and it may mean the land over which the water flows".[59]

This dictum, which refers to artificial watercourses, applies to both a pipe and an open channel. Therefore, where there is a grant of "free and uninterrupted passage of water" as in *Rance v Elvin*,[60] or "rights of passage of water soil, gas, electricity and telephone communications" as in *Duffy v Lamb*,[61] the right granted may be merely to receive such water as runs through the pipe; however, it may amount to a conveyance of the pipe itself coupled with a right to receive water through it or it may involve a conveyance of the three-dimensional space itself through which the pipe runs, together with the ownership of the pipe. The resolution of which category the particular grant comes within is a matter of construction. In *Taylor v St Helens Corp*[62] it was decided that the grant was of a corporeal hereditament but this decision was made before the compulsory registration of land. In modern times it seems likely that the courts would be reluctant to find that a right to a watercourse involved ownership of the space since this would then have to be registered as a separate estate. In *Simmons v Midford* this construction was excluded by the express grant of a right to use the pipe, which was inconsistent with a conveyance of the space itself.

21.17 The basic rule is that when you place something permanently on someone else's land then it becomes part of the land. Thus if someone builds a house on another's land the house becomes the property of that other person. However, when a person is granted a right to install a pipe to take his water supply (or his drains) he does not usually intend to cede that pipe to the owner of the land. The point has been the subject of considerable dispute, but it appears to have been decided in *Simmons v Midford*[63] that even where the space itself is not conveyed the pipes will usually remain the property of the dominant owner coupled with an easement entitling him to use it. Accordingly, he is entitled to stop the servient owner from breaking into the pipes for his own purposes. If he should wish to replace the pipe he would be able to do so providing that he could obtain access for this purpose, such a right normally being implied.

Although rights which involve exclusive possession are not usually the subject matter of easements, the courts have consistently refused to treat this as a rigid rule and, in the case of a pipe right, it is clear that the right to install and maintain the pipe, even where it is exclusive, is not the same

---

[59] per Jessel M.R. at 271.
[60] (1985) 50 P. & C.R. 9.
[61] (1998) 75 P. & C.R. 364, a case about electricity where *Rance v Elvin* (1985) 50 P. & C.R. 9 was specifically followed.
[62] (1877) L.R. 6 Ch. D. 264.
[63] [1969] 2 Ch. 415; [1969] 3 W.L.R. 168.

thing as ownership of the space filled by the pipe. There is therefore, it seems, no need in such cases to register title to the space through which the pipe runs.

It must be remembered that the right to use a pipe is not the same as the right to a supply of water. The right to a natural supply is dealt with in the next section, whereas a right to a supply of water from the mains is dependent on the customer's rights and the water company's duties under the Water Industry Act 1991. All that the pipe easement entails is a right to use the pipe for such water as you can obtain.

This gives rise to considerable problems in relation to services, including electricity cables, gas pipes and telephone connections, as well as water and soil pipes. In respect of natural flows which the dominant owner does not have to pay for it is simple to state that he must not interfere with the flow. However, the dominant owner may often have to pay for the supply of water or other services. He might expect in such circumstances to be able to switch them off if he wishes. In *Rance v Elvin*[64] the Court of Appeal made a distinction between refusing to pay for the supply, in which case the water supply company could cut it off, and taking specific action to block it. Although the distinction may appear rather artificial, it ensures that if the dominant owner decides not to pay the relevant charges, he has to put up with having his own supply cut off as well.[65] Browne-Wilkinson L.J. added obiter[66] that in his view the servient owner would have a quasi-contractual right to recover a fair share of the payment due to the water company.

(2) Right to receive water

Although most properties get their water supplies from the mains there **21.18** are still many private supplies coming from underground springs. An easement cannot be obtained entitling the dominant owner to percolating water and accordingly the only right will be to such water as emerges from the spring. If the servient owner does things on the land which cause the spring to dry up then there is no right of action. Equally a right can be obtained to use a pump or a well, but this does not guarantee a supply of water in the well. A supply of water can also be obtained by diverting part of the flow of an existing watercourse, which may or may not run along your land or by drawing water from a watercourse in respect of which you are a riparian owner. The rights and obligations where the watercourse is a natural one have been considered above,[67] but

---

[64] (1985) 50 P. & C.R. 9.
[65] See *Duffy v Lamb* (1998) 75 P. & C.R. 364, which related to electricity. The result was that the supply had to be kept on even though the servient owner had failed to pay his share.
[66] *Rance v Elvin* (1985) 50 P. & C.R. 9 at 17.
[67] See above para.21.02 et seq.

where the watercourse is artificial any riparian rights must depend on easements whether created by grant or prescription.

Whether or not the right to the water supply is exclusive is a matter of construction.[68] In cases where the right is in common with others difficulties can arise over their respective rights. In respect of a piped supply the initial position seems to be that the person with the first branch of the pipe can draw as much as he wants, leaving any residue to the next and so on down the line, *Beauchamp v Frome Rural District Council*,[69] but the first owner is not entitled to extend the pipe to supply other sources. This decision, however, was before *Jelbert v Davis*[70] which developed the concept of excessive use of easements and it may be that excessive use of the supply by the upper owner could be prevented. In any event in *John White & Sons v J & M White*[71] it was stated that the right to the "first water" from an artificial watercourse did not justify the use of the whole of the water.

21.19   In the absence of an express grant it is necessary to decide whether there is an implied grant or reservation under s.62 of the Law of Property Act 1925 created when the watercourse and the land claiming the right ceased to be in common ownership or prescriptive rights under the Prescription Act 1832 or the doctrine of lost modern grant.[72] In deciding whether a prescriptive easement arises and if so what its extent is, the court will look not only at what has actually happened, but also what was the probable purpose of the creation of the watercourse in the first place. In *Baily & Co v Clark Son & Morland*[73] there was an ancient artificial watercourse of unknown origin, it was held that the proper inference was that the riparian owners had the same rights as if it had been a natural watercourse. This principle was extended in *Lewis v Meredith*[74] to a watercourse leading to a mill. However, to reach this decision it was necessary to distinguish *Burrows v Lang*.[75] In *Burrows v Lang* it was held that there could be no such implication where the watercourse was "temporary" which was construed to mean for a specific purpose such as a mill race. The point was clearly made that the persons constructing the watercourse could not have intended to place on the mill owner an obligation to maintain the mill race after the mill had closed simply to provide drinking water for the riparian owners' cattle. More doubtfully the court concluded from that that there could also be no right to use what water there was for

[68] *Taylor v St Helens Corp* (1877) L.R. 6 Ch. D. 264, 274.
[69] [1938] 1 All E.R. 595.
[70] [1968] 1 W.L.R. 589; [1968] 1 All E.R. 1182.
[71] [1906] A.C. 72.
[72] *Bosomworth v Faber* (1995) 69 P. & C.R. 288.
[73] [1902] 1 Ch. 649.
[74] [1913] 1 Ch. 571.
[75] [1901] 2 Ch. 502.

that purpose. Where the use originated from a grant which proves to be void, the Court will look at the actual use and not the purpose of the void grant.[76]

Even if there is an easement it will not necessarily include a right to have the flow maintained as opposed to a right to such flow as there is. The right to claim the continuous discharge onto your land of a watercourse is very difficult to establish.[77]

"It is difficult for the lower proprietor to establish a right to have the flow continued just as it would be very difficult to make out that because for 20 years my pump has dripped on to a neighbour's ground, therefore he has a right at the end of 20 years to say that my pump must go on leaking."[78]

This was indeed what happened in *Bartlett v Tottenham*[79] where it was held that just because your water tanks overflow for 20 years this does not give the lower owner a right to expect the overflow to continue.

It is not, therefore, always easy to predict in what circumstances actual **21.20** extraction of water for a period will give rise to a right firstly to continue to extract what there is and secondly to have the flow maintained.

It seems that any right obtained will not be to take so many gallons of water, but a right to take what water is needed for the purposes of the dominant tenement. The volume of water may vary with different agricultural practices.[80]

While it is possible to show a right to receive water from a specific watercourse it will be impossible to show a right to receive water by seepage[81] though there can be a right to receive the water from a spring.

Private water supplies can be the subject of contract or covenants rather than easements.[82] In this way rights can be obtained which could not be obtained by an easement.

An easement to abstract water is always subject to the restrictions on abstraction imposed by the Water Resources Act 1991[83] which applies to anyone who wishes to "abstract water from any source of supply". As stated above, *Cargill v Gotts*[84] makes clear that no prescriptive rights can be acquired where the user is illegal in that it is in breach of the statutory limits.

---

[76] *Bosomworth v Faber* (1995) 69 P. & C.R. 288.
[77] *Chamber Colliery v Hopwood* (1886) L.R. 32 Ch. D. 549.
[78] *Burrows v Lang* [1901] 2 Ch. 502 at 558.
[79] [1932] 1 Ch. 114.
[80] *Cargill v Gotts* [1981] 1 W.L.R. 441; [1981] 1 All E.R. 682.
[81] *Bradford Corp v Pickles* [1895] A.C. 587; *Roberts v Fellowes* (1906) 94 L.T. 279.
[82] e.g. *Shayler v Woolf* [1946] Ch. 320; [1946] 2 All E.R. 54.
[83] As amended by the Water Act 2003.
[84] [1981] 1 All E.R. 682.

(3)   Right of drainage

21.21   A right of drainage through pipes leading to the public sewer is the corollary of a right to receive water from the water mains. In the standard cases such as *Simmons v Midford*[85] and *Duffy v Lamb*[86] both rights are granted together. The same problems about ownership of the pipe and of the space through which the pipe runs, therefore, apply to drainage as to receiving water.

Equally the existence of a pipe used for this purpose for the requisite period of 20 years will normally be sufficient to prove prescription without needing any further evidence to show that the use is as of right.

A right can also be obtained to drain by means of a ditch or water-course.[87] A right to drain through a watercourse will often be granted expressly but it may also be obtained by prescription:

> "The mere discharge of water by an upper proprietor upon the land of a lower may easily establish a right on the part of the upper proprietor to go on discharging because so long as the discharge continues there is submission on the part of the lower proprietor to proceedings which indicate a claim of right on the part of the proprietor above."[88]

Although this dictum seems, on the face of it, sufficient to include a right of seepage, it seems clear that a right to receive water by seepage is not capable of being the subject matter of an easement[89] nor has the lower owner a right to complain if the natural drainage is stopped up.[90]

The correct analysis is that a right to drain onto lower land by seepage is part of the natural rights of a landowner,

> "the common law rule is that the lower occupier has no ground of complaint and no cause of action against the higher occupier for permitting the natural, unconcentrated flow of water, whether on or under the surface, to pass from the higher to the lower land, but that at the same time the lower occupier is under no obligation to receive it."[91]

The corollary of this is that the owner of the upper land has no right to require the owner of the lower land to do any work on his own land to

---

[85] [1969] 2 Ch. 415; [1969] 3 W.L.R. 168.
[86] (1998) 75 P. & C.R. 364.
[87] As in *Green v Lord Somerleyton* [2003] EWCA Civ 198.
[88] *Chamber Colliery Co v Hopwood* (1886) L.R. 32 Ch. D 549 at 558.
[89] *Bradford Corp v Pickles* [1895] A.C. 587; *Roberts v Fellowes* (1906) 94 L.T. 279.
[90] *Home Brewery Co v William Davis & Co* (Leicester) [1987] Q.B. 339; [1987] 2 W.L.R. 117.
[91] per Piers Ashworth Q.C. in *Home Brewery Co v William Davis & Co* (Leicester) [1987] Q.B. 339 at 364E.

ease that drainage. So, if the owner of the lower land neglects his ditches, thereby affecting the drainage of the upper land by seepage, the owner of the upper land has no easement by lost modern grant to enable him to clear out the ditches,[92] but it would certainly include water flowing back from an osier bed.[93]

However, a right of drainage will not permit the dominant tenement to cause a nuisance and the wide definition of nuisance in *Holbeck Hall Hotel Ltd v Scarborough BC*[94] is sufficient to cover acts or omissions by the upper owner which materially affect the lower land or vice versa.[95]

These might include, for example, filling in a clay pit for development[96] or failing to clear a dyke which then flooded.[97]

(4) The right to a mooring

A right to a mooring is a riparian right which automatically goes with the land. However, it is clear that it can be qualified by easements, in particular where properties in common ownership are divided. Therefore moorings used by riparian land in common ownership, can be divided, when the land passes into different ownership by reference to the existing enjoyment and the intention of the parties, rather than the precise parcel of land to which the mooring applies.[98] Equally, the courts have accepted in principle that an easement of mooring can arise by prescription,[99] since all rights which can arise by grant, can also arise by prescription.[100]

(5) Right of eavesdrop

In so far as it is a right to drop water on your neighbour the easement **21.22** of eavesdrop is akin to a right of drainage. The specific easement, however, normally relates to houses and the right to send off the contents of your gutter to your neighbour. It is rarely granted by express grant and will usually exist by prescription. It is permissible for the dominant owner to raise his roof and thereby change his guttering as long as he does not increase the burden on the servient owner.[101]

---

[92] *Palmer v Bowman* [2000] 1 W.L.R. 842.
[93] *Home Brewery Co v William Davis & Co* (Leicester) [1987] Q.B. 339.
[94] [2000] Q.B. 836; [2000] 2 All E.R. 705.
[95] *Green v Lord Somerleyton* [2003] EWCA Civ 198; [2004] 1 P. & C.R. 33.
[96] *Home Brewery Co v William Davis & Co* (Leicester) [1987] Q.B. 339, though this case pre-dated *Holbeck Hall Hotel Ltd v Scarborough BC* [2000] Q.B. 836; [2000] 2 All E.R. 705.
[97] *Green v Lord Somerleyton* [2003] EWCA Civ 198, where, in the end, the claimant failed.
[98] *P&S Platt Ltd v Crouch* [2004] 1 P. & C.R. 18.
[99] *Port of London Authority v Ashmore* [2010] EWCA Civ 30; [2010] 1 All E.R. 1139.
[100] *Moncrieff v Jamieson* [2007] UKHL 42; [2007] 1 W.L.R. 2620.
[101] *Harvey v Walters* (1872–73) L.R. 8 C.P. 162.

4. Navigation

21.23   The right of navigation of a river is not an incident of riparian ownership, but a public right akin to a public right of way.[102] It was held in
Attorney General Ex rel Yorkshire Derwent Trust Ltd v Brotherton[103] that a
public right of navigation is not a right of way for the purposes of the
Public Rights of Way Act 1932, now contained in s.31 of the Highways Act
1980. As a result it is not a public highway and cannot be obtained by 20
years' user under that Act. As the right is not an incident of the ownership
of land, but a free-standing public right, it is not strictly within the ambit
of this book and only a brief resumé will be attempted.

There is a common law public right of navigation over a tidal river.[104]
However, a public right of navigation can only be obtained over a non-
tidal river by statute or by common-law prescription. Where there has
been a statutory right of navigation which has been repealed it is still
possible to show a public right of navigation whether by showing that the
right existed before the statute or that it has arisen since the statute has
been repealed.[105]

While the House of Lords in *Attorney General Ex rel Yorkshire Derwent
Trust Ltd v Brotherton*[106] expressly rejected the proposition that a public
right of navigation was a public highway, it was made quite clear that a
public right of navigation can still be obtained by common law
prescription:

> "The rights of the public (including, of course, public rights of navi-
> gation) could be established either from express dedication or from
> dedication presumed from long-continued user."[107]

There is no clear authority about what length of user is sufficient to show
a common law public right of navigation. Presumably the common law
cases as to public highways would apply, which means that the length of
user would depend on the circumstances.

21.24   It is not clear whether use for pleasure purposes is use under a right of
navigation. It was only in the latter part of the nineteenth century that use
of boats for pleasure, rather than as a means of transport became

---

[102] *Tate & Lyle Industries Ltd v Greater London Council* [1983] 2 A.C. 509; [1983] 2 W.L.R. 649.
[103] [1992] 1 A.C. 425; [1992] 1 All E.R. 230.
[104] The meaning of "tidal river" is explained in Ch. 8.
[105] *Attorney General Ex rel Yorkshire Derwent Trust Ltd v Brotherton* [1990] Ch. 136; [1989] 2
 W.L.R. 938, appealed on other grounds sub nom. *Attorney General Ex rel Yorkshire Derwent
 Trust Ltd v Brotherton* [1992] 1 A.C. 425; [1992] 1 All E.R. 230.
[106] [1992] A.C. 425; [1992] 1 All E.R. 230.
[107] per Lord Oliver in *Attorney General Ex rel Yorkshire Derwent Trust Ltd v Brotherton* [1992]
 A.C. 425; [1992] 1 All E.R. 230 at 248j.

popular.[108] There are many places where pleasure boats have in practice used waterways where there is an acknowledged right of navigation on the basis that such right includes all vessels. However, there are indications in *Simpson v Attorney General*[109] that use for pleasure should be regarded with extreme caution in considering whether a right of navigation has been proved. The basis of this view is that a landowner may extend a privilege to a person who is using a river for pleasure, but would take a different view if the use were commercial. In the personal injuries case of *Curtis v Wild*[110] it was held that "messing about in boats" is not using water for "navigation" within the Merchant Shipping Act 1984. However, in *Attorney General Ex rel Yorkshire Derwent Trust Ltd v Brotherton*[111] Vinelott J. refused to find that non-commercial use could not be relevant in deciding whether a right of navigation had been dedicated, but he made it clear that evidence of such user must be treated with caution:

> "To infer an intention to dedicate the river as a public navigation from the failure of the riparian owners to prevent user of the navigation by non-commercial vessels would be not only to force them to be churlish about their rights, it would put on them the intolerable burden of policing the river to see that user permitted by the undertakers did not extend beyond its proper limits".

However, in *Dyfed CC v Secretary of State for Wales*[112] a similar problem was faced in respect of a public footpath over land used for recreation. In that case the Court of Appeal held that "pure walking", i.e. recreational walking, as opposed to, say, picnicking or playing games in an area, could give rise to a public right of way over land. There seems no good reason why use of a waterway, as of right and openly over a long period, by pleasure boats should not give rise to a similar public right of navigation.

The public right of navigation in tidal water depends on the tidal river or creek being realistically navigable:

> "If it is a petty stream, navigable only at certain period of the tide and then only for a very short time and by very small boats, it is difficult to suppose it has ever been a public navigable channel."[113]

---

[108] See *Simpson v Attorney General* [1904] A.C. 476 at 492 per Lord Macnaghten.

[109] [1904] A.C. 476.

[110] [1991] 4 All E.R. 172.

[111] (1990) 59 P.& C.R. 60, reported in part [1990] Ch. 136; [1989] 2 All E.R. 423, appealed on another point sub nom. *Attorney General Ex rel Yorkshire Derwent Trust Ltd v Brotherton* [1992] A.C. 425; [1992] 1 All E.R. 230.

[112] (1990) 59 P. & C.R. 275.

[113] per Bayley J. in *R. v Montague* (1825) 4 B. & C. 598 approved in *Sim E Bak v Ang Yong Huat* [1923] A.C. 429.

Once a public right of navigation is established on a non-tidal part of a river, it cannot be lost by disuse.[114] Equally continuous use as private water whether for 20 years of any other period does not cause the public right to be forfeited.[115]

5.   Fisheries

21.25   A right for an individual or body corporate to fish a particular stretch of non-tidal water is a profit à prendre, whether or not the benefit of that right is annexed to land. Profits à prendre are dealt with below, and a full consideration of fishing law is outside the scope of this book. It can also be a franchise granted expressly or by implied dedication by the Crown and either owned by an individual as an incorporeal hereditament in gross or attached to a manor.[116] Prescription is at common law, which probably means 20 years continuous exercise. However, it appears that any franchise which seeks to prevent the public from exercising it is excluded by Magna Carta and therefore only applies to a grant made before that date as stated below.

There is also a public right to fish in the sea and in tidal waters including the foreshore, creeks and tidal rivers. The right applies to tidal waters, whether navigable or not, but not to non-tidal waters even if they are navigable.[117] A public right of sea fishing includes, as an ancillary right, the right to dig for worms on the foreshore, but not for sale or in an unreasonable manner.[118] Such fishing rights are, however, circumscribed by a body of statute law. They are also circumscribed by the common law which requires that such rights be exercised in a reasonable manner using the normal methods of fishing by net or line, etc. (as opposed to fixed engines[119] or dynamite). The right does not imply any right to use river banks or the seashore above the foreshore unless there is a customary right in favour of local inhabitants.[120]

The public right of sea fishing is also subject to various several fisheries which have been granted to individuals or particular groups. To prove such a right it is necessary to show an express or implied Royal grant before Magna Carta which prevented such Crown Grants.[121] The exercise of the public fishing right is also subject to the public right of navigation which takes priority.[122]

---

[114] *Rowland v Environment Agency* [2005] Ch. 1 per Peter Gibson L.J. at [49].

[115] ibid. at [60].

[116] *Crown Estates Commissioners v Roberts* [2008] EWCA Civ 98; [2008] Ch. 439.

[117] *Attorney General of British Columbia v Attorney General of Canada* [1914] A.C. 153.

[118] *Anderson v Alnwick DC* [1993] 3 All E.R. 613.

[119] *Bevins v Bird* (1865) 6 New Rep. 111.

[120] *Earl Iveagh v Martin* [1961] 1 Q.B. 232; *Mercer v Denne* [1905] 2 Ch. 538.

[121] *Blount v Layard* [1891] 2 Ch. 681 at 685; *Stephens v Snell* [1939] 3 All E.R. 622.

[122] *Gann v Free Fishers of Whitstable* (1865) 11 H.L. Cas. 192.

Chapter Twenty Two
Fencing

It is the common law obligation of every owner of cattle or other **22.01**
animals to fence his land to prevent them escaping onto the land of his
neighbour. If the cattle escape this gives rise to an action for cattle trespass. However, this obligation can be qualified in certain cases by an
obligation placed on the neighbour to fence his own land. This obligation
gives rise in turn to a corresponding right in the adjoining owner to have
his neighbour's land fenced.

There are two different origins for such a right. It can arise by prescription, in which case it is a right incidental to the land of an individual, or
it can arise by custom, in which case it is a right attached to a particular
section of the population such as the inhabitants of a village or the
commoners of a common.[1] An obligation to fence can also arise by statute,
for example in Inclosure Acts[2] or in respect of railways.[3]

The obligation most frequently arises where there is common land or
waste of the manor which is used for pasture. The commoners cannot
fence land which does not belong to them and accordingly the owners of
land adjoining the common may be expected to maintain their fences
against the common. One explanation of how such a right arises is where
the waste of the manor has been enclosed and there is a grant by copyhold. It is then implied that when the lord of the manor granted the copyhold he would naturally have included an obligation to fence.[4]

This obligation is ancient and has proved difficult to fit into a jurispru- **22.02**
dential framework. It was called in the early editions of Gale on Easements
"a spurious easement". In *Jones v Price*[5] it was described as a "quasi-
easement". The reason for this reticence about accepting it as a true

---

[1] See *R. v Oxfordshire CC Ex p. Sunningwell Parish Council* [2000] 1 A.C. 335; [1999] 3 W.L.R.
160 for a discussion of the meaning of customary rights.
[2] See *Smith v Muller* [2008] EWCA Civ 1425.
[3] Under the Railway Clause Consolidation Act 1845. While the obligation on Network Rail
to fence railway property is in practice universal, the obligation emanates from the
various private Acts of Parliament by which the existing railways were created.
[4] *Barber v Whitely* (1865) 34 L.J.Q.B. 212.
[5] [1965] 2 Q.B. 618; [1965] 2 All E.R. 625.

easement is that, unlike other easements, it involves the owner of the servient tenement in positive action.

The right and obligation has been considered in three comparatively recent cases. In *Jones v Price* the claim was made between neighbours without any suggestion of communal rights. Although the Court of Appeal decided that there was no such right in that case, there was a clear decision that such a right can arise by prescription and therefore must be regarded as being in the nature of an easement.

In *Crow v Wood*[6] this principle was upheld and extended by a finding that the right could also arise by implied grant under s.62 of the Law of Property Act 1925. This is a logical conclusion from the decision that it can arise by prescription since, as Diplock L.J. pointed out in *Jones v Price,*[7] prescription rests on a presumed grant.[8]

The whole issue was then considered in *Egerton v Harding.*[9] In that case the judge at first instance had held that the duty arose by custom. The Court of Appeal held that it did not really matter whether it arose by custom or by prescription. There was no need to delve into the jurisprudential origin. "A duty to fence against another's land could arise by grant or custom."[10] If it could arise by grant then it can arise by prescription or presumed grant. If the right and obligation can arise by prescription or presumed grant and can attach to the land or other hereditament of the plaintiff it does not greatly matter whether it is a true easement or just a right in the nature of an easement.

22.03   It is not clear whether the immemorial usage can be defeated in the same way as common law prescription by showing that it could not have been in operation for some time after 1189. In *Jones v Price*[11] Diplock L.J. specifically refused to decide whether it could arise by lost modern grant. However, if it can arise by implied grant it would seem to follow that it could arise by lost modern grant and it is submitted that this is what the decisions in *Barber v Whitely*[12] and *Egerton v Harding*[13] amount to. Although Scarman L.J. is careful not to refer in terms to the doctrine of lost modern grant this must be the presumed lawful origin to which he refers. If this is so then only 20 years' user is required and not user from time immemorial.

It is crucial that the usage should be as a matter of obligation. Obviously an owner will normally fence his land against a common or against his

---

[6] [1971] 1 Q.B. 77; [1970] 3 All E.R. 425.
[7] [1965] 2 Q.B. 618; [1965] 2 All E.R. 625 at 634B cited with approval in *Crow v Wood* [1971] 1 Q.B. 77, [1970] 3 All E.R. 425 at 429a.
[8] This passage was approved in *Sugarman v Porter* [2006] EWHC 331 (Ch).
[9] [1975] 1 Q.B. 62; [1974] 3 All E.R. 689.
[10] *Egerton v Harding* [1975] 1 Q.B. 62; [1974] 3 All E.R. 689 per Scarman L.J. at 694c.
[11] [1965] 2 Q.B. 618; [1965] 2 All E.R. 625.
[12] (1865) 34 L.J.Q.B. 212 which was before *Dalton v Angus* (1880–81) L.R. 6 App. Cas. 740 where the doctrine of lost modern grant was finally accepted.
[13] [1975] 1 Q.B. 62; [1974] 3 All E.R. 689.

neighbour's land for his own benefit. It is only if it can be shown that people have been required by their neighbours to fence that the right can be shown. There is, however, no need to show that the individual owner has been required to fence. It is sufficient if other owners adjoining the common have been required to keep their fences in repair.

The obligation can go beyond fencing against cattle to include an obligation to maintain a sea wall.[14] Any such prescriptive obligations are over and above the Crown's obligations contained in the Coast Protection Act 1949. The basis of the decision was customary obligation. Although the reported cases are old, there is no reason to think that the prescriptive obligations of this kind have ceased to exist.

The duty is an absolute one. It does not matter that the servient owner has no notice of the breach.[15] The only defences are act of God and force majeure. The extent of the obligation is to fence against the animals normally to be expected on the land. Therefore, for example, a Dartmoor farmer cannot be expected to fence against high jumping Scotch sheep.[16]

An easement of fencing is very similar to a covenant to fence. However, where a covenant to fence is granted it cannot be treated as an easement in order to ensure that the burden passes.[17]

The Law Commission[18] recommends that it should cease to be possible to create or acquire an easement of fencing. If, therefore, the draft Bill[19] is adopted, the right will be limited to existing rights, which have not been abandoned.

---

[14] *L.N.W.R. v Fobbing Levels Sewers Commissioners* (1897) 75 L.T. 629.

[15] *Lawrence v Jenkins* (1872–73) L.R. 8 Q.B. 274.

[16] *Coaker v Willcocks* [1911] 2 K.B. 124.

[17] *Sugarman v Porter* [2006] EWHC 331 (Ch).

[18] Law Commission, *Making Land Work: Easements, Covenants and Profits à Prendre* (London: Stationery Office, 2011), Law Com. No.327.

[19] Draft Law of Property Bill Cl.27.

Chapter Twenty Three
Profits à Prendre

1. Meaning of profit à prendre

"A profit à prendre confers a right to take from the servient tenement **23.01** some part of the soil of that tenement or minerals under it or some part of its natural produce, or the animals *ferae naturae* existing on it".[1]

Profits à prendre are closely related to easements and most of the law of easements relates also to profits. Like easements they are incorporeal hereditaments, but unlike easements they are not necessarily annexed to property, but can exist in gross.[2] This means that whereas a person cannot own a right of way except as an incident to a dominant tenement a person can own a right to fish a river without owning any land in the area.

The history of profits is linked with the history of customary rights mainly in respect of common land. It was common in villages for particular rights to be attached to particular land, such as the right to put out pigs among the acorns ("pannage"), the right to cut litter,[3] to cut peat or turves ("turbary") and above all to pasture sheep ("sheepwalk") or cattle. These customary rights now only exist in so far as they have been registered under the Commons Registration Act 1965 or have come into existence subsequently. Most other customary rights, which were annexed to or in respect of copyhold land, were abolished as a result of copyhold enfranchisement under the Law of Property Act 1922. It is now established[4] that these rights are not necessarily appurtenant to adjoining land and can be traded providing that their exercise is not related specifically to the adjoining land. Under the 1965 Act a right of common levant and couchant (which depends on the number of cattle the dominant land can

---

[1] per Winn L.J. in *Alfred F Beckett Ltd v Lyons* [1967] Ch. 449; [1967] 1 All E.R. 833 at 851c.
[2] *Bettison v Langton* [2001] UKHL 24; [2002] 1 A.C. 27; [2001] 2 W.L.R. 1605 at 1618 per Lord Scott of Foscote.
[3] *Earl de la Warr v Miles* (1881) L.R. 17 Ch. D. 535.
[4] *Bettison v Langton* [2001] UKHL 24; [2002] 1 A.C. 27; [2001] 2 W.L.R. 1605.

support in winter) became a right of pasturage for a fixed number of cattle. If this is disposed of separately from the land it survives as a profit in gross.

23.02   There are also still prescriptive profits which are appurtenant to land, but these are comparatively rare. What has become much more important is sporting rights, particularly fishing and shooting game. While these may be appurtenant to land, they usually exist in gross, which means that they become a proprietary right like any other and can be bought and sold and inherited in accordance with the normal property law.

Because profits à prendre allow the dominant owner to take something from the land, whether by actually carrying it away or by allowing his animals to consume it, they create special problems and the intention in this chapter is to deal with the problems which arise particularly in respect of profits. In so far as the law of profits coincides with that of easements, it is covered by the preceding chapters on easements in general. The difficulty with dealing with the law of profits is that many of the cases are somewhat ancient, whereas there are often more modern cases dealing with easements. It is dangerous, in such cases, to assume that the law of profits differs from the law of easements even when the relevant case seems to indicate such a difference. There is always the risk that the court will take the view that the profits case has been superseded by a more modern easement case.

2.   Profits à prendre appurtenant

23.03   A profit à prendre exists either in gross or as appurtenant to land. It is essential to distinguish between these two because a profit appurtenant passes automatically on the sale of land, whereas a profit in gross passes as separate property by sale or inheritance. Accordingly the registration régime is different. Profits à prendre appurtenant are dependant interests under s.27(2)(d) of the Land Registration Act 2002 and, accordingly, are registered in the same way as easements under rr.73 and 74 of the Land Registration Rules 2003.[5] On the other hand, profits à prendre in gross can be registered under s.3. Failure to register does not affect the validity of the grant. There are also profits à prendre appendant, which can only exist if they were created before 1290 when the statute *Quia Emptores* came into force. A profit à prendre appurtenant can be either several, so that it excludes the use by the servient tenement, or in common, so that both can use it together.

Just like an easement, a profit must be for the benefit of the dominant tenement[6] or, in other words, "accommodate" the dominant tenement.

---

[5] See 12.12 above.
[6] See para.10.06 et seq.

However, this does not mean that it has to be necessary for the dominant tenement or that the dominant tenement has to get real or appreciable benefit from it. "Accommodation depends on a connection between the right and the normal enjoyment of the dominant tenement". This is the latest expression of the law from *Polo Woods Foundation v Sheldon-Agar.*[7] It qualifies the phrase "related to the needs and use of the dominant tenement". All that is needed is a real connection.

So a profit à prendre appurtenant does not permit the dominant owner to exploit the right for commercial purposes unconnected with his use of the dominant land. This is so whether the right is claimed by prescription,[8] or by express grant.[9] The position therefore is that an unlimited right of grazing cannot pass as appurtenant on a conveyance of the dominant tenement because, being unlimited, it is unrelated to the needs and use of the dominant tenement.[10]

Clearly the grazing of sheep on a moor (unlike a right to gather litter to feed the pigs on your farm) is not related to the use of the dominant tenement as such, but is an additional right connected with the farming operation, which will allow the owner of the dominant tenement to pasture more sheep. As such it has a real connection with the farm.

The essential point in *Anderson v Bostoc,*[11] also emphasised in *Polo Woods Foundation v Sheldon-Agar,*[12] was that there could be no grant of an unlimited right. In *White v Taylor (No.2)*[13] a right to pasture a specific number of sheep on the servient land was considered potentially valid, regardless of whether pasturing that number of sheep was necessary for the benefit of the dominant farms. Many such rights were created under the Commons Registration Act 1965 which required the number of cattle to be identified in cases where there was a general right of pasturage appurtenant to particular land. Once the number of cattle has been identified, the right remains appurtenant to the land until such time as it is specifically disposed of separately.[14]

This aspect is particularly important where the right claimed is actually **23.04** to take something away, such as a right to take timber or to fish. It was said in *Bailey v Stephens*[15] that a right to cut timber could only exist if it was "to be used upon the land of the party claiming the profit", but in *Harris v Earl of Chesterfield*[16] the right claimed was a right to fish. Clearly

---

[7] [2009] EWHC 1361 (Ch); [2010] 1 All E.R. 539.
[8] *Harris v Earl of Chesterfield* [1911] A.C. 623.
[9] *Staffordshire & Worcestershire Canal Navigation v Bradley* [1912] 1 Ch. 91.
[10] *Anderson v Bostock* [1976] Ch. 312; [1976] 1 All E.R. 560.
[11] [1976] Ch. 312; [1976] 1 All E.R. 560.
[12] [2009] EWHC 1361 (Ch); [2010] 1 All E.R. 539.
[13] [1969] 1 Ch. 150; [1967] 3 All E.R. 349.
[14] *Bettison v Langton* [2001] UKHL 24; [2002] 1 A.C. 27.
[15] (1862) 12 C.B. N.S. 91.
[16] [1911] A.C. 623.

the fish caught would not be used on the farm, but would be sold or eaten. They did not decide that there can be no profit à prendre appurtenant to fish.

The position, therefore, seems to be that an appurtenant profit can include rights to gather material for the dominant farm, pasturage rights that benefit the farm and sporting rights for the dominant owner. The significance of whether the use is "commercial" or not has been somewhat diminished by *Bettison v Langton*.[17] There is no doubt that many customary rights were commercial, in the sense that the people owning them were commercial farmers. Equally, sporting rights are often of greater commercial value than agricultural rights. Despite dicta in *Harris v Earl of Chesterfield*[18] it now seems that the issue is not whether the rights are commercial, but whether the rights are truly in connection with the dominant land, in which case they are appurtenant to that land and cannot be alienated from it, or whether they have become so crystallised that they can be alienated without putting an additional burden on the servient land. Once alienated they can be exploited commercially.

As the right is appurtenant, it passes to each owner under s.62 of the Law of Property Act 1925.[19] Furthermore, the right can be sub-divided if the dominant tenement is split up into different parcels.[20] If the deed sub-dividing the profit does not expressly state how it is to be divided, it is apportioned on a pro rata basis. Logically, this means that if a parcel of land has the right to pasture nine sheep, a sale of a third of it will carry with it the right to pasture three sheep but, in *Owen v Blathwayt*,[21] a right to graze sheep on a common "in common with the other tenants of the Lessor" was interpreted as giving each lessee pro rata entitlement in accordance with "the number of sheep which could be maintained on each farm" a concept fraught with potential arguments about intensive farming methods.

As what is created is an incorporeal hereditament at law, it can only be expressly created by deed,[22] though it can also be created in equity by signed contract.[23]

23.05   An appurtenant profit can also be created by prescription. Where the prescription is under the Prescription Act 1832 the profit has to be exercised for 30 years prior to action brought. The 40-year period is also extended in the case of profits, to 60 years. However, it has been held in

---

[17] [2001] UKHL 24; [2002] 1 A.C. 27.
[18] [1911] A.C. 623.
[19] *White v Williams* [1922] 1 K.B. 727.
[20] *White v Taylor* (No.2) [1969] 1 Ch. 150; [1967] 3 All E.R. 349.
[21] [2002] EWHC 2231 (Ch); [2003] 1 P. & C.R. 28.
[22] *Webber v Lee* (1881–82) L.R. 9 Q.B.D. 315.
[23] Law of Property Act 1925 s.40, as amended by Law of Property (Miscellaneous Provisions) Act 1989.

Lord Dynevor v Richardson[24] that under the doctrine of lost modern grant the period is 20 years, the same as for easements. The Law Commission[25] recommends that prescription for easements and profits should be under a single regime, abolishing common law prescription, prescription under the Prescription Act 1832 and the doctrine of lost modern grant. As such the period for profits would be the same as for easements, namely 20 years.[26]

The profit will normally be for the same estate (i.e. freehold or leasehold) as the dominant land and will be enjoyed by the tenant or occupier of the dominant land in the same way as an easement. As it has to be used in connection with the dominant land, it seems that it cannot be let off by the owner of the dominant land separately from the dominant land itself.

Where the claim is by prescription there may well be difficulties over the extent of the dominant tenement to be benefited. Essentially the problem is the same as with easements, but there are particular problems in cases such as fisheries where the fishery is exercised by the owner of the land in title to his land over such parts of the river as he wishes.[27] Weirs were often built not just to control the flow of water, but to provide specific fishing areas and a right of fishing from particular weirs can be separated off from other parts of the river.[28]

3. Profits in gross

Unlike easements, a profit à prendre can exist in gross.[29] It nevertheless **23.06** remains an interest in land and not a mere licence.[30] As such it can be created as a freehold or a leasehold and is subject to the usual formalities required for dispositions of land.[31] The Land Registration Act 2002[32] has introduced provision for voluntary registration of profits à prendre. The process is set out in rr.2, 7, 24 and Sch.6 of the Land Registration Rules 2003. This, however, does not affect the validity of unregistered profits. The apparent requirement of registration in r.2 does not override the voluntary nature of registration in s.3 of the Act.

Logically, if a right can be created by express grant, it can also be created by prescription, since prescription is based on the presumption of a lawful

---

[24] [1995] Ch. 173; [1994] 3 W.L.R. 1091.
[25] Law Commission, *Making Land Work: Easements, Covenants and Profits à Prendre* (London: The Stationery Office, 2011), Law Com. No.327.
[26] Law Commission, *Making Land Work: Easements, Covenants and Profits à Prendre* (London: The Stationery Office, 2011), Law Com. No.327. The draft Law of Property Bill appears to repeal the existing law of easements and profits, but only to bring in a new principle for easements.
[27] *Lord Advocate v Lord Lovat* (1879–80) L.R. 5 App. Cas. 273.
[28] *Neill v Duke of Devonshire* (1882–83) L.R. 8 App. Cas. 135.
[29] *Bettison v Langton* [2002] 1 A.C. 27 at [49] per Lord Scott.
[30] *Fitzgerald v Firbank* [1897] 2 Ch. 96.
[31] *Webber v Lee* (1881–82) L.R. 9 Q.B.D. 315.
[32] Land Registration Act 2002 s.3.

origin. In *Barton v Church Commissioners for England*[33] a prescriptive right to a several fishery on the River Wye was upheld on the basis of long use. In that case the law was fully explained and it is clear that prescriptive rights to profits in gross can be obtained in the same way as any other prescriptive rights. Thus, it has been held that a "sole and several pasturage" can exist in gross having been exercised from time immemorial.[34] "Instances of sole pasturage are to be found in the South Downs in Sussex and they are frequently transferred in gross" per Lord Abinger C.B.[35] There was some doubt in that case whether such a right can arise under the Prescription Act 1832,[36] despite the express reference to profits in the Act, but this is of little importance since, if the Prescription Act does not apply, there seems no reason why the doctrine of lost modern grant should not be used. As it is not annexed to land it cannot be created by implied grant under s.62 of the Law of Property Act 1925.

It has also been claimed that a body of persons, such as the inhabitants of an area, have exercised a profit by custom. In *Alfred F Beckett Ltd v Lyons*,[37] people had collected sea coal from the beaches between Seaham and Hartlepool for generations. One of the ways the claim was put before the Court of Appeal was that it was a local custom, but it was held that a fluctuating body cannot obtain a prescriptive right of this nature. There is, however, authority for a specific body of people, such as the corporation of a borough, being entitled to an immemorial exclusive right of pasturage.[38]

4. Profits and licences

23.07   A profit in gross must be distinguished from a licence. It is perfectly possible to grant a licence to exercise rights such as fishing or shooting over land. Perhaps the most obvious example is that of a person who takes a licence to fish for a day or a week. There could be no suggestion that this would give rise to a profit à prendre. The main difference in practice between a licence and a profit is that a profit is alienable whereas a licence will normally be personal to the licensee. In *Re Vickers Lease*[39] the lessor of fishing rights on a stretch of the river Test had reserved "for her own use a rod in the said fishing". The Court of Appeal, reversing Roxburgh J., held that this was not the re-grant of a profit, but simply a licence personal to the lessor. Accordingly on her death it lapsed. The

---

[33] [2008] EWHC 3091 (Ch).
[34] *Welcome v Upton* (1840) 6 M. & W. 536.
[35] At 541.
[36] *Shuttleworth v Le Fleming* (1865) 19 C.B. N.S. 687, based apparently on the fact that profits in gross are not rights in common.
[37] [1967] Ch. 449.
[38] *Johnson v Barnes* (1872–73) L.R. 8 C.P. 527.
[39] [1947] Ch. 420.

principles distinguishing a licence from a profit are similar to those which distinguish licences from other interests in land and it is more helpful to apply those authorities by analogy than to try to use old cases specifically about profits.[40] Essentially the issue is a question of construction depending on whether what is effectively created is an interest in land or a mere contractual right.

5. Exercise of rights of profit

Unless the grant expressly says so a right of profit is not an exclusive **23.08** right.[41] The person who owns it may exercise it either in person or by his employees. Usually express grants of sporting rights make clear the limitations, for example, to a certain number of rods or guns. There is no reason in principle why a grant of a profit in gross should be limited. It could, for example, include a right to take all the wood and grass from the grantor's land,[42] but such a right cannot be claimed by prescription.[43]

One of the most difficult problems encountered with profits is the extent of the obligation on the servient owner to maintain the land. A person granted rights to fish or shoot, or to collect timber or to pasture sheep can only do so if the land is kept in a state where it can support the subject matter. A right to pasture sheep over land that has since been developed as a building estate is of little value. On the other hand, the servient owner can hardly be expected to expend large sums maintaining the game or stocking the river and, without changing the use to which his land is put, he may wish to cut down copses used as cover for game or alter the management of the river in a way which affects the fishing.

This problem was confronted in *Peech v Best*.[44] There the Claimant had sporting rights over some land on a 14-year lease. The servient owner built houses on it. It was held that he had infringed the dominant owner's right. It was decided that it is clearly an interference with a profit à prendre wilfully to destroy the game, though the servient owner, if he has not entered into a covenant to do his best to keep up the head of game (as he had in that case), may change his cultivation methods or cut down the cover:

"So long as the tenant [or the servient owner] is bona fide and reasonably managing and cultivating his holding the landlord [i.e. the dominant owner] must (as a general rule) be content to exercise

---

[40] See *Street v Mountford* [1985] A.C. 809; [1985] 2 W.L.R. 877.
[41] *Duke of Sutherland v Heathcote* [1892] 1 Ch. 475.
[42] *Sir Francis Barrington* 8 Co. Rep. 136, cited with approval in *Bailey v Stephens* (1862) 12 C.B. N.S. 91.
[43] *Bailey v Stephens* (1862) 12 C.B. N.S. 91.
[44] [1931] 1 K.B. 1.

his sporting rights upon the lands as he finds them from time to time."[45]

It was held that the building of the houses did amount to an infringement of the sporting rights.

The same principle was applied in *Pole v Peake*,[46] where it was affirmed that a person with sporting rights to game including rearing them had the right to enter the land to rear pheasants, was not liable for the normal damage caused by pheasants and the owner of the land, while entitled to use it for agricultural purposes would not be able to change the use of the land in such a way as to render the sporting right unexercisable.

However, in *Well Barn Shoot Ltd v Shackleton*,[47] the decision went the other way. A declaration was granted allowing the development providing that it did not interfere with the shooting rights. The crucial questions were:

- whether the changes amounted to a substantial interference with the sporting rights; and, if so,

- whether it amounted to a fundamental change in the character of the neighbourhood.

6. Extinguishment of profits

23.09   Essentially, profits à prendre are extinguished in the same way as easements.[48] As there are more modern cases about easements it is safer to assume that the rule as to easements applies than to make use of a venerable case which may seem to indicate that there is a difference.

The substantial difference between an easement and a profit, however, is that a profit can be exhausted. If the exhaustion is due to a change in the character of the servient tenement which has been acquiesced in by the owner of the profit, then this may be regarded as abandonment, but it is always possible that the exhaustion of the profit may occur for natural reasons unrelated to the actions of the servient owner. In these circumstances, the profit may be extinguished if the exhaustion is permanent, though not if it is temporary. Whether cessation of user by the dominant owner coupled with a change of use by the servient owner gives rise to

---

[45] *Peech v Best* [1931] 1 K.B. 1 at 8, per Scrutton L.J. quoting Barton J. in *Caldwell v Kilkelly* [1905] 1 I.R. 434 at 447.
[46] [1998] E.G. 125 (C.S.).
[47] [2003] EWCA Civ 2.
[48] See para.17.01, et seq.

abandonment is a question of fact.[49] There is some doubt as to whether a several fishery created by deed can be abandoned.[50]

7. Enforcement of profits

It has been said that interference with a profit is a trespass and accord- **23.10** ingly can be enforced without proof of pecuniary loss, *Nicholls v Ely Beet Sugar Factory Ltd (No.2)*.[51] However, in that case the court said that in this respect it was just like an easement, but an action for interference with an easement is in nuisance and only arises if there is a substantial interference with the convenient exercise of the right. That case concerned pollution of a fishing river, which could not be shown to cause pecuniary loss to the fishermen who exercised their rights for sport. A similar claim to infringement of an easement (for example a right of way to a pond used for fishing) could also be pursued without proof of commercial loss and there is no reason to consider that the enforcement of profits is any different from that of easements.

---

[49] *Carr v Lambert* (1865–66) L.R. 1 Ex. 168; *Scrutton v Stone* (1893) 9 T.L.R. 478.
[50] *Neill v Duke of Devonshire* (1882–83) 8 App. Cas. 135.
[51] [1936] 1 Ch. 343.

Part III:
Remedies

Chapter Twenty Four
Remedies

CAUSES OF ACTION

As a rule, the cause of action in boundary disputes is trespass to land, **24.01** whereas the cause of action where there is disturbance of an easement is nuisance. It has always been possible to join more than one cause of action in a single claim and, although there is nothing specific about this in the Civil Procedure Rules 1998, there is no reason to doubt that this is still possible. Accordingly it is very common for claims for trespass to land to be coupled with claims for disturbance of an easement, such as a right of way, or for trespass to goods or, in all too many cases, trespass to the person, where the emotional strain, which so frequently occurs in boundary or easement disputes, erupts into violence.

The remedy for trespass or nuisance is damages which may be coupled with a declaration or an injunction. In appropriate cases, declarations and injunction can be claimed on their own without proof of damage.[1]

Trespass is actionable per se, which means that it is not necessary to prove damage or the threat of damage in order to bring the action. This means that if a claimant proves that the defendant has encroached on his land, even if he has since withdrawn, he is entitled to a small sum by way of damages. This may have relevance in relation to costs. A claimant who pursues a claim but succeeds only to a limited degree may be unable to persuade the court to award him costs, but he may be able to prevent an order for costs being made against him. The court has a wide discretion in costs, but it is only in exceptional circumstances that an order for costs should be made against a successful defendant[2] and presumably the same applies to a successful claimant, at least where the damages awarded are more than nominal.[3] For this reason it is not uncommon, where there is a possibility that a minor trespass has occurred, for the defendant to pay a small sum into court, in the hope that if the judgment is for less than this sum he will be able to claim costs against the claimant.

---

[1] See below, para.24.05 et seq. and para.24.22.
[2] *Knight v Clifton* [1971] Ch. 700; [1971] 2 W.L.R. 564.
[3] *Gupta v Klita, The Times*, November 23, 1989.

The move towards conciliation and alternative dispute resolution has led to the much discussed case of *Halsey v Milton Keynes General NHS Trust*,[4] where the Court of Appeal upheld a decision to refuse costs to the successful party who had refused offers of mediation.

The main form of alternative dispute resolution is by mediation by a third party, often from a court-based mediation service. This is specifically dealt with in Chapter 17 of the Chancery Guide.

> "There are too many calamitous neighbour disputes in the courts. Greater use should be made of the services of local mediators, who have specialist legal and surveying skills and are experienced in alternative dispute resolution. An attempt at mediation should be made right at the beginning of the dispute and certainly well before things turn nasty and become expensive. By the time neighbours get to court it is often too late for court-based ADR and mediation schemes to have much impact. Litigation hardens attitudes. Costs become an additional aggravating issue. Almost by its own momentum the case that cried out for compromise moves onwards and upwards to a conclusion that is disastrous for one of the parties, possibly for both".[5]

Mediation costs may in principle be recoverable from the unsuccessful party.[6] The Court went so far as to consider whether they could order a party to submit to mediation, but decided that this would not be appropriate (particularly under art.6 of the European Convention on Human Rights). However, they concluded that costs sanctions were appropriate where the successful party had acted unreasonably in refusing mediation, based on the nature of the dispute, the merits of the case, whether other settlement methods have been attempted, the proportionality of the costs of mediation, the delay caused by mediation and whether mediation had a reasonable prospect of success. All these issues are very relevant to boundary disputes.

24.02   Although boundary disputes and easement claims do arise where the financial value of the claim is less that £5,000, it is not normal to allocate such claims to the small claims track. By r.26.8 a relevant matter in the allocation to a track is "the likely complexity of the facts, law or evidence" and "the views expressed by the parties". The Practice Direction provides that,

> "the small claims track is intended to provide a proportionate procedure by which most straightforward claims of a financial value of not more than £5,000 can be decided".[7]

---

[4] [2004] EWCA Civ 576; [2004] 1 W.L.R. 3002.
[5] per Mummery L.J. in *Bradford v James* [2008] EWCA Civ 837.
[6] *National Westminster Bank v Feeney* [2006] EWHC 90066 (Costs) at [20].
[7] CPR PD 26–8.1(1)(a).

It would be a true optimist who would embark on a boundary dispute in the belief that it is likely to be straightforward. Accordingly, costs are likely to be an issue in most boundary/easement disputes.

In order to found an action in trespass, the claimant has to prove either possession which has been interfered with or a right to possession. Usually in boundary disputes this presents no problem. A party is either relying on a paper title or adverse possession. However, where there is waste land, with no obvious owner and no-one in possession a person may wish to assert possession and then exclude his neighbour. In *Marsden v Miller*,[8] it was made clear that this is not possible if the neighbour is alert. The taking of possession must be effective to exclude others. It is not, therefore, enough to erect a fence which is promptly pulled down by the neighbour.

Where there is disturbance of an easement the position is different. The claimant has to show that his user of the easement has been materially affected. The principle was put thus in *West v Sharp*[9]:

"Not every actionable interference with an easement, such as a right of way, is actionable. There must be a substantial interference with the enjoyment of it. There is no actionable interference with a right of way if it can be substantially and practically exercised as conveniently after as before the occurrence of the alleged obstruction. Thus, the grant of a right of way in law in respect of every part of a defined area does not involve the proposition that the grantee can in fact object to anything done on any part of the area which would obstruct passage over that part. He can only object to such activities, including obstruction, as substantially interfere with the exercise of the defined right as for the time being is reasonably required by him."

This principle cannot, however, be taken too far:

"(1) The test of an actionable interference is not whether what the grantee is left with is reasonable, but whether his insistence on being able to continue the use of the whole of what he contracted for is reasonable; (2) it is not open to the grantor to deprive the grantee of his preferred modus operandi and then argue that someone else would prefer to do things differently, unless the grantee's preference is unreasonable or perverse."[10]

The same applies to all easements. There can be no technical disturbance of a right of support or a right of light or of any other easement. If the

---

[8] (1992) 64 P. & C.R. 239.
[9] (2000) 79 P. & C.R. 327 at 332, per Mummery L.J.
[10] per Blackburne J. in *B&Q v Liverpool & Lancashire Properties* (2001) 81 P. & C.R. 20 at [45].

disturbance alleged does not cause some abridgement of the right the action fails. It is not, however, necessary to show any pecuniary loss.

24.03   In boundary disputes it is not uncommon to find, particularly in the less well-drawn pleadings, a claim for possession. The claim for possession, which originates from the action in ejectment, is normally used in landlord and tenant or other cases where the main issue is not the boundary of the land but whether the person in occupation has a right to be there. There is, however, no reason in principle why it should not be used in a boundary dispute as it is a claim against a person "in possession of land",[11] even though the procedure in Pt 55 of the Civil Procedure Rules 1998 is clearly designed principally to be used against people who are in possession of a property.

There is a further obscure cause of action that can be useful in certain cases. This is slander of title. The action lies where someone falsely and maliciously disparages a person's title to land causing the other person special damage. The circumstances in which it can arise are where a person is seeking to sell property and a neighbour challenges either the boundary or an easement, but neither takes any steps to interfere with the land or easement nor threatens to do so. In such a case the claimant should be able to succeed in obtaining a declaration of his rights[12] but if he has lost a sale as a result of the allegations it is difficult to find a cause of action on which to peg a claim for damages.

To give an example, if at an auction sale the adjoining owner attends and states that he owns part of the land the auction sale may collapse, but the adjoining owner has not committed trespass nor necessarily threatened to do so. In these circumstances an action for slander of title may lie, but this cause of action is rarely used because of the need to prove malice and special damage.

REMEDIES

24.04   Most boundary disputes and easement claims are commenced in the county court and the procedure described is based on that presumption.

A.   Declarations

24.05   What most people want when they commence a boundary dispute or an action about an easement is a final decision on who owns the land in dispute or the existence or extent of the easement. Sometimes the person commencing the proceedings has suffered substantial damage which cannot be solved by a declaration or an injunction, but in most cases the

---

[11] CPR r.55.1.
[12] *Re Lewis's Declaration of Trust* [1953] Ch. 423.

basic remedy, and often the only remedy eventually obtained, is a declaration as to the true ownership of the land or the existence or otherwise and extent of the easement.

There has been some doubt about the origin of declarations. Declarator claims have existed for hundreds of years in Scotland[13] and declarations were granted consequent upon other claims in Courts of Chancery before 1850. The Court of Chancery Act 1851[14] (extended to all divisions of the High Court by the Judicature Act 1873), amended the powers of the Court of Chancery and appears to have extended these powers to allow declarations to be made alone and not simply annexed to other relief as had previously been the practice. In *Guaranty Trust Co of New York v Hannay & Co*[15] the rules allowing declarations to be made without being annexed to other claims were challenged, but despite the fact that the Chancery Procedure Acts were repealed in 1883 it was nevertheless held that the rules were intra vires.

The power to make declaratory judgments is contained in r.40.20 of the Civil Procedure Rules 1998,[16] which makes it clear that the court may make binding declarations whether or not any other remedy is claimed. The power applies equally to the High Court and the county court. By s.38(1) of the County Courts Act 1984 the county court can make any order which the High Court could make (except for certiorari and mandamus and any prescribed powers[17]) and by s.21 it can deal with actions where title is in question.

Despite the existence of the power of the courts to grant declarations, right up to the 1920s the courts showed an antipathy to declarations as a new-fangled idea and there was doubt about their origin: **24.06**

> "In truth these abstract declarations, whatever else they may be, are neither law nor equity. Perhaps when that is more clearly recognised they will, to the general advantage, be less promiscuously employed."[18]

This was only the most acerbic of numerous pronouncements to the effect that declarations should be ordered "sparingly", "with great care and jealousy", etc. but such views are now of historical interest only. The modern law is as set out by Viscount Radcliffe in *Ibeneweka v Egbuna*[19]:

---

[13] per Lord Dunedin in Russian Commercial and *Russian Commercial and Industrial Bank v British Bank for Foreign Trade Ltd* [1921] 2 A.C. 438.

[14] s.14 generalised by s.50 of the Chancery Procedure Act 1852.

[15] [1915] 2 K.B. 535.

[16] As amended by Civil Procedure Amendment Rules 2001 (SI 2001/256) r.13.

[17] County Courts (Remedies Regulations) 1991 and the County Court (Remedies) Amendment Regulations 1995, neither of which are directly relevant to boundary or easement disputes.

[18] *Gray v Spyer* [1921] 2 Ch. 549 at 557 overruled on appeal [1922] 2 Ch. 22.

[19] [1964] 1 W.L.R. 219 PC (Nigeria).

"Beyond the fact that the power to grant a declaration should be exercised with a proper sense of responsibility and a full realisation that judicial pronouncements ought not to be issued unless there were circumstances that called for their making, there was no legal restriction on the award of a declaration."

This approach is the one pursued in practice and it is now realised that a declaration is a very useful way of setting out the rights of the parties without making any penal order in the form of an injunction.

In *Greenwich Healthcare NHS Trust v London & Quadrant Housing Trust*,[20] Lightman J. summarised the general law on declarations. The conditions are,

"that the question under consideration is a real question; that the person seeking the declaration has a real interest; and that there has been proper argument".

He took the unusual step of granting a declaration that the defendants would not be entitled to an injunction if and when the development takes place.[21]

24.07   The remedy is discretionary.[22] However, it is not clear whether it is equitable. There seems little doubt that its English origins were in the Courts of Chancery and that the now repealed statutes simply extended powers which had been earlier exercised in equity. The point was, however, considered by the Court of Appeal in *Chapman v Michaelson*[23] and it was decided, without any meticulous historical analysis, that,

"the considerations which affect an action for true equitable relief . . . do not necessarily apply to an action for a mere declaration of rights."[24]

This case makes it clear, therefore, that the discretion exercised in granting or refusing a declaration is not exercised on the same equitable principles as in granting or refusing an injunction. Whatever its historical origin, therefore, no clear guidance has been given on the circumstances in which a declaration will be refused on discretionary grounds. It is

---

[20] [1998] 1 W.L.R. 1749; (1999) 77 P. & C.R. 133 at 138.
[21] *Greenwich Healthcare NHS Trust v London & Quadrant Housing Trust* [1998] 1 W.L.R. 1749; (1999) 77 P. & C.R. 133 per Lightman J. at 240, approved in *Well Barn Shoot Ltd v Shackleton* [2003] EWCA Civ 2.
[22] *Gray v Spyer* [1922] 2 Ch. 22; *Russian Commercial and Industrial Bank v British Bank for Foreign Trade Ltd* [1921] 2 A.C. 438.
[23] [1909] 1 Ch. 238.
[24] *Chapman v Michaelson* [1909] 1 Ch. 238 per Fletcher Moulton L.J. at 242.

certainly the case that on many occasions a declaration has been granted when the court has refused an injunction in exercise of its discretion, because, for example, of the conduct of the claimant.[25] It has not been specifically decided, however, whether the court has a discretion to refuse even a declaration because of the conduct of the claimant. Courts tend to recognise that once a decision has been made it is binding on the parties by virtue of issue estoppel and that a declaration is the best way of setting that decision out in clear terms however badly the parties have conducted themselves. Accordingly, unlike an injunction, a declaration may be ordered whether or not the action is trivial.[26]

The concern commonly expressed about declarations was that they would be used to answer hypothetical problems. This concern has proved to be largely unjustified. In terms of boundary disputes a dispute sometimes arises where an adjoining owner claims that the apparent boundary is incorrect but does not take any positive steps to alter it. The claimant may choose to start proceedings based on the trespass of the person who he claims to be in wrongful possession of part of his land. Such a claim may be solely for a declaration, but will more often involve a claim for an injunction to have the boundary fence moved and damages for any loss incurred as a result of the trespass.

However, the person making the claim may, instead, restrict himself **24.08** to letters and other assertions of title. The person receiving these assertions then has the choice of either sitting back and waiting to see what happens or taking the initiative by commencing proceedings himself. He will be particularly keen to start proceedings if he is thinking of selling and fears that the existence of a dispute, which would have to be disclosed in the replies to the preliminary inquiries, may jeopardize his sale. In such circumstances the only remedy available may be a declaration.

A very similar problem may arise in an easement case. A person asserting a right may be subject to challenge from the owner of the servient tenement which consists not of any physical obstruction or even threats of such obstruction, but just letters or remarks challenging the existence of the alleged right. He may wish to ensure that the right he is exercising is proved in court. Where there is a genuine dispute the court will be prepared to grant a declaration in circumstances where there is neither a claim to damages or to an injunction.

The difficulty that the claimant has in such circumstances is that he has no real cause of action. Simply writing letters does not amount to trespass and slander of title can only be claimed if it is malicious. However, if there is a real dispute then it will still be appropriate to make

---

[25] *St Mary, Islington v Hornsey Urban DC* [1900] 1 Ch. 695.
[26] *Llandudno Urban DC v Woods* [1899] 2 Ch. 705.

a claim for a declaration alone (or coupled with a quia timet injunction if the other party has threatened trespass). This is an occasion where the court will make a declaration even though there is no cause of action in existence.[27]

24.09   Another situation is where a person who is proposing some development which might or might not amount to disturbance of an easement (e.g. a right of light) may wish to have the matter resolved before embarking on development expenditure.[28] He may then commence an action claiming a declaration thereby forcing the other party to accept or resist the proposals before they are put into effect. Despite relatively recent pronouncements by the Court of Appeal that the court should grant such declarations "with considerable reserve",[29] in *Greenwich Healthcare NHS Trust v London & Quadrant Housing Trust*.[30] Lightman J. was happy to make a declaration that the defendants would not be entitled to an injunction or damages if and when the development took place and this approach was followed by the Court of Appeal in *Wellbarn Shoot Ltd v Shackleton*.[31]

A declaration is only binding on the parties to the decision and their successors in title. Accordingly it is desirable that all parties with an interest in the proceedings should be joined and the court may insist on this.[32] Otherwise a person who has not been made a party to the proceedings may re-open the issue. Rule 19.8A of the Civil Procedure Rules 1998 gives the court power to make judgments binding on non-parties in claims in the High Court relating to the estate of a deceased person or property subject to a trust or the sale of any property.

In terms of a boundary dispute, this means that it is normally desirable for both the owners and the tenants of the disputed land to be joined, together with any other person who has actually been involved in the trespass. Equally where the dispute involves an easement it is desirable that the owners and occupiers of the dominant and the servient tenements should be parties. The person who caused the obstruction should also be made a party since, unless he is acting as agent for someone else, any claim for damages will be against him. Whether to include a particular person as a party is, however, a matter of judgment. Sometimes including a person as a defendant who is on the fringes of the dispute will be more trouble than it is worth.

---

[27] *Louden v Ryder (No.2)* [1953] Ch. 423; [1953] 2 W.L.R. 863.
[28] *HKRUK II (CHC) Ltd v Heaney* [2010] EWHC 2245 (Ch).
[29] See generally *Thorne Rural DC v Bunting (No.1)* [1972] Ch. 470; [1972] 2 W.L.R. 517 and *Mellstrom v Garner* [1970] 1 W.L.R. 603.
[30] [1998] 1 W.L.R. 1749; (1999) 77 P. & C.R. 133.
[31] [2003] EWCA Civ 2.
[32] *Ibeneweka v Egbuna* [1964] 1 W.L.R. 219; *London Passenger Transport Board v Moscrop* [1942] A.C. 332.

The true ownership of the property may only emerge on disclosure, at **24.10** which point application should be made to amend to add additional parties. This can only be done with the permission of the court.[33] In boundary and easement disputes it is common to find that one individual is the prime mover in the dispute, but not the sole owner of the adjacent property or of the dominant or servient tenement. His or her spouse may be the other joint owner, or the property may be owned by parents or may be part of a deceased's estate, or the person causing the problems may be only a tenant or a licensee. There is nothing to prevent action being brought against any person who trespasses on land or who disturbs an easement, whether or not he has any interest in the adjoining land or in the dominant tenement, but a declaration will only normally be obtained where all the persons with an interest are joined. It is not, however, normal to join mortgagees unless the claim will have a substantial effect on the value of their security. They should, however, be informed of the dispute.

It is important to ensure that the correct parties are joined in the action before the limitation period expires. By s.35(1) of the Limitation Act 1980, any amendment adding a new party or a new cause of action relates back to the date the proceedings were originally commenced, but this in turn means that normally the court will not order the addition of a new party if the application to amend is made after the expiry of the limitation period, s.35(3) of the Limitation Act 1980. There are exceptions to this contained in s.35(4) and (5) which allow for rules of court to provide for the addition of further parties after the expiry of the limitation period where the addition or substitution of the new party is necessary for the determination of the original action, which means either that the original party name was included by mistake or that the action against the original party cannot be maintained unless the new party is joined.[34] The relevant rule is 19.5(3)(b). The Court may add a party where,

"the claim cannot properly be carried on by or against the original party unless the new party is added or substituted as claimant or defendant".

Although this does not specifically refer to the addition of a party for the purposes of a declaration, this is plainly intended.

Applications to amend to add or substitute a new party are by definition made before the proposed new party is a party to the proceedings. Accordingly if an order is made adding a new party and the new party claims that the limitation period has expired or for some other reason he should not be joined he has to apply to have the leave to amend rescinded.

---

[33] CPR r.19.2(2).
[34] Limitation Act 1980 s.35(6).

24.11   A claim for a declaration should be pleaded and should set out the terms claimed. However, properly drafted Particulars of Claim should set out the precise nature of the claimant's case in the main body of the pleading and, if this is done, it is not necessary for the claim to a declaration set out in the Claim itself to go beyond asking for a declaration that the claimant is entitled to the property claimed in the Particulars of Claim.

If the pleadings do not include a claim for a declaration this makes the situation "very awkward" for the court, but in the end the court may decide to grant a declaration which sets out the true position rather than decide the issue and then make no order or a nominal order for damages.[35]

It is easy at the end of a hard fought case to attach little importance to the form of the declaration. However, it must be remembered that the decision should constitute a final resolution of the respective rights of the parties and that it should be kept with the deeds. It is important to ensure, therefore, that the form of the declaration sets out clearly the Court's decision and does not leave room for further argument at some time in the future about the meaning of the decision. A declaration that the Claimant is "entitled to the land claimed in the Particulars of Claim" for example, though perfectly proper in the Claim Form itself may beg questions if incorporated in the final order and in any case will require the pleadings to be stored with the decision. The ideal is for the declaration to include a map setting out the precise boundary line, but this may not always be sufficient. Frequently the judgment refers to particular features, such as a tree or a fence, which may not remain there for ever. The declaration should, therefore, contain a sufficiently precise verbal description of the boundary. There is nothing to prevent photographs being referred to in the declaration. It is, nevertheless, the practice for the declaration to be comparatively short and succinct.

In *Dicker v Scammell*,[36] the consent declaration by which the original boundary dispute was settled was so imprecise that one party brought fresh proceedings to have it declared void for uncertainty. This was partly because the line was drawn on a small-scale map with a wide pen. The claimant won before the County Court, but the Court of Appeal overturned that decision, holding that, given the Court's powers to assist in working out or clarifying orders, the Declaration was not void. However, the uncertainty, no doubt, added considerably to the costs.

24.12   In an easement dispute, the form of the declaration will obviously depend on the nature of the easement in dispute and, in the case of a right of way, will also depend on whether it is the route of the way, or the extent of the user that is in dispute. However, as with boundary disputes

---

[35] *Harrison Broadley v Smith* [1964] 1 W.L.R. 456.
[36] *Dicker v Scammell* [2005] EWCA Civ 405; [2006] 1 P. & C.R. 4.

the general rule is that the declaration should consist of a short, succinct statement of the rights as found, backed by a map and/or photographs.

The other important factor is to ensure that a proper record of the decision is kept. County courts keep records of their orders for an absurdly short time and frequently boundary and easement disputes, previously resolved by the courts, re-emerge decades later. In these circumstances a proper record of the decision kept with the deeds can be invaluable in resolving or preventing further disputes.

Normally a declaration will only be made at the end of the hearing and not on an interim order.[37] There is jurisdiction to make a final declaration on an interim application, but this jurisdiction should be exercised sparingly.[38] The reason for this is that a declaration is a formal order which is intended to finalise the proceedings and it is undesirable to make a declaration at an interim stage when there is the possibility that the final order would be inconsistent with it. If, however, the parties have reached agreement on one separate aspect of the claim there is no reason why that aspect should not be settled by a declaration leaving other aspects to be tried.

There is a provision in r.25(1)(b) of the Civil Procedure Rules 1998 for **24.13** an interim declaration as an alternative to an interim injunction. It is not clear to what extent this will be useful in boundary and easement disputes.

Where the defendant does not enter an Acknowledgment of Service or a Defence the claimant can proceed to obtain a default judgment.[39] Where the claim is for a declaration or an injunction this involves an application for a Court Order.[40] The court may deal with such an application without a hearing[41] or by telephone,[42] but it must be a judicial act and not an administrative exercise.[43] In the Chancery Division it is necessary to follow the Chancery Guide, Ch.9.

A declaration, unlike an injunction, is binding on the successors in title to the parties to the action. It is not, however, a contempt of court to refuse or fail to comply with a declaration.[44] If the defendant does not comply the correct course is to go back to the court to ask for an injunction. It seems clear that if a declaration is made and not complied with it is open

---

[37] *Wallersteiner v Moir* [1974] 1 W.L.R. 991; [1974] 3 All E.R. 217; *Meade v Haringey LBC* [1979] 1 W.L.R. 637; [1979] 2 All E.R. 1016.
[38] *Clarke v Chadburn* [1985] 1 W.L.R. 78; [1985] 1 All E.R. 211.
[39] CPR Pt 12.
[40] CPR Pt 23.
[41] CPR Pt 23.8.
[42] CPR PD 23A (Applications) para.6.2.
[43] CPR r.23.8(3).
[44] *Webster v Southwark LBC* [1983] Q.B. 698; [1983] 2 W.L.R. 217.

to the party aggrieved to return to issue an application in the same action to obtain an injunction to enforce it.

Therefore, if the judge, having decided the line of the boundary or the existence and extent of the easement, feels that no injunction is necessary, because he believes that the parties will accept the decision made without a penal order, it is desirable, if he cannot be persuaded to grant an injunction, to ask for liberty to apply for an injunction should the declaration not be complied with. This should be sufficient to keep the action alive.

In respect of registered it may well be desirable to apply for registration of a fixed boundary under r.119(2) of the Land Registration Rules 2003.[45]

B.   Injunctions

(1)   Generally

24.14   When a boundary or easement dispute arises it is usually important to take prompt action. Sometimes the first the adjoining owner knows of the boundary dispute or the claim or objection to the easement is when his neighbour takes direct action, either in erecting or pulling down a boundary fence or wall, or blocking a right of way, or removing an obstruction to an alleged right of way, or otherwise asserting his claimed rights.

Very often the first advice given when a person visits his solicitor to complain about an alleged infringement of his rights is to take direct action to remove the offending fence or re-erect what has been pulled down. However this can give rise to an unseemly battle with parties setting out in the middle of the night to stake their claims and, occasionally, with violence ensuing.

The alternative to direct action is either to take immediate action to preserve the status quo by interim injunction and then to proceed through the courts to obtain a final injunction preventing further trespass and/or remedying the breaches which have occurred, or to stand by and allow the alleged breach to take place temporarily and then bring an action for damages and a permanent injunction without first seeking interim relief.

An injunction is by far the most effective remedy in a boundary or easement dispute but, because of its draconian nature, the courts may be reluctant to order it. It is, in short, the claimant's most effective remedy and the one which the defendant most fears. Though, no doubt, civilised boundary and easement disputes do exist where the parties simply want the court to decide on the merits, will do nothing pending the trial and will abide by the decision once made, all too often either or both parties are convinced that they are right and are unwilling or reluctant to accept the court's verdict unless it is backed up by an injunction.

---

[45] As amended by the 2005 rules, see para.4.32 above.

(2)   Interim injunctions

The Civil Procedure Rules specifically refer to the court's entitlement to **24.15** make interim injunctions.[46] The jurisdiction of the High Court derives from s.37(1) of the Supreme Court Act 1981 and that of the county court from s.38 of the County Courts Act 1984. A master or district judge may usually only grant injunctions in agreed terms.[47]

An interim injunction can be granted with or without notice.[48] In either case the party obtaining the interim injunction will be required to give an undertaking in damages,[49] which can be extended to other potential defendants.[50] The form of undertaking given in the Civil Court Practice Forms[51] is as follows:

> "The claimant gave an undertaking (through his counsel or solicitor) promising to pay any damages ordered by the court if it later decides that the defendant has suffered loss or damage as a result of this order."

This undertaking means that the claimant has to weigh up whether to put up with the trespass, obstruction or interference until the hearing, (which may be months or years) or to risk the possibility, if he loses his action, of having to pay out substantial damages to the defendant by reason of the undertaking.

Unfortunately for the claimant the court has shown itself unwilling to allow him always to make a free choice. In *Gafford v Graham*[52] Nourse L.J. set out the position:

> "As a general rule, someone who, with the knowledge that he has clearly enforceable rights and the ability to enforce them, stands by while a permanent structure"

is built, ought not to have an injunction.

However, *Mortimer v Bailey*[53] made it clear that this was just an example of the exercise of judicial discretion and upheld the grant of an injunction, in a breach of covenant case, where the claimant had made it clear that he intended to bring a claim:

---

[46] CPR r.25.1(1)(a).
[47] CPR PD 25A (Interim Injunctions) para.1.2.
[48] ibid., CPR r.25.3(1).
[49] ibid., CPR PD 25A (Interim Injunctions) para.5.1.
[50] CCR PD 25A.1A.
[51] Civil Court Practice Forms, Form N16.
[52] [1999] 3 E.G.L.R. 75.
[53] [2004] EWCA Civ 1514; [2005] 2 P. & C.R. 9.

"It may be entirely reasonable for the claimant, having put the defendant on notice, to proceed to trial rather than to take the risk of expending money wastefully by seeking interim relief."

It seems, therefore, that the decision whether to grant a final mandatory injunction to pull down a building where no interim injunction has been applied for before the work is done, will very much depend on the particular facts of the case.

24.16 In any event, this pressure on the claimant to apply for interim relief only arises where the defendant is in the process of carrying out a development which will be costly to delay and even more costly to pull down. In such cases, the court in deciding on the final remedy, or even in deciding whether the case should proceed to trial at all, will take into account the claimant's action in applying for or refraining from applying for an interim injunction. It will also take into account a failure to object when notified of the proposed development as part of the planning application process.[54]

Where the absence of an interim injunction will not cause the defendant to take an irrevocable step the question of whether to apply for an interim injunction is a matter within the claimant's discretion. He has to decide whether he would rather put up with the breach until trial or have it stopped immediately but risk having to pay out under the undertaking as to damages if he loses. His decision (like that of the court if he does decide to apply) will involve balancing the inconvenience to him against the loss the defendant will suffer if the injunction is granted. He will also have to consider the possibility that an interim injunction will in practice dispose of the action because the defendant will decide to concede the issue.

There is a general feeling among practitioners that, despite the risk, it is usually desirable to bring the matter to a head at the interim stage, if only to force the defendant to consider the possible consequences of his actions if he loses.

(a) Injunctions obtained without notice

24.17 The Civil Procedure Rules[55] make no specific distinction between applications made on notice or without notice, except that if no notice is given the application must explain why.[56] However, it is clear from the Civil Court Practice[57] that the practice is essentially unchanged. The first duty

---

[54] *Greenwich Healthcare NHS Trust v London & Quadrant Housing Trust* [1998] 1 W.L.R. 1749; (1999) 77 P. & C.R. 133.
[55] CPR r.25.3.
[56] CCR 25.3.3.
[57] CPR r.25.3[1], [2] and [3].

is the claimant's duty of disclosure. There is an obligation on the party applying for the injunction to lay all the facts before the court, not just those which favour the claimant, and not to mislead the court, *R. v Kensington Income Tax Commissioners Ex p. Princess Edmond de Polignac.*[58] That case did not concern an application without notice, but the court expressed the view that, if the remedy was obtained by deception then,

"the court ought for its own protection and to prevent an abuse of its process to refuse to proceed any further with the examination of the merits".

However, more recent authorities have taken a less stringent approach and have sought to balance the prejudice to the claimant in discharging the injunction as a penalty when it might otherwise be continued on the merits, against the seriousness of the non-disclosure.[59] Thus failing by mistake to disclose a relevant legal authority which was against his claim may not be fatal.[60]

The Rules make clear that an injunction can be granted at any time, including before proceedings are started and after judgment has been given.[61] However, it is still the case that an interim injunction will usually only be ordered after the claim form has been issued and, if for some specific reason it needs to be done before that, the claimant's solicitor will be obliged to give an undertaking to issue one. The court can give directions to this effect.[62] Failure to comply with the undertaking will be regarded not only as a grave breach by the claimant but also a grave breach of the solicitor's duty to the court.[63] An order made before the issue of the claim form should be headed with the names of the parties as "the claimant and defendant in an intended action".

It has also been found that the court administration will be reluctant to find time for an injunction application until the claim form has been issued and a number obtained. Accordingly it will only be in cases of extreme urgency, particularly when events happen over the weekend, that orders will be made before the process is issued. Although court offices are not open on Saturdays, Sundays or Bank Holidays, judges can issue injunctions at any time or place, including a Sunday, traditionally a *dies non juridicus.*[64] All courts have a duty judge who is available at weekends and the evenings, but this service is mainly intended for urgent

[58] [1917] 1 K.B. 486.
[59] *Network Multimedia Television Ltd v Jobserve Ltd, The Times,* January 25, 2001.
[60] *Memory Corp v Sidue, The Times,* May 31, 1999.
[61] CPR r.25.2.1.
[62] CPR r.25.23.
[63] *PS Refson & Co Ltd v Saggers* [1984] 1 W.L.R. 1025; [1984] 3 All E.R. 111.
[64] *Re N. (Infants) (No.2)* [1967] Ch. 512.

applications concerning children and should be used sparingly in relation to boundary or easement disputes. Such applications are normally dealt with at a court hearing, but cases of extreme urgency may be dealt with by telephone.[65] If it is dealt with by telephone the judge will require a draft order to be faxed to him. The application and order must then be filed with the court on the first working day after the order together with two copies for sealing.

24.18 The principles on which an injunction will be granted without notice are either that it is extremely urgent or

> "that the party to be restrained will, if put on notice, do the act which it is intended to restrain before any appropriate remedy is granted by the court"

(though this is no longer expressly stated in the Rules).

An application for interim injunction must be supported by evidence (unless the court orders otherwise).[66] Where there is no notice, the evidence must explain why no notice has been given. The evidence must be verified by a statement of truth. It is very rare that this requirement will be dispensed with. It may, however, be sufficient to provide a statement of case, verified by the statement of truth. The order must specifically set out the respondent's right to apply for it to be set aside.[67] No specific provisions are contained in the rules as to injunctions made without notice. However, the Practice Direction makes clear that wherever possible a draft of the order sought should be filed with the application and a disk containing the draft should also be available. This is all the more important in respect of an application without notice, which is bound to be urgent. While mandatory interim injunctions may be granted, it is almost unprecedented for such an injunction to be granted without notice.[68] Normally the application will be by the claimant. A defendant can apply for an interim injunction once he has filed an acknowledgment of service or a defence[69] (though there is discretion to override this requirement). This would only arise where the claimant is threatening to do something and, if given notice, will carry out his threat before the remedy can be obtained. Once an order is made and served it is open to the defendant to apply to have it set aside, but it will in any event contain a return date for an inter partes hearing.[70]

---

[65] CPR PD 25A (Interim Injunctions) para.4.2.
[66] CPR r.25.3(2).
[67] CPR r.23.9(3).
[68] See *Ansah v Ansah* [1977] Fam. 138, a matrimonial case.
[69] CPR r.25.2(2)(c).
[70] CPR PD 25A (Interim Injunctions) para.5.1(3).

It is open to the court to make a summary assessment of costs on any **24.19** application. However, where the application is made without notice, the court will be reluctant to make an immediate order and is likely to follow the former practice and reserve the costs to the hearing.

The same practice applies in all courts, including the Chancery Division, the Queens's Bench Division and the county court.

(b) Injunctions obtained on notice

(i) Procedure

The procedure for applying for an interim injunction is set out in the **24.20** Civil Procedure Rules 1998 and in the accompanying Practice Direction. The procedure is the same in the High Court as in the county court. Any differences in the Chancery Division are set out in the Chancery Guide.

The application is made by an application notice to the court where the claim was started or to which it has been transferred.[71] An application notice must say what order the applicant is seeking and briefly why he is doing so.[72] The application must be filed with any evidence in support and served as soon as practicable and, in any event, at least three days before the court is to deal with it.[73] On service it must be accompanied by a copy of the evidence in support. This may consist of the application verified by a statement of truth. If the court is to serve the application sufficient copies for service must be supplied. A draft Order should be prepared together with a copy on disk so that the court officer can arrange for amendments and seal it.

Where a respondent to an application wishes to rely on evidence he must serve it and file it with the court as soon as possible[74] and the same applies to any evidence in reply.

On claims for interim injunctions the court will not usually be resolving **24.21** issues of fact and accordingly it is not normally necessary for witnesses who have submitted statements of fact to be present to be cross-examined. If, for some specific reason, it is desired to cross-examine a witness, application should be made to the court for permission to do so.[75] If the court gives permission and the person does not attend his evidence may not be used.[76]

The interim injunction when granted will be subject to an undertaking in damages. The Practice Direction no longer sets out a prescribed form but the old form in the following terms:

[71] CPR r.23.2.
[72] CPR r.23.6.
[73] CPR r.23.7.
[74] CPR PD 23A (Applications) para.9.4.
[75] CPR r.32.7(1).
[76] ibid., CPR r.32.7(2).

"The claimant gave an undertaking (through his counsel or solicitor) promising to pay any damages ordered by the court if it later decides that the defendant has suffered loss or damage as a result of this order."[77]

The injunction may be either until the trial or for a fixed period. The claimant will only be required to pay damages when the injunction should not have been granted in the first place.[78] If an interim injunction is granted initially but then discharged, the usual practice is to adjourn the question of whether damages should be paid to the trial. A district judge may only make an injunction in agreed terms.[79] A county court judge can make any order which could be made by the High Court.

(ii) Types of Injunction

24.22 An injunction will either be prohibitory or mandatory. A prohibitory injunction orders someone not to do something whereas a mandatory injunction orders him to do something. This distinction is dealt with more fully later.[80] A prohibitory injunction may be granted either to prevent further breaches by the other party or quia timet to prevent him from doing something that he is threatening to do. In order to obtain a quia timet injunction the applicant must show that there is imminent danger that the other party will do something that will have a serious effect on him. It is not enough for him simply to fear that there is some possibility. He must show real evidence that the other party is likely to do what is suggested if not prevented by injunction. However, in such a situation the other party is put into a difficult situation. If he refuses to give an undertaking to the court not to do what is suggested then the court may be tempted to conclude that he does intend to do what is alleged.

Generally, therefore, the difference between a quia timet and other kinds of prohibitory injunction is merely that the court is naturally more reluctant to grant an injunction, with its penal provisions in the case of breach, where the other part has not actually done anything to damage the applicant than it is where the other part has actually done something and is likely to continue.

In theory at least, mandatory injunctions can be granted at the interim stage, but such an order will only be made in exceptional circumstances. The court will require evidence that severe problems will be caused to the applicant if the injunction is not granted and a high degree of assurance

---

[77] CPR PD 25A (Interim Injunctions) para.5.1.
[78] *Ushers Brewery v PS King & Co* [1972] Ch. 148; [1971] 2 W.L.R. 1411.
[79] CPR PD 25A (Interim Injunctions) para.1.2.
[80] See below, para.24.41.

that at the trial it will appear that the injunction was rightly granted.[81] This, therefore, is an exception to the general rule that the comparative strength of the parties' cases is the last factor to be considered in granting or refusing an interim injunction,[82] but this does not mean that the court will be prepared to embark on a full assessment of the respective merits of the cases. It will only be in a case where the merits seem clear that a mandatory injunction will be granted at the interim stage.

The kind of circumstances in which mandatory injunctions will be **24.23** granted at an interim stage in boundary or easement cases is where one party is seeking to steal a march on another.[83] Perhaps the simplest example is the removal of a fence. If the court feels that one party has removed the fence just in order to establish a tactical advantage it may order that the fence be reinstated pending the trial even though this involves a mandatory injunction. Such decisions depend very much on their own facts, but one important factor will be the expense involved in carrying out the order. The more expensive it is to reinstate the fence the less likely that a mandatory interim injunction will be granted.

(iii)   Principles for grant of interim injunction

The leading case setting out the principles on which the court will grant **24.24** or refuse an interim injunction is *American Cyanamid Co v Ethicon Ltd*,[84] where Lord Diplock gave the judgment of the court. This case decides that it is not necessary for the party claiming an interim injunction to show that he has a strong prima facie case. All he need show is that "there is a serious question to be tried"[85]:

> ". . . the governing principle is that the court should first consider whether if the claimant were to succeed at the trial in establishing his right to a permanent injunction he would be adequately compensated by an award of damages for the loss he would have sustained as a result of the defendant's continuing to do what was sought to be enjoined between the time of the application and the time of the trial. If damages in the measure recoverable at common law would be adequate remedy and the defendant would be in a financial position to pay them, no interim injunction should normally be granted,

---

[81] *Shepherd Homes Ltd v Sandham* [1971] Ch. 340; [1970] 3 W.L.R. 348, approved in *Locobail International Finance Ltd v Agroexport and Atlanta (UK) Ltd* [1986] 1 W.L.R. 657; [1986] 1 All E.R. 901 at 906g.

[82] [1975] A.C. 396; [1975] 2 W.L.R. 316.

[83] See *Locobail International Finance Ltd v Agroexport and Atlanta (UK) Ltd* [1986] 1 W.L.R. 657; [1986] 1 All E.R. 901 at 906g.

[84] *American Cyanamid Co v Ethicon Ltd* [1975] A.C. 396; [1975] 2 W.L.R. 316.

[85] per Lord Diplock, at 510f.

however strong the claimant's claim appears to be at that stage. If, on the other hand, damages would not provide an adequate remedy for the claimant in the event of his succeeding at the trial, the court should then consider, whether, on the contrary hypothesis that the defendant were to succeed at the trial in establishing his right to do that which was sought to be enjoined, he would be adequately compensated under the claimant's undertaking as to damages for the loss he would have sustained by being prevented from doing so between the time of the application and the time of the trial. If damages in the measure recoverable under such an undertaking would be an adequate remedy and the claimant would be in a financial position to pay them, there would be no reason on this ground to refuse an interim injunction.

It is where there is doubt as to the adequacy of the respective remedies in damages available to either party or to both, that the question of balance of convenience arises. It would be unwise to attempt even to list all the various matters which may need to be taken into consideration in deciding where the balance lies, let alone to suggest the relative weights to be attached to them. These will vary from case to case.

Where other factors appear to be evenly balanced it is a counsel of prudence to take such measures as are calculated to preserve the status quo. If the defendant is enjoined temporarily from doing something that he has not done before, the only effect of the interim injunction in the event of his succeeding at the trial is to postpone the date at which he is able to embark on a course of action which he has not previously found it necessary to undertake; whereas to interrupt him in his conduct of an established enterprise would cause much greater inconvenience to him since he would have to start again to establish it in the event of his succeeding at the trial.

24.25   Save in the simplest case, the decision to grant or to refuse an interim injunction will cause to whichever party is unsuccessful in the application some disadvantage which his ultimate success at the trial may show he ought to have been spared. And the disadvantage may be such that the recovery of damages to which he would then be entitled, either in the action or under the claimant's undertaking, would not be sufficient to compensate him fully for all of them. The extent to which the disadvantages to each party would be incapable of being compensated in damages in the event of his succeeding at the trial is always a significant factor in assessing where the balance of convenience lies; and if the extent of the uncompensatable disadvantage to each party would not differ widely, it may not be improper to take into account in tipping the balance the relative strength of each party's case as revealed by the affidavit evidence adduced on the hearing of the application. This, however, should be done only where it is apparent on the facts disclosed by evidence as to which there is no credible dispute that the strength of one party's case is disproportionate to that of the other party. The court is not justified in embarking on anything resembling a trial of the action on conflicting affidavits in order to evaluate the strength of the either party's case."

This authoritative statement of the law sets out a number of principles, each of which raises some difficulties. The requirements for an injunction to be granted are:

(1) that there is a serious question to be tried;

(2) that damages would not be an adequate remedy;

(3) that the defendant would be adequately compensated by the claimant's undertaking as to damages;

(4) that the balance of convenience favours an injunction;

(5) that all other things being equal the status quo should be maintained; and

(6) that in certain cases the merits may be relied on as tipping the balance in either direction.

These principles merit further consideration.

(1) Serious question to be tried

Lord Diplock said that: **24.26**

"The court no doubt must be satisfied that the claim is not frivolous or vexatious; in other words, that there is a serious question to be tried."[86]

This suggests that it will only be in very rare cases, where the claimant's claim is virtually capable of being struck out as frivolous or vexatious, that the claimant will be unable to show a sufficient case to get beyond this stage. In practice, however, there are several reported cases,[87] where the court has held that there is no serious question to be tried even though there is no question of the claim being struck out as frivolous:

---

[86] *American Cyanamid Co v Ethicon Ltd* [1975] A.C. 396; [1975] 1 All E.R. 504 at 510d.
[87] e.g. *Re Lord Cable (deceased)* [1977] 1 W.L.R. 7; [1976] 3 All E.R. 417; *Smith v Inner London Education Authority* [1978] 1 All E.R. 411.

"It is still necessary for any claimant who is seeking interim relief to adduce sufficiently precise factual evidence to satisfy the court that he has a real prospect of succeeding in his claim for a permanent injunction at the trial."[88]

In reality, however much they seek to ignore the merits, courts are influenced in their decisions on whether or not to grant an interim injunction by their initial reaction to the merits of the case.

Normally the "serious question" issue is raised against the claimant's claim, but it can also be put forward by the claimant who claims that, though the balance of convenience may favour the defendant, the defendant has no serious defence and therefore that there should be an interim injunction to prevent him from continuing, despite the fact that the damage to the claimant would be slight if no injunction were granted.[89]

(2)   Damages an inadequate remedy

24.27   This concept is not very clearly analysed in the *American Cyanamid* case. Reported cases since the decision have always paid lip service to this principle, but in most of the reported cases the court has found, at the interim stage, that damages are not an adequate remedy.[90]

It is for the claimant to adduce evidence as to the effect on him if an injunction is refused.[91]

Despite the frequent judicial assertion of this principle, the reality is that in any case of pure economic loss damages can be an adequate remedy (though not perhaps where the principle of free speech is at stake).[92] Even the loss caused by having to close your business due to the alleged breach can be compensated by a large award of damages. It is, therefore, rather difficult to see what is really meant by the principle. What the courts have done in practice is to balance the degree of financial loss which the claimant is likely to suffer if the injunction is not granted against the degree of loss that the defendant will suffer if the injunction is granted. In effect, therefore, it is submitted that this equation is part of the assessment of the balance of convenience.

24.28   This problem has a particular significance in boundary and easement disputes. The reported cases on the grant or refusal of interim injunctions often involve commercial situations where the grant or refusal of an

---

[88]   per Slade J. in *Re Lord Cable (deceased)* [1977] 1 W.L.R. 7; [1976] 3 All E.R. 417 at 431b.

[89]   *Patel v WH Smith* [1987] 1 W.L.R. 853; [1987] 2 All E.R. 569.

[90]   Cf. *Garden Cottage Foods Ltd v Milk Marketing Board* [1984] A.C. 130; [1983] 2 All E.R. 770, where the House of Lords overruled the Court of Appeal and upheld the judge's decision that damages would be an adequate remedy.

[91]   *Fellowes v Fisher* [1976] Q.B. 122; [1975] 3 W.L.R. 184.

[92]   *Cambridge Nutrition Ltd v BBC* [1990] 3 All E.R. 523.

injunction will involve the preservation or loss of large sums of money. Boundary and easement cases tend to involve much lesser sums of potential loss, which in principle ought to be more easily compensated in damages, but this has not stopped the courts in practice from granting injunctions in such cases. If a person seeks to pull down a fence between two properties, no doubt the loss suffered by the other party, if it is proved that he did so wrongly, can be compensated in damages. However, the practice of the courts is to give a fairly liberal interpretation of what is meant by damages not constituting an adequate remedy and to concentrate much more on the balance of convenience than on the extent and nature of the damage which would be suffered by the applicant should the other party continue to do what the injunction seeks to prevent him from doing.

(3) Adequacy of undertaking in damages

It is the universal rule that the claimant who obtains an interim injunc- **24.29** tion must give an undertaking as to damages in the form set out above, or similar.[93] If such an undertaking is omitted from the order by mistake it will be inserted under the slip rule.[94] The practice in such cases is that if the defendant wishes to suggest that such an undertaking is worthless he should file evidence to this effect and without such evidence the court will not make any such assumption. Normally in boundary and easement cases the claimant is the owner, or at least the lessee, of land and may be assumed to have some basis for paying any sums eventually found to be due.

(4) Balance of convenience

The most important principle to emerge from *American Cyanamid Co v* **24.30** *Ethicon Ltd*[95] is that the court will usually decide on the grant or refusal of an injunction on the balance of convenience rather than the respective strength of the parties' contentions. Such a balance can include an infinite variety of factors. Usually, as discussed below, the most important is maintaining the status quo, but the court will take into account such matters as economic loss suffered by either party in the event of the grant or refusal of the injunction and personal inconvenience suffered, for example in cases of excessive user of a right of way.

One of the most common and difficult problems faced in boundary and easement cases is where one party has embarked on a development which the other party claims will affect his rights. In such a case the

---

[93] See above para.24.21.
[94] *Colledge v Crossley, The Times*, March 18, 1975.
[95] [1975] A.C. 396; [1975] 2 W.L.R. 316.

defendant can contend that if he is prevented from completing his development he will suffer severe loss, whereas if the claimant eventually succeeds the claimant's additional loss will be small since the defendant will be obliged to pull down the building. In practice, however, a court may well be reluctant to order the pulling down of a building that has been erected, even if the work was completed with knowledge of the dispute. Despite the strict logic that suggests that the injunction be refused and that the defendant should be allowed to complete the building at his own risk, the tendency is to grant an injunction halting building, providing that this can be done without causing physical damage to the part which has already been constructed by exposing it to the weather for the duration of the dispute.

Where the practical effect of the grant of an injunction will be to put an end to the action the court will be reluctant to grant an injunction whatever the balance of convenience, unless the merits of the case strongly favour the claimant.[96]

A court may refuse to allow a servient owner to erect a gate on the way pending the hearing, even if this means that other people, who are not alleging a right of way, can continue to use the way.[97]

(5)   Status quo

24.31   It is one of the fundamental principles of interim injunctions that their primary purpose is to maintain the status quo. This is the basis on which an injunction may be granted to restrain construction works even though the immediate damage to the claimant will be small.

The fact is that it is much easier for a court to freeze the situation pending hearing than to allow the situation to change and then be obliged to unravel it when the respective rights are finally established. The status quo referred to is that at the time of issue of particulars or, if there is unreasonable delay between the issue of the claim and injunction, the period immediately preceding the claim and the application for an interim application.[98]

(6)   The merits of the respective cases

24.32   The Court of Appeal has established the principles applying to trespass cases in *Patel v WH Smith,*[99] namely that where the claimant's title is not in issue and the defendant puts forward a claim to an easement he must

---

[96] *Cayne v Global Natural Resources Plc* [1984] 1 All E.R. 225; *Lansing Linde Ltd v Kerr* [1991] 1 W.L.R. 251; [1991] 1 All E.R. 418.
[97] *Rafique v Trustees of Walton Estate* (1993) 65 P. & C.R. 356.
[98] *Garden Cottage Foods Ltd v Milk Marketing Board* [1984] A.C. 130; [1983] 3 W.L.R. 143.
[99] [1987] 1 W.L.R. 853; [1987] 2 All E.R. 569.

show that he has a serious claim to an easement which would justify the defence. However, as emphasised by Lord Diplock, the Court will not embark on a detailed assessment of the respective cases of the parties, particularly in cases where there is a dispute as to fact. At the interim stage, therefore, the court will not normally allow cross-examination aimed at establishing that the contentions put forward by the other party are false.

(iv) Discretion

An injunction is an equitable remedy and is discretionary. The princi- **24.33**
ples on which the court exercises its discretion to grant an interim injunction are generally the same as the principles on which it grants a permanent injunction and these principles are dealt with below,[100] except with regard to delay.

It is a basic requirement of interim relief that application should be made promptly. This is particularly the case where the defendant is carrying out works which will be costly to demolish. In some circumstances, interim relief will be refused on the grounds that it has been applied for too late[101] and this will mean that a final mandatory injunction may be refused to demolish the building even where the claimant proves his case.[102] The problem in relation to permanent injunction is dealt with fully below.[103] Differing views have been expressed on whether it is essential to apply for interim relief, rather than just threaten or commence proceedings,[104] with the latest Court of Appeal judgment indicating a more liberal line.

It seems clear, however, that a claimant is not automatically entitled to stand by while the proposed defendant carries out works which amount to a breach of his right, if those works involve considerable expenditure. If the claimant wishes to obtain a permanent injunction as opposed to damages in lieu of an injunction he must act promptly. If he does not apply for an interim injunction, he takes the chance that final relief will be refused for this reason.

This, in truth, puts a heavy burden on the claimant, because, as stated **24.34**
above, a claimant who obtains an interim injunction is obliged to give an undertaking as to damages.[105] This means that if his contentions prove to be incorrect the defendant may obtain damages from him representing

---

[100] See below, para.24.37, et seq.
[101] As in *Mortimer v Bailey* [2004] EWCA Civ 1514; [2005] 2 P. & C.R. 9.
[102] However, this will not always be the case: *Mortimer v Bailey* [2004] EWCA Civ 1514; [2005] 2 P. & C.R. 9; *Jacklin v Chief Constable of West Yorkshire* [2007] EWCA Civ 181.
[103] See below, para.24.39 et seq.
[104] *Mortimer v Bailey* [2004] EWCA Civ 1514; [2005] 2 P. & C.R. 9.
[105] In the form set out above.

the loss he has suffered by reason of being unable to carry out the works that he intended (or in the case of a mandatory injunction the cost of the works he carried out under the order).

A person who sees his neighbour carrying out building works which he considers constitute a trespass or an interference with his easement is therefore in a dilemma. If there is any doubt about his rights he may be tempted to inform the other person of the rights he claims, to threaten proceedings and then sit back and allow the defendant to carry on with the building, in the full knowledge of the claimant's claim. It might be thought that if the defendant chooses to carry on and is proved to be in the wrong, then he should be obliged to remove his building. That seems to be the way in which the law is moving, with an increased willingness to take drastic action where the defendant has carried on regardless of the dispute[106] and so the claimant is then obliged to choose between risking substantial sums payable under the undertaking as to damages if his contentions prove to be unfounded and losing his right to an injunction by reason of his acquiescence. It will, however, depend very much on the facts of the case. In *Greenwich Healthcare NHS Trust v London & Quadrant Housing Trust*[107] the claimant had failed to object to planning applications and, in *Shaw v Applegate*,[108] the delay had been over several years. By contrast, in *Mortimer v Bailey*,[109] the claimant had made his intentions clear from the start, had challenged the planning application and applied for an interim injunction within two months of construction beginning, albeit the building work was almost complete by then. Although an interim injunction was refused the Court of Appeal upheld the grant of a mandatory injunction to remove the extension. In any event the principle is clear that applications for interim injunctions should be made promptly, as soon as it becomes apparent what the defendant is doing, and that failure to act promptly may lose the claimant his injunction even if the other factors set out in *American Cyanamid Co v Ethicon Ltd*[110] indicate that an injunction should be granted.

Where an interim injunction is granted, costs will normally be ordered in the cause, since, if the claimant loses the case in the end, it follows that the interim injunction should not have been granted. Where an injunction is refused, costs can be awarded against the claimant, since, whatever the outcome of the action, it is clear that he is not entitled to the relief he claims.

---

[106] *Jacklin v Chief Constable of West Yorkshire* [2007] EWCA Civ 181; *HKRUK II (CHC) Ltd v Heaney* [2010] EWHC 2245 (Ch).
[107] [1998] 1 W.L.R. 1749; (1999) 77 P. & C.R. 133.
[108] [1977] 1 W.L.R. 970.
[109] [2004] EWCA Civ 1514; [2005] 2 P. & C.R. 9.
[110] [1975] A.C. 396; [1975] 2 W.L.R. 316.

(v)   Inquiry as to damages

Where there has been an undertaking as to damages and the claimant **24.35** eventually loses the claim or fails to obtain a permanent injunction the court has a discretion whether to order an inquiry as to damages.

Firstly, it is necessary for the defendant to show that he has suffered damage resulting directly from the grant of the interim injunction.[111] Secondly it is necessary for him to act promptly. The correct time for applying for an inquiry as to damages is shortly after the trial of the action when the full injunction is refused. Applying before the full hearing is premature.[112]

It is now established, however, that, subject to the normal discretionary reasons for refusal, an inquiry as to damages will normally be granted to any defendant who has suffered loss as a result of an interim injunction wrongly granted whether or not the claimant has been guilty of any misrepresentation in setting out the grounds for obtaining his injunction. Jessel M.R. suggested in *Smith v Day*[113] that as the object of the undertaking was to protect the defendant and the court from improper applications, an inquiry would only be ordered where the claimant had "suppressed or misrepresented the facts" and not, for example, where the judge had made a mistake of law in granting the injunction. However, this approach was specifically rejected by the Court of Appeal in *Griffith v Blake*[114] and has not been followed since.[115]

If, therefore, there has been an interim injunction, but no permanent injunction is granted at the trial, whether because the judge at the trial finds the facts not to be as set out in the claimant's affidavit or because he takes a different view of the law, a defendant who has suffered financial loss as a result of the injunction, should apply promptly for an inquiry as to damages. Such an inquiry will be conducted by the master or the district judge.

(3)   Permanent Injunctions

An injunction granted at the end of the trial will usually be a permanent **24.36** injunction. It will either be prohibitory or mandatory, i.e. it will either prevent the defendant from doing something in future or it will order him to do something, for example remove an obstruction. The order is discretionary and it is made against named individuals. Failure to comply with an injunction is a contempt of court. It cannot usually be set aside.

---

[111] *Smith v Day* (1882) L.R. 21 Ch. D. 421.
[112] *Ushers Brewery v PS King & Co* [1972] Ch. 148.
[113] (1882) L.R. 21 Ch. D. 421 at 424.
[114] (1884) L.R. 27 Ch. D. 474.
[115] *Digital Equipment Corp v Darkcrest Ltd* [1984] Ch. 512; [1984] 3 W.L.R. 617.

(a) Discretion

24.37 Although the court has a discretion whether or not to grant an injunction such discretion must be exercised judicially and if the judge does not exercise his discretion in a judicial manner his decision can be altered on appeal. This does mean, however, that the judge hearing the case has a degree of latitude and that an appellant will have to show a failure to apply the law properly.[116]

The basic principles, derived from the classic exposition in *Shelfer v City of London Electric Lighting Co*[117] were summarised in *Jaggard v Sawyer*[118] by Bingham M.R.:

> "In any instance in which a case for an injunction has been made out, if the plaintiff by his act or laches had disentitled himself to an injunction the court may award damages in its place. So again, whether the case be for a mandatory injunction or to restrain a continuing nuisance, the appropriate remedy may be damages in lieu of an injunction, assuming a case for an injunction has been made out. In my opinion it may be stated as a good working rule that; (1) if the injury to the plaintiff's legal rights is small; (2) and is one which is capable of being estimated in money; (3) and is one which can be compensated by a small money payment, (4) and the case is one in which it would be oppressive to the defendant to grant an injunction; then damages in substitution for an injunction may be given."

The basic rule in trespass is that if a defendant threatens to continue a trespass an injunction will be granted to prevent him, whether or not the claimant suffers any substantial damage as a result of the trespass. This applies for example to a crane which is hanging over a person's airspace during the course of building works next door[119] or a defendant who persistently parks cars on the claimants' land.[120] The fact that the damage suffered is trivial is nevertheless a factor to be taken into consideration[121] and may, for example, be one reason for postponing the operation of the injunction to allow the defendant time to finish the work.[122]

For an action in respect of an easement to succeed at all it is necessary to show a substantial interference with the claimant's rights. The principle

---

[116] *Jacklin v Chief Constable of West Yorkshire* [2007] EWCA Civ 181.
[117] [1895] 1 Ch. 287.
[118] [1995] 1 W.L.R. 269.
[119] *Woollerton & Wilson Ltd v Richard Costain Ltd* [1970] 1 W.L.R. 411; *John Trenberth v National Westminster Bank Ltd* (1980) 39 P. & C.R. 104.
[120] *Patel v WH Smith* [1987] 1 W.L.R. 853; [1987] 2 All E.R. 569.
[121] *Armstrong v Sheppard & Short* [1959] 2 Q.B. 384; [1959] 3 W.L.R. 84.
[122] *Woollerton & Wilson Ltd v Richard Costain Ltd* [1970] 1 W.L.R. 411.

set out above does not, therefore, apply to claims for interference with an easement.

The authorities on the circumstances in which the Court award damages **24.38** in lieu of an injunction, rather than granting an injunction were fully considered by the Court of Appeal in *Regan v Paul Properties*[123] and re-asserted in *Jacklin v Chief Constable of West Yorkshire*[124] In the former case the Court overturned the court of first instance which had refused a mandatory injunction in a right of light case and in the latter case the judge's permanent injunction was upheld despite considerable inconvenience to the defendants. Even though the Court emphasised that the grant of an injunction is discretionary and that these principles are only a working rule and not an exhaustive statement of the law, the principles in *Shelfer* were upheld and an injunction was granted.

It has been stated that the court is not entitled to take into account the public interest in deciding whether to exercise its discretion to grant an injunction in a case of nuisance. This proposition was upheld by the Court of Appeal in *Kennaway v Thompson.*[125] However, in *Das v Linden Mews,*[126] the Court of Appeal referred the grant of an injunction back to the judge requiring him to consider that,

> "the use of the way gives access to and unlocks a valuable asset held by the owner, but does not necessarily place any burden on LM Ltd"

and also to consider the delay by the claimant. This seemed to reinstate the public interest approach against the principle of strict enforcement of rights. However, this contrasts with the more recent assessment in *Regan v Paul Properties*[127] where the Court rejected the suggestion that the "expropriation factor" was overdone and stated that "the defendants must take the natural consequence of their acts in interfering with the right of light" and in *Jacklin v Chief Constable of West Yorkshire*[128] the Court of Appeal took a similar approach where the defendants should have realised that there would be a right of way over their land. The proposition that the public interest in releasing land for office development was rejected as a proper basis for opposing a mandatory injunction in *HKRUK II (CHC) Ltd v Heaney.*[129]

---

[123] [2006] EWCA Civ 1391; [2007] Ch. 135.
[124] [2007] EWCA Civ 181.
[125] [1981] Q.B. 88; [1980] 3 All E.R. 329.
[126] [2002] EWCA Civ 590; [2003] 2 P. & C.R. 4.
[127] [2006] EWCA Civ 1391; [2007] Ch. 135.
[128] [2007] EWCA Civ 181.
[129] [2010] EWHC 2245 (Ch).

24.39 The court will refuse to exercise its discretion to grant an injunction where there is no serious risk of the defendant repeating the acts alleged, where the claimant has been guilty of undue delay and where the claimant has, by his conduct, forfeited the right to an injunction.

It is very irritating to be refused an injunction after succeeding in a case, because it raises the risk of the defendant continuing or repeating his breaches which will require a further application to the court and possibly a fresh action. Where an injunction is refused because the judge believes that the defendant has learnt his lesson then it may be possible to come back to the court and apply for an injunction if the declaration proves insufficient. In these circumstances it is sensible to request that a specific liberty to apply for an injunction is included in the final order.

A refusal of an injunction on the ground of delay creates a different situation. Normally the result will be an order for damages in lieu of injunction.[130] Such damages are intended to represent the value of the right and accordingly it follows that the claimant cannot come back to the court to ask for a further remedy or bring a fresh action claiming continuing breach.

One of the reasons for refusing a final mandatory injunction is that the claimant has not taken steps to prevent the defendant from carrying out the actions which amounted to a breach. The best way of ensuring that substantial works are not carried out by the defendant is to apply for an interim injunction preventing him from doing so pending trial.[131] However, this involves an undertaking as to damages and the claimant may be reluctant to take this risk, especially where a delay in the works will involve economic loss to the defendant.

In *Mortimer v Bailey*,[132] the grant of a mandatory injunction to pull down an extension was upheld despite delay in applying for an interim injunction. This involved distinguishing *Gafford v Graham*[133] where Nourse L.J. suggested that if a claimant fails to apply for an interim injunction he should not get a permanent mandatory injunction. The key is the extent to which the claimant has stood by and allowed it to happen, rather than, as in *Mortimer v Bailey* making his position clear, challenging the planning application and, albeit after some delay, applying for an interim injunction. This is consistent with the approach in *Regan v Paul Properties*[134] and *Jacklin v Chief Constable of West Yorkshire*.[135]

24.40 It is open to the court to refuse an injunction by reason of the conduct of the claimant alone.[136] However, this power will only rarely be used

---

[130] See below, para.24.57.
[131] See above, para.24.14 et seq.
[132] [2004] EWCA Civ 1514; [2005] 2 P. & C.R. 9.
[133] (1999) 77 P. & C.R. 73.
[134] [2006] EWCA Civ 1391; [2007] Ch. 135.
[135] [2007] EWCA Civ 181.
[136] *Armstrong v Sheppard & Short* [1959] 2 Q.B. 384; [1959] 3 W.L.R. 84.

where all that is required is a prohibitory injunction which amounts to no more than ensuring that the defendants respects the claimant's right in future.

(b) Prohibitory and mandatory injunctions

Injunctions may be prohibitory or mandatory. A prohibitory injunction **24.41** orders someone not to do something. A mandatory injunction orders a person to do something.

It is well established that the court will be more reluctant to order a mandatory injunction than a prohibitory one, particularly at an interim stage.[137] Most of the matters which are taken into account are the same whether the injunction is prohibitory or mandatory. Such matters include the degree of damage suffered by the claimant if the injunction is not granted, delay in applying, etc. There are, however, matters which apply only to mandatory injunctions.

With a mandatory injunction it is important that the defendant should know exactly what he is required to do. Simply requiring him to restore the claimant to the position he was in before may not be enough.[138] This is particularly the case where there may be more than one way of remedying the breach, e.g. where support has been removed there may be several possible ways of restoring it.

As stated above, the court is also entitled to take into account the cost **24.42** to the defendant of carrying out the proposed work balanced against the damage suffered to date by the claimant and the damage which is likely to occur in the future, not forgetting that he will have a separate claim in damages in respect of further damage. In short, the court will be reluctant to order expensive works when it is not certain what loss the claimant is likely to suffer or what work will be required to prevent it.[139] The court will be even more reluctant to make such an order when the demolition involves the destruction of something useful and of substantial value, for example the demolition of housing.[140] There are, however, signs of a change of heart from the Courts in cases such as *Regan v Paul Properties*[141] and *HKRUK II (CHC) Ltd v Heaney*[142] where mandatory injunctions were granted when developers had deliberately continued work in the knowledge of the probable right and of the potential proceedings.

---

[137] *Shepherd Homes Ltd v Sandham (No.1)* [1971] Ch. 340; [1970] 3 W.L.R. 348.
[138] *Redland Bricks v Morris* [1970] A.C. 652; [1969] 2 W.L.R. 1437.
[139] ibid.
[140] *Wrotham Park Estate Co Ltd v Parkside Homes Ltd* [1974] 1 W.L.R. 798; [1974] 2 All E.R. 321; *Regan v Paul Properties Ltd* [2006] EWCA Civ 1391; [2007] Ch. 135.
[141] [2006] EWCA Civ 1391; [2007] Ch. 135.
[142] [2010] EWHC 2245 (Ch).

In carrying out this balancing act the court will also consider the nature of the defendant's conduct.

> "There may also be cases in which, though the four . . . requirements exist, the defendant by his conduct, as, for instance, hurrying up his buildings so as if possible to avoid an injunction, or otherwise acting with reckless disregard to the plaintiff's rights, has disentitled himself from asking that damages may be assessed in substitution for an injunction."[143]

Another factor is that the court will be reluctant to order a mandatory injunction if the work ordered will require supervision. In terms of boundary disputes the obvious example is a wall. If a trespasser has erected a wall on his neighbour's land the court can either order him to remove it or award the neighbour damages representing the cost of removing it. Either of such orders can be coupled with a prohibitory injunction restraining further trespass. It will not necessarily be in the claimant's interest to obtain a mandatory injunction rather than damages. The defendant while demolishing the wall is unlikely to take as much care as a contractor engaged by the claimant. On the other hand the defendant may have limited funds and it may be easier to get him to do the work of demolishing it himself than to pay for a contractor and then try to recover the cost.

24.43   Where it is a question of demolition it is fairly easy to obtain a mandatory injunction. It is much more difficult to obtain an order requiring the defendant to construct something, such as a wall which he has demolished. Unless he is prepared to engage agreed contractors there is a danger that the new wall will not be as well constructed as the old one and this may give rise to further litigation about whether the injunction has been complied with.

Similar situations arise over easements but in such cases the work involved will usually have to be carried out on the defendant's land. This makes it more appropriate to make a mandatory order. Thus with rights of light the obstruction will be on the defendant's land and so there is little difficulty about requiring him to remove it. With a right of way it is usually going to be a matter of removing something like an obstruction or a ramp, rather than replacing something which has been removed, but again the work is likely to be carried out on the defendant's land albeit land which is subject to the claimant's right of way. However, in respect of boundary walls this will now be dealt with by the Party Wall, etc. Act 1996.

---

[143] per Bingham M.R., in *Jaggard v Sawyer* [1995] 1 W.L.R. 269.

These are, nevertheless, matters of discretion. The court has an unfettered discretion to make mandatory injunctions requiring the defendant to do positive acts and will do so in any case where this seems the simplest and most convenient way of obtaining the desired effect.

The court also has a discretion as to when the injunction should be carried out, but this does not entitle the judge to postpone the mandatory injunction for a long period, such as three years, in an attempt to force a settlement on the parties.[144]

(c) Quia timet injunctions

A *quia timet* injunction is one granted because the claimant fears that the **24.44** defendant will do something. Of course, all prohibitory injunctions are granted because of the fear that the defendant will repeat his breach. The significance of a *quia timet* injunction is that it may be granted before the claimant has actually suffered any damage at all.

There are obvious dangers in the exercise of such a jurisdiction. It is not right that a defendant should have to come to court to defend his right to do something he never intended to do in the first place. Furthermore it is necessary that the nature of the proposed action should be sufficiently precise for the court to gauge its likely effect. If a person proposes to build something nearby it is impossible to know whether it will interfere with the claimant's right of light unless it is known with some precision what is proposed. Equally if the servient owner threatens to do something on a right of way it may not be possible to know whether the proposed action will substantially affect the claimant's user. For these reasons the courts have always warned about the dangers of such injunctions.

> "As Lord Dunedin said it is not sufficient to say 'timeo'. It is a jurisdiction to be exercised sparingly and with caution but, in a proper case, unhesitatingly."[145]

Where the issue is as to entitlement, the alternative to a preventive injunction is a declaration. This leaves open the opposite alternative available to the developer of a declaration that no injunction will be granted if a certain course, which may be a technical trespass or nuisance, is followed.[146]

The claimant therefore has to decide whether to apply promptly and **24.45** risk being told that he has not proved that the defendant is going to do

---

[144] *Charrington v Simons & Co Ltd* [1971] 1 W.L.R. 598; [1971] 2 All E.R. 588.
[145] per Lord Upjohn, *Redland Bricks v Morris* [1970] A.C. 652; [1969] 2 All E.R. 576 at 579, quoting Lord Dunedin in *Attorney General for Canada v Ritchie Contracting & Supply Co Ltd* [1919] A.C. 999 at 1005.
[146] *Greenwich Healthcare NHS Trust v London & Quadrant Housing Trust* [1998] 1 W.L.R. 1749; (1999) 77 P. &. C.R. 133.

the act complained of, or to wait and risk being told that he has lost his right of injunction due to delay. Generally, the best advice is to act promptly. If the defendant does not intend to do what the claimant believes he intends, then he can be asked to give an undertaking not to do it. If he refuses there must be suspicion that he really does intend to do so. On the other hand it is unwise to act on mere rumour. A planning application to build on the disputed land or the arrival of building materials is one thing. A rumour overheard in the pub is another.

It was pointed out by Lord Upjohn, in *Redland Bricks v Morris*,[147] that there are two kinds of quia timet injunctions, those where the defendant is threatening to do acts and those where the defendant has already done an act which may cause further damage in future. The former gives rise to prohibitory injunctions, but there can also be a mandatory quia timet injunction in the latter case. This latter case differs from a mandatory injunction to remove a wall or an obstruction which is already causing damage to the claimant. The example he was dealing with was an order to restore support where it was uncertain what further damage would occur if the works were not carried out. Lord Upjohn pointed out that the court should be even more cautious about ordering defendants to expend large sums of money carrying out works unless it is absolutely clear that the feared damage really will occur.

(d)   Undertaking to the court

24.46   An injunction may be refused where the defendant gives an undertaking to the court to refrain from doing the acts he is accused of. Such an undertaking has the same effect as an injunction.[148] The procedure is that a copy of the document recording the undertaking shall be delivered to the person giving the undertaking either by handing it to him before he leaves the court or posting it to his residence or through his solicitor or personally.[149] This is a prerequisite of enforcement. It is therefore no longer the case, at least in the county court, that an undertaking is enforceable without being served. The previous rule, however, still it seems applies in the High Court.[150] In general, courts are anxious to deal with matters by way of undertaking rather than injunction since it is felt that a defendant is more likely to abide by a promise he has made to the court than to comply with an order made without his agreement. It may therefore be possible to escape with an undertaking in less strict terms than the injunction would have been.

---

[147] [1970] A.C. 652; [1969] 2 All E.R. 576 at 578C.
[148] *Gandolfo v Gandolfo* [1981] Q.B. 359; [1980] 2 W.L.R. 680.
[149] CCR Ord.29 r.1A.
[150] *Hussain v Hussain* [1986] Fam. 134; [1986] 1 All E.R. 961.

It is important to be clear that such an undertaking only takes effect if it is given to the court. This form confirms the usual practice that the undertaking is given in court either by the defendant or his counsel or solicitor, and that the judge explains its meaning and effect. The form makes it clear that breach can lead to prison for contempt of court. Even if this form is not followed it may be that an undertaking given to the court will still be valid. There is no comparable High Court form but the same principles apply.

An undertaking given to the other party or his solicitor, and not to the court, is not enforceable as an injunction, though if it is given for valuable consideration it may be enforceable as a contract which may result in a mandatory injunction.[151]

If an undertaking is given as part of a final order it cannot normally be discharged unless the purpose for which it was given comes to an end.[152] An undertaking given in the course of interim proceedings "until trial or further order" can be discharged before trial if the defendant is able to raise fresh matters and particularly if he has intimated this intention at the time of the undertaking.[153] As an undertaking is not an order of the court it cannot strictly be varied. If the person giving the undertaking wants to vary it he has to apply for its release and then give a fresh undertaking in the varied terms.[154]

(e)   Enforcement of injunctions

An injunction is an order made against one or more named persons and **24.47** not against the land. Once granted it is not valid until it is served on the defendant with a penal notice.[155] The penal notice must be prominently displayed on the front of the order and the court has no power to dispense with this requirement.[156] Breach of an injunction is a contempt of court. While the court has power to order damages in lieu of an injunction, once an injunction is ordered damages cannot be ordered for its breach,[157] unless the breach of undertaking or injunction amounts to a breach of contract in which case it is possible to award damages at the hearing of the application for committal.[158]

If the defendant fails to comply with an injunction which has been served on him, whether it is interim or permanent, whether with or without notice, whether prohibitory or mandatory, the usual remedy is to

---

[151] See e.g. *Bourne v McDonald* [1950] 2 K.B. 422.
[152] *Chanel Ltd v FW Woolworth & Co Ltd* [1981] 1 W.L.R. 485.
[153] *Butt v Butt* [1987] 1 W.L.R. 1351; [1987] 3 All E.R. 657.
[154] *Cutler v Wandsworth Stadium* [1945] 1 All E.R. 103.
[155] CCR Ord.29 r.1; RSC Ord.45 r.7(2).
[156] *Moerman Lenglet v Henshaw, The Times*, November 23, 1992.
[157] *Chapman v Honig* [1963] 2 Q.B. 502; [1963] 3 W.L.R. 19.
[158] *Midland Marts Ltd v Hobday* [1989] 1 W.L.R. 1143; [1989] 3 All E.R. 246.

apply to the court for committal for contempt. The Civil Procedure Rules 1998 have not, as yet, superseded the Rules of the Supreme Court and the County Court Rules with regard to contempt proceedings. Accordingly the procedure is still set out in Order 29 of the County Court Rules 1981 and Order 52 of the Rules of the Supreme Court. However, both procedures are now governed by a practice direction.[159] All such applications are made in public before a High Court judge or circuit judge (or appropriate deputy). A certificate of truth is not sufficient. The evidence must be given on affidavit. In an urgent case the court can give leave for evidence to be given orally. Despite the urgency of such applications, the Rules now take increased notice of the defendant's basic human rights in view of the possibility that he will lose his liberty. Accordingly the hearing is usually at least 14 clear days after the application and legal advice should be made available to the defendant if he is unrepresented. He will be given information about the Community Legal Service.

The County Court Rules make a specific distinction between mandatory and prohibitory injunctions. A person may be held in contempt of a prohibitory injunction, even if he has not been served with it, if he was present when the order was made or has been notified of the order by telephone, fax or email or otherwise.[160] A mandatory injunction, on the other hand, can only be enforced once it has been served, indorsed with a penal notice. Where it proves impossible to serve the injunction the court may dispense with service.[161] Although this distinction between prohibitory and mandatory injunctions is not set out in the Rules of the Supreme Court the same principles apply in the High Court.[162]

24.48   If the defendant is found to be in contempt the judge has discretion either to accept his apology and make no order, or to make a suspended committal order or to commit him to prison immediately. The High Court and the county court both have power to commit a person in contempt for a fixed period of up to two years.[163] This power can be exercised by a judge or a district judge.[164] However, after a person has been committed to prison the court may discharge him on application under Order 29 r.3.[165] There are two separate elements in a sentence of imprisonment for failure to comply with an injunction. There is a punitive element which involves punishing the defendant for defying the court and a coercive element aimed at persuading him to see sense and purge his contempt. Where the defendant is continuing his defiance it may be appropriate to pass a long

---

[159] RSC PD 52, CCR PD 29.
[160] CCR Ord.29 r.1(6).
[161] ibid., r.1(7).
[162] *Ronson Products Ltd v Ronson Furniture Ltd* [1966] Ch. 603.
[163] Contempt of Court Act 1981 ss.14(1) and 14(4A).
[164] County Courts Act 1984 s.118, as amended by Courts and Legal Services Act 1990 s.74.
[165] Order 52 r.8; CCR Ord.29 r.3.

sentence of 18 months or so and wait for him to apply to purge his contempt.

> "If the contemnor was aggrieved he could seek his immediate release by ceasing his defiance, complying with the order and thereby purging his contempt."[166]

If there is a real possibility that a person will be committed for prison court bailiffs should be available to take him into custody when the order is made.

When a person fails to comply with an injunction or an undertaking courts are faced with a difficult problem. Committal to prison even for a short time is a draconian measure and there is an inevitable reluctance to make such an order. For this reason the application itself should set out as precisely as possible the exact facts relied upon.[167] Whether a committal order is made will very much depend on the attitude of the person in contempt himself. If he apologises and seeks to purge his contempt he is unlikely to end up in gaol, but even a person who is proving difficult is likely to be given a little time to think things over. In an extreme case a course sometimes taken is to pass a very short prison sentence and hope that it will be sufficient. Despite the severity of the threat, however, substantial prison sentences are not infrequently passed against people who persistently disregard injunctions.

An injunction can only be granted against parties. The form of the order is usually "it is ordered that the defendants be restrained whether by themselves their servants or agents or otherwise" from carrying out the prohibited acts. This order can be enforced against one defendant acting independently[168] though it is perhaps desirable to add "or either of them" after "defendants".

The order can also be enforced against a person who is not a party **24.49** who knowingly aids and abets the breach. However, it is only in cases of criminal contempt, brought by the Attorney General, that a person who is aware of the order but not a party to the proceedings can be liable.[169]

Apart from committal there are two other remedies for contempt of court. One is a fine. The High Court power to fine for contempt is limited to £2,500 on any occasion.[170] Section 118 of the County Court Act 1984 applies only to insults and interruptions in court. Whether or not the

---

[166] per Donaldson M.R. in *Lightfoot v Lightfoot* (1988) *The Times*, December 12, 1988.
[167] *Dorrell v Dorrell* [1985] F.L.R. 1089.
[168] *Lenton v Tregoning* [1960] 1 W.L.R. 333.
[169] *Attorney General v Newspaper Publishing Plc* [1988] Ch. 333; [1987] 3 All E.R. 276.
[170] Contempt of Court Act 1981 s.14(1) as amended.

county court has power to fine for breach of an injunction this is not usually appropriate in boundary or easements cases because a fine does not benefit the party who suffers the damage since the court cannot order the fine to be paid to the other party.[171]

The other remedy is sequestration. A writ of sequestration can be issued by order of the court.[172] The application is made under Pt 23 of the Civil Procedure Rules and must be heard by a judge. The procedure has been used to good effect in industrial cases and is a particularly effective procedure where a defendant has failed to carry out a mandatory injunction. It may then be possible to carry out the required act and charge him for it. Although it is usually used against companies or other corporate bodies it can apply to individuals as well. There is no express provision for a writ of sequestration in the County Court Rules but as a result of s.38 of the County Courts Act 1984, the county court nevertheless has power to order sequestration.[173] There may well be boundary and easements cases, therefore, where sequestration is a more effective remedy than committal to prison. It is particularly useful where the defendant is a limited company and it is difficult to identify the person responsible for the breach of injunction.

24.50   One of the major shortcomings of an injunction is that it binds the person and not the land. As a result, if the defendant disposes of his property or dies the injunction cannot be enforced against his successor in title. This is one reason why it is important to obtain a declaration as well as an injunction. Whether or not a declaration has been obtained, issue estoppel will apply to any action involving land and this should prevent a new owner from re-opening issues resolved in a previous action. It will, however, be necessary to start fresh proceedings for an injunction to prevent any new trespass or interference with the easement. It seems that the new owner cannot be committed for contempt just by showing that he had notice of the injunction.[174]

C.   Damages

(a)   Common law damages

24.51   Although damages are the primary remedy for all actions in tort, they have rather less significance in respect of boundary and easement disputes. Usually the parties are principally concerned to establish their rights for the future and the damages for trespass or nuisance are often a

---

[171] *Midland Marts Ltd v Hobday* [1989] 1 W.L.R. 1143; [1989] 3 All E.R. 246.
[172] RSC Ord.46 r.5.
[173] *Re Rose* [1990] 1 Q.B. 562; [1989] 3 W.L.R. 873.
[174] *Attorney General v Newspaper Publishing Plc* [1988] Ch. 333; [1987] 3 All E.R. 276 at 299j.

comparatively minor aspect of the final judgment. Nevertheless there are cases where the claimant has suffered substantial damage.

Damages at common law are awarded only for damage which the claimant has already suffered and not for loss which he may suffer in the future. The cut-off date is the date that the proceedings were commenced.

The basic principle on which damages for trespass or nuisance are assessed is that damages are awarded to compensate the claimant for the loss he has suffered as a result of the defendant's tort:

> "The general rule is that a successful claimant in an action in tort recovers damages equivalent to the loss which he has suffered, no more and no less. If he has suffered no loss the most he can recover are nominal damages."[175]

This will depend not only on the nature of the damage, but also on the effect on the claimant's activities and plans, sometimes called economic loss. Thus where a defendant has occupied the land of the claimant or has interfered with the claimant's easement the claimant is entitled to damages both for any direct damage to his land or property and for the loss which he has suffered by reason of not being able to use his land or exercise his rights.

Where there has been direct damage to the claimant's property, for example by the demolition of a boundary wall or damage to a building either caused by the direct action of the defendant or, for example, by withdrawal of support or even the silting up of the claimant's wharf,[176] the question arises whether the claimant is entitled to the cost of reinstatement or only to the reduction in the value of his land. **24.52**

Where a wall or fence is demolished this may have only a marginal effect on the value of the claimant's land, but may cost a lot of money to re-build. Providing that the claimant genuinely intends to use the money to re-build and providing that the cost is reasonable in relation to the benefit to the claimant gained by re-building, the court will order the cost of re-building.[177]

If, for example, the claimant had no love of his wall or outbuilding and intended to demolish it anyway in due course, there is no reason why he should receive damages for the cost of reinstatement which he will probably just pocket.[178] In such circumstances it may be that the loss of the wall or outbuilding has not reduced the value of the property at all,[179]

---

[175] per Nourse L.J. in *Stoke on Trent City Council v W&J Wass Ltd (No.1)* [1988] 1 W.L.R. 1406; [1988] 3 All E.R. 394 at 397j.

[176] See *Tate & Lyle Industries Ltd v Greater London Council* [1983] 2 A.C. 509; [1983] 2 W.L.R. 649.

[177] *Bernadt v Dhataruya* [1990] 10 C.L. 213.

[178] *Hole & Sons v Harrisons of Thurnscoe Ltd* [1973] 1 Lloyd's Rep. 345.

[179] *CR Taylor Ltd v Hepworths Ltd* [1977] 1 W.L.R. 659; [1977] 2 All E.R. 784.

though it is usual to make some award of damages when there has been damage to the claimant's property even if the loss to the claimant is slight.

24.53   Another possibility is that the cost of re-building the wall will be out of all proportion to its value to the claimant. The cost of restoring a unique feature which the claimant genuinely wishes to reinstate may be reasonable,[180] but not if it is out of all proportion to the value.[181] Where the claimant intended to restore the property, but as a result of the defendants' action it has been demolished he may claim diminution in value of the basis of what it would have been worth restored less the cost of restoration, i.e. a value based on development potential. This is not future loss; it is a realistic assessment of the loss of value.[182]

If the court decides that reinstatement is appropriate there is no reason to make any allowance for the resulting betterment.[183] The reverse situation is where even complete reparation is not enough to prevent the value of the land being affected. The factual example was radioactive contamination. Even an expensive exercise in de-contamination was not enough to prevent the land being blighted.[184] An example more directly related to boundary disputes might be where a boundary feature had historical value which was greater than any replacement.

Quite apart from damages for the physical damage to the land, the claimant is entitled to damages for the loss suffered by being unable to use his land or exercise his rights. Often in boundary or easement cases this loss may be unquantifiable. The temporary loss of part of the garden or the inability to use the particular right of way may not result in any direct financial loss, especially if the claimant's property is a private house. On the other hand he will have suffered inconvenience and it would be wrong in principle for the defendant to have to pay nothing for his breach. Damages will therefore be awarded for inconvenience caused by the defendant's breach even where the value of the land affected is small and there is no quantifiable financial loss.

Where the loss is permanent, for example where trees are cut down, the claimant may be awarded substantial sums for distress, inconvenience and loss of amenity.[185]

24.54   Where the defendant has occupied land belonging to the claimant the normal principle is that he should be ordered to pay a sum representing

---

[180] *Hollebone v Midhurst & Fenhurst Builders* [1968] 1 Lloyd's Rep. 38.

[181] *Farmer Giles v Wessex Water Authority* [1990] 18 E.G. 102.

[182] *Farmer Giles v Wessex Water Authority* [1990] 18 E.G. 102 at 105, per Russell L.J.

[183] *Hollebone v Midhurst & Fenhurst Builders* [1968] 1 Lloyd's Rep. 38; *Harbutts Plasticine Ltd v Wayne Tank & Pump Co Ltd* [1970] 1 Q.B. 447 overruled on other grounds *Photo Production Ltd v Securicor Transport Ltd* [1980] A.C. 827; [1980] 1 All E.R. 556.

[184] *Blue Circle Industries Plc v Ministry of Defence* (1998) 76 P. & C.R. 251.

[185] *Haque v Chopra* [1993] C.L.Y. 1383.

the loss of use of the land. If the land could have been let, e.g. a field, the loss may be of the rental value, even if the claimant had no intention of letting it, though this might not be appropriate if the land was just derelict land.[186]

Sometimes, however, the defendant has gained considerable advantage out of his actions, but the claimant has suffered little financial loss. In such cases it may be appropriate to assess the loss on the basis of the benefit to the trespasser rather than on the loss to the claimant. This figure may be what a reasonable claimant would have charged for the benefit gained[187] but in some cases it is better to look at what the defendant has gained than at what the claimant would have charged. Thus a widow staying on in a mansion because she cannot find other accommodation may only be charged the reasonable cost of such accommodation and a services wife staying on in married quarters after her husband has left may be charged only what comparable local authority housing would have cost rather than the full open market charge.[188]

This method of assessment is an exception to the general principle that damages are for the loss suffered by the claimant. The application of the rule, therefore, is limited. It was held in *Stoke on Trent City Council v W &J Wass Ltd*[189] that this rule does not apply to the infringement of a right to hold a market where the claimant, who held the market franchise, had suffered no loss as a result of the market. It would appear that this decision was on the basis that the rule set out above applies only to trespass, where damages can be awarded without proof of loss. The principle on which such awards were made was debated in *Ministry of Defence v Ashman*.[190] The majority of the Court of Appeal treated it as an anomalous form of damages in trespass and Lloyd L.J. specifically rejected the suggestion that it was an example of the remedy of restitution, but Hoffman L.J. maintained that it was an alternative remedy. The key difference is whether the right to damages assessed on the basis of benefit to the defendant rather than loss to the claimant is an alternative open to election by the claimant, as Hoffman L.J. thought, or an alternative method of assessment which can be decided upon by the court in circumstances where it is considered to meet the justice of the case.

Quite apart from the direct damage to the claimant's property and the **24.55** inconvenience caused by being unable to make use of his land or

---

[186] *CR Taylor Ltd v Hepworths Ltd* [1977] 1 W.L.R. 659; [1977] 2 All E.R. 784.
[187] *Whitwham v Westminster Brymbo Coal & Coke Co* [1896] 2 Ch. 538; *Penarth Dock Engineering Co v Pounds* [1963] 1 Lloyd's Rep. 359; *Swordheath Properties Ltd v Tabet* [1979] 1 W.L.R. 285; [1979] 1 All E.R. 240.
[188] *Ministry of Defence v Ashman* (1993) 66 P. & C.R. 195.
[189] [1988] 1 W.L.R. 1406; [1988] 3 All E.R. 394, not cited in *Ministry of Defence v Ashman* (1993) 66 P. & C.R. 195.
[190] (1993) 66 P. & C.R. 195.

easement the claimant may have suffered consequential loss. If he uses his premises for business purposes the obstruction of a right of way or other easement may cause him financial loss.[191] Such losses are recoverable under the general tortious principles that all loss of the type that is foreseeable will be recoverable.[192] However:

"It is not necessary that the precise concatenation of circumstances should be envisaged. If the consequence was one which was within the general range which any reasonable person might foresee (and was not of an entirely different kind which no-one would anticipate) then it is within the rule that a person who has been guilty of negligence is liable for the consequences."[193]

It seems that the same principle applies to both nuisance and trespass.

As stated above, even where there is no damage to the claimant's land nor any financial loss caused by the trespass or interference with the easement the claimant is entitled to damages for the inconvenience caused by the breach. In addition, where the defendant's conduct has gone beyond asserting his perceived rights in a reasonable manner the court may award aggravated damages for "stress worry and anxiety".[194] These are essentially compensatory in their nature but will only be awarded where the defendant's conduct has been improper and the defendant has suffered unnecessary anxiety as a result. The concept of aggravated damages sits uneasily between compensatory and exemplary damages. As Stuart-Smith L.J. said in *AB v South West Water Services Ltd*,[195] "anger and indignation is not a proper subject for compensation: it is neither pain nor suffering". Most of the reported cases concern people being evicted from their homes, but actions short of eviction can still cause considerable stress, worry and anxiety. A person asserting a boundary claim or challenging a person's right to an easement may be better advised to bring proceedings to assert his claim rather than to take the law into his own hands and enter his neighbour's land or obstruct his easement by force. If he tries direct action and his claim fails he may find himself paying a substantial sum for the upset and distress he causes. Whether this is described as aggravated damages or just general damages, the sums can be considerable. However, aggravated damages should not just be awarded as a symbol of the court's disapproval of the defendant.

---

[191] *Rose v Groves* (1843) 5 Man. & G. 613.
[192] *Overseas Tankship (UK) Ltd v Morts Dock & Engineering Co (The Wagon Mound)* [1961] A.C. 388; *Overseas Tankship (UK) Ltd v Miller Steamship Co Pty Ltd (The Wagon Mound)* [1967] 1 A.C. 617.
[193] per Lord Denning M.R., *Stewart v West African Terminals* [1964] 2 Lloyd's Rep. 371 at 375 quoted with approval in *Meah v McCreamer (No. 2)* [1986] 1 All E.R. 943.
[194] *Drane v Evangelou* [1978] 1 W.L.R. 455; [1978] 2 All E.R. 437.
[195] [1993] Q.B. 507 at 528A.

Aggravated damages will be sufficient to deal with most cases of trespass or interference with easements. However, there is a further category of exemplary damages. It has been held (prior to the Civil Procedure Rules 1998) that in the county court such damages do not have to be specifically pleaded.[196] The correct procedure is for the court first to consider the normal compensatory damages, then to consider whether it is appropriate to award aggravated damages for stress worry and anxiety and finally to consider whether to award exemplary damages which may exceed the loss which the claimant has suffered.[197] The total damages can then be awarded as a global sum.[198]

The basis for an award of exemplary damages is, however, limited to **24.56** the specific categories set out in *Rookes v Barnard*.[199] It is only the second category which really applies to boundary and easement cases, namely, where the defendant stands to make a financial gain from his actions. This might be seen as an extension of the principle of way-leave set out above.[200] If a person acts in cynical disregard of another's rights in order to make a profit for himself the court may award exemplary damages to reduce or wipe out his profit. If, for example, a landowner can only develop his land by taking plant over his neighbour's land and decides to do so regardless of his neighbour's rights it is open to the court to order him to pay a sum representing all or part of his profit from the development[201] or even in excess of his profit in an appropriate case.[202] There is, however, a requirement that the defendant was aware that he had no right to do what he has done, but went ahead in the belief that he would gain more than he would be ordered to pay in damages. Exemplary damages are not an appropriate remedy merely because the defendant has shown reckless disregard for the claimant's rights where there is no substantial permanent damage.[203] An application for the equitable remedy of an account of profits was refused in *Forsyth-Grant v Allen*.[204]

(b) Damages in lieu of injunction

The court has jurisdiction in equity to award damages in addition to or **24.57** in substitution for other relief. Equitable damages originated from Lord Cairns Act[205] which was passed before the Court of Chancery was

---

[196] *Drane v Evangelou* [1978] 1 W.L.R. 455; [1978] 2 All E.R. 437.
[197] *McMillan v Singh* (1985) 17 H.L.R. 120.
[198] *Guppys Ltd v Brookling* (1984) 14 H.L.R. 1.
[199] [1964] A.C. 1129. See AB *v South West Water Ltd* [1993] Q.B. 507.
[200] See above para.11.13 et seq.
[201] Cf. *Guppys Ltd v Brookling* (1984) 14 H.L.R. 1.
[202] *McMillan v Singh* (1985) 17 H.L.R. 120.
[203] *Ketley v Gooden* (1997) 73 P. & C.R. 305.
[204] [2008] EWCA Civ 505.
[205] Chancery Amendment Act 1858.

assimilated into the Supreme Court of Judicature. Its original aim was to enable a party in the Court of Chancery to obtain damages as well as an equitable remedy instead of having to bring a separate action in the common law courts.[206]

Ever since 1873 it has been possible for any court to award damages at common law as well as equitable remedies such as an injunction and accordingly the jurisdiction to award damages in equity is no longer needed for this purpose and indeed Lord Cairns Act has been repealed. However, damages at common law can only be awarded for loss which has actually occurred and so the primary importance of the equitable power to award damages in lieu of injunction (which has survived the repeal of the Act) is that it allows damages to be awarded for prospective loss which will be caused by the continuation of the trespass or nuisance which would otherwise have been stopped by the injunction. This is the case even where the action was quia timet and, therefore, no damage has been suffered at all at the date of the hearing.[207] However, aggravated damages cannot be awarded in lieu of an injunction.[208]

In *Wrotham Park Estate Co Ltd v Parkside Homes Ltd*[209] an award of damages was made in lieu of injunction where the defendant had developed land in breach of a restrictive covenant and the court decided not to make a mandatory injunction requiring the houses to be pulled down "for social and economic reasons"[210] but nevertheless awarded damages representing a proportion of the profit the developer would make in circumstances where the claimant had suffered no quantifiable loss. This award was stated to be in lieu of injunction, but the authorities relied upon included *Whitwham v Westminster Brymbo Coal & Coke Co*,[211] which was a case of common law damages and there seems no reason why Brightman J. could not have awarded the same sum as common law damages.

24.58   In *Wrotham Park Estate Co Ltd v Parkside Homes Ltd*[212] there was a once and for all breach of the covenant. Although the buildings built in breach of covenant remained, there was no continuing trespass and therefore it would not have been open to the claimant to bring a further common law action for damages in the future. However, cases may arise where the offending building constitutes a continuing trespass or infringement of a right of light or the actions of the defendants in using a way or other easement to which they are not entitled will continue in the future unless

---

[206] *Leeds Industrial Cooperative Society v Slack* [1924] A.C. 851 at 857, per Viscount Finlay.
[207] ibid. [1924] A.C. 851.
[208] *Cardwell v Walker* [2003] EWHC 3117 (Ch); [2004] 2 P. & C.R. 9.
[209] [1974] 1 W.L.R. 798; [1974] 2 All E.R. 321.
[210] per Brightman J. at 339d.
[211] [1896] 2 Ch. 538, see above.
[212] [1974] 1 W.L.R. 798; [1974] 2 All E.R. 321.

prevented by injunction. Even in these circumstances it is still open to the court to refuse an injunction and to award damages in lieu.

Perhaps the best summary is that of Mummery L.J. in *Regan v Paul Properties*[213]:

> ". . . the reported cases are merely illustrations of the circumstances in which particular judges have exercised their discretion. In particular all the circumstances of the case have to be considered".

In these circumstances there could be no award of damages at common law beyond the damage which had already been incurred but the equitable jurisdiction referred to above allows the court to award damages not only for the loss which has already been suffered but for prospective loss in respect of continuing trespass or nuisance which will occur in the future.

Such damages will be assessed on the basis of what a reasonable landowner would have charged for the right that the defendant has seized. In general a person will not be permitted to purchase by his wrongdoing a right which he could not have obtained by legitimate means.[214] But nevertheless on several occasions, particularly where the claimant has failed to apply for an interim injunction in good time, defendants have in effect been allowed to obtain rights to which they were not entitled by paying the sums awarded as damages in lieu of injunction.[215]

One of the problems in trespass and nuisance cases is what would happen should the claimant start a new common law action for damages.[216] In theory a new cause of action accrues each time the way is used or each day the obstruction to the claimant's right of light continues, but once an award of damages in lieu of injunction has been made it would be unjust for the claimant to be entitled to bring a fresh action, even if this meant that the defendant was, in effect, being granted an easement by the court.

This point was made and was used as an argument for granting an **24.59** injunction in *Anchor Brewhouse v Berkeley House*[217] where the principle set out in *Bracewell v Appleby*[218] was doubted. However, it was firmly rejected by the Court of Appeal in *Jaggard v Sawyer*[219] where Bingham M.R. made

---

[213] [2006] EWCA Civ 1391 at [59].
[214] *Cowper v Laidler* [1903] 2 Ch. 337 at 341.
[215] *Bracewell v Appleby* [1975] Ch. 408; [1975] 2 W.L.R. 282; *Carr-Saunders v Dick McNeil Associates Ltd* [1986] 1 W.L.R. 922; [1986] 2 All E.R. 888; *Das v Linden Mews Ltd* [2002] EWCA Civ 590.
[216] See Lord Sumner's dissenting judgment in *Leeds Industrial Cooperative Society v Slack* [1924] A.C. 851 at 870.
[217] (1987) 38 B.L.R. 82.
[218] [1975] Ch. 408; [1975] 2 W.L.R. 282.
[219] [1995] 1 W.L.R. 269; [1995] 2 All E.R. 189.

it clear that, in his view, any attempt to bring a further action for damages would be struck out. He did not, however, set out the principle of law on which any such striking out might be ordered. Presumably it would be on the basis of equitable estoppel.

The basis of the assessment will be not the whole profit made by the defendant but a reasonable sum for the purchase of the right bearing in mind the profit made.[220] In *Wrotham Park Estate Co Ltd v Parkside Homes Ltd*[221] this was assessed on the basis of five per cent of the anticipated profit of £50,000. In the most recent case on this issue, *HKRUK II (CHC) Ltd v Heaney*[222] Judge Langan helpfully set out a number of issues which the Court would take into account:

> "1) The overall principle is that the Court must attempt to find out what would be a 'fair' result of a hypothetical negotiation between the parties;
>
> (2) The context, including the nature and seriousness of the breach, must be kept in mind;
>
> (3) The right to prevent a development (or part) gives the owner of the right a significant bargaining position;
>
> (4) The owner of the right with such a bargaining position will normally be expected to receive some part of the likely profit from the development (or relevant part);
>
> (5) If there is no evidence of the likely size of the profit, the Court can do its best by awarding a suitable multiple of the damages for loss of amenity;
>
> (6) If there is evidence of the likely size of the profit, the Court should normally award a sum which takes into account a fair percentage of the profit;
>
> (7) The size of the award should not in any event be so large that the development (or relevant part) would not have taken place had such a sum been payable;
>
> (8) After arriving at a figure which takes into account all the above and any other relevant factors, the Court needs to consider whether the 'deal feels right'."

Over the years appeal courts have come to various proportions of the potential profit to the defendant and the potential loss to the claimant and there is, therefore, considerable scope for the court to reflect its views

---

[220] *Wrotham Park Estate Co Ltd v Parkside Homes Ltd* [1974] 1 W.L.R. 798; *Bracewell v Appleby* [1975] Ch. 408; *Carr-Saunders v Dick McNeil Associates* [1986] 1 W.L.R. 922.
[221] [1974] 2 All E.R. 321.
[222] [2010] EWHC 2245 (Ch).

about the conduct of the defendant and the claimant in assessing the quantum of damages in lieu of injunction.[223]

(c) Account of profits

In *Forsyth-Grant v Allen*[224] the claimant put forward an innovative claim for the equitable remedy of an account of profits. The Court of Appeal accepted that such a remedy still exists, particularly where there is a fiduciary relationship between the claimant and the defendant. In *Attorney General v Blake*[225] the House of Lords held that this remedy could be available (perhaps properly described as "restitutionary damages") in, for example, cases of conversion, but the Court of Appeal doubted that it applies to nuisance and, in any event, held that it only applies in "exceptional circumstances".

D. Self-Help

As a matter of general principle a person is entitled to do whatever he **24.60** wants on his own property, providing that it does not breach any general laws or cause a nuisance to his neighbour. However, if he goes on his neighbour's land, he is liable to be sued in trespass. The right of abatement of a nuisance is therefore a specific right and remedy. As pointed out in *Leakey v National Trust for Places of Historic Interest or Natural Beauty*,[226] it can only arise where there is a cause of action and, even then, it is a very unsatisfactory remedy. In essence, the right of abatement has been supplanted by the power of the court to make a mandatory injunction ordering the defendant to do works on his own land to abate the nuisance.[227]

The position in respect of trespass might be seen as different. If a neighbour erects a fence on your land you can remove it. However, the time must come when the law intervenes to prevent the matter dissolving into a battle. In *Burton v Winters*[228] the claimant had proved her case that the defendant had built a building encroaching four inches onto her land, but she had been refused a mandatory injunction. She set about removing the building herself and an injunction was granted against her, which resulted in turn in contempt of court proceedings and her eventual imprisonment for two years. The matter was considered by the Court of Appeal, since if she had the absolute right to remove the trespassing building she could not be enjoined to stop doing so. The Court of Appeal

---

[223] See above, para.24.56.
[224] [2008] EWCA Civ 505.
[225] [2001] 1 A.C. 268; [2000] 3 W.L.R. 625.
[226] [1980] Q.B. 485; [1980] 1 All E.R. 17 at 34f, per Megaw L.J.
[227] *Burton v Winters* [1993] 1 W.L.R. 1077; [1993] 3 All E.R. 847 at 851e.
[228] [1993] 1 W.L.R. 1077; [1993] 3 All E.R. 847.

made clear that self-help or abatement was not a natural right, but was a specific alternative remedy and was confined to simple cases such as an overhanging branch or an encroaching root which would not justify the expense of legal proceedings. It was further specifically decided that the refusal of a mandatory injunction in itself meant that the remedy of self-help was not available.

This is an obviously sensible decision, but it does raise some further questions. Clearly an encroaching building cannot be removed without affecting other parts of the building which are not encroaching, but what of something portable? The problem is the same as that faced in *Bracewell v Appleby*.[229] When an equitable remedy is refused, the breach does not go away.

[229] [1975] Ch. 408; [1975] 2 W.L.R. 282.

Part IV:
Precedents

Part IV: Precedents

I

CLAIM FORM

IN THE HIGH COURT OF JUSTICE **25.01**
Chancery Division
[District Registry]
Claim No
Claimant

[IN THE . . . . COUNTY COURT
Chancery Business[1]
Claim No. . . .]

First Defendant
Second Defendant

BRIEF DETAILS OF CLAIM

(1) A declaration that the Claimant is the owner of the land shown on the plan annexed to the Statement of Claim and thereon coloured brown.

(2) An injunction restraining the Defendant by himself his servants or agents or otherwise from entering upon the said land or otherwise interfering with the Claimant's occupation thereof.

(3) An order that the Claimant do remove forthwith the fence between the points "X" and "Y" on plan annexed to the Statement of Claim and the motor car and tarmac on the said land and reinstate the same to its former condition.

(4) Damages[2] [including aggravated damages] together with interest thereon pursuant to section 35A of the Supreme Court Act 1981 at the rate of 15 per cent. per annum [i.e. the current permitted rate] from the . . . . to the date hereof.

(5) Costs.

(6) Further or other relief.

---

[1] If this is included, the claim will be treated as Chancery Business in the county court and will be allocated accordingly. The Chancery Guide will then apply.

[2] Although cases should only be commenced in the High Court where the value of the claim exceeds £25,000, it is not necessary to issue a Statement of Value until the Summons for Directions.

Value

The value of the claim is not quantified but exceeds £15,000[3]

Does, or will your claim include any issues under the Human Rights Act 1998? No

Signature of legal representative

DATED ....

STATEMENT OF TRUTH

The claimant believes that the facts stated in these particulars of claim are true.

I am duly authorised by the claimant to sign this statement as the claimant's solicitor.

Full name, address, signature etc.

[3] This should put the claim into multi-track.

II

CLAIM TO OWNERSHIP OF UNREGISTERED LAND THE SUBJECT OF A BOUNDARY DISPUTE

IN THE . . . . COUNTY COURT **25.02**
[Chancery Business][1]
Claim No . . . .
Claim form issued . . . .

Claimant

First Defendant
Second Defendant

PARTICULARS OF CLAIM

1. The Claimant is and was at all material times the freehold owner[2] in possession of the property known as Greenacre [address] (hereinafter called "Greenacre" [or "the red land"]) which is shown on the plan annexed hereto edged red. The western boundary of Greenacre is marked by a fence shown on the plan between the points "A" and "B".

2. By a conveyance [root of title] dated . . . . and made between . . . . . and . . . . Greenacre was conveyed to . . . . in fee simple. The property conveyed included all of the land coloured red on the plan including the area hatched brown (hereinafter called "the disputed land"'). A copy of this conveyance is attached. The Claimant is the successor in title of . . .

3. The first Defendant is in possession of the neighbouring property known as Whiteacre [address] (hereinafter called "Whiteacre") which is shown on the plan annexed hereto coloured blue.

4. On numerous occasions since . . . . the Defendants and each of them have trespassed upon the disputed land.

---

1 If this is included, the claim will be treated as Chancery Business in the county court and will be allocated accordingly. The Chancery Guide will then apply.
2 This is done under CPR Pt 19.

PARTICULARS

(1) On or about . . . . the first Defendant and/or the second Defendant entered upon the disputed land and removed the fence shown on the plan between the points "A" and "B".

(2) On or about . . . . the first Defendant and/or the second Defendant entered upon the disputed land and uprooted cabbages belonging to the Claimant growing on the disputed land.

(3) On or about . . . . the second Defendant swore at the Claimant and threatened him, saying "Get off my land or I'll get you" thereby causing the Claimant fear and distress.

(4) On various dates between . . . . the first Defendant and/or the second Defendant have erected a fence on the disputed land between the points "X" and "Y" on the said land and claims that his fence represents the boundary between Greenacre and Whiteacre.

(5) Since the said date the first Defendant has entered into possession of the disputed land, has laid tarmac on it and has frequently parked his car there.

5. By letter dated . . . . the Claimant requested the first Defendant and/or the second Defendant to remove his fence, the tarmac and the car but the Defendants have failed or refused to do so and threaten and intend to remain in possession of the disputed land.

6. By reason of the Defendants' trespass the Claimant has suffered distress, inconvenience, loss and damage.

PARTICULARS OF SPECIAL DAMAGE

(1) Cost of removal of the tarmac and reinstatement of the Claimant's garden estimated at £. . . . . .

(2) Cost of reinstatement of the Claimant's fence estimated at £. . . . .

(3) Loss of the Claimant's growing produce estimated at £. . . . . .

(4) Loss of use of the disputed land from . . . . to date at £. . . . . . . per week continuing.

7. The Claimant has (not) complied with Sections III or IV of the Practice Direction (Pre-Action Conduct).

AND the Claimant claims:

(1) Against the first Defendant a declaration that the Claimant is the owner of the disputed land.

(2) Against both Defendants an injunction restraining the Defendants or either of them (whether by himself or by instructing or encouraging any other person) from entering upon the disputed land or otherwise interfering with the Claimant's occupation thereof.

(3) Against both Defendants an order that they remove forthwith the said fence between the points "X" and "Y" and the said motor car and tarmac and reinstate the same to its former condition.

(4) Damages including aggravated damages together with interest thereon pursuant to section 69 County Courts Act 1984 at the rate allowed on judgments in the High Court.

Signature of legal representative

DATED . . . .

STATEMENT OF TRUTH

The claimant believes that the facts stated in these particulars of claim are true.
I am duly authorised by the claimant to sign this statement as the claimant's solicitor.

Full name . . . .
Name of claimant's solicitor's firm . . . .
Signed . . . . (position or office held)
Address

III

CLAIM FOR DECLARATION
AND RECTIFICATION IN RESPECT
OF REGISTERED LAND[1]

25.03

IN THE . . . . COUNTY COURT
[Chancery Business]
Claim No . . . .
Claim form issued . . . .

Claimant

First Defendant
Second Defendant

PARTICULARS OF CLAIM

1. The Claimant is and was at all material times the registered owner of the property known as Greenacre [*address*] (hereinafter called "Greenacre") the title of which is registered at . . . . District Land Registry as title number . . . . The Claimant's predecessor in title . . . . was registered as first proprietor of Greenacre on . . . . and the Claimant was registered as proprietor on . . . . The property is shown on the plan annexed hereto edged red. A copy of the Land Certificate is attached.

2. The Defendant is the registered owner of Whiteacre [*address*] (hereinafter called "Whiteacre") which is registered at . . . . . District Land Registry as title number . . . . . . Whiteacre is shown on the said plan edged blue.

3. When Whiteacre was registered, a piece of land forming part of O.S. Number . . . . on the . . . . Edition of the Ordnance Survey map (hereinafter called "the disputed land") was wrongly included in the said title. The disputed land forms part of Greenacre and had formerly been registered as part of title number . . . . The disputed land is shown on the plan hatched brown.

4. Further or in the alternative the precise boundary between Greenacre and Whiteacre is marked by a fence between the points "A" and "B" on the plan.

---

[1] If this is included, the claim will be treated as Chancery Business in the county court and will be allocated accordingly. The Chancery Guide will then apply.

5. On or about . . . . the Defendant claimed that the disputed land was his property and since that date by letters and conduct has threatened to take possession of the disputed land.

AND the Claimant claims:

(1) A declaration that the Claimant is the absolute owner of the disputed land, hatched brown on the plan.

(2) Rectification[2] of the register to remove the disputed land from title number . . . .

(3) An injunction to restrain the Defendant (whether by himself or by instructing or encouraging any other person) from entering upon or otherwise interfering with the Claimant's possession of the disputed land.

(4) Costs.

Signature of legal representative

DATED . . . .

STATEMENT OF TRUTH

The claimant believes that the facts stated in these particulars of claim are true.
I am duly authorised by the claimant to sign this statement as the claimant's solicitor.

Full name . . . .
Name of claimant's solicitor's firm . . . .
Signed . . . . (position or office held)
Address

---

[2] For the distinction between rectification and "alteration" see Land Registration Act 2002 Sch.4 para.1.

IV

CLAIM TO DRAINAGE RIGHTS

25.04

IN THE . . . . COUNTY COURT
[Chancery Business][1]
Claim No . . . .
Claim form issued . . . .

Claimant

First Defendant
Second Defendant

PARTICULARS OF CLAIM

1. The Claimant is and was at all material times the owner in possession of the property known as Greenacre [*address*] (hereinafter called "Greenacre") which is shown on the plan annexed hereto edged red.[2]

2. The Defendant is in possession of the property known as Whiteacre [*address*] (hereinafter called "Whiteacre") which is shown on the plan edged blue.

3. A drainage pipe runs from Greenacre across Whiteacre and joins to the public sewer at the point marked "X" on the plan. The route of the pipe is shown on the plan by a brown line between the points marked "X" and "Y" on the plan.

4. By a conveyance dated . . . . and made between the Defendant's predecessor in title [*name*] and the Claimant's predecessor in title [*name*] the said . . . . granted to the said . . . . a right to install a pipe across Whiteacre, to attach the same to the public sewer and to use it to drain Greenacre. A copy of the Conveyance is attached hereto. The Conveyance refers [does not refer] to residential land.

5. In or about . . . . the said . . . . installed a pipe between the point X and Y and has ever thereafter used the same to drain Greenacre.

6. It was an implied term of the grant that the said . . . . . . and his successors in title were entitled to enter upon Whiteacre and to carry out thereon all necessary repairs and replacements. The right is claimed as an

---

[1] If this is included, the claim will be treated as Chancery Business in the county court and will be allocated accordingly. The Chancery Guide will then apply.
[2] If land is registered, insert registration details as per Precedent II.

implied easement under section 62 Law of Property Act 1925 and under the rule in *Wheeldon v Burrows*.

7. On or about . . . . the pipe became blocked and the Claimant gave notice to the Defendant of his intention to exercise his right to carry out repairs to the pipe and to replace a section thereof but the Defendant refused the Claimant access thereto.

8. By reason of the Defendant's interference with the Claimant's right the Claimant has suffered inconvenience, loss and damage.

<u>PARTICULARS OF SPECIAL DAMAGE</u>

(1) Cost of abortive visit by drainage contractors £ . . . .

(2) Cost of temporary piping to Claimant's
alternative drain £ . . . .

9. The Claimant has (not) complied with Sections III or IV of the Practice Direction (Pre-Action Conduct).

AND the Claimant claims:

(1) A declaration that the Claimant is the owner of the said pipe and/or is entitled to install and maintain a pipe on Whiteacre.

(2) A declaration that the Claimant is entitled by himself his servants or agents to enter upon Whiteacre and to carry out necessary repairs and replacements on the said pipe.

(3) An injunction to restrain the Defendant (whether by himself or by instructing or encouraging any other person) from interfering with the Claimant, his servants or agents in exercising their said right.

(4) Damages together with interest thereon pursuant to section 69 County Courts Act 1984 at the rate allowed on judgments in the High Court.

Signature of legal representative

DATED . . . .

STATEMENT OF TRUTH

The claimant believes that the facts stated in these particulars of claim are true.

I am duly authorised by the claimant to sign this statement as the claimant's solicitor.

Full name . . . .

Name of claimant's solicitor's firm . . . .

Signed . . . . (position or office held)

Address

V

CLAIM TO A RIGHT OF WAY BY EXPRESS GRANT

IN THE . . . . COUNTY COURT **25.05**
[Chancery Business]¹
Claim No . . . .
Claim form issued . . . .

Claimant

First Defendant
Second Defendant

PARTICULARS OF CLAIM

1. The Claimant is and was at all material times the owner in fee simple in possession of the property known as Greenacre [*address*] (hereinafter called "Greenacre") which is shown on the plan annexed hereto edged red

2. The Defendant is in possession of the property known as Whiteacre [*address*] (hereinafter called 'Whiteacre") which is shown on the plan edged blue.

3. By a conveyance dated . . . . and made between . . . . and . . . . Greenacre was conveyed to . . . . TOGETHER with a right of way in favour of . . . . his servants or agents for all purposes to pass and re-pass over Whiteacre for the purpose of access to and egress from Greenacre to the public highway known as . . . . Lane. A copy of the Conveyance is attached hereto. The Conveyance refers [does not refer] to residential land.

4. The Claimant is the successor in title of the said. . . . . The said right of way is shown on the plan coloured brown.

5. The Defendant has on numerous occasions obstructed the said way and has interfered with the Claimant and his visitors seeking to exercise the right of way.

PARTICULARS

(1) On or about . . . . the Defendant told the milkman who was delivering milk to the Claimant not to use the way.

¹ If this is included, the claim will be treated as Chancery Business in the county court and will be allocated accordingly. The Chancery Guide will then apply.

(2) On or about . . . . the Defendant stood in the way of the Claimant who was driving his lorry along the way and threatened to hit him if he continued any further. Thereafter the Defendant has on numerous occasions abused the Claimant.

(3) On or about . . . . the Defendant his servants or agents placed boulders on the way thereby preventing the Claimant from using the same.

6. By letters dated . . . . the Claimant's solicitors have requested the Defendant to remove the obstructions and to stop interfering with the Claimant's use of the way but the Defendant has refused or neglected to do so.

7. By reason of the Defendant's said acts the Claimant has suffered distress, inconvenience loss and damage.

PARTICULARS OF SPECIAL DAMAGE

The Claimant carries on a haulage business from his premises. He has been unable to use the premises for this purpose since . . . . and has thereby suffered loss of profit estimated at £. . . . . . per month for a period of . . . . months to date continuing £. . . . . .

PARTICULARS OF DISTRESS AND INCONVENIENCE

The Claimant is of a nervous disposition and as a result of the Defendant's persistent abuse and threats has been obliged to obtain medical treatment in the form of drugs.

8 The Claimant has (not) complied with Sections III or IV of the Practice Direction (Pre-Action Conduct).

AND the Claimant claims:

(1) A declaration that he is entitled to the said right of way coloured brown on the terms and for the purposes set out in the conveyance dated.

(2) An order that the Defendant do remove forthwith the boulders strewn across the way.

(3) An injunction restraining the Defendant (whether by himself or by instructing or encouraging any other person) from obstructing the way or from interfering with the Claimant and his visitors' use thereof.

(4) Damages together with interest thereon pursuant to section 69 County Courts Act 1984 at the rate allowed on judgments in the High Court.

Signature of legal representative

DATED . . . .

STATEMENT OF TRUTH

The claimant believes that the facts stated in these particulars of claim are true.

I am duly authorised by the claimant to sign this statement as the claimant's solicitor.

Full name . . . .

Name of claimant's solicitor's firm . . . .

Signed . . . . (position or office held)

Address

VI

CLAIM TO A RIGHT OF WAY BASED ON IMPLIED GRANT AND/OR PRESCRIPTION

25.06

IN THE . . . . . . COUNTY COURT
[Chancery Business][1]
Claim No . . . .
Claim form issued . . . .

Claimant

First Defendant
Second Defendant

PARTICULARS OF CLAIM

1. The Claimant is and was at all material times the owner in fee simple in possession of the property known as Greenacre [address] (hereinafter called "Greenacre") which is shown on the plan annexed edged red.

2. The Defendant is in possession of the property known as Whiteacre [address] (hereinafer called "Whiteacre") which is shown on the plan edged blue.

3. By a conveyance dated . . . . . . and made between . . . . . [vendor] of the one part and . . . . [purchaser] of the other part Greenacre was conveyed to . . . . [purchaser] in fee simple. The . . . . [vendor] was also the owner of Whiteacre. The Claimant is the successor in title of . . . . [purchaser]. Copies of the relevant conveyances are attached hereto[2]. The Conveyances relates [does not relate] to residential land. .

4. At the time of the conveyance and at all material times thereafter there has been a path running across Whiteacre leading from Greenacre to the public highway known as . . . . This path ("the disputed way") is shown on the plan marked brown. This path was enjoyed with and was appurtenant to Greenacre and the conveyance contained an implied grant of a right of way for all purposes over and along the disputed way as a means of access and egress to and from Greenacre under the provisions of section 62 Law of Property Act 1925.

---

[1] If this is included, the claim will be treated as Chancery Business in the county court and will be allocated accordingly. The Chancery Guide will then apply.

[2] If the land is registered, insert registration details.

5. Further or in the alternative the disputed way was a usual and apparent easement and the Claimant claims that there was an implied grant of a right of way by virtue of the rule in *Wheeldon v Burrows*.

6. Further or in the further alternative the Claimant and his predecessors in title owners and occupiers for the time being of Greenacre have for the full period of 20 years and more up to the date of these proceedings used the disputed way as of right and without interruption at all times and for all purposes in connection with their occupation of Greenacre and the right is claimed as a right of way under section 2 Prescription Act 1832. Alternatively the right is claimed by virtue of the doctrine of lost modern grant and/or as a common law right having been exercised from time immemorial.

7. Further or in the further alternative the disputed way is the only access to the public highway from Greenacre and the claimant claims a right of way over the disputed way as a way of necessity.

8. The Defendant has on numerous occasions obstructed the way and has interfered with the Claimant and his visitors seeking to exercise the right of way.

PARTICULARS

(1) On or about . . . . the Defendant told the milkman who was delivering milk to the Claimant not to use the way.

(2) On or about . . . . the Defendant stood in the way of the Claimant who was driving his car along the way and threatened to hit him if he continued any further. Thereafter the defendant has on numerous occasions abused the Claimant.

(3) On or about . . . . the Defendant his servants or agents placed boulders on the way thereby preventing the Claimant from using the same.

9. By letters dated . . . . the Claimant's solicitors have requested the Defendant to remove the obstructions and to stop interfering with the Claimant's use of the way but the Defendant has refused or neglected to do so.

10. By reason of the Defendant's acts the Claimant has suffered distress, inconvenience loss and damage.

PARTICULARS

The Claimant has been unable to use the disputed way since. . . . . The disputed way is the only vehicular access to Greenacre and the Claimant his wife, family and visitors have been forced to park his car on the highway and walk to his property.

11. The Claimant has (not) complied with Sections III or IV of the Practice Direction (Pre-Action Conduct).

AND the Claimant claims:

(1) A declaration that he is entitled to the right of way for himself his family and visitors at all times and for all purposes over and along the disputed way as a means of access and egress to and from Greenacre.

(2) An order that the Defendant do remove forthwith the boulders strewn across the way.

(3) An injunction restraining the Defendant (whether by himself or by instructing or encouraging any other person) from obstructing the way or from interfering with the Claimant and his visitors' use thereof.

(4) Damages together with interest thereon pursuant to section 69 County Court Act 1984 at the rate allowed on judgments in the High Court.

Signature of legal representative

DATED . . . .

STATEMENT OF TRUTH

The claimant believes that the facts stated in these particulars of claim are true.
I am duly authorised by the claimant to sign this statement as the claimant's solicitor.

Full name . . . .
Name of claimant's solicitor's firm . . . .
Signed . . . . (position or office held)
Address

VII

CLAIM TO OWNERSHIP OF LAND WITH RIGHT OF WAY AND PARKING IN THE ALTERNATIVE

IN THE . . . . . . COUNTY COURT **25.07**
[Chancery Business][1]
Claim No . . . .
Claim form issued . . . .

Claimant

First Defendant
Second Defendant

PARTICULARS OF CLAIM

1. The Claimant is and was at all material times the owner in fee simple in possession of the property known as Greenacre [address] (hereinafter called "Greenacre") which is shown on the plan annexed hereto edged red.

2. The Defendant is in possession of the property known as Whiteacre [address] (hereinafter called "Whiteacre") which is shown on the plan edged blue.

3. Between Greenacre and Whiteacre there is a driveway which leads to the rear gardens of the two properties and to the Claimant's garage. This path (hereinafter called "the disputed path") is shown on the plan coloured brown. By a conveyance [root of title] dated . . . . . and made between . . . . . . and . . . . Greenacre was conveyed to the said . . . . in fee simple. The property conveyed included the disputed path. Copies of the relevant conveyances are attached hereto. The Conveyance relates [does not relate] to residential land. The Claimant is the successor in title of the . . . .[2]

[4. In the alternative the Claimant and his predecessors in title have been in undisturbed possession of the disputed path since at least . . . . and title is claimed pursuant to the Limitation Act 1980.[3]]

---

[1] If this is included, the claim will be treated as Chancery Business in the county court and will be allocated accordingly. The Chancery Guide will then apply.

[2] If land is registered, insert registration details as per Precedent II.

[3] This can only be used for unregistered land. For registered land the procedures under Part IX of the Land Registration Act 2002 must be used.

5. Further or in the further alternative the Claimant and his predecessors in title owners and occupiers for the time being of Greenacre have for the full period of 20 years and more up to the date of these proceedings used the disputed path as of right and without interruption at all times and for all purposes as a means of access to and egress from the said garage and the rear garden of Greenacre and the said right is claimed as a right of way under section 2 Prescription Act 1832. Alternatively the said right is claimed by virtue of the doctrine of lost modern grant and/or as a common law right having been exercised from time immemorial.

6. The disputed path has for the full period referred to in paragraph 5 been used for the purpose of parking vehicles and the Claimant claims that the right of way includes an easement of parking for the benefit of the Claimant, his servants, agents and visitors.[4]

7. The Defendant has on numerous occasions trespassed upon the said path and interfered with the Claimant seeking to exercise the right of way.

PARTICULARS

(1) On or about . . . . the Defendant stood in the way of the Claimant who was driving his car along the path and threatened to hit him if he continued any further. Thereafter the Defendant has on numerous occasions abused the Claimant.

(2) On or about . . . . the Defendant his servants or agents placed a fence along the middle of the path thereby preventing the Claimant from using the same as a means of access to his garage.

8. By letters dated . . . . the Claimant's solicitors have requested the defendant to stop trespassing on the Claimant's land to remove the obstructions and to stop interfering with the Claimant's use of the way but the Defendant has refused or neglected to do so.

9. By reason of the Defendant's said acts the Claimant has suffered distress, inconvenience loss and damage.

PARTICULARS

(1) The Claimant has been unable to use the disputed way since. . . . . The disputed way is the only access to his garage and the Claimant his wife, family and visitors have been forced to park his car on the highway and walk to his property.

---

[4] See *Moncrieff v Jamieson* [2008] 1 P. & C.R. 349.

    (2) The Claimant has a second vehicle which he regularly parks on the disputed way in the area outside his house. His family, tradesmen and visitors regularly park in the same area. The Claimant, his family, and his tradesmen and visitors now have to park on the public highway and walk to his property.

10. The Claimant has (not) complied with Sections III or IV of the Practice Direction (Pre-Action Conduct).

AND the Claimant claims:

    (1) A declaration that he is the owner in fee simple of the disputed path and that the same forms part of Greenacre.

    (2) In the alternative a declaration that he is entitled to a right of way for himself his family and visitors at all times and for all purposes over and also the disputed way as a means of access to and egress from his garage and rear garden and/or a right of parking for himself, his family and visitors on the disputed way.

    (3) An order that the Defendant do remove forthwith the said fence.

    (4) An injunction restraining the Defendant (whether by himself or by instructing or encouraging any other person) from obstructing the way or from interfering with the Plaintiff and his visitors' use thereof.

    (5) Damages together with interest thereon pursuant to section 69 County Courts Act 1984 at the rate allowed on judgments in the High Court.

Signature of legal representative

DATED . . . .

STATEMENT OF TRUTH

The claimant believes that the facts stated in these particulars of claim are true.
I am duly authorised by the claimant to sign this statement as the claimant's solicitor.

Full name . . . .
Name of claimant's solicitor's firm . . . .
Signed . . . . (position or office held)
Address

VIII

CLAIM TO NATURAL RIGHT OF SUPPORT WITH EASEMENT IN THE ALTERNATIVE

25.08

IN THE . . . . . . COUNTY COURT
[Chancery Business][1]
Claim No . . . .
Claim form issued . . . .

Claimant

First Defendant
Second Defendant

PARTICULARS OF CLAIM

1. The Claimant is and was at all material times the freehold owner in possession of the property known as Greenacre [address] (hereinafter called "Greenacre") which is shown on the plan annexed hereto edged red.[2] A copy of the Conveyance is attached hereto. The Conveyance relates [does not relate] to residential land.

2. The Defendant is in possession of the property known as Whiteacre [address] (hereinafter called "Whiteacre") which is shown on the plan edged blue.

3. There is an outbuilding on Greenacre, shown on the plan hatched brown. This outbuilding has for a period in excess of 20 years prior to the commencement of these proceedings enjoyed the support of an outbuilding on Whiteacre shown on the plan hatched yellow. The Claimant claims an easement of support in respect of the outbuilding hatched brown under section 2 Prescription Act 1832 and/or by virtue of the doctrine of lost modern grant. Further or in the alternative Greenacre and the said outbuilding constructed thereon is entitled to a natural right of support from Whiteacre.[3]

4. On or about . . . . the Defendant began demolishing his outbuilding and excavating his land. The Claimant orally and by letter dated . . . . protested that the said excavations were

---

[1] If this is included, the claim will be treated as Chancery Business in the county court and will be allocated accordingly. The Chancery Guide will then apply.

[2] If the land is registered, insert registration details.

[3] See *Holbeck Hall v Scarborough B.C.* [2000] Q.B. 836, which extends the principle of natural rights of support as discussed in Chapter 19.

withdrawing support from his own outbuildings and also from other parts of his land, but the Defendant has failed or refused to stop his excavations or to restore the said support.

PARTICULARS

(1) On or about .... contractors started demolishing the Defendant's outbuilding.

(2) On or about .... the Claimant protested orally to the Defendant that these works were likely to damage his property.

(3) On or about .... the Claimant noticed cracks appearing in his outbuilding.

(4) By letter dated .... the Claimant requested the Defendant to stop the excavations and restore support to the Claimant's outbuildings and to the rest of Whiteacre.

(5) On or about .... the Defendants' contractors started excavating between the points "X" and "Y" on the plan. To date the excavations have reached a depth of about four feet.

(6) On or about .... part of Greenacre fell into the excavation at or about the point marked "A" on the plan.

5. By reason of the Defendant's said breaches of the Claimant's natural rights of support and his said easement of support the Claimant has suffered loss and damage.

PARTICULARS OF SPECIAL DAMAGE

(1) There has been subsidence of the Claimant's outbuilding which will continue unless and until support is restored. This may require the demolition and re-construction of the outbuilding at an approximate cost of £. ....

(2) The Claimant has been unable to use his outbuilding since .... He has suffered loss of use at the rate of £. ..... per week continuing.

(3) Part of the Claimant"s garden has fallen into the excavation including part of an ornamental rosebed. The cost of restoring this will be approximately £. ....

6. Unless restrained by this court the Defendant threatens and intends to continue his said excavations and to continue with the withdrawal of support.

7. The Claimant has (not) complied with Sections III or IV of the Practice Direction (Pre-Action Conduct).

AND the Claimant claims:

(1) A declaration that he is entitled to the said easement of support.

(2) An order that the Defendant do forthwith restore support to the Claimant's land by filling in the excavation and providing adequate shoring to the Claimant's outbuilding.

(3) An injunction restraining the Defendant (whether by himself or by instructing or encouraging any other person) from further withdrawing support from Greenacre or any part thereof and/or from the Claimant's outbuilding.

(4) Damages together with interest thereon pursuant to section 69 County Courts Act 1984 at the rate allowed on judgments in the High Court.

Signature of legal representative

DATED ......

STATEMENT OF TRUTH

The claimant believes that the facts stated in these particulars of claim are true.
I am duly authorised by the claimant to sign this statement as the claimant's solicitor.

Full name ....
Name of claimant's solicitor's firm ....
Signed .... (position or office held)
Address

IX

CLAIM TO A RIGHT OF LIGHT[1]

IN THE . . . . . . COUNTY COURT **25.09**
[Chancery Business][2]
Claim No . . . .
Claim form issued . . . .

Claimant

First Defendant
Second Defendant

PARTICULARS OF CLAIM

1. The Claimant is and was at all material times the freehold owner in possession of the property known as Greenacre [address] (hereinafter called "Greenacre") which is shown on the plan annexed hereto edged red.[3] A copies of the relevant conveyance is attached hereto. The Conveyance relates [does not relate] to residential land.

2. There is a bungalow built on Greenacre where the Claimant lives. This bungalow was built in . . . . . . and is shown on the plan hatched yellow. There are two windows facing in a westerly direction which have both been in their present position since the bungalow was built. These windows are shown on the plan marked "X" and "Y" respectively. The Claimant has an easement of light in respect of both these windows under section 4 Prescription Act 1832 and by virtue of the doctrine of lost modern grant.

3. The Defendant is in possession of the property known as Whiteacre [address] (hereinafter called "Whiteacre") which is shown on the plan edged blue.

4. On or about . . . . the Defendant applied for planning permission to construct a four storey block of flats on Whiteacre. The location of the proposed block of flats is shown on the plan hatched brown. If this block of flats were to be constructed it would materially diminish the

---

[1] This is a preventive action. If the offending building has already been commenced the Claimant should claim a mandatory injunction and damages.

[2] If this is included, the claim will be treated as Chancery Business in the county court and will be allocated accordingly. The Chancery Guide will then apply.

[3] If land is registered, insert registration details as per Precedent II.

light flowing into the Claimant's bungalow and in particular the light flowing through the window marked "X" and "Y," and would materially affect the Claimant's reasonable enjoyment of Greenacre.

5. By letter dated . . . . the Claimant requested the Defendant to abandon his plans, but the Defendant threatens and intends to construct the block of flats in accordance with the plans.

6. The Claimant has (not) complied with Sections III or IV of the Practice Direction (Pre-Action Conduct).

AND the Claimant claims:

(1) A declaration that he is entitled to the said easement of light and that the Claimant's proposed development would be an interference therewith.

(2) An injunction restraining the Defendant (whether by himself or by instructing or encouraging any other person) from constructing the proposed building or otherwise from interfering with the Claimant's rights of light.

Signature of legal representative

DATED . . . .

STATEMENT OF TRUTH

The claimant believes that the facts stated in these particulars of claim are true.
I am duly authorised by the claimant to sign this statement as the claimant's solicitor.

Full name . . . .
Name of claimant's solicitor's firm . . . .
Signed . . . . (position or office held)
Address

X

CLAIM TO SHOOTING RIGHTS

IN THE . . . . . . COUNTY COURT **25.10**
[Chancery Business][1]
Claim No . . . .
Claim form issued . . . .

Claimant

First Defendant
Second Defendant

PARTICULARS OF CLAIM

1. By a deed of grant made . . . . between . . . . of the one part and the Claimant of the other part the shooting rights over the property known as Whiteacre [address] (hereinafter called "Whiteacre") were granted to the Claimant for a term of 21 years at a rent of £. . . . . per annum. A copy of this deed is attached hereto. The Defendant is the successor in title of the said . . . . Whiteacre is shown on the plan annexed hereto edged blue.[2]

2. On or about . . . . the Defendant, his servants or agents cut down a copse which formed cover for the game birds on the said land. The copse is shown on the plan coloured brown.

3. Cutting down the said copse materially affected the availability of game birds for the season. In the premises it constituted a substantial interference with the Claimant's rights and the Claimant has thereby suffered loss and damage.

PARTICULARS OF SPECIAL DAMAGE

For the . . . . season the number of birds shot has reduced from . . . . brace to . . . . brace. At a price of £. . . . . per brace this amounts to a loss for the season of £. . . . . . This loss will continue annually and the value of the Claimant's shooting rights have been

---

[1] If this is included, the claim will be treated as Chancery Business in the county court and will be allocated accordingly. The Chancery Guide will then apply.
[2] Such rights will be voluntarily registrable under the Land Registration Act 2002.

549

substantially affected. The Claimant estimates that the value of his shooting rights has been reduced by £. . . . .

4. The Defendant threatens and intends to carry out further coppicing work on his land.

5. The Claimant has [not] complied with Sections III or IV of the Practice Direction (Pre-Action Conduct).

AND the Claimant claims:

    (1) A declaration that he is entitled to the said shooting rights and that the Defendant's actions constitute a substantial interference therewith.

    (2) An injunction restraining the Defendant (whether by himself or by instructing or encouraging any other person) from further interfering with the Claimant's said rights.

    (3) Damages together with interest thereon pursuant to section 69 County Courts Act 1984.

Signature of legal representative

DATED . . . .

STATEMENT OF TRUTH

The claimant believes that the facts stated in these particulars of claim are true.
I am duly authorised by the claimant to sign this statement as the claimant's solicitor.

Full name . . . .
Name of claimant's solicitor's firm . . . .
Signed . . . . (position or office held)
Address

XI

DEFENCE AND COUNTERCLAIM ALLEGING OWNERSHIP WITH ADVERSE POSSESSION IN THE ALTERNATIVE[1]

(This pleading is in answer to Particulars of Claim No. II)

IN THE . . . . . . COUNTY COURT **25.11**
[Chancery Business][2]
Claim No . . . .
Claim form issued . . . .

Claimant

First Defendant
Second Defendant

DEFENCE AND COUNTERCLAIM OF BOTH DEFENDANTS

1. No admission is made as to the Claimant's title. In particular it is denied that the Claimant is the owner of the disputed land.

2. By a conveyance dated . . . . and made between . . . . and . . . . Whiteacre together with the disputed land was conveyed to the said . . . . in fee simple. The first Defendant is the successor in title of the said . . . .[3] A copy of this Conveyance is attached. The conveyance relates [does not relate] to residential land.

[3. In the alternative the first Defendant and his predecessors in title have been in undisputed possession of the disputed land for a period in excess of 12 years before these proceedings and accordingly any title

---

[1] There is now a prescribed "Admission Defence and Counterclaim" (N9C) which should be filled in. However, only a small space is provided under "What are your reasons for disputing the claim?" and it is still appropriate to set out the Defence and Counterclaim in a separate document.

[2] If this is included, the claim will be treated as Chancery Business in the county court and will be allocated accordingly. The Chancery Guide will then apply.

[3] If this is registered land, set out the title details.

551

of the Claimant's has been extinguished by virtue of the Limitation Act 1980.[4]][5]

4. It is admitted and averred, as alleged in paragraph 4 of the Particulars of Claim, that the Defendants have on numerous occasions entered upon the disputed land. The Defendants have done so in right of the first Defendant's ownership of the said land as hereinbefore averred.

PARTICULARS

(1) It is admitted that on or about .... the Defendants entered upon the disputed land and removed the fence wrongly placed there by the Claimant. No admission is made as to the exact line of this fence.

(2) It is admitted that on or about .... the Defendants entered upon the disputed land and uprooted cabbages wrongly planted thereon by the Claimant.

(3) It is denied that the second Defendant swore at the Claimant as alleged or at all.

(4) It is admitted and averred that the Defendants have erected a fence on the disputed land between the points marked "X" and "Y" on the plan annexed to the Particulars of Claim. This fence represents the true boundary between the Claimant's and the first Defendant's land.

(5) It is admitted that the Defendants have laid tarmac on the disputed land and parked their car there. It is averred that they are entitled to do so.

5. It is admitted that the Claimant has sent letters to the Defendants claiming ownership of the disputed land, but it is averred that the disputed land belongs to the first Defendant.

6. No admission is made as to the alleged or any damage.

7. Save in so far as hereinbefore expressly admitted each and every allegation contained in the Particulars of Claim is hereby denied.

---

[4] The Defendant should consider the provisions of Sch.6 of the Land Registration Act 2002. Providing he has been in possession for 10 years he can apply for registration as a person in adverse possession. However, he may not wish to pursue this procedure until the court proceedings are completed.

[5] This can only be pleaded if both properties are unregistered. If either title is registered the process under the Land Registration Act 2002 should be sued.

COUNTERCLAIM

8. The Defendants repeat paragraphs 1 to 4 of the Defence as Particulars of the Counterclaim.

9. The Claimant or his predecessors in title have on numerous occasions trespassed upon the disputed land.

PARTICULARS

(1) On a date unknown to the Defendants in or about. . . . . .the Claimant or his predecessor in title entered upon the disputed land and erected thereon the fence referred to in paragraph 4(1) of the Particulars of Claim.

(2) On a date unknown to the Defendants in or about. . . . . .the Claimant entered upon the disputed land and planted the cabbages referred to in paragraph 4(2) of the Particulars of Claim.

9. The Defendants have, by reason of the Claimant's trespasses suffered loss and damage.

10. The Claimant threatens and intends, unless restrained by this court, to continue to trespass upon the disputed land.

AND the first Claimant counterclaims:

(1) A declaration that the first Defendant is the owner of the disputed land.[6]

(2) An injunction restraining the Claimant (whether by himself or by instructing or encouraging any other person) upon the disputed land or otherwise interfering with the first Defendant's occupation thereof.

(3) Damages together with interest thereon pursuant to section 69 County Courts Act 1984.

Signature of legal representative

DATED . . . .

---

[6] If the land is registered land, the defendant may wish to apply for rectification of the register.

STATEMENT OF TRUTH

The claimant believes that the facts stated in these particulars of claim are true.

I am duly authorised by the claimant to sign this statement as the claimant's solicitor.

Full name . . . .
Name of claimant's solicitor's firm . . . .
Signed . . . . (position or office held)
Address

XII

DEFENCE AND COUNTERCLAIM ALLEGING RIGHT OF WAY[1]

IN THE . . . . . . COUNTY COURT **25.12**
[Chancery Business][2]
Claim No . . . .
Claim form issued . . . .

Claimant

First Defendant
Second Defendant

DEFENCE AND COUNTERCLAIM

1. Subject to proof of the Claimant's title paragraph 1 of the Particulars of Claim is admitted.

2. It is admitted and averred that the Defendant is the owner of Whiteacre. The Defendant and his predecessors in title owners and occupiers for the time being of Whiteacre have for the full period of 20 years and more up to the date of these proceedings used the disputed land as of right and without interruption at all times and for all purposes in connection with their occupation of Whiteacre as a means of access to the public highway known as. . . . . .and the said right is claimed as a right of way under section 2 Prescription Act 1832. Alternatively the said right is claimed by virtue of the doctrine of lost modern grant and/or as a common law right having been exercised from time immemorial.

3. It is admitted and averred that the Defendant and his visitors have on numerous occasions entered on the disputed land. It is denied that such actions constitute trespass. The Defendant's use of the disputed land has been in pursuance of the right of way set out in paragraph 2 above.

---

[1] There is now a prescribed "Admission Defence and Counterclaim" (N9 C) which should be filled in. However, only a small space is provided under "What are your reasons for disputing the claim?" and it is still appropriate to set out the Defence and Counterclaim in a separate document.

[2] If this is included, the claim will be treated as Chancery Business in the county court and will be allocated accordingly. The Chancery Guide will then apply.

PARTICULARS

(1) It is admitted that on or about..............the Defendant entered upon the disputed land and removed the fence placed there by the Claimant. This fence was materially obstructing the Defendant's said right of way.

(2) It is admitted that the Defendant has laid tarmac on the disputed land and parked his car there. The car has only been parked there for the purpose of loading and unloading.

4. It is admitted that the Claimant has sent letters to the Defendant claiming ownership of the disputed land, but it is averred that the Defendant has never disputed the Claimant's ownership.

5. No admission is made as to the alleged or any damage.

6. Save in so far as hereinbefore expressly admitted each and every allegation contained in the Particulars of Claim is hereby denied.

COUNTERCLAIM

7. The Defendant repeats paragraph 2 of the Defence as Particulars of the Counterclaim.

8. The Claimant or his predecessors in title have on numerous occasions interfered with the lawful use of the said right of way by the Defendant and his visitors.

PARTICULARS

(1) On a date unknown to the Defendants in or about.........the Claimant or his predecessor in title erected the fence referred to in paragraph 3(1) of above.

(2) On or about..............the Claimant told the Defendant's milkman that he was not to use the disputed land to deliver milk to Whiteacre.

(3) The Claimant his servants or agents have on numerous other occasions tried to stop the Defendant and his visitors from using the way by barring their way.

9. The Defendant has, by reason of the Claimant's said trespasses suffered loss and damage.

10. The Claimant threatens and intends, unless restrained by this court, to continue to trespass upon the disputed land.

AND the Defendant counterclaims:

(1) A declaration that the Defendant is entitled to the said right of way.

(2) An injunction restraining the Claimant (whether by himself or by instructing or encouraging any other person) from interfering with the lawful use of the right of way by the Defendant and his visitors.

(3) Damages together with interest thereon pursuant to section 69 County Courts Act 1984.

Signature of legal representative

DATED . . . .

STATEMENT OF TRUTH

The claimant believes that the facts stated in these particulars of claim are true.
I am duly authorised by the claimant to sign this statement as the claimant's solicitor.

Full name . . . .
Name of claimant's solicitor's firm . . . .
Signed . . . . (position or office held)
Address

XIII

DEFENCE AND COUNTERCLAIM ALLEGING UNITY OF POSSESSION AND IMPLIED RELEASE[1]

IN THE . . . . . . COUNTY COURT **25.13**
[Chancery Business][2]
Claim No . . . .
Claim form issued . . . .

Claimant

First Defendant
Second Defendant

DEFENCE AND COUNTERCLAIM

1. Subject to proof of the Claimant's title paragraph 1 of the Particulars of Claim is admitted. It is further admitted that an express right of way over the way coloured brown on the plan was granted to the Claimant by the conveyance referred to in paragraph 2 of the Particulars of Claim.
2. It is admitted and averred that the Defendant is the owner of Whiteacre.

3. By a conveyance dated . . . . and made between . . . . of the one part and . . . . of the other part Whiteacre was conveyed to the said . . . . A copy of this Conveyance is attached. The Conveyance relates [does not relate] to residential land. The said . . . . remained the owner of Whiteacre until . . . . when he conveyed it to the Defendant's predecessor in title. For all or part of the said period the said . . . . was also the owner of Greenacre. In the premises the right of way referred to in paragraph 2 of the Particulars of Claim has been extinguished by unity of ownership.[3]

4. Further or in the alternative the alleged right of way was not used for a period of 20 years between . . . . and . . . . when the Claimant began to claim a right to do so. The Claimant and his

---

[1] There is now a prescribed "Admission Defence and Counterclaim" (N9C) which should be filled in. However, only a small space is provided under "What are your reasons for disputing the claim?" and it is still appropriate to set out the Defence and Counterclaim in a separate document.
[2] If this is included, the claim will be treated as Chancery Business in the county court and will be allocated accordingly. The Chancery Guide will then apply.
[3] If this is registered land, insert registration details.

predecessors in title have done acts indicating their intention to abandon the said right.

PARTICULARS

(1) In or about . . . . the Claimant's predecessor in title moved his fence so as to make it impossible for vehicles to gain access to the alleged way.

(2) In or about . . . . the Defendant's predecessor in title built a fence across the alleged way in between the points marked "X" and "Y" on the plan annexed hereto. The Claimant and his predecessors in title acquiesced in the said obstruction until . . . . . . when the Claimant attempted to assert the alleged right of way.

(3) In or about . . . . the Claimant's predecessor in title one . . . . told the Defendant's predecessor in title one . . . . that she no longer intended to use the way.

5. It is alleged that the said acts and omissions of the Claimant and his predecessors in title constituted an implied release of the said way and that thereafter the right of way was extinguished.

6. No admission is made as to the alleged or any damage.

7. Save in so far as hereinbefore expressly admitted each and every allegation contained in the Particulars of Claim is hereby denied.

COUNTERCLAIM

8. The Defendant repeats paragraph 2 of the Defence as Particulars of the Counterclaim.

9. On or about . . . . and on numerous occasions thereafter the Claimant has trespassed upon Whiteacre and has caused damage thereto.

PARTICULARS

(1) On or about . . . . the Claimant removed the fence referred to in paragraph 4(2) above and shown on the plan between the points "X" and "Y."

(2) On or about . . . . the Claimant drove his motor car along the said way.

(3) On numerous occasions thereafter, despite the protests of the Defendant the Claimant has continued to use the alleged way on foot and with vehicles.

10. The Defendant has, by reason of the Claimant's said trespasses suffered loss and damage.

PARTICULARS OF SPECIAL DAMAGE

Estimated cost of replacing the said fence £

11. The Claimant threatens and intends, unless restrained by this court, to continue to use the alleged way.

AND the Defendant counterclaims:

(1) A declaration that the Claimant is not entitled to the said right of way.

(2) An injunction restraining the Claimant (whether by himself or by instructing or encouraging any other person) from trespassing on Whiteacre or any part thereof including the alleged way.

(3) Damages together with interest thereon pursuant to section 69 County Courts Act 1984.

Signature of legal representative

DATED . . . .

STATEMENT OF TRUTH

The claimant believes that the facts stated in these particulars of claim are true.

I am duly authorised by the claimant to sign this statement as the claimant's solicitor.

Full name . . . .
Name of claimant's solicitor's firm . . . .
Signed . . . . (position or office held)
Address

XIV

DEFENCE AND COUNTERCLAIM ALLEGING PARKING AND/OR EXCESSIVE USER[1]

IN THE . . . . . . COUNTY COURT **25.14**
[Chancery Business][2]
Claim No . . . .
Claim form issued . . . .

Claimant

First Defendant
Second Defendant

DEFENCE AND COUNTERCLAIM

1. Subject to proof of the Claimant's title paragraph 1 of the Particulars of Claim is admitted. It is further admitted that an express right of way over the way coloured brown on the plan was granted to the Claimant by the conveyance referred to in paragraph 2 of the Particulars of Claim.

2. It is admitted and averred that the Defendant is the owner of Whiteacre.

3. The said right of way does not include a right of parking, but the Claimant his servants and agents have on numerous occasions parked on the right of way. Such user constitutes a trespass on the Defendant's said land.

PARTICULARS

(1) On or about .... there was a blue Ford Sierra motor car parked on the way at or about the point marked "X" on the plan annexed hereto between the hours of ..... and ....

(2) [Set out details of further infringements]

---

[1] There is now a prescribed "Admission Defence and Counterclaim" (N9C) which should be filled in. However, only a small space is provided under "What are your reasons for disputing the claim?" and it is still appropriate to set out the Defence and Counterclaim in a separate document.

[2] If this is included, the claim will be treated as Chancery Business in the county court and will be allocated accordingly. The Chancery Guide will then apply.

4. Further or in the alternative the Claimant has made excessive use of the said right of way.

PARTICULARS

The right of way is over an unmetalled track but the Claimant has on occasions too numerous further to particularise used the way in connection with his business as a haulage contractor. The way is used at all times of the day and night by heavy lorries and other commercial vehicles. The way is being used up to 20 times a day.

5. No admission is made as to the alleged or any damage.

6. Save in so far as hereinbefore expressly admitted each and every allegation contained in the Particulars of Claim is hereby denied.

COUNTERCLAIM

7. The Defendant repeats paragraphs 1 to 4 of the Defence as Particulars of the Counterclaim.

8. By reason of the Claimant's said trespass and excessive user of the way the defendant has suffered loss and damage, distress and inconvenience.

PARTICULARS OF SPECIAL DAMAGE

(1) The way has been damaged by the excessive user and will have to be repaired. Estimated cost £ ....

(2) The way has become so rutted that the Defendant has been unable to use the way himself for access to his own property.

(3) The noise and smell of the vehicles has caused the Defendant and his family distress and inconvenience.

9. Unless restrained by this court the Claimant threatens and intends to continue to use the way for parking his vehicles and/or to use the way excessively.

AND the Defendant counterclaims:

(1) An injunction restraining the Claimant (whether by himself or by instructing or encouraging any other person) from causing or permitting motor vehicles to park on the said way.

(2) An injunction restraining the Claimant by himself his servants or agents or otherwise from using the said way for the purposes of his business or otherwise making excessive use of the way.

(3) Damages together with interest thereon pursuant to section 69 County Courts Act 1984.

Signature of legal representative

DATED ....

STATEMENT OF TRUTH

The claimant believes that the facts stated in these particulars of claim are true.

I am duly authorised by the claimant to sign this statement as the claimant's solicitor.

Full name . . . .
Name of claimant's solicitor's firm . . . .
Signed . . . . (position or office held)
Address

XV

WITNESS STATEMENT CLAIMING INJUNCTION WITHOUT NOTICE

25.15
                                IN THE . . . . . . COUNTY COURT
                                [Chancery Business][1]
                                Claim No . . . .
                                Claim form issued . . . .

Claimant

First Defendant
Second Defendant

I, [name] of [address] the above-named Claimant state as follows:

1. Save where the context otherwise makes clear this statement refers to matters which are within my own personal knowledge.

2. By a conveyance dated .... and made between .... of the one part and myself of the other part the property known as [address] .... (hereinafter called "Greenacre") was conveyed to me in fee simple. A true copy of the said conveyance is now produced and shown to me marked "AB1".[2] The property conveyed to me included the land shown on the plan annexed to the Particulars of Claim and thereon hatched brown (hereinafter called "the disputed land").[3]

3. As set out in paragraph 4 of the Particulars of Claim [set out briefly the facts as known to the Claimant].

4. There has been correspondence passing between myself and the Defendant about the disputed land. In this correspondence I have set out my claim, based on the conveyance referred to in paragraph 2 above, and the Defendant has alleged that he is entitled to the land by virtue of measurements he says he has made from his deeds of title. A bundle consisting of true copies of the correspondence passing between us is now produced and shown to me marked "AB2".

---

[1] If this is included, the claim will be treated as Chancery Business in the county court and will be allocated accordingly. The Chancery Guide will then apply.
[2] The document should be identified by the initials of the deponent.
[3] If the land is registered land, set out details of the registration.

5. On .... the Defendant began to dig foundations on the disputed land. I approached him about this work and he said that he was going to build a garage on the land, that it was his land and he could do what he liked with it.

6. The area on which the Defendant is building is an ornamental garden which I have developed over a number of years of hard work. Unless the Claimant is prevented from continuing with his plans all of my hard work over the past 10 years will be destroyed for ever.

7. In the past the Defendant has taken no notice of my requests that he keep away from the disputed land and I believe that unless an injunction is granted he will continue with the works, causing irreparable damage to the disputed land. I submit that it is desirable that the status quo should remain until the dispute over the ownership of the land has been resolved.

8. I have written to the Defendant informing him that I intend to apply to this court for an injunction. I submit that by the time a hearing can be arranged the Defendant will have caused the damage which I am seeking to prevent.

9. In these circumstances I apply to the court for an injunction in the form of the draft injunction supplied herewith.

Signature of legal representative

DATED.................

STATEMENT OF TRUTH

The claimant believes that the facts stated in these particulars of claim are true.
I am duly authorised by the claimant to sign this statement as the claimant's solicitor.

Full name . . . .
Name of claimant's solicitor's firm . . . .
Signed . . . . (position or office held)
Address

XVI

APPLICATION FOR INTERIM INJUNCTION ON NOTICE[1]

25.16

In The .... County Court
Case Number
Claimant's ref.
Defendant's ref.

BETWEEN

.... **Claimant**

and

.... **Defendant**

1. *Insert name or, if a solicitor, the name of firm).*

2. I am the claimant [or solicitor for the claimant and I represent the claimant].

3. I am asking the court to make the following order–

That the Defendant be forbidden (whether by himself or by instructing or encouraging any other person) from entering upon the disputed land situated at [*address*] and coloured brown on the plan annexed to the Particulars of Claim or otherwise interfering with the Claimant"s occupation thereof.

4. The grounds of this application are set out in the written evidence of [set out names of witnesses]

---

[1] This form is taken from Form 16A. It is no longer necessary to submit a separate blank Notice of Application when applying for an injunction since the notice of hearing is incorporated in the draft injunction (see Form XVII). If there has been no application without notice then there should be evidence in support of this application in similar form to Form XIV, but omitting the final paragraph.

5. I have [not] attached a draft of the order I am applying for.

6. I wish to have this application dealt with [at a hearing *or* without a hearing *or* at a telephone hearing].[5]

7. The time estimate is .... The time estimate is [not] agreed by all parties.

8. This hearing should be dealt with by a (*level of judge*).

9. The parties to be served are ....

10. I will be relying on [the attached witness statement *or* the statement of case *or* the evidence set out in the box below (*if necessary, continue on separate sheet*).[6]

STATEMENT OF TRUTH

The claimant believes that the facts stated in these particulars of claim are true.
I am duly authorised by the claimant to sign this statement as the claimant's solicitor.

Signed .... (position or office held)
Address

XVII

DRAFT INTERIM INJUNCTION[1]

25.17 Injunction Order ....

In the .... County Court
Case No. ....
Claimant's Ref. ....
Defendant's Ref. ....

For completion by the Court
Issued on ....

BETWEEN

.... **Claimant**

and

.... **Defendant**

Before His Honour Judge .....

To

If you do not obey this order you may be guilty of contempt of court and you may be sent to prison

On the .... of .... 199..... the court considered an application for an injunction

The Court ordered that [the name of the person the order is directed to] is forbidden (whether by himself or by instructing or encouraging any other person) from entering upon the disputed land situated at [address] and coloured brown on the plan annexed to the Particulars of Claim or otherwise interfering with the Claimant's occupation thereof

This order shall remain in force until (the __of __ at __ o'clock unless before then it is revoked by a further order of the court.

The Claimant gave an undertaking (through his counsel or solicitor) promising to pay any damages ordered by the court if it later decides that the defendant has suffered loss or damage as a result of this order.

[1] This draft application is taken from Form N16A. It should be submitted with an application for an interim injunction_whether with or without notice.

It is further ordered that the costs shall be reserved.

Notice of further hearing

The court will re-consider the application and whether the order should continue at a further hearing at

on .... the .... day of .... 199.... at .... o'clock.

If you do not attend at the time shown the court may make an injunction order in your absence

You are entitled to apply to the court to re-consider the order before that day [*Delete if order made on notice*]

If you do not understand anything in this order you should go to a Solicitor, Legal Advice Centre or Citizens' Advice Bureau.

The Court Office at ....

is open from 10 am to 4 pm. When corresponding with the court, address all forms and letter to the Chief Clerk and quote the claim number.

XVIII

DRAFT INTERIM INJUNCTION ON NOTICE[1]

25.18 Injunction Order ....

In the .... County Court
Case No. ....
Claimant's Ref. ....
Defendant's Ref. ....

For completion by the Court
Issued on ....

BETWEEN

.... **Claimant**

and

.... **Defendant**

To

If you do not obey this order you will be guilty of contempt of court and you may be sent to prison

On the .... of .... 199..... the court considered an application for an injunction

The Court ordered that [*the name of the person the order is directed to*]

is forbidden (whether by himself or by instructing or encouraging any other person) from entering upon the disputed land situated at [address] and coloured brown on the plan annexed to the Particulars of Claim or otherwise interfering with the Claimant"s occupation thereof until the day after the day upon which this action shall be heard, or until further order in the meantime

It is further ordered that the costs of this application be in the cause

If you do not understand anything in this order you should go to a Solicitor, Legal Advice Centre or Citizen's Advice Bureau.

_____

The Court Office at ....

is open from 10 am to 4 pm. When corresponding with the court, address all forms and letter to the Chief Clerk and quote the case number.

[1] This draft application is taken from Form N16. It should be submitted with an application for an injunction whether with or without notice.

XIX

25.19

Who owns that Property?

Form **313**

Would you like to discover who is the owner of a property but do not know where to start? The Land Registry can provide you with information about the ownership of registered land in England and Wales. The majority of properties are registered but some are not. Where property is unregistered the Land Registry will not have any details of the owners.

If you would like a **copy** of a registered title, you can obtain a free leaflet and an application form by writing to the Land Registry at the address below. A copy of a registered title will show details of ownership, extent and the rights which benefit or burden the land.

However, **if you wish simply to know the name and address of the registered owner of any freehold or leasehold property identified by a single postal address (e.g. 21 SMITH STREET, ANYTOWN AN3 4TZ), please complete Panels A and B below and Panel C overleaf and send this form to our HARROW office at the following address:**

> The Chief Land Registrar
> The Customer Information Centre, Room 105
> The Harrow District Land Registry
> Lyon House, Lyon Road
> Harrow, Middx.   (For DX members, the Harrow no. is
> HA1 2EU   DX: 4299 HARROW (4))

This form may NOT be used to obtain the name and address of the owner of a piece of land or building which does not have a postal address (e.g. "LAND ADJOINING 21 SMITH STREET" or "GARAGE AT REAR OF 21 SMITH STREET"). If you wish to enquire about the owners of this type of property you should contact the Land Registry at the above address for the appropriate forms.

1. I/We enclose a cheque/postal order for £4 (made payable to "HM Land Registry") which is the fee for this service. I/We understand that if the investigation reveals that there is no registered owner then the fee will be refunded. (Applicants who wish to pay the fee using their Land Registry Credit Account should complete Panel D overleaf.)

2. I/We understand that this form can be used for a single postal address only, and a separate fee and form is needed for any other postal address for which information is required.

3. I/We understand that a name and address of a registered owner (proprietor) given by the Land Registry in Panel E will be that actually recorded on the registered title at the date stated and that there may have been changes in the ownership which have yet to result in a new owner being registered. I/We also understand that no account will be taken of any uncompleted application to register freehold and leasehold property for the first time.

Signature _____   Telephone no. for **day time** contact _____

Panel A Please insert in this panel the single postal address of the property to which this enquiry relates

Full postal address

Postcode

Panel B Please complete this panel with your name, address and postcode

Reference:

IMPORTANT
Please complete Panels A and B fully as this part of the form will be used to notify you of the result.

Please turn over

Panel C Please enter the name and address of the person or firm making the application

I/We

of

request you to supply me/us with the name and address of the registered owner of the property described in Panel A overleaf.

Panel D To be completed by Land Registry Credit Account holders only

Please debit the Credit Account mentioned below with the £4 fee payable under the current Land Registration Fees Order.

YOUR KEY NUMBER:-

YOUR REFERENCE:- Any reference quoted should be limited to 25 characters (including oblique strokes and punctuation).

NB. If the investigation reveals that there is no registered owner, the £4 fee will be refunded.

For official use only

Fees

Record of Fee paid

Fee Debited £

Referral *(Complete when form sent on to another DLR)*

☐ Referred to _____ DLR

☐ Title no. cannot be identified from CPD

☐ Form 313 includes plan to identify the property

☐

Remarks (if any):

Name: DLR:
Date:

Result obtained

☐ CPD ☐ Index Map

☐ Title no(s) _____

☐ Ownership unregistered

Description *(complete when property is unregistered so that application can be identified should there be a follow up enquiry)*

Name: Date:

For official use only Form 313 (Result)

Panel E Result of investigation

1 The property is registered under Title No. _____
The name and address of the registered owner is:

Land Registry Stamp/ Date of Information

2 The ownership of the property is not registered.

(Revised 12/99 Internet)

XX

APPLICATION TO SEARCH INDEX MAP

Land Registry
Application for an official search of the
index map

SIM

25.20

If you need more room than is provided for in a panel, and your software allows, you can expand any panel in the form. Alternatively use continuation sheet CS and attach it to this form.

Land Registry is unable to give legal advice but our website www1.landregistry.gov.uk provides guidance on Land Registry applications. This includes public guides and practice guides (aimed at conveyancers) that can also be obtained from any Land Registry office.

See www1.landregistry.gov.uk/regional if you are unsure which Land Registry office to send this application to.

LAND REGISTRY USE ONLY
Record of fees paid
Particulars of under/over payments
Reference number
Fees debited £

Where there is more than one local authority serving an area, enter the one to which council tax or business rates are normally paid.

If no postal address insert description, for example 'land adjoining 2 Acacia Avenue'.

1	Local authority serving the property:

2	Property to be searched
	Flat/unit number:
	Postal number or description:
	Name of road:
	Name of locality:
	Town:
	Postcode:
	Ordnance Survey map reference (if known):
	Known title number:

3	Application and fee	
	Application	Fee paid (£)
	Search of the index map	

See fees calculator at www1.landregistry.gov.uk/fees

Place 'X' in the appropriate box.

The fee will be charged to the account specified in panel 4.

Fee payment method

☐ cheque made payable to 'Land Registry'

☐ Land Registry credit account

☐ direct debit, under an agreement with Land Registry

If you are paying by direct debit, this will be the account charged.	**4** This application is sent to Land Registry by
	Key number (if applicable):
	Name: Address or UK DX box number:
	Email address: Reference:
	Phone no: Fax no:

Please note that the facility of issuing results electronically is not available at present. When it is, a direction will appear on our website and details will be given in Public Guide 1 and Practice Guide 10. Until there is a direction, you do not need to complete this panel to obtain an official copy in paper format. Official copies issued electronically are in 'Portable Document Format' (PDF) which replicates the appearance of the hard copy version. You will need Adobe Acrobat Reader (which you can install free from www.adobe.com) to open the document. Place 'X' in the box if applicable.	**5** Issue of certificate of result of search in paper format where an email address has been supplied If you have supplied an email address in panel 4, then, unless you complete the box below, any certificate of result of search of the index map will be issued electronically to that address, if there is a direction under section 100(4) of the Land Registration Act 2002 by the registrar covering such issuing. ☐ I have supplied an email address but require the certificate of result of search to be issued in paper format instead of being issued electronically
Any attached plan must contain sufficient details of the surrounding roads and other features to enable the land to be identified satisfactorily on the Ordnance Survey map. A plan may be unnecessary if the land can be identified by postal description.	**6** I apply for an official search of the index map in respect of the land referred to in panel 2 shown on the attached plan

	7
	
	     Signature of applicant: --
	
	     Date:

WARNING
If you dishonestly enter information or make a statement that you know is, or might be, untrue or misleading, and intend by doing so to make a gain for yourself or another person, or to cause loss or the risk of loss to another person, you may commit the offence of fraud under section 1 of the Fraud Act 2006, the maximum penalty for which is 10 years' imprisonment or an unlimited fine, or both.

Failure to complete this form with proper care may result in a loss of protection under the Land Registration Act 2002 if, as a result, a mistake is made in the register.

Under section 66 of the Land Registration Act 2002 most documents (including this form) kept by the registrar relating to an application to the registrar or referred to in the register are open to public inspection and copying. If you believe a document contains prejudicial information, you may apply for that part of the document to be made exempt using Form EX1, under rule 136 of the Land Registration Rules 2003.

574

XXI

APPLICATION FOR A SEARCH IN THE INDEX OF PROPRIETORS' NAMES

Land Registry
Application for a search in the index of
proprietors' names

PN1 25.21

```
Land Registry
Seaton Court
2 William Prance Road
Plymouth PL6 5WS

DX 8249 Plymouth 3
```

If you need more room than is provided for in a panel, and your software allows, you can expand any panel in the form. Alternatively use continuation sheet CS and attach it to this form.

Land Registry is unable to give legal advice but our website www1.landregistry.gov.uk provides guidance on Land Registry applications. This includes public guides and practice guides (aimed at conveyancers) that can also be obtained from any Land Registry office.

'Conveyancer' is a term used in this form. It is defined in rule 217(1) of the Land Registration Rules 2003 and includes, among others, solicitor, licensed conveyancer and fellow of the Institute of Legal Executives.

LAND REGISTRY USE ONLY
Record of fees paid
Particulars of under/over payments
Reference number Fees debited £

See fees calculator at www1.landregistry.gov.uk/fees

Place 'X' in the appropriate box.

The fee will be charged to the account specified in panel 3.

Provide the full name(s) of the person(s) making the application.

If you are paying by direct debit, this will be the account charged.

1	Application and fee	
	Application	Fee paid (£)
	Search in the index of proprietors' names	

Fee payment method

☐ cheque made payable to 'Land Registry'

☐ Land Registry credit account

☐ direct debit, under an agreement with Land Registry

2	The applicant:

3	This application is sent to Land Registry by

Key number (if applicable):

Name:
Address or UK DX box number:

Email address:
Reference:

Phone no:	Fax no:

List the documents lodged with this form. Copy documents should be listed separately. If you supply a certified copy of an original document we will return the original; if a certified copy is not supplied, we may retain the original document and it may be destroyed.	**4** Documents lodged with this form:
Enter the full name (in forename – surname order) of the person in respect of whom the search is to be made. Only one name per form – a separate form should be used in respect of any former or alternative name(s).	**5** The applicant applies for a search to be made in the index of proprietors' names in respect of:
Every address that may have been entered in the register should be stated.	**6** Enter the address of the person named in panel 5:
Place 'X' in the appropriate box. Enclose evidence of death or a conveyancer's certificate to that effect. State reasons.	**7** Entitlement to search The applicant is ☐ searching against their own name ☐ searching against a company or other corporation aggregate ☐ a personal representative of name searched ☐ a trustee in bankruptcy of name searched ☐ otherwise interested generally within the meaning of rule 11(3) of the Land Registration Rules 2003:
If a conveyancer is acting for the applicant, that conveyancer must sign. If no conveyancer is acting, the applicant (and if more than one person then each of them) must sign.	**8** Signature of applicant(s) or their conveyancer: -- Date:

WARNING
If you dishonestly enter information or make a statement that you know is, or might be, untrue or misleading, and intend by doing so to make a gain for yourself or another person, or to cause loss or the risk of loss to another person, you may commit the offence of fraud under section 1 of the Fraud Act 2006, the maximum penalty for which is 10 years' imprisonment or an unlimited fine, or both.

Failure to complete this form with proper care may result in a loss of protection under the Land Registration Act 2002 if, as a result, a mistake is made in the register.

Under section 66 of the Land Registration Act 2002 most documents (including this form) kept by the registrar relating to an application to the registrar or referred to in the register are open to public inspection and copying. If you believe a document contains prejudicial information, you may apply for that part of the document to be made exempt using Form EX1, under rule 136 of the Land Registration Rules 2003.

© Crown copyright (ref: LR/HO) 02/11

576

XXII

APPLICATION FOR OFFICIAL COPIES OF REGISTER/PLAN OR CERTIFICATE IN FORM C1

Land Registry
Application for official copies of register/
plan or certificate in Form CI

OC1 25.22

Use one form per title.

If you need more room than is provided for in a panel, and your software allows, you can expand any panel in the form. Alternatively use continuation sheet CS and attach it to this form.

Land Registry is unable to give legal advice but our website www1.landregistry.gov.uk provides guidance on Land Registry applications. This includes public guides and practice guides (aimed at conveyancers) that can also be obtained from any Land Registry office.

See www1.landregistry.gov.uk/regional if you are unsure which Land Registry office to send this application to.

LAND REGISTRY USE ONLY
Record of fees paid
Particulars of under/over payments
Reference number
Fees debited £

Where there is more than one local authority serving an area, enter the one to which council tax or business rates are normally paid.

Use a separate form for each registered title.

Place 'X' in the appropriate box.

1   Local authority serving the property:

2   Details of estate

    (a) Title number if known:

    (b) (Where the title number is unknown) this application relates to

    ☐ freehold   ☐ leasehold   ☐ manor

    ☐ franchise   ☐ caution against first registration

    ☐ rentcharge   ☐ profit a prendre in gross

3   Property

    Flat/unit number:

    Postal number or description:

    Name of road:

    Name of locality:

    Town:

    Postcode:

4	Application and fee		
	Application	Total number of all copies or certificates requested in panel 7	Fee paid (£)
	Official copy of register /plan or certificate of inspection of title plan		

See fees calculator at www1.landregistry.gov.uk/fees

Fee payment method

☐ cheque made payable to 'Land Registry'

Place 'X' in the appropriate box.

☐ Land Registry credit account

The fee will be charged to the account specified in panel 5.

☐ direct debit, under an agreement with Land Registry

5	This application is sent to Land Registry by

If you are paying by credit account or direct debit, this will be the account charged.

Key number (if applicable):

Name:
Address or UK DX box number:

Email address:
Reference:

Phone no: | Fax no:

Please note that the facility of issuing copies electronically is not available at present. When it is, a direction will appear on our website and details will be given in Public Guide 1 and Practice Guide 11. Until there is a direction, you do not need to complete this panel to obtain an official copy in paper format.

6 Issue of official copies in paper format where an email address has been supplied

If you have supplied an email address in panel 5, then, unless you complete the box below, any official copy will be issued electronically to that address, if there is a direction under section 100(4) of the Land Registration Act 2002 by the registrar covering such issuing.

Official copies issued electronically are in 'Portable Document Format' (PDF) which replicates the appearance of the hard copy version. You will need Adobe Acrobat Reader (which you can install free from www.adobe.com) to open the document.

Place 'X' in the box if applicable.

☐ I have supplied an email address but require the official copy(ies) to be issued in paper format instead of being issued electronically

7	I apply for

Indicate how many copies of each are required.

——— official copy(ies) of the register of the above mentioned property

——— official copy(ies) of the title plan or caution plan of the above mentioned property

——— certificate(s) of inspection of title plan, in which case either

Place 'X' in the appropriate box.

i. ☐ an estate plan has been approved and the plot number is:

or

State reference, for example 'edged red'.

ii. ☐ no estate plan has been approved and a certificate is to be issued in respect of the land shown on the attached plan and copy

Land Registry
Application for official copies of register/
plan or certificate in Form CI

Use one form per title.

If you need more room than is provided for in a panel, and your
software allows, you can expand any panel in the form.
Alternatively use continuation sheet CS and attach it to this form.

Land Registry is unable to give legal advice but our website
www1.landregistry.gov.uk provides guidance on Land Registry
applications. This includes public guides and practice guides
(aimed at conveyancers) that can also be obtained from any Land
Registry office.

See www1.landregistry.gov.uk/regional if you are unsure which
Land Registry office to send this application to.

LAND REGISTRY USE ONLY
Record of fees paid

Particulars of under/over payments

Reference number
Fees debited £

579

XXIII

APPLICATION FOR OFFICIAL COPY OF AN EXEMPT INFORMATION DOCUMENT

25.23 Land Registry
Application for official copy of an
exempt information document

Use one form per document.	LAND REGISTRY USE ONLY
	Record of fees paid

If you need more room than is provided for in a panel, and your software allows, you can expand any panel in the form. Alternatively use continuation sheet CS and attach it to this form.

Land Registry is unable to give legal advice but our website www1.landregistry.gov.uk provides guidance on Land Registry applications. This includes public guides and practice guides (aimed at conveyancers) that can also be obtained from any Land Registry office.

See www1.landregistry.gov.uk/regional if you are unsure which Land Registry office to send this application to.

'Conveyancer' is a term used in this form. It is defined in rule 217(1) of the Land Registration Rules 2003 and includes, among others, solicitor, licensed conveyancer and fellow of the Institute of Legal Executives.

Particulars of under/over payments

Reference number
Fees debited £

Where there is more than one local authority serving an area, enter the one to which council tax and business rates are normally paid.	1	Local authority serving the property:
If the document relates to many titles, you only need to quote one.	2	Title number(s) of the registered estate(s) to which the document relates:
Insert address including postcode (if any) or other description of the property, for example 'land adjoining 2 Acacia Avenue'.	3	Property:
If the document relates to many properties, you only need to quote the property relating to the title number quoted in panel 2.		
Some register entries refer to documents being filed under a different title number.	4	Title number under which this document is filed:

	5	Application and fee

Application	Fee paid (£)
Official copy of an exempt information document	

Fee payment method

See fees calculator at www1.landregistry.gov.uk/fees

Place 'X' in the appropriate box.

The fee will be charged to the account specified in panel 7.

☐ cheque made payable to 'Land Registry'

☐ Land Registry credit account

☐ direct debit, under an agreement with Land Registry

Provide the full name(s) of the person(s) applying for an official copy of the exempt document. Where a conveyancer lodges the application, this must be the name of the client(s), not the conveyancer.

6	The applicant:

If you are paying by direct debit, this will be the account charged.

This is the address to which we will normally send requisitions and return documents. However if you insert an email address, we will use this whenever possible.

7	This application is sent to Land Registry by

Key number (if applicable):

Name:
Address or UK DX box number:

Email address:
Reference:

Phone no:	Fax no:

Insert date, parties and nature of document.

8	The applicant applies for an official copy of the following document that has been designated an exempt information document:

9	State the reason(s) why you consider an official copy of the edited information document is not sufficient for your purposes:

10 State why you consider that none of the information omitted from the edited information document is prejudicial information:

OR

If you accept that some or all of the information is prejudicial information, give details and state why you consider that the public interest in providing an official copy of the exempt information document outweighs the public interest in not doing so:

If a conveyancer is acting for the applicant, that conveyancer must sign. If no conveyancer is acting, the applicant (and if more than one person then each of them) must sign.

11

Signature of applicant or their conveyancer: --

Date:

WARNING
If you dishonestly enter information or make a statement that you know is, or might be, untrue or misleading, and intend by doing so to make a gain for yourself or another person, or to cause loss or the risk of loss to another person, you may commit the offence of fraud under section 1 of the Fraud Act 2006, the maximum penalty for which is 10 years' imprisonment or an unlimited fine, or both.

Failure to complete this form with proper care may result in a loss of protection under the Land Registration Act 2002 if, as a result, a mistake is made in the register.

Under section 66 of the Land Registration Act 2002 most documents (including this form) kept by the registrar relating to an application to the registrar or referred to in the register are open to public inspection and copying. If you believe a document contains prejudicial information, you may apply for that part of the document to be made exempt using Form EX1, under rule 136 of the Land Registration Rules 2003.

© Crown copyright (ref: LR/HO) 07/08

583

XXIV

APPLICATION FOR REGISTRATION OF A PERSON IN ADVERSE POSSESSION UNDER SCHEDULE 6 TO THE LAND REGISTRATION ACT 2002

25.24

Land Registry

Application for registration of a person in adverse possession under Schedule 6 to the Land Registration Act 2002

If you need more room than is provided for in a panel, and your software allows, you can expand any panel in the form. Alternatively use continuation sheet CS and attach it to this form.

Land Registry is unable to give legal advice but our website www1.landregistry.gov.uk provides guidance on Land Registry applications. This includes public guides and practice guides (aimed at conveyancers) that can also be obtained from any Land Registry office.

See www1.landregistry.gov.uk/regional if you are unsure which Land Registry office to send this application to.

'Conveyancer' is a term used in this form. It is defined in rule 217(1) of the Land Registration Rules 2003 and includes, among others, solicitor, licensed conveyancer and fellow of the Institute of Legal Executives.

LAND REGISTRY USE ONLY
Record of fees paid
Particulars of under/over payments
Reference number
Fees debited £

Where there is more than one local authority serving an area, enter the one to which council tax or business rates are normally paid.	**1**	Local authority serving the property:
	2	Title number(s) of property:
Insert address including postcode (if any) or other description of the property, for example 'land adjoining 2 Acacia Avenue'. Place 'X' in the appropriate box. Give a brief description of the part affected, for example 'edged red on the plan to the statutory declaration dated ....'. The statutory declaration or statement of truth must exhibit a plan identifying clearly the extent of the part, unless one of the exceptions in rule 188 of the Land Registration Rules 2003 applies.	**3**	Property: The application relates to ☐ the whole of the title(s) ☐ part of the title(s) as shown:

4 Application and fee

Application	Fee paid (£)
Registration of a person in adverse possession	

See fees calculator at www1.landregistry.gov.uk/fees

Place 'X' in the appropriate box.

The fee will be charged to the account specified in panel 8.

Fee payment method

☐ cheque made payable to 'Land Registry'

☐ direct debit, under an agreement with Land Registry

List the documents lodged with this form. Copy documents should be listed separately. If you supply a certified copy of an original document we will return the original; if a certified copy is not supplied, we may retain the original document and it may be destroyed.	5	Documents lodged with this form: 1. Statutory declaration/ Statement of truth
Provide the full name(s) of the person(s) applying to be registered. Where a conveyancer lodges the application, this must be the name(s) of the client(s), not the conveyancer.	6	The applicant:
Complete as appropriate where the applicant is a company. Also, for an overseas company, unless an arrangement with Land Registry exists, lodge either a certificate in Form 7 in Schedule 3 to the Land Registration Rules 2003 or a certified copy of the constitution in English or Welsh, or other evidence permitted by rule 183 of the Land Registration Rules 2003.		**For UK incorporated companies/LLPs** Registered number of company or limited liability partnership including any prefix: **For overseas companies** (a) Territory of incorporation: (b) Registered number in the United Kingdom including any prefix:
Each proprietor may give up to three addresses for service, one of which must be a postal address whether or not in the UK (including the postcode, if any). The others can be any combination of a postal address, a UK DX box number or an electronic address.	7	Applicant's intended address(es) for service (including postcode) for entry in the register:
	8	This application is sent to Land Registry by
If you are paying by direct debit, this will be the account charged.		Key number (if applicable):
		Name: Address or UK DX box number:
This is the address to which we will normally send requisitions and return documents. However if you insert an email address, we will use this whenever possible.		
		Email address: Reference:
		Phone no: Fax no:
Where there is more than one applicant, place 'X' in the appropriate box.	9	Declaration of trust. The applicant is more than one person and ☐ they are to hold the property on trust for themselves as joint tenants ☐ they are to hold the property on trust for themselves as tenants in common in equal shares
Complete as necessary.		☐ they are to hold the property on trust:
Place 'X' in the appropriate box.	10	This application is made under ☐ Paragraph 1 of Schedule 6 to the Land Registration Act 2002 ☐ Paragraph 6(1) of Schedule 6 to the Land Registration Act 2002
Please confirm which, if any, of these conditions the applicant intends to rely on, if a counter notice under paragraph 3 of Schedule 6 is lodged in response to the application.	11	If applying under Paragraph 1 of Schedule 6 to the Land Registration Act 2002 confirm which, if any, of the following conditions you intend to rely on ☐ Paragraph 5(2) of Schedule 6 ☐ Paragraph 5(3) of Schedule 6 ☐ Paragraph 5(4) of Schedule 6

If a conveyancer is acting for the applicant, that conveyancer must sign. If no conveyancer is acting, the applicant (and if more than one person then each of them) must sign.

12	
Signature of applicant or their conveyancer:	-------------------------------------
Date:	

WARNING
If you dishonestly enter information or make a statement that you know is, or might be, untrue or misleading, and intend by doing so to make a gain for yourself or another person, or to cause loss or the risk of loss to another person, you may commit the offence of fraud under section 1 of the Fraud Act 2006, the maximum penalty for which is 10 years' imprisonment or an unlimited fine, or both.

Failure to complete this form with proper care may result in a loss of protection under the Land Registration Act 2002 if, as a result, a mistake is made in the register.

Under section 66 of the Land Registration Act 2002 most documents (including this form) kept by the registrar relating to an application to the registrar or referred to in the register are open to public inspection and copying. If you believe a document contains prejudicial information, you may apply for that part of the document to be made exempt using Form EX1, under rule 136 of the Land Registration Rules 2003.

© Crown copyright (ref: LR/HO) 07/09

XXV

APPLICATION TO BE REGISTERED TO BE NOTIFIED OF AN APPLICATION FOR ADVERSE POSSESSION

Land Registry
Application to be registered as a
person to be notified of an
application for adverse possession

ADV2   25.25

If you need more room than is provided for in a panel, and your software allows, you can expand any panel in the form. Alternatively use continuation sheet CS and attach it to this form.

Land Registry is unable to give legal advice but our website www1.landregistry.gov.uk provides guidance on Land Registry applications. This includes public guides and practice guides (aimed at conveyancers) that can also be obtained from any Land Registry office.

See www1.landregistry.gov.uk/regional if you are unsure which Land Registry office to send this application to.

'Conveyancer' is a term used in this form. It is defined in rule 217(1) of the Land Registration Rules 2003 and includes, among others, solicitor, licensed conveyancer and fellow of the Institute of Legal Executives.

LAND REGISTRY USE ONLY
Record of fees paid
Particulars of under/over payments
Reference number
Fees debited £

Where there is more than one local authority serving an area, enter the one to which council tax or business rates are normally paid.	1	Local authority serving the property:
	2	Title number(s) of property:
Insert address including postcode (if any) or other description of the property, for example 'land adjoining 2 Acacia Avenue'. Place 'X' in the appropriate box. Give a description by reference to an attached plan enabling the land to be identified on the Ordnance Survey map.	3	Property: The application relates to ☐ the whole of the title(s) ☐ part of the title(s) as shown:

4   Application and fee

Application	Fee paid (£)
Registration of a person to be notified of an application for adverse possession	

See fees calculator at www1.landregistry.gov.uk/fees

Place 'X' in the appropriate box.

The fee will be charged to the account specified in panel 7.

Fee payment method
☐ cheque made payable to 'Land Registry'
☐ direct debit, under an agreement with Land Registry

Provide the full name(s) of the person(s) making this application. Where a conveyancer lodges the application, this must be the name(s) of the client(s), not the conveyancer.

5   The applicant:

Each applicant may give up to three addresses for service, one of which must be a postal address whether or not in the UK (including the postcode, if any). The others can be any combination of a postal address, a UK DX box number or an electronic address.	6	Applicant's intended address(es) for service (including postcode) for entry in the register:
If you are paying by direct debit, this will be the account charged. This is the address to which we will normally send requisitions and return documents. However if you insert an email address, we will use this whenever possible.	7	This application is sent to Land Registry by Key number (if applicable): Name: Address or UK DX box number: Email address: Reference:
		Phone no: | Fax no:
Place 'X' in the appropriate box.	8	Confirmation of interest and application I/We confirm that the applicant has an interest in the ☐ registered estate ☐ registered rentcharge being the title as entered in panel 2 which would be prejudiced by the registration of any other person as proprietor of that estate/rentcharge under Schedule 6 to the Land Registration Act 2002. The applicant hereby applies to the registrar to be registered as a person or persons to be notified of any application under paragraph 1 of Schedule 6 to the Land Registration Act 2002.
Place 'X' in the appropriate box.	9	Identity of person making the statement of truth in panel 10 ☐ The statement is made by (one of) the applicant(s). The full name of the person making the statement is: ☐ The statement is made on behalf (one of) of the applicant(s), who cannot make this statement for the following reasons: The full name of the person making the statement is: Address: ☐ The statement is made by a conveyancer acting for the applicant(s). The conveyancer's full name is: Firm name (if any): Address or UK DX box number:

588

This panel must set out the nature of the applicant's interest. Do not attach any documents.

See the warnings at the end of this form.

If a joint statement is made by two or more persons, consequential amendments can be made to the text in this panel (for example, 'I' can be changed to 'we').

| 10 | Statement of truth |

I state that the applicant is interested in the property described in panel 3 as:

I believe that the facts and matters contained in this statement are true.

If the person making the statement is unable to sign it, this wording will need to be amended to comply with rule 215A(5) and (6) of the Land Registration Rules 2003. In addition, and in cases where the person making the statement is unable to read, there will need to be an appropriate certificate: see rule 215A(4) and (5).

Signature: _____

Print full name:

Date:

| If a conveyancer is acting for the applicant, that conveyancer must sign. If no conveyancer is acting, the applicant (and if more than one person then each of them) must sign. | 11 Signature of applicant or their conveyancer: _____ Date: |

WARNING
If you dishonestly enter information or make a statement that you know is, or might be, untrue or misleading, and intend by doing so to make a gain for yourself or another person, or to cause loss or the risk of loss to another person, you may commit the offence of fraud under section 1 of the Fraud Act 2006, the maximum penalty for which is 10 years' imprisonment or an unlimited fine, or both.

Failure to complete this form with proper care may result in a loss of protection under the Land Registration Act 2002 if, as a result, a mistake is made in the register.

Under section 66 of the Land Registration Act 2002 most documents (including this form) kept by the registrar relating to an application to the registrar or referred to in the register are open to public inspection and copying. If you believe a document contains prejudicial information, you may apply for that part of the document to be made exempt using Form EX1, under rule 136 of the Land Registration Rules 2003.

XXVI

APPLICATION TO DETERMINE THE EXACT LINE OF A BOUNDARY

Land Registry
Application to determine the
exact line of a boundary

DB   25.26

If you need more room than is provided for in a panel, and your software allows, you can expand any panel in the form. Alternatively use continuation sheet CS and attach it to this form.

Land Registry is unable to give legal advice but our website www1.landregistry.gov.uk provides guidance on Land Registry applications. This includes public guides and practice guides (aimed at conveyancers) that can also be obtained from any Land Registry office.

See www1.landregistry.gov.uk/regional if you are unsure which Land Registry office to send this application to.

'Conveyancer' is a term used in this form. It is defined in rule 217(1) of the Land Registration Rules 2003 and includes, among others, solicitor, licensed conveyancer and fellow of the Institute of Legal Executives.

LAND REGISTRY USE ONLY
Record of fees paid
Particulars of under/over payments
Reference number
Fees debited £

Where there is more than one local authority serving an area, enter the one to which council tax or business rates are normally paid.

1   Local authority serving the property:

2   Title number(s) of the property:

Title number(s) of affected adjoining property:

Insert address including postcode (if any) or other description of the property, for example 'land adjoining 2 Acacia Avenue'.

3   Property:

See fees calculator at www1.landregistry.gov.uk/fees

4   Application and fee

Application	Fee paid (£)
Determination of the exact line of a boundary	

Fee payment method

Place 'X' in the appropriate box.

The fee will be charged to the account specified in panel 7.

☐ cheque made payable to 'Land Registry'

☐ direct debit, under an agreement with Land Registry

5   Documents lodged with this form

Place 'X' in the appropriate box.

☐ A plan identifying the exact line of the boundary

The plan must show sufficient surrounding physical features to allow the general position of the boundary to be drawn on the Ordnance Survey map.

☐ A plan and a verbal description (on the plan) identifying the exact line of the boundary

The following documents are lodged as evidence relied on to establish the exact line of the boundary:

List the documents lodged with this form. Copy documents should be listed separately. If you supply a certified copy of an original document we will return the original; if a certified copy is not supplied, we may retain the original document and it may be destroyed.

Provide the full name(s) of the person(s) making the application to determine the line of the boundary. Where a conveyancer lodges the application, this must be the name(s) of the client(s), not the conveyancer.

6	The applicant:

If you are paying by direct debit, this will be the account charged.

This is the address to which we will normally send requisitions and return documents. However if you insert an email address, we will use this whenever possible.

7	This application is sent to Land Registry by

Key number (if applicable):

Name:
Address or UK DX box number:

Email address:
Reference:

Phone no:	Fax no:

You do not need to supply details of owners (whether freehold or leasehold) whose title is registered.

8	Name(s) and address(es) of those with an interest in yours or the adjoining property, to the best of your knowledge

Property	Freehold owner(s)	Leasehold owner(s) (if any)
Your property		
Neighbouring property adjoining the property which is the subject of your application		

592

All adjoining owner(s) should complete and sign this statement.	9	Where the application is being made with the agreement of adjoining owner(s) I/We: (full name(s) in block capitals) as owners of: (title number or address of property) agree that the accompanying plan/plan and verbal description signed by me/us shows the exact line of the boundary and I/we consent to this application Signed: _____ Signed: _____ Date:
If a conveyancer is acting for the applicant, that conveyancer must sign. If no conveyancer is acting, the applicant (and if more than one person then each of them) must sign.	10	Signature of applicant or their conveyancer: _____ Date:

XXVII

APPLICATION FOR COPIES OF HISTORICAL EDITION(S) OF THE REGISTER/TITLE PLAN HELD IN ELECTRONIC FORM

25.27 Land Registry
Application for copies of historical
edition(s) of the register/title plan
held in electronic form

Use one form per title.

If you need more room than is provided for in a panel, and your software allows, you can expand any panel in the form. Alternatively use continuation sheet CS and attach it to this form.

Land Registry is unable to give legal advice but our website www1.landregistry.gov.uk provides guidance on Land Registry applications. This includes public guides and practice guides (aimed at conveyancers) that can also be obtained from any Land Registry office.

See www1.landregistry.gov.uk/regional if you are unsure which Land Registry office to send this application to.

LAND REGISTRY USE ONLY
Record of fees paid
Particulars of under/over payments
Reference number
Fees debited £

Where there is more than one local authority serving an area, enter the one to which council tax or business rates are normally paid.	**1** Local authority serving the property:
Use a separate form for each registered title. Place 'X' in the appropriate box.	**2** Details of estate (a) Title number if known: (b) (where the title number is unknown) this application relates to ☐ freehold ☐ leasehold ☐ manor ☐ franchise ☐ caution against first registration ☐ rentcharge ☐ profit a prendre in gross
Insert address including postcode (if any) or other description of the property, for example 'land adjoining 2 Acacia Avenue'.	**3** Property address including postcode (if any):

4   Application and fee

Application	Fee paid (£)
Historical copy of register /title plan	

See fees calculator at www1.landregistry.gov.uk/fees

Place 'X' in the appropriate box.

The fee will be charged to the account specified in panel 5.

Fee payment method
☐ cheque made payable to 'Land Registry'
☐ Land Registry credit account
☐ direct debit, under an agreement with Land Registry

594

	5	This application is sent to Land Registry by

If you are paying by credit account or direct debit, this will be the account charged.

Key number (if applicable):

Name:
Address or UK DX box number:

Email address:
Reference:

Phone no:	Fax no:

Indicate how many copies of each are required and insert the required date.

Complete in format DD/MM/YYYY.

6   I apply for:

____ copy(ies) of the last historical edition of the register for

/   /

____ copy(ies) of the last historical edition of the title plan for

/   /

____ copy(ies) of every historical edition of the register for

/   /

____ copy(ies) of every historical edition of the title plan for

/   /

Warning

Normally only one edition of a register or a title plan is issued on a single day. In rare cases more than one will be produced. If you want historical copies of the last edition issued on a specific day you must complete either or both of the first and second boxes. If you want historical copies of all editions issued on a specific day you must complete either or both of the third and fourth boxes. You cannot apply for editions spanning a period. For example you cannot apply for "every edition in May 2007". Applications without a single specific day/month/year date will be rejected.

7

Signature of applicant: --

Date:

XXVIII

APPLICATION FOR REGISTRATION OF A PENDING ACTION

25.28

Important: Please read the notes overleaf before completing the form.	**Form K3** **Land Charges Act 1972** **Application for registration of a Pending Action** Application is hereby made for the registration of a Pending Action in respect of the following particulars	**Fee panel** *Place "X" in the appropriate box. See Note 1 overleaf.* ☐ A cheque or postal order for the correct fee accompanies this application. ☐ Please debit our Credit Account with the appropriate fee payable. ☐ Please debit our Direct Debit under an authorised agreement with Land Registry.
Enter full name(s) and address(es) of chargee(s) *(See Notes 2 and 3 overleaf)*	**Particulars of chargee(s)** *Continue on form K10 (if necessary)*	
	Particulars of action or proceeding Nature of action or proceeding Name of court and official reference number Title of action or proceeding Date commenced or filed	
	PA	If application is made pursuant to a Priority Notice please state its official reference number	
	Particulars of land affected County District Short description	
(See Notes 4 and 5 overleaf)		

Only one individual or body to be entered. *(See Note 6 overleaf)*	**Particulars of estate owner** Forename(s) **Surname** Title, trade or profession Address	**For official use only**
(See Note 7 overleaf)	Key number	

Solicitor's name and address (including postcode) If no Solicitor is acting enter applicant's name and address (including postcode) *(See Note 8 overleaf)*	Solicitor's reference:	1	2	3
		*C		
		4	5	6

I/We certify that the estate owner's title is not registered at the Land Registry.

Signature of solicitor or applicant   Date
(See Note 9 overleaf)

Explanatory Notes

The following notes are supplied for assistance in making the application overleaf. Detailed information for the making of all kinds of applications to the Land Charges Department is contained in Practice Guide *63 – Land Charges – Applications for registration, official search, office copy and cancellation* which is obtainable on application at the address shown below.

Fee payable

1. Fees must be paid by credit account, by Direct Debit under an authorised agreement with Land Registry or by cheque or postal order made payable to "Land Registry" (see the Practice Guide referred to above).

Form completion

2. Please complete the form in block letters in writing or typewriting using black ink not liable to smear. No covering letter is required and no plan or other document should be lodged in support of the application. If the application is not made by a practising solicitor, it must be accompanied by a statutory declaration form K14.

Chargee's name(s)

3. Please give the full name(s) and address(es) of the person(s) and on whose behalf the application is being made.

County and District

4. Enter as "County" the appropriate name as set out in Practice Guide *63 – Land Charges – Applications for registration, official search, office copy and cancellation*. As stated therein, if the land referred to in the application lies within the Greater London Area, then "Greater London" should be stated as the county name.

Short description

5. A short description, identifying the land as far as may be practicable, should be furnished.

Estate owner

6. Please give the full name, address and description of the estate owner as defined in the Law of Property Act 1925 against whom registration is to be effected. A separate form is required for each full name. Enter forename(s) and surname on separate lines. The name of the company or other body should commence on the forename line and may continue on the surname line (the words "Forename(s) and "Surname" should be deleted).

Key number

7. If you have been allocated a key number, please take care to enter this in the space provided overleaf, whether or not you are paying fees through your credit account or by Direct Debit.

Solicitor's reference

8. Any reference should be limited to 25 characters (including oblique strokes and punctuation).

Signature and certificate

9. An application will be rejected if it is not signed or if the certificate that it does not affect registered land has been deleted. However, in a case of extreme urgency where it is not practicable for the applicant first to ascertain whether or not the land is registered, the Department will accept an application with the certificate deleted provided that it is accompanied by a letter to the following effect. The letter must certify that the applicant has applied for an official search of the index map at the appropriate Land Registry office. It must also contain an undertaking that he will apply to cancel this registration if he discovers from the result of search that the title to the land is registered.

Despatch of form

10. When completed, this application form should be despatched to the address shown below which is printed in a position to fit within a standard envelope.

The Superintendent
Land Charges Department
Registration Section
Plumer House, Tailyour Road,
Crownhill, PLYMOUTH PL6 5HY
DX 8249 PLYMOUTH (3)

597

XXIX

APPLICATION FOR REGISTRATION OF A WRIT OF ORDER

25.29

Important: Please read the notes overleaf before completing the form.	**Form K4** **Land Charges Act 1972** **Application for registration of a Writ or Order** Application is hereby made for the registration of a Writ or Order in respect of the following particulars	**Fee panel** *Place "X" in the appropriate box. See Note 1 overleaf.* ☐ A cheque or postal order for the correct fee accompanies this application. ☐ Please debit our Credit Account with the appropriate fee payable. ☐ Please debit our Direct Debit under an authorised agreement with Land Registry.
Enter full name(s) and address(es) of chargee(s) *(See Notes 2 and 3 overleaf)*	**Particulars of chargee(s)** *Continue on form K10 (if necessary)*	
	Particulars of action or matter Nature of writ or order Name of court and official reference number Title of action Date of Writ or order	
	WO If application is made pursuant to a Priority Notice please state its official reference number	
(See Notes 4 and 5 overleaf)	**Particulars of land affected** County District Short description	
Only one individual or body to be entered. *(See Note 6 overleaf)*	**Particulars of estate owner** Forename(s) **Surname** Title, trade or profession Address	**For official use only**
(See Note 7 overleaf)	Key number	
Solicitor's name and address (including postcode) If no Solicitor is acting enter applicant's name and address (including postcode) *(See Note 8 overleaf)*	 Solicitor's reference:	1 2 3 *C 4 5 6

I/We certify that the estate owner's title is not registered at the Land Registry.

Signature of solicitor or applicant ————————————————— Date
(See Note 9 overleaf)

Explanatory Notes

The following notes are supplied for assistance in making the application overleaf. Detailed information for the making of all kinds of applications to the Land Charges Department is contained in Practice Guide 63 – *Land Charges – Applications for registration, official search, office copy and cancellation* which is obtainable on application at the address shown below.

Fee payable

1. Fees must be paid by credit account, by Direct Debit under an authorised agreement with Land Registry or by cheque or postal order made payable to "Land Registry" (see the Practice Guide referred to above).

Form completion

2. Please complete the form in block letters in writing or typewriting using black ink not liable to smear. No covering letter is required and no plan or other document should be lodged in support of the application. If the application is not made by a practising solicitor, it must be accompanied by a statutory declaration form K14.

Chargee's name(s)

3. Please give the full name(s) and address(es) of the person(s) and on whose behalf the application is being made.

County and District

4. Enter as "County" the appropriate name as set out in Practice Guide 63 – *Land Charges – Applications for registration, official search, office copy and cancellation*. As stated therein, if the land referred to in the application lies within the Greater London Area, then "Greater London" should be stated as the county name.

Short description

5. A short description, identifying the land as far as may be practicable, should be furnished.

Estate owner

6. Please give the full name, address and description of the estate owner as defined in the Law of Property Act 1925 against whom registration is to be effected. A separate form is required for each full name. Enter forename(s) and surname on separate lines. The name of the company or other body should commence on the forename line and may continue on the surname line (the words "Forename(s)" and "Surname" should be deleted).

Key number

7. If you have been allocated a key number, please take care to enter this in the space provided overleaf, whether or not you are paying fees through your credit account or by Direct Debit.

Solicitor's reference

8. Any reference should be limited to 25 characters (including oblique strokes and punctuation).

Signature and certificate

9. An application will be rejected if it is not signed or if the certificate that it does not affect registered land has been deleted. However, in a case of extreme urgency where it is not practicable for the applicant first to ascertain whether or not the land is registered, the Department will accept an application with the certificate deleted provided that it is accompanied by a letter to the following effect. The letter must certify that the applicant has applied for an official search of the index map at the appropriate Land Registry office. It must also contain an undertaking that he will apply to cancel this registration if he discovers from the result of search that the title to the land is registered.

Despatch of form

10. When completed, this application form should be despatched to the address shown below which is printed in a position to fit within a standard envelope.

The Superintendent
Land Charges Department
Registration Section
Plumer House, Tailyour Road,
Crownhill, PLYMOUTH PL6 5HY
DX 8249 PLYMOUTH (3)

Crown copyright (ref: LR/HO) 2/07

599

XXXI

APPLICATION FOR RECTIFICATION OF THE REGISTER[1]

25.30 *ALRForm.dot*

The Adjudicator to HM Land Registry

RECTIFICATION APPLICATION TO THE ADJUDICATOR TO RECTIFY OR SET ASIDE DOCUMENTS

Part 1 Details of Applicant
Name
Address
Post Code
Telephone (work)
Telephone (home)
Telephone (mobile)
Fax
Email

ALRFORM.dot
Part 2 Details of Applicant s Solicitor or Other Representative
If applicable, please fill in the details of the applicant s solicitor.
Name
Address
Post Code
Telephone
Fax
Email
In the case of a lay representative (i.e. someone who is not a qualified solicitor or barrister),
the Applicant s signature is required below to authorise the lay representative to act on their
behalf.
Signature: Date:

ALRFORM.dot
Part 3 Details of Person(s) Against Whom an Order is Sought

[1] This form should be attached as a Continuation Page to Form AP1.

Please enter the contact details of the person(s) against whom you are seeking an order.

Name
Address
Post Code
Telephone (work)
Telephone (home)
Telephone (mobile)
Fax
Email

Part 4 Details of Application
Please enter the details of the application, including the Land Registry Title Number.
Description/Address
Title Number
Remedy SoughtRectification of the register by omitting therefrom the piece of land shown on the plan annexed hereto and thereon coloured brown.
Grounds on which
Application is Based
See below

ALRFORM.dot
Part 5 List of Documents
Please list any documents on which you intend to rely to support your application.
[Please continue on a separate sheet if necessary]

Part 6 List of Witnesses
Please list any witnesses that you intend to call to give evidence to support your application.
[Please continue on a separate sheet if necessary]

ALRFORM.dot
Part 7 Copy Documents to Include With Your Application
Pursuant to rule 16(1) of The Adjudicator to HM Land Registry (Practice and Procedure)
Rules 2003, which is reproduced overleaf, you are required to include the following with your
application:
A copy of each of the documents you have listed in Part 5
A copy of the document to which this application relates

Part 8 Signature and Date
The application must be signed and dated below before it can be accepted.

601

Signed:
Date:
I am the Applicant / Applicant s Representative (delete as applicable)

Part 9 Where to Send This Form
Please return the completed form and copy documents to:
The Adjudicator to HM Land Registry
Procession House
55 Ludgate Hill
London EC4M 7JW
Telephone: 020 7029 9780
October

The grounds for this application are as follows:

1. The Applicant is and was at all material times the registered owner of the property known as Greenacre [address] (hereinafter called "Greenacre") the title of which is registered at .... District Land Registry as title number ....
The Applicant's predecessor in title .... was registered as first proprietor of Greenacre on .... and the Claimant was registered as proprietor on .... .The said property is shown on the plan annexed hereto edged red.

2. [Name] is the registered proprietor of Whiteacre [address] (hereinafter called "Whiteacre") which is registered at .... District Land Registry as title number .... Whiteacre is shown on the said plan edged blue.

3. When Whiteacre was registered a piece of land forming part of O.S. Number .... on the .... Edition of the Ordnance Survey map was wrongly included in the said title. The disputed land forms part of Greenacre and had formerly been registered as part of title number .... The disputed land is shown on the plan hatched brown.

4. The applicant accordingly applies to the Chief Land Registrar to rectify the register and filed plan under title no. [Whiteacre's title no.] in the manner aforesaid under section 82(1)(g) and (h) of the Land Registration Act 1925 and rule 14 of the Land Registration Rules 1925 on the grounds that he is the only person entitled to the disputed land.

5. The Land Certificate [An office copy of the entry] relating to title no. .... is enclosed with this application.

Part V:
Appendix One

Part V: Statutes

PRESCRIPTION ACT 1832 c. 71

An Act for shortening the time of prescription in certain cases.   **A1.1.001**

[1st August 1832]

Whereas the expression "time immemorial, or time whereof the memory of man runneth not to the contrary," is now by the Law of England in many cases considered to include and denote the whole period of time from the Reign of King Richard the First, whereby the title to matters that have been long enjoyed is sometimes defeated by shewing the commencement of such enjoyment, which is in many cases productive of inconvenience and injustice;

1. Claims to right of common and other profits à prendre, not to be defeated after thirty years enjoyment by merely showing the commencement; after sixty years enjoyment the right to be absolute, unless had by consent or agreement

No claim which may be lawfully made at the common law, by custom, **A1.1.002** prescription, or grant, to any right of common or other profit or benefit to be taken and enjoyed from or upon any land of our sovereign lord the King, or any land being parcel of the duchy of Lancaster or of the duchy of Cornwall, or of any ecclesiastical or lay person, or body corporate, except such matters and things as are herein specially provided for, and except tithes, rent, and services, shall, where such right, profit, or benefit shall have been actually taken and enjoyed by any person claiming right thereto without interruption for the full period of thirty years, be defeated or destroyed by showing only that such right, profit, or benefit was first taken or enjoyed at any time prior to such period of thirty years, but nevertheless such claim may be defeated in any other way by which the same is now liable to be defeated; and when such right, profit, or benefit shall have been so taken and enjoyed as aforesaid for the full period of sixty years, the right thereto shall be deemed absolute and indefeasible, unless it shall appear that the same was taken and enjoyed by some consent or agreement expressly made or given for that purpose by deed or writing.

2. In claims of right of way or other easement the periods to be twenty years and forty years

No claim which may be lawfully made at the common law, by custom, **A1.1.003** prescription, or grant, to any way or other easement, or to any watercourse, or the use of any water, to be enjoyed or derived upon, over, or from any land or water of our said lord the King, or being parcel of the duchy of Lancaster or of the duchy of Cornwall, or being the property of any ecclesiastical or lay person, or body corporate, when such way or other matter as herein last before mentioned shall have been actually enjoyed by any person claiming right thereto without interruption for the full period of twenty years, shall be defeated or destroyed by showing only that such way or other matter was first enjoyed at any time prior to such period of twenty years, but nevertheless such claim may be defeated in any other way by which the same is now liable to be defeated; and where such way or other matter as herein last before mentioned shall have been so enjoyed as aforesaid for the full period of forty years, the right thereto shall be deemed absolute and indefeasible, unless it shall appear that the same was enjoyed by some consent or agreement expressly given or made for that purpose by deed or writing.

3. Claim to the use of light enjoyed for 20 years

A1.1.004   When the access and use of light to and for any dwelling house, work-shop, or other building shall have been actually enjoyed therewith for the full period of twenty years without interruption, the right thereto shall be deemed absolute and indefeasible, any local usage or custom to the contrary notwithstanding, unless it shall appear that the same was enjoyed by some consent or agreement expressly made or given for that purpose by deed or writing.

4. Before mentioned periods to be deemed those next before suits

A1.1.005   Each of the respective periods of years herein-before mentioned shall be deemed and taken to be the period next before some suit or action wherein the claim or matter to which such period may relate shall have been or shall be brought into question and that no act or other matter shall be deemed to be an interruption, within the meaning of this statute, unless the same shall have been or shall be submitted to or acquiesced in for one year after the party interrupted shall have had or shall have notice thereof, and of the person making or authorizing the same to be made.

5. In actions on the case, the claimant may allege his right generally, as at present. In pleas to trespass and certain other pleadings, the period mentioned in this Act may be alleged. Exceptions, &c. to be replied to specially

A1.1.006   In all actions upon the case and other pleadings, wherein the party claiming may now by law allege his right generally, without averring the existence of such right from time immemorial, such general allegation shall still be deemed sufficient, and if the same shall be denied, all and every the matters in this Act mentioned and provided, which shall be applicable to the case, shall be admissible in evidence to sustain or rebut such allegation; and that in all pleadings to actions of trespass, and in all other pleadings wherein before the passing of this Act it would have been necessary to allege the right to have existed from time immemorial, it shall be sufficient to allege the enjoyment thereof as of right by the occupiers of the tenement in respect whereof the same is claimed for and during such of the periods mentioned in this Act as may be applicable to the case, and without claiming in the name or right of the owner of the fee, as is now usually done; and if the other party shall intend to rely on any proviso, exception, incapacity, disability, contract, agreement, or other matter herein-before mentioned, or on any cause or matter of fact or of law not inconsistent with the simple fact of enjoyment, the same shall be specially alleged and set forth in answer to the allegation of the party claiming, and shall not be received in evidence on any general traverse or denial of such allegation.

6. Presumption to be allowed in claims herein provided for

In the several cases mentioned in and provided for by this Act, no **A1.1.007** presumption shall be allowed or made in favour or support of any claim, upon proof of the exercise or enjoyment of the right or matter claimed for any less period of time or number of years than for such period or number mentioned in this Act as may be applicable to the case and to the nature of the claim.

7. Proviso for infants, &c.

Provided also, that the time during which any person otherwise capable **A1.1.008** of resisting any claim to any of the matters before mentioned shall have been or shall be an infant, idiot, non compos mentis, feme covert, or tenant for life, or during which any action or suit shall have been pending, and which shall have been diligently prosecuted, until abated by the death of any party or parties thereto, shall be excluded in the computation of the periods herein-before mentioned, except only in cases where the right or claim is hereby declared to be absolute and indefeasible.

8. What time to be excluded in computing the term of forty years appointed by this Act

Provided always, that when any land or water upon, over, or from **A1.1.009** which any such way or other convenient watercourse or use of water shall have been or shall be enjoyed or derived hath been or shall be held under or by virtue of any term of life, or any term of years exceeding three years from the granting thereof, the time of the enjoyment of any such way or other matter as herein last before mentioned, during the continuance of such term, shall be excluded in the computation of the said period of forty years, in case the claim shall within three years next after the end or sooner determination of such term be resisted by any person entitled to any reversion expectant on the determination thereof.

8A.—Exclusion of time because of mediation in certain cross-border disputes

A1.1.010   (1) In this section—

    (a)   "Mediation Directive" means Directive 2008/52/EC of the European Parliament and of the Council of 21 May 2008 on certain aspects of mediation in civil and commercial matters;

    (b)   "mediation" has the meaning given by article 3(a) of the Mediation Directive;

    (c)   "mediator" has the meaning given by article 3(b) of the Mediation Directive;

    (d)   "relevant dispute" means a dispute to which article 8(1) of the Mediation Directive applies (certain cross-border disputes).

(2) Where a period is prescribed by this Act in relation to the subject of the whole or part of a relevant dispute, any time after the start of a mediation in relation to the relevant dispute is to be excluded in the computation of that period, but only if—

    (a)   the time when the period must end by virtue of section 4 falls before the mediation ends or less than eight weeks after it ends, or

    (b)   a further mediation in relation to the relevant dispute starts less than eight weeks after the previous mediation ends, and the time when the period must end by virtue of section 4 falls before the further mediation ends or less than eight weeks after it ends.

(3) Any time excluded under subsection (2) is also to be excluded in the computation of the second period of three years mentioned in section 8 (period within which claim is resisted).

(4) For the purposes of this section, a mediation starts on the date of the agreement to mediate that is entered into by the parties and the mediator.

(5) For the purposes of this section, a mediation ends on the date of the first of these to occur—

(a) the parties reach an agreement in resolution of the relevant dispute;

(b) a party completes the notification of the other parties that it has withdrawn from the mediation;

(c) a party to whom a qualifying request is made fails to give a response reaching the other parties within 14 days of the request;

(d) the parties, after being notified that the mediator's appointment has ended (by death, resignation or otherwise), fail to agree within 14 days to seek to appoint a replacement mediator;

(e) the mediation otherwise comes to an end pursuant to the terms of the agreement to mediate.

(6) For the purpose of subsection (5), a qualifying request is a request by a party that another (A) confirm to all parties that A is continuing with the mediation.

(7) In the case of any relevant dispute, references in this section to a mediation are references to the mediation so far as it relates to that dispute, and references to a party are to be read accordingly.

9. Limitation

This Act shall not extend to Scotland . . .   **A1.1.011**

10, 11 [Repealed by Statute Law Revision Act 1874 (c. 35)]

ACCESS TO NEIGHBOURING LAND ACT 1992 c. 23

1.—Access orders

A1.2.001   (1) A person—

  (a) who, for the purpose of carrying out works to any land (the "dominant land"), desires to enter upon any adjoining or adjacent land (the "servient land"), and

  (b) who needs, but does not have, the consent of some other person to that entry,

may make an application to the court for an order under this section ("an access order") against that other person.

(2) On an application under this section, the court shall make an access order if, and only if, it is satisfied—

  (a) that the works are reasonably necessary for the preservation of the whole or any part of the dominant land; and

  (b) that they cannot be carried out, or would be substantially more difficult to carry out, without entry upon the servient land;

but this subsection is subject to subsection (3) below.

(3) The court shall not make an access order in any case where it is satisfied that, were it to make such an order—

  (a) the respondent or any other person would suffer interference with, or disturbance of, his use or enjoyment of the servient land, or

  (b) the respondent, or any other person (whether of full age or capacity or not) in occupation of the whole or any part of the servient land, would suffer hardship,

to such a degree by reason of the entry (notwithstanding any requirement of this Act or any term or condition that may be imposed under it) that it would be unreasonable to make the order.

(4) Where the court is satisfied on an application under this section that it is reasonably necessary to carry out any basic preservation works to the dominant land, those works shall be taken for the purposes of this Act to be reasonably necessary for the preservation of the land; and in this subsection "basic preservation works" means any of the following, that is to say—(a) the maintenance, repair or renewal of any part of a building or other structure comprised in, or situate on, the dominant land;

(b) the clearance, repair or renewal of any drain, sewer, pipe or cable so comprised or situate;

(c) the treatment, cutting back, felling, removal or replacement of any hedge, tree, shrub or other growing thing which is so comprised and which is, or is in danger of becoming, damaged, diseased, dangerous, insecurely rooted or dead;

(d) the filling in, or clearance, of any ditch so comprised;

but this subsection is without prejudice to the generality of the works which may, apart from it, be regarded by the court as reasonably necessary for the preservation of any land.

(5) If the court considers it fair and reasonable in all the circumstances of the case, works may be regarded for the purposes of this Act as being reasonably necessary for the preservation of any land (or, for the purposes of subsection (4) above, as being basic preservation works which it is reasonably necessary to carry out to any land) notwithstanding that the works incidentally involve—

(a) the making of some alteration, adjustment or improvement to the land, or

(b) the demolition of the whole or any part of a building or structure comprised in or situate upon the land.

(6) Where any works are reasonably necessary for the preservation of the whole or any part of the dominant land, the doing to the dominant land of anything which is requisite for, incidental to, or consequential on, the carrying out of those works shall be treated for the purposes of this Act as the carrying out of works which are reasonably necessary for the preservation of that land; and references in this Act to works, or to the carrying out of works, shall be construed accordingly.

(7) Without prejudice to the generality of subsection (6) above, if it is reasonably necessary for a person to inspect the dominant land—

(a) for the purpose of ascertaining whether any works may be reasonably necessary for the preservation of the whole or any part of that land,

(b) for the purpose of making any map or plan, or ascertaining the course of any drain, sewer, pipe or cable, in preparation for, or otherwise in connection with, the carrying out of works which are so reasonably necessary, or

(c) otherwise in connection with the carrying out of any such works, the making of such an inspection shall be taken for the purposes of this Act to be the carrying out to the dominant land of works which are reasonably necessary for the preservation of that land; and references in this Act to works, or to the carrying out of works, shall be construed accordingly.

2.—Terms and conditions of access orders

A1.2.002   (1) An access order shall specify—

(a) the works to the dominant land that may be carried out by entering upon the servient land in pursuance of the order;

(b) the particular area of servient land that may be entered upon by virtue of the order for the purpose of carrying out those works to the dominant land; and

(c) the date on which, or the period during which, the land may be so entered upon;

and in the following provisions of this Act any reference to the servient land is a reference to the area specified in the order in pursuance of paragraph (b) above.

(2) An access order may impose upon the applicant or the respondent such terms and conditions as appear to the court to be reasonably necessary for the purpose of avoiding or restricting—

(a) any loss, damage, or injury which might otherwise be caused to the respondent or any other person by reason of the entry authorised by the order; or

(b) any inconvenience or loss of privacy that might otherwise be so caused to the respondent or any other person.

(3) Without prejudice to the generality of subsection (2) above, the terms and conditions which may be imposed under that subsection include provisions with respect to—

(a) the manner in which the specified works are to be carried out;

(b) the days on which, and the hours between which, the work involved may be executed;

(c) the persons who may undertake the carrying out of the specified works or enter upon the servient land under or by virtue of the order;

(d) the taking of any such precautions by the applicant as may be specified in the order.

(4) An access order may also impose terms and conditions—

    (a) requiring the applicant to pay, or to secure that such person connected with him as may be specified in the order pays, compensation for—

        (i) any loss, damage or injury, or

        (ii) any substantial loss of privacy or other substantial inconvenience,

which will, or might, be caused to the respondent or any other person by reason of the entry authorised by the order;

    (b) requiring the applicant to secure that he, or such person connected with him as may be specified in the order, is insured against any such risks as may be so specified; or

    (c) requiring such a record to be made of the condition of the servient land, or of such part of it as may be so specified, as the court may consider expedient with a view to facilitating the determination of any question that may arise concerning damage to that land.

(5) An access order may include provision requiring the applicant to pay the respondent such sum by way of consideration for the privilege of entering the servient land in pursuance of the order as appears to the court to be fair and reasonable having regard to all the circumstances of the case, including, in particular—

    (a) the likely financial advantage of the order to the applicant and any persons connected with him; and

    (b) the degree of inconvenience likely to be caused to the respondent or any other person by the entry;

but no payment shall be ordered under this subsection if and to the extent that the works which the applicant desires to carry out by means of the entry are works to residential land.

(6) For the purposes of subsection (5)(a) above, the likely financial advantage of an access order to the applicant and any persons connected with him shall in all cases be taken to be a sum of money equal to the greater of the following amounts, that is to say—

    (a) the amount (if any) by which so much of any likely increase in the value of any land—

(i) which consists of or includes the dominant land, and

(ii) which is owned or occupied by the same person as the dominant land,

as may reasonably be regarded as attributable to the carrying out of the specified works exceeds the likely cost of carrying out those works with the benefit of the access order; and

(b) the difference (if it would have been possible to carry out the specified works without entering upon the servient land) between—

(i) the likely cost of carrying out those works without entering upon the servient land; and

(ii) the likely cost of carrying them out with the benefit of the access order.

(7) For the purposes of subsection (5) above, "residential land" means so much of any land as consists of— (a) a dwelling or part of a dwelling;

(b) a garden, yard, private garage or outbuilding which is used and enjoyed wholly or mainly with a dwelling; or

(c) in the case of a building which includes one or more dwellings, any part of the building which is used and enjoyed wholly or mainly with those dwellings or any of them.

(8) The persons who are to be regarded for the purposes of this section as "connected with" the applicant are—

(a) the owner of any estate or interest in, or right over, the whole or any part of the dominant land;

(b) the occupier of the whole or any part of the dominant land; and

(c) any person whom the applicant may authorise under section 3(7) below to exercise the power of entry conferred by the access order.

(9) The court may make provision—

(a) for the reimbursement by the applicant of any expenses reasonably incurred by the respondent in connection with the application which are not otherwise recoverable as costs;

(b) for the giving of security by the applicant for any sum that might become payable to the respondent or any other person by virtue of this section or section 3 below.

3.—Effect of access order

(1) An access order requires the respondent, so far as he has power to **A1.2.003** do so, to permit the applicant or any of his associates to do anything which the applicant or associate is authorised or required to do under or by virtue of the order or this section.

(2) Except as otherwise provided by or under this Act, an access order authorises the applicant or any of his associates, without the consent of the respondent,—

(a) to enter upon the servient land for the purpose of carrying out the specified works;

(b) to bring on to that land, leave there during the period permitted by the order and, before the end of that period, remove, such materials, plant and equipment as are reasonably necessary for the carrying out of those works; and

(c) to bring on to that land any waste arising from the carrying out of those works, if it is reasonably necessary to do so in the course of removing it from the dominant land;

but nothing in this Act or in any access order shall authorise the applicant or any of his associates to leave anything in, on or over the servient land (otherwise than in discharge of their duty to make good that land) after their entry for the purpose of carrying out works to the dominant land ceases to be authorised under or by virtue of the order.

(3) An access order requires the applicant—

(a) to secure that any waste arising from the carrying out of the specified works is removed from the servient land forthwith;

(b) to secure that, before the entry ceases to be authorised under or by virtue of the order, the servient land is, so far as reasonably practicable, made good; and

(c) to indemnify the respondent against any damage which may be caused to the servient land or any goods by the applicant or any of his associates which would not have been so caused had the order not been made;

but this subsection is subject to subsections (4) and (5) below.

(4) In making an access order, the court may vary or exclude, in whole or in part,—

(a) any authorisation that would otherwise be conferred by subsection (2)(b) or (c) above; or

(b) any requirement that would otherwise be imposed by subsection (3) above.

(5) Without prejudice to the generality of subsection (4) above, if the court is satisfied that it is reasonably necessary for any such waste as may arise from the carrying out of the specified works to be left on the servient land for some period before removal, the access order may, in place of subsection (3)(a) above, include provision—

(a) authorising the waste to be left on that land for such period as may be permitted by the order; and

(b) requiring the applicant to secure that the waste is removed before the end of that period.

(6) Where the applicant or any of his associates is authorised or required under or by virtue of an access order or this section to enter, or do any other thing, upon the servient land, he shall not (as respects that access order) be taken to be a trespasser from the beginning on account of his, or any other person's, subsequent conduct.

(7) For the purposes of this section, the applicant's "associates" are such number of persons (whether or not servants or agents of his) whom he may reasonably authorise under this subsection to exercise the power of entry conferred by the access order as may be reasonably necessary for carrying out the specified works.

4.—Persons bound by access order, unidentified persons and bar on contracting out

A1.2.004 (1) In addition to the respondent, an access order shall, subject to the provisions of the Land Charges Act 1972 and the [Land Registration Act 2002], be binding on—

(a) any of his successors in title to the servient land; and

(b) any person who has an estate or interest in, or right over, the whole or any part of the servient land which was created after the making of the order and who derives his title to that estate, interest or right under the respondent;

and references to the respondent shall be construed accordingly.

(2) If and to the extent that the court considers it just and equitable to allow him to do so, a person on whom an access order becomes binding by virtue of subsection (1)(a) or (b) above shall be entitled, as respects anything falling to be done after the order becomes binding on him, to

enforce the order or any of its terms or conditions as if he were the respondent, and references to the respondent shall be construed accordingly.

(3) Rules of court may—

    (a) provide a procedure which may be followed where the applicant does not know, and cannot reasonably ascertain, the name of any person whom he desires to make respondent to the application; and

    (b) make provision enabling such an applicant to make such a person respondent by description instead of by name;

and in this subsection "applicant" includes a person who proposes to make an application for an access order.

(4) Any agreement, whenever made, shall be void if and to the extent that it would, apart from this subsection, prevent a person from applying for an access order or restrict his right to do so.

5.—Registration of access orders and of applications for such orders

(1) In section 6(1) of the Land Charges Act 1972 (which specifies the **A1.2.005** writs and orders affecting land that may be entered in the register) after paragraph (c) there shall be added—

"(d) any access order under the Access to Neighbouring Land Act 1992."

. . .

(4) In any case where—

    (a) an access order is discharged under section 6(1)(a) below, and

    (b) the order has been protected by an entry registered under the Land Charges Act 1972 or by a notice under the Land Registration Act 2002,

the court may by order direct that the entry or notice shall be cancelled.

(5) The rights conferred on a person by or under an access order shall not be capable of falling within paragraph 2 of Schedule 1 or 3 to the Land Registration Act 2002 (overriding status of interest of person in actual occupation).

(6) An application for an access order shall be regarded as a pending land action for the purposes of the Land Charges Act 1972 and the Land Registration Act 2002.

6.—Variation of orders and damages for breach

A1.2.006   (1) Where an access order or an order under this subsection has been made, the court may, on the application of any party to the proceedings in which the order was made or of any other person on whom the order is binding—

    (a) discharge or vary the order or any of its terms or conditions;

    (b) suspend any of its terms or conditions; or

    (c) revive any term or condition suspended under paragraph (b) above;

and in the application of subsections (1) and (2) of section 4 above in relation to an access order, any order under this subsection which relates to the access order shall be treated for the purposes of those subsections as included in the access order.

(2) If any person contravenes or fails to comply with any requirement, term or condition imposed upon him by or under this Act, the court may, without prejudice to any other remedy available, make an order for the payment of damages by him to any other person affected by the contravention or failure who makes an application for relief under this subsection.

7.—Jurisdiction over, and allocation of, proceedings

A1.2.007   (1) The High Court and the county courts shall both have jurisdiction under this Act.

(2) In article 4 of the High Court and County Courts Jurisdiction Order 1991 (which provides that proceedings in which the county courts and the High Court both have jurisdiction may, subject to articles 5 and 6, be commenced either in a county court or in the High Court) for the words "and 6" there shall be substituted the words", 6 and 6A"; and after article 6 of that Order there shall be inserted—

    "6A.–Applications under section 1 of the Access to Neighbouring Land Act 1992 shall be commenced in a county court."

(3) The amendment by subsection (2) above of provisions contained in an order shall not be taken to have prejudiced any power to make further orders revoking or amending those provisions.

8.—Interpretation and application

A1.2.008   (1) Any reference in this Act to an "entry" upon any servient land includes a reference to the doing on that land of anything necessary for carrying out the works to the dominant land which are reasonably necessary for its preservation; and "enter" shall be construed accordingly.

(2) This Act applies in relation to any obstruction of, or other interference with, a right over, or interest in, any land as it applies in relation to an entry upon that land; and "enter" and "entry" shall be construed accordingly.

(3) In this Act—

"access order" has the meaning given by section 1(1) above;

"applicant" means a person making an application for an access order and, subject to section 4 above, "the respondent" means the respondent, or any of the respondents, to such an application;

"the court" means the High Court or a county court;

"the dominant land" and "the servient land" respectively have the meanings given by section 1(1) above, but subject, in the case of servient land, to section 2(1) above;

"land" does not include a highway;

"the specified works" means the works specified in the access order in pursuance of section 2(1)(a) above.

9.—Short title, commencement and extent

(1) This Act may be cited as the Access to Neighbouring Land Act 1992. **A1.2.009**

(2) This Act shall come into force on such day as the Lord Chancellor may by order made by statutory instrument appoint.

(3) This Act extends to England and Wales only.

HUMAN RIGHTS ACT 1998 c. 42

1.—The Convention Rights

A1.3.001   (1) In this Act "the Convention rights" means the rights and fundamental freedoms set out in—(a) Articles 2 to 12 and 14 of the Convention,

> (b)   Articles 1 to 3 of the First Protocol, and

> (c)   Article 1 of the Thirteenth Protocol,

as read with Articles 16 to 18 of the Convention.

(2) Those Articles are to have effect for the purposes of this Act subject to any designated derogation or reservation (as to which see sections 14 and 15).

(3) The Articles are set out in Schedule 1.

(4) The Secretary of State may by order make such amendments to this Act as he considers appropriate to reflect the effect, in relation to the United Kingdom, of a protocol.

(5) In subsection (4) "protocol" means a protocol to the Convention— (a) which the United Kingdom has ratified; or

> (b)   which the United Kingdom has signed with a view to ratification.

(6) No amendment may be made by an order under subsection (4) so as to come into force before the protocol concerned is in force in relation to the United Kingdom.

2.—Interpretation of Convention rights

A1.3.002   (1) A court or tribunal determining a question which has arisen in connection with a Convention right must take into account any—

> (a)   judgment, decision, declaration or advisory opinion of the European Court of Human Rights,

> (b)   opinion of the Commission given in a report adopted under Article 31 of the Convention,

> (c)   decision of the Commission in connection with Article 26 or 27(2) of the Convention, or

> (d)   decision of the Committee of Ministers taken under Article 46 of the Convention,

whenever made or given, so far as, in the opinion of the court or tribunal, it is relevant to the proceedings in which that question has arisen.

(2) Evidence of any judgment, decision, declaration or opinion of which account may have to be taken under this section is to be given in proceedings before any court or tribunal in such manner as may be provided by rules.

(3) In this section "rules" means rules of court or, in the case of proceedings before a tribunal, rules made for the purposes of this section—(a) by the Lord Chancellor or ... the Secretary of State, in relation to any proceedings outside Scotland;

- (b) by the Secretary of State, in relation to proceedings in Scotland; or

- (c) by a Northern Ireland department, in relation to proceedings before a tribunal in Northern Ireland—

  - (i) which deals with transferred matters; and
  - (ii) for which no rules made under paragraph (a) are in force.

3.—Interpretation of legislation

(1) So far as it is possible to do so, primary legislation and subordinate **A1.3.003** legislation must be read and given effect in a way which is compatible with the Convention rights.

(2) This section—

- (a) applies to primary legislation and subordinate legislation whenever enacted;

- (b) does not affect the validity, continuing operation or enforcement of any incompatible primary legislation; and

- (c) does not affect the validity, continuing operation or enforcement of any incompatible subordinate legislation if (disregarding any possibility of revocation) primary legislation prevents removal of the incompatibility.

4.—Declaration of incompatibility

(1) Subsection (2) applies in any proceedings in which a court deter- **A1.3.004** mines whether a provision of primary legislation is compatible with a Convention right.

(2) If the court is satisfied that the provision is incompatible with a Convention right, it may make a declaration of that incompatibility.

(3) Subsection (4) applies in any proceedings in which a court determines whether a provision of subordinate legislation, made in the exercise of a power conferred by primary legislation, is compatible with a Convention right.

(4) If the court is satisfied—

(a) that the provision is incompatible with a Convention right, and

(b) that (disregarding any possibility of revocation) the primary legislation concerned prevents removal of the incompatibility,

it may make a declaration of that incompatibility.

(5) In this section "court" means —(a) the Supreme Court;

(b) the Judicial Committee of the Privy Council;

(c) the Court Martial Appeal Court;

(d) in Scotland, the High Court of Justiciary sitting otherwise than as a trial court or the Court of Session;

(e) in England and Wales or Northern Ireland, the High Court or the Court of Appeal;

(f) the Court of Protection, in any matter being dealt with by the President of the Family Division, the Vice-Chancellor or a puisne judge of the High Court.

(6) A declaration under this section ("a declaration of incompatibility")—

(a) does not affect the validity, continuing operation or enforcement of the provision in respect of which it is given; and

(b) is not binding on the parties to the proceedings in which it is made.

5.—Right of Crown to intervene

A1.3.005 (1) Where a court is considering whether to make a declaration of incompatibility, the Crown is entitled to notice in accordance with rules of court.

(2) In any case to which subsection (1) applies—

(a) a Minister of the Crown (or a person nominated by him),

(b) a member of the Scottish Executive,

(c) a Northern Ireland Minister,

(d) a Northern Ireland department,

is entitled, on giving notice in accordance with rules of court, to be joined as a party to the proceedings.

(3) Notice under subsection (2) may be given at any time during the proceedings.

(4) A person who has been made a party to criminal proceedings (other than in Scotland) as the result of a notice under subsection (2) may, with leave, appeal to the Supreme Court against any declaration of incompatibility made in the proceedings.

(5) In subsection (4)—

"criminal proceedings" includes all proceedings before the Court Martial Appeal Court; and

"leave" means leave granted by the court making the declaration of incompatibility or by the [Supreme Court].

6.—Acts of public authorities

(1) It is unlawful for a public authority to act in a way which is incompatible with a Convention right.   **A1.3.006**

(2) Subsection (1) does not apply to an act if—

(a) as the result of one or more provisions of primary legislation, the authority could not have acted differently; or

(b) in the case of one or more provisions of, or made under, primary legislation which cannot be read or given effect in a way which is compatible with the Convention rights, the authority was acting so as to give effect to or enforce those provisions.

(3) In this section "public authority" includes—(a) a court or tribunal, and

(b) any person certain of whose functions are functions of a public nature,

but does not include either House of Parliament or a person exercising functions in connection with proceedings in Parliament.

. . .

(5) In relation to a particular act, a person is not a public authority by virtue only of subsection (3)(b) if the nature of the act is private.

(6) "An act" includes a failure to act but does not include a failure to—(a) introduce in, or lay before, Parliament a proposal for legislation; or

(b) make any primary legislation or remedial order.

7.—Proceedings

A1.3.007   (1) A person who claims that a public authority has acted (or proposes to act) in a way which is made unlawful by section 6(1) may—

(a) bring proceedings against the authority under this Act in the appropriate court or tribunal, or

(b) rely on the Convention right or rights concerned in any legal proceedings,

but only if he is (or would be) a victim of the unlawful act.

(2) In subsection (1)(a) "appropriate court or tribunal" means such court or tribunal as may be determined in accordance with rules; and proceedings against an authority include a counterclaim or similar proceedings.

(3) If the proceedings are brought on an application for judicial review, the applicant is to be taken to have a sufficient interest in relation to the unlawful act only if he is, or would be, a victim of that act.

(4) If the proceedings are made by way of a petition for judicial review in Scotland, the applicant shall be taken to have title and interest to sue in relation to the unlawful act only if he is, or would be, a victim of that act.

(5) Proceedings under subsection (1)(a) must be brought before the end of—

(a) the period of one year beginning with the date on which the act complained of took place; or

(b) such longer period as the court or tribunal considers equitable having regard to all the circumstances,

but that is subject to any rule imposing a stricter time limit in relation to the procedure in question.

(6) In subsection (1)(b) "legal proceedings" includes—(a) proceedings brought by or at the instigation of a public authority; and

(b) an appeal against the decision of a court or tribunal.

(7) For the purposes of this section, a person is a victim of an unlawful act only if he would be a victim for the purposes of Article 34 of the Convention if proceedings were brought in the European Court of Human Rights in respect of that act.

(8) Nothing in this Act creates a criminal offence.

(9) In this section "rules" means —(a) in relation to proceedings before a court or tribunal outside Scotland, rules made by . . . the the Lord

Chancellor or Secretary of State for the purposes of this section or rules of court,

(b)   in relation to proceedings before a court or tribunal in Scotland, rules made by the Secretary of State for those purposes,

(c)   in relation to proceedings before a tribunal in Northern Ireland—

(i)   which deals with transferred matters; and
(ii)   for which no rules made under paragraph (a) are in force,
rules made by a Northern Ireland department for those purposes,

and includes provision made by order under section 1 of the Courts and Legal Services Act 1990.

(10) In making rules, regard must be had to section 9.

(11) The Minister who has power to make rules in relation to a particular tribunal may, to the extent he considers it necessary to ensure that the tribunal can provide an appropriate remedy in relation to an act (or proposed act) of a public authority which is (or would be) unlawful as a result of section 6(1), by order add to—

(a)   the relief or remedies which the tribunal may grant; or

(b)   the grounds on which it may grant any of them.

(12) An order made under subsection (11) may contain such incidental, supplemental, consequential or transitional provision as the Minister making it considers appropriate.

(13) "The Minister" includes the Northern Ireland department concerned.

8.—Judicial remedies

(1) In relation to any act (or proposed act) of a public authority which **A1.3.008** the court finds is (or would be) unlawful, it may grant such relief or remedy, or make such order, within its powers as it considers just and appropriate.

(2) But damages may be awarded only by a court which has power to award damages, or to order the payment of compensation, in civil proceedings.

(3) No award of damages is to be made unless, taking account of all the circumstances of the case, including—

(a)   any other relief or remedy granted, or order made, in relation to the act in question (by that or any other court), and

(b) the consequences of any decision (of that or any other court) in respect of that act,

the court is satisfied that the award is necessary to afford just satisfaction to the person in whose favour it is made.

(4) In determining—

(a) whether to award damages, or

(b) the amount of an award,

the court must take into account the principles applied by the European Court of Human Rights in relation to the award of compensation under Article 41 of the Convention.

(5) A public authority against which damages are awarded is to be treated—

(a) in Scotland, for the purposes of section 3 of the Law Reform (Miscellaneous Provisions) (Scotland) Act 1940 as if the award were made in an action of damages in which the authority has been found liable in respect of loss or damage to the person to whom the award is made;

(b) for the purposes of the Civil Liability (Contribution) Act 1978 as liable in respect of damage suffered by the person to whom the award is made.

(6) In this section—

"court" includes a tribunal;

"damages" means damages for an unlawful act of a public authority; and

"unlawful" means unlawful under section 6(1).

9.—Judicial acts

A1.3.009   (1) Proceedings under section 7(1)(a) in respect of a judicial act may be brought only—

(a) by exercising a right of appeal;

(b) on an application (in Scotland a petition) for judicial review; or

(c) in such other forum as may be prescribed by rules.

(2) That does not affect any rule of law which prevents a court from being the subject of judicial review.

(3) In proceedings under this Act in respect of a judicial act done in good faith, damages may not be awarded otherwise than to compensate a person to the extent required by Article 5(5) of the Convention.

(4) An award of damages permitted by subsection (3) is to be made against the Crown; but no award may be made unless the appropriate person, if not a party to the proceedings, is joined.

(5) In this section—

"appropriate person" means the Minister responsible for the court concerned, or a person or government department nominated by him;

"court" includes a tribunal;

"judge" includes a member of a tribunal, a justice of the peace and a clerk or other officer entitled to exercise the jurisdiction of a court;

"judicial act" means a judicial act of a court and includes an act done on the instructions, or on behalf, of a judge; and

"rules" has the same meaning as in section 7(9).

Schedule 1

PART II

THE FIRST PROTOCOL

ARTICLE 1

Protection of property

A1.3.010 Every natural or legal person is entitled to the peaceful enjoyment of his possessions. No one shall be deprived of his possessions except in the public interest and subject to the conditions provided for by law and by the general principles of international law.

The preceding provisions shall not, however, in any way impair the right of a State to enforce such laws as it deems necessary to control the use of property in accordance with the general interest or to secure the payment of taxes or other contributions or penalties.

ARTICLE 2

Right to education

No person shall be denied the right to education. In the exercise of any functions which it assumes in relation to education and to teaching, the State shall respect the right of parents to ensure such education and teaching in conformity with their own religious and philosophical convictions.

ARTICLE 3

Right to free elections

The High Contracting Parties undertake to hold free elections at reasonable intervals by secret ballot, under conditions which will ensure the free expression of the opinion of the people in the choice of the legislature.

COUNTRYSIDE AND RIGHTS OF WAY ACT 2000 c. 37

Chapter I

Right of access

1.—Principal definitions for Part I

(1) In this Part "access land" means any land which—(a) is shown as **A1.4.001** open country on a map in conclusive form issued by the appropriate countryside body for the purposes of this Part,

    (b) is shown on such a map as registered common land,

    (c) is registered common land in any area outside Inner London for which no such map relating to registered common land has been issued,

    (d) is situated more than 600 metres above sea level in any area for which no such map relating to open country has been issued, . . .

    (da) is coastal margin, or

    (e) is dedicated for the purposes of this Part under section 16,

but does not (in any of those cases) include excepted land or land which is treated by section 15(1) as being accessible to the public apart from this Act.

(2) In this Part—

"access authority"—(a) in relation to land in a National Park, means the National Park authority, and

    (b) in relation to any other land, means the local highway authority in whose area the land is situated;

"the appropriate countryside body" means—(a) in relation to England, Natural England, and

(b)   in relation to Wales, the Countryside Council for Wales;

"coastal margin" means land which is of a description specified by an order under section 3A;

"excepted land" means land which is for the time being of any of the descriptions specified in Part I of Schedule 1, those descriptions having effect subject to Part II of that Schedule;

"mountain" includes, subject to the following definition, any land situated more than 600 metres above sea level;

"mountain, moor, heath or down" does not include land which appears to the appropriate countryside body to consist of improved or semi-improved grassland;

"open country" means land which—(a) appears to the appropriate countryside body to consist wholly or predominantly of mountain, moor, heath or down, and

(b)   is not registered common land or coastal margin.

(3) In this Part "registered common land" means—(a) land which is registered as common land under the Commons Registration Act 1965 (in this section referred to as "the 1965 Act") and whose registration under that Act has become final, or

(b)   subject to subsection (4), land which fell within paragraph (a) on the day on which this Act is passed or at any time after that day but has subsequently ceased to be registered as common land under the 1965 Act on the register of common land in which it was included being amended by reason of the land having ceased to be common land within the meaning of that Act.

(4) Subsection (3)(b) does not apply where—

(a)   the amendment of the register of common land was made in pursuance of an application made before the day on which this Act is passed, or

(b)   the land ceased to be common land by reason of the exercise of—

(i)   any power of compulsory purchase, of appropriation or of sale which is conferred by an enactment,
(ii)   any power so conferred under which land may be made common land within the meaning of the 1965 Act in substitution for other land.

2.—Rights of public in relation to access land

(1) Any person is entitled by virtue of this subsection to enter and **A1.4.002** remain on any access land for the purposes of open-air recreation, if and so long as—

(a) he does so without breaking or damaging any wall, fence, hedge, stile or gate, and

(b) he observes the general restrictions in Schedule 2 and any other restrictions imposed in relation to the land under Chapter II.

(2) Subsection (1) has effect subject to subsections (3) and (4) and to the provisions of Chapter II.

(3) Subsection (1) does not entitle a person to enter or be on any land, or do anything on any land, in contravention of any relevant statutory prohibition.

(3A) In subsection (3) "relevant statutory prohibition" means—(a) in the case of land which is coastal margin, a prohibition contained in or having effect under any enactment, and

(b) in any other case, a prohibition contained in or having effect under any enactment other than an enactment contained in a local or private Act.

(4) If a person becomes a trespasser on any access land by failing to comply with—

(a) subsection (1)(a),

(b) the general restrictions in Schedule 2, or

(c) any other restrictions imposed in relation to the land under Chapter II,

he may not, within 72 hours after leaving that land, exercise his right under subsection (1) to enter that land again or to enter other land in the same ownership.

(5) In this section "owner", in relation to any land which is subject to a farm business tenancy within the meaning of the Agricultural Tenancies Act 1995 or a tenancy to which the Agricultural Holdings Act 1986 applies, means the tenant under that tenancy, and "ownership" shall be construed accordingly.

3.—Power to extend to coastal land: Wales

A1.4.003   (1) The Welsh Ministers may by order amend the definition of " "open country" " in section 1(2) so as to include as respects Wales a reference to coastal land or to coastal land of any description.

(2) An order under this section may—

> (a) make consequential amendments of other provisions of this Part, and

> (b) modify the provisions of this Part in their application to land which is open country merely because it is coastal land.

(3) In this section "coastal land" means—(a) the foreshore, and

> (b) land adjacent to the foreshore (including in particular any cliff, bank, barrier, dune, beach or flat which is adjacent to the foreshore).

Part II

Public Rights Of Way And Road Traffic

Public rights of way and definitive maps and statements

47.—Redesignation of roads used as public paths

A1.4.004   (1) In the Wildlife and Countryside Act 1981 (in this Act referred to as "the 1981 Act"), section 54 (duty to reclassify roads used as public paths) shall cease to have effect.

(2) Every way which, immediately before the commencement of this section, is shown in any definitive map and statement as a road used as a public path shall be treated instead as shown as a restricted byway; and the expression "road used as a public path" shall not be used in any definitive map and statement to describe any way.

48.—Restricted byway rights

A1.4.005   (1) Subject to subsections (2) and (3), the public shall have restricted byway rights over any way which, immediately before the commencement of section 47, is shown in a definitive map and statement as a road used as a public path.

(2) Subsection (1) has effect subject to the operation of any enactment or instrument (whether coming into operation before or after the

commencement of section 47), and to the effect of any event otherwise within section 53(3)(a) of the 1981 Act, whereby a highway—

(a) is authorised to be stopped up, diverted, widened or extended, or

(b) becomes a public path;

and subsection (1) applies accordingly to any way as so diverted, widened or extended.

(3) Subsection (1) does not apply to any way, or part of a way, over which immediately before the commencement of section 47 there was no public right of way.

(4) In this Part—

"restricted byway rights" means—(a) a right of way on foot,

(b) a right of way on horseback or leading a horse, and

(c) a right of way for vehicles other than mechanically propelled vehicles; and

"restricted byway" means a highway over which the public have restricted byway rights, with or without a right to drive animals of any description along the highway, but no other rights of way.

(5) A highway at the side of a river, canal or other inland navigation is not excluded from the definition of "restricted byway" in subsection (4) merely because the public have a right to use the highway for purposes of navigation, if the highway would fall within that definition if the public had no such right over it.

(6) Subsection (1) is without prejudice to any question whether the public have over any way, in addition to restricted byway rights, a right of way for mechanically propelled vehicles or any other right.

(7) In subsections (4) and (6) "mechanically propelled vehicle" does not include a vehicle falling within paragraph (c) of section 189(1) of the Road Traffic Act 1988.

(8) Every surveying authority shall take such steps as they consider expedient for bringing to the attention of the public the effect of section 47(2) and this section.

(9) The powers conferred by section 103(5) must be so exercised as to secure that nothing in section 47 or this section affects the operation of section 53 or 54 of, or Schedule 14 or 15 to, the 1981 Act in relation to—

(a) a relevant order made before the commencement of section 47, or

(b) an application made before that commencement for a relevant order.

(10) In subsection (9) "relevant order" means an order which relates to a way shown in a definitive map and statement as a road used as a public path and which—(a) is made under section 53 of the 1981 Act and contains modifications relating to that way by virtue of subsection (3)(c) (ii) of that section, or

(b) is made under section 54 of the 1981 Act.

(11) Where—

(a) by virtue of an order under subsection (3) of section 103 ("the commencement order") containing such provision as is mentioned in subsection (5) of that section, an order under Part III of the 1981 Act ("the Part III order") takes effect, after the commencement of section 47, in relation to any way which, immediately before that commencement, was shown in a definitive map and statement as a road used as a public path,

(b) the commencement order does not prevent subsection (1) from having effect on that commencement in relation to that way, and

(c) if the Part III order had taken effect before that commencement, that way would not have fallen within subsection (1),

all rights over that way which exist only by virtue of subsection (1) shall be extinguished when the Part III order takes effect.

49.—Provisions supplementary to ss.47 and 48

A1.4.006   (1) Every way over which the public have restricted byway rights by virtue of subsection (1) of section 48 (whether or not they also have a right of way for mechanically propelled vehicles or any other right) shall, as from the commencement of that section, be a highway maintainable at the public expense.

(2) As from the commencement of that section, any liability, under a special enactment (within the meaning of the Highways Act 1980) or by reason of tenure, enclosure or prescription, to maintain, otherwise than as a highway maintainable at the public expense, a restricted byway to which subsection (1) applies is extinguished.

(3) Every way which, in pursuance of—

(a) paragraph 9 of Part III of Schedule 3 to the Countryside Act 1968, or

(b) any order made under section 54(1) of the 1981 Act before the coming into force of section 47, is shown in any definitive map and statement as a byway open to all traffic, a bridleway or a footpath, shall continue to be maintainable at the public expense.

(4) Nothing in subsections (1) and (3) or in section 48(1) obliges a highway authority to provide on any way a metalled carriage-way or a carriage-way which is by any other means provided with a surface suitable for cycles or other vehicles.

(5) Nothing in section 48, or in section 53 of the 1981 Act, limits the operation of orders under the Road Traffic Regulation Act 1984 or the operation of any byelaws.

(6) Section 67 of the 1981 Act (application to the Crown) has effect as if this section and sections 47, 48 and 50 were contained in Part III of that Act.

50.—Private rights over restricted byways

(1) Restricted byway rights over any way by virtue of subsection (1) of **A1.4.007** section 48 are subject to any condition or limitation to which public rights of way over that way were subject immediately before the commencement of that section.

(2) Any owner or lessee of premises adjoining or adjacent to a relevant highway shall, so far as is necessary for the reasonable enjoyment and occupation of the premises, have a right of way for vehicular and all other kinds of traffic over the relevant highway.

(3) In subsection (2), in its application to the owner of any premises, "relevant highway" means so much of any highway maintainable at the public expense by virtue of section 49(1) as was, immediately before it became so maintainable, owned by the person who then owned the premises.

(4) In subsection (2), in its application to the lessee of any premises, "relevant highway" means so much of any highway maintainable at the public expense by virtue of section 49(1) as was, immediately before it became so maintainable, included in the lease on which the premises are held.

(5) In this section—

"lease" and "lessee" have the same meaning as in the 1980 Act;

"owner", in relation to any premises, means a person, other than a mortgagee not in possession, who is for the time being entitled to dispose of the fee simple of the premises, whether in possession or in reversion, and "owned" shall be construed accordingly; and

"premises" has the same meaning as in the 1980 Act.

51.–Amendments relating to definitive maps and statements and restricted byways

A1.4.008   Schedule 5 to this Act (which contains amendments relating to definitive maps and statements and restricted byways) has effect.

52.—Restricted byways: power to amend existing legislation

A1.4.009   (1) The Secretary of State may by regulations—

> (a)   provide for any relevant provision which relates—
>
>> (i)   to highways or highways of a particular description,
>> (ii) to things done on or in connection with highways or highways of a particular description, or
>> (iii) to the creation, stopping up or diversion of highways or highways of a particular description,
>
> not to apply, or to apply with or without modification, in relation to restricted byways or to ways shown in a definitive map and statement as restricted byways, and
>
> (b)   make in any relevant provision such amendments, repeals or revocations as appear to him appropriate in consequence of the coming into force of sections 47 to 50 or provision made by virtue of paragraph (a) or subsection (6)(a).

(2) In this section—

"relevant provision" means a provision contained—(a) in an Act passed before or in the same Session as this Act, or

> (b)   in any subordinate legislation made before the passing of this Act;

"relevant Welsh provision" means a provision contained—(a) in a local or private Act passed before or in the same Session as this Act and relating only to areas in Wales, or

> (b)   in any subordinate legislation which was made before the passing of this Act and which the National Assembly for Wales has power to amend or revoke as respects Wales.

(3) In exercising the power to make regulations under subsection (1), the Secretary of State—

(a) may not make provision which has effect in relation to Wales unless he has consulted the National Assembly for Wales, and

(b) may not without the consent of the National Assembly for Wales make any provision which (otherwise than merely by virtue of the amendment or repeal of a provision contained in an Act) amends or revokes subordinate legislation made by the Assembly.

(4) The National Assembly for Wales may submit to the Secretary of State proposals for the exercise by the Secretary of State of the power conferred by subsection (1).

(5) The powers conferred by subsection (1) may be exercised in relation to a relevant provision even though the provision is amended or inserted by this Act.

(6) As respects Wales, the National Assembly for Wales may by regulations—

(a) provide for any relevant Welsh provision which relates—

(i) to highways or highways of a particular description,
(ii) to things done on or in connection with highways or highways of a particular description, or
(iii) to the creation, stopping up or diversion of highways or highways of a particular description,

not to apply, or to apply with or without modification, in relation to restricted byways or to ways shown in a definitive map and statement as restricted byways, and

(b) make in any relevant Welsh provision such amendments, repeals or revocations as appear to the Assembly appropriate in consequence of the coming into force of sections 47 to 50 or provision made by virtue of subsection (1)(a) or paragraph (a).

(7) Regulations under this section shall be made by statutory instrument, but no such regulations shall be made by the Secretary of State unless a draft of the instrument containing them has been laid before, and approved by a resolution of, each House of Parliament.

(8) Where the Secretary of State lays before Parliament the draft of an instrument containing regulations under subsection (1) in respect of which consultation with the National Assembly for Wales is required by subsection (3)(a), he shall also lay before each House of Parliament a document giving details of the consultation and setting out any representations received from the Assembly.

53.—Extinguishment of unrecorded rights of way

A1.4.010

(1) Subsection (2) applies to a highway if—

(a) it was on 1st January 1949 a footpath or a bridleway, is on the cut-off date (in either case) a footpath or a bridleway, and between those dates has not been a highway of any other description,

(b) it is not on the cut-off date shown in a definitive map and statement as a highway of any description, and

(c) it is not on the cut-off date an excepted highway, as defined by section 54(1).

(2) All public rights of way over a highway to which this subsection applies shall be extinguished immediately after the cut-off date.

(3) Where a public right of way created before 1949—

(a) falls within subsection (4) on the cut-off date, and

(b) is not on that date an excepted right of way, as defined by section 54(5),

that right of way shall be extinguished immediately after the cut-off date.

(4) A public right of way falls within this subsection if it is—

(a) a public right of way on horseback, leading a horse or for vehicles over a bridleway, restricted byway or byway open to all traffic which is shown in a definitive map and statement as a footpath;

(b) a right for the public to drive animals of any description along a bridleway, restricted byway or byway open to all traffic which is shown in a definitive map and statement as a footpath;

(c) a public right of way for vehicles over a restricted byway or byway open to all traffic which is shown in a definitive map and statement as a bridleway; or

(d) a public right of way for mechanically propelled vehicles over a byway open to all traffic which is shown in a definitive map and statement as a restricted byway.

(5) Where by virtue of subsection (3) a highway ceases to be a bridleway, the right of way created over it by section 30 of the Countryside Act 1968 (riding of pedal cycles on bridleways) is also extinguished.

(6) In determining—

(a) for the purposes of subsection (1) whether any part of a highway was on 1st January 1949 a footpath or bridleway, or

(b) for the purposes of subsection (3) whether a public right of way over any part of a highway was created before 1st January 1949,

any diversion, widening or extension of the highway on or after that date (and not later than the cut-off date) is to be treated as having occurred before 1st January 1949.

(7) Where a way shown on the cut-off date in a definitive map and statement has at any time been diverted, widened or extended, it is to be treated for the purposes of subsections (1) to (5) as shown as so diverted, widened or extended, whether or not it is so shown.

(8) In this section—

"cut-off date" has the meaning given in section 56, and

"mechanically propelled vehicle" does not include a vehicle does not include a vehicle falling within paragraph (c) of section 189(1) of the Road Traffic Act 1988.

54.—Excepted highways and rights of way

(1) A footpath or bridleway is an excepted highway for the purposes of **A1.4.011** section 53(1) if—

(a) it is a footpath or bridleway which satisfies either of the conditions in subsections (2) and (3),

(b) it is, or is part of, a footpath or bridleway any part of which is in an area which, immediately before 1st April 1965, formed part of the administrative county of London,

(c) it is a footpath or bridleway—

(i) at the side of (whether or not contiguous with) a carriageway constituting or comprised in another highway, or

(ii) between two carriageways comprised in the same highway (whether or not the footpath or bridleway is contiguous with either carriageway),

(d) it is a footpath or bridleway of such other description as may be specified in regulations made (as respects England) by the Secretary of State or (as respects Wales) by the National Assembly for Wales, or

(e) it is a footpath or bridleway so specified.

(2) A footpath or bridleway ("the relevant highway") satisfies the first condition if—

(a) it became a footpath or bridleway on or after 1st January 1949 by the diversion, widening or extension of a footpath or, as the case may be, of a bridleway by virtue of an event within section 53(3)(a) of the 1981 Act,

(b) it became a footpath on or after 1st January 1949 by the stopping up of a bridleway,

(c) it was on 1st January 1949 a footpath and is on the cut-off date a bridleway,

(d) it is so much of a footpath or bridleway as on or after 1st January 1949 has been stopped up as respects part only of its width, or

(e) it is so much of a footpath or bridleway as passes over a bridge or through a tunnel,

and it communicates with a retained highway, either directly or by means of one or more footpaths or bridleways each of which forms part of the same highway as the relevant highway and each of which either falls within any of paragraphs (a) to (e) or satisfies the condition in subsection (3).

(3) A footpath or bridleway satisfies the second condition if—

(a) it extends from a footpath or bridleway ("the relevant highway") which—

(i) falls within any of paragraphs (a) to (e) of subsection (2), or
(ii) is an excepted highway by virtue of subsection (1)(c),

to, but not beyond, a retained highway, and

(b) it forms part of the same highway as the relevant highway.

(4) A retained highway for the purposes of subsections (2) and (3) is any highway over which, otherwise than by virtue of subsection (1)(a), section 53(2) does not extinguish rights of way.

(5) A public right of way is an excepted right of way for the purposes of section 53(3) if—

(a) it subsists over land over which there subsists on the cut-off date any public right of way created on or after 1st January 1949 otherwise than by virtue of section 30 of the Countryside Act 1968 (riding of pedal cycles on bridleways),

(b) it subsists over the whole or part of a way any part of which is in an area which, immediately before 1st April 1965, formed part of the administrative county of London,

(c) it is a public right of way of such other description as may be specified in regulations made (as respects England) by the Secretary of State or (as respects Wales) by the National Assembly for Wales, or

(d) it subsists over land so specified.

(6) Regulations under subsection (1)(d) or (e) or (5)(c) or (d) shall be made by statutory instrument, and a statutory instrument containing such regulations made by the Secretary of State shall be subject to annulment in pursuance of a resolution of either House of Parliament.

55.—Bridleway rights over ways shown as bridleways

(1) Subject to subsections (2) and (3), the public shall, as from the day **A1.4.012** after the cut-off date, have a right of way on horseback or leading a horse over any way which—

(a) was immediately before 1st January 1949 either a footpath or a bridleway, and

(b) is, throughout the period beginning with the commencement of this section and ending with the cut-off date,

a footpath which is shown in a definitive map and statement as a bridleway.

(2) Subsection (1) has effect subject to the operation of any enactment or instrument (whether coming into operation before or after the cut-off date), and to the effect of any event otherwise within section 53(3)(a) of the 1981 Act, whereby a highway is authorised to be stopped up, diverted, widened or extended; and subsection (1) applies accordingly to any way as so diverted, widened or extended.

(3) Subsection (1) does not apply in relation to any way which is, or is part of, a footpath any part of which is in an area which, immediately before 1st April 1965, formed part of the administrative county of London.

(4) Any right of way over a way by virtue of subsection (1) is subject to any condition or limitation to which the public right of way on foot over that way was subject on the cut-off date.

(5) Where—

(a) by virtue of regulations under section 56(2) an order under Part III of the 1981 Act takes effect after the cut-off date in relation to any footpath which, at the cut-off date was shown in a definitive map and statement as a bridleway,

(b) the regulations do not prevent subsection (1) from having effect after the cut-off date in relation to that footpath, and

(c) if the order had taken effect before that date, that footpath would not have fallen within subsection (1),

all rights over that way which exist only by virtue of subsection (1) shall be extinguished when the order takes effect.

(6) In this section "cut-off date" has the meaning given in section 56.

56.—Cut-off date for extinguishment etc.

A1.4.013 (1) The cut-off date for the purposes of sections 53 and 55 is, subject to regulations under subsection (2), 1st January 2026.

(2) The Secretary of State (as respects England) or the National Assembly for Wales (as respects Wales) may make regulations—

(a) substituting as the cut-off date for the purposes of those sections a date later than the date specified in subsection (1) or for the time being substituted under this paragraph;

(b) containing such transitional provisions or savings as appear to the Secretary of State or the National Assembly for Wales (as the case may be) to be necessary or expedient in connection with the operation of those sections, including in particular their operation in relation to any way as respects which—

(i) on the cut-off date an application for an order under section 53(2) of the 1981 Act is pending,

(ii) on that date an order under Part III of that Act has been made but not confirmed, or

(iii) after that date such an order or any provision of such an order is to any extent quashed.

(3) Regulations under subsection (2)(a)—

(a) may specify different dates for different areas; but

(b) may not specify a date later than 1st January 2031, except as respects an area within subsection (4).

(4) An area is within this subsection if it is in—

(a) the Isles of Scilly, or

(b) an area which, at any time before the repeal by section 73 of the 1981 Act of sections 27 to 34 of the National Parks and Access to the Countryside Act 1949—

(i) was excluded from the operation of those sections by virtue of any provision of the 1949 Act, or

(ii) would have been so excluded but for a resolution having effect under section 35(2) of that Act.

(5) Where by virtue of regulations under subsection (2) there are different cut-off dates for areas into which different parts of any highway extend, the cut-off date in relation to that highway is the later or latest of those dates.

(6) Regulations under this section shall be made by statutory instrument, and a statutory instrument containing such regulations made by the Secretary of State shall be subject to annulment in pursuance of a resolution of either House of Parliament.

57.—Creation, stopping up and diversion of highways

The Highways Act 1980 (in this Act referred to as "the 1980 Act") has **A1.4.014** effect subject to the amendments in Part I of Schedule 6 (which relate to the creation, stopping up and diversion of highways); and Part II of that Schedule (which contains consequential amendments of other Acts) has effect.

58.—Application for path creation order for purposes of Part I

(1) An application for the making of a public path creation order under **A1.4.015** section 26(2) of the 1980 Act may be made–

(a) by Natural England to the Secretary of State, or

(b) for the purpose of enabling the public to obtain access to any access land (within the meaning of Part 1) or of facilitating such access, by the Countryside Council for Wales to the National Assembly for Wales.

(2) Before making a request under subsection (1), the body making the request shall have regard to any rights of way improvement plan prepared by any local highway authority whose area includes land over which the proposed footpath or bridleway would be created.

59.—Effect of Part I on powers to stop up or divert highways

A1.4.016   (1) This section applies to any power to stop up or divert a highway of any description or to make or confirm an order authorising the stopping up or diversion of a highway of any description; and in the following provisions of this section—

(a) "the relevant authority" means the person exercising the power, and

(b) "the existing highway" means the highway to be stopped up or diverted.

(2) Where the relevant authority is required (expressly or by implication) to consider—

(a) whether the existing highway is unnecessary, or is needed for public use,

(b) whether an alternative highway should be provided, or

(c) whether any public right of way should be reserved,

the relevant authority, in considering that question, is not to regard the fact that any land is access land in respect of which the right conferred by section 2(1) is exercisable as reducing the need for the existing highway, for the provision of an alternative highway or for the reservation of a public right of way.

(3) Where—

(a) the existing highway is situated on, or in the vicinity of, any access land, and

(b) the relevant authority is required (expressly or by implication) to consider the extent (if any) to which the existing highway would, apart from the exercise of the power, be likely to be used by the public,

the relevant authority, in considering that question, is to have regard, in particular, to the extent to which the highway would be likely to be used by the public at any time when the right conferred by section 2(1) is not exercisable in relation to the access land.

(4) In this section "access land" has the same meaning as in Part I.

LAND REGISTRATION ACT 2002 c. 9

PART 1

PRELIMINARY

1.—Register of title

(1) There is to continue to be a register of title kept by the registrar. **A1.5.001**

(2) Rules may make provision about how the register is to be kept and may, in particular, make provision about—

(a) the information to be included in the register,

(b) the form in which information included in the register is to be kept, and

(c) the arrangement of that information.

2.—Scope of title registration

This Act makes provision about the registration of title to— **A1.5.002**

(a) unregistered legal estates which are interests of any of the following kinds—

  (i)   an estate in land,
  (ii) a rentcharge,
  (iii) a franchise,
  (iv) a profit a prendre in gross, and
  (v)   any other interest or charge which subsists for the benefit of, or is a charge on, an interest the title to which is registered; and

(b) interests capable of subsisting at law which are created by a disposition of an interest the title to which is registered.

PART 2

FIRST REGISTRATION OF TITLE

CHAPTER 1

FIRST REGISTRATION

Voluntary registration

3.—When title may be registered

A1.5.003   (1) This section applies to any unregistered legal estate which is an interest of any of the following kinds—

   (a)   an estate in land,

   (b)   a rentcharge,

   (c)   a franchise, and

   (d)   a profit a prendre in gross.

(2) Subject to the following provisions, a person may apply to the registrar to be registered as the proprietor of an unregistered legal estate to which this section applies if—

   (a)   the estate is vested in him, or

   (b)   he is entitled to require the estate to be vested in him.

(3) Subject to subsection (4), an application under subsection (2) in respect of a leasehold estate may only be made if the estate was granted for a term of which more than seven years are unexpired.

(4) In the case of an estate in land, subsection (3) does not apply if the right to possession under the lease is discontinuous.

(5) A person may not make an application under subsection (2)(a) in respect of a leasehold estate vested in him as a mortgagee where there is a subsisting right of redemption.

(6) A person may not make an application under subsection (2)(b) if his entitlement is as a person who has contracted to buy under a contract.

(7) If a person holds in the same right both—

   (a)   a lease in possession, and

   (b)   a lease to take effect in possession on, or within a month of, the end of the lease in possession, then, to the extent that they relate to the same land, they are to be treated for the purposes of this section as creating one continuous term.

Compulsory registration

4.—When title must be registered

(1) The requirement of registration applies on the occurrence of any of **A1.5.004** the following events—

(a) the transfer of a qualifying estate—

    (i)   for valuable or other consideration, by way of gift or in pursuance of an order of any court, . . .

    (ii) by means of an assent (including a vesting assent); or

    (iii) giving effect to a partition of land subject to a trust of land;

(aa) the transfer of a qualifying estate—

    (i)   by a deed that appoints, or by virtue of section 83 of the Charities Act 1993 has effect as if it appointed, a new trustee or is made in consequence of the appointment of a new trustee, or

    (ii) by a vesting order under section 44 of the Trustee Act 1925 that is consequential on the appointment of a new trustee;

(b) the transfer of an unregistered legal estate in land in circumstances where section 171A of the Housing Act 1985 (c. 68) applies (disposal by landlord which leads to a person no longer being a secure tenant);

(c) the grant out of a qualifying estate of an estate in land—

    (i)   for a term of years absolute of more than seven years from the date of the grant, and

    (ii) for valuable or other consideration, by way of gift or in pursuance of an order of any court;

(d) the grant out of a qualifying estate of an estate in land for a term of years absolute to take effect in possession after the end of the period of three months beginning with the date of the grant;

(e) the grant of a lease in pursuance of Part 5 of the Housing Act 1985 (the right to buy) out of an unregistered legal estate in land;

(f) the grant of a lease out of an unregistered legal estate in land in such circumstances as are mentioned in paragraph (b);

(g) the creation of a protected first legal mortgage of a qualifying estate.

(2) For the purposes of subsection (1), a qualifying estate is an unregistered legal estate which is—

(a) a freehold estate in land, or

(b) a leasehold estate in land for a term which, at the time of the transfer, grant or creation, has more than seven years to run.

(3) In subsection (1)(a), the reference to transfer does not include transfer by operation of law.

(4) Subsection (1)(a) does not apply to—

(a) the assignment of a mortgage term, or

(b) the assignment or surrender of a lease to the owner of the immediate reversion where the term is to merge in that reversion.

(5) Subsection (1)(c) does not apply to the grant of an estate to a person as a mortgagee.

(6) For the purposes of subsection (1)(a) and (c), if the estate transferred or granted has a negative value, it is to be regarded as transferred or granted for valuable or other consideration.

(7) In subsection (1)(a) and (c), references to transfer or grant by way of gift include transfer or grant for the purpose of—

(a) constituting a trust under which the settlor does not retain the whole of the beneficial interest, or

(b) uniting the bare legal title and the beneficial interest in property held under a trust under which the settlor did not, on constitution, retain the whole of the beneficial interest.

(8) For the purposes of subsection (1)(g)—

(a) a legal mortgage is protected if it takes effect on its creation as a mortgage to be protected by the deposit of documents relating to the mortgaged estate, and

(b) a first legal mortgage is one which, on its creation, ranks in priority ahead of any other mortgages then affecting the mortgaged estate.

(9) In this section—

"land" does not include mines and minerals held apart from the surface;

"vesting assent" has the same meaning as in the Settled Land Act 1925 (c. 18).

5.—Power to extend section 4

(1) The Lord Chancellor may by order—   A1.5.005

  (a) amend section 4 so as to add to the events on the occurrence of which the requirement of registration applies such relevant event as he may specify in the order, and

  (b) make such consequential amendments of any provision of, or having effect under, any Act as he thinks appropriate.

(2) For the purposes of subsection (1)(a), a relevant event is an event relating to an unregistered legal estate which is an interest of any of the following kinds—

  (a) an estate in land,

  (b) a rentcharge,

  (c) a franchise, and

  (d) a profit a prendre in gross.

(3) The power conferred by subsection (1) may not be exercised so as to require the title to an estate granted to a person as a mortgagee to be registered.

(4) Before making an order under this section the Lord Chancellor must consult such persons as he considers appropriate.

6.—Duty to apply for registration of title

(1) If the requirement of registration applies, the responsible estate A1.5.006
owner, or his successor in title, must, before the end of the period for registration, apply to the registrar to be registered as the proprietor of the registrable estate.

(2) If the requirement of registration applies because of section 4(1)(g)—

  (a) the registrable estate is the estate charged by the mortgage, and

  (b) the responsible estate owner is the owner of that estate.

(3) If the requirement of registration applies otherwise than because of section 4(1)(g)—

    (a) the registrable estate is the estate which is transferred or granted, and

    (b) the responsible estate owner is the transferee or grantee of that estate.

(4) The period for registration is 2 months beginning with the date on which the relevant event occurs, or such longer period as the registrar may provide under subsection (5).

(5) If on the application of any interested person the registrar is satisfied that there is good reason for doing so, he may by order provide that the period for registration ends on such later date as he may specify in the order.

(6) Rules may make provision enabling the mortgagee under any mortgage falling within section 4(1)(g) to require the estate charged by the mortgage to be registered whether or not the mortgagor consents.

7.—Effect of non-compliance with section 6

A1.5.007   (1) If the requirement of registration is not complied with, the transfer, grant or creation becomes void as regards the transfer, grant or creation of a legal estate.

(2) On the application of subsection (1)—

    (a) in a case falling within section 4(1)(a) or (b) , the title to the legal estate reverts to the transferor who holds it on a bare trust for the transferee, . . .

    (aa) in a case fallling within section 4(1)(aa), the title to the legal estate reverts to the person in whom it was vested immediately before the transfer, and

    (b) in a case falling within section 4(1)(c) to (g), the grant or creation has effect as a contract made for valuable consideration to grant or create the legal estate concerned.

(3) If an order under section 6(5) is made in a case where subsection (1) has already applied, that application of the subsection is to be treated as not having occurred.

(4) The possibility of reverter under subsection (1) is to be disregarded for the purposes of determining whether a fee simple is a fee simple absolute.

8.—Liability for making good void transfers etc

If a legal estate is retransferred, regranted or recreated because of a **A1.5.008** failure to comply with the requirement of registration, the transferee, grantee or, as the case may be, the mortgagor—

(a) is liable to the other party for all the proper costs of an incidental to the retransfer, regrant or recreation of the legal estate, and

(b) is liable to indemnify the other party in respect of any other liability reasonably incurred by him because of the failure to comply with the requirement of registration.

Classes of title

9.—Titles to freehold estates

(1) In the case of an application for registration under this Chapter of a **A1.5.009** freehold estate, the classes of title with which the applicant may be registered as proprietor are—

(a) absolute title,

(b) qualified title, and

(c) possessory title;

and the following provisions deal with when each of the classes of title is available.

(2) A person may be registered with absolute title if the registrar is of the opinion that the person's title to the estate is such as a willing buyer could properly be advised by a competent professional adviser to accept.

(3) In applying subsection (2), the registrar may disregard the fact that a person's title appears to him to be open to objection if he is of the opinion that the defect will not cause the holding under the title to be disturbed.

(4) A person may be registered with qualified title if the registrar is of the opinion that the person's title to the estate has been established only for a limited period or subject to certain reservations which cannot be disregarded under subsection (3).

(5) A person may be registered with possessory title if the registrar is of the opinion—

(a) that the person is in actual possession of the land, or in receipt of the rents and profits of the land, by virtue of the estate, and

    (b) that there is no other class of title with which he may be registered.

10.—Titles to leasehold estates

A1.5.010   (1) In the case of an application for registration under this Chapter of a leasehold estate, the classes of title with which the applicant may be registered as proprietor are—

    (a) absolute title,

    (b) good leasehold title,

    (c) qualified title, and

    (d) possessory title;

and the following provisions deal with when each of the classes of title is available.

    (2) A person may be registered with absolute title if—

    (a) the registrar is of the opinion that the person's title to the estate is such as a willing buyer could properly be advised by a competent professional adviser to accept, and

    (b) the registrar approves the lessor's title to grant the lease.

    (3) A person may be registered with good leasehold title if the registrar is of the opinion that the person's title to the estate is such as a willing buyer could properly be advised by a competent professional adviser to accept.

    (4) In applying subsection (2) or (3), the registrar may disregard the fact that a person's title appears to him to be open to objection if he is of the opinion that the defect will not cause the holding under the title to be disturbed.

    (5) A person may be registered with qualified title if the registrar is of the opinion that the person's title to the estate, or the lessor's title to the reversion, has been established only for a limited period or subject to certain reservations which cannot be disregarded under subsection (4).

    (6) A person may be registered with possessory title if the registrar is of the opinion—

    (a) that the person is in actual possession of the land, or in receipt of the rents and profits of the land, by virtue of the estate, and

    (b) that there is no other class of title with which he may be registered.

Effect of first registration

11.—Freehold estates

(1) This section is concerned with the registration of a person under **A1.5.011** this Chapter as the proprietor of a freehold estate.

(2) Registration with absolute title has the effect described in subsections (3) to (5).

(3) The estate is vested in the proprietor together with all interests subsisting for the benefit of the estate.

(4) The estate is vested in the proprietor subject only to the following interests affecting the estate at the time of registration—

(a) interests which are the subject of an entry in the register in relation to the estate,

(b) unregistered interests which fall within any of the paragraphs of Schedule 1, and

(c) interests acquired under the Limitation Act 1980 (c. 58) of which the proprietor has notice.

(5) If the proprietor is not entitled to the estate for his own benefit, or not entitled solely for his own benefit, then, as between himself and the persons beneficially entitled to the estate, the estate is vested in him subject to such of their interests as he has notice of.

(6) Registration with qualified title has the same effect as registration with absolute title, except that it does not affect the enforcement of any estate, right or interest which appears from the register to be excepted from the effect of registration.

(7) Registration with possessory title has the same effect as registration with absolute title, except that it does not affect the enforcement of any estate, right or interest adverse to, or in derogation of, the proprietor's title subsisting at the time of registration or then capable of arising.

12.—Leasehold estates

(1) This section is concerned with the registration of a person under **A1.5.012** this Chapter as the proprietor of a leasehold estate.

(2) Registration with absolute title has the effect described in subsections (3) to (5).

(3) The estate is vested in the proprietor together with all interests subsisting for the benefit of the estate.

(4) The estate is vested subject only to the following interests affecting the estate at the time of registration—

(a) implied and express covenants, obligations and liabilities incident to the estate,

(b) interests which are the subject of an entry in the register in relation to the estate,

(c) unregistered interests which fall within any of the paragraphs of Schedule 1, and

(d) interests acquired under the Limitation Act 1980 (c. 58) of which the proprietor has notice.

(5) If the proprietor is not entitled to the estate for his own benefit, or not entitled solely for his own benefit, then, as between himself and the persons beneficially entitled to the estate, the estate is vested in him subject to such of their interests as he has notice of.

(6) Registration with good leasehold title has the same effect as registration with absolute title, except that it does not affect the enforcement of any estate, right or interest affecting, or in derogation of, the title of the lessor to grant the lease.

(7) Registration with qualified title has the same effect as registration with absolute title except that it does not affect the enforcement of any estate, right or interest which appears from the register to be excepted from the effect of registration.

(8) Registration with possessory title has the same effect as registration with absolute title, except that it does not affect the enforcement of any estate, right or interest adverse to, or in derogation of, the proprietor's title subsisting at the time of registration or then capable of arising.

Dependent estates

13.—Appurtenant rights and charges

A1.5.013   Rules may—

(a) make provision for the registration of the proprietor of a registered estate as the proprietor of an unregistered legal estate which subsists for the benefit of the registered estate;

(b) make provision for the registration of a person as the proprietor of an unregistered legal estate which is a charge on a registered estate.

Supplementary

14.—Rules about first registration

Rules may— A1.5.014

(a) make provision about the making of applications for registration under this Chapter;

(b) make provision about the functions of the registrar following the making of such an application, including provision about—

    (i) the examination of title, and

    (ii) the entries to be made in the register where such an application is approved;

(c) make provision about the effect of any entry made in the register in pursuance of such an application.

CHAPTER 2

Cautions Against First Registration

15.—Right to lodge

(1) Subject to subsection (3), a person may lodge a caution against the A1.5.015
registration of title to an unregistered legal estate if he claims to be—

(a) the owner of a qualifying estate, or

(b) entitled to an interest affecting a qualifying estate.

(2) For the purposes of subsection (1), a qualifying estate is a legal estate which—

(a) relates to land to which the caution relates, and

(b) is an interest of any of the following kinds—

    (i) an estate in land,

    (ii) a rentcharge,

    (iii) a franchise, and

    (iv) a profit a prendre in gross.

(3) No caution may be lodged under subsection (1)—

(a) in the case of paragraph (a), by virtue of ownership of—

> > (i) a freehold estate in land, or
> > (ii) a leasehold estate in land granted for a term of which more than seven years are unexpired;
> >
> > (b) in the case of paragraph (b), by virtue of entitlement to such a leasehold estate as is mentioned in paragraph (a)(ii) of this subsection.

(4) The right under subsection (1) is exercisable by application to the registrar.

16.—Effect

A1.5.016 (1) Where an application for registration under this Part relates to a legal estate which is the subject of a caution against first registration, the registrar must give the cautioner notice of the application and of his right to object to it.

(2) The registrar may not determine an application to which subsection (1) applies before the end of such period as rules may provide, unless the cautioner has exercised his right to object to the application or given the registrar notice that he does not intend to do so.

(3) Except as provided by this section, a caution against first registration has no effect and, in particular, has no effect on the validity or priority of any interest of the cautioner in the legal estate to which the caution relates.

(4) For the purposes of subsection (1), notice given by a person acting on behalf of an applicant for registration under this Part is to be treated as given by the registrar if—

> (a) the person is of a description provided by rules, and

> (b) notice is given in such circumstances as rules may provide.

17.—Withdrawal

A1.5.017 The cautioner may withdraw a caution against first registration by application to the registrar.

18.—Cancellation

A1.5.018 (1) A person may apply to the registrar for cancellation of a caution against first registration if he is—

> (a) the owner of the legal estate to which the caution relates, or

> (b) a person of such other description as rules may provide.

(2) Subject to rules, no application under subsection (1)(a) may be made by a person who—

(a) consented in such manner as rules may provide to the lodging of the caution, or

(b) derives title to the legal estate by operation of law from a person who did so.

(3) Where an application is made under subsection (1), the registrar must give the cautioner notice of the application and of the effect of subsection (4).

(4) If the cautioner does not exercise his right to object to the application before the end of such period as rules may provide, the registrar must cancel the caution.

19.—Cautions register

(1) The registrar must keep a register of cautions against first **A1.5.019** registration.

(2) Rules may make provision about how the cautions register is to be kept and may, in particular, make provision about—

(a) the information to be included in the register,

(b) the form in which information included in the register is to be kept, and

(c) the arrangement of that information.

20.—Alteration of register by court

(1) The court may make an order for alteration of the cautions register **A1.5.020** for the purpose of—

(a) correcting a mistake, or

(b) bringing the register up to date.

(2) An order under subsection (1) has effect when served on the registrar to impose a duty on him to give effect to it.

(3) Rules may make provision about—

(a) the circumstances in which there is a duty to exercise the power under subsection (1),

(b) the form of an order under that subsection, and

(c) service of such an order.

21.—Alteration of register by registrar

A1.5.021 (1) The registrar may alter the cautions register for the purpose of—

> (a) correcting a mistake, or

> (b) bringing the register up to date.

(2) Rules may make provision about—

> (a) the circumstances in which there is a duty to exercise the power under subsection (1),

> (b) how the cautions register is to be altered in exercise of that power,

> (c) applications for the exercise of that power, and

> (d) procedure in relation to the exercise of that power, whether on application or otherwise.

(3) Where an alteration is made under this section, the registrar may pay such amount as he thinks fit in respect of any costs reasonably incurred by a person in connection with the alteration.

22.—Supplementary

A1.5.022 In this Chapter, "the cautioner", in relation to a caution against first registration, means the person who lodged the caution, or such other person as rules may provide.

PART 3

DISPOSITIONS OF REGISTERED LAND

Powers of disposition

23.—Owner's powers

A1.5.023 (1) Owner's powers in relation to a registered estate consist of—

> (a) power to make a disposition of any kind permitted by the general law in relation to an interest of that description, other than a mortgage by demise or sub-demise, and

> (b) power to charge the estate at law with the payment of money.

(2) Owner's powers in relation to a registered charge consist of—

    (a) power to make a disposition of any kind permitted by the general law in relation to an interest of that description, other than a legal sub-mortgage, and

    (b) power to charge at law with the payment of money indebtedness secured by the registered charge.

(3) In subsection (2)(a), "legal sub-mortgage" means—(a) a transfer by way of mortgage,

    (b) a sub-mortgage by sub-demise, and

    (c) a charge by way of legal mortgage.

24.—Right to exercise owner's powers

A person is entitled to exercise owner's powers in relation to a regis- **A1.5.024** tered estate or charge if he is—

    (a) the registered proprietor, or

    (b) entitled to be registered as the proprietor.

25.—Mode of exercise

(1) A registrable disposition of a registered estate or charge only has **A1.5.025** effect if it complies with such requirements as to form and content as rules may provide.

(2) Rules may apply subsection (1) to any other kind of disposition which depends for its effect on registration.

26.—Protection of disponees

(1) Subject to subsection (2), a person's right to exercise owner's **A1.5.026** powers in relation to a registered estate or charge is to be taken to be free from any limitation affecting the validity of a disposition.

(2) Subsection (1) does not apply to a limitation—

    (a) reflected by an entry in the register, or

    (b) imposed by, or under, this Act.

(3) This section has effect only for the purpose of preventing the title of a disponee being questioned (and so does not affect the lawfulness of a disposition).

Registrable dispositions

27.—Dispositions required to be registered

A1.5.027   (1) If a disposition of a registered estate or registered charge is required to be completed by registration, it does not operate at law until the relevant registration requirements are met.

(2) In the case of a registered estate, the following are the dispositions which are required to be completed by registration—

   (a)   a transfer,

   (b)   where the registered estate is an estate in land, the grant of a term of years absolute—

   (i)   for a term of more than seven years from the date of the grant,
   (ii)   to take effect in possession after the end of the period of three months beginning with the date of the grant,
   (iii) under which the right to possession is discontinuous,
   (iv)   in pursuance of Part 5 of the Housing Act 1985 (c. 68) (the right to buy), or
   (v)   in circumstances where section 171A of that Act applies (disposal by landlord which leads to a person no longer being a secure tenant),

   (c)   where the registered estate is a franchise or manor, the grant of a lease,

   (d)   the express grant or reservation of an interest of a kind falling within section 1(2)(a) of the Law of Property Act 1925 (c. 20), other than one which is capable of being registered under the Commons Registration Act 1965 (c. 64),

   (e)   the express grant or reservation of an interest of a kind falling within section 1(2)(b) or (e) of the Law of Property Act 1925, and

   (f)   the grant of a legal charge.

(3) In the case of a registered charge, the following are the dispositions which are required to be completed by registration—

   (a)   a transfer, and

   (b)   the grant of a sub-charge.

(4) Schedule 2 to this Act (which deals with the relevant registration requirements) has effect.

(5) This section applies to dispositions by operation of law as it applies to other dispositions, but with the exception of the following—

    (a) a transfer on the death or bankruptcy of an individual proprietor,

    (b) a transfer on the dissolution of a corporate proprietor, and

    (c) the creation of a legal charge which is a local land charge.

(6) Rules may make provision about applications to the registrar for the purpose of meeting registration requirements under this section.

(7) In subsection (2)(d), the reference to express grant does not include grant as a result of the operation of section 62 of the Law of Property Act 1925 (c. 20).

Effect of dispositions on priority

28.—Basic rule

(1) Except as provided by sections 29 and 30, the priority of an interest **A1.5.028** affecting a registered estate or charge is not affected by a disposition of the estate or charge.

(2) It makes no difference for the purposes of this section whether the interest or disposition is registered.

29.—Effect of registered dispositions: estates

(1) If a registrable disposition of a registered estate is made for valu- **A1.5.029** able consideration, completion of the disposition by registration has the effect of postponing to the interest under the disposition any interest affecting the estate immediately before the disposition whose priority is not protected at the time of registration.

(2) For the purposes of subsection (1), the priority of an interest is protected—

    (a) in any case, if the interest—

        (i) is a registered charge or the subject of a notice in the register,

        (ii) falls within any of the paragraphs of Schedule 3, or

        (iii) appears from the register to be excepted from the effect of registration, and

    (b) in the case of a disposition of a leasehold estate, if the burden of the interest is incident to the estate.

(3) Subsection (2)(a)(ii) does not apply to an interest which has been the subject of a notice in the register at any time since the coming into force of this section.

(4) Where the grant of a leasehold estate in land out of a registered estate does not involve a registrable disposition, this section has effect as if—

(a) the grant involved such a disposition, and

(b) the disposition were registered at the time of the grant.

30.—Effect of registered dispositions: charges

A1.5.030   (1) If a registrable disposition of a registered charge is made for valuable consideration, completion of the disposition by registration has the effect of postponing to the interest under the disposition any interest affecting the charge immediately before the disposition whose priority is not protected at the time of registration.

(2) For the purposes of subsection (1), the priority of an interest is protected—

(a) in any case, if the interest—

(i)   is a registered charge or the subject of a notice in the register,
(ii) falls within any of the paragraphs of Schedule 3, or
(iii) appears from the register to be excepted from the effect of registration, and

(b) in the case of a disposition of a charge which relates to a leasehold estate, if the burden of the interest is incident to the estate.

(3) Subsection (2)(a)(ii) does not apply to an interest which has been the subject of a notice in the register at any time since the coming into force of this section.

31.—Inland Revenue charges

A1.5.031   The effect of a disposition of a registered estate or charge on a charge under section 237 of the Inheritance Tax Act 1984 (c. 51) (charge for unpaid tax) is to be determined, not in accordance with sections 28 to 30 above, but in accordance with sections 237(6) and 238 of that Act (under which a purchaser in good faith for money or money's worth takes free from the charge in the absence of registration).

PART 4

NOTICES AND RESTRICTIONS

Notices

32.—Nature and effect

(1) A notice is an entry in the register in respect of the burden of an **A1.5.032**
interest affecting a registered estate or charge.

(2) The entry of a notice is to be made in relation to the registered estate
or charge affected by the interest concerned.

(3) The fact that an interest is the subject of a notice does not necessarily mean that the interest is valid, but does mean that the priority of
the interest, if valid, is protected for the purposes of sections 29 and 30.

33.—Excluded interests

No notice may be entered in the register in respect of any of the **A1.5.033**
following—

    (a) an interest under—

        (i) a trust of land, or
        (ii) a settlement under the Settled Land Act 1925 (c. 18),

    (b) a leasehold estate in land which—

        (i) is granted for a term of years of three years or less from the
           date of the grant, and
        (ii) is not required to be registered,

    (c) a restrictive covenant made between a lessor and lessee, so far as
        relating to the demised premises,

    (d) an interest which is capable of being registered under the
        Commons Registration Act 1965 (c. 64), and

    (e) an interest in any coal or coal mine, the rights attached to any
        such interest and the rights of any person under section 38, 49 or
        51 of the Coal Industry Act 1994 (c. 21).

34.—Entry on application

(1) A person who claims to be entitled to the benefit of an interest **A1.5.034**
affecting a registered estate or charge may, if the interest is not excluded
by section 33, apply to the registrar for the entry in the register of a notice
in respect of the interest.

(2) Subject to rules, an application under this section may be for—

    (a) an agreed notice, or

    (b) a unilateral notice.

(3) The registrar may only approve an application for an agreed notice if—

    (a) the applicant is the relevant registered proprietor, or a person entitled to be registered as such proprietor,

    (b) the relevant registered proprietor, or a person entitled to be registered as such proprietor, consents to the entry of the notice, or

    (c) the registrar is satisfied as to the validity of the applicant's claim.

(4) In subsection (3), references to the relevant registered proprietor are to the proprietor of the registered estate or charge affected by the interest to which the application relates.

35.—Unilateral notices

A1.5.035   (1) If the registrar enters a notice in the register in pursuance of an application under section 34(2)(b) ("a unilateral notice"), he must give notice of the entry to—

    (a) the proprietor of the registered estate or charge to which it relates, and

    (b) such other persons as rules may provide.

(2) A unilateral notice must—

    (a) indicate that it is such a notice, and

    (b) identify who is the beneficiary of the notice.

(3) The person shown in the register as the beneficiary of a unilateral notice, or such other person as rules may provide, may apply to the registrar for the removal of the notice from the register.

36.—Cancellation of unilateral notices

A1.5.036   (1) A person may apply to the registrar for the cancellation of a unilateral notice if he is—

(a) the registered proprietor of the estate or charge to which the notice relates, or

(b) a person entitled to be registered as the proprietor of that estate or charge.

(2) Where an application is made under subsection (1), the registrar must give the beneficiary of the notice notice of the application and of the effect of subsection (3).

(3) If the beneficiary of the notice does not exercise his right to object to the application before the end of such period as rules may provide, the registrar must cancel the notice.

(4) In this section—

"beneficiary", in relation to a unilateral notice, means the person shown in the register as the beneficiary of the notice, or such other person as rules may provide;

"unilateral notice" means a notice entered in the register in pursuance of an application under section 34(2)(b).

37.—Unregistered interests

(1) If it appears to the registrar that a registered estate is subject to an **A1.5.037** unregistered interest which—

(a) falls within any of the paragraphs of Schedule 1, and

(b) is not excluded by section 33,

he may enter a notice in the register in respect of the interest.

(2) The registrar must give notice of an entry under this section to such persons as rules may provide.

38.—Registrable dispositions

Where a person is entered in the register as the proprietor of an interest **A1.5.038** under a disposition falling within section 27(2)(b) to (e), the registrar must also enter a notice in the register in respect of that interest.

39.—Supplementary

Rules may make provision about the form and content of notices in the **A1.5.039** register.

Restrictions

40.—Nature

A1.5.040 (1) A restriction is an entry in the register regulating the circumstances in which a disposition of a registered estate or charge may be the subject of an entry in the register.

(2) A restriction may, in particular—

(a) prohibit the making of an entry in respect of any disposition, or a disposition of a kind specified in the restriction;

(b) prohibit the making of an entry—

(i) indefinitely,
(ii) for a period specified in the restriction, or
(iii) until the occurrence of an event so specified.

(3) Without prejudice to the generality of subsection (2)(b)(iii), the events which may be specified include—

(a) the giving of notice,

(b) the obtaining of consent, and

(c) the making of an order by the court or registrar.

(4) The entry of a restriction is to be made in relation to the registered estate or charge to which it relates.

41.—Effect

A1.5.041 (1) Where a restriction is entered in the register, no entry in respect of a disposition to which the restriction applies may be made in the register otherwise than in accordance with the terms of the restriction, subject to any order under subsection (2).

(2) The registrar may by order—

(a) disapply a restriction in relation to a disposition specified in the order or dispositions of a kind so specified, or

(b) provide that a restriction has effect, in relation to a disposition specified in the order or dispositions of a kind so specified, with modifications so specified.

(3) The power under subsection (2) is exercisable only on the application of a person who appears to the registrar to have a sufficient interest in the restriction.

42.—Power of registrar to enter

(1) The registrar may enter a restriction in the register if it appears to **A1.5.042** him that it is necessary or desirable to do so for the purpose of—

    (a) preventing invalidity or unlawfulness in relation to dispositions of a registered estate or charge,

    (b) securing that interests which are capable of being overreached on a disposition of a registered estate or charge are overreached, or

    (c) protecting a right or claim in relation to a registered estate or charge.

(2) No restriction may be entered under subsection (1)(c) for the purpose of protecting the priority of an interest which is, or could be, the subject of a notice.

(3) The registrar must give notice of any entry made under this section to the proprietor of the registered estate or charge concerned, except where the entry is made in pursuance of an application under section 43.

(4) For the purposes of subsection (1)(c), a person entitled to the benefit of a charging order relating to an interest under a trust shall be treated as having a right or claim in relation to the trust property.

43.—Applications

(1) A person may apply to the registrar for the entry of a restriction **A1.5.043** under section 42(1) if—

    (a) he is the relevant registered proprietor, or a person entitled to be registered as such proprietor,

    (b) the relevant registered proprietor, or a person entitled to be registered as such proprietor, consents to the application, or

    (c) he otherwise has a sufficient interest in the making of the entry.

(2) Rules may—

    (a) require the making of an application under subsection (1) in such circumstances, and by such person, as the rules may provide;

    (b) make provision about the form of consent for the purposes of subsection (1)(b);

    (c)   provide for classes of person to be regarded as included in subsection (1)(c);

    (d)   specify standard forms of restriction.

(3) If an application under subsection (1) is made for the entry of a restriction which is not in a form specified under subsection (2)(d), the registrar may only approve the application if it appears to him—

    (a)   that the terms of the proposed restriction are reasonable, and

    (b)   that applying the proposed restriction would—

        (i)   be straightforward, and
        (ii) not place an unreasonable burden on him.

(4) In subsection (1), references to the relevant registered proprietor are to the proprietor of the registered estate or charge to which the application relates.

44.—Obligatory restrictions

A1.5.044   (1) If the registrar enters two or more persons in the register as the proprietor of a registered estate in land, he must also enter in the register such restrictions as rules may provide for the purpose of securing that interests which are capable of being overreached on a disposition of the estate are overreached.

(2) Where under any enactment the registrar is required to enter a restriction without application, the form of the restriction shall be such as rules may provide.

45.—Notifiable applications

A1.5.045   (1) Where an application under section 43(1) is notifiable, the registrar must give notice of the application, and of the right to object to it, to—

    (a)   the proprietor of the registered estate or charge to which it relates, and

    (b)   such other persons as rules may provide.

(2) The registrar may not determine an application to which subsection (1) applies before the end of such period as rules may provide, unless the person, or each of the persons, notified under that subsection has exercised his right to object to the application or given the registrar notice that he does not intend to do so.

(3) For the purposes of this section, an application under section 43(1) is notifiable unless it is—

(a) made by or with the consent of the proprietor of the registered estate or charge to which the application relates, or a person entitled to be registered as such proprietor,

(b) made in pursuance of rules under section 43(2)(a), or

(c) an application for the entry of a restriction reflecting a limitation under an order of the court or registrar, or an undertaking given in place of such an order.

46.—Power of court to order entry

(1) If it appears to the court that it is necessary or desirable to do so for the purpose of protecting a right or claim in relation to a registered estate or charge, it may make an order requiring the registrar to enter a restriction in the register. **A1.5.046**

(2) No order under this section may be made for the purpose of protecting the priority of an interest which is, or could be, the subject of a notice.

(3) The court may include in an order under this section a direction that an entry made in pursuance of the order is to have overriding priority.

(4) If an order under this section includes a direction under subsection (3), the registrar must make such entry in the register as rules may provide.

(5) The court may make the exercise of its power under subsection (3) subject to such terms and conditions as it thinks fit.

47.—Withdrawal

A person may apply to the registrar for the withdrawal of a restriction if— **A1.5.047**

(a) the restriction was entered in such circumstances as rules may provide, and

(b) he is of such a description as rules may provide.

PART 6

REGISTRATION: GENERAL

Registration as proprietor

58.—Conclusiveness

A1.5.048   (1) If, on the entry of a person in the register as the proprietor of a legal estate, the legal estate would not otherwise be vested in him, it shall be deemed to be vested in him as a result of the registration.

(2) Subsection (1) does not apply where the entry is made in pursuance of a registrable disposition in relation to which some other registration requirement remains to be met.

59.—Dependent estates

A1.5.049   (1) The entry of a person in the register as the proprietor of a legal estate which subsists for the benefit of a registered estate must be made in relation to the registered estate.

(2) The entry of a person in the register as the proprietor of a charge on a registered estate must be made in relation to that estate.

(3) The entry of a person in the register as the proprietor of a sub-charge on a registered charge must be made in relation to that charge.

Boundaries

60.—Boundaries

A1.5.050   (1) The boundary of a registered estate as shown for the purposes of the register is a general boundary, unless shown as determined under this section.

(2) A general boundary does not determine the exact line of the boundary.

(3) Rules may make provision enabling or requiring the exact line of the boundary of a registered estate to be determined and may, in particular, make provision about—

(a) the circumstances in which the exact line of a boundary may or must be determined,

(b) how the exact line of a boundary may be determined,

(c) procedure in relation to applications for determination, and

(d) the recording of the fact of determination in the register or the index maintained under section 68.

(4) Rules under this section must provide for applications for determination to be made to the registrar.

61.—Accretion and diluvion

(1) The fact that a registered estate in land is shown in the register as **A1.5.051** having a particular boundary does not affect the operation of accretion or diluvion.

(2) An agreement about the operation of accretion or diluvion in relation to a registered estate in land has effect only if registered in accordance with rules.

Quality of title

62.—Power to upgrade title

(1) Where the title to a freehold estate is entered in the register as **A1.5.052** possessory or qualified, the registrar may enter it as absolute if he is satisfied as to the title to the estate.

(2) Where the title to a leasehold estate is entered in the register as good leasehold, the registrar may enter it as absolute if he is satisfied as to the superior title.

(3) Where the title to a leasehold estate is entered in the register as possessory or qualified the registrar may—

  (a) enter it as good leasehold if he is satisfied as to the title to the estate, and

  (b) enter it as absolute if he is satisfied both as to the title to the estate and as to the superior title.

(4) Where the title to a freehold estate in land has been entered in the register as possessory for at least twelve years, the registrar may enter it as absolute if he is satisfied that the proprietor is in possession of the land.

(5) Where the title to a leasehold estate in land has been entered in the register as possessory for at least twelve years, the registrar may enter it as good leasehold if he is satisfied that the proprietor is in possession of the land.

(6) None of the powers under subsections (1) to (5) is exercisable if there is outstanding any claim adverse to the title of the registered proprietor which is made by virtue of an estate, right or interest whose enforceability is preserved by virtue of the existing entry about the class of title.

(7) The only persons who may apply to the registrar for the exercise of any of the powers under subsections (1) to (5) are—

(a) the proprietor of the estate to which the application relates,

(b) a person entitled to be registered as the proprietor of that estate,

(c) the proprietor of a registered charge affecting that estate, and

(d) a person interested in a registered estate which derives from that estate.

(8) In determining for the purposes of this section whether he is satisfied as to any title, the registrar is to apply the same standards as those which apply under section 9 or 10 to first registration of title.

(9) The Lord Chancellor may by order amend subsection (4) or (5) by substituting for the number of years for the time being specified in that subsection such number of years as the order may provide.

63.—Effect of upgrading title

A1.5.053   (1) On the title to a registered freehold or leasehold estate being entered under section 62 as absolute, the proprietor ceases to hold the estate subject to any estate, right or interest whose enforceability was preserved by virtue of the previous entry about the class of title.

(2) Subsection (1) also applies on the title to a registered leasehold estate being entered under section 62 as good leasehold, except that the entry does not affect or prejudice the enforcement of any estate, right or interest affecting, or in derogation of, the title of the lessor to grant the lease.

64.—Use of register to record defects in title

A1.5.054   (1) If it appears to the registrar that a right to determine a registered estate in land is exercisable, he may enter the fact in the register.

(2) Rules may make provision about entries under subsection (1) and may, in particular, make provision about—

(a) the circumstances in which there is a duty to exercise the power conferred by that subsection,

(b) how entries under that subsection are to be made, and

(c) the removal of such entries.

65.—Alteration of register

A1.5.055   Schedule 4 (which makes provision about alteration of the register) has effect.

Information etc.

66.—Inspection of the registers etc

(1) Any person may inspect and make copies of, or of any part of— **A1.5.056**

    (a) the register of title,

    (b) any document kept by the registrar which is referred to in the register of title,

    (c) any other document kept by the registrar which relates to an application to him, or

    (d) the register of cautions against first registration.

(2) The right under subsection (1) is subject to rules which may, in particular—

    (a) provide for exceptions to the right, and

    (b) impose conditions on its exercise, including conditions requiring the payment of fees.

67.—Official copies of the registers etc

(1) An official copy of, or of a part of— **A1.5.057**

    (a) the register of title,

    (b) any document which is referred to in the register of title and kept by the registrar,

    (c) any other document kept by the registrar which relates to an application to him, or

    (d) the register of cautions against first registration,

is admissible in evidence to the same extent as the original.

(2) A person who relies on an official copy in which there is a mistake is not liable for loss suffered by another by reason of the mistake.

(3) Rules may make provision for the issue of official copies and may, in particular, make provision about—

    (a) the form of official copies,

    (b) who may issue official copies,

    (c) applications for official copies, and

(d) the conditions to be met by applicants for official copies, including conditions requiring the payment of fees.

68.—Index

A1.5.058 (1) The registrar must keep an index for the purpose of enabling the following matters to be ascertained in relation to any parcel of land—

    (a) whether any registered estate relates to the land,

    (b) how any registered estate which relates to the land is identified for the purposes of the register,

    (c) whether the land is affected by any, and, if so what, caution against first registration, and

    (d) such other matters as rules may provide.

(2) Rules may—

    (a) make provision about how the index is to be kept and may, in particular, make provision about—

        (i) the information to be included in the index,
        (ii) the form in which information included in the index is to be kept, and
        (iii) the arrangement of that information;

    (b) make provision about official searches of the index.

69.—Historical information

A1.5.059 (1) The registrar may on application provide information about the history of a registered title.

(2) Rules may make provision about applications for the exercise of the power conferred by subsection (1).

(3) The registrar may—

    (a) arrange for the provision of information about the history of registered titles, and

    (b) authorise anyone who has the function of providing information under paragraph (a) to have access on such terms as the registrar thinks fit to any relevant information kept by him.

70.—Official searches

Rules may make provision for official searches of the register, including **A1.5.060** searches of pending applications for first registration, and may, in particular, make provision about—

    (a) the form of applications for searches,

    (b) the manner in which such applications may be made,

    (c) the form of official search certificates, and

    (d) the manner in which such certificates may be issued.

Applications

71.—Duty to disclose unregistered interests

Where rules so provide— **A1.5.061**

    (a) a person applying for registration under Chapter 1 of Part 2 must provide to the registrar such information as the rules may provide about any interest affecting the estate to which the application relates which—

        (i)   falls within any of the paragraphs of Schedule 1, and
        (ii) is of a description specified by the rules;

    (b) a person applying to register a registrable disposition of a registered estate must provide to the registrar such information as the rules may provide about any unregistered interest affecting the estate which—

        (i)   falls within any of the paragraphs of Schedule 3, and
        (ii) is of description specified by the rules.

72.—Priority protection

(1) For the purposes of this section, an application for an entry in the **A1.5.062** register is protected if—

    (a) it is one to which a priority period relates, and

    (b) it is made before the end of that period.

(2) Where an application for an entry in the register is protected, any entry made in the register during the priority period relating to the application is postponed to any entry made in pursuance of it.

(3) Subsection (2) does not apply if—

    (a) the earlier entry was made in pursuance of a protected application, and

    (b) the priority period relating to that application ranks ahead of the one relating to the application for the other entry.

(4) Subsection (2) does not apply if the earlier entry is one to which a direction under section 46(3) applies.

(5) The registrar may defer dealing with an application for an entry in the register if it appears to him that subsection (2) might apply to the entry were he to make it.

(6) Rules may—

    (a) make provision for priority periods in connection with—

        (i)   official searches of the register, including searches of pending applications for first registration, or
        (ii) the noting in the register of a contract for the making of a registrable disposition of a registered estate or charge;

    (b) make provision for the keeping of records in relation to priority periods and the inspection of such records.

(7) Rules under subsection (6)(a) may, in particular, make provision about—

    (a) the commencement and length of a priority period,

    (b) the applications for registration to which such a period relates,

    (c) the order in which competing priority periods rank, and

    (d) the application of subsections (2) and (3) in cases where more than one priority period relates to the same application.

73.—Objections

A1.5.063   (1) Subject to subsections (2) and (3), anyone may object to an application to the registrar.

(2) In the case of an application under section 18, only the person who lodged the caution to which the application relates, or such other person as rules may provide, may object.

(3) In the case of an application under section 36, only the person shown in the register as the beneficiary of the notice to which the application relates, or such other person as rules may provide, may object.

(4) The right to object under this section is subject to rules.

(5) Where an objection is made under this section, the registrar—

    (a) must give notice of the objection to the applicant, and

    (b) may not determine the application until the objection has been disposed of.

(6) Subsection (5) does not apply if the objection is one which the registrar is satisfied is groundless.

(7) If it is not possible to dispose by agreement of an objection to which subsection (5) applies, the registrar must refer the matter to the adjudicator.

(8) Rules may make provision about references under subsection (7).

74.—Effective date of registration

An entry made in the register in pursuance of—   **A1.5.064**

    (a) an application for registration of an unregistered legal estate, or

    (b) an application for registration in relation to a disposition required to be completed by registration,

has effect from the time of the making of the application.

Proceedings before the registrar

75.—Production of documents

(1) The registrar may require a person to produce a document for the **A1.5.065** purposes of proceedings before him.

(2) The power under subsection (1) is subject to rules.

(3) A requirement under subsection (1) shall be enforceable as an order of the court.

(4) A person aggrieved by a requirement under subsection (1) may appeal to a county court, which may make any order which appears appropriate.

76.—Costs

(1) The registrar may make orders about costs in relation to proceed- **A1.5.066** ings before him.

(2) The power under subsection (1) is subject to rules which may, in particular, make provision about—

(a) who may be required to pay costs,

(b) whose costs a person may be required to pay,

(c) the kind of costs which a person may be required to pay, and

(d) the assessment of costs.

(3) Without prejudice to the generality of subsection (2), rules under that subsection may include provision about—

(a) costs of the registrar, and

(b) liability for costs thrown away as the result of neglect or delay by a legal representative of a party to proceedings.

(4) An order under subsection (1) shall be enforceable as an order of the court.

(5) A person aggrieved by an order under subsection (1) may appeal to a county court, which may make any order which appears appropriate.

Miscellaneous

77.—Duty to act reasonably

A1.5.067   (1) A person must not exercise any of the following rights without reasonable cause—

(a) the right to lodge a caution under section 15,

(b) the right to apply for the entry of a notice or restriction, and

(c) the right to object to an application to the registrar.

(2) The duty under this section is owed to any person who suffers damage in consequence of its breach.

78.—Notice of trust not to affect registrar

A1.5.068   The registrar shall not be affected with notice of a trust.

PART 7

SPECIAL CASES

Pending actions etc.

87.—Pending land actions, writs, orders and deeds of arrangement

(1) Subject to the following provisions, references in this Act to an **A1.5.069** interest affecting an estate or charge include—

  (a) a pending land action within the meaning of the Land Charges Act 1972,

  (b) a writ or order of the kind mentioned in section 6(1)(a) of that Act (writ or order affecting land issued or made by any court for the purposes of enforcing a judgment or recognisance),

  (c) an order appointing a receiver or sequestrator, and

  (d) a deed of arrangement.

(2) No notice may be entered in the register in respect of—

  (a) an order appointing a receiver or sequestrator, or

  (b) a deed of arrangement.

(3) None of the matters mentioned in subsection (1) shall be capable of falling within paragraph 2 of Schedule 1 or 3.

(4) In its application to any of the matters mentioned in subsection (1), this Act shall have effect subject to such modifications as rules may provide.

(5) In this section, "deed of arrangement" has the same meaning as in the Deeds of Arrangement Act 1914 (c. 47).

Miscellaneous

88.—Incorporeal hereditaments

In its application to—   **A1.5.070**

  (a) rentcharges,

  (b) franchises,

(c) profits a prendre in gross, or

(d) manors,

this Act shall have effect subject to such modification as rules may provide.

PART 9

ADVERSE POSSESSION

96.—Disapplication of periods of limitation

A1.5.071 (1) No period of limitation under section 15 of the Limitation Act 1980 (c. 58) (time limits in relation to recovery of land) shall run against any person, other than a chargee, in relation to an estate in land or rentcharge the title to which is registered.

(2) No period of limitation under section 16 of that Act (time limits in relation to redemption of land) shall run against any person in relation to such an estate in land or rentcharge.

(3) Accordingly, section 17 of that Act (extinction of title on expiry of time limit) does not operate to extinguish the title of any person where, by virtue of this section, a period of limitation does not run against him.

97.—Registration of adverse possessor

A1.5.072 Schedule 6 (which makes provision about the registration of an adverse possessor of an estate in land or rentcharge) has effect.

98.—Defences

A1.5.073 (1) A person has a defence to an action for possession of land if—

(a) on the day immediately preceding that on which the action was brought he was entitled to make an application under paragraph 1 of Schedule 6 to be registered as the proprietor of an estate in the land, and

(b) had he made such an application on that day, the condition in paragraph 5(4) of that Schedule would have been satisfied.

(2) A judgment for possession of land ceases to be enforceable at the end of the period of two years beginning with the date of the judgment if the proceedings in which the judgment is given were commenced against a person who was at that time entitled to make an application under paragraph 1 of Schedule 6.

(3) A person has a defence to an action for possession of land if on the day immediately preceding that on which the action was brought he was entitled to make an application under paragraph 6 of Schedule 6 to be registered as the proprietor of an estate in the land.

(4) A judgment for possession of land ceases to be enforceable at the end of the period of two years beginning with the date of the judgment if, at the end of that period, the person against whom the judgment was given is entitled to make an application under paragraph 6 of Schedule 6 to be registered as the proprietor of an estate in the land.

(5) Where in any proceedings a court determines that—

(a) a person is entitled to a defence under this section, or

(b) a judgment for possession has ceased to be enforceable against a person by virtue of subsection (4),

the court must order the registrar to register him as the proprietor of the estate in relation to which he is entitled to make an application under Schedule 6.

(6) The defences under this section are additional to any other defences a person may have.

(7) Rules may make provision to prohibit the recovery of rent due under a rentcharge from a person who has been in adverse possession of the rentcharge.

PART 11

ADJUDICATION

107.—The adjudicator

(1) The Lord Chancellor shall appoint a person to be the Adjudicator to Her Majesty's Land Registry. **A1.5.074**

(2) To be qualified for appointment under subsection (1), a person must satisfy the judicial-appointment eligibility condition on a 7-year basis.

(3) Schedule 9 (which makes further provision about the adjudicator) has effect.

108.—Jurisdiction

(1) The adjudicator has the following functions— **A1.5.075**

(a) determining matters referred to him under section 73(7), and

(b) determining appeals under paragraph 4 of Schedule 5.

(2) Also, the adjudicator may, on application, make any order which the High Court could make for the rectification or setting aside of a document which—

(a) effects a qualifying disposition of a registered estate or charge,

(b) is a contract to make such a disposition, or

(c) effects a transfer of an interest which is the subject of a notice in the register.

(3) For the purposes of subsection (2)(a), a qualifying disposition is—

(a) a registrable disposition, or

(b) a disposition which creates an interest which may be the subject of a notice in the register.

(4) The general law about the effect of an order of the High Court for the rectification or setting aside of a document shall apply to an order under this section.

109.—Procedure

A1.5.076   (1) Hearings before the adjudicator shall be held in public, except where he is satisfied that exclusion of the public is just and reasonable.

(2) Subject to that, rules may regulate the practice and procedure to be followed with respect to proceedings before the adjudicator and matters incidental to or consequential on such proceedings.

(3) Rules under subsection (2) may, in particular, make provision about—

(a) when hearings are to be held,

(b) requiring persons to attend hearings to give evidence or to produce documents,

(c) the form in which any decision of the adjudicator is to be given,

(d) payment of costs of a party to proceedings by another party to the proceedings, and

(e) liability for costs thrown away as the result of neglect or delay by a legal representative of a party to proceedings.

110.—Functions in relation to disputes

A1.5.077   (1) In proceedings on a reference under section 73(7), the adjudicator may, instead of deciding a matter himself, direct a party to the proceedings to commence proceedings within a specified time in the court for the purpose of obtaining the court's decision on the matter.

(2) Rules may make provision about the reference under subsection (1) of matters to the court and may, in particular, make provision about—

(a) adjournment of the proceedings before the adjudicator pending the outcome of the proceedings before the court, and

(b) the powers of the adjudicator in the event of failure to comply with a direction under subsection (1).

(3) Rules may make provision about the functions of the adjudicator in consequence of a decision on a reference under section 73(7) and may, in particular, make provision enabling the adjudicator to determine, or give directions about the determination of—

(a) the application to which the reference relates, or

(b) such other present or future application to the registrar as the rules may provide.

(4) If, in the case of a reference under section 73(7) relating to an application under paragraph 1 of Schedule 6, the adjudicator determines that it would be unconscionable because of an equity by estoppel for the registered proprietor to seek to dispossess the applicant, but that the circumstances are not such that the applicant ought to be registered as proprietor, the adjudicator—

(a) must determine how the equity due to the applicant is to be satisfied, and

(b) may for that purpose make any order that the High Court could make in the exercise of its equitable jurisdiction.

111.—Appeals

(1) Subject to subsection (2), a person aggrieved by a decision of the **A1.5.078** adjudicator may appeal to the High Court.

(2) In the case of a decision on an appeal under paragraph 4 of Schedule 5, only appeal on a point of law is possible.

(3) If on an appeal under this section relating to an application under paragraph 1 of Schedule 6 the court determines that it would be unconscionable because of an equity by estoppel for the registered proprietor to seek to dispossess the applicant, but that the circumstances are not such that the applicant ought to be registered as proprietor, the court must determine how the equity due to the applicant is to be satisfied.

112.—Enforcement of orders etc

A1.5.079 A requirement of the adjudicator shall be enforceable as an order of the court.

113.—Fees

A1.5.080 The Lord Chancellor may by order—

(a) prescribe fees to be paid in respect of proceedings before the adjudicator;

(b) make provision about the payment of prescribed fees.

114.—Supplementary

A1.5.081 Power to make rules under this Part is exercisable by the Lord Chancellor.

PART 12

MISCELLANEOUS AND GENERAL

Miscellaneous

115.—Rights of pre-emption

A1.5.082 (1) A right of pre-emption in relation to registered land has effect from the time of creation as an interest capable of binding successors in title (subject to the rules about the effect of dispositions on priority).

(2) This section has effect in relation to rights of pre-emption created on or after the day on which this section comes into force.

116.—Proprietary estoppel and mere equities

A1.5.083 It is hereby declared for the avoidance of doubt that, in relation to registered land, each of the following—

(a) an equity by estoppel, and

(b) a mere equity,

has effect from the time the equity arises as an interest capable of binding successors in title (subject to the rules about the effect of dispositions on priority).

117.—Reduction in unregistered interests with automatic protection

(1) Paragraphs 10 to 14 of Schedules 1 and 3 shall cease to have effect **A1.5.084** at the end of the period of ten years beginning with the day on which those Schedules come into force.

(2) If made before the end of the period mentioned in subsection (1), no fee may be charged for—

   (a) an application to lodge a caution against first registration by virtue of an interest falling within any of paragraphs 10 to 14 of Schedule 1, or

   (b) an application for the entry in the register of a notice in respect of an interest falling within any of paragraphs 10 to 14 of Schedule 3.

118.—Power to reduce qualifying term

(1) The Lord Chancellor may by order substitute for the term specified **A1.5.085** in any of the following provisions—

   (a) section 3(3),

   (b) section 4(1)(c)(i) and (2)(b),

   (c) section 15(3)(a)(ii),

   (d) section 27(2)(b)(i),

   (e) section 80(1)(b)(i),

   (f) paragraph 1 of Schedule 1,

   (g) paragraphs 4(1), 5(1) and 6(1) of Schedule 2, and

   (h) paragraph 1 of Schedule 3,

such shorter term as he thinks fit.

(2) An order under this section may contain such transitional provision as the Lord Chancellor thinks fit.

(3) Before making an order under this section, the Lord Chancellor must consult such persons as he considers appropriate.

119.—Power to deregister manors

On the application of the proprietor of a registered manor, the registrar **A1.5.086** may remove the title to the manor from the register.

120.—Conclusiveness of filed copies etc

A1.5.087 (1) This section applies where—

    (a) a disposition relates to land to which a registered estate relates, and

    (b) an entry in the register relating to the registered estate refers to a document kept by the registrar which is not an original.

(2) As between the parties to the disposition, the document kept by the registrar is to be taken—

    (a) to be correct, and

    (b) to contain all the material parts of the original document.

(3) No party to the disposition may require production of the original document.

(4) No party to the disposition is to be affected by any provision of the original document which is not contained in the document kept by the registrar.

Offences etc.

123.—Suppression of information

A1.5.088 (1) A person commits an offence if in the course of proceedings relating to registration under this Act he suppresses information with the intention of—

    (a) concealing a person's right or claim, or

    (b) substantiating a false claim.

(2) A person guilty of an offence under this section is liable—

    (a) on conviction on indictment, to imprisonment for a term not exceeding two years or to a fine;

    (b) on summary conviction, to imprisonment for a term not exceeding six months or to a fine not exceeding the statutory maximum, or to both.

124.—Improper alteration of the registers

(1) A person commits an offence if he dishonestly induces another— **A1.5.089**

  (a) to change the register of title or cautions register, or

  (b) to authorise the making of such a change.

(2) A person commits an offence if he intentionally or recklessly makes an unauthorised change in the register of title or cautions register.
(3) A person guilty of an offence under this section is liable—

  (a) on conviction on indictment, to imprisonment for a term not exceeding 2 years or to a fine;

  (b) on summary conviction, to imprisonment for a term not exceeding six months or to a fine not exceeding the statutory maximum, or to both.

(4) In this section, references to changing the register of title include changing a document referred to in it.

125.—Privilege against self-incrimination

(1) The privilege against self-incrimination, so far as relating to offences **A1.5.090** under this Act, shall not entitle a person to refuse to answer any question or produce any document or thing in any legal proceedings other than criminal proceedings.
(2) No evidence obtained under subsection (1) shall be admissible in any criminal proceedings under this Act against the person from whom it was obtained or that person's spouse or civil partner.

Supplementary

129.—Crown application

This Act binds the Crown. **A1.5.091**

130.—Application to internal waters

This Act applies to land covered by internal waters of the United **A1.5.092** Kingdom which are—

  (a) within England or Wales, or

  (b) adjacent to England or Wales and specified for the purposes of this section by order made by the Lord Chancellor.

131.—"Proprietor in possession"

A1.5.093 (1) For the purposes of this Act, land is in the possession of the proprietor of a registered estate in land if it is physically in his possession, or in that of a person who is entitled to be registered as the proprietor of the registered estate.

(2) In the case of the following relationships, land which is (or is treated as being) in the possession of the second-mentioned person is to be treated for the purposes of subsection (1) as in the possession of the first-mentioned person—

(a) landlord and tenant;

(b) mortgagor and mortgagee;

(c) licensor and licensee;

(d) trustee and beneficiary.

(3) In subsection (1), the reference to entitlement does not include entitlement under Schedule 6.

132.—General interpretation

A1.5.094 (1) In this Act—

"adjudicator" means the Adjudicator to Her Majesty's Land Registry;
"caution against first registration" means a caution lodged under section 15;
"cautions register" means the register kept under section 19(1);
"charge" means any mortgage, charge or lien for securing money or money's worth;
"demesne land" means land belonging to Her Majesty in right of the Crown which is not held for an estate in fee simple absolute in possession;
"land" includes—(a) buildings and other structures,

(b) land covered with water, and
(c) mines and minerals, whether or not held with the surface;

"land registration rules" means any rules under this Act, other than rules under section 93, Part 11, section 121 or paragraph 1, 2 or 3 of Schedule 5;
"legal estate" has the same meaning as in the Law of Property Act 1925 (c. 20);
"legal mortgage" has the same meaning as in the Law of Property Act 1925;

"mines and minerals" includes any strata or seam of minerals or substances in or under any land, and powers of working and getting any such minerals or substances;

"registrar" means the Chief Land Registrar;

"register" means the register of title, except in the context of cautions against first registration;

"registered" means entered in the register;

"registered charge" means a charge the title to which is entered in the register;

"registered estate" means a legal estate the title to which is entered in the register, other than a registered charge;

"registered land" means a registered estate or registered charge;

"registrable disposition" means a disposition which is required to be completed by registration under section 27;

"requirement of registration" means the requirement of registration under section 4;

"sub-charge" means a charge under section 23(2)(b);

"term of years absolute" has the same meaning as in the Law of Property Act 1925 (c. 20);

"valuable consideration" does not include marriage consideration or a nominal consideration in money.

(2) In subsection (1), in the definition of "demesne land", the reference to land belonging to Her Majesty does not include land in relation to which a freehold estate in land has determined, but in relation to which there has been no act of entry or management by the Crown.

(3) In this Act—

(a) references to the court are to the High Court or a county court,

(b) references to an interest affecting an estate or charge are to an adverse right affecting the title to the estate or charge, and

(c) references to the right to object to an application to the registrar are to the right under section 73.

Schedule 1

Unregistered Interests Which Override First Registration

Leasehold estates in land

1.—A leasehold estate in land granted for a term not exceeding seven **A1.5.095** years from the date of the grant, except for a lease the grant of which falls within section 4(1)(d), (e) or (f).

Interests of persons in actual occupation

2.—An interest belonging to a person in actual occupation, so far as relating to land of which he is in actual occupation, except for an interest under a settlement under the Settled Land Act 1925 (c. 18).

Easements and profits a prendre

3.—A legal easement or profit a prendre.

Customary and public rights

4.—A customary right.
5.—A public right.

Local land charges

6.—A local land charge.

Mines and minerals

7.—An interest in any coal or coal mine, the rights attached to any such interest and the rights of any person under section 38, 49 or 51 of the Coal Industry Act 1994 (c. 21).

8.—In the case of land to which title was registered before 1898, rights to mines and minerals (and incidental rights) created before 1898.

9.—In the case of land to which title was registered between 1898 and 1925 inclusive, rights to mines and minerals (and incidental rights) created before the date of registration of the title.

Miscellaneous

10.—A franchise.

11.—A manorial right.

12.—A right to rent which was reserved to the Crown on the granting of any freehold estate (whether or not the right is still vested in the Crown).

13.—A non-statutory right in respect of an embankment or sea or river wall.

14.—A right to payment in lieu of tithe.

... 15–[Repealed by Land Registration Act 2002 c.9 Sch.12 para.7]

16.—A right in respect of the repair of a church chancel.

Schedule 2

Registrable Dispositions: Registration Requirements

Part 1

Registered Estates

Introductory

1.—This Part deals with the registration requirements relating to those **A1.5.096** dispositions of registered estates which are required to be completed by registration.

Transfer

2.—(1) In the case of a transfer of whole or part, the transferee, or his successor in title, must be entered in the register as the proprietor.

(2) In the case of a transfer of part, such details of the transfer as rules may provide must be entered in the register in relation to the registered estate out of which the transfer is made.

Lease of estate in land

3.—(1) This paragraph applies to a disposition consisting of the grant out of an estate in land of a term of years absolute.

(2) In the case of a disposition to which this paragraph applies—

(a) the grantee, or his successor in title, must be entered in the register as the proprietor of the lease, and

(b) a notice in respect of the lease must be entered in the register.

Lease of franchise or manor

4.—(1) This paragraph applies to a disposition consisting of the grant out of a franchise or manor of a lease for a term of more than seven years from the date of the grant.

(2) In the case of a disposition to which this paragraph applies—

(a) the grantee, or his successor in title, must be entered in the register as the proprietor of the lease, and

(b) a notice in respect of the lease must be entered in the register.

5.—(1) This paragraph applies to a disposition consisting of the grant out of a franchise or manor of a lease for a term not exceeding seven years from the date of the grant.

(2) In the case of a disposition to which this paragraph applies, a notice in respect of the lease must be entered in the register.

Creation of independently registrable legal interest

6.—(1) This paragraph applies to a disposition consisting of the creation of a legal rentcharge or profit a prendre in gross, other than one created for, or for an interest equivalent to, a term of years absolute not exceeding seven years from the date of creation.

(2) In the case of a disposition to which this paragraph applies—

    (a)   the grantee, or his successor in title, must be entered in the register as the proprietor of the interest created, and

    (b)   a notice in respect of the interest created must be entered in the register.

(3) In sub-paragraph (1), the reference to a legal rentcharge or profit a prendre in gross is to one falling within section 1(2) of the Law of Property Act 1925 (c. 20).

Creation of other legal interest

7.—(1) This paragraph applies to a disposition which—

    (a)   consists of the creation of an interest of a kind falling within section 1(2)(a), (b) or (e) of the Law of Property Act 1925, and

    (b)   is not a disposition to which paragraph 4, 5 or 6 applies.

(2) In the case of a disposition to which this paragraph applies—

    (a)   a notice in respect of the interest created must be entered in the register, and

    (b)   if the interest is created for the benefit of a registered estate, the proprietor of the registered estate must be entered in the register as its proprietor.

(3) Rules may provide for sub-paragraph (2) to have effect with modifications in relation to a right of entry over or in respect of a term of years absolute.

Creation of legal charge

8.—In the case of the creation of a charge, the chargee, or his successor in title, must be entered in the register as the proprietor of the charge.

PART 2

Registered Charges

Introductory

9.—This Part deals with the registration requirements relating to those dispositions of registered charges which are required to be completed by registration.

Transfer

10.—In the case of a transfer, the transferee, or his successor in title, must be entered in the register as the proprietor.

Creation of sub-charge

11.—In the case of the creation of a sub-charge, the sub-chargee, or his successor in title, must be entered in the register as the proprietor of the sub-charge.

SCHEDULE 3

Unregistered Interests Which Override Registered Dispositions

Leasehold estates in land

1.—A leasehold estate in land granted for a term not exceeding seven **A1.5.097** years from the date of the grant, except for—

(a) a lease the grant of which falls within section 4(1)(d), (e) or (f);

(b) a lease the grant of which constitutes a registrable disposition.

Interests of persons in actual occupation

2.—An interest belonging at the time of the disposition to a person in actual occupation, so far as relating to land of which he is in actual occupation, except for—

(a) an interest under a settlement under the Settled Land Act 1925 (c. 18);

(b) an interest of a person of whom inquiry was made before the disposition and who failed to disclose the right when he could reasonably have been expected to do so;

(c) an interest—

    (i) which belongs to a person whose occupation would not have been obvious on a reasonably careful inspection of the land at the time of the disposition, and

    (ii) of which the person to whom the disposition is made does not have actual knowledge at that time;

(d) a leasehold estate in land granted to take effect in possession after the end of the period of three months beginning with the date of the grant and which has not taken effect in possession at the time of the disposition.

Easements and profits a prendre

3.—(1) A legal easement or profit a prendre, except for an easement, or a profit a prendre which is not registered under the Commons Registration Act 1965 (c. 64), which at the time of the disposition—

(a) is not within the actual knowledge of the person to whom the disposition is made, and

(b) would not have been obvious on a reasonably careful inspection of the land over which the easement or profit is exercisable.

(2) The exception in sub-paragraph (1) does not apply if the person entitled to the easement or profit proves that it has been exercised in the period of one year ending with the day of the disposition.

Customary and public rights

4.—A customary right.
5.—A public right.

Local land charges

6.—A local land charge.

Mines and minerals

7.—An interest in any coal or coal mine, the rights attached to any such interest and the rights of any person under section 38, 49 or 51 of the Coal Industry Act 1994 (c. 21).

8.—In the case of land to which title was registered before 1898, rights to mines and minerals (and incidental rights) created before 1898.

9.—In the case of land to which title was registered between 1898 and 1925 inclusive, rights to mines and minerals (and incidental rights) created before the date of registration of the title.

Miscellaneous

10.—A franchise.

11.—A manorial right.

12.—A right to rent which was reserved to the Crown on the granting of any freehold estate (whether or not the right is still vested in the Crown).

13.—A non-statutory right in respect of an embankment or sea or river wall.

14.—A right to payment in lieu of tithe.

15.—[Repealed by Land Registration Act 2002 c. 9 Sch.12 para.11]

16.—A right in respect of the repair of a church chancel.

SCHEDULE 4

Alteration Of The Register

Introductory

1.—In this Schedule, references to rectification, in relation to alteration **A1.5.098** of the register, are to alteration which—

(a) involves the correction of a mistake, and

(b) prejudicially affects the title of a registered proprietor.

Alteration pursuant to a court order

2.—(1) The court may make an order for alteration of the register for the purpose of—

(a) correcting a mistake,

(b) bringing the register up to date, or

(c) giving effect to any estate, right or interest excepted from the effect of registration.

(2) An order under this paragraph has effect when served on the registrar to impose a duty on him to give effect to it.

3.—(1) This paragraph applies to the power under paragraph 2, so far as relating to rectification.

(2) If alteration affects the title of the proprietor of a registered estate in land, no order may be made under paragraph 2 without the proprietor's consent in relation to land in his possession unless—

> (a) he has by fraud or lack of proper care caused or substantially contributed to the mistake, or
>
> (b) it would for any other reason be unjust for the alteration not to be made.

(3) If in any proceedings the court has power to make an order under paragraph 2, it must do so, unless there are exceptional circumstances which justify its not doing so.

(4) In sub-paragraph (2), the reference to the title of the proprietor of a registered estate in land includes his title to any registered estate which subsists for the benefit of the estate in land.

4.—Rules may—

> (a) make provision about the circumstances in which there is a duty to exercise the power under paragraph 2, so far as not relating to rectification;
>
> (b) make provision about the form of an order under paragraph 2;
>
> (c) make provision about service of such an order.

Alteration otherwise than pursuant to a court order

5.—The registrar may alter the register for the purpose of—

> (a) correcting a mistake,
>
> (b) bringing the register up to date,
>
> (c) giving effect to any estate, right or interest excepted from the effect of registration, or
>
> (d) removing a superfluous entry.

6.—(1) This paragraph applies to the power under paragraph 5, so far as relating to rectification.

(2) No alteration affecting the title of the proprietor of a registered estate in land may be made under paragraph 5 without the proprietor's consent in relation to land in his possession unless—

    (a) he has by fraud or lack of proper care caused or substantially contributed to the mistake, or

    (b) it would for any other reason be unjust for the alteration not to be made.

(3) If on an application for alteration under paragraph 5 the registrar has power to make the alteration, the application must be approved, unless there are exceptional circumstances which justify not making the alteration.

(4) In sub-paragraph (2), the reference to the title of the proprietor of a registered estate in land includes his title to any registered estate which subsists for the benefit of the estate in land.

7.—Rules may—

    (a) make provision about the circumstances in which there is a duty to exercise the power under paragraph 5, so far as not relating to rectification;

    (b) make provision about how the register is to be altered in exercise of that power;

    (c) make provision about applications for alteration under that paragraph, including provision requiring the making of such applications;

    (d) make provision about procedure in relation to the exercise of that power, whether on application or otherwise.

Rectification and derivative interests

8.—The powers under this Schedule to alter the register, so far as relating to rectification, extend to changing for the future the priority of any interest affecting the registered estate or charge concerned.

Costs in non-rectification cases

9.—(1) If the register is altered under this Schedule in a case not involving rectification, the registrar may pay such amount as he thinks fit in respect of any costs or expenses reasonably incurred by a person in connection with the alteration which have been incurred with the consent of the registrar.

(2) The registrar may make a payment under sub-paragraph (1) notwithstanding the absence of consent if—

(a) it appears to him—

    (i) that the costs or expenses had to be incurred urgently, and

    (ii) that it was not reasonably practicable to apply for his consent, or

(b) he has subsequently approved the incurring of the costs or expenses.

SCHEDULE 6

Registration Of Adverse Possessor

Right to apply for registration

A1.5.099   1.—(1) Subject to paragraph 16, a person may apply to the registrar to be registered as the proprietor of a registered estate in land if he has been in adverse possession of the estate for the period of ten years ending on the date of the application.

(2) Subject to paragraph 16, a person may also apply to the registrar to be registered as the proprietor of a registered estate in land if—

(a) he has in the period of six months ending on the date of the application ceased to be in adverse possession of the estate because of eviction by the registered proprietor, or a person claiming under the registered proprietor,

(b) on the day before his eviction he was entitled to make an application under sub-paragraph (1), and

(c) the eviction was not pursuant to a judgment for possession.

(3) However, a person may not make an application under this paragraph if—

(a) he is a defendant in proceedings which involve asserting a right to possession of the land, or

(b) judgment for possession of the land has been given against him in the last two years.

(4) For the purposes of sub-paragraph (1), the estate need not have been registered throughout the period of adverse possession.

Notification of application

2.—(1) The registrar must give notice of an application under paragraph 1 to—

(a) the proprietor of the estate to which the application relates,

(b) the proprietor of any registered charge on the estate,

(c) where the estate is leasehold, the proprietor of any superior registered estate,

(d) any person who is registered in accordance with rules as a person to be notified under this paragraph, and

(e) such other persons as rules may provide.

(2) Notice under this paragraph shall include notice of the effect of paragraph 4.

Treatment of application

3.—(1) A person given notice under paragraph 2 may require that the application to which the notice relates be dealt with under paragraph 5.

(2) The right under this paragraph is exercisable by notice to the registrar given before the end of such period as rules may provide.

4.—If an application under paragraph 1 is not required to be dealt with under paragraph 5, the applicant is entitled to be entered in the register as the new proprietor of the estate.

5.—(1) If an application under paragraph 1 is required to be dealt with under this paragraph, the applicant is only entitled to be registered as the new proprietor of the estate if any of the following conditions is met.

(2) The first condition is that—

(a) it would be unconscionable because of an equity by estoppel for the registered proprietor to seek to dispossess the applicant, and

(b) the circumstances are such that the applicant ought to be registered as the proprietor.

(3) The second condition is that the applicant is for some other reason entitled to be registered as the proprietor of the estate.

(4) The third condition is that—

(a) the land to which the application relates is adjacent to land belonging to the applicant,

(b) the exact line of the boundary between the two has not been determined under rules under section 60,

(c) for at least ten years of the period of adverse possession ending on the date of the application, the applicant (or any predecessor in title) reasonably believed that the land to which the application relates belonged to him, and

(d) the estate to which the application relates was registered more than one year prior to the date of the application.

(5) In relation to an application under paragraph 1(2), this paragraph has effect as if the reference in sub-paragraph (4)(c) to the date of the application were to the day before the date of the applicant's eviction.

Right to make further application for registration

6.—(1) Where a person's application under paragraph 1 is rejected, he may make a further application to be registered as the proprietor of the estate if he is in adverse possession of the estate from the date of the application until the last day of the period of two years beginning with the date of its rejection.

(1A) Sub-paragraph (1) is subject to paragraph 16,

(2) However, a person may not make an application under this paragraph if—

(a) he is a defendant in proceedings which involve asserting a right to possession of the land,

(b) judgment for possession of the land has been given against him in the last two years, or

(c) he has been evicted from the land pursuant to a judgment for possession.

7.—If a person makes an application under paragraph 6, he is entitled to be entered in the register as the new proprietor of the estate.

Restriction on applications

8.—(1) No one may apply under this Schedule to be registered as the proprietor of an estate in land during, or before the end of twelve months after the end of, any period in which the existing registered proprietor is for the purposes of the Limitation (Enemies and War Prisoners) Act 1945 (8 & 9 Geo. 6 c. 16)—

(a) an enemy, or

(b) detained in enemy territory.

(2) No-one may apply under this Schedule to be registered as the proprietor of an estate in land during any period in which the existing registered proprietor is—

(a) unable because of mental disability to make decisions about issues of the kind to which such an application would give rise, or

(b) unable to communicate such decisions because of mental disability or physical impairment.

(3) For the purposes of sub-paragraph (2), "mental disability" means a disability or disorder of the mind or brain, whether permanent or temporary, which results in an impairment or disturbance of mental functioning.

(4) Where it appears to the registrar that sub-paragraph (1) or (2) applies in relation to an estate in land, he may include a note to that effect in the register.

Effect of registration

9.—(1) Where a person is registered as the proprietor of an estate in land in pursuance of an application under this Schedule, the title by virtue of adverse possession which he had at the time of the application is extinguished.

(2) Subject to sub-paragraph (3), the registration of a person under this Schedule as the proprietor of an estate in land does not affect the priority of any interest affecting the estate.

(3) Subject to sub-paragraph (4), where a person is registered under this Schedule as the proprietor of an estate, the estate is vested in him free of any registered charge affecting the estate immediately before his registration.

(4) Sub-paragraph (3) does not apply where registration as proprietor is in pursuance of an application determined by reference to whether any of the conditions in paragraph 5 applies.

Apportionment and discharge of charges

10.—(1) Where—

(a) a registered estate continues to be subject to a charge notwithstanding the registration of a person under this Schedule as the proprietor, and

(b) the charge affects property other than the estate,

the proprietor of the estate may require the chargee to apportion the amount secured by the charge at that time between the estate and the other property on the basis of their respective values.

(2) The person requiring the apportionment is entitled to a discharge of his estate from the charge on payment of—

    (a) the amount apportioned to the estate, and

    (b) the costs incurred by the chargee as a result of the apportionment.

(3) On a discharge under this paragraph, the liability of the chargor to the chargee is reduced by the amount apportioned to the estate.

(4) Rules may make provision about apportionment under this paragraph, in particular, provision about—

    (a) procedure,

    (b) valuation,

    (c) calculation of costs payable under sub-paragraph (2)(b), and

    (d) payment of the costs of the chargor.

Meaning of "adverse possession"

11.—(1) A person is in adverse possession of an estate in land for the purposes of this Schedule if, but for section 96, a period of limitation under section 15 of the Limitation Act 1980 (c. 58) would run in his favour in relation to the estate.

(2) A person is also to be regarded for those purposes as having been in adverse possession of an estate in land—

    (a) where he is the successor in title to an estate in the land, during any period of adverse possession by a predecessor in title to that estate, or

    (b) during any period of adverse possession by another person which comes between, and is continuous with, periods of adverse possession of his own.

(3) In determining whether for the purposes of this paragraph a period of limitation would run under section 15 of the Limitation Act 1980, there are to be disregarded—

    (a) the commencement of any legal proceedings, and

    (b) paragraph 6 of Schedule 1 to that Act.

Trusts

12.—A person is not to be regarded as being in adverse possession of an estate for the purposes of this Schedule at any time when the estate is subject to a trust, unless the interest of each of the beneficiaries in the estate is an interest in possession.

Crown foreshore

13.—(1) Where—

(a) a person is in adverse possession of an estate in land,

(b) the estate belongs to Her Majesty in right of the Crown or the Duchy of Lancaster or to the Duchy of Cornwall, and

(c) the land consists of foreshore,

paragraph 1(1) is to have effect as if the reference to ten years were to sixty years.

(2) For the purposes of sub-paragraph (1), land is to be treated as foreshore if it has been foreshore at any time in the previous ten years.

(3) In this paragraph, "foreshore" means the shore and bed of the sea and of any tidal water, below the line of the medium high tide between the spring and neap tides.

Rentcharges

14.—Rules must make provision to apply the preceding provisions of this Schedule to registered rentcharges, subject to such modifications and exceptions as the rules may provide.

Procedure

15.—Rules may make provision about the procedure to be followed pursuant to an application under this Schedule.

Extension of time limits because of mediation in certain cross-border disputes

16.—(1) In this paragraph—

(a) "Mediation Directive" means Directive 2008/52/EC of the European Parliament and of the Council of 21 May 2008 on certain aspects of mediation in civil and commercial matters,

(b) "mediation" has the meaning given by article 3(a) of the Mediation Directive,

(c) "mediator" has the meaning given by article 3(b) of the Mediation Directive, and

(d) "relevant dispute" means a dispute to which article 8(1) of the Mediation Directive applies (certain cross-border disputes).

(2) Sub-paragraph (3) applies where—

(a) a period of time is prescribed by paragraph 1(1), 1(2)(a) or 6(1) in relation to the whole or part of a relevant dispute,

(b) a mediation in relation to the relevant dispute starts before the period expires, and

(c) if not extended by this paragraph, the period would expire before the mediation ends or less than eight weeks after it ends.

(3) The period expires instead at the end of eight weeks after the mediation ends (subject to sub-paragraph (4)).

(4) If a period has been extended by this paragraph, sub-paragraphs (2) and (3) apply to the extended period as they apply to a period mentioned in sub-paragraph (2)(a).

(5) Where more than one period applies in relation to a relevant dispute, the extension by sub-paragraph (3) of one of those periods does not affect the others.

(6) For the purposes of this paragraph, a mediation starts on the date of the agreement to mediate that is entered into by the parties and the mediator.

(7) For the purposes of this paragraph, a mediation ends on date of the first of these to occur—

(a) the parties reach an agreement in resolution of the relevant dispute,

(b) a party completes the notification of the other parties that it has withdrawn from the mediation,

(c) a party to whom a qualifying request is made fails to give a response reaching the other parties within 14 days of the request,

(d) the parties, after being notified that the mediator's appointment has ended (by death, resignation or otherwise), fail to agree within 14 days to seek to appoint a replacement mediator,

(e) the mediation otherwise comes to an end pursuant to the terms of the agreement to mediate.

(8) For the purpose of sub-paragraph (7), a qualifying request is a request by a party that another (A) confirm to all parties that A is continuing with the mediation.

(9) In the case of any relevant dispute, references in this paragraph to a mediation are references to the mediation so far as it relates to that dispute, and references to a party are to be read accordingly.

SCHEDULE 8

Indemnities

Entitlement

1.—(1) A person is entitled to be indemnified by the registrar if he **A1.5.100** suffers loss by reason of—

(a) rectification of the register,

(b) a mistake whose correction would involve rectification of the register,

(c) a mistake in an official search,

(d) a mistake in an official copy,

(e) a mistake in a document kept by the registrar which is not an original and is referred to in the register,

(f) the loss or destruction of a document lodged at the registry for inspection or safe custody,

(g) a mistake in the cautions register, or

(h) failure by the registrar to perform his duty under section 50.

(2) For the purposes of sub-paragraph (1)(a)—

(a) any person who suffers loss by reason of the change of title under section 62 is to be regarded as having suffered loss by reason of rectification of the register, and

(b) the proprietor of a registered estate or charge claiming in good faith under a forged disposition is, where the register is rectified, to be regarded as having suffered loss by reason of such rectification as if the disposition had not been forged.

(3) No indemnity under sub-paragraph (1)(b) is payable until a decision has been made about whether to alter the register for the purpose of correcting the mistake; and the loss suffered by reason of the mistake is to be determined in the light of that decision.

Mines and minerals

2.—No indemnity is payable under this Schedule on account of—

    (a) any mines or minerals, or

    (b) the existence of any right to work or get mines or minerals,

unless it is noted in the register that the title to the registered estate concerned includes the mines or minerals.

Costs

3.—(1) In respect of loss consisting of costs or expenses incurred by the claimant in relation to the matter, an indemnity under this Schedule is payable only on account of costs or expenses reasonably incurred by the claimant with the consent of the registrar.

(2) The requirement of consent does not apply where—

    (a) the costs or expenses must be incurred by the claimant urgently, and

    (b) it is not reasonably practicable to apply for the registrar's consent.

(3) If the registrar approves the incurring of costs or expenses after they have been incurred, they shall be treated for the purposes of this paragraph as having been incurred with his consent.

4.—(1) If no indemnity is payable to a claimant under this Schedule, the registrar may pay such amount as he thinks fit in respect of any costs or expenses reasonably incurred by the claimant in connection with the claim which have been incurred with the consent of the registrar.

(2) The registrar may make a payment under sub-paragraph (1) notwithstanding the absence of consent if—

    (a) it appears to him—

        (i) that the costs or expenses had to be incurred urgently, and

        (ii) that it was not reasonably practicable to apply for his consent, or

    (b) he has subsequently approved the incurring of the costs or expenses.

Claimant's fraud or lack of care

5.—(1) No indemnity is payable under this Schedule on account of any loss suffered by a claimant—

(a) wholly or partly as a result of his own fraud, or

(b) wholly as a result of his own lack of proper care.

(2) Where any loss is suffered by a claimant partly as a result of his own lack of proper care, any indemnity payable to him is to be reduced to such extent as is fair having regard to his share in the responsibility for the loss.

(3) For the purposes of this paragraph any fraud or lack of care on the part of a person from whom the claimant derives title (otherwise than under a disposition for valuable consideration which is registered or protected by an entry in the register) is to be treated as if it were fraud or lack of care on the part of the claimant.

Valuation of estates etc.

6.—Where an indemnity is payable in respect of the loss of an estate, interest or charge, the value of the estate, interest or charge for the purposes of the indemnity is to be regarded as not exceeding—

(a) in the case of an indemnity under paragraph 1(1)(a), its value immediately before rectification of the register (but as if there were to be no rectification), and

(b) in the case of an indemnity under paragraph 1(1)(b), its value at the time when the mistake which caused the loss was made.

Determination of indemnity by court

7.—(1) A person may apply to the court for the determination of any question as to—

(a) whether he is entitled to an indemnity under this Schedule, or

(b) the amount of such an indemnity.

(2) Paragraph 3(1) does not apply to the costs of an application to the court under this paragraph or of any legal proceedings arising out of such an application.

Time limits

8.—For the purposes of the Limitation Act 1980 (c. 58)—

(a) a liability to pay an indemnity under this Schedule is a simple contract debt, and

(b) the cause of action arises at the time when the claimant knows, or but for his own default might have known, of the existence of his claim.

Interest

9.—Rules may make provision about the payment of interest on an indemnity under this Schedule, including—

(a) the circumstances in which interest is payable, and

(b) the periods for and rates at which it is payable.

Recovery of indemnity by registrar

10.—(1) Where an indemnity under this Schedule is paid to a claimant in respect of any loss, the registrar is entitled (without prejudice to any other rights he may have)—

(a) to recover the amount paid from any person who caused or substantially contributed to the loss by his fraud, or

(b) for the purpose of recovering the amount paid, to enforce the rights of action referred to in sub-paragraph (2).

(2) Those rights of action are—

(a) any right of action (of whatever nature and however arising) which the claimant would have been entitled to enforce had the indemnity not been paid, and

(b) where the register has been rectified, any right of action (of whatever nature and however arising) which the person in whose favour the register has been rectified would have been entitled to enforce had it not been rectified.

(3) References in this paragraph to an indemnity include interest paid on an indemnity under rules under paragraph 9.

Interpretation

11.—(1) For the purposes of this Schedule, references to a mistake in something include anything mistakenly omitted from it as well as anything mistakenly included in it.

(2) In this Schedule, references to rectification of the register are to alteration of the register which—

(a) involves the correction of a mistake, and

(b) prejudicially affects the title of a registered proprietor.

SCHEDULE 9

The Adjudicator

Holding of office

1.—(1) The adjudicator may at any time resign his office by written **A1.5.101** notice to the Lord Chancellor.

(2) The Lord Chancellor may, with the concurrence of the Lord Chief Justice, remove the adjudicator from office on the ground of incapacity or misbehaviour.

(3) Section 26 of the Judicial Pensions and Retirement Act 1993 (c. 8) (compulsory retirement at 70, subject to the possibility of annual extension up to 75) applies to the adjudicator.

(4) Subject to the above, a person appointed to be the adjudicator is to hold and vacate office in accordance with the terms of his appointment and, on ceasing to hold office, is eligible for reappointment.

Remuneration

2.—(1) The Lord Chancellor shall pay the adjudicator such remuneration, and such other allowances, as the Lord Chancellor may determine.

(2) The Lord Chancellor shall—

(a) pay such pension, allowances or gratuities as he may determine to or in respect of a person who is or has been the adjudicator, or

(b) make such payments as he may determine towards provision for the payment of a pension, allowances or gratuities to or in respect of such a person.

(3) Sub-paragraph (2) does not apply if the office of adjudicator is a qualifying judicial office within the meaning of the Judicial Pensions and Retirement Act 1993.

(4) If, when a person ceases to be the adjudicator, the Lord Chancellor determines that there are special circumstances which make it right that the person should receive compensation, the Lord Chancellor may pay to the person by way of compensation a sum of such amount as he may determine.

Staff

3.—(1) The adjudicator may appoint such staff as he thinks fit.

(2) The terms and conditions of appointments under this paragraph shall be such as the adjudicator, with the approval of the Minister for the Civil Service, thinks fit.

Conduct of business

4.—(1) Subject to sub-paragraph (2), any function of the adjudicator may be carried out by any member of his staff who is authorised by him for the purpose.

(2) In the case of functions which are not of an administrative character, sub-paragraph (1) only applies if the member of staff satisfies the judicial-appointment eligibility condition on a 7-year basis.

5.—The Lord Chancellor may by regulations make provision about the carrying out of functions during any vacancy in the office of adjudicator.

Finances

6.—The Lord Chancellor shall be liable to reimburse expenditure incurred by the adjudicator in the discharge of his functions.

7.—The Lord Chancellor may require the registrar to make payments towards expenses of the Lord Chancellor under this Schedule.

Application of Tribunals and Inquiries Act 1992

8.—In Schedule 1 to the Tribunal and Inquiries Act 1992 (c. 53) (tribunals under the supervision of the Council on Tribunals), after paragraph 27 there is inserted—

"Land Registration 27B. The Adjudicator to Her Majesty's Land Registry."

Parliamentary disqualification

9.—In Part 1 of Schedule 1 to the House of Commons Disqualification Act 1975 (c. 24) (judicial offices), there is inserted at the end—

"Adjudicator to Her Majesty's Land Registry.";

and a corresponding amendment is made in Part 1 of Schedule 1 to the Northern Ireland Assembly Disqualification Act 1975 (c. 25).

COMMONS ACT 2006 c. 26

PART 1

REGISTRATION

INTRODUCTORY

1.—Registers of common land and greens

Each commons registration authority shall continue to keep– **A1.6.001**

    (a) a register known as a register of common land; and

    (b) a register known as a register of town or village greens.

2.—Purpose of registers

(1) The purpose of a register of common land is– **A1.6.002**

    (a) to register land as common land; and

    (b) to register rights of common exercisable over land registered as common land.

(2) The purpose of a register of town or village greens is–

    (a) to register land as a town or village green; and

    (b) to register rights of common exercisable over land registered as a town or village green.

3.—Content of registers

(1) The land registered as common land in a register of common land **A1.6.003** is, subject to this Part, to be–

    (a) the land so registered in it at the commencement of this section; and

    (b) such other land as may be so registered in it under this Part.

(2) The land registered as a town or village green in a register of town or village greens is, subject to this Part, to be–

    (a) the land so registered in it at the commencement of this section; and

    (b) such other land as may be so registered in it under this Part.

(3) The rights of common registered in a register of common land or town or village greens are, subject to this Part, to be–

(a) the rights registered in it at the commencement of this section; and

(b) such other rights as may be so registered in it under this Part.

(4) The following information is to be registered in a register of common land or town or village greens in respect of a right of common registered in it–

(a) the nature of the right;

(b) if the right is attached to any land, the land to which it is attached;

(c) if the right is not so attached, the owner of the right.

(5) Regulations may–

(a) require or permit other information to be included in a register of common land or town or village greens;

(b) make provision as to the form in which any information is to be presented in such a register.

(6) Except as provided under this Part or any other enactment–

(a) no land registered as common land or as a town or village green is to be removed from the register in which it is so registered;

(b) no right of common registered in a register of common land or town or village greens is to be removed from that register.

(7) No right of common over land to which this Part applies is to be registered in the register of title.

4.—Commons registration authorities

A1.6.004   (1) The following are commons registration authorities–

(a) a county council in England;

(b) a district council in England for an area without a county council;

(c) a London borough council; and

(d) a county or county borough council in Wales.

(2) For the purposes of this Part, the commons registration authority in relation to any land is the authority in whose area the land is situated.

(3) Where any land falls within the area of two or more commons registration authorities, the authorities may by agreement provide for one of them to be the commons registration authority in relation to the whole of the land.

5.—Land to which Part 1 applies

(1) This Part applies to all land in England and Wales, subject as **A1.6.005** follows.

(2) This Part does not apply to–

(a) the New Forest; or

(b) Epping Forest.

(3) This Part shall not be taken to apply to the Forest of Dean.

(4) If any question arises under this Part whether any land is part of the forests mentioned in this section it is to be referred to and decided by the appropriate national authority.

6.—Creation

(1) A right of common cannot at any time after the commencement of **A1.6.006** this section be created over land to which this Part applies by virtue of prescription.

(2) A right of common cannot at any time after the commencement of this section be created in any other way over land to which this Part applies except–

(a) as specified in subsection (3); or

(b) pursuant to any other enactment.

(3) A right of common may be created over land to which this Part applies by way of express grant if–

(a) the land is not registered as a town or village green; and

(b) the right is attached to land.

(4) The creation of a right of common in accordance with subsection (3) only has effect if it complies with such requirements as to form and content as regulations may provide.

(5) The creation of a right of common in accordance with subsection (3) does not operate at law until on an application under this section–

(a)　the right is registered in a register of common land; and

(b)　if the right is created over land not registered as common land, the land is registered in a register of common land.

(6) An application under this section to register the creation of a right of common consisting of a right to graze any animal is to be refused if in the opinion of the commons registration authority the land over which it is created would be unable to sustain the exercise of–

(a)　that right; and

(b)　if the land is already registered as common land, any other rights of common registered as exercisable over the land.

7.—Variation

A1.6.007　(1) For the purposes of this section a right of common is varied if by virtue of any disposition–

(a)　the right becomes exercisable over new land to which this Part applies instead of all or part of the land over which it was exercisable;

(b)　the right becomes exercisable over new land to which this Part applies in addition to the land over which it is already exercisable;

(c)　there is any other alteration in what can be done by virtue of the right.

(2) A right of common which is registered in a register of common land or town or village greens cannot at any time after the commencement of this section be varied so as to become exercisable over new land if that land is at the time registered as a town or village green.

(3) A right of common which is registered in a register of town or village greens cannot at any time after the commencement of this section be varied so as to extend what can be done by virtue of the right.

(4) The variation of a right of common which is registered in a register of common land or town or village greens–

(a)　only has effect if it complies with such requirements as to form and content as regulations may provide; and

(b)　does not operate at law until, on an application under this section, the register is amended so as to record the variation.

(5) An application under this section to record a variation of a right of common consisting of a right to graze any animal is to be refused if in the opinion of the commons registration authority the land over which the right is or is to be exercisable would, in consequence of the variation, be unable to sustain the exercise of–

(a) that right; and

(b) if the land is already registered as common land, any other rights of common registered as exercisable over the land.

8.—Apportionment

(1) Regulations may make provision as to the amendments to be made **A1.6.008** to a register of common land or town or village greens where a right of common which is registered in a register of common land or town or village greens as attached to any land is apportioned by virtue of any disposition affecting the land.

(2) Regulations under subsection (1) may provide that a register is only to be amended when–

(a) a disposition relating to an apportioned right itself falls to be registered under this Part; or

(b) the register falls to be amended under section 11.

(3) Where at any time–

(a) a right of common which is registered in a register of common land or town or village greens as attached to any land has been apportioned by virtue of any disposition affecting the land, and

(b) no amendments have been made under subsection (1) in respect of the apportionment of that right,

the rights of common subsisting as a result of the apportionment shall be regarded as rights which are registered in that register as attached to the land to which they attach as a result of the apportionment.

9.—Severance

(1) This section applies to a right of common which– **A1.6.009**

(a) is registered in a register of common land or town or village greens as attached to any land; and

(b) would, apart from this section, be capable of being severed from that land.

(2) A right of common to which this section applies is not at any time on or after the day on which this section comes into force capable of being severed from the land to which it is attached, except–

(a) where the severance is authorised by or under Schedule 1; or

(b) where the severance is authorised by or under any other Act.

(3) Where any instrument made on or after the day on which this section comes into force would effect a disposition in relation to a right of common to which this section applies in contravention of subsection (2), the instrument is void to the extent that it would effect such a disposition.

(4) Where by virtue of any instrument made on or after the day on which this section comes into force–

(a) a disposition takes effect in relation to land to which a right of common to which this section applies is attached, and

(b) the disposition would have the effect of contravening subsection (2),

the disposition also has effect in relation to the right notwithstanding anything in the instrument to the contrary.

(5) Where by virtue of any instrument made on or after the day on which this section comes into force a right of common to which this section applies falls to be apportioned between different parts of the land to which it is attached, the instrument is void to the extent that it purports to apportion the right otherwise than rateably.

(6) Nothing in this section affects any instrument made before, or made pursuant to a contract made in writing before, the day on which this section comes into force.

(7) This section and Schedule 1 shall be deemed to have come into force on 28 June 2005 (and an order under paragraph 2 of that Schedule may have effect as from that date).

10.—Attachment

A1.6.010   (1) This section applies to any right of common which is registered in a register of common land or town or village greens but is not registered as attached to any land.

(2) The owner of the right may apply to the commons registration authority for the right to be registered in that register as attached to any land, provided that–

(a) he is entitled to occupy the land; or

(b) the person entitled to occupy the land has consented to the application.

11.—Re-allocation of attached rights

(1) Where–   **A1.6.011**

(a) a right of common is registered in a register of common land or town or village greens as attached to any land, and

(b) subsection (2), (3) or (4) applies in relation to part of the land ("the relevant part"),

the owner of the land may apply to the commons registration authority for the register to be amended so as to secure that the right does not attach to the relevant part.

(2) This subsection applies where the relevant part is not used for agricultural purposes.

(3) This subsection applies where planning permission has been granted for use of the relevant part for purposes which are not agricultural purposes.

(4) This subsection applies where–

(a) an order authorising the compulsory purchase of the relevant part by any authority has been made in accordance with the Acquisition of Land Act 1981 (c. 67) (and, if the order requires to be confirmed under Part 2 of that Act, has been so confirmed);

(b) the relevant part has not vested in the authority; and

(c) the relevant part is required for use other than use for agricultural purposes.

(5) Regulations may for the purposes of subsections (2) to (4) make provision as to what is or is not to be regarded as use of land for agricultural purposes.

(6) Regulations may provide that an application under this section is not to be granted without the consent of any person specified in the regulations.

12.—Transfer of rights in gross

The transfer of a right of common which is registered in a register of **A1.6.012** common land or town or village greens but is not registered as attached to any land–

(a) only has effect if it complies with such requirements as to form and content as regulations may provide; and

(b) does not operate at law until, on an application under this section, the transferee is registered in the register as the owner of the right.

13.—Surrender and extinguishment

A1.6.013 (1) The surrender to any extent of a right of common which is registered in a register of common land or town or village greens–

(a) only has effect if it complies with such requirements as to form and content as regulations may provide; and

(b) does not operate at law until, on an application under this section, the right is removed from the register.

(2) The reference in subsection (1) to a surrender of a right of common does not include a disposition having the effect referred to in section 7(1)(a).

(3) A right of common which is registered in a register of common land or town or village greens cannot be extinguished by operation of common law.

Registration, deregistration and exchange of land

14.—Statutory dispositions

A1.6.014 (1) Regulations may make provision as to the amendment of a register of common land or town or village greens where by virtue of any relevant instrument–

(a) a disposition is made in relation to land registered in it as common land or as a town or village green; or

(b) a disposition is made in relation to a right of common registered in it.

(2) Regulations may provide that, where–

(a) by virtue of any relevant instrument a disposition is made in relation to land registered as common land or as a town or village green,

(b) by virtue of regulations under subsection (1) the land ceases to be so registered, and

(c) in connection with the disposition other land is given in exchange,

the land given in exchange is to be registered as common land or as a town or village green.

(3) In this section, "relevant instrument" means–(a) any order, deed or other instrument made under or pursuant to the Acquisition of Land Act 1981 (c. 67);

(b) a conveyance made for the purposes of section 13 of the New Parishes Measure 1943 (No. 1);

(c) any other instrument made under or pursuant to any enactment.

(4) Regulations under this section may require the making of an application to a commons registration authority for amendment of a register of common land or town or village greens.

(5) Regulations under this section may provide that a relevant instrument, so far as relating to land registered as common land or as a town or village green or to any right of common, is not to operate at law until any requirement for which they provide is complied with.

15.—Registration of greens

(1) Any person may apply to the commons registration authority to **A1.6.015** register land to which this Part applies as a town or village green in a case where subsection (2), (3) or (4) applies.

(2) This subsection applies where–

(a) a significant number of the inhabitants of any locality, or of any neighbourhood within a locality, have indulged as of right in lawful sports and pastimes on the land for a period of at least 20 years; and

(b) they continue to do so at the time of the application.

(3) This subsection applies where–

(a) a significant number of the inhabitants of any locality, or of any neighbourhood within a locality, indulged as of right in lawful sports and pastimes on the land for a period of at least 20 years;

(b) they ceased to do so before the time of the application but after the commencement of this section; and

(c) the application is made within the period of two years beginning with the cessation referred to in paragraph (b).

(4) This subsection applies (subject to subsection (5)) where–

(a) a significant number of the inhabitants of any locality, or of any neighbourhood within a locality, indulged as of right in lawful sports and pastimes on the land for a period of at least 20 years;

(b) they ceased to do so before the commencement of this section; and

(c) the application is made within the period of five years beginning with the cessation referred to in paragraph (b).

(5) Subsection (4) does not apply in relation to any land where–

(a) planning permission was granted before 23 June 2006 in respect of the land;

(b) construction works were commenced before that date in accordance with that planning permission on the land or any other land in respect of which the permission was granted; and

(c) the land–

(i) has by reason of any works carried out in accordance with that planning permission become permanently unusable by members of the public for the purposes of lawful sports and pastimes; or

(ii) will by reason of any works proposed to be carried out in accordance with that planning permission become permanently unusable by members of the public for those purposes.

(6) In determining the period of 20 years referred to in subsections (2) (a), (3)(a) and (4)(a), there is to be disregarded any period during which access to the land was prohibited to members of the public by reason of any enactment.

(7) For the purposes of subsection (2)(b) in a case where the condition in subsection (2)(a) is satisfied–

(a) where persons indulge as of right in lawful sports and pastimes immediately before access to the land is prohibited as specified in subsection (6), those persons are to be regarded as continuing so to indulge; and

(b) where permission is granted in respect of use of the land for the purposes of lawful sports and pastimes, the permission is to be disregarded in determining whether persons continue to indulge in lawful sports and pastimes on the land "as of right".

(8) The owner of any land may apply to the commons registration authority to register the land as a town or village green.

(9) An application under subsection (8) may only be made with the consent of any relevant leaseholder of, and the proprietor of any relevant charge over, the land.

(10) In subsection (9)

"relevant charge" means–

(a) in relation to land which is registered in the register of title, a registered charge within the meaning of the Land Registration Act 2002 (c. 9);

(b) in relation to land which is not so registered–

(i) a charge registered under the Land Charges Act 1972 (c. 61); or

(ii) a legal mortgage, within the meaning of the Law of Property Act 1925 (c. 20), which is not registered under the Land Charges Act 1972;

"relevant leaseholder" means a leaseholder under a lease for a term of more than seven years from the date on which the lease was granted.

16.—Deregistration and exchange: applications

(1) The owner of any land registered as common land or as a town or **A1.6.016** village green may apply to the appropriate national authority for the land ("the release land") to cease to be so registered.

(2) If the release land is more than 200 square metres in area, the application must include a proposal under subsection (3).

(3) A proposal under this subsection is a proposal that land specified in the application ("replacement land") be registered as common land or as a town or village green in place of the release land.

(4) If the release land is not more than 200 square metres in area, the application may include a proposal under subsection (3).

(5) Where the application includes a proposal under subsection (3)

(a) the replacement land must be land to which this Part applies;

(b) the replacement land must not already be registered as common land or as a town or village green; and

(c) if the owner of the release land does not own the replacement land, the owner of the replacement land must join in the application.

(6) In determining the application, the appropriate national authority shall have regard to–

    (a) the interests of persons having rights in relation to, or occupying, the release land (and in particular persons exercising rights of common over it);

    (b) the interests of the neighbourhood;

    (c) the public interest;

    (d) any other matter considered to be relevant.

(7) The appropriate national authority shall in a case where–

    (a) the release land is not more than 200 square metres in area, and

    (b) the application does not include a proposal under subsection (3),

have particular regard under subsection (6) to the extent to which the absence of such a proposal is prejudicial to the interests specified in paragraphs (a) to (c) of that subsection.

(8) The reference in subsection (6)(c) to the public interest includes the public interest in–

    (a) nature conservation;

    (b) the conservation of the landscape;

    (c) the protection of public rights of access to any area of land; and

    (d) the protection of archaeological remains and features of historic interest.

(9) An application under this section may only be made with the consent of any relevant leaseholder of, and the proprietor of any relevant charge over–

    (a) the release land;

    (b) any replacement land.

(10) In subsection (9) "relevant charge" and "relevant leaseholder" have the meanings given by section 15(10).

17.—Deregistration and exchange: orders

A1.6.017   (1) Where the appropriate national authority grants an application under section 16 it must make an order requiring the commons registration authority to remove the release land from its register of common land or town or village greens.

(2) Where the application included a proposal to register replacement land, the order shall also require the commons registration authority–

- (a) to register the replacement land as common land or as a town or village green in place of the release land; and

- (b) to register as exercisable over the replacement land any rights of common which, immediately before the relevant date, are registered as exercisable over the release land.

(3) A commons registration authority must take such other steps on receiving an order under this section as regulations may require.

(4) Where immediately before the relevant date any rights of common are registered as exercisable over the release land, those rights are on that date extinguished in relation to that land.

(5) Where immediately before the relevant date any rights are exercisable over the release land by virtue of its being, or being part of, a town or village green–

- (a) those rights are extinguished on that date in respect of the release land; and

- (b) where any replacement land is registered in its place, those rights shall become exercisable as from that date over the replacement land instead.

(6) Where immediately before the relevant date the release land was registered as common land and any relevant provision applied in relation to it–

- (a) the provision shall on that date cease to apply to the release land; and

- (b) where any replacement land is registered in its place, the provision shall on that date apply to the replacement land instead.

(7) An order under this section may contain–

- (a) provision disapplying the effect of subsection (5)(b) or (6)(b) in relation to any replacement land;

- (b) supplementary provision as to the effect in relation to any replacement land of–

(i) any rights exercisable over the release land by virtue of its being, or being part of, a town or village green;

(ii) any relevant provision;

(c) supplementary provision as to the effect in relation to the release land or any replacement land of any local or personal Act.

(8) In subsections (6) and (7) "relevant provision" means a provision contained in, or made under–(a) section 193 of the Law of Property Act 1925 (c. 20);

(b) a scheme under the Metropolitan Commons Act 1866 (c. 122);

(c) an Act under the Commons Act 1876 (c. 56) confirming a provisional order of the Inclosure Commissioners;

(d) a scheme under the Commons Act 1899 (c. 30);

(e) section 1 of the Commons Act 1908 (c. 44).

(9) In this section, "relevant date" means the date on which the commons registration authority amends its register as required under subsections (1) and (2).

(10) Regulations may make provision for the publication of an order under this section.

Conclusiveness and correction of the registers

18.—Conclusiveness

A1.6.018   (1) This section applies to land registered as common land, or as a town or village green, which is registered as being subject to a right of common.

(2) If the land would not otherwise have been subject to that right, it shall be deemed to have become subject to that right, as specified in the register, upon its registration.

(3) If the right is registered as attached to any land, the right shall, if it would not otherwise have attached to that land, be deemed to have become so attached upon registration of its attachment.

(4) If the right is not registered as attached to any land, the person registered as the owner of the right shall, if he would not otherwise have been its owner, be deemed to have become its owner upon his registration.

(5) Nothing in subsection (2) affects any constraint on the exercise of a right of common where the constraint does not appear in the register.

(6) It is immaterial whether the registration referred to in subsection (2), (3) or (4) occurred before or after the commencement of this section.

19.—Correction

(1) A commons registration authority may amend its register of **A1.6.019** common land or town or village greens for any purpose referred to in subsection (2).

(2) Those purposes are–

(a) correcting a mistake made by the commons registration authority in making or amending an entry in the register;

(b) correcting any other mistake, where the amendment would not affect–

(i) the extent of any land registered as common land or as a town or village green; or

(ii) what can be done by virtue of a right of common;

(c) removing a duplicate entry from the register;

(d) updating the details of any name or address referred to in an entry;

(e) updating any entry in the register relating to land registered as common land or as a town or village green to take account of accretion or diluvion.

(3) References in this section to a mistake include–

(a) a mistaken omission, and

(b) an unclear or ambiguous description,

and it is immaterial for the purposes of this section whether a mistake was made before or after the commencement of this section.

(4) An amendment may be made by a commons registration authority–

(a) on its own initiative; or

(b) on the application of any person.

(5) A mistake in a register may not be corrected under this section if the authority considers that, by reason of reliance reasonably placed on the register by any person or for any other reason, it would in all the circumstances be unfair to do so.

(6) Regulations may make further provision as to the criteria to be applied in determining an application or proposal under this section.

(7) The High Court may order a commons registration authority to amend its register of common land or town or village greens if the High Court is satisfied that–

(a) any entry in the register, or any information in an entry, was at any time included in the register as a result of fraud; and

(b) it would be just to amend the register.

Part VI:
Appendix Two

Part VI: Statutory Instruments

LAND REGISTRATION RULES 2003

SI 2003/1417

1.—Citation and commencement

These rules may be cited as the Land Registration Rules 2003 and shall **A2.1.001** come into force on the day that section 1 of the Act comes into force.

PART 1

THE REGISTER OF TITLE

2.—Form and arrangement of the register of title

(1) The register of title may be kept in electronic or paper form, or **A2.1.002** partly in one form and partly in the other.

(2) Subject to rule 3, the register of title must include an individual register for each registered estate which is–

(a) an estate in land, or

(b) a rentcharge, franchise, manor or profit a prendre in gross, vested in a proprietor.

3.—Individual registers and more than one registered estate, division and amalgamation

(1) The registrar may include more than one registered estate in an **A2.1.003** individual register if the estates are of the same kind and are vested in the same proprietor.

(2) On first registration of a registered estate, the registrar may open an individual register for each separate area of land affected by the proprietor's registered estate as he designates.

(3) Subsequently, the registrar may open an individual register for part of the registered estate in a registered title and retain the existing individual register for the remainder–

(a) on the application of the proprietor of the registered estate and of any registered charge over it, or

(b) if he considers it desirable for the keeping of the register of title, or

(c) on the registration of a charge of part of the registered estate comprised in the registered title.

733

(4) The registrar may amalgamate two or more registered titles, or add an estate which is being registered for the first time to an existing registered title, if the estates are of the same kind and are vested in the same proprietor–

    (a) on the application of the proprietor of the registered estate and of any registered charge over it, or

    (b) if he considers it desirable for the keeping of the register of title.

(5) Where the registrar has divided a registered title under paragraph (3)(b) or amalgamated registered titles or an estate on first registration with a registered title under paragraph (4)(b) he–

    (a) must notify the proprietor of the registered estate and any registered charge, unless they have agreed to such action, and

    (b) may make a new edition of any individual register or make entries on any individual register to reflect the division or amalgamation.

4.—Arrangement of individual registers

A2.1.004   (1) Each individual register must have a distinguishing number, or series of letters and numbers, known as the title number.

(2) Each individual register must consist of a property register, a proprietorship register and, where necessary, a charges register.

(3) An entry in an individual register may be made by reference to a plan or other document; in which case the registrar must keep the original or a copy of the document.

(4) Whenever the registrar considers it desirable, he may make a new edition of any individual register so that it contains only the subsisting entries, rearrange the entries in the register or alter its title number.

5.—Contents of the property register

A2.1.005   Except where otherwise permitted, the property register of a registered estate must contain–

    (a) a description of the registered estate which in the case of a registered estate in land, rentcharge or registered franchise which is an affecting franchise must refer to a plan based on the Ordnance Survey map and known as the title plan;

    (b) where appropriate, details of–

(i) the inclusion or exclusion of mines and minerals in or from the registration under rule 32,

(ii) easements, rights and privileges benefiting the registered estate and other similar matters,

(iii) all exceptions or reservations arising on enfranchisement of formerly copyhold land, and

(iv) any . . . matter otherwise required to be entered in any other part of the register which the registrar considers may more conveniently be entered in the property register, and

(c) such other matters as are required to be entered in the property register by these rules.

6.—Property register of a registered leasehold estate

(1) The property register of a registered leasehold estate must also **A2.1.006** contain sufficient particulars of the registered lease to enable that lease to be identified.

(2) Subject to rule 72A(3), if the lease contains a provision that prohibits or restricts dispositions of the leasehold estate, the registrar must make an entry in the property register stating that the lease prohibits or restricts dispositions of the estate.

7.—Property register of a registered estate in a rentcharge, a franchise or a profit a prendre in gross

Where practicable, the property register of a registered estate in a **A2.1.007** rentcharge, franchise or a profit a prendre in gross must, if the estate was created by an instrument, also contain sufficient particulars of the instrument to enable it to be identified.

8.—Contents of the proprietorship register

(1) The proprietorship register of a registered estate must contain, **A2.1.008** where appropriate–

(a) the class of title,

(b) the name of the proprietor of the registered estate including, where the proprietor is a company registered under the Companies Acts, or a limited liability partnership incorporated under the Limited Liability Partnerships Act 2000, its registered number,

(c) an address for service of the proprietor of the registered estate in accordance with rule 198,

(d) restrictions under section 40 of the Act, including one entered under section 86(4) of the Act, in relation to the registered estate,

(e) notices under section 86(2) of the Act in relation to the registered estate,

(f) positive covenants by a transferor or transferee and indemnity convenants by a transferee entered under rules 64 or 65,

(g) details of any modification of the covenants implied by paragraphs 20(2) and (3) of Schedule 12 to the Act entered under rule 66,

(h) details of any modification of the covenants implied under the Law of Property (Miscellaneous Provisions) Act 1994 entered under rule 67(6), and

. . .

(j) such other matters as are required to be entered in the proprietorship register by these rules.

(2) Where practicable, the registrar must enter in the proprietorship register—

(a) on first registration of a registered estate,

(b) following completion by registration of a lease which is a registrable disposition, and

(c) on a subsequent change of proprietor of a registered estate,

the price paid or value declared for the registered estate.

(3) An entry made under paragraph (2) must remain until there is a change of proprietor, or some other change in the register of title which the registrar considers would result in the entry being misleading.

A2.1.009 9.—Contents of the charges register

Except where otherwise permitted, the charges register of a registered estate must contain, where appropriate–

(a) details of leases, charges, and any other interests which adversely affect the registered estate subsisting at the time of first registration of the estate or created thereafter,

(b) any dealings with the interests referred to in paragraph (a), or affecting their priority, which are capable of being noted on the register,

(c) sufficient details to enable any registered charge to be identified,

(d) the name of the proprietor of any registered charge including, where the proprietor is a company registered under the Companies Acts, or a limited liability partnership incorporated under the Limited Liability Partnerships Act 2000, its registered number,

(e) an address for service of the proprietor of any registered charge in accordance with rule 198,

(f) restrictions under section 40 of the Act, including one entered under section 86(4) of the Act, in relation to a registered charge,

(g) notices under section 86(2) of the Act in relation to a registered charge, . . .

(h) such other matters affecting the registered estate or any registered charge as are required to be entered in the charges register by these rules, and

(i) any matter otherwise required to be entered in any other part of the register which the registrar considers may more conveniently be entered in the charges register.

PART 2

INDICES

1.010 10.—Index to be kept under section 68 of the Act

(1) The index to be kept under section 68 of the Act must comprise–

(a) an index map from which it is possible to ascertain, in relation to a parcel of land, whether there is–

(i) a pending application for first registration (other than of title to a relating franchise),
(ii) a pending application for a caution against first registration (other than where the subject of the caution is a relating franchise),
(iii) a registered estate in land,
(iv) a registered rentcharge,
(v) a registered profit a prendre in gross,
(vi) a registered affecting franchise, or
(vii) a caution against first registration (other than where the subject of the caution is a relating franchise),

and, if there is such a registered estate or caution, the title number, and

737

(b) an index of verbal descriptions of–

(i) pending applications for first registration of title to relating franchises,

(ii) pending applications for cautions against first registration where the subject of the caution is a relating franchise,

(iii) registered franchises which are relating franchises,

(iv) registered manors, and

(v) cautions against first registration where the subject of the caution is a relating franchise,

and the title numbers of any such registered estates and cautions, arranged by administrative area.

(2) The information required to be shown in the index to be kept under section 68 is to be entered by the registrar in the index as soon as practicable.

11.—Index of proprietors' names

A2.1.011   (1) Subject to paragraph (2), the registrar must keep an index of proprietors' names, showing for each individual register the name of the proprietor of the registered estate and the proprietor of any registered charge together with the title number.

(2) Until every individual register is held in electronic form, the index need not contain the name of any corporate or joint proprietor of an estate or of a charge registered as proprietor prior to 1st May 1972.

(3) A person may apply in Form PN1 for a search to be made in the index in respect of—

(a) his own name,

(b) the name of a corporation aggregate, or

(c) the name of some other person in whose property he can satisfy the registrar that he is interested generally (for instance as trustee in bankruptcy or personal representative).

(4) On receipt of such an application the registrar must make the search and supply the applicant with details of every entry in the index relating to the particulars given in the application.

12.—The day list

A2.1.012   (1) The registrar must keep a record (known as the day list) showing the date and time at which every pending application under the Act or these rules was made and of every application for an official search with priority under rule 147.

(2) The entry of notice of an application for an official search with priority must remain on the day list until the priority period conferred by the entry has ceased to have effect.

(3) Where the registrar proposes to alter the register without having received an application he must enter his proposal on the day list and, when so entered, the proposal will have the same effect for the purposes of rules 15 and 20 as if it were an application to the registrar made at the date and time of its entry.

(4) In this rule the term "pending application" does not include [an application for a network access agreement under paragraph 1(4) of Schedule 5 to the Act, or] an application within Part 13, other than an application that the registrar designate a document an exempt information document under rule 136.

Part 3

Applications: General Provisions

13.—Form AP1

(1) Any application made under the Act or these rules for which no **A2.1.013** other application form is prescribed must be made in Form AP1.

(2) Paragraph (1) does not apply to–

(a) an application to remove from the register the name of a deceased joint registered proprietor,

(b) applications made under rule 14, or

(c) outline applications as defined in rule 54.

14.—Electronic delivery of applications

Any application to which rule 15 applies (other than an outline applica- **A2.1.014** tion under rule 54) may during the currency of any notice given under Schedule 2, and subject to and in accordance with the limitations contained in that notice, be delivered by electronic means and the applicant shall provide, in such order as may be required by that notice, such of the particulars required for an application of that type as are appropriate in the circumstances and as are required by the notice.

15.—Time at which applications are taken to be made

(1) An application received on a business day is to be taken as made at **A2.1.015** the earlier of–

(a) the time of the day that notice of it is entered in the day list, or

(b) (i) midnight marking the end of the day it was received if the application was received before 12 noon, or
(ii) midnight marking the end of the next business day after the day it was received if the application was received at or after 12 noon.

(2) An application received on a day which is not a business day is to be taken as made at the earlier of–

(a) the time of [the] day that notice of it is entered in the day list, or

(b) midnight marking the end of the next business day after the day it was received.

(3) In this rule an application is received when it is delivered–

(a) to the designated proper office in accordance with an order under section 100(3) of the Act, or

(b) to the registrar in accordance with a written arrangement as to delivery made between the registrar and the applicant or between the registrar and the applicant's conveyancer, or

(c) to the registrar under the provisions of any relevant notice given under Schedule 2.

(4) This rule does not apply to applications under Part 13, other than an application that the registrar designate a document an exempt information document under rule 136.

16.—Applications not in order

A2.1.016 (1) If an application is not in order the registrar may raise such requisitions as he considers necessary, specifying a period (being not less than twenty business days) within which the applicant must comply with the requisitions.

(2) If the applicant fails to comply with the requisitions within that period, the registrar may cancel the application or may extend the period when this appears to him to be reasonable in the circumstances.

(3) If an application appears to the registrar to be substantially defective, he may reject it on delivery or he may cancel it at any time thereafter.

(4) Where a fee for an application is paid by means of a cheque and the registrar becomes aware, before that application has been completed, that the cheque has not been honoured, the application may be cancelled.

17.—Additional evidence and enquiries

If the registrar at any time considers that the production of any further **A2.1.017** documents or evidence or the giving of any notice is necessary or desirable, he may refuse to complete or proceed with an application, or to do any act or make any entry, until such documents, evidence or notices have been supplied or given.

18.—Continuation of application on a transfer by operation of law

If, before an application has been completed, the whole of the appli- **A2.1.018** cant's interest is transferred by operation of law, the application may be continued by the person entitled to that interest in consequence of that transfer.

19.—Objections

(1) Subject to paragraph (5), an objection under section 73 of the Act to **A2.1.019** an application must be made by delivering to the registrar at the appropriate office a written statement signed by the objector or his conveyancer.

(2) The statement must–

(a) state that the objector objects to the application,

(b) state the grounds for the objection, and

(c) give the full name of the objector and an address for service in accordance with rule 198.

(3) Subject to paragraph (5), the written statement referred to in paragraph (1) must be delivered–

(a) in paper form, or

(b) to the electronic address, or

(c) to the fax number.

(4) In paragraph (3) the reference to the electronic address and the fax number is to the electronic address or fax number for the appropriate office specified in a direction by the registrar under section 100(4) of the Act as that to be used for delivery of objections.

(5) Where a person is objecting to an application in response to a notice given by the registrar, he may alternatively do so in the manner and to the address stated in the notice as provided by rule 197(1)(c).

(6) In this rule the appropriate office is the same office as the proper office, designated under an order under section 100(3) of the Act, for the receipt of an application relating to the land in respect of which the objection is made, but on the assumption that if the order contains exceptions none of the exceptions apply to that application.

20.—Completion of applications

A2.1.020 (1) Any entry in, removal of an entry from or alteration of the register pursuant to an application under the Act or these rules has effect from the time of the making of the application.

(2)—This rule does not apply to the applications mentioned in section 74 of the Act.

Part 4

FIRST REGISTRATION

A2.1.021 ## 31.—First registration-foreshore

(1) Where it appears to the registrar that any land included in an application for first registration comprises foreshore, he must serve a notice of that application on–

    (a) the Crown Estate Commissioners in every case,

    (b) the Chancellor of the Duchy of Lancaster in the case of land in the county palatine of Lancaster,

    (c) the appropriate person in the case of land in the counties of Devon and Cornwall and in the Isles of Scilly and in the case of land within the jurisdiction of the Port of London Authority, and

    (d) the Port of London Authority in the case of land within its jurisdiction.

(2) A notice under paragraph (1) must provide a period ending at 12 noon on the twentieth business day after the date of issue of the notice in which to object to the application.

(3) A notice need not be served under paragraph (1) where, if it was served, it would result in it being served on the applicant for first registration.

(4) In this rule–

    "the appropriate person" means such person as the Duke of Cornwall, or the possessor for the time being of the Duchy of Cornwall, appoints, "foreshore" has the meaning given by paragraph 13(3) of Schedule 6 to the Act.

32.—Mines and minerals-note as to inclusion or exclusion   A2.1.022

Where, on first registration of an estate in land which comprises or includes the land beneath the surface, the registrar is satisfied that the mines and minerals are included in or excluded from the applicant's title he must make an appropriate note in the register.

33.—First registration-entry of beneficial rights   A2.1.023

(1) The benefit of an appurtenant right may be entered in the register at the time of first registration if–

   (a) on examination of the title, or

   (b) on receipt of a written application providing details of the right and evidence of its existence,

      the registrar is satisfied that the right subsists as a legal estate and benefits the registered estate.

(2) If the registrar is not satisfied that the right subsists as a legal interest benefiting the registered estate, he may enter details of the right claimed in the property register with such qualification as he considers appropriate.

(3) The evidence referred to in paragraph (1)(b) may consist of, or include, a statement of truth, which may be made in Form ST4 if appropriate.

34.—First registration-registration of a proprietor of a legal mortgage not within rule 22 or rule 38

(1) The registrar must enter the mortgagee of a legal mortgage to   **A2.1.024** which this rule applies as the proprietor of that charge if on first registration of the legal estate charged by that charge he is satisfied of that person's entitlement.

(2) This rule applies to a legal mortgage–

   (a) which is either–

      (i) a charge on the legal estate that is being registered, or
      (ii) is a charge on such charge, and

   (b) which is not a charge falling within rule 22 or rule 38.

35.—First registration-entry of burdens

A2.1.025 (1) On first registration the registrar must enter a notice in the register of the burden of any interest which appears from his examination of the title to affect the registered estate.

(2) This rule does not apply to–

(a) an interest that under section 33 or 90(4) of the Act cannot be protected by notice,

(b) a public right,

(c) a local land charge,

(d) an interest which appears to the registrar to be of a trivial or obvious character, or the entry of a notice in respect of which would be likely to cause confusion or inconvenience.

36.—First registration-note as to rights of light and air

A2.1.026 On first registration, if it appears to the registrar that an agreement prevents the acquisition of rights of light or air for the benefit of the registered estate, he may make an entry in the property register of that estate.

Part 5

CAUTIONS AGAINST FIRST REGISTRATION

39.—Definitions

A2.1.027 In this Part–

"cautioner" has the same meaning as in section 22 of the Act (read with rule 52),

"cautioner's register" is the register so named in rule 41(2) the contents of which are described in rule 41(5),

"relevant interest" means the interest claimed by the cautioner in the unregistered legal estate to which the caution against first registration relates.

40.—Form and arrangement of the cautions register

A2.1.028 (1) The cautions register may be kept in electronic or paper form, or partly in one form and partly in the other.

(2) Subject to paragraph (3), the cautions register will comprise an individual caution register for each caution against the registration of title to an unregistered estate.

(3) On registration of a caution, the registrar may open an individual caution register for each separate area of land affected by the caution as he designates.

41.—Arrangement of individual caution registers

(1) Each individual caution register will have a distinguishing number, **A2.1.029** or series of letters and numbers, known as the caution title number.

(2) Each individual caution register will be in two parts called the caution property register and the cautioner's register.

(3) The caution property register will contain–

    (a)   a description of the legal estate to which the caution relates, and

    (b)   a description of the relevant interest.

(4) Where the legal estate to which the caution relates is an estate in land, a rentcharge, or an affecting franchise, the description will refer to a caution plan, which plan will be based on the Ordnance Survey map.

(5) The cautioner's register will contain–

    (a)   the name of the cautioner including, where the cautioner is a company registered under the Companies Acts, or a limited liability partnership incorporated under the Limited Liability Partnerships Act 2000, its registered number,

    (b)   an address for service in accordance with rule 198, and

    (c)   where appropriate, details of any person consenting to the lodging of the caution under rule 47.

42.—Caution against first registration-application

An application for a caution against first registration must be made in **A2.1.030** Form CT1 and contain sufficient details, by plan or otherwise, so that the extent of the land to which the caution relates can be identified clearly on the Ordnance Survey map.

43.—Withdrawal of a caution against first registration-application

An application to withdraw a caution against first registration must be **A2.1.031** made in Form WCT and, if the application is made in respect of part only of the land to which the individual caution register relates, it must contain sufficient details, by plan or otherwise, so that the extent of that part can be identified clearly on the Ordnance Survey map.

44.—Cancellation of a caution against first registration-application

A2.1.032 (1) Subject to paragraph (5), an application for the cancellation of a caution against first registration must be in Form CCT.

(2) Where the application is made in respect of part only of the land to which the individual caution register relates, it must contain sufficient details, by plan or otherwise, so that the extent of that part can be identified clearly on the Ordnance Survey map.

(3) Where a person applies under section 18(1)(a) of the Act or rule 45(a) or (b)(ii), evidence to satisfy the registrar that he is entitled to apply must accompany the application.

(4) Where the applicant, or a person from whom the applicant derives title to the legal estate by operation of law, has consented to the lodging of the caution, evidence of the facts referred to in rule 46 must accompany the application.

(5) Where an application is made for the cancellation of a caution against first registration by Her Majesty by virtue of rule 45(b)(i), Form CCT must be used with such modifications to it as are appropriate and have been approved by the registrar.

45.—Other persons who may apply to cancel a caution against first registration

A2.1.033 In addition to the owner of the legal estate to which the caution relates–

    (a) the owner of a legal estate derived out of that estate, and

    (b) where the land to which the caution relates is demesne land,

        (i) Her Majesty, or
        (ii) the owner of a legal estate affecting the demesne land,

may apply under section 18(1)(b) of the Act for cancellation of a caution against first registration.

46.—Application for cancellation of a caution against first registration by a person who originally consented

A2.1.034 A person to whom section 18(2) of the Act applies may make an application for cancellation of a caution against first registration only if–

    (a) the relevant interest has come to an end, or

    (b) the consent referred to in section 18(2) was induced by fraud, misrepresentation, mistake or undue influence or given under duress.

47.—Consent to registration of a caution against first registration

For the purposes of section 18(2) of the Act a person consents to the **A2.1.035** lodging of a caution against first registration if before the caution is entered in the cautions register–

(a) he has confirmed in writing that he consents to the lodging of the caution, and

(b) that consent is produced to the registrar.

48.—Alteration of the cautions register by the court

(1) If in any proceedings the court decides that the cautioner does not **A2.1.036** own the relevant interest, or only owns part, or that such interest either wholly or in part did not exist or has come to an end, the court must make an order for alteration of the cautions register under section 20(1) of the Act.

(2) An order for alteration of the cautions register must state the caution title number of the individual caution register affected, describe the alteration that is to be made, and direct the registrar to make the alteration.

(3) For the purposes of section 20(2) of the Act an order for alteration of the cautions register may only be served on the registrar by making an application for him to give effect to the order.

49.—Alteration of the cautions register by the registrar

(1) Subject to paragraph (2), if the registrar is satisfied that the cautioner **A2.1.037** does not own the relevant interest, or only owns part, or that such interest did not exist or has come to an end wholly or in part, he must on application alter the cautions register under section 21(1) of the Act.

(2) The registrar is not obliged to alter the cautions register under section 21(1) of the Act to substitute another person for the cautioner in the cautioner's register unless the whole of the relevant interest is vested in that other person by operation of law.

50.—Applications to the registrar to alter the cautions register and service of notice

(1) A person who wishes the registrar to alter the cautions register **A2.1.038** under section 21(1) of the Act must request the registrar to do so by an application, which must include–

    (a) written details of the alteration required and of the grounds on which the application is made, and

    (b) any supporting document.

(2) Before the registrar alters the cautions register under section 21(1) of the Act he must serve a notice on the cautioner giving details of the application, unless the registrar is satisfied that service of the notice is unnecessary.

51.—Alteration of the cautions register — alteration of cautioner

A2.1.039   (1) A person who claims that the whole of the relevant interest described in an individual caution register is vested in him by operation of law as successor to the cautioner may apply for the register to be altered under section 21(1) of the Act to substitute him for the cautioner in the cautioner's register. . . .

(2) If the registrar does not serve notice under rule 50(2) or if the cautioner does not object within the time specified in the notice, the registrar must give effect to the application.

52.—Definition of "the cautioner"

A2.1.040   (1) The other person referred to in sections 22 and 73(2) of the Act shall be the person for the time being shown as cautioner in the cautioner's register, where that person is not the person who lodged the caution against first registration.

(2) Where the cautioner shown in the cautioner's register comprises more than one person, then each such person has a separate right to object to an application made under section 18 of the Act.

53.—The prescribed periods under section 16(2) and section 18(4) of the Act

A2.1.041   (1) The period for the purpose of section 16(2) and section 18(4) of the Act is the period ending at 12 noon on the fifteenth business day after the date of issue of the notice under section 16(1) or section 18(3) of the Act, as the case may be, or such longer period as the registrar may allow following a request under paragraph (2), provided that the longer period never exceeds a period ending at 12 noon on the thirtieth business day after the date of issue of the notice.

(2) The request referred to in paragraph (1) is one by the cautioner to the registrar setting out why the longer period referred to in that paragraph should be allowed.

(3) If a request is received under paragraph (2), the registrar may, if he considers it appropriate, seek the views of the person who applied for registration or cancellation, as the case may be, and if, after considering any such views and all other relevant matters, he is satisfied that a longer period should be allowed he may allow such period (not exceeding a period ending at 12 noon on the thirtieth business day after the date of issue of the notice) as he considers appropriate, whether or not the period is the same as any period requested by the cautioner.

(4) A request under paragraph (2) must be made before the period ending at 12 noon on the fifteenth business day after the date of issue of the notice has expired.

Part 6

REGISTERED LAND: APPLICATIONS,
DISPOSITIONS AND MISCELLANEOUS ENTRIES

Mines or minerals

70.—Description of land where mines or minerals situated

Where the registrar is describing a registered estate in land in the **A2.1.042** property register by reference to land where mines or minerals are or may be situated, he may make an entry to the effect that the description is an entry made under rule 5(a) and is not a note that the registered estate includes the mines or minerals for the purposes of paragraph 2 of Schedule 8 to the Act.

71.—Note as to inclusion of mines or minerals in the registered estate

(1) An application for a note to be entered that a registered estate **A2.1.043** includes the mines or minerals, or specified mines or minerals, must be accompanied by evidence to satisfy the registrar that those mines or minerals are included in the registered estate.

(2) If the registrar is satisfied that those mines or minerals are included in the registered estate, he must enter the appropriate note.

Miscellaneous entries

72.—Register entries arising from transfers and charges of part

A2.1.044   (1) Subject to paragraphs (2) and (3), on registration of a transfer or charge of part of the registered estate in a registered title the registrar must make an entry in the property register of that registered title referring to the removal of the estate comprised in the transfer or charge.

(2) The registrar may, instead of making the entry referred to in paragraph (1), make a new edition of the registered title out of which the transfer or charge is made and, if the registrar considers it desirable, he may allot a new title number to that registered title.

(3) Paragraph (1) only applies to a charge of part of a registered estate in a registered title if the registrar decides that the charged part will be comprised in a separate registered title from the uncharged part.

(4) Subject to paragraph (5), on registration of a transfer or charge of part of the registered estate in a registered title the registrar must (where appropriate) make entries in the relevant individual registers in respect of any rights, restrictive covenants, provisions and other matters created by the transfer or charge which are capable of being entered in an individual register.

(5) The registrar need make no entries under paragraph (4) in individual registers where the title numbers of those registers in which entries are to be made have not been given in panel 2 of the Form AP1 lodged for the purpose of registering the transfer or charge, unless separate application is made in respect of the rights, restrictive covenants, provisions or other matters.

(6) Unless the Form AP1 contains a specific application, the registrar need not complete under paragraph 6 of Schedule 2 to the Act the registration of an interest of a kind falling within section 1(2)(b) of the Law of Property Act 1925 contained in a transfer or charge of part of the registered estate in a registered title.

72A.—Register entries arising in respect of leases within section 27(2)(b) of the Act granted on or after 19 June 2006

A2.1.045   (1) This rule applies to leases within section 27(2)(b) of the Act granted on or after 19 June 2006.

(2) Subject to paragraphs (3), (4) and (6), on completion of the lease by registration the registrar must (where appropriate) make entries in the

relevant individual register in respect of interests contained in that lease which are of the nature referred to in clauses LR9, LR10, LR11 or LR12.

(3) Subject to rule 58A(3), where the lease is a prescribed clauses lease and contains a prohibition or restriction on disposal of the nature referred to in clause LR8 or contains interests of the nature referred to in clauses LR9, LR10, LR11 or LR12, but the prohibition or restriction or interests are not specified or referred to in those clauses or the lease does not contain the required wording in relation to them, then the registrar need take no action in respect of them unless separate application is made.

(4) The registrar need make no entries in individual registers in respect of interests of the nature referred to in clauses LR9, LR10 or LR11 or a restriction set out in clause LR13 where—

(a) in the case of a prescribed clauses lease, the title numbers of the individual registers have not been given in clause LR2.2, or

(b) in any other case, the title numbers of the individual registers required by clause LR2.2 have not been given in panel 2 of the Form AP1 lodged for the purpose of completing the lease by registration,

unless separate application is made in respect of the interests or restriction.

(5) Where a separate application required by paragraphs (3) or (4) is made in Form AP1 and is in respect of either a prohibition or restriction on disposal of the lease or the grant or reservation of an easement, the Form AP1 must specify the particular clause, schedule or paragraph of a schedule where the prohibition or restriction or easement is contained in the lease.

(6) The requirement under paragraph (2) to make an entry in respect of an interest of the nature referred to in clause LR12 is satisfied by entry (where appropriate) of notice of the interest created.

(7) In this rule—

(a) a reference to a clause with the prefix "LR" followed by a number is to the clause so prefixed and numbered in Schedule 1A, and

(b) "prescribed clauses lease" and "required wording" have the same meanings as in rule 58A(4).

72B.—Entries in the tenant's registered title in respect of notices in the landlord's registered title

On completion of a lease within section 27(2)(b) or (c) of the Act by **A2.1.046** registration, the registrar must enter a notice or make another entry, as appropriate, in the individual register of the registered lease in respect of any interest which—

(a) at the time of registration, is the subject of a notice in the individual register of the registered estate out of which the lease is granted, and

(b) the registrar considers may affect the registered lease.

72C.—Register entries arising from other registrable dispositions

A2.1.047   (1) This rule applies to dispositions of registered estates within section 27(2) of the Act, to which rules 72 and 72A do not apply.

(2) Subject to paragraph (3), on registration of a disposition within paragraph (1), the registrar must (where appropriate) make entries in the relevant individual registers in respect of any rights, restrictive covenants, provisions and other matters created by the disposition which are capable of being entered in an individual register.

(3) The registrar need make no entries in individual registers under paragraph (2) where the title numbers of those registers have not been given in panel 2 of the Form AP1 lodged for the purpose of registering the disposition, unless separate application is made in respect of the rights, restrictive covenants, provisions or other matters.

(4) Unless the Form AP1 contains a specific application, the registrar need not complete under paragraph 6 of Schedule 2 to the Act the registration of an interest of a kind falling within section 1(2)(b) of the Law of Property Act 1925 contained in a disposition within paragraph (1).

73A.—Application for register entries for legal easements and profits a prendre[1]

A2.1.048   (1) A proprietor of a registered estate may apply to be registered as the proprietor of a legal easement or profit a prendre which—

(a) has been expressly granted or reserved over an unregistered estate, or

(b) has been acquired otherwise than by express grant or reservation.

(2) The application must be accompanied by evidence to satisfy the registrar that the easement or profit a prendre is a legal estate which subsists for the benefit of the applicant's registered estate.

(3) In paragraph (1)(a) the reference to express grant does not include a grant as a result of the operation of section 62 of the Law of Property Act 1925, but the reference in paragraph (1)(b) to acquisition otherwise than

---

[1] Rule 73A was substituted for rr.73–75 by Land Registration (Amendment) Rules 2008 (SI 2008/1919).

by express grant does include an acquisition as a result of the operation of that section.

(4) The evidence referred to in paragraph (2) may consist of, or include, a statement of truth, which may be made in Form ST4, if appropriate.

(5) Where the registrar is not satisfied that the right claimed is a legal estate which subsists for the benefit of the applicant's registered estate, the registrar may enter details of the right claimed in the property register with such qualification as he considers appropriate.

76.—Note as to rights of light or air

If it appears to the registrar that an agreement prevents the acquisition **A2.1.049** of rights of light or air for the benefit of the registered estate, he may make an entry in the property register of that estate.

77.—No entry in the register of a right of entry in certain leases

(1) This rule applies to a right of entry created in a grant of a term of **A2.1.050** years absolute, the right being exercisable over or in respect of that term of years.

(2) Where the grant is completed by registration, the disposition which consists of the creation of the right of entry is also completed by registration, without any specific entry relating to it being made in the register.

Part 7

NOTICES

80.—Certain interests to be protected by agreed notices

A person who applies for the entry of a notice in the register must apply **A2.1.051** for the entry of an agreed notice where the application is for–

(a) a ... home rights notice,

(b) an inheritance tax notice,

(c) a notice in respect of an order under the Access to Neighbouring Land Act 1992,

(d) a notice of any variation of a lease effected by or under an order under section 38 of the Landlord and Tenant Act 1987 (including any variation as modified by an order under section 39(4) of that Act),

(e) a notice in respect of a–

    (i) public right, or

    (ii) customary right.

81.—Application for an agreed notice

A2.1.052 (1) Subject to paragraph (2), an application for the entry in the register of an agreed notice (including an agreed notice in respect of any variation of an interest protected by a notice) must be–

(a) made in Form AN1,

(b) accompanied by the order or instrument (if any) giving rise to the interest claimed or, if there is no such order or instrument, such other details of the interest claimed as satisfy the registrar as to the nature of the applicant's claim, and

(c) accompanied, where appropriate, by–

    (i) the consent referred to in section 34(3)(b) of the Act, and, where appropriate, evidence to satisfy the registrar that the person applying for, or consenting to the entry of, the notice is entitled to be registered as the proprietor of the registered estate or charge affected by the interest to which the application relates, or

    (ii) evidence to satisfy the registrar as to the validity of the applicant's claim.

(2) Paragraph (1) does not apply to an application for the entry of a . . . home rights notice made under rule 82.

82.—Application for a . . . home rights notice or its renewal

A2.1.053 (1) An application under section 31(10)(a) or section 32 of, and paragraph 4(3)(b) of Schedule 4 to, the Family Law Act 1996 for the entry of an agreed notice in the register must be in Form HR1.

(2) An application to renew the registration of a . . . home rights notice or a matrimonial home rights caution under section 32 of, and paragraph 4(3)(a) of Schedule 4 to, the Family Law Act 1996 must be in Form HR2.

(3) An application in Form HR1, where the application is made under section 32 of, and paragraph 4(3)(b) of Schedule 4 to, the Family Law Act 1996 , or in Form HR2 must be accompanied by–

(a) an office copy of the section 33(5) order, or

(b) a conveyancer's certificate that he holds an office copy of the section 33(5) order.

83.—Application for entry of a unilateral notice

An application for the entry in the register of a unilateral notice must **A2.1.054**
be in Form UN1.

84.—Entry of a notice in the register

(1) A notice under section 32 of the Act must be entered in the charges **A2.1.055**
register of the registered title affected.

(2) The entry must identify the registered estate or registered charge
affected and, where the interest protected by the notice only affects part
of the registered estate in a registered title, it must contain sufficient
details, by reference to a plan or otherwise, to identify clearly that part.

(3) In the case of a notice (other than a unilateral notice), the entry must
give details of the interest protected.

(4) In the case of a notice (other than a unilateral notice) of a variation
of an interest protected by a notice, the entry must give details of the
variation.

(5) In the case of a unilateral notice, the entry must give such details of
the interest protected as the registrar considers appropriate.

85.—Removal of a unilateral notice

(1) An application for the removal of a unilateral notice from the **A2.1.056**
register under section 35(3) of the Act must be in Form UN2.

(2) The personal representative or trustee in bankruptcy of the person
shown in the register as the beneficiary of a unilateral notice may apply
under section 35(3) of the Act; and if he does he must provide evidence to
satisfy the registrar as to his appointment as personal representative or
trustee in bankruptcy.

(3) If the registrar is satisfied that the application is in order he must
remove the notice.

86.—Cancellation of a unilateral notice

(1) An application to cancel a unilateral notice under section 36 of the **A2.1.057**
Act must be made in Form UN4.

(2) An application made under section 36(1)(b) of the Act must be
accompanied by–

    (a) evidence to satisfy the registrar of the applicant's entitlement
        to be registered as the proprietor of the estate or charge to
        which the unilateral notice the subject of the application
        relates, or

(b) a conveyancer's certificate that the conveyancer is satisfied that the applicant is entitled to be registered as the proprietor of the estate or charge to which the unilateral notice the subject of the application relates.

(3) The period referred to in section 36(3) of the Act is the period ending at 12 noon on the fifteenth business day after the date of issue of the notice or such longer period as the registrar may allow following a request under paragraph (4), provided that the longer period never exceeds a period ending at 12 noon on the thirtieth business day after the issue of the notice.

(4) The request referred to in paragraph (3) is one by the beneficiary to the registrar setting out why the longer period referred to in that paragraph should be allowed.

(5) If a request is received under paragraph (4) the registrar may, if he considers it appropriate, seek the views of the person who applied for cancellation and if after considering any such views and all other relevant matters he is satisfied that a longer period should be allowed he may allow such period (not exceeding a period ending at 12 noon on the thirtieth business day after the issue of the notice) as he considers appropriate, whether or not the period is the same as any period requested by the beneficiary.

(6) A request under paragraph (4) must be made before the period ending at 12 noon on the fifteenth business day after the date of issue of the notice under section 36(2) of the Act has expired.

(7) A person entitled to be registered as the beneficiary of a notice under rule 88 may object to an application under section 36(1) of the Act for cancellation of that notice and the reference to the beneficiary in section 36(3) includes such a person.

(8) Where there are two or more persons—

(a) shown in the register as the beneficiary of the notice, or

(b) to whom paragraph (7) applies,

each such person is a beneficiary of the notice for the purpose of section 36(3) of the Act.

87.—Cancellation of a notice (other than a unilateral notice or a . . . home rights notice)

A2.1.058   (1) An application for the cancellation of a notice (other than a unilateral notice or a . . . home rights notice) must be in Form CN1 and be accompanied by evidence to satisfy the registrar of the determination of the interest.

(2) Where a person applies for cancellation of a notice in accordance with paragraph (1) and the registrar is satisfied that the interest protected by the notice has come to an end, he must cancel the notice or make an entry in the register that the interest so protected has come to an end.

(3) If the interest protected by the notice has only come to an end in part, the registrar must make an appropriate entry.

(4) If the registrar is not satisfied that the interest protected by the notice has come to an end, he may enter in the register details of the circumstances in which the applicant claims the interest has determined.

87A.—Cancellation of a home rights notice

An application for the cancellation of a home rights notice must be made in Form HR4. **A2.1.059**

88.—Registration of a new or additional beneficiary of a unilateral notice

(1) A person entitled to the benefit of an interest protected by a unilateral notice may apply to be entered in the register in place of, or in addition to, the registered beneficiary. **A2.1.060**

(2) An application under paragraph (1) must be–

   (a) in Form UN3, and

   (b) accompanied by evidence to satisfy the registrar of the applicant's title to the interest protected by the unilateral notice.

(3) Subject to paragraph (4), if an application is made in accordance with paragraph (2) and the registrar is satisfied that the interest protected by the unilateral notice is vested–

   (a) in the applicant, the registrar must enter the applicant in the register in place of the registered beneficiary, or

   (b) in the applicant and the registered beneficiary, the registrar must enter the applicant in addition to the registered beneficiary.

(4) Except where one of the circumstances specified in paragraph (5) applies, the registrar must serve notice of the application on the registered beneficiary before entering the applicant in the register.

(5) The registrar is not obliged to serve notice on the registered beneficiary if–

(a) the registered beneficiary signs Form UN3 or otherwise consents to the application, or

(b) the applicant is the registered beneficiary's personal representative and evidence of his title to act accompanies the application.

(6) In this rule, "registered beneficiary" means the person shown in the register as the beneficiary of the notice at the time an application is made under paragraph (1).

89.—Notice of unregistered interests

A2.1.061 (1) If the registrar enters a notice of an unregistered interest under section 37(1) of the Act, he must give notice–

(a) subject to paragraph (2), to the registered proprietor, and

(b) subject to paragraph (3), to any person who appears to the registrar to be entitled to the interest protected by the notice or whom the registrar otherwise considers appropriate.

(2) The registrar is not obliged to give notice to a registered proprietor under paragraph (1)(a) who applies for entry of the notice or otherwise consents to an application to enter the notice.

(3) The registrar is not obliged to give notice to a person referred to in paragraph (1)(b) if–

(a) that person applied for the entry of the notice or consented to the entry of the notice, or

(b) that person's name and his address for service under rule 198 are not set out in the individual register in which the notice is entered.

90.—Application for entry of a notice under paragraph 5(2) or, in certain cases, paragraph 7(2)(a) of Part 1 of Schedule 2 to the Act

A2.1.062 An application to meet the registration requirements under–

(a) paragraph 5(2) of Part 1 of Schedule 2 to the Act, or

(b) paragraph 7(2)(a) of that Part, where the interest is created for the benefit of an unregistered estate,

must be made in Form AP1.

Part 8

RESTRICTIONS

91.—Standard forms of restriction

(1) The forms of restriction set out in Schedule 4 (varied, where appro- **A2.1.063** priate, as permitted by rule 91A) are standard forms of restriction prescribed under section 43(2)(d) of the Act.

(2) The word "conveyancer", where it appears in any of the standard forms of restriction, has the same meaning as in these rules.

(3) The word "registered", where it appears in any of the standard forms of restriction in relation to a disposition, means completion of the registration of that disposition by meeting the relevant registration requirements under section 27 of the Act.

91A.—Completion of standard forms of restriction

(1) Subject to paragraphs (2) and (3), if a standard form of restriction is **A2.1.064** to affect part only of the registered estate, then, where it refers to a disposition, or to a disposition of a specified type, to which it applies, that reference may be followed by the words "of the part of the registered estate" together with a sufficient description, by reference to a plan or otherwise, to identify clearly the part so affected.

(2) The words incorporated under paragraph (1) shall be in place of the words "of the registered estate" where those latter words appear in a standard form of restriction and are referring to a disposition, or to a disposition of a specified type, to which the restriction applies.

(3) The registrar may alter the words of any restriction affecting part of the registered estate . . . that he intends to enter in the register so that such part is described by reference to the relevant title plan or in another appropriate way.

(4) A restriction in Form L, N, S, T, II, NN or OO may commence with—

(a) the words "Until the death of [*name*]",

(b) the words "Until the death of the survivor of [*names of two or more persons*]", or

(c) the word "Until" followed by a calendar date.

(5) A restriction in Form M, O, P or PP may commence with the word "Until" followed by a calendar date.

(6) Where a restriction in Form J, K, Q, S, T, BB, DD, FF, HH, JJ, LL or OO relates to a registered charge, which is one of two or more registered charges bearing the same date and affecting the same registered estate,

the words "in favour of" followed by the name of the registered proprietor of the charge must be inserted in the restriction after the date of the charge.

(7) Where in a standard form of restriction the word "they" or "their" refers to a person named in the restriction, it may be replaced as appropriate by the word "he", "she", "it", "his", "her" or "its".

(8) Where a standard form of restriction permits a type of disposition to be specified in place of the word "disposition", the types of disposition that may be specified are "transfer", "lease", "charge" or "sub-charge", or any appropriate combination of those types.

91B.—Where a certificate or consent under a restriction is given by a corporation

A2.1.065　(1) Subject to paragraphs (2), (3) and (4), where a certificate or written consent required by the terms of a restriction is given by a corporation aggregate, it must be signed on its behalf by—

   (a) its clerk, secretary or other permanent officer,

   (b) a member of its board of directors, council or other governing body,

   (c) its conveyancer, or

   (d) its duly authorised employee or agent.

(2) This rule does not apply where the certificate or written consent is given in a deed executed by the company or in a document to which section 91 of the Act applies.

(3) Paragraph (1) does not apply if a contrary intention appears in the restriction, except where paragraph (4) applies.

(4) Where a restriction requires a certificate or consent to be signed on behalf of a corporation aggregate by its secretary (whether or not it also permits signature by its conveyancer), and the corporation has no secretary, the certificate or consent must be signed on its behalf by a person specified in paragraph (1).

(5) A document signed on behalf of a corporation in accordance with this rule must state the full name of the signatory and the capacity in which the signatory signs.

92.—Application for a restriction and the prescribed period under section 45(2) of the Act

A2.1.066　(1) Subject to paragraphs (5), (6), (7) and (8) an application for a restriction to be entered in the register must be made in Form RX1.

(2) The application must be accompanied by–

    (a) full details of the required restriction,

    (b) where rule 198(2)(d) applies, the address for service of the person named in the restriction,

    (c) if the application is made with the consent of the relevant registered proprietor, or a person entitled to be registered as such proprietor, and that consent is not given in Form RX1, the relevant consent,

    (d) if the application is made by or with the consent of a person entitled to be registered as the relevant registered proprietor, evidence to satisfy the registrar of his entitlement, and

    (e) if the application is made by a person who claims that he has a sufficient interest in the making of the entry, the statement referred to in paragraph (3) signed by the applicant or his conveyancer.

(3) The statement required under paragraph (2)(e) must—

    (a) give details of the nature of the applicant's interest in the making of the entry of the required restriction, and

    (b) give details of how the applicant's interest arose.

(4) If requested to do so, an applicant within paragraph (2)(e) must supply further evidence to satisfy the registrar that he has a sufficient interest.

(5) The registrar may accept a certificate given by a conveyancer that the conveyancer is satisfied that the person making or consenting to the application is entitled to be registered as the relevant proprietor, and that either–

    (a) the conveyancer holds the originals of the documents that contain evidence of that person's entitlement, or

    (b) an application for registration of that person as proprietor is pending at the land registry.

(6) If an application is made with the consent of the relevant registered proprietor, or a person entitled to be registered as such proprietor, the registrar may accept a certificate given by a conveyancer that the conveyancer holds the relevant consent.

(7) Paragraph (1) of this rule does not apply where a person applies for the entry of a standard form of restriction—

(a) in the additional provisions panel of Form TP1, TP2, TR1, TR2, TR4, TR5, AS1, AS2 or AS3,

(b) in panel 8 of Form CH1 or in an electronic legal charge,

(c) in an approved charge,

(d) in clause LR13 (as set out in Schedule 1A) of a relevant lease, or

(e) in Form A, using Form SEV.

(8) This rule does not apply to an application to the registrar to give effect to an order of the court made under section 46 of the Act.

(9) The period for the purpose of section 45(2) of the Act is the period ending at 12 noon on the fifteenth business day after the date of issue of the notice under section 45(1) or, if more than one such notice is issued, the date of issue of the latest notice.

(10) In this rule—

"approved charge" means a charge the form of which (including the application for the restriction) has first been approved by the registrar, and

"relevant lease" means—(a) a prescribed clauses lease as defined in rule 58A(4), or

(b) any other lease which complies with the requirements as to form and content set out in rule 58A(1) and which either is required to be completed by registration under section 27(2)(b) of the Act or is the subject of an application for first registration of the title to it.

93.—Persons regarded as having a sufficient interest to apply for a restriction

A2.1.067 The following persons are to be regarded as included in section 43(1)(c) of the Act–

(a) any person who has an interest in a registered estate held under a trust of land where a sole proprietor or a survivor of joint proprietors (unless a trust corporation) will not be able to give a valid receipt for capital money, and who is applying for a restriction in Form A to be entered in the register of that registered estate,

(b) any person who has a sufficient interest in preventing a contravention of section 6(6) or section 6(8) of the Trusts of Land and

Appointment of Trustees Act 1996 and who is applying for a restriction in order to prevent such a contravention,

(c) any person who has an interest in a registered estate held under a trust of land where the powers of the trustees are limited by section 8 of the Trusts of Land and Appointment of Trustees Act 1996, and who is applying for a restriction in Form B to be entered in the register of that registered estate,

(d) any person who has an interest in the due administration of the estate of a deceased person, where–

   (i) the personal representatives of the deceased hold a registered estate on a trust of land created by the deceased's will and the personal representatives' powers are limited by section 8 of the Trusts of Land and Appointment of Trustees Act 1996, and

   (ii) he is applying for a restriction in Form C to be entered in the register of that registered estate,

(e) the donee of a special power of appointment in relation to registered land affected by that power,

(f) the Charity Commissioners in relation to registered land held upon charitable trusts,

(g) the Church Commissioners, the Parsonages Board or the Diocesan Board of Finance if applying for a restriction–

   (i) to give effect to any arrangement which is made under any enactment or Measure administered by or relating to the Church Commissioners, the Parsonages Board or the Diocesan Board of Finance, or

   (ii) to protect any interest in registered land arising under any such arrangement or statute,

(h) any person with the benefit of a freezing order or an undertaking given in place of a freezing order, who is applying for a restriction in Form AA or BB,

(i) any person who has applied for a freezing order and who is applying for a restriction in Form CC or DD,

(j) a trustee in bankruptcy in whom a beneficial interest in registered land held under a trust of land has vested, and who is applying for a restriction in Form J to be entered in the register of that land,

(k) any person with the benefit of a charging order over a beneficial interest in registered land held under a trust of land who is applying for a restriction in Form K to be entered in the register of that land,

(l) a person who has obtained a restraint order under–

   (i) paragraph 5(1) or 5(2) of Schedule 4 to the Terrorism Act 2000, or
   (ii) section 41 of the Proceeds of Crime Act 2002,

   and who is applying for a restriction in Form EE or FF,

(m) a person who has applied for a restraint order under the provisions referred to in paragraph (1) and who is applying for a restriction in Form GG or HH,

(n) a person who has obtained an acquisition order under section 28 of the Landlord and Tenant Act 1987 and who is applying for a restriction in Form L or N,

(o) a person who has applied for an acquisition order under section 28 of the Landlord and Tenant Act 1987 and who is applying for a restriction in Form N,

(p) a person who has obtained a vesting order under section 26(1) or 50(1) of the Leasehold Reform, Housing and Urban Development Act 1993 and who is applying for a restriction in Form L or N,

(q) a person who has applied for a vesting order under section 26(1) or 50(1) of the Leasehold Reform, Housing and Urban Development Act 1993 and who is applying for a restriction in Form N,

(r) the International Criminal Court where it applies for a restriction–

   (i) in Form AA or BB to give effect to a freezing order under Schedule 6 to the International Criminal Court Act 2001, or
   (ii) in Form CC or DD to protect an application for such a freezing order,

(s) a receiver or a sequestrator appointed by order who applies for a restriction in Form L or N,

(t) a trustee under a deed of arrangement who applies for a restriction in Form L or N,

(u) a person who has obtained an interim receiving order under section 246 of the Proceeds of Crime Act 2002 and who is applying for a restriction in Form EE or FF, . . .

(v) a person who has applied for an interim receiving order under section 246 of the Proceeds of Crime Act 2002 and who is applying for a restriction in Form GG or HH [, . . .

(w) the Legal Services Commission where it has a statutory charge, created by section 16(6) of the Legal Aid Act 1988 or by section 10(7) of the Access to Justice Act 1999 , over a beneficial interest in registered land held under a trust of land and is applying for a restriction in Form JJ to be entered in the register of that land, and

(x) a local authority where it has a statutory charge created under section 22 of the Health and Social Services and Social Security Adjudications Act 1983 on the beneficial interest of an equitable joint tenant in a registered estate and is applying for a restriction in Form MM to be entered in the register of that estate.

94.—When an application for a restriction must be made

(1) Subject to paragraph (9), a proprietor of a registered estate must **A2.1.068** apply for a restriction in Form A where–

(a) the estate becomes subject to a trust of land, other than on a registrable disposition, and the proprietor or the survivor of joint proprietors will not be able to give a valid receipt for capital money, or

(b) the estate is held on a trust of land and, as a result of a change in the trusts, the proprietor or the survivor of joint proprietors will not be able to give a valid receipt for capital money.

(2) A sole or last surviving trustee of land held on a trust of land must, when applying to register a disposition of a registered estate in his favour or to be registered as proprietor of an unregistered estate, at the same time apply for a restriction in Form A.

(2A) Where two or more persons apply to register a disposition of a registered estate in their favour or to be registered as proprietors of an unregistered estate, they must at the same time apply for a restriction in Form A if—

(a) the estate is a rentcharge, profit a prendre in gross, franchise or manor, and

(b) a sole proprietor or the survivor of joint proprietors will not be able to give a valid receipt for capital money.

(3) Subject to paragraphs (6) and (10), a personal representative of a deceased person who holds a registered estate on a trust of land created by the deceased's will, or on a trust of land arising under the laws of intestacy which is subsequently varied, and whose powers have been

limited by section 8 of the Trusts of Land and Appointment of Trustees Act 1996, must apply for a restriction in Form C.

(4) Subject to paragraphs (6), (7) and (9), a proprietor of a registered estate must apply for a restriction in Form B where–

    (a) a declaration of trust of that estate imposes limitations on the powers of the trustees under section 8 of the Trusts of Land and Appointment of Trustees Act 1996, or

    (b) a change in the trusts on which that estate is held imposes limitations or changes the limitations on the powers of the trustees under section 8 of the Trusts of Land and Appointment of Trustees Act 1996.

(5) Subject to paragraphs (6) and (7), an applicant for first registration of a legal estate held on a trust of land where the powers of the trustees are limited by section 8 of the Trusts of Land and Appointment of Trustees Act 1996 must at the same time apply for a restriction in Form B.

(6) Paragraphs (3), (4) and (5) do not apply to legal estates held on charitable, ecclesiastical or public trusts.

(7) Paragraphs (4) and (5) apply not only where the legal estate is held by the trustees, but also where it is vested in the personal representatives of a sole or last surviving trustee.

(8) An application for a restriction must be made where required by paragraphs (2) or (3) of rule 176 or paragraph (2) of rule 178.

(9) Where there are two or more persons entered in the register as the proprietor of a registered estate, an application for the appropriate restriction by one or more of them satisfies the obligation in paragraph (1) or (4).

(10) Where there are two or more personal representatives of a deceased proprietor, an application for a restriction in Form C by one or more of them satisfies the obligation in paragraph (3).

95.—Form of obligatory restrictions

A2.1.069   (1) The form of any restriction that the registrar is obliged to enter under any enactment shall be–

    (a) as specified in these rules,

    (b) as required by the relevant enactment, or

    (c) in other cases, such form as the registrar may direct having regard to the provisions of the relevant enactment.

(2) The form of the restriction required under–

(a) section 44(1) of the Act is Form A,

(b) section 37(5A) of the Housing Act 1985 is Form U,

(c) section 157(7) of the Housing Act 1985 is Form V,

(d) section 81(10) of the Housing Act 1988 is Form X,

(e) section 133 of the Housing Act 1988 is Form X,

(f) paragraph 4 of Schedule 9A to the Housing Act 1985 is Form W,

(g) section 173(9) of the Local Government and Housing Act 1989 is Form X, and

(h) section 13(5) of the Housing Act 1996 is Form Y.

96.—Application for an order that a restriction be disapplied or modified

(1) An application to the registrar for an order under section 41(2) of **A2.1.070** the Act must be made in Form RX2.

(2) The application must–

(a) state whether the application is to disapply or to modify the restriction and, if the latter, give details of the modification requested,

(b) explain why the applicant has a sufficient interest in the restriction to make the application,

(c) give details of the disposition or the kind of dispositions that will be affected by the order, and

(d) state why the applicant considers that the registrar should make the order.

(3) If requested to do so, the applicant must supply further evidence to satisfy the registrar that he should make the order.

(4) The registrar may make such enquiries and serve such notices as he thinks fit in order to determine the application.

(5) A note of the terms of any order made by the registrar under section 41(2) of the Act must, if appropriate, be entered in the register.

97.—Application to cancel a restriction

1.071   (1) An application to cancel a restriction must be made in Form RX3.

(2) The application must be accompanied by evidence to satisfy the registrar that the restriction is no longer required.

(3) If the registrar is satisfied that the restriction is no longer required, he must cancel the restriction.

98.—Applications to withdraw a restriction from the register

A2.1.072
(1) An application to withdraw a restriction must be made in Form RX4 and be accompanied by the required consent.

(2) The required consent is—

(a) where the restriction requires the consent of a specified person, the consent of that person,

(b) where the restriction requires a certificate to be given by a specified person, the consent of that person,

(c) where the restriction requires notice to be given to a specified person, the consent of that person,

(d) where the restriction requires the consent of a specified person, or alternatively a certificate to be given by a specified person, the consent of all such persons,

(e) in any other case, the consent of all persons who appear to the registrar to have an interest in the restriction.

(3) No application may be made to withdraw a restriction—

(a) that is entered under section 42(1)(a) of the Act and reflects some limitation on the registered proprietor's powers of disposition imposed by statute or the general law,

(b) that is entered in the register following an application under rule 94,

(c) that the registrar is under an obligation to enter in the register,

(d) that reflects a limitation under an order of the court or registrar, or an undertaking given in place of such an order,

(e) that is entered pursuant to a court order under section 46 of the Act.

(4) The registrar may accept a certificate given by a conveyancer that the conveyancer holds a required consent.

99.—Two Cancellation of a restriction relating to a trust

When registering a disposition of a registered estate, the registrar must **A2.1.073** cancel a restriction entered for the purpose of protecting an interest, right or claim arising under a trust of land if he is satisfied that the registered estate is no longer subject to that trust of land.

100.—Entry following a direction of the court regarding overriding priority in connection with a restriction

(1) Any entry in the register required under section 46(4) of the Act **A2.1.074** shall be in such form as the registrar may determine so as to ensure that the priority of the restriction ordered by the court is apparent from the register.

(2) Where the making of the entry is completed by the registrar during the priority period of an official search which was delivered before the making of the application for the entry, he must give notice of the entry to the person who applied for the official search or, if a conveyancer or other agent applied on behalf of that person, to that agent, unless he is satisfied that such notice is unnecessary.

Part 10

BOUNDARIES

117.—Definition

In this Part, except in rule 121, "boundary" includes part only of a **A2.1.075** boundary.

118.—Application for the determination of the exact line of a boundary

(1) A proprietor of a registered estate may apply to the registrar **A2.1.076** for the exact line of the boundary of that registered estate to be determined.

(2) An application under paragraph (1) must be made in Form DB and be accompanied by–

(a) a plan, or a plan and a verbal description, identifying the exact line of the boundary claimed and showing sufficient surrounding physical features to allow the general position of the boundary to be drawn on the Ordnance Survey map, and

(b) evidence to establish the exact line of the boundary.

119.—Procedure on an application for the determination of the exact line of a boundary

A2.1.077   (1) Subject to paragraph (2), where the registrar is satisfied that–

(a)   the plan, or plan and verbal description, supplied in accordance with rule 118(2)(a) identifies the exact line of the boundary claimed,

(b)   the applicant has shown an arguable case that the exact line of the boundary is in the position shown on the plan, or plan and verbal description, supplied in accordance with rule 118(2)(a), and

(c)   he can identify all the owners of the land adjoining the boundary to be determined and has an address at which each owner may be given notice,

he must give the owners of the land adjoining the boundary to be determined (except the applicant) notice of the application . . . and of the effect of paragraph (6).

(2) The registrar need not give notice of the application to an owner of the land adjoining the boundary to be determined where the evidence supplied in accordance with rule 118(2)(b) includes—

(a)   an agreement in writing with that owner as to the line of the boundary, or

(b)   a court order determining the line of the boundary.

(3) Subject to paragraph (4), the time fixed by the notice to the owner of the land to object to the application shall be the period ending at 12 noon on the twentieth business day after the date of issue of the notice or such longer period as the registrar may decide before the issue of the notice.

(4) The period set for the notice under paragraph (3) may be extended for a particular recipient of the notice by the registrar following a request by that recipient, received by the registrar before that period has expired, setting out why an extension should be allowed.

(5) If a request is received under paragraph (4) the registrar may, if he considers it appropriate, seek the views of the applicant and if, after considering any such views and all other relevant matters, he is satisfied that a longer period should be allowed he may allow such period as he considers appropriate, whether or not the period is the same as any period requested by the recipient of the notice.

(6) Unless any recipient of the notice objects to the application to determine the exact line of the boundary within the time fixed by the notice (as

extended under paragraph (5), if applicable), the registrar must complete the application.

(7) Where the registrar is not satisfied as to paragraph (1)(a), (b) and (c), he must cancel the application.

(8) In this rule, the "owner of the land" means–

    (a) a person entitled to apply to be registered as the proprietor of an unregistered legal estate in land under section 3 of the Act,

    (b) the proprietor of any registered estate or charge affecting the land, or

    (c) if the land is demesne land, Her Majesty.

120.—Completion of application for the exact line of a boundary to be determined

(1) Where the registrar completes an application under rule 118, he must– **A2.1.078**

    (a) make an entry in the individual register of the applicant's registered title and, if appropriate, in the individual register of any superior or inferior registered title, and any registered title affecting the other land adjoining the determined boundary, stating that the exact line of the boundary is determined under section 60 of the Act, and

    (b) subject to paragraph (2), add to the title plan of the applicant's registered title and, if appropriate, to the title plan of any superior or inferior registered title, and any registered title affecting the other land adjoining the determined boundary, such particulars of the exact line of the boundary as he considers appropriate.

(2) Instead of, or as well as, adding particulars of the exact line of the boundary to the title plans mentioned in paragraph (1)(b), the registrar may make an entry in the individual registers mentioned in paragraph (1)(a) referring to any other plan showing the exact line of the boundary.

121.—Relationship between determined and undetermined parts of a boundary

A2.1.079

Where the exact line of part of the boundary of a registered estate has been determined, the ends of that part of the boundary are not to be treated as determined for the purposes of adjoining parts of the boundary the exact line of which has not been determined.

122.—Determination of the exact line of a boundary without application

A2.1.080　(1) This rule applies where–

(a) there is–

(i) a transfer of part of a registered estate in land, or
(ii) the grant of a term of years absolute which is a registrable disposition of part of a registered estate in land,

(b) there is a common boundary, and

(c) there is sufficient information in the disposition to enable the registrar to determine the exact line of the common boundary.

(2) The registrar may determine the exact line of the common boundary and if he does he must–

(a) make an entry in the individual registers of the affected registered titles stating that the exact line of the common boundary is determined under section 60 of the Act, and

(b) subject to paragraph (3), add to the title plan of the disponor's affected registered title (whether or not the disponor is still the proprietor of that title, or still entitled to be registered as proprietor of that title) and to the title plan of the registered title under which the disposition is being registered, such particulars of the exact line of the common boundary as he considers appropriate.

(3) Instead of, or as well as, adding particulars of the exact line of the common boundary to the title plans mentioned in paragraph (2)(b), the registrar may make an entry in the individual registers of the affected registered titles referring to the description of the common boundary in the disposition.

(4) In this rule–

"common boundary" means any boundary of the land disposed of by a disposition which adjoins land in which the disponor at the date of the disposition had a registered estate in land or of which such disponor was entitled to be registered as proprietor, and

"disposition" means a transfer or grant mentioned in paragraph (1)(a).

123.—Agreement about accretion or diluvion

(1) An application to register an agreement about the operation of **A2.1.081** accretion or diluvion in relation to a registered estate in land must be made by, or be accompanied by the consent of, the proprietor of the registered estate and of any registered charge, except that no such consent is required from a person who is party to the agreement.

(2) On registration of such an agreement the registrar must make a note in the property register that the agreement is registered for the purposes of section 61(2) of the Act.

PART 11

QUALITY OF TITLE

124.—Application to upgrade title under section 62 of the Act

(1) An application for the registrar to upgrade title under section 62 of **A2.1.082** the Act must be made in Form UT1.

(2) An application referred to in paragraph (1) must, except where made under sections 62(2), (4) or (5) of the Act, be accompanied by such documents as will satisfy the registrar as to the title.

(3) An application under section 62(2) of the Act must be accompanied by–

    (a) such documents as will satisfy the registrar as to any superior title which is not registered,

    (b) where any superior title is registered with possessory, qualified or good leasehold title, such evidence as will satisfy the registrar that that title qualifies for upgrading to absolute title, and

    (c) evidence of any consent to the grant of the lease required from–

        (i) any chargee of any superior title, and
        (ii) any superior lessor.

(4) An application under section 62(3)(b) of the Act must, in addition to the documents referred to in paragraph (2), be accompanied by the documents listed at paragraph (3)(a) to (c).

(5) An application by a person entitled to be registered as the proprietor of the estate to which the application relates must be accompanied by evidence of that entitlement.

(6) An application by a person interested in a registered estate which derives from the estate to which the application relates must be accompanied by–

(a) details of the interest, and

(b) where the interest is not apparent from the register, evidence to satisfy the registrar of the applicant's interest.

125.—Use of register to record defects in title

A2.1.083 (1) An entry under section 64 of the Act that a right to determine a registered estate in land is exercisable shall be made in the property register.

(2) An application for such an entry must be supported by evidence to satisfy the registrar that the applicant has the right to determine the registered estate and that the right is exercisable.

(3) Subject to paragraph (4), the registrar must make the entry on receipt of an application which relates to a right to determine the registered estate on non-payment of a rentcharge.

(4) Before making an entry under this rule the registrar must give notice of the application to the proprietor of the registered estate to which the application relates and the proprietor of any registered charge on that estate.

(5) A person may apply to the registrar for removal of the entry if he is–

(a) the person entitled to determine the registered estate,

(b) the proprietor of the registered estate to which the entry relates,

(c) a person entitled to be registered as proprietor of that estate, or

(d) any other person whom the registrar is satisfied has an interest in the removal of the entry.

(6) An application for removal of the entry must be supported by evidence to satisfy the registrar that the right to determine the registered estate is not exercisable.

PART 12

ALTERATIONS AND CORRECTIONS

126.—Alteration under a court order — not rectification

A2.1.084 (1) Subject to paragraphs (2) and (3), if in any proceedings the court decides that–

(a) there is a mistake in the register,

(b) the register is not up to date, or

(c)   there is an estate, right or interest excepted from the effect of registration that should be given effect to,

it must make an order for alteration of the register under the power given by paragraph 2(1) of Schedule 4 to the Act.

(2) The court is not obliged to make an order if there are exceptional circumstances that justify not doing so.

(3) This rule does not apply to an alteration of the register that amounts to rectification.

127.—Court order for alteration of the register — form and service

(1) An order for alteration of the register must state the title number of **A2.1.085** the title affected and the alteration that is to be made, and must direct the registrar to make the alteration.

(2) Service on the registrar of an order for alteration of the register must be made by making an application for the registrar to give effect to the order, accompanied by the order.

128.—Alteration otherwise than pursuant to a court order — notice and enquiries

(1) Subject to paragraph (5), this rule applies where an application **A2.1.086** for alteration of the register has been made, or where the registrar is considering altering the register without an application having been made.

(2) The registrar must give notice of the proposed alteration to–

(a)   the registered proprietor of any registered estate,

(b)   the registered proprietor of any registered charge, and

(c)   subject to paragraph (3), any person who appears to the registrar to be entitled to an interest protected by a notice,

where that estate, charge or interest would be affected by the proposed alteration, unless he is satisfied that such notice is unnecessary.

(3) The registrar is not obliged to give notice to a person referred to in paragraph (2)(c) if that person's name and his address for service under rule 198 are not set out in the individual register in which the notice is entered.

(4) The registrar may make such enquiries as he thinks fit.

(5) This rule does not apply to alteration of the register in the specific circumstances covered by any other rule.

129.—Alteration otherwise than under a court order — evidence

A2.1.087   Unless otherwise provided in these rules, an application for alteration of the register (otherwise than under a court order) must be supported by evidence to justify the alteration.

130.—Correction of mistakes in an application or accompanying document

A2.1.088   (1) This rule applies to any alteration made by the registrar for the purpose of correcting a mistake in any application or accompanying document.

(2) The alteration will have effect as if made by the applicant or other interested party or parties–

    (a) in the case of a mistake of a clerical or like nature, in all circumstances,

    (b) in the case of any other mistake, only if the applicant and every other interested party has requested, or consented to, the alteration.

PART 13

INFORMATION ETC

Interpretation of this Part

131.—Definitions

A2.1.089   In this Part–

"commencement date" means the date of commencement of this Part,

"edited information document" means, where the registrar has designated a document an exempt information document, the edited copy of that document lodged under rule 136(2)(b) [or the document prepared by the registrar under either rule 136(6) or rule 138(4)],

"exempt information document" means the original and copies of a document so designated under rule 136(3),

"prejudicial information" means–

    (a) information that relates to an individual who is the applicant under rule 136 and if disclosed to other persons (whether to the public generally or specific persons) would, or would be likely to, cause substantial unwarranted damage or substantial unwarranted distress to the applicant or another, or

(b) information that if disclosed to other persons (whether to the public generally or specific persons) would, or would be likely to, prejudice the commercial interests of the applicant under rule 136,

"priority period" means–

(a) where the application for an official search is entered on the day list before the date referred to in rule 216(3), the period beginning at the time when that application is entered on the day list and ending at midnight marking the end of the thirtieth business day thereafter, and

(b) where the application for an official search is entered on the day list on or after the date referred to in rule 216(3), the period beginning at the time when that application is entered on the day list and ending at midnight marking the end of the thirty sixth business day thereafter,

"protectable disposition" means a registrable disposition (including one by virtue of rule 38) of a registered estate or registered charge made for valuable consideration,

"purchaser" means a person who has entered into or intends to enter into a protectable disposition as disponee,

"registrable estate or charge" means the legal estate and any charge which is sought to be registered as a registered estate or registered charge in an application for first registration,

"search from date" means–

(a) the date stated on an official copy of the individual register of the relevant registered title, as the date on which the entries shown on that official copy were subsisting,

(b) the date stated at the time of an access by remote terminal, where provided for under these rules, to the individual register of the relevant registered title as the date on which the entries accessed were subsisting.

. . .

132.—Delivery of applications and issuing of certificates by electronic and other means

(1) During the currency of a relevant notice given under Schedule 2, **A2.1.090** and subject to and in accordance with the limitations contained in that notice, any application under this Part may be made by delivering the application to the registrar by any means of communication other than

post, document exchange or personal delivery, and the applicant must provide, in such order as may be required by that notice, such of the particulars required for an application of that type as are appropriate in the circumstances and as are required by the notice.

(2) During the currency of a relevant notice given under Schedule 2, and subject to and in accordance with the limitations contained in that notice, any certificates and other results of applications and searches under this Part may be issued by any means of communication other than post, document exchange or personal delivery.

(3) Except where otherwise provided in this Part, where information is issued under paragraph (2) it must be to like effect to that which would have been provided had the information been issued in paper form.

133.—Inspection and copying

A2.1.091 (1) This rule applies to the right to inspect and make copies of the registers and documents under section 66(1) of the Act.

(2) Excepted documents are excepted from the right.

(3) Subject to rule 132(1), an application under section 66 of the Act must be in Form PIC.

(4) Where inspection and copying under this rule takes place at an office of the land registry it must be undertaken in the presence of a member of the land registry.

(5) In paragraph (2), an "excepted document" is—

(a) an exempt information document,

(b) an edited information document which has been replaced by another edited information document under rule 136(6),

(c) a Form EX1A,

(d) a Form CIT,

(e) any form to which a Form CIT has been attached under rule 140(3) or (4),

(f) any document or copy of any document prepared by the registrar in connection with an application in a form to which Form CIT has been attached under rule 140(3) or (4),

(g) any document relating to an application for a network access agreement under paragraph 1(4) of Schedule 5 to the Act,

(h) an identity document, and

(i) an investigation of crime document.

(6) Subject to paragraph (7), in paragraph (5)(h) an "identity document" means any document within section 66(1)(c) of the Act provided to the registrar as evidence of identity of any person or prepared or obtained by the registrar in connection with such identity.

(7) Forms AP1, DS2 and FR1 are not identity documents.

(8) In paragraph 5(i), an "investigation of crime document" is any document within section 66(1)(c) of the Act (other than an identity document) which relates to the prevention or detection of crime and is not—

(a) a document received by the registrar as part of or in support of an application to the registrar,

(b) a document received by the registrar as part of or in support of an objection made under section 73 of the Act, or

(c) a document to which paragraph (9) applies.

(9) This paragraph applies to a document if—

(a) it is a document prepared by, or at the request of, the registrar as part of the process of considering an application or objection, and

(b) it is not so prepared principally in connection with the prevention or detection of crime.

(10) In paragraph (5), the references to Form EX1A and Form CIT and forms to which Form CIT has been attached include any equivalent information provided under rule 132 and the reference to an application in a form to which Form CIT has been attached includes an equivalent application made by virtue of rule 132.

Official Copies

134.—Application for official copies of a registered title, the cautions register or for a certificate of inspection of the title plan

(1) A person may apply for–   A2.1.092

(a) an official copy of an individual register,

(b) an official copy of any title plan referred to in an individual register,

(c) an official copy of an individual caution register and any caution plan referred to in it, and

(d) a certificate of inspection of any title plan.

(2) Subject to rule 132(1), an application under paragraph (1) must be in Form OC1.

(3) A separate application must be made in respect of each registered title or individual caution register.

(4) Where, notwithstanding paragraph (3), an application is in respect of more than one registered title or individual caution register, but the applicant fails to provide a title number, or the title number provided does not relate to any part of the property in respect of which the application is made, the registrar may–

    (a) deal with the application as if it referred only to one of the title numbers relating to the property,

    (b) deal with the application as if it referred to all of the title numbers relating to the property, or

    (c) cancel the application.

(5) In paragraph (4) the reference to title number includes in the case of an individual caution register a caution title number.

(6) Where the registrar deals with the application under paragraph (4) (b), the applicant is to be treated as having made a separate application in respect of each of the registered titles or each of the individual caution registers.

(7) An official copy of an individual caution register and any caution plan referred to in it must be issued disregarding any application or matter that may affect the subsistence of the caution.

135.—Application for official copies of documents referred to in the register of title and other documents kept by the registrar

A2.1.093   (1) Subject to paragraph (2), a person may apply for an official copy of—

    (a) any document referred to in the register of title and kept by the registrar,

    (b) any other document kept by the registrar that relates to an application to the registrar.

(2) Excepted documents are excepted from paragraph (1).

(3) Subject to rule 132(1), an application under paragraph (1) must be made in Form OC2.

(4) In this rule, "excepted document" has the same meaning as in rule 133.

Exempt information documents

136.—Application that the registrar designate a document an exempt information document

(1) A person may apply for the registrar to designate a relevant docu- **A2.1.094** ment an exempt information document if he claims that the document contains prejudicial information.

(2) Subject to rule 132(1), an application under paragraph (1) must be made in Form EX1 and EX1A and include a copy of the relevant document which—

(a) excludes the prejudicial information,

(b) includes the words "excluded information" where the prejudicial information has been excluded, and

(c) is certified as being a true copy of the relevant document, except that it does not include the prejudicial information and includes the words required by sub-paragraph (b).

(3) Subject to paragraph (4), provided that the registrar is satisfied that the applicant's claim is not groundless he must designate the relevant document an exempt information document.

(4) Where the registrar considers that designating the document an exempt information document could prejudice the keeping of the register, he may cancel the application.

(5) Where a document is an exempt information document, the registrar may make an appropriate entry in the individual register of any affected registered title.

(6) Where a document is an exempt information document and a further application is made under paragraph (1) which would, but for the existing designation, have resulted in its being so designated, the registrar must prepare another edited information document which excludes–

(a) the information excluded from the existing edited information document, and

(b) any further information excluded from the edited information document lodged by the applicant.

(7) In this rule a "relevant document" is a document–

(a) referred to in the register of title, or one that relates to an application to the registrar, the original or a copy of which is kept by the registrar, or

(b) that will be referred to in the register of title as a result of an application (the "accompanying application") made at the same time as an application under this rule, or that relates to the accompanying application, the original or a copy of which will be or is for the time being kept by the registrar.

137.—Application for an official copy of an exempt information document

A2.1.095 (1) A person may apply for an official copy of an exempt information document.

(2) Subject to rule 132(1), application under paragraph (1) must be made in Form EX2.

(3) The registrar must give notice of an application under paragraph (1) to the person who made the relevant application under rule 136(1) unless he is satisfied that such notice is unnecessary or impracticable.

(4) If the registrar decides that–

(a) none of the information excluded from the edited information document is prejudicial information, or

(b) although all or some of the information excluded is prejudicial information, the public interest in providing an official copy of the exempt information document to the applicant outweighs the public interest in not doing so,

then he must provide an official copy of the exempt information document to the applicant.

(5) Where the registrar has decided an application under paragraph (1) on the basis that none of the information is prejudicial information, he must remove the designation of the document as an exempt information document and any entry made in respect of the document under rule 136(5).

138.—Application for removal of the designation of a document as an exempt information document

A2.1.096 (1) Where a document is an exempt information document, the person who applied for designation under rule 136(1) may apply for the designation to be removed.

(2) Subject to rule 132(1), an application made under paragraph (1) must be in Form EX3.

(3) Subject to paragraph (4), where the registrar is satisfied that the application is in order, he must remove the designation of the document as an exempt information document and remove any entry made in respect of the document under rule 136(5).

(4) Where–

(a) the document has been made an exempt information document under more than one application,

(b) an application under paragraph (1) is made by fewer than all of the applicants under rule 136(1), and

(c) the registrar is satisfied that the application is in order,

the registrar must replace the existing edited information document with one that excludes only the information excluded both from that edited information document and the edited information documents lodged under rule 136(2)(b) by those applicants not applying under paragraph (1).

Inspection, official copies and searches of the index of proprietors' names in connection with court proceedings, insolvency and tax liability

140.—Application in connection with court proceedings, insolvency and tax liability

(1) In this rule, a qualifying applicant is a person referred to in column **A2.1.097** 1 of Schedule 5 who gives the registrar the appropriate certificate referred to in column 2 of the Schedule or, where rule 132 applies, an equivalent certificate in accordance with a notice given under Schedule 2.

(2) A qualifying applicant may apply–

(a) to inspect or make copies of any document (including a form) within rule 133(2) . . .,

(b) for official copies of any document (including a form) within rule 135(2) . . ., and

(c) for a search in the index of proprietors' names in respect of the name of a person specified in the application.

(3) Subject to rule 132(1), an application under paragraph (2) must be made in Form PIC, OC2 or PN1, as appropriate, with Form CIT attached.

(4) A qualifying applicant who applies–

(a) to inspect and make copies of registers and documents not within paragraph (2)(a) under section 66 of the Act,

(b) for official copies of registers and plans under rule 134(1) and of documents not within paragraph (2)(b) under rule 135,

(c) for an historical edition of a registered title under rule 144,

(d) for an official search of the index map under rule 145, or

(e) for an official search of the index of relating franchises and manors under rule 146,

may attach Form CIT to the Form PIC, OC1, OC2, HC1, SIM or SIF, as appropriate, used in the application.

(4A) A qualifying applicant who applies for a search in the index of proprietors' names under paragraph (2) may apply at the same time in the Form CIT attached to the Form PN1 for official copies of every individual register referred to in the entries (if any) in the index relating to the particulars given in the search application.

(5) In Form CIT and Schedule 5, references to tax are references to any of the taxes mentioned in the definition of tax in section 118(1) of the Taxes Management Act 1970.

Information about the day list, electronic discharges of registered charges and title plans

141.—Day list information

A2.1.098 (1) In this rule "day list information" means information kept by the registrar under rule 12.

(2) A person may only apply for the day list information relating to a specified title number during the currency of a relevant notice given under Schedule 2, and subject to and in accordance with the limitations contained in the notice.

(3) The registrar must provide the day list information in the manner specified in the relevant notice.

(4) Unless otherwise stated by the registrar, the day list information provided must be based on the entries subsisting in the day list immediately before the information is provided.

(5) The registrar is not required to disclose under this rule details of an application under rule 136.

142.—Enquiry as to discharge of a charge by electronic means

A2.1.099 (1) A person may apply in respect of a specified registered title for confirmation of receipt by the registrar of notification of–

(a) the discharge of a registered charge given by electronic means, or

(b) the release of part of a registered estate from a registered charge given by electronic means.

(2) An application under paragraph (1) may only be made during the currency of a relevant notice given under Schedule 2, and subject to and in accordance with the limitations contained in the notice.

(3) The registrar is not required to disclose under this rule any information concerning a notification once the entries of the registered charge to which it relates have been cancelled from the relevant registered title, or the affected part of it.

143.—Certificate of inspection of title plan

(1) Where a person has applied under rule 134 for a certificate of **A2.1.100** inspection of a title plan, on completion of the inspection the registrar must issue a certificate of inspection.

(2) Subject to rule 132(2), the certificate of inspection must be issued by the registrar in Form CI or to like effect.

Historical information

144.—Application for an historical edition of a registered title kept by the registrar in electronic form

(1) A person may apply for a copy of–   **A2.1.101**

(a) the last edition for a specified day, or

(b) every edition for a specified day,

of a registered title, and of a registered title that has been closed, kept by the registrar in electronic form.

(2) Subject to rule 132(1), an application under paragraph (1) must be made in Form HC1.

(3) Subject to paragraph (4), if an application under paragraph (1) is in order and the registrar is keeping in electronic form an edition of the registered title for the day specified in the application, he must issue–

(a) if the application is under paragraph (1)(a), subject to rule 132(2), a paper copy of the edition of the registered title at the end of that day, or

(b) if the application is under paragraph (1)(b), subject to rule 132(2), a paper copy of the edition of the registered title at the end of that day and any prior edition kept in electronic form of the registered title for that day.

(4) Where only part of the edition of the registered title requested is kept by the registrar in electronic form he must issue, subject to rule 132(2), a paper copy of that part.

Official searches of the index kept under section 68 of the Act

145.—Searches of the index map

A2.1.102   (1) Any person may apply for an official search of the index map.

(2) Subject to rule 132(1), an application under paragraph (1) must be made in Form SIM.

(3) If the registrar so requires, an applicant must provide a copy of an extract from the Ordnance Survey map on the largest scale published showing the land to which the application relates.

(4) If an application under paragraph (1) is in order, subject to rule 132(2), a paper certificate must be issued including such information specified in Part 1 of Schedule 6 as the case may require.

146.—Searches of the index of relating franchises and manors

A2.1.103   (1) Any person may apply for an official search of the index of relating franchises and manors.

(2) Subject to rule 132(1), an application under paragraph (1) must be made in Form SIF.

(3) If an application under paragraph (1) is in order, subject to rule 132(2), a paper certificate must be issued including such information specified in Part 2 of Schedule 6 as the case may require.

Official searches with priority

147.—Application for official search with priority by purchaser

A2.1.104   (1) A purchaser may apply for an official search with priority of the individual register of a registered title to which the protectable disposition relates.

(2) Where there is a pending application for first registration, the purchaser of a protectable disposition which relates to that pending application may apply for an official search with priority in relation to that pending application.

(3) Subject to rule 132(1), an application for an official search with priority must be made in Form OS1 or Form OS2, as appropriate.

(4) Where the application is made in Form OS2 and an accompanying plan is required, unless the registrar allows otherwise, the plan must be delivered in duplicate.

148.—Entry on day list of application for official search with priority

(1) An application for an official search with priority is to be taken as **A2.1.105** having been made on the date and at the time of the day notice of it is entered on the day list.

(2) Paragraph (3) has effect where–

(a) an application for an official search is in order, and

(b) the applicant has not withdrawn the official search.

(3) Subject to paragraph (4), the entry on the day list of notice of an application for an official search with priority confers a priority period on an application for an entry in the register in respect of the protectable disposition to which the official search relates.

(4) Paragraph (3) does not apply if the application for an official search with priority is cancelled subsequently because it is not in order.

149.—Issue of official search certificate with priority

(1) If an application for an official search with priority is in order an **A2.1.106** official search certificate with priority must be issued giving the result of the search as at the date and time that the application was entered on the day list.

(2) An official search certificate with priority relating to a registered estate or to a pending application for first registration may, at the registrar's discretion, be issued in one or both of the following ways–

(a) in paper form, or

(b) under rule 132(2).

(3) Subject to paragraph (4), an official search certificate issued under paragraph (2) must include such information as specified in Part 3 or Part 4 of Schedule 6 as the case may require and may be issued by reference to an official copy of the individual register of the relevant registered title.

(4) If an official search certificate is to be, or has been, issued in paper form under paragraph (2)(a), another official search certificate issued under paragraph (2)(b) in respect of the same application need only include the information specified at A, F, G and H of Part 3 and A, H and I of Part 4 of Schedule 6, as the case may require.

150.—Withdrawal of official search with priority

A2.1.107 (1) Subject to paragraph (2), a person who has made an application for an official search with priority of a registered title or in relation to a pending first registration application, may withdraw that official search by application to the registrar.

(2) An application under paragraph (1) cannot be made if an application for an entry in the register in respect of the protectable disposition made pursuant to the official search has been made and completed.

(3) Once an official search has been withdrawn under paragraph (1) rule 148(3) shall cease to apply in relation to it.

151.—Protection of an application on which a protected application is dependent

A2.1.108 (1) Subject to paragraph (4), paragraph (2) has effect where an application for an entry in the register is one on which an official search certificate confers a priority period and there is a prior registrable disposition affecting the same registered land, on which that application is dependent.

(2) An application for an entry in the register in relation to that prior registrable disposition is for the purpose of section 72(1)(a) of the Act an application to which a priority period relates.

(3) The priority period referred to in paragraph (2) is a period expiring at the same time as the priority period conferred by the official search referred to in paragraph (1).

(4) Paragraph (2) does not have effect unless both the application referred to in paragraph (1) and the application referred to in paragraph (2) are–

(a) made before the end of that priority period, and

(b) in due course completed by registration.

152.—Protection of an application relating to a pending application for first registration on which a protected application is dependent

A2.1.109 (1) Subject to paragraphs (4) and (5), paragraph (2) has effect where–

(a) there is a pending application for first registration,

(b) there is a pending application for an entry in the register on which an official search confers a priority period,

(c) there is an application for registration of a prior registrable disposition affecting the same registrable estate or charge as the pending application referred to in sub-paragraph (b),

(d) the pending application referred to in sub-paragraph (b) is dependent on the application referred to in sub-paragraph (c), and

(e) the application referred to in sub-paragraph (c) is subject to the pending application for first registration referred to in sub-paragraph (a).

(2) An application for an entry in the register in relation to the prior registrable disposition referred to in paragraph (1)(c) is for the purpose of section 72(1)(a) of the Act an application to which a priority period relates.

(3) The priority period referred to in paragraph (2) is a period expiring at the same time as the priority period conferred by the official search referred to in paragraph (1)(b).

(4) Paragraph (2) does not have effect unless the pending application for first registration referred to in paragraph (1)(a) is in due course completed by registration of all or any part of the registrable estate.

(5) Paragraph (2) does not have effect unless both the pending application on which an official search confers priority referred to in paragraph (1)(b) and the application relating to the prior registrable disposition referred to in paragraph (1)(c) are–

(a) made before the end of that priority period, and

(b) in due course completed by registration.

153.—Priority of concurrent applications for official searches with priority and concurrent official search certificates with priority

(1) Where two or more official search certificates with priority relating to the same registrable estate or charge or to the same registered land have been issued and are in operation, the certificates take effect, as far as relates to the priority conferred, in the order of the times at which the applications for official search with priority were entered on the day list, unless the applicants agree otherwise. **A2.1.110**

(2) Where one transaction is dependent upon another the registrar must assume (unless the contrary appears) that the applicants for official search with priority have agreed that their applications have priority so as to give effect to the sequence of the documents effecting the transactions.

154.—Applications lodged at the same time as the priority period expires

(1) Where an official search with priority has been made in respect of a registered title and an application relating to that title is taken as having **A2.1.111**

been made at the same time as the expiry of the priority period relating to that search, the time of the making of that application is to be taken as within that priority period.

(2) Where an official search with priority has been made in respect of a pending application for first registration and a subsequent application relating to a registrable estate which is subject to that pending application for first registration, or was so subject before completion of the registration of that registrable estate, is taken as having been made at the same time as the expiry of the priority period relating to that search, the time of the making of that subsequent application is to be taken as within that priority period.

155.—Application for official search without priority

A2.1.112   (1) A person may apply for an official search without priority of an individual register of a registered title.

(2) Subject to rule 132(1), an application for an official search without priority must be made in Form OS3.

(3) Where the application is in Form OS3 and an accompanying plan is required, unless the registrar allows otherwise, the plan must be delivered in duplicate.

156.—Issue of official search certificate without priority

A2.1.113   (1) If an application for an official search without priority is in order, an official search certificate without priority must be issued.

(2) An official search certificate without priority may, at the registrar's discretion, be issued in one or both of the following ways–

(a)   in paper form, or

(b)   under rule 132(2).

(3) Subject to paragraph (4), an official search certificate without priority issued under paragraph (2) must include such information specified in Part 3 of Schedule 6 as the case may require and may be issued by reference to an official copy of the individual register of the relevant registered title.

(4) If an official certificate of search is to be, or has been, issued in paper form under paragraph (2)(a), another official search certificate issued under paragraph (2)(b) in respect of the same application need only include the information specified at A, F, G and H of Part 3 of Schedule 6, as the case may require.

Request for information

157.—Information requested by telephone, oral or remote terminal application for an official search

(1) If an application under rule 147(3) or rule 155(2) has been made by **A2.1.114** telephone or orally by virtue of rule 132(1) in respect of a registered title, the registrar may, before or after the official search has been completed, at his discretion, inform the applicant, by telephone or orally, whether or not–

- (a) there have been any relevant adverse entries made in the individual register since the search from date given in the application, or

- (b) there is any relevant entry subsisting on the day list.

(2) If an application under rule 147(3) has been made by telephone or orally by virtue of rule 132(1) in respect of a legal estate subject to a pending application for first registration, the registrar may, before or after the official search has been completed, at his discretion, inform the applicant, by telephone or orally, whether or not there is any relevant entry subsisting on the day list.

(3) If an application under rule 147(3) or rule 155(2) has been made to the land registry computer system from a remote terminal by virtue of rule 132(1), the registrar may, before or after the official search has been completed, at his discretion, inform the applicant, by a transmission to the remote terminal, whether or not–

- (a) in the case of an official search of a registered title, there have been any relevant entries of the kind referred to in paragraph (1) (a) or (b), or

- (b) in the case of an official search of a legal estate subject to a pending application for first registration, there have been any relevant entries of the kind referred to in paragraph (2).

(4) Under this rule the registrar need not provide the applicant with details of any relevant entries.

Part 14

MISCELLANEOUS AND SPECIAL CASES

Pending land actions, writs and orders

172.—Benefit of pending land actions, writs and orders

A2.1.115 (1) For the purposes of section 34(1) of the Act, a relevant person shall be treated as having the benefit of the pending land action, writ or order, as appropriate.

(2) In determining whether a person has a sufficient interest in the making of an entry of a restriction under section 43(1)(c) of the Act, a relevant person shall be treated as having the benefit of the pending land action, writ or order, as appropriate.

(3) In this rule, "a relevant person" means a person (or his assignee or chargee, if appropriate) who is taking any action or proceedings which are within section 87(1)(a) of the Act, or who has obtained a writ or order within section 87(1)(b) of the Act.

The Crown

173.—Escheat etc

A2.1.116 (1) Where a registered freehold estate in land has determined, the registrar may enter a note of that fact in the property register and in the property register of any inferior affected registered title.

(2) Where the registrar considers that there is doubt as to whether a registered freehold estate in land has determined, the entry under paragraph (1) must be modified by a statement to that effect.

Adverse Possession

187.—Interpretation

A2.1.117 (1) Where the application is to be registered as proprietor of a registered rentcharge, the references in rules 188, 188A, 189, 190, 192, 193, 194A, 194B, 194C, 194F, and 194G to Schedule 6 to the Act are to Schedule 6 as applied by rule 191.

(2) In rules 194A, 194B and 194F, "post" means pre-paid delivery by a postal service which seeks to deliver documents within the United Kingdom no later than the next working day in all or the majority of cases, and to deliver outside the United Kingdom within such period as is reasonable in all the circumstances.

(3) In rules 194A, 194B, 194C, 194F and 194G, "qualified surveyor" means a fellow or professional associate of the Royal Institution of Chartered Surveyors.

188.—Applications for registration — procedure

(1) An application under paragraphs 1 or 6 of Schedule 6 to the Act **A2.1.118** must be in Form ADV1 and be accompanied by–

(a) a statutory declaration or statement of truth made by the applicant not more than one month before the application is taken to have been made, together with any supporting statutory declarations or statements of truth, to provide evidence of adverse possession of the registered estate in land or rentcharge against which the application is made for a period which if it were to continue from the date of the applicant's statutory declaration or statement of truth to the date of the application would be–

　　(i) where the application is under paragraph 1, of not less than ten years (or sixty years, if paragraph 13 of Schedule 6 to the Act applies) ending on the date of the application, or

　　(ii) where the application is under paragraph 6, of not less than two years beginning with the date of rejection of the original application under paragraph 1 and ending on the date of the application,

(b) any additional evidence which the applicant considers necessary to support the claim.

(2) The statutory declaration or statement of truth by an applicant in support of an application under paragraph 1 of Schedule 6 to the Act must also–

(a) if the application relates to part only of the land in a registered title, exhibit a plan which enables that part to be identified on the Ordnance Survey map, unless that part is referred to in the statutory declaration or statement of truth by reference to the title plan and this enables that part to be so identified,

(b) if reliance is placed on paragraph 1(2) of Schedule 6 to the Act, contain the facts relied upon with any appropriate exhibits,

(c) contain confirmation that paragraph 1(3) of Schedule 6 to the Act does not apply,

(d) where the application is to be registered as proprietor of a registered rentcharge, contain confirmation that the proprietor of the registered rentcharge has not re-entered the land out of which the rentcharge issues,

(e) contain confirmation that to the best of his knowledge the restriction on applications in paragraph 8 of Schedule 6 to the Act does not apply,

(f) contain confirmation that to the best of his knowledge the estate or rentcharge is not, and has not been during any of the period of alleged adverse possession, subject to a trust (other than one where the interest of each of the beneficiaries is an interest in possession),

(g) if, should a person given notice under paragraph 2 of Schedule 6 to the Act require the application to be dealt with under paragraph 5 of that Schedule, it is intended to rely on one or more of the conditions set out in paragraph 5 of Schedule 6 to the Act, contain the facts supporting such reliance.

(3) The statutory declaration or statement of truth by an applicant in support of an application under paragraph 6 of Schedule 6 to the Act must also–

(a) if the application relates to part only of the land in a registered title, exhibit a plan which enables that part to be identified clearly on the Ordnance Survey map, unless the previous rejected application related only to that part, or that part is referred to in the statutory declaration or statement of truth by reference to the title plan and this enables that part to be so identified,

(b) contain full details of the previous rejected application,

(c) contain confirmation that to the best of his knowledge the restriction on applications in paragraph 8 of Schedule 6 to the Act does not apply,

(d) contain confirmation that to the best of his knowledge the estate or rentcharge is not, and has not been during any of the period of alleged adverse possession, subject to a trust (other than one where the interest of each of the beneficiaries is an interest in possession),

(e) contain confirmation that paragraph 6(2) of Schedule 6 to the Act does not apply, and

(f) where the application is to be registered as proprietor of a registered rentcharge, contain confirmation that the proprietor of the registered rentcharge has not re-entered the land out of which the rentcharge issues.

(4) A statement of truth by an applicant under paragraphs 1 or 6 of Schedule 6 to the Act, and any supporting statements of truth, may be made in Form ST1 or Form ST2, as appropriate.

188A.—Notification of application where registered proprietor is a dissolved company

(1) This rule applies where an application under paragraph 1 of Schedule 6 to the Act is made. **A2.1.119**

(2) Where the registrar considers that the proprietor of the estate to which the application relates is, or may be, a company which is dissolved and that its last registered office was, or may have been, situated in the county palatine of Lancaster, the registrar must give notice of the application to the Solicitor for the affairs of the Duchy of Lancaster.

(3) Where the registrar considers that the proprietor of the estate to which the application relates is, or may be, a company which is dissolved and that its last registered office was, or may have been, situated in the county of Cornwall or in the Isles of Scilly, the registrar must give notice of the application to the Duke of Cornwall or the possessor for the time being of the Duchy of Cornwall.

(4) Where the registrar considers that the proprietor of the estate to which the application relates is, or may be, a company which is dissolved and that its last registered office was, or may have been, situated outside the areas referred to in paragraphs (2) and (3), the registrar must give notice of the application to the Treasury Solicitor.

(5) The notice referred to in paragraphs (2) to (4) is notice under paragraph 2 of Schedule 6 to the Act.

(6) In this rule, "company" means a company incorporated in any part of the United Kingdom under the Companies Acts.

189.—Time limit for reply to a notice of an application

The period for the purpose of paragraph 3(2) of Schedule 6 to the Act is the period ending at 12 noon on the sixty-fifth business day after the date of issue of the notice. **A2.1.120**

190.—Notice under paragraph 3(2) of Schedule 6 to the Act

(1) A notice to the registrar under paragraph 3(2) of Schedule 6 to the Act from a person given a registrar's notice must be– **A2.1.121**

(a) in Form NAP, and

(b) given to the registrar in the manner and at the address stated in the registrar's notice.

(2) Form NAP must accompany a registrar's notice.

(3) In this rule a "registrar's notice" is a notice given by the registrar under paragraph 2 of Schedule 6 to the Act.

191.—Adverse possession of rentcharges

A2.1.122   Schedule 6 to the Act applies to the registration of an adverse possessor of a registered rentcharge in the modified form set out in Schedule 8.

192.—Adverse possession of a rentcharge; non-payment of rent

A2.1.123   (1) This rule applies where–

(a)   a person is entitled to be registered as proprietor of a registered rentcharge under Schedule 6 to the Act, and

(b)   if that person were so registered he would not be subject to a registered charge or registered lease or other interest protected in the register, and

(c)   that person's adverse possession is based on non-payment of rent due under the registered rentcharge.

(2) Where paragraph (1) applies the registrar must–

(a)   close the whole of the registered title of the registered rentcharge, or

(b)   cancel the registered rentcharge, if the registered title to it also comprises other rentcharges.

193.—Prohibition of recovery of rent after adverse possession of a rentcharge

A2.1.124   (1) When–

(a)   a person has been registered as proprietor of a rentcharge, or

(b)   the registered title to a rentcharge has been closed, or

(c)   a registered rentcharge has been cancelled, where the registered title also comprises other rentcharges,

following an application made under Schedule 6 to the Act, and, if appropriate, closure or cancellation under rule 192, no previous registered proprietor of the rentcharge may recover any rent due under the rentcharge from a person who has been in adverse possession of the rentcharge.

(2) Paragraph (1) applies whether the adverse possession arose either as a result of non-payment of the rent or by receipt of the rent from the person liable to pay it.

194.—Registration as a person entitled to be notified of an application for adverse possession

(1) Any person who can satisfy the registrar that he has an interest in a **A2.1.125** registered estate in land or a registered rentcharge which would be prejudiced by the registration of any other person as proprietor of that estate under Schedule 6 to the Act or as proprietor of a registered rentcharge under that Schedule as applied by rule 191 may apply to be registered as a person to be notified under paragraph 2(1)(d) of Schedule 6.

(2) An application under paragraph (1) must be made in Form ADV2.

(3) The registrar must enter the name of the applicant in the proprietorship register as a person entitled to be notified under paragraph 2 of Schedule 6 to the Act.

194A.—Arbitration requested by proprietor

(1) This rule applies where a proprietor with the right under para- **A2.1.126** graph 10(1) of Schedule 6 to the Act to require apportionment has given the chargor notice in accordance with paragraph (2).

(2) The notice referred to in paragraph (1) must—

(a) identify the proprietor and give an address for communications to the proprietor from the chargor,

(b) make proposals as to the values of the registered estate and the other property subject to the charge,

(c) state the proprietor's intention, in the absence of agreement on the respective values of the registered estate and the other property subject to the charge, to request the President of the Royal Institution of Chartered Surveyors to appoint a qualified surveyor to determine these values, and

(d) be served by post to, or by leaving the notice at, any postal address or by electronic transmission to an electronic address (if there is one) entered in the register as an address for service for the chargor.

(3) If the chargor does not provide the proprietor with the chargor's written agreement to the values referred to in paragraph (2)(b), or to any

other valuations acceptable to the proprietor, within one month of when the notice was received, the proprietor may make the request referred to in paragraph (2)(c).

(4) Where a qualified surveyor has been appointed pursuant to a request under paragraph (3)—

    (a) the proprietor shall be liable for the costs of that appointment,

    (b) the qualified surveyor shall act as an arbitrator and the provisions of the Arbitration Act 1996 shall apply,

    (c) the proprietor and the chargor shall be parties to the arbitration,

    (d) the chargee may elect to be joined as a party to the arbitration, and the qualified surveyor must ascertain whether the chargee so elects, and

    (e) the proprietor and the chargor must allow the qualified surveyor access to the land any estate in which is subject to the charge.

(5) In this rule, "an address for communications" means a postal address but if additionally the proprietor provides an e-mail address then that is also an address for communications.

194B.—Notice of required apportionment

A2.1.127   (1) The right of the proprietor of a registered estate under paragraph 10(1) of Schedule 6 to the Act to require a chargee to apportion the amount secured by a charge is exercisable by notice being given by the proprietor to the chargee.

(2) The notice referred to in paragraph (1) must—

    (a) identify the proprietor and give an address for communications to him from the chargee,

    (b) state that apportionment is required under paragraph 10 of Schedule 6 to the Act,

    (c) identify the chargor and the date of the charge,

    (d) state whether the valuations accompanying the notice were by a qualified surveyor appointed pursuant to a request under rule 194A and, if they were, state the effect of rule 194C(1), and

    (e) be served by post to, or by leaving the notice at, any postal address or by electronic transmission to an electronic address (if there is one) entered in the register as an address for service for the chargee.

(3) Subject to paragraph (4), the notice referred to in paragraph (1) must be accompanied by—

    (a) valuations of the registered estate and of the other property subject to the charge by a qualified surveyor dated no earlier than two months before the notice is sent,

    (b) the chargor's written agreement to the valuations,

    (c) an official copy of the individual register and title plan of the registered estate, and

    (d) a copy of the individual register and title plan, supplied in response to an application under rule 144, in respect of the registered title which immediately before the registration under Schedule 6 to the Act comprised the registered estate, unless such a copy is unavailable.

(4) If the valuations of the registered estate and of the other property subject to the charge are by a qualified surveyor appointed pursuant to a request under rule 194A, the requirements in paragraph (3)(b), (c) and (d) do not apply.

(5) In this rule, "an address for communications" means a postal address but if additionally the proprietor provides an e-mail address then that is also an address for communications.

194C.—Apportionment

(1) If the valuations accompanying the notice referred to in rule 194B(1) **A2.1.128** are by a qualified surveyor appointed pursuant to a request under rule 194A, the chargee must, within two months of when the notice was received, apportion the amount secured by the charge at the time referred to in paragraph 10(1) of Schedule 6 to the Act on the basis of these valuations.

(2) If the valuations accompanying the notice referred to in rule 194B(1) are not by a qualified surveyor pursuant to a request under rule 194A, the chargee must, within two months of when the notice was received, either—

    (a) apportion the amount secured by the charge at the time referred to in paragraph 10(1) of Schedule 6 to the Act on the basis of the valuations accompanying the notice, or on the basis of other valuations agreed by the proprietor and the chargor, or

    (b) request the President of the Royal Institution of Chartered Surveyors to appoint a qualified surveyor to value the registered estate and the other property subject to the charge.

(3) Where a qualified surveyor has been appointed pursuant to a request under paragraph (2)(b)—

(a) the chargee shall be liable for the costs of that appointment,

(b) the qualified surveyor shall act as an arbitrator and the provisions of the Arbitration Act 1996 shall apply,

(c) the proprietor and the chargee shall be parties to the arbitration,

(d) the chargor may elect to be joined as a party to the arbitration, and the qualified surveyor must ascertain whether the chargor so elects, and

(e) the proprietor and the chargor must allow the qualified surveyor access to the land any estate in which is subject to the charge.

(4) Where a qualified surveyor has been appointed pursuant to a request under paragraph (2)(b), the chargee must, within two months of when the valuations by the qualified surveyor were received, apportion the amount secured by the charge at the time referred to in paragraph 10(1) of Schedule 6 to the Act on the basis of those valuations.

194D.—Basis of valuation

A2.1.129 (1) For the purposes of rules 194A, 194B and 194C, where the other property affected by the charge includes an estate in land, the value of the proprietor's registered estate shall be the diminution in value of that other property as determined in accordance with paragraph (2).

(2) The diminution in value of the other property is the difference between—

(a) the value of all the property subject to the charge if the chargor were the proprietor and in possession of the proprietor's registered estate, and

(b) the value of the property subject to the charge without the proprietor's registered estate.

194E.—Receipt of notice etc

A2.1.130 (1) Notices and valuations shall be treated as received for the purposes of rules 194A(3) and 194C(1), (2) and (4) on—

(a) the second working day after posting, where the notice is posted to an address in the United Kingdom,

(b) the working day after it was left, where the notice is left at a postal address,

(c) the seventh working day after posting, where the notice is posted to an address outside the United Kingdom, and

(d) the second working day after transmission, where the notice is sent by electronic transmission (including email).

194F.—Notice of apportionment

(1) Within ten working days of any apportionment under rule 194C, **A2.1.131** the chargee must issue notice of the apportionment to the proprietor and to the chargor.

(2) The notice referred to in paragraph (1) must state—

(a) the amount secured by the charge at the time referred to in paragraph 10(1) of Schedule 6 to the Act,

(b) the amount apportioned to the registered estate, and

(c) the costs incurred by the chargee as a result of the apportionment and payable under paragraph 10(2)(b) of Schedule 6 to the Act.

(3) The notice referred to in paragraph (1) which is issued to the proprietor must be served by post to, or by leaving the notice at, the postal address or by electronic transmission to any e-mail address given in the notice of required apportionment under rule 194B(1) or at another postal or e-mail address agreed in writing by the chargee and the proprietor.

194G.—Costs

(1) Where in the award under rule 194A(4) or rule 194C(3) the qualified **A2.1.132** surveyor decides that the chargee shall be responsible for payment of the costs incurred by the chargee or any other party to the arbitration, such costs shall be excluded from the costs payable under paragraph 10(2)(b) of Schedule 6 to the Act.

(2) Subject to paragraph (3), the chargor shall be entitled to be paid by the proprietor those costs reasonably incurred by the chargor in the apportionment and, in particular, those in relation to valuations obtained for the purpose of the apportionment.

(3) Where in the award the qualified surveyor decides that the chargor shall be responsible for payment of the costs incurred by the chargor or any other party to the arbitration, such costs shall be excluded from the costs payable under paragraph (2).

Indemnity; interest on

195.—Payment of interest on an indemnity

A2.1.133   (1) Subject to paragraph (3), interest is payable in accordance with paragraph (4) on the amount of any indemnity paid under Schedule 8 to the Act—

(a) where paragraph 1(1)(a) of Schedule 8 applies other than in respect of any indemnity on account of costs or expenses, from the date of the rectification to the date of payment,

(b) where any other sub-paragraph of paragraph 1(1) of Schedule 8 applies other than in respect of any indemnity on account of costs or expenses, from the date the loss is suffered by reason of the relevant mistake, loss, destruction or failure to the date of payment,

(c) in respect of an indemnity on account of costs or expenses within paragraph 3 of Schedule 8, from the date when the claimant pays them to the date of payment.

(2) A reference in this rule to a period from a date to the date of payment excludes the former date but includes the latter date.

(3) No interest is payable under paragraph (1) for any period or periods where the registrar or the court is satisfied that the claimant has not taken reasonable steps to pursue with due diligence the claim for indemnity or, where relevant, the application for rectification.

(4) Simple interest is payable—

(a) where the period specified in paragraph (1) starts on or after 10 November 2008, at one percent above the applicable Bank of England base rate or rates, or

(b) where the period specified in paragraph (1) starts before that date,

(i) for the part of the period before that date, at the applicable rate or rates set for court judgment debts, and

(ii) for the part of the period on or after that date, at one percent above the applicable Bank of England base rate or rates.

(5) In this rule "Bank of England base rate" means—

(a) the rate announced from time to time by the Monetary Policy Committee of the Bank of England as the official dealing rate, being the rate at which the Bank is willing to enter into transactions for providing short term liquidity in the money markets, or

(b)   where an order under section 19 of the Bank of England Act 1998 is in force, any equivalent rate determined by the Treasury under that section.

Statements under the Leasehold Reform, Housing and Urban Development Act 1993

196.—Statements in transfers or conveyances and leases under the Leasehold Reform, Housing and Urban Development Act 1993

(1) The statement required by section 34(10) of the Leasehold Reform, **A2.1.134** Housing and Urban Development Act 1993 to be contained in a conveyance executed for the purposes of Chapter I of Part I of that Act must be in the following form:

"(Form not available in online format. Please see original printed copy.)".

(2) The statement required by section 57(11) of the Leasehold Reform, Housing and Urban Development Act 1993 to be contained in any new lease granted under section 56 of that Act must be in the following form:

"This lease is granted under section 56 of the Leasehold Reform, Housing and Urban Development Act 1993.".

Modification of Parts 2 and 3 of the Act in their application to incorporeal hereditaments

196A.—Possessory titles to rentcharges

In their application to rentcharges, sections 9(5) and 10(6) of the Act **A2.1.135** have effect as if for the words "in actual possession of the land, or in receipt of the rents and profits of the land," there were substituted the words "in receipt of the rent".

196B.—Application of sections 11, 12 and 29 of the Act to franchises

(1) In their application to franchises, sections 11(4) and 12(4) of the Act **A2.1.136** have effect without prejudice to any right of the Crown to forfeit the franchise.

(2) In its application to franchises, section 29(2)(a) of the Act has effect with the deletion of the word "or" at the end of sub-paragraph (ii) and

with the insertion between the words "registration," and "and" at the end of sub-paragraph (iii) of—

"or

(iv) is a right of the Crown to forfeit the franchise,".

Part 15

GENERAL PROVISIONS

Notices and Addresses for Service

197.—Content of notice

A2.1.137   (1) Every notice given by the registrar must–

(a) fix the time within which the recipient is to take any action required by the notice,

(b) state what the consequence will be of a failure to take such action as is required by the notice within the time fixed,

(c) state the manner in which any reply to the notice must be given and the address to which it must be sent.

(2) Except where otherwise provided by these rules, the time fixed by the notice will be the period ending at 12 noon on the fifteenth business day after the date of issue of the notice.

198.—Address for service of notice

A2.1.138   (1) A person who is (or will as a result of an application be) a person within paragraph (2) must give the registrar an address for service to which all notices and other communications to him by the registrar may be sent, as provided by paragraph (3).

(2) The persons referred to in paragraph (1) are–

(a) the registered proprietor of a registered estate or registered charge,

(b) the registered beneficiary of a unilateral notice,

(c) a cautioner named in an individual caution register,

(d) a person named in—

(i) a standard form of restriction set out in Schedule 4, whose address is required by that restriction, or

(ii) any other restriction, whose consent or certificate is required, or to whom notice is required to be given by the registrar or another person,

except where the registrar is required to enter the restriction without application,

(e) a person entitled to be notified of an application for adverse possession under rule 194,

(f) a person who objects to an application under section 73 of the Act,

(g) a person who gives notice to the registrar under paragraph 3(2) of Schedule 6 to the Act, and

(h) any person who while dealing with the registrar in connection with registered land or a caution against first registration is requested by the registrar to give an address for service.

(3) A person within paragraph (1) must give the registrar an address for service which is a postal address, whether or not in the United Kingdom.

(4) A person within paragraph (1) may give the registrar one or two additional addresses for service, provided that he may not have more than three addresses for service, and the address or addresses must be–

(a) a postal address, whether or not in the United Kingdom, or

(b) subject to paragraph (7), a box number at a United Kingdom document exchange, or

(c) an electronic address.

(5) Subject to paragraphs (3) and (4) a person within paragraph (1) may give the registrar a replacement address for service.

(6) A cautioner who is entered in the register of title in respect of a caution against dealings under section 54 of the Land Registration Act 1925 may give the registrar a replacement or additional address for service provided that–

(a) he may not have more than three addresses for service,

(b) one of his addresses for service must be a postal address, whether or not in the United Kingdom, and

(c) all of his addresses for service must be such addresses as are mentioned in paragraph (4).

(6A) Where a cautioner who is shown in the register of title as having been entered in that register in respect of a caution against dealings under section 54 of the Land Registration Act 1925 has died, his personal representative may apply to the registrar for the entry of a replacement or additional address for service provided that—

(a) there may not be more than three addresses for service,

(b) one of the addresses for service must be a postal address, whether or not in the United Kingdom,

(c) all of the addresses for service must be such addresses as are mentioned in paragraph (4), and

(d) the application must be accompanied by—

(i)   the original grant of probate of the deceased proprietor and, where section 7 of the Administration of Justice Act 1925 applies, the original grant of probate showing the chain of representation, to prove that the transferor is his personal representative,

(ii) the original letters of administration of the deceased proprietor showing the transferor as his personal representative,

(iii) a court order appointing the applicant as the deceased's personal representative, or

(iv) (where a conveyancer is acting for the applicant) a certificate given by a conveyancer that he holds the original or a certified office copy of such grant of probate, letters of administration or court order.

(7) The box number referred to at paragraph (4)(b) must be at a United Kingdom document exchange to which delivery can be made on behalf of the land registry under arrangements already in existence between the land registry and a service provider at the time the box number details are provided to the registrar under this rule.

(8) In this rule an electronic address means–

(a) an e-mail address, or

(b) any other form of electronic address specified in a direction under paragraph (9).

(9) If the registrar is satisfied that a form of electronic address, other than an e-mail address, is a suitable form of address for service he may issue a direction to that effect.

(10) A direction under paragraph (9) may contain such conditions or limitations or both as the registrar considers appropriate.

(11) A person within paragraph (2)(d) shall be treated as having complied with any duty imposed on him under paragraph (1) where rule 92(2)(b) has been complied with.

199.—Service of notice

(1) All notices which the registrar is required to give may be served– **A2.1.139**

    (a) by post, to any postal address in the United Kingdom entered in the register as an address for service,

    (b) by post, to any postal address outside the United Kingdom entered in the register as an address for service,

    (c) by leaving the notice at any postal address in the United Kingdom entered in the register as an address for service,

    (d) by directing the notice to the relevant box number at any document exchange entered in the register as an address for service,

    (e) by electronic transmission to the electronic address entered in the register as an address for service,

    (f)   subject to paragraph (3), by fax, or

    (g) by any of the methods of service given in sub-paragraphs (a), (b), (c) and (d) to any other address where the registrar believes the addressee is likely to receive it.

(2) In paragraph (1) references to an address or box number "entered in the register as an address for service" include an address for service given under rule 198(2)(h), whether or not it is entered in the register.

(3) The notice may be served by fax if the recipient has informed the registrar in writing–

    (a)   that the recipient is willing to accept service of the notice by fax, and

    (b)   of the fax number to which it should be sent.

(4) Service of a notice which is served in accordance with this rule shall be regarded as having taken place at the time shown in the table below–

Method of service	Time of service
Post to an address in the United Kingdom	The second working day after posting
Leaving at a postal address	The working day after it was left
Post to an address outside the United Kingdom	The seventh working day after posting
Document exchange	On the second working day after it was left at the registrar's document exchange
Fax	The working day after transmission
Electronic transmission to an electronic address	The second working day after transmission

(5) In this rule "post" means pre-paid delivery by a postal service which seeks to deliver documents within the United Kingdom no later than the next working day in all or the majority of cases, and to deliver outside the United Kingdom within such a period as is reasonable in all the circumstances.

. . .

Specialist assistance

200.—Use of specialist assistance by the registrar

A2.1.140   (1) The registrar may refer to an appropriate specialist–

(a)   the examination of the whole or part of any title lodged with an application for first registration, or

(b)   any question or other matter which arises in the course of any proceedings before the registrar and which, in his opinion, requires the advice of an appropriate specialist.

(2) The registrar may act upon the advice or opinion of an appropriate specialist to whom he has referred a matter under paragraph (1).

(3) In this rule, "appropriate specialist" means a person who the registrar considers has the appropriate knowledge, experience and expertise to advise on the matter referred to him.

Proceedings before the registrar

201.—Production of documents

(1) The registrar may only exercise the power conferred on him by **A2.1.141** section 75(1) of the Act if he receives from a person who is a party to proceedings before him a request that he should require a document holder to produce a document for the purpose of those proceedings.

(2) The request must be made–

(a) in paper form in Form PRD1 delivered to such office of the land registry as the registrar may direct, or

(b) during the currency of a relevant notice given under Schedule 2, and subject to and in accordance with the limitations contained in the notice, by delivering the request to the registrar, by any means of communication, other than as mentioned in sub-paragraph (a).

(3) The registrar must give notice of the request to the document holder.

(4) The address for the document holder provided in Form PRD1 is to be regarded for the purpose of rule 199 as an address for service given under rule 198(2)(h).

(5) The notice must give the document holder a period ending at 12 noon on the twentieth business day after the issue of the notice, or such other period as the registrar thinks appropriate, to deliver a written response to the registrar by the method and to the address stated in the notice.

(6) The response must–

(a) state whether or not the document holder opposes the request,

(b) if he does, state in full the grounds for that opposition,

(c) give an address to which communications may be sent, and

(d) be signed by the document holder or his conveyancer.

(7) The registrar must determine the matter on the basis of the request and any response submitted to him and, subject to paragraph (8), he may make the requirement by sending a notice in Form PRD2 to the document holder if he is satisfied that–

(a) the document is in the control of the document holder, and

(b) the document may be relevant to the proceedings, and

(c) disclosure of the document is necessary in order to dispose fairly of the proceedings or to save costs,

and he is not aware of any valid ground entitling the document holder to withhold the document.

(8) The registrar may, as a condition of making the requirement, provide that the person who has made the request should pay the reasonable costs incurred in complying with the requirement by the document holder.

(9) In this rule, "document holder" means the person who is alleged to have control of a document which is the subject of a request under paragraph (1).

202.—Costs

A2.1.142 (1) A person who has incurred costs in relation to proceedings before the registrar may request the registrar to make an order requiring a party to those proceedings to pay the whole or part of those costs.

(2) The registrar may only order a party to proceedings before him to pay costs where those costs have been occasioned by the unreasonable conduct of that party in relation to the proceedings.

(3) Subject to paragraph (5), a request for the payment of costs must be made by delivering to the registrar a written statement in paper form by 12 noon on the twentieth business day after the completion of the proceedings to which the request relates.

(4) The statement must–

(a) identify the party against whom the order is sought and include an address where notice may be served on that party,

(b) state in full the grounds for the request,

(c) give an address to which communications may be sent, and

(d) be signed by the person making the request or his conveyancer.

(5) During the currency of a relevant notice given under Schedule 2, and subject to and in accordance with the limitations contained in the notice, a request under this rule may also be made by delivering the written statement to the registrar, by any means of communication, other than as mentioned in paragraph (3).

(6) The registrar must give notice of the request to the party against whom the order is sought at the address provided under paragraph (4)(a) and if that party has an address for service in an individual register that relates to the proceedings, at that address.

(7) An address for a party provided under paragraph (4)(a) is to be regarded for the purpose of rule 199 as if it was an address for service given under rule 198(2)(h).

(8) The notice must give the recipient a period ending at 12 noon on the twentieth business day after the issue of the notice, or such other period as the registrar thinks appropriate, to deliver a written response to the registrar by the method and to the address stated in the notice.

(9) The response must–

(a) state whether or not the recipient opposes the request,

(b) if he does, state in full the grounds for that opposition,

(c) give an address to which communications may be sent, and

(d) be signed by the recipient or his conveyancer.

(10) The registrar must determine the matter on the basis of: the written request and any response submitted to him, all the circumstances including the conduct of the parties, and the result of any enquiries he considers it necessary to make.

(11) The registrar must send to all parties his written reasons for any order he makes under paragraph (1).

(12) An order under paragraph (1) may–

(a) require a party against whom it is made to pay to the requesting party the whole or such part as the registrar thinks fit of the costs incurred in the proceedings by the requesting party,

(b) specify the sum to be paid or require the costs to be assessed by the court (if not otherwise agreed), and specify the basis of the assessment to be used by the court.

Retention and return of documents

203.—Retention of documents on completion of an application

(1) Subject to paragraphs (2) to (5), on completion of any application **A2.1.143** the registrar may retain all or any of the documents that accompanied the application and must return all other such documents to the applicant or as otherwise specified in the application.

(2) When making an application, an applicant or his conveyancer may request the return of all or any of the documents accompanying the application.

(3) Except on an application for first registration, a person making a request under paragraph (2) must deliver with the application certified copies of the documents which are the subject of the request.

(4) On an application for first registration, a person making a request under paragraph (2) for the return of any statutory declaration, statement of truth, subsisting lease, subsisting charge, a certificate relating to stamp duty land tax as required by section 79 of the Finance Act 2003, or the latest document of title must deliver with the application certified copies of any such documents as are the subject of the request, but shall not be required to deliver copies of any other documents.

(5) Subject to the delivery of any certified copies required under paragraphs (3) or (4), the registrar must comply with any request made under paragraph (2).

(6) The registrar may destroy any document retained under paragraph (1) if he is satisfied that either–

(a) he has made and retained a sufficient copy of the document, or

(b) further retention of the document is unnecessary.

(7) If the registrar considers that he no longer requires delivery of certified copies of documents, or classes of documents, under this rule he may, in such manner as he thinks appropriate for informing persons who wish to make applications, give notice to that effect and on and after the date specified in such notice–

(a) the requirement under this rule to deliver certified copies of the documents covered by the notice no longer applies, and

(b) the registrar may amend any Schedule 1 form to reflect that fact.

(8) In paragraph (4) the "latest document of title" means the document vesting the estate sought to be registered in the applicant or where the estate vested in the applicant by operation of law the most recent document that vested the estate in a predecessor of the applicant.

204.—Request for the return of certain documents

A2.1.144   (1) This rule applies to all documents on which any entry in the register of title is or was founded and which are kept by the registrar on the relevant date.

(2) During the period of 5 years beginning with the relevant date any person who delivered a document to the registrar may request the return of that document.

(3) Where at the time of the delivery of the document the person delivering the document was the registered proprietor, or was applying to

become the registered proprietor, of any registered estate or registered charge in respect of which the entry referred to in paragraph (1) was made, a person who is at the date of the request the registered proprietor of any part of the same registered estate or registered charge may make a request under paragraph (2) for the document to be returned to him.

(4) Subject to paragraph (5), if, at the date of the request under paragraph (2), the document is kept by the registrar he must return it to the person making the request.

(5) If the registrar receives more than one request under paragraph (2) in respect of the same document, he may either retain the document or, in his discretion, return it to one of the persons making a request.

(6) At the end of the period mentioned in paragraph (2) if there is no outstanding request in relation to the document the registrar may destroy any document if he is satisfied that–

(a) he has retained a copy of the document, or

(b) further retention of the document is unnecessary.

(7) Where a request is made for the return of a document after the end of the period mentioned in paragraph (2), the registrar may treat the request as a request under paragraph (2).

(8) The "relevant date" for the purpose of this rule is the date on which these rules come into force.

205.—Release of documents kept by the registrar

The registrar may release any document retained under rule 203(1) or **A2.1.145** to which rule 204 applies upon such terms, if any, for its return as he considers appropriate.

Forms

206.—Use of forms

(1) Subject to paragraph (4) and to [rules 207A, 208 and 209, the **A2.1.146** Schedule 1] forms must be used where required by these rules and must be prepared in accordance with the requirements of rules 210 and 211.

(2) Subject to paragraph (4) and to rules 208 and 209, except where these rules require the use of a Schedule 1 form, the Schedule 3 forms must be used in all matters to which they refer, or are capable of being applied or adapted, with such alterations and additions as are desired and the registrar allows.

(3) Subject to rule 208(2), the forms of execution in Schedule 9 must be used in the execution of dispositions in the scheduled forms in the cases

for which they are provided, or are capable of being applied or adapted, with such alterations and additions, if any, as the registrar may allow.

(4) A requirement in these rules to use a scheduled form is subject, where appropriate, to the provisions in these rules relating to the making of applications and issuing results of applications other than in paper form, during the currency of a notice given under Schedule 2.

A2.1.147 **207** [Revoked by Land Registration (Amendment) Rules 2008/1919]

207A.—Amendment of certain Schedule 1 forms to provide for explanatory information to be altered

A2.1.148   (1) In order to assist applicants in completing a form or in making an application in relation to a form, the registrar may remove, add to, or alter any explanatory information outside the panels of a Schedule 1 form.

(2) Any amendment under paragraph (1) must not alter the name and description of the form at the top of the first page or instructions as to what must be entered in the form.

(3) Where a form has been amended under paragraph (1) a person may use the form for the purposes of these rules as amended or as unamended.

208.—Welsh language forms

A2.1.149   (1) Where the registrar, in exercise of his powers under section 100(4) of the Act, publishes an instrument as the Welsh language version of a scheduled form, the instrument shall be regarded as being in the scheduled form.

(2) In place of the form of execution provided by Schedule 9, an instrument referred to in paragraph (1) may be executed using a form of execution approved by the registrar as the Welsh language version of the Schedule 9 form.

(3) An instrument containing a statement approved by the registrar as the Welsh language version of a statement prescribed by these rules shall be regarded as containing the prescribed statement.

(4) An instrument containing a provision approved by the registrar as the Welsh language version of a provision prescribed by these rules shall be regarded as containing the prescribed provision.

209.—Use of non-prescribed forms

A2.1.150   (1) This rule applies where–

(a)   an application should be accompanied by a scheduled form and a person wishes to make an application relying instead upon an alternative document that is not the relevant scheduled form, and

(b) it is not possible for that person to obtain and lodge the relevant scheduled form (duly executed, if appropriate) at the land registry or it is only possible to do so at unreasonable expense.

(2) Such a person may make a request to the registrar, either before or at the time of making the application which should be accompanied by the relevant scheduled form, that he be permitted to rely upon the alternative document.

(3) The request must contain evidence to satisfy the registrar as mentioned in paragraph (1)(b) and include the original, or, if the request is made before the application, a copy, of the alternative document.

(4) If, after considering the request, the registrar is satisfied as mentioned at paragraph (1)(b) and that neither the rights of any person nor the keeping of the register are likely to be materially prejudiced by allowing the alternative document to be relied upon instead of the relevant scheduled form, he may permit such reliance.

(5) If the registrar allows the request it may be on condition that the person making the request provides other documents or evidence in support of the application.

(6) This rule is without prejudice to any of the registrar's powers under the Act.

210.—Documents in a Schedule 1 form

(1) Subject to rule 211, any application or document in one of the **A2.1.151** Schedule 1 forms must–

(a) be printed on durable A4 size paper,

(b) subject to rule 215A(4) and (5), be reproduced as set out in the Schedule as to its wording, layout, ruling, font and point size, and

(c) contain all the information required in an easily legible form.

(2) Where on a Schedule 1 form (other than Form DL) any panel is insufficient in size to contain the required insertions, and the method of production of the form does not allow the depth of the panel to be increased, the information to be inserted in the panel must be continued on a continuation sheet in Form CS.

(3) When completing a Schedule 1 form containing an additional provisions panel, any statement, certificate or application required or permitted by these rules to be included in the form for which the form

does not otherwise provide and any additional provisions desired by the parties must be inserted in that panel or a continuation of it.

(4) Where the form consists of more than one sheet of paper, or refers to an attached plan or a continuation sheet, all the sheets and any plan must be securely fastened together.

211.—Electronically produced forms

A2.1.152   Where the method of production of a Schedule 1 form permits–

(a)   the depth of a panel may be increased or reduced to fit the material to be comprised in it, and a panel may be divided at a page break,

(b)   the text outside the panels of a Schedule 1 form, other than—

(i)   the name and description of the form at the top of the first page, and
(ii)   any text after the final panel,

may be omitted,

(c)   inapplicable certificates and statements may be omitted,

(d)   the plural may be used instead of the singular and the singular instead of the plural,

(e)   panels which would contain only the panel number and the panel heading may be omitted, but such omission must not affect the numbering of subsequent panels,

(f)   "X" boxes may be omitted where all inapplicable statements and certificates have been omitted,

(g)   the sub-headings in an additional provisions panel may be added to, amended, repositioned or omitted,

(h)   "Seller" may be substituted for "Transferor" and "Buyer" for "Transferee" in a transfer on sale,

(i)   the vertical lines which define the left and right boundaries of the panel may be omitted.

212.—Documents where no form is prescribed

A2.1.153   (1) Documents for which no form is prescribed must be in such form as the registrar may direct or allow.

(2) A document prepared under this rule must not bear the number of a Schedule 1 form.

(3) A document affecting a registered title must refer to the title number.

Documents accompanying applications

213.—Identification of part of the registered title dealt with

(1) Subject to paragraphs (4) and (5) of this rule, a document lodged at **A2.1.154** the land registry dealing with part of the land in a registered title must have attached to it a plan identifying clearly the land dealt with.

(2) Where the document is a disposition, the disponor must sign the plan.

(3) Where the document is an application, the applicant must sign the plan.

(4) If the land dealt with is identified clearly on the title plan of the registered title, it may instead be described by reference to that title plan.

(5) Where a disposition complies with this rule, the application lodged in respect of it need not.

214.—Lodging of copy instead of an original document

(1) Subject to paragraphs (2), (3) and (4), where a rule requires that an **A2.1.155** application be accompanied by an original document (for instance, a grant of representation) the applicant may, instead of lodging the original, lodge a certified or office copy of that document.

(2) This rule does not apply to–

    (a) any document required to be lodged under Part 4,

    (b) a scheduled form,

    (c) a document that is a registrable disposition.

(3) This rule does not apply also where the registrar considers that the circumstances are such that the original of a document should be lodged and the applicant has possession, or the right to possession, of that original document.

(4) Where this rule permits a certified or office copy of a document to be lodged the registrar may permit an uncertified copy of the document to be lodged instead.

215.—Documents and other evidence in support of an application

2.1.156 (1) This rule applies where–

    (a) the lodging of a document (not being a scheduled form) or other evidence in support of an application is required by these rules, and

817

(b) the document or other evidence is in the particular case unnecessary or the purpose of the lodging of the document or other evidence can be achieved by another document or other evidence.

(2) An applicant may request the registrar to be relieved of the requirement.

(3) The request must contain evidence to satisfy the registrar as mentioned in paragraph (1)(b).

(4) If, after considering the request, the registrar is satisfied as mentioned at paragraph (1)(b) and that neither the rights of any person nor the keeping of the register are likely to be materially prejudiced by relieving the applicant of the requirement, he may so relieve the applicant.

(5) If the registrar allows the request it may be on condition that the applicant provides other documents or evidence in support of the application.

(6) This rule is without prejudice to any of the registrar's powers under the Act.

215A.—Statements of truth

A2.1.157 (1) In these rules, a statement of truth means a statement which—

(a) is made by an individual in writing,

(b) contains a declaration of truth in the following form—
'I believe that the facts and matters contained in this statement are true', and

(c) is signed in accordance with paragraphs (2) to (6).

(2) Subject to paragraph (5), a statement of truth must be signed by the individual making the statement.

(3) The full name of the individual who signs a statement of truth must be printed clearly beneath his signature.

(4) Where a statement of truth is to be signed by an individual who is unable to read, it must—

(a) be signed in the presence of a conveyancer, and

(b) contain a certificate made and signed by that conveyancer in the following form—

'I [name and address of conveyancer] certify that I have read over the contents of this statement of truth and explained the nature and effect of any documents referred to in it and the consequences of making a false declaration to the person making this statement who signed it or made [his]*or*[her] mark in my presence having first (a) appeared to me to understand the statement (b) approved its content as accurate and (c) appeared to me to understand the declaration of truth and the consequences of making a false declaration.'.

(5) Where a statement of truth is to be made by an individual who is unable to sign it, it must—

(a) state that individual's full name,

(b) be signed by a conveyancer at the direction and on behalf of that individual, and

(c) contain a certificate made and signed by that conveyancer in the following form—
'I [*name and address of conveyancer*] certify that [the person making this statement of truth has read it in my presence, approved its content as accurate and directed me to sign it on [his]*or*[her] behalf]*or*[I have read over the contents of this statement of truth and explained the nature and effect of any documents referred to in it and the consequences of making a false declaration to the person making this statement who directed me to sign it on [his]*or*[her] behalf] having first (a) appeared to me to understand the statement (b) approved its content as accurate and (c) appeared to me to understand the declaration of truth and the consequences of making a false declaration.'.

(6) Where a statement of truth, or a certificate under paragraph (4) or (5), is signed by a conveyancer—

(a) the conveyancer must sign in their own name and not that of their firm or employer, and

(b) the conveyancer must state the capacity in which they sign and where appropriate the name of their firm or employer.

Land Registry-when open to public

216.—Days on which the Land Registry is open to the public

(1) Subject to paragraph (2), the land registry shall be open to the **A2.1.158** public daily except on—

(a) Saturdays, Sundays, Christmas Day and Good Friday, or

(b) any other day—

(i) specified or declared by proclamation under section 1 of the Banking and Financial Dealings Act 1971,

(ii) appointed by the Lord Chancellor, or

(iii) certified as an interrupted day under paragraph (6).

(2) If the registrar is satisfied that adequate arrangements have been made or will be in place for opening the land registry to the public on Saturdays, he may, in such manner as he considers appropriate, give notice to that effect.

(3) On and after the date specified in any notice given pursuant to paragraph (2), paragraph (1) shall have effect as though the word "Saturdays" had been omitted.

(4) The date referred to in paragraph (3) must be at least eight weeks after the date of the notice.

(5) On and after the date specified in any notice given pursuant to paragraph (2), the periods in column 3 in the table below are substituted for the periods in column 2 in that table in the rules to which they relate.

(1) Rule	(2) Prescribed period before any notice given under rule 216(2) takes effect	(3) Prescribed period after any notice given under rule 216(2) takes effect
16(1)	Twenty business days	twenty-four business days
31(2)	the twentieth business day	the twenty-fourth business day
53(1)	the fifteenth business day	the eighteenth business day
53(1)	the thirtieth business day	the thirty-sixth business day
53(3)	the thirtieth business day	the thirty-sixth business day
53(4)	the fifteenth business day	the eighteenth business day
54(9)	the fourth business day	the fourth business day
55(4)	fifteen business days	Eighteen business days
86(3)	the fifteenth business day	the eighteenth business day
86(3)	the thirtieth business day	the thirty-sixth business day
86(5)	the thirtieth business day	the thirty-sixth business day
86(6)	the fifteenth business day	the eighteenth business day
92(9)	the fifteenth business day	the eighteenth business day

119(3)	the twentieth business day	the twenty-fourth business day
189	the sixty-fifth business day	the seventy-eighth business day
197(2)	the fifteenth business day	the eighteenth business day
201(5)	the twentieth business day	the twenty-fourth business day
202(3)	the twentieth business day	the twenty-fourth business day
202(8)	the twentieth business day	the twenty-fourth business day
218	the fifteenth business day	the eighteenth business day

(6) The registrar may certify any day as an interrupted day if he is satisfied that on that day there is likely to be—

(a) a general delay in, or failure of, a communication service in England and Wales, or

(b) any other event or circumstance,

causing a substantial interruption in the normal operation of the land registry.

(7) The registrar must give notice of any certification under paragraph (6) in such manner as he considers appropriate.

(8) Any certification under paragraph (6) must take place before the start of the day being certified.

(9) In this rule, "communication service" means a service by which documents may be sent and delivered and includes a post service, a document exchange service and electronic communications.

Interpretation

217.—General Interpretation

(1) In these rules–   **A2.1.159**

"the Act" means the Land Registration Act 2002,

"affecting franchise" means a franchise which relates to a defined area of land and is an adverse right affecting, or capable of affecting, the title to an estate or charge,

"business day" means a day when the land registry is open to the public under rule 216, "caution plan" has the meaning given by rule 41(4),

"caution title number" has the meaning given by rule 41(1),

"certified copy" means a copy of a document which a conveyancer, or such other person as the registrar may permit, has certified on its face to be a true copy of the original and endorsed with his name and address, and the reference to a conveyancer includes where the document is one referred to in– (a) rule 168(2)(a) or 168(3), the bankrupt's trustee in bankruptcy or the official receiver,

(b) rule 184(2), the company's administrator,

(c) rule 184(5), the company's liquidator,

"charges register" is the register so named in rule 4 the contents of which are described in rule 9,

"charity" and "charity trustees" have the same meaning as in sections 96 and 97(1) of the Charities Act 1993 respectively,

"Companies Acts" means—(a) the Companies Act 2006 and any Act amending or replacing that Act,

(b) the provisions of the Companies Act 1985, the Companies Consolidation (Consequential Provisions) Act 1985, Part 2 of the Companies (Audit, Investigations and Community Enterprise) Act 2004 and the Companies (N.I.) Order 1986 that remain in force, and

(c) any former enactment relating to companies,

"control" in relation to a document of which a person has control means physical possession, or the right to possession, or right to take copies of the document,

"conveyancer" means—

(a) a solicitor,

(b) a licensed conveyancer within the meaning of section 11(2) of the Administration of Justice Act 1985,

(c) a fellow of the Institute of Legal Executives,

(d) a barrister,

(e) a duly certificated notary public, or

(f) a registered European lawyer within the meaning of the European Communities (Lawyer's Practice) Regulations 2000 who by virtue of regulations 6 and 12 of those Regulations is entitled to prepare for remuneration an instrument creating or transferring an interest in land in England and Wales, "day list" has the same meaning given by rule 12,

"electronic legal charge" has the same meaning as in the Land Registration (Electronic Conveyancing) Rules 2008,

"exempt charity" has the same meaning as in section 96 of the Charities Act 1993 and "non-exempt charity" means a charity which is not an exempt charity,

"home rights notice" means a notice registered under section 31(10)(a) or section 32 of, and paragraph 4(3)(a) or 4(3)(b) of Schedule 4 to, the Family Law Act 1996, or section 2(8) or section 5(3)(b) of the Matrimonial Homes Act 1983, or section 2(7) or section 5(3)(b) of the Matrimonial Homes Act 1967,

"index map" has the meaning given by rule 10(1)(a),

"index of proprietors' names" has the meaning given by rule 11(1),

"index of relating franchises and manors" is the index described in rule 10(1)(b),

"individual caution register" is the register so named in rule 41(1) the arrangement of which is described in rule 41(2),

"individual register" is the register so named in rule 2 the contents and arrangement of which are described in rules 3 and 4,

"inheritance tax notice" means a notice in respect of an Inland Revenue charge arising under Part III of the Finance Act 1975 or section 237 of the Inheritance Tax Act 1984,

"matrimonial home rights caution" means a caution registered under the Matrimonial Homes Act 1967 before 14 February 1983,

. . .

"official custodian" means the official custodian for charities,

"old tenancy" means a tenancy as defined in section 28 of the Landlord and Tenant (Covenants) Act 1995 which is not a new tenancy as defined in section 1 of that Act,

"overseas company" means a company incorporated outside the United Kingdom,

"property register" is the register so named in rule 4 the contents of which are described in rules 5, 6 and 7,

"proprietorship register" is the register so named in rule 4 the contents of which are described in rule 8,

"registered title" means an individual register and any title plan referred to in that register, "relating franchise" means a franchise which is not an affecting franchise,

"Schedule 1 form" means a form in Schedule 1,

"Schedule 3 form" means a form in Schedule 3,

"scheduled form" means a Schedule 1 form or a Schedule 3 form,

"section 33(5) order" means an order made under section 33(5) of the Family Law Act 1996,

"statement of truth" has the meaning given by rule 215A,

"statutory declaration" includes affidavit,

"title number" has the meaning given by rule 4,

"title plan" has the meaning given by rule 5,

"trust corporation" has the same meaning as in the Settled Land Act 1925,

"trusts" in relation to a charity has the same meaning as in section 97(1) of the Charities Act 1993,

"unregistered company" means a body corporate to which section 718(1) of the Companies Act 1985 applies,

"working day" means any day from Monday to Friday (inclusive) which is not Christmas Day, Good Friday or any other day either specified or declared by proclamation under section 1 of the Banking and Financial Dealings Act 1971 or appointed by the Lord Chancellor.

(2) Subject to paragraph (3), a reference in these rules to a form by letter, or by number, or by a combination of both is to a scheduled form.

(3) A reference in these rules to Forms A to Y and Forms AA to PP (in each case inclusive) is to the standard form of restriction bearing that letter in Schedule 4.

Part 16

TRANSITIONAL

Cautions against dealings

218.—Definitions

A2.1.160   In this Part–

"the 1925 Act" means the Land Registration Act 1925,

"caution" means a caution entered in the register of title under section 54 of the 1925 Act,

"cautioner" includes his personal representative,

"the notice period" is the period ending at 12 noon on the fifteenth business day, or ending at 12 noon on such later business day as the registrar may allow, after the date of issue of the notice.

219.—Consent under a caution

Any consent given under section 55 or 56 of the 1925 Act must be in writing signed by the person giving it or his conveyancer. **A2.1.161**

220.—Notice under section 55(1) of the 1925 Act and under rule 223(3)

(1) Rule 199 applies to the method of service of a notice under section 55(1) of the 1925 Act and under rule 223(3). **A2.1.162**

(2) The notice period applies to a notice served under section 55(1) of the 1925 Act and to one served under rule 223(3).

221.—Cautioner showing cause

(1) This rule applies where notice is served under section 55(1) of the 1925 Act or rule 223(3). **A2.1.163**

(2) At any time before expiry of the notice period, the cautioner may show cause why the registrar should not give effect to the application that resulted in the notice being served.

(3) To show cause, the cautioner must–

    (a) deliver to the registrar, in the manner and to the address stated in the notice, a written statement signed by the cautioner or his conveyancer setting out the grounds relied upon, and

    (b) show that he has a fairly arguable case for the registrar not to give effect to the application that resulted in the notice being served.

(4) If, after reading the written statement, and after making any enquiries he thinks necessary, the registrar is satisfied that cause has been shown, he must order that the caution is to continue until withdrawn or otherwise disposed of under these rules or the Act.

(5) Where the registrar makes an order under paragraph (4)–

(a)   the registrar must give notice to the applicant and the cautioner that he has made the order and of the effect of sub-paragraph (b),

(b)   the cautioner is to be treated as having objected under section 73 of the Act to the application that resulted in notice being served, and

(c)   the notice given by the registrar under sub-paragraph (a) to the applicant is to be treated as notice given under section 73(5)(a) of the Act.

(6) If after service of the notice under section 55(1) of the 1925 Act or rule 223(3) the application that resulted in the notice being served is cancelled, withdrawn or otherwise does not proceed, the registrar must make an order that the caution will continue to have effect, unless he has already done so or the caution has been cancelled.

222.—Withdrawal of a caution by the cautioner

A2.1.164   (1) The cautioner may at any time apply to withdraw his caution in Form WCT.

(2) The form must be signed by the cautioner or his conveyancer.

223.—Cancellation of a caution — application by the proprietor etc

A2.1.165   (1) A person may apply to the registrar for the cancellation of a caution if he is–

(a)   the proprietor of the registered estate or a registered charge to which the caution relates, or

(b)   a person who is, or but for the existence of the caution would be, entitled to be registered as the proprietor of that estate or charge.

(2) An application for the cancellation of a caution must be in Form CCD.

(3) Where application is made under this rule, the registrar must give the cautioner notice of the application.

(4) Following the expiry of the notice period, unless the registrar makes an order under rule 221(4), the registrar must cancel the entry of the caution.

Rentcharges and adverse possession

224.—Registered rentcharges held in trust under section 75(1) of the 1925 Act on commencement

Where a rentcharge is held in trust under section 75(1) of the Land **A2.1.166** Registration Act 1925 immediately before the coming into force of section 97 of the Act, the beneficiary of the trust may apply–

(a) to be registered as proprietor of the rentcharge, or

(b) for the registration of the rentcharge to be cancelled.

ADJUDICATOR TO HER MAJESTY'S LAND REGISTRY (PRACTICE AND PROCEDURE) RULES 2003

SI 2003/2117

1.—Citation and Commencement

A2.2.001 These Rules may be cited as the Adjudicator to Her Majesty's Land Registry (Practice and Procedure) Rules 2003 and shall come into force on 13th October 2003.

Part 1

INTRODUCTION

2.—Interpretation

A2.2.002 (1) In these Rules–

"applicant" means the party whom the adjudicator designates as such under rule 5 or under rule 24, or the party who makes a rectification application;

"document" means anything in which information is recorded in any form, and an obligation in these Rules to provide or allow access to a document or a copy of a document for any purpose means, unless the adjudicator directs otherwise, an obligation to provide access to such document or copy in a legible form or in a form which can be readily made into a legible form;

"hearing" means a sitting of the adjudicator for the purpose of enabling the adjudicator to reach or announce a substantive decision, but does not include a sitting of the adjudicator solely in the exercise of one or more of the following powers–

    (a) to consider an application, representation or objection made in the interim part of the proceedings;

    (b) to reach a substantive decision without an oral hearing; or

    (c) to consider whether to grant permission to appeal a decision or to stay the implementation of a decision pending the outcome of an appeal;

"matter" means the subject of either a reference or a rectification application;

"office copy" means an official copy of a document held or issued by a public authority;

"original application" means the application originally made to the registrar that resulted in a reference;

"proceedings" means, except in the expression "court proceedings", the proceedings of the matter before the adjudicator but does not include any negotiations, communications or proceedings that occurred prior to the reference or rectification application;

"record of matters" means a record of references, rectification applications and certain other applications and decisions, kept in accordance with these Rules and in particular in accordance with rule 46;

"rectification application" means an application made to rectify or set aside a document under section 108(2) for determination of the matter by the adjudicator;

"reference" means a reference from the registrar to the adjudicator under section 73(7) for determination of the matter by the adjudicator;

"respondent" means the party or parties who the adjudicator designates as such under rule 5 or rule 24, or the party or parties making an objection to a rectification application;

"statement of truth" means—

(a) in the case of a witness statement, a statement signed by the maker of the statement that the maker of the statement believes that the facts stated in the witness statement are true; or

(b) in the case of other documents, a statement that the party by whom or on whose behalf the document is submitted believes the facts stated in the document are true, signed by either—

    (i) the party by whom or on whose behalf the document is submitted; or

    (ii) that party's authorised representative, in which case the statement of truth must state the name of the representative and the relationship of the representative to the party;

"substantive decision" means a decision of the adjudicator on the matter or on any substantive issue that arises in it but does not include any direction in interim parts of the proceedings, any order made under rule 8(4) or 9(4), or any order as to costs or any order as to costs thrown away;

"substantive order" means an order or direction that records and gives effect to a substantive decision;

"the Act" means the Land Registration Act 2002 and a reference to a section by number alone is a reference to a section of the Act;

"witness statement" means a written statement . . . containing the evidence that the witness intends to give and verified by a statement of truth; and

"working day" means any day other than a Saturday or Sunday, Christmas Day, Good Friday or any other bank holiday.

(2) For the purposes of these Rules a person has a document . . . in his possession or control if–

(a) it is in his physical possession;

(b) he has a right to possession of it; or

(c) he has a right to inspect or take copies of it.

3.—The overriding objective

A2.2.003 (1) The overriding objective of these Rules is to enable the adjudicator to deal with matters justly.
(2) Dealing with a matter justly includes, so far as is practicable–

(a) ensuring that the parties are on an equal footing;

(b) saving expense;

(c) dealing with the matter in ways that are proportionate–

(i) to the value of the land or other interests involved;
(ii) to the importance of the matter;
(iii) to the complexity of the issues in the matter; and
(iv) to the financial position of each party; and

(d) ensuring that the matter is dealt with expeditiously and fairly.

(3) The adjudicator must seek to give effect to the overriding objective when he–

(a) exercises any power given to him by these Rules; or

(b) interprets these Rules.

(4) The parties are required to help the adjudicator to further the overriding objective.

PART 2

REFERENCES TO THE ADJUDICATOR

4.—Scope of this Part

The rules in this Part apply to references.   A2.2.004

5.—Notice of receipt by the adjudicator of a reference

Following receipt by the adjudicator of a reference, the adjudicator **A2.2.005**
must–

(a) enter the particulars of the reference in the record of matters; and

(b) serve on the parties notice in writing of–

    (i) the fact that the reference has been received by the adjudicator;

    (ii) the date when the adjudicator received the reference;

    (iii) the matter number allocated to the reference;

    (iv) the name and any known address and address for service of the parties to the proceedings; and

    (v) which party will be the applicant for the purposes of the proceedings and which party or parties will be the respondent.

6.—Direction to commence court proceedings under section 110(1)

Where the adjudicator intends to direct a party to commence court **A2.2.006**
proceedings under section 110(1), the parties may make representations
or objections but any representations or objections must be concerned
with one or more of the following–

(a) whether the adjudicator should make such a direction;

(b) which party should be directed to commence court proceedings;

(c) the time within which court proceedings should commence; and

(d) the questions the court should determine.

7.—Notification to the adjudicator of court proceedings following a direction to commence court proceedings under section 110(1)

A2.2.007   (1) In this Part–

"the date that the matter before the court is finally disposed of" means the earliest date by which the court proceedings relating to the matter or on the relevant part (including any court proceedings on or in consequence of an appeal) have been determined and any time for appealing or further appealing has expired;

"the relevant part" means the part of the matter in relation to which the adjudicator has directed a party under section 110(1) to commence court proceedings; and

"the final court order" means the order made by the court that records the court's final determination (on appeal or otherwise).

(2) A party who has been directed to commence court proceedings under section 110(1) must serve on the adjudicator–

  (a) within 14 days of the commencement of the court proceedings, a written notice stating–

  (i) that court proceedings have been issued in accordance with directions given by the adjudicator;
  (ii) the date of issue of the court proceedings;
  (iii) the names and any known addresses of the parties to the court proceedings;
  (iv) the name of the court at which the court proceedings will be heard; and
  (v) the case number allocated to the court proceedings;

  (b) within 14 days of the date of the court's decision on any application for an extension of time, a copy of that decision; and

  (c) within 14 days of the date that the matter before the court is finally disposed of, a copy of the final court order.

8.—Adjournment of proceedings before the adjudicator following a direction to commence court proceedings on the whole of the matter under section 110(1)

A2.2.008   (1) This rule applies where the adjudicator has directed a party under section 110(1) to commence court proceedings for the court's decision on the whole of the matter.

(2) Once he has received notice under rule 7(2)(a) that court proceedings have been issued, the adjudicator must adjourn all of the proceedings before him pending the outcome of the court proceedings.

(3) Subject to paragraph (4), once the adjudicator has received a copy of the final court order in accordance with rule 7(2)(c) and unless the court directs otherwise, the adjudicator must close the proceedings before him without making a substantive decision.

(4) Before closing the proceedings in accordance with paragraph (3) the adjudicator may make an order either with or without a hearing and either with or without giving prior notice to the parties if—

(a) such order is necessary, in addition to the final court order, to implement the decision of the court; and

(b) the adjudicator would have had the power to make such order if the adjudicator had made a substantive decision in relation to the proceedings.

9.—Adjournment of proceedings before the adjudicator following a direction to commence court proceedings on part of the matter under section 110(1)

(1) This rule applies where the adjudicator has directed a party under section 110(1) to commence court proceedings for the court's decision on the relevant part. **A2.2.009**

(2) Once the adjudicator has received notice under rule 7(2)(a) that court proceedings have been issued in relation to the relevant part, the adjudicator must adjourn the proceedings brought under these Rules in relation to that part, pending the outcome of the court proceedings.

(3) Subject to paragraph (4), once the adjudicator has received a copy of the final court order on the relevant part in accordance with rule 7(2)(c) and unless the court directs otherwise, the adjudicator must close the proceedings before him in relation to the relevant part without making a substantive decision on that relevant part.

(3A) Before closing the proceedings in relation to the relevant part in accordance with paragraph (3) the adjudicator may make an order either with or without a hearing and either with or without giving prior notice to the parties if—

(a) such order is necessary, in addition to the final court order, to implement the decision of the court; and

(b) the adjudicator would have had the power to make such order if the adjudicator had made a substantive decision in relation to the relevant part.

(4) The adjudicator may adjourn the proceedings in relation to any other part of the matter before him pending the outcome of the court proceedings.

(5) While the court proceedings are still ongoing, the party directed to commence court proceedings must notify the court of any substantive decision made by the adjudicator within 14 days of service on that party of the substantive decision.

10.—Notification where court proceedings are commenced otherwise than following a direction to commence court proceedings under section 110(1)

A2.2.010 Where a party commences or has commenced court proceedings otherwise than following a direction under section 110(1) and those court proceedings concern or relate to the matter before the adjudicator, that party must serve–

(a) on the adjudicator within 14 days of the commencement of the court proceedings or, if later, within 7 days of service on that party of notification of the reference under rule 5(b), a written notice stating–

(i) that court proceedings have been issued;

(ii) the way and the extent to which the court proceedings concern or relate to the matter before the adjudicator;

(iii) the date of issue of the court proceedings;

(iv) the names and any known addresses of the parties to the court proceedings;

(v) the name of the court at which the court proceedings will be heard; and

(vi) the case number allocated to the court proceedings;

(b) on the adjudicator within 14 days of the date that the matter before the court is finally disposed of, a copy of the final court order; and

(c) on the court within 14 days of service on that party of such a decision, a copy of any substantive decision made by the adjudicator on the matter.

11.—Adjournment of proceedings before the adjudicator where court proceedings are commenced otherwise than following a direction to commence court proceedings under section 110(1)

A2.2.011 Where court proceedings are commenced otherwise than following a direction to commence court proceedings under section 110(1), the adjudicator may adjourn the whole or part of the proceedings before him pending the outcome of the court proceedings.

12.—Applicant's statement of case and documents

Unless otherwise directed by the adjudicator, the applicant must serve **A2.2.012** on the adjudicator and each of the other parties within 28 days of service of the notification of the reference under rule 5(b)–

(a) his statement of case which must be in accordance with rule 14; and

(b) copies of any documents in the applicant's possession or control which—

    (i) are central to the applicant's case; or

    (ii) the adjudicator or any other party to the proceedings will require in order properly to understand the applicant's statement of case.

13.—Respondent's statement of case and documents

The respondent must serve on the adjudicator and each of the other **A2.2.013** parties within 28 days of service of the applicant's statement of case–

(a) his statement of case which must be in accordance with rule 14; and

(b) copies of any documents in the respondent's possession or control which—

    (i) are central to the respondent's case; or

    (ii) the adjudicator or any other party to the proceedings will require in order properly to understand the respondent's statement of case.

14.—Statement of case

(1) Where under these Rules a party is required to provide a statement **A2.2.014** of case, that statement of case must be in writing, be verified by a statement of truth and include–

(a) the name of the party and confirmation of the party's address for service;

(b) the party's reasons for supporting or objecting to the original application;

(c) the facts on which the party intends to rely in the proceedings; and

. . .

(e) a list of witnesses that the party intends to call to give evidence in support of the party's case.

(2) If in relation to part only of the matter–

(a) a party has been directed to commence or has commenced court proceedings; or

(b) the adjudicator has adjourned proceedings before him,

the adjudicator may direct that the statement of case should contain the information specified in paragraphs (1)(b) to (1)(e) inclusive only in relation to the part of the matter that is not before the court for the court's decision or has not been adjourned before the adjudicator.

Part 3

Rectification Application to the Adjudicator to Rectify or set Aside Documents

15.—Scope of this Part

A2.2.015   The rules in this Part apply to rectification applications.

16.—Form and contents of a rectification application

A2.2.016   (1) A rectification application must–

(a) be made in writing;

(b) be dated and verified by a statement of truth;

(c) be addressed to the adjudicator;

(d) include the following information–

(i) the name and address of the person or persons against whom the order is sought;

(ii) details of the remedy being sought;

(iii) the grounds on which the rectification application is based;

. . .

(v) a list of witnesses that the party intends to call to give evidence in support of the rectification application; and

(vi) the applicant's name and address for service;

(e) include the following copies–

    (i) copies of any documents in the applicant's possession or control which—

        (aa) are central to the applicant's case; or

        (bb) the adjudicator or any other party to the proceedings will require in order properly to understand the rectification application; and

    (ii) a copy of the document to which the rectification application relates, or if a copy is not available, details of the document, which must include if available, its nature, its date, the parties to it and any version number or other similar identification number or code that it has; and

(f) be served on the adjudicator.

(2) Following receipt by the adjudicator of a rectification application, the adjudicator must enter the particulars of the rectification application in the record of matters.

(3) If, having considered the rectification application and made any enquiries he thinks necessary, the adjudicator is satisfied that it is groundless, he must reject the rectification application.

17.—Notice of a rectification application

(1) This rule does not apply where the adjudicator has rejected a rectification application under rule 16(3).   **A2.2.017**

(2) Where a rectification application has been received by the adjudicator, he must either serve, or direct the applicant to serve on the person against whom the order is sought and on any other person who, in the opinion of the adjudicator, should be a party to the proceedings–

(a) written notice of the rectification application; and

(b) a copy of the rectification application.

(3) The . . . notice under paragraph (2)(a) [must specify that if a party receiving the notice has any objection to the rectification application and that party wishes to lodge an objection, he must lodge his objection within 28 days of service of the notice under paragraph (2)(a).

18.—Objection to a rectification application

A person lodges an objection under rule 17(3) if within 28 days of   **A2.2.018**
service of the notice under rule 17(2)(a) he serves–

(a) on the adjudicator–

> (i) a written statement addressed to the adjudicator, dated and verified by a statement of truth, setting out the grounds for the objection;

> . . .

> (iii) copies of any documents in the party's possession or control which—

>> (aa) are central to the party's case; or
>> (bb) the adjudicator or any other party to the proceedings will require in order properly to understand the party's written statement;

> (iv) a written list of witnesses that the party intends to call to give evidence in support of the objection; and
> (v) written confirmation of his name and address for service; and

(b) on the other parties a copy of all the information and documents served on the adjudicator under sub-paragraph (a).

PART 4

PREPARATION FOR DETERMINATION OF REFERENCES AND RECTIFICATION APPLICATIONS

19.—Scope of this Part

A2.2.019   This Part sets out the procedure for the preparation for the determination of references and rectification applications.

20.—Directions

A2.2.020   (1) The adjudicator may at any time, on the application of a party or otherwise, give directions to enable the parties to prepare for a hearing, or to assist the adjudicator to conduct the proceedings or determine any question in the proceedings with or without a hearing.

(2) Such directions may include, but are not limited to—

(a) a direction that the parties attend a case management conference or a pre-hearing review; and

(b) such other directions as are provided for in these Rules.

21.—Form of directions

A2.2.021   (1) Any direction made by the adjudicator must be–

(a)   in writing;

(b)   dated; and

(c)   except in the case of requirement notices under rule 28, served by him on–

    (i)   every party to the proceedings;

    (ii)   where the person who made the application, representation or objection that resulted in the direction was not a party, that person; and

    (iii)   where the direction requires the registrar to take action, the registrar.

(2) Directions containing a requirement must, where appropriate, include a statement of the possible consequences of failure to comply with the requirement within any time limit specified by these Rules, or imposed by the adjudicator.

(3) Directions requiring a party to provide or produce a document ... may require the party to provide or produce it to the adjudicator or to another party or both.

22.—Consolidating proceedings

Where a reference or rectification application is related to another refer- **A2.2.022** ence or rectification application and in the opinion of the adjudicator it is appropriate or practicable to do so, the adjudicator may direct that any or all of those related references or rectification applications be dealt with together.

23.—Intention to appear

The adjudicator may give directions requiring a party to state whether **A2.2.023** that party intends to–

(a)   attend or be represented at the hearing; and

(b)   call witnesses.

24.—Addition and substitution of parties

(1) The adjudicator may give one or more of the following **A2.2.024** directions–

(a)   that any person be added as a new party to the proceedings, if it appears to the adjudicator desirable for that person to be made a party;

    (b) that any person cease to be a party to the proceedings, if it appears to the adjudicator that it is not desirable for that person to remain a party; and

    (c) that a new party be substituted for an existing party, if–

        (i) the existing party's interest or liability has passed to the new party; and

        (ii) it appears to the adjudicator desirable to do this to enable him to resolve the whole or part of the matter or any question of dispute in the proceedings.

(2) If the adjudicator directs that a new party is to be added to the proceedings, the adjudicator must specify–

    (a) whether the new party is added as an applicant or a respondent; and

    (b) how the new party is to be referred to.

(3) Each new party must be given a single identification that should be in accordance with the order in which they joined the proceedings, for example "second applicant" or "second respondent".

(4) If the adjudicator directs that a new party is to be substituted for an existing party, the adjudicator must specify which party the new party is to substitute, for example "respondent" or "second applicant".

(5) The adjudicator must either serve, or direct one or more of the existing parties to serve on each new party a copy of each of the following–

    (a) the applicant's statement of case and copy documents served on the adjudicator under rule 12 or the applicant's rectification application served on the adjudicator under rule 16(1); and

    (b) the respondent's statement of case and copy documents served on the adjudicator under rule 13 or the documents and information served by the respondent on the adjudicator under rule 18(a).

(6) If the new party is added to or substituted for parties to proceedings on a reference, the new party must serve on the adjudicator and each of the other parties within 28 days of service on him of the documents specified in paragraph (5)–

    (a) his statement of case which must be in accordance with rule 14; and

    (b) copies of any documents in the new party's possession or control which—

(i) are central to the new party's case; or

(ii) the adjudicator or any other party to the proceedings will require in order properly to understand the new party's statement of case.

(7) If the new party is added to or substituted for parties to proceedings on a rectification application, the new party must serve on the adjudicator and each of the other parties, within 28 days of service on him of the documents specified in paragraph (5)–

(a) if the new party is added or substituted as an applicant, his rectification application which must be in accordance with rule 16(1); or

(b) if the new party is added or substituted as a respondent, his objection to the rectification application which must be in accordance with rule 18(a).

(8) If a continuing party wishes to respond to the documents specified in paragraph (6) or (7), he may apply to the adjudicator for leave to do so.

(9) If the adjudicator grants the requested leave to respond, the adjudicator must require the party requesting leave to respond to serve a copy of his response on the adjudicator and all other parties.

(10) When directing the addition or substitution of parties or at any time thereafter and if it is necessary to do so, the adjudicator may give consequential directions, including for–

(a) the preparation and updating of a list of parties;

(b) the delivery and service of documents; and

(c) the waiver of the requirement to supply copies of documents under paragraph (6)(b) where copies have already been served by or on the adjudicator and each of the other parties in the course of the proceedings.

25.—Further information, supplementary statements and further responses to statements of case

The adjudicator may give directions requiring a party to provide one or more of the following– **A2.2.025**

(a) a statement of the facts in dispute or issues to be decided;

(b) a statement of the facts on which that party intends to rely and the allegations he intends to make;

(c) a summary of the arguments on which that party intends to rely; and

(d) such further information, responses to statements of case or supplementary statements as may reasonably be required for the determination of the whole or part of the matter or any question in dispute in the proceedings.

26.—Witness statements

A2.2.026   The adjudicator may give directions requiring a party to provide a witness statement made by any witness on whose evidence that party intends to rely in the proceedings.

27.—Disclosure and inspection of documents

A2.2.027   (1) Any document ... supplied to the adjudicator or to a party under this rule or under rule 28 may only be used for the purpose of the proceedings in which it was disclosed.

(2) Within 28 days after service of the respondent's statement of case under rule 13 or the lodging of an objection under rule 18, each party must—

(a) serve on the adjudicator and each of the other parties a list, which complies with rule 47, of all documents in that party's possession or control which—

(i) that party intends to rely upon in the proceedings;
(ii) adversely affect that party's own case;
(iii) adversely affect another party's case; or
(iv) support another party's case; and

(b) send to the adjudicator copies of all documents in the list served under sub-paragraph (a).

(3) Paragraph (4) applies to documents—

(a) referred to in a party's—

(i) statement of case;
(ii) rectification application under rule 16(1); or
(iii) written statement under rule 18(a)(i); or

(b) appearing on a list served by a party under paragraph (2).

(4) In addition to any other requirement in these rules to disclose or provide copies of documents, in relation to any document referred to in paragraph (3) each party must—

(a) permit any other party to inspect and take copies on reasonable notice and at a reasonable time and place; and

(b) provide a copy if requested by another party on payment by such other party of reasonable copying costs.

(5) Paragraphs (2), (3) and (4) are subject to any direction of the adjudicator to the contrary.

(6) The adjudicator may at any time give directions requiring a party to state whether that party has any particular document, or class of documents, in its possession or control and, if so, to comply with the requirements of paragraphs (2), (3) and (4) in relation to such documents as if one of the categories at paragraph (2)(a) applied to them.

28.—Requirement notices

(1) The adjudicator may, at any time, require the attendance of any **A2.2.028** person to give evidence or to produce any document . . . specified by the adjudicator which is in that person's possession or control.

(2) The adjudicator must make any such requirement in a requirement notice.

(3) The requirement notice must be in the form specified by the adjudicator provided that the requirement notice–

(a) is in writing;

(b) identifies the person who must comply with the requirement;

(c) identifies the matter to which the requirement relates;

(d) states the nature of the requirement being imposed by the adjudicator;

(e) specifies the time and place at which the adjudicator requires the person to attend and, if appropriate, produce any document . . .; and

(f) includes a statement of the possible consequences of failure to comply with the requirement notice.

(4) The party on whose behalf it is issued must serve the requirement notice.

(5) Subject to paragraph (6) a requirement notice will be binding only if, not less than 7 working days before the time that the person is required to attend–

(a) the requirement notice is served on that person; and

(b) except in the case where that person is a party to the proceedings, the necessary expenses of his attendance are offered and (unless he has refused the offer of payment of his expenses) paid to him.

(6) At any time before the time that the person is required to attend, that person and the party on whose behalf the requirement notice is issued may substitute a shorter period for the period of 7 working days specified in paragraph (5) by–

(a) agreeing in writing such shorter period; and

(b) before the time that the person is required to attend, serving a copy of that agreement on the adjudicator.

(7) Where a requirement has been imposed on a person under paragraph (1), that person may apply to the adjudicator for the requirement to be varied or set aside.

(8) Any application made under paragraph (7) must be made to the adjudicator before the time when the person is to comply with the requirement to which the application under paragraph (7) relates.

29.—Estimate of length of hearing

A2.2.029   The adjudicator may require the parties to provide an estimate of the length of the hearing.

30.—Site inspections

A2.2.030   (1) In this rule–

"the appropriate party" is the party who is in occupation or has ownership or control of the property;

"the property" is the land or premises that the adjudicator wishes to inspect for the purposes of determining the whole or part of the matter; and

"a request for entry" is a written request from the adjudicator to the appropriate party, requesting permission for the adjudicator to enter onto and inspect the property and such a request may include a request to be accompanied by one or more of–

(a) another party;

(b) such number of the adjudicator's officers or staff as he considers necessary; and

(c) if a member of the [Administrative Justice and Tribunals Council] informs the adjudicator that he wishes to attend the inspection, that member.

(2) The adjudicator, at any time for the purpose of determining the whole or part of the matter, may serve a request for entry on an appropriate party.

(3) The request for entry must specify a time for the entry that, unless otherwise agreed in writing by the appropriate party, must be not earlier than 7 days after the date of service of the request for entry.

(4) The adjudicator must serve a copy of the request for entry on any party (other than the appropriate party) and any member of the [Administrative Justice and Tribunals Council] named in the request for entry and, if reasonably practicable to do so in the circumstances, must notify them of any change in the time specified.

(5) If the adjudicator makes a request for entry and the appropriate party withholds or refuses his consent to the whole or part of the request without reasonable excuse, the adjudicator may take such refusal into account when making his substantive decision.

(6) If a request for entry includes a request for a member of the Administrative Justice and Tribunals Council to accompany the adjudicator and the appropriate party consents to the presence of that member, then that member shall be entitled to attend the site inspection but must not take an active part in the inspection.

31.—Preliminary issues

(1) At any time and on the application of a party or of his own motion, **A2.2.031** the adjudicator may dispose of any matter or matters that are in dispute as a preliminary issue.

(2) If in the opinion of the adjudicator the decision on the preliminary issue will dispose of the whole of the matter then the decision on the preliminary issue must be–

(a) made in accordance with the provisions in these Rules on substantive decisions; and

(b) treated as a substantive decision.

PART 5

HEARINGS AND SUBSTANTIVE DECISIONS

32.—Scope of this Part

A2.2.032   This Part sets out the procedure for determination of references and rectification applications, the format of substantive decisions and substantive orders and rules on costs.

32A.—Summary disposal

A2.2.033   (1) The adjudicator may summarily dispose of the proceedings or any particular issue in the proceedings on an application by a party or of its own motion if—

> (a) the adjudicator considers that the applicant or respondent has no real prospect of succeeding in the proceedings or on the issue; and
>
> (b) there is no other compelling reason why the proceedings or issue should not be disposed of summarily.

(2) Except with the permission of the adjudicator, an applicant may not apply for summary disposal until the respondent has served a statement of case or lodged an objection (as appropriate), or the respondent's time to do so has expired.

(3) A respondent may apply for summary disposal at any time after the applicant has served a statement of case or rectification application (as appropriate), or (in the case of service of a statement of case) the applicant's time to do so has expired.

(4) Paragraph (5) applies where—

> (a) a respondent applies for summary disposal before serving a statement of case or lodging an objection (as appropriate) and before the time to do so has expired; and
>
> (b) that application does not result in the disposal of the entire proceedings.

(5) In the circumstances described in paragraph (4) the respondent's time for serving a statement of case or lodging an objection is extended to—

> (a) 28 days after service on the respondent of the adjudicator's decision in relation to the application for summary disposal; or
>
> (b) such other time as the adjudicator directs.

(6) An application for summary disposal must include a witness statement in support of the application. That witness statement must state that the party making the application—

(a) believes that the other party has no real prospect of succeeding on the proceedings or on the issue to which the application relates; and

(b) knows of no other reason why the disposal of the proceedings or issue should not be disposed of summarily.

(7) When serving a notice under rule 51(5) or (7), or directing the party making the application to serve a notice under rule 51(5), and such notice relates in whole or in part to summary disposal, the adjudicator must give directions for the service of evidence by the parties and for the determination of the issue of summary disposal.

(8) When the adjudicator determines the issue of summary disposal the adjudicator may make an order—

(a) disposing of the proceedings or of any issue; or

(b) dismissing the application for or intention to consider summary disposal.

(9) Where an order made under paragraph (8) does not dispose of the entire proceedings, the adjudicator must give case management directions as to the future conduct of the proceedings.

33.—Substantive decision without a hearing

(1) There is a presumption that a substantive decision is made following a hearing. **A2.2.034**

(2) Subject to paragraph (1), the adjudicator may make a substantive decision without a hearing if–

(a) he is satisfied that there is no important public interest consideration that requires a hearing in public; and

(b) unless paragraph (3) applies, he has served written notice on the parties in accordance with these Rules that he intends to make a substantive decision without a hearing or that he has received an application requesting that the substantive decision be made without a hearing and–

(i) the parties agree to the substantive decision being made without a hearing; or

(ii) the parties fail to object within the specified period for objection to the substantive decision being made without a hearing.

(3) The adjudicator is not required to serve notice under paragraph (2) (b) if all parties have requested the adjudicator to make the substantive decision without a hearing.

34.—Notice of hearing

A2.2.035   (1) Where the adjudicator is to hold a hearing, he must serve written notice of his intention to hear on such parties as he considers necessary.

(2) The adjudicator must specify in the notice under paragraph (1), the date, time and location of the hearing.

(3) The adjudicator must serve the notice under paragraph (1)–

(a) no later than 28 days before the hearing; or

(b) before the expiry of such shorter notice period as agreed by all the parties on whom he intends to serve notice under paragraph (1).

35.—Representation at the hearing

A2.2.036   (1) At the hearing a party may conduct his case himself or, subject to paragraph (2), be represented or assisted by any person, whether or not legally qualified.

(2) If, in any particular case, the adjudicator is satisfied that there is sufficient reason for doing so, he may refuse to permit a particular person to represent or assist a party at the hearing.

36.—Publication of hearings

A2.2.037   The adjudicator must publish details of all listed hearings at the office of the adjudicator and, if different, the venue at which the hearing is to take place.

A2.2.038 **37.**—[Revoked by Adjudicator to Her Majesty's Land Registry (Practice and Procedure) (Amendment) Rules 2008/1731 rule 21 (July 25, 2008)]

38.—Absence of parties

A2.2.039   (1) If any party does not attend and is not represented at any hearing of which notice has been served on him in accordance with these Rules, the adjudicator–

(a) may proceed with the hearing and reach a substantive decision in that party's absence if–

    (i) the adjudicator is not satisfied that any reasons given for the absence are justified;

    (ii) the absent party consents; or

    (iii) it would be unjust to adjourn the hearing; or

(b) must otherwise adjourn the hearing.

(2) Following a decision by the adjudicator under paragraph (1) to proceed with or adjourn the hearing, the adjudicator may make such consequential directions as he sees fit.

39.—Substantive decision of the adjudicator

(1) Where there is a hearing, the substantive decision of the adjudicator **A2.2.040** may be given orally at the end of the hearing or reserved.

(2) A substantive decision of the adjudicator, whether made at a hearing or without a hearing, must be recorded in a substantive order.

(3) The adjudicator may not vary or set aside a substantive decision.

40.—Substantive orders and written reasons

(1) A substantive order must–   **A2.2.041**

(a) be dated;

(b) be in writing;

(c) be sealed and state the name of the person making the order;

(d) state the substantive decision that has been reached;

(e) state any steps that must be taken to give effect to that substantive decision; and

(f) where appropriate, state the possible consequences of a party's failure to comply with the substantive order within any specified time limits.

(2) The substantive order must be served by the adjudicator on–

(a) every party to the proceedings; and

(b) where the substantive order requires the registrar to take action, the registrar.

(3) A substantive order requiring a party to provide or produce a document . . . may require the party to provide or produce it to any or all of the adjudicator, the registrar or another party.

(4) Unless the adjudicator directs otherwise, the substantive order must be publicly available.

(5) Where the substantive order is publicly available, the adjudicator may provide copies of it to the public on request.

(6) The adjudicator must give in writing to all parties his reasons for–

(a) his substantive decision; and

(b) any steps that must be taken to give effect to that substantive decision.

(7) The adjudicator's reasons referred to in paragraph (6) need not be given in the substantive order.

41.—Substantive orders on a reference that include requirements on the registrar

A2.2.042 (1) Where the adjudicator has made a substantive decision on a reference, the substantive order giving effect to that substantive decision may include a requirement on the registrar to–

(a) give effect to the original application in whole or in part as if the objection to that original application had not been made; or

(b) cancel the original application in whole or in part.

(2) A requirement on the registrar under this rule may include–

(a) a condition that a specified entry be made on the register of any title affected; or

(b) a requirement to reject any future application of a specified kind by a named party to the proceedings–

(i) unconditionally; or

(ii) unless that party satisfies specified conditions.

41A.—Orders under rule 8(4) or 9(4)

A2.2.043 An order made under rule 8(4) or 9(4) must—

(a) comply with the requirements of rule 40(1)(a), (b), (c) and (f), (2), (3), (4) and (5) as if it were a substantive order;

(b) identify the decision of the court which the order implements; and

(c) state the reasons why the order complies with rule 8(4)(a) or 9(4)(a).

42.—Costs

(1) In this rule— **A2.2.044**

(a) "all the circumstances" are all the circumstances of the proceedings and include—

(i) the conduct of the parties—

(aa) in respect of proceedings commenced by a reference, during (but not prior to) the proceedings; or

(bb) in respect of proceedings commenced by a rectification application, before and during the proceedings;

(ii) whether a party has succeeded on part of his case, even if he has not been wholly successful; and

(iii) any representations made to the adjudicator by the parties; and

(b) the conduct of the parties . . . includes—

(i) whether it was reasonable for a party to raise, pursue or contest a particular allegation or issue;

(ii) the manner in which a party has pursued or defended his case or a particular allegation or issue; and

(iii) whether a party who has succeeded in his case in whole or in part exaggerated his case.

(2) The adjudicator may, on the application of a party or of his own motion, make an order as to costs.

(3) In deciding what order as to costs (if any) to make, the adjudicator must have regard to all the circumstances.

(4) An order as to costs may, without limitation—

(a) require a party to pay the whole or a part of the costs of another party and—

(i) specify a fixed sum or proportion to be paid; or

(ii) specify that costs from or until a certain date are to be paid;

(b) if the adjudicator considers it impracticable to make an order in respect of the relevant part of a party's costs under paragraph (a), specify that costs relating to a distinct part of the proceedings are to be paid;

(c) specify an amount to be paid on account before costs are agreed or assessed; or

(d) specify the time within which costs are to be paid.

(5) The adjudicator may—

(a) summarily assess the whole or a part of a party's costs; or

(b) specify that, if the parties are unable to reach agreement on an amount to be paid, the whole or a part of a party's costs be assessed in a specified manner.

(6) An order as to costs must be recorded in a costs order and must–

(a) be in writing;

(b) be dated;

(c) be sealed and state the name of the person making the order;

(d) state the order as to costs; and

(e) be served by the adjudicator on the parties.

(7) Where the costs are to be assessed by the adjudicator, he may assess the costs–

(a) on the standard basis; or

(b) on the indemnity basis,

but in either case the adjudicator will not allow costs that have been unreasonably incurred or are unreasonable in amount.

(8) The adjudicator must inform the parties of the basis on which he will be assessing the costs.

(9) Where the amount of the costs are to be assessed on the standard basis, the adjudicator must–

(a) only allow costs which are proportionate to the matters in issue; and

(b) resolve any doubt that he may have as to whether costs were reasonably incurred or reasonable and proportionate in favour of the paying party.

(10) In deciding whether costs assessed on the standard basis were either proportionately and reasonably incurred or proportionate and reasonable in amount, the adjudicator must have regard to all the circumstances.

(11) Where costs are to be assessed on the indemnity basis, the adjudicator must resolve in favour of the receiving party any doubt as to the reasonableness of the incurring or the amount of the costs.

(12) In deciding whether costs assessed on the indemnity basis were either reasonably incurred or reasonable in amount, the adjudicator must have regard to all the circumstances.

(13) Once the adjudicator has assessed the costs, he must serve on the parties written notice–

(a) of the amount which must be paid;

(b) by whom and to whom the amount must be paid; and

(c) if appropriate, the time by when the amount must be paid.

43.—Costs thrown away

(1) In this rule–   A2.2.045

"costs thrown away" means costs of the proceedings resulting from any neglect or delay of the legal representative during (but not prior to) the proceedings and which–

(a) have been incurred by a party; or
(b) have been–

(i)   paid by a party to another party; or
(ii) awarded to a party,

under an order made under rule 42;

"an order as to costs thrown away" means an order requiring the legal representative concerned to meet the whole or part of the costs thrown away; and

"the legal representative" means the legally qualified representative of a party.

(2) The adjudicator may, on the application of a party or otherwise, make an order as to costs thrown away provided the adjudicator is satisfied that–

(a) a party has incurred costs of the proceedings unnecessarily as a result of the neglect or delay of the legal representative; and

(b) it is just in all the circumstances for the legal representative to compensate the party who has incurred or paid the costs thrown away, for the whole or part of those costs.

(3) If the adjudicator has received an application for or proposes to make an order as to costs thrown away, he may give directions to the parties and the legal representative about the procedure to be followed to ensure that the issues are dealt with in a way that is fair and as simple and summary as the circumstances permit.

(4) An order as to costs thrown away may–

(a) specify the amount of costs to be paid by the legal representative; and

(b) if the adjudicator considers it appropriate, specify the time within which the costs are to be paid.

(5) An order as to costs thrown away must be recorded in a costs thrown away order.

(6) A costs thrown away order must–

(a) be in writing;

(b) be dated;

(c) be sealed and state the name of the person making the order;

(d) state the order as to costs thrown away; and

(e) be served by the adjudicator on the parties and the legal representative.

PART 6

APPEALS FROM ADJUDICATOR

44.—Scope of this Part

A2.2.046   This Part contains provisions in relation to appeals to the High Court of decisions by the adjudicator and includes provisions about the adjudicator staying implementation of his decision pending the outcome of an appeal.

45.—Appeals to the High Court

(1) Where a party is granted permission to appeal, the adjudicator may, **A2.2.047** of his own motion or on the application of a party, stay the implementation of the whole or part of his decision pending the outcome of the appeal.

(2) A party who wishes to apply to the adjudicator to stay the implementation of the whole or part of a decision pending the outcome of the appeal must make such an application to the adjudicator at the same time that he applies to the adjudicator for permission to appeal.

(3) Where a party applies under paragraph (2) to the adjudicator to stay implementation of the whole or part of a decision, that party must at the same time provide reasons for the application.

(4) Before reaching a decision as to whether to grant permission to appeal a decision or to stay implementation of a decision, the adjudicator must allow the parties the opportunity to make representations or objections.

(5) The adjudicator must serve written notice on the parties of any decision that he makes as to whether to grant permission to appeal or to stay the implementation of the whole or part of his decision pending the outcome of the appeal.

(6) Where the adjudicator's decision to grant permission to appeal or to stay implementation of a decision relates to a decision contained in a substantive order, the adjudicator must serve on the registrar a copy of the notice under paragraph (5).

(7) The notice under paragraph (5) must–

(a) be in writing;

(b) be dated;

(c) specify the decision made by the adjudicator;

(d) include the adjudicator's reasons for his decision; and

(e) be sealed and state the name of the person making the order.

PART 7

GENERAL

46.—Record of matters

(1) The adjudicator must keep at his principal office a record of matters **A2.2.048** that records the particulars of all–

(a) references;

(b) rectification applications;

(c) substantive decisions; and

(d) all applications and decisions made under rule 45.

(2) Subject to paragraph (3), the record of matters must be open to the inspection of any person without charge at all reasonable hours on working days.

(3) Where the adjudicator is satisfied that it is just and reasonable to do so, the adjudicator may exclude from inspection any information contained in the record of matters.

(4) Depending on all the circumstances, it may be just and reasonable for the adjudicator to exclude from inspection any information contained in the record of matters if it is in the interest of morals, public order, national security, juveniles or the protection of the private lives of the parties to the proceedings, or where the adjudicator considers that publicity would prejudice the interests of justice.

47.—List of documents and documents

A2.2.049   (1) For the purposes of these Rules, a list of documents must be in writing and, subject to paragraph (1A), must contain the following information where available in relation to each document–

(a) a brief description of the nature of the document;

. . .

(c) whether the document is an original, a copy certified to be a true copy of the original, an office copy or another type of copy;

(d) the date of the document;

(e) the document parties or the original author and recipient of the document; and

(f) the version number or similar identification number or code of the document.

(1A) If a large number of documents fall into a particular class, that class of documents may be listed in accordance with paragraph (1) as if it were an individual document.

(1B) If a class of documents is listed in accordance with paragraph (1A), the description of the class of documents must be sufficiently clear and precise to enable any party receiving the list to identify—

(a) the nature of the contents of each document included within that class of documents; and

(b) whether any particular document which exists is included within that class of documents.

(2) Unless the adjudicator otherwise permits, where a document provided for the purposes of the proceedings is or contains a coloured map, plan or drawing, any copy provided of that map, plan or drawing must be in the same colours as the map, plan or drawing of which it is a copy (so for example, where a plan shows the boundary of a property in red, a copy of the plan must also show the boundary in red).

48.—Evidence

(1) The adjudicator may require any witness to give evidence on oath **A2.2.050** or affirmation and for that purpose there may be administered an oath or affirmation in due form.

(2) No person may be compelled to give any evidence or produce any document [. . .] that that person could not be compelled to give or produce on a trial of an action in a court of law in England and Wales.

49.—Expert evidence

No party may call an expert, or submit an expert's report as evidence, **A2.2.051** without the adjudicator's permission.

50.—Service of documents

(1) A party's address for service must be a postal address in England **A2.2.052** and Wales.

(2) The address for service in paragraph (1) must be either that of the party or of the party's representative who has been appointed as his representative for the purposes of the proceedings.

(3) A party's address for service remains that party's address for service for the purposes of these Rules unless and until he serves on the adjudicator and the other parties notice of a different address for service.

(4) Any document to be served on or delivered to any person (other than the adjudicator) under these Rules may only be served–

(a) by first class post to his postal address given as his address for service;

(b) by leaving it at his address for service;

(c) . . . by document exchange;

(d) subject to paragraph (6), by fax;

(e) subject to paragraph (7), by email; or

(f) where no address for service has been given, by post to or leaving it at his registered office, principal place of business, head or main office or last known address, as appropriate.

. . .

(6) A document may be served by fax on any person other than the adjudicator, to a fax number at the address for service for that person if, in advance, the recipient has informed the adjudicator and all parties in writing–

(a) that the recipient is willing to accept service by fax; and

(b) of the fax number to which the documents should be sent.

(7) A document may be served by email on any person other than the adjudicator, if, in advance, the recipient has informed the adjudicator and all parties in writing–

(a) that the recipient is willing to accept service by email;

(b) of the email address to which documents should be sent, which shall be deemed to be at the recipient's address for service; and

(c) if the recipient wishes to so specify, the format in which documents must be sent.

(8) Any document addressed to the adjudicator must be sent–

(a) by first class post to an address specified by the adjudicator; or

(b) by such other method as the adjudicator may specify, including document exchange, fax or email.

(9) Where under paragraph (8)(b) the adjudicator specifies another method of service, the adjudicator may–

(a) specify that that method may be used generally or only in relation to a certain document or documents;

(b) specify that the specified method is no longer available or substitute that specified method with another specified method; and

(c) make such directions in relation to the use of the specified method as he deems appropriate.

(10) Any document served on an unincorporated body may be sent to its secretary, manager or similar officer duly authorised to accept such service.

(11) Any document which is served in accordance with this rule shall be regarded as having been served on the day shown in the table below–

Method of service	Day of service
First class post to a postal address within England and Wales	The second working day after it was posted.
Leaving it at a postal address within England and Wales	The working day after it was left.
Document exchange within England and Wales	The second working day after it was left at the document exchange.
Fax	The working day after it was transmitted.
Email	The working day after it was transmitted.

(12) The adjudicator may direct that service under these Rules of any document may be dispensed with and in those circumstances may make such consequential directions as he deems appropriate.

51.—Applications, actions by the adjudicator of his own motion, notification, representations and objections

(1) This rule does not apply to Part 3 and rule 45. A2.2.053

(2) An application to the adjudicator must–

(a) be in writing;

(b) state the name of the person applying or on whose behalf the application is made;

(c) be addressed to the adjudicator;

(d) state the nature of the application;

(e) state the reason or reasons for the application; and

(f) if any of the parties or persons who would be affected by the application consent to it, either–

(i) be signed by all the parties or persons who consent or their duly authorised representatives; or

(ii) have attached to it a copy of their written consent.

(3) The adjudicator may dispense with any or all of the requirements under paragraph (2)–

(a) in relation to an application made to the adjudicator at a time when all persons who would be affected by the application are present before the adjudicator; or

(b) if the adjudicator otherwise considers it appropriate or practicable to do so.

(4) For the purposes of paragraph (2)(f), the written consent referred to in that paragraph may be in the form of a letter, fax or email.

(5) If an application is not consented to by all persons who will be affected by the application then, subject to paragraph (10), the adjudicator must either serve, or direct the party making the application to serve written notice on persons who have not consented to the application but who would be affected by it, and any such direction to the party making the application must include the information to be included in the notice under paragraph (6)(d).

(6) The notice under paragraph (5) . . . must state–

(a) that the application has been made;

(b) details of the application;

(c) that the person has a right to make written objections to or representations about the application; and

(d) the period within which such objections or representations must be lodged with the adjudicator.

(7) If the adjudicator intends to act of his own motion under these Rules then, subject to paragraph (10), he must serve written notice of his intention on all persons who will be affected by the action.

(8) In the notice under paragraph (7) the adjudicator must state–

(a) that the adjudicator intends to take action of his own motion;

(b) the action the adjudicator intends to take;

(c) that a person has a right to make written objections or representations to the action that the adjudicator intends to take; and

(d) the period within which such objections or representations must be lodged with the adjudicator.

(9) A person lodges an objection or representation if within the specified period he serves–

    (a) on the adjudicator a written statement setting out the grounds for his objection or representation; and

    (b) on all the other persons who will be affected by the action a copy of the written statement served on the adjudicator under sub-paragraph (a).

(10) The adjudicator shall not be required to serve, or direct the applicant to serve notice under paragraphs (5) and (7) if, in the circumstances, he does not consider it appropriate or practicable to do so.

(11) Paragraph (10) does not apply to notices—

    (a) under paragraphs (5) or (7) which relate to a proposal that the adjudicator exercise the power under rule 32A(1); or

    (b) required to be served by rule 33.

52.—Consideration by the adjudicator of applications (including applications for directions), representations and objections

(1) In relation to any application, representation or objection made to the adjudicator, unless– **A2.2.054**

    (a) the adjudicator is satisfied that it is frivolous or vexatious; or

    (b) it is received by the adjudicator after the expiry of any time limit specified for making that application, representation or objection,

the adjudicator must consider all applications, representations or objections made to him.

(2) If an application, representation or objection is received by the adjudicator after the expiry of any time limit specified for making it, the adjudicator may consider the application, representation or objection, but he is not bound to do so.

(3) In considering any application, representation or objection, the adjudicator must make all enquiries he thinks necessary and must, if required by these Rules or if he considers it necessary, give the person making the application, representation or objection and the parties or other persons who will be affected by it the opportunity to appear before him or to submit written representations.

(4) The adjudicator may decide to accept or reject an application, representation or objection in whole or in part.

(5) Following his consideration of any applications, representations or objections that are made to him, the adjudicator must notify the person who made the application, representation or objection and the parties and any other persons who will be affected by it, of his decision in accordance with these Rules.

53.—Adjournment

A2.2.055 In addition to the powers and obligations to adjourn proceedings contained in Part 2 and rule 38, the adjudicator may adjourn the whole or part of the proceedings when and to the extent that he feels it reasonable to do so.

54.—Power to vary or set aside directions

A2.2.056 Subject to these Rules, the adjudicator may at any time, on the application of a party or otherwise, vary or set aside directions made under these Rules.

55.—Failure to comply with a direction

A2.2.057 (1) Where a party has failed to comply with a direction given by the adjudicator (including a direction to commence court proceedings under section 110(1)) the adjudicator may impose a sanction on the defaulting party–

(a) on the application of any other party; or

(b) of his own motion.

(2) Where the defaulting party was the person who made (or has been substituted for or added to the party who made) the original application, the sanction may include requiring the registrar to cancel the original application in whole or in part.

(3) Where the defaulting party was a person who objected to (or has been substituted for or added to the party who objected to) the original application, the sanction may include requiring the registrar to give effect to the original application in whole or in part as if the objection had not been made.

(4) A sanction that includes either of the requirements on the registrar under paragraph (2) or (3) shall be treated as the substantive decision on that matter.

(5) If the sanction does not include either of the requirements on the registrar under paragraph (2) or (3), the adjudicator must serve written

notice on the parties of his decision as to what if any sanctions are imposed, and he may make consequential directions.

56.—Errors of procedure

Where, before the adjudicator has made his final substantive order in **A2.2.058** relation to a matter, there has been an error of procedure such as a failure to comply with a rule–

(a) the error does not invalidate any step taken in the proceedings, unless the adjudicator so orders; and

(b) the adjudicator may make an order or take any other step that he considers appropriate to remedy the error.

57.—Accidental slips or omissions

The adjudicator may at any time amend an order or direction to correct **A2.2.059** a clerical error or other accidental slip or omission.

58.—Time and place

If the adjudicator deems it appropriate to do so, he may alter–   **A2.2.060**

(a) any time limit specified in these Rules;

(b) any time limit set by the adjudicator; or

(c) the date, time or location appointed for a hearing or for any other appearance of the parties before him.

59.—Calculation of time

(1) Where a period of time for doing an act is specified by these **A2.2.061** Rules or by a direction of the adjudicator, that period is to be calculated–

(a) excluding the day on which the period begins; and

(b) unless otherwise specified, by reference to calendar days.

(2) Where the time specified by these Rules or by a direction of the adjudicator for doing an act ends on a day which is not a working day, that act is done in time if it is done on the next working day.

60.—Representation of parties

A2.2.062   (1) If a party who was previously unrepresented appoints a representative or, having been represented, appoints a replacement representative, that party must, as soon as reasonably practicable following the appointment, notify the adjudicator and the other parties in writing–

   (a) of the fact that he has appointed a representative or replacement representative;

   (b) the name and contact details of the representative or replacement representative;

   (c) whether the representative or replacement representative has been authorised by the party to accept service of documents; and

   (d) if the representative or replacement representative has been authorised to accept service, the address for service.

   (2) If a party who was previously represented ceases to be represented, that party must, as soon as reasonably practicable following the ending of his representation, notify the adjudicator and the other parties in writing–

   (a) of the fact that he is no longer represented; and

   (b) where the party's address for service had previously been the address of the representative, the party's new address for service.

61.—Independence of adjudicator's staff

A2.2.063   When undertaking a non-administrative function of the adjudicator on the adjudicator's authorisation, a member of the adjudicator's staff is not subject to the direction of the Lord Chancellor or any other person or body.

LAND REGISTRATION (REFERRAL TO THE ADJUDICATOR TO HM LAND REGISTRY) RULES

SI (2003/2114)

1.—Citation and commencement

These rules may be cited as the Land Registration (Referral to the **A2.3.001** Adjudicator to HM Land Registry) Rules 2003 and shall come into force on 13 October 2003.

2.—Interpretation

In these rules– **A2.3.002**

"the Act" means the Land Registration Act 2002;

"business day" means a day when the land registry is open to the public under rule 216 of the Land Registration Rules 2003;

"disputed application" means an application to the registrar under the Act to which an objection has been made;

"objection" means an objection made under section 73 of the Act;

"the parties" means the person who has made the disputed application and the person who has made an objection to that application.

3.—Procedure for referral to the adjudicator

(1) When the registrar is obliged to refer a matter to the adjudicator **A2.3.003** under section 73(7) of the Act, he must as soon as practicable–

(a) prepare a case summary containing the information set out in paragraph (2),

(b) send a copy of the case summary to the parties,

(c) give the parties an opportunity to make comments on the contents of the case summary in the manner, to the address, and within the time specified by him, and

(d) inform the parties in writing that the case summary together with copies of the documents listed in it will be sent to the adjudicator with the notice referred to in rule 5(2).

(2) The case summary must contain the following information–

    (a)   the names of the parties,

    (b)   the addresses of the parties,

    (c)   details of their legal or other representatives (if any),

    (d)   a summary of the core facts,

    (e)   details of the disputed application,

    (f)   details of the objection to that application,

    (g)   a list of any documents that will be copied to the adjudicator, and

    (h)   anything else that the registrar may consider to be appropriate.

(3) The registrar may amend the case summary as he considers appropriate having considered any written comments made to him by the parties under paragraph (1)(c).

4.—Parties' addresses

A2.3.004   (1) If the address of a party set out in the case summary does not comply with paragraph (2), that party must provide the registrar with one that does.

    (2) An address complies with this paragraph if it–

    (a)   is a postal address in England and Wales, and

    (b)   is either that of the party or of his representative.

5.—Notice of referral to the adjudicator

A2.3.005   (1) This rule applies–

    (a)   when the registrar has considered any written comments made by the parties under rule 3(1)(c), or

    (b)   if he has not received any comments from the parties within the time specified under rule 3(1)(c), on the expiry of that period, and

    (c)   when he has amended the case summary, if appropriate, under rule 3(3).

    (2) The registrar must as soon as practicable–

    (a)   send to the adjudicator a written notice, accompanied by the documents set out in paragraph (3), informing him that the matter is referred to him under section 73(7) of the Act,

(b) inform the parties in writing that the matter has been referred to the adjudicator, and

(c) send the parties a copy of the case summary prepared under rule 3 in the form sent to the adjudicator.

(3) The notice sent to the adjudicator under paragraph (2)(a) must be accompanied by–

(a) the case summary prepared under rule 3 amended, if appropriate, by the registrar under rule 3(3), and

(b) copies of the documents listed in that case summary.

6.—Specified time periods

(1) For the purposes of rule 3(1)(c), the time specified by the registrar **A2.3.006** must not end before 12 noon on the fifteenth business day after the date on which the registrar sends the copy of the case summary to the relevant party under rule 3(1)(b) or such earlier time as the parties may agree.

(2) On and after the date specified in any notice given pursuant to rule 216(2) of the Land Registration Rules 2003, paragraph (1) shall have effect with the substitution of the words "eighteenth business day" for the words "fifteenth business day".

Index

FROM SWEET & MAXWELL

This index has been prepared using Sweet & Maxwell's Legal Taxonomy. Main index entries conform to keywords provided by the Legal Taxonomy except where references to specific documents or non-standard terms (denoted by quotation marks) have been included. These keywords provide a means of identifying similar concepts in other Sweet & Maxwell publications and online services to which keywords from the Legal Taxonomy have been applied. Readers may find some minor differences between terms used in the text and those which appear in the index. Suggestions to *sweet&maxwell.taxonomy@thomson.com*.

(All references are to paragraph number)